Doing Business 2008

COMPARING REGULATION IN 178 ECONOMIES

A copublication of the World Bank and the International Finance Corporation

1818 H Street NW
Washington, D.C. 20433
Telephone 202-473-1000
Internet www.worldbank.org
E-mail feedback@worldbank.org

1 2 3 4 5 09 08 07

A copublication of the World Bank and the International Finance Corporation.

This volume is a product of the staff of the World Bank Group. The findings, interpretations and conclusions expressed in this volume do not necessarily reflect the views of the Executive Directors of The World Bank or the governments they represent. The World Bank Group does not guarantee the accuracy of the data included in this work.

Additional copies of *Doing Business 2008, Doing Business 2007: How to Reform, Doing Business in 2006: Creating Jobs, Doing Business in 2005: Removing Obstacles to Growth* and *Doing Business in 2004: Understanding Regulation* may be purchased at www.doingbusiness.org.

ISBN: 978-0-8213-7231-9
E-ISBN: 978-0-8213-7232-6
DOI: 10.1596/978-0-8213-7231-9
ISSN: 1729-2638

Library of Congress Cataloging-in-Publication data has been applied for.

Contents

Doing Business 2008 is the fifth in a series of annual reports investigating the regulations that enhance business activity and those that constrain it. *Doing Business* presents quantitative indicators on business regulations and the protection of property rights that can be compared across 178 economies—from Afghanistan to Zimbabwe—and over time.

Regulations affecting 10 stages of a business's life are measured: starting a business, dealing with licenses, employing workers, registering property, getting credit, protecting investors, paying taxes, trading across borders, enforcing contracts and closing a business. Data in *Doing Business 2008* are current as of June 1, 2007. The indicators are used to analyze economic outcomes and identify what reforms have worked, where, and why.

The *Doing Business* methodology has limitations. Other areas important to business—such as a country's proximity to large markets, the quality of its infrastructure services (other than those related to trading across borders), the security of property from theft and looting, the transparency of government procurement, macroeconomic conditions or the underlying strength of institutions—are not studied directly by *Doing Business*. To make the data comparable across countries, the indicators refer to a specific type of business—generally a limited liability company operating in the largest business city.

The methodology for 3 of the *Doing Business* topics changed for *Doing Business 2008:* dealing with licenses, employing workers and enforcing contracts. See Data notes for details. Three new topics—not paying bribes, opportunities for women and infrastructure—are under development. The analysis is described in What to expect.

Overview 1

Starting a business 9
Dealing with licenses 14
Employing workers 19
Registering property 24
Getting credit 29
Protecting investors 34
Paying taxes 39
Trading across borders 44
Enforcing contracts 49
Closing a business 54
What to expect 59

References 63
Data notes 67
Ease of doing business 82
Doing Business indicators 87
Country tables 103

Acknowledgments 163

Overview

This year Eastern Europe and the former Soviet Union surpassed East Asia in the ease of doing business (figure 1.1). Several of the region's countries have gone even further, surpassing many Western European economies. Estonia, the most business friendly of the former socialist bloc, ranks 17 on the ease of doing business. Georgia and Latvia are also in the top 25.

The result is a boom in new businesses. Georgia now has 15 registered businesses per 100 people (same as Malaysia). The Czech Republic and Slovakia have 13 (same as Singapore). Estonia and Poland have 12 (same as Hong Kong, China). Some of these new businesses have become global leaders in their field—for example, the Estonian-born software company Skype and the Czech carmaker Škoda.

As in previous years, Eastern European countries dominate the list of top reformers in 2006/07, with Croatia, FYR Macedonia, Georgia and Bulgaria reforming the most. Croatia is a top reformer for the second year running, Georgia for the third.

Many others are reforming too. Two hundred reforms —in 98 economies—were introduced between April 2006 and June 2007. Reformers simplified business regulations, strengthened property rights, eased tax burdens, increased access to credit and reduced the cost of exporting and importing.

Across regions, Eastern Europe and Central Asia reformed the most, followed by South Asia and rich countries (figure 1.2). Latin America reformed the least. The pickup in South Asia was led by India, which rose 12 ranks on the ease of doing business. The slowdown in Latin America could be a result of a busy election year:

FIGURE 1.1
Which region is the most business friendly in 2007?

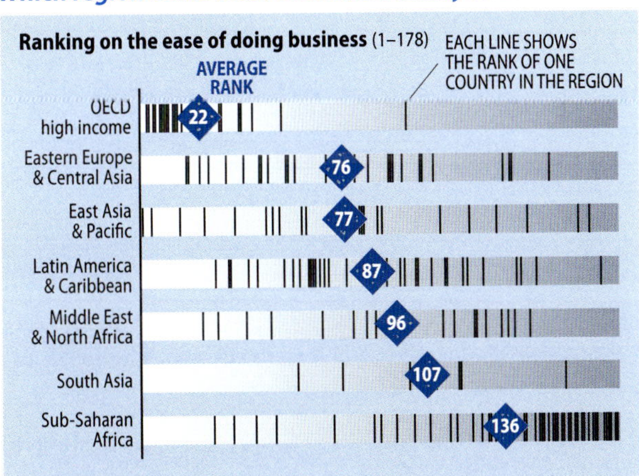

Source: Doing Business database.

FIGURE 1.2
Most reform in Eastern Europe & Central Asia—again

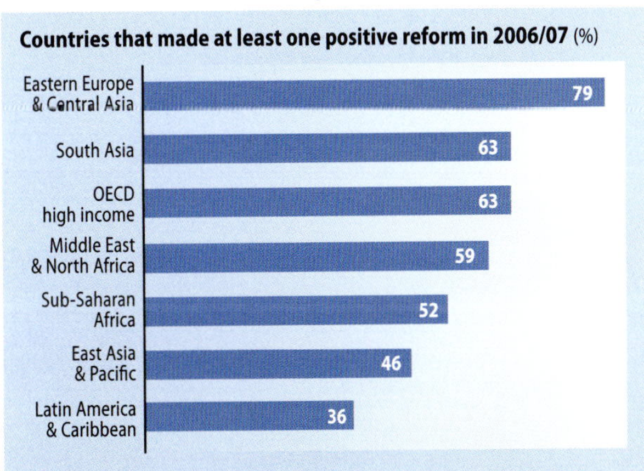

Source: Doing Business database.

TABLE 1.1
The top 10 reformers in 2006/07

Economy	Starting a business	Dealing with licenses	Employing workers	Registering property	Getting credit	Protecting investors	Paying taxes	Trading across borders	Enforcing contracts	Closing a business
Egypt	✓	✓		✓	✓			✓		
Croatia	✓			✓	✓					✓
Ghana	✓			✓	✓			✓	✓	
Macedonia, FYR	✓	✓					✓			
Georgia	✓	✓		✓	✓	✓				✓
Colombia						✓	✓	✓		
Saudi Arabia	✓				✓			✓		
Kenya	✓	✓		✓	✓					
China		✓			✓					✓
Bulgaria		✓					✓		✓	

Note: Economies are ranked on the number and impact of reforms. First, *Doing Business* selects the economies that reformed in 3 or more of the *Doing Business* topics. Second, it ranks these economies on the increase in rank on the ease of doing business from the previous year. The larger the improvement, the higher the ranking as a reformer.
Source: Doing Business database.

13 countries saw new governments sworn in. Earlier analysis suggests that the region might experience a reform boom next year, as nearly 85% of reforms take place in the first 15 months of a new government.[1]

Egypt is the top reformer for 2006/07, improving in 5 of the 10 areas studied by *Doing Business* (table 1.1). Egypt's reforms went deep. They made starting a business easier, slashing the minimum capital requirement from 50,000 Egyptian pounds to 1,000 and halving start-up time and cost. Fees for registering property were reduced from 3% of the property value to a low fixed fee. With more properties registered and less evasion, revenue from title registrations jumped by 39% in the 6 months after the reform. New one-stop shops were launched for traders at the ports, cutting the time to import by 7 days and the time to export by 5. The first private credit bureau was established. And builders now face less bureaucracy in getting construction permits.

FIGURE 1.3
Making trade easier in India

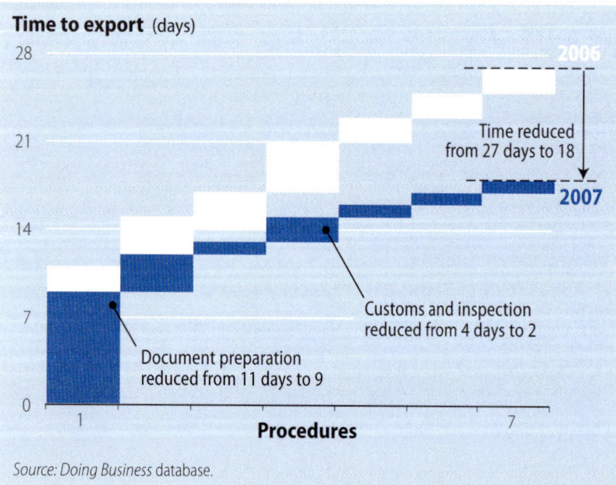

Source: Doing Business database.

Croatia is the runner-up, with reforms in 4 of the *Doing Business* areas. Two years ago registering a property in Croatia took 956 days. Now it takes 174. Croatia also sped company start-up, consolidating procedures at the one-stop shop and allowing pension and health services registration online. Two procedures and 5 days were cut from the process. Credit became easier to access: a new credit bureau got off the ground, and a unified registry now records all charges against movable property in one place. In the first 2 months €1.4 billion of credit was registered. Finally, amendments to the Croatian insolvency law introduced professional requirements for bankruptcy trustees and shortened timelines.

Large emerging economies—fast reformers

China, Egypt, India, Indonesia, Turkey and Vietnam all improved in the ease of doing business.

In China a new property law put private property rights on equal footing with state property rights. The law also expanded the range of assets that can be used as collateral to include inventory and accounts receivable. China also passed a new bankruptcy law. The law gives secured creditors priority to the proceeds from their collateral. And construction became easier, with electronic processing of building permits reducing delays by 2 weeks.

India rivaled this pace of reform. Traders can now submit customs declarations and pay customs fees online before the cargo arrives in port. It takes 18 days to meet all the administrative requirements to export—in 2006 it took 27 (figure 1.3). The credit bureau expanded to include payment histories on businesses as well as individuals. And reformers introduced an electronic collateral registry for security rights granted by companies.

Other big emerging markets also made large reforms. Russia established a new credit bureau. Indonesia strengthened investor protections and expanded credit information by removing the minimum size cutoff for loans covered by the public credit registry.

Vietnam also strengthened investor protections, with a new enterprise law and securities act. A secured transactions decree allows businesses to use a wider range of assets as collateral, easing access to credit. Nigeria introduced electronic procedures at the company registry and sped start-up time by 9 days. And reforms reduced the time to obtain building permits from 90 days to 30. Turkey cut its corporate income tax from 30% to 20% and introduced electronic customs procedures, reducing the time to export by 6 days and the time to import by 10.

Investors are taking note. They look for upside potential, and they find it in economies that are reforming—regardless of the starting point. Indeed, equity returns are highest in countries that are reforming the most (figure 1.4). With emerging markets aggressively improving their business regulations, there has hardly been a better time to invest.

Reform in Africa—uneven

Some African countries have reformed, led by Ghana and Kenya—both top 10 reformers. In southern Africa several have reformed, with Madagascar, Mauritius and Mozambique taking the lead (figure 1.5). Mauritius now ranks 27 on the ease of doing business, the highest among African countries. In West and Central Africa, however, little reform took place outside Burkina Faso and Ghana.

FIGURE 1.4

Shareholders benefit from reform

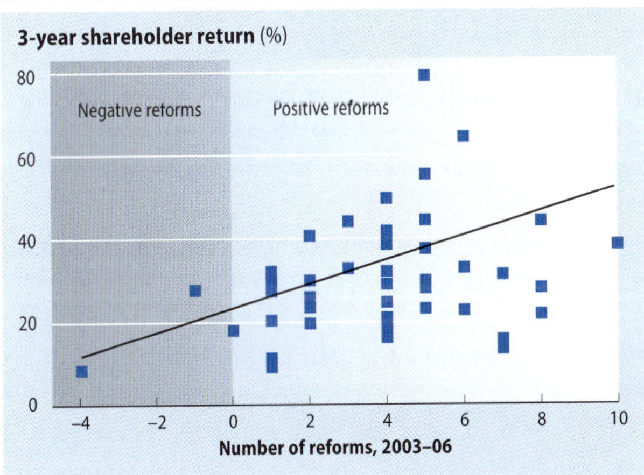

Source: Doing Business database, Morgan Stanley Capital International data.

Easing business entry—the most popular reform

Reforms to ease the entry of new firms were the most popular in 2006/07 (figure 1.6). Thirty-nine countries made start-up simpler, faster or cheaper. The second most popular were reforms to cut taxes and simplify their administration. Some reforms are harder, requiring new legislation and the political tradeoffs that come with it. Only 10 countries revised their bankruptcy laws. And the fewest positive reforms took place in the area of employing workers. Eight countries increased the flexibility of labor regulations; 4 made them more rigid.

The 3 boldest reforms, driving the biggest improvements in the *Doing Business* indicators:

- Saudi Arabia's easing of business start-up.
- Georgia's increase in investor protections.
- Russia's opening of its new credit bureau.

Saudi Arabia eliminated layers of bureaucracy that had previously made it one of the toughest places in the world to start a business. The reforms cut 6 procedures for forming a new company—speeding processes at the Ministry of Commerce, merging publication requirements and allowing social security registration online. The time for start-up dropped from 39 days to 15.

But most dramatic was Saudi Arabia's elimination of the minimum capital requirement. Saudi entrepreneurs once had to set aside $124,464—the fifth largest minimum capital requirement in the world. No more. New business owners can now put that capital to work immediately—hiring staff, renting office space and marketing new products.

Georgia made investing safer. Amendments to its securities law eliminated loopholes that allowed corporate insiders to expropriate minority investors. Reform-

FIGURE 1.5

Who reformed the most in Africa in 2006/07?

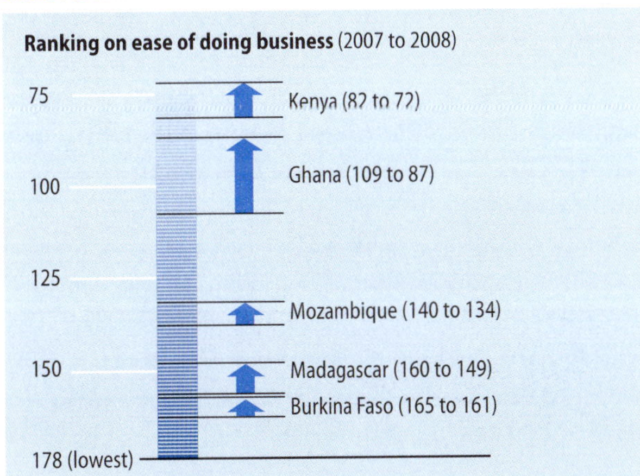

Source: Doing Business database.

FIGURE 1.6

200 reforms made business easier—27 made it more difficult

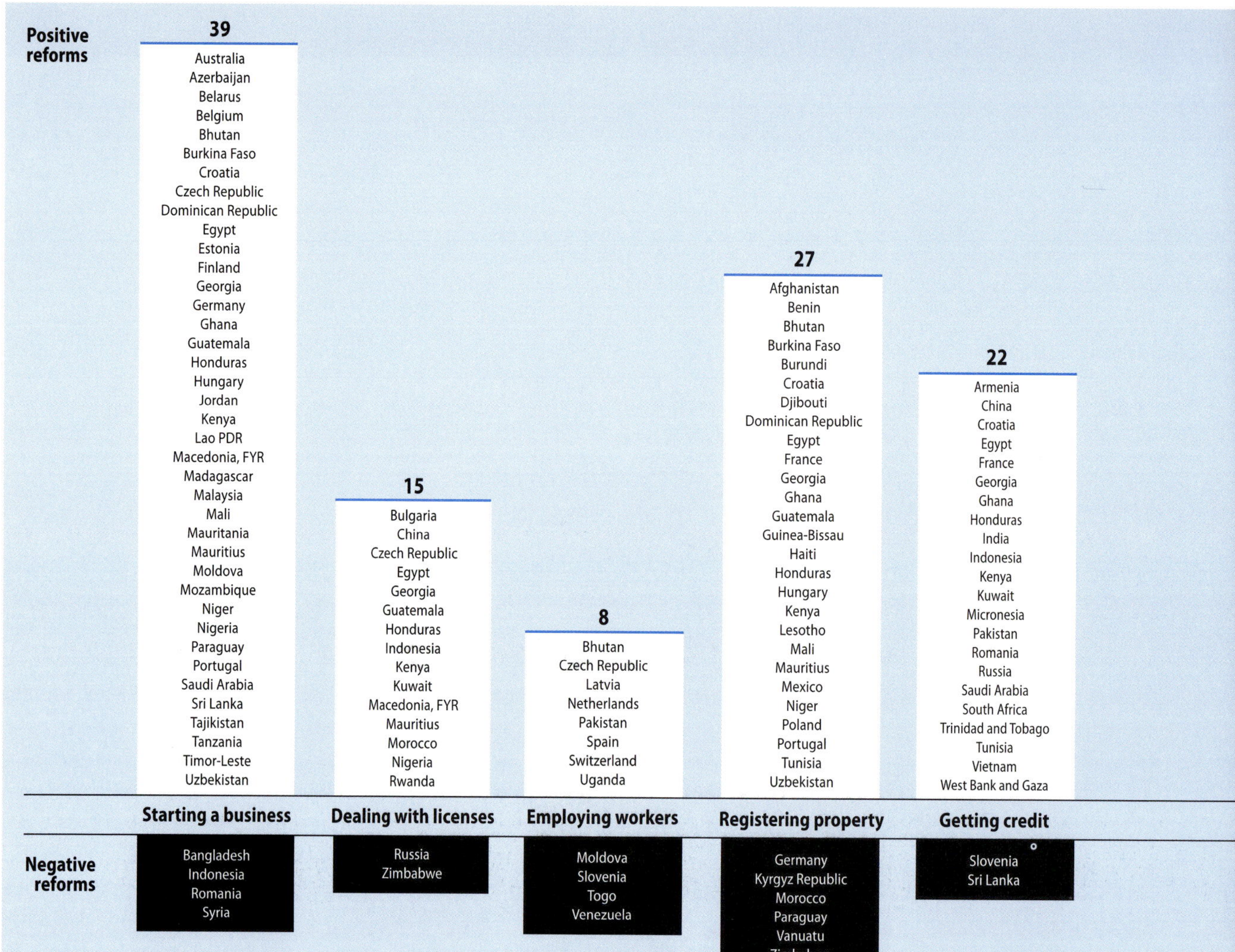

Source: Doing Business database.

ers increased disclosure requirements for directors' conflicts of interest, detailed stricter duties to the firm for directors and heightened penalties for self-dealing.

Russia's first credit bureau started up in 2006 and by July 2007 had extended its coverage to more than 6 million people. Before, banks had no central database to tap when judging a client's creditworthiness. Now they can turn to the new bureau for data on both individuals and firms—and for positive as well as negative information (for example, on payment history and number and frequency of late payments).

Some countries slipped backward. Venezuela had the largest negative reforms. Doing business there was already hard. In 2006/07 it got harder. Exporters now need a separate license for each transaction. To get the license, they must submit proof of identity and solvency—documents that themselves must be frequently renewed. The time to export stretched to 45 days, barely faster than in landlocked Burundi. But slow clerks need not worry about losing their job: Venezuela also expanded its ban on firing workers to cover anyone who earns less than 3 times the minimum wage.

Singapore—number 1, again

For the second year running, Singapore tops the rankings on the ease of doing business (table 1.2). New Zealand, the United States and Hong Kong (China) follow close behind. Denmark is next, demonstrating that countries can be business friendly and provide strong social protections.

Georgia and Saudi Arabia entered the top 25. Many countries with the most business-friendly regulations continued to reform, such as Australia, Denmark, the Netherlands, Norway and Switzerland. Some stopped—and slipped in the rankings. The message: if you are not reforming, another country will overtake you.

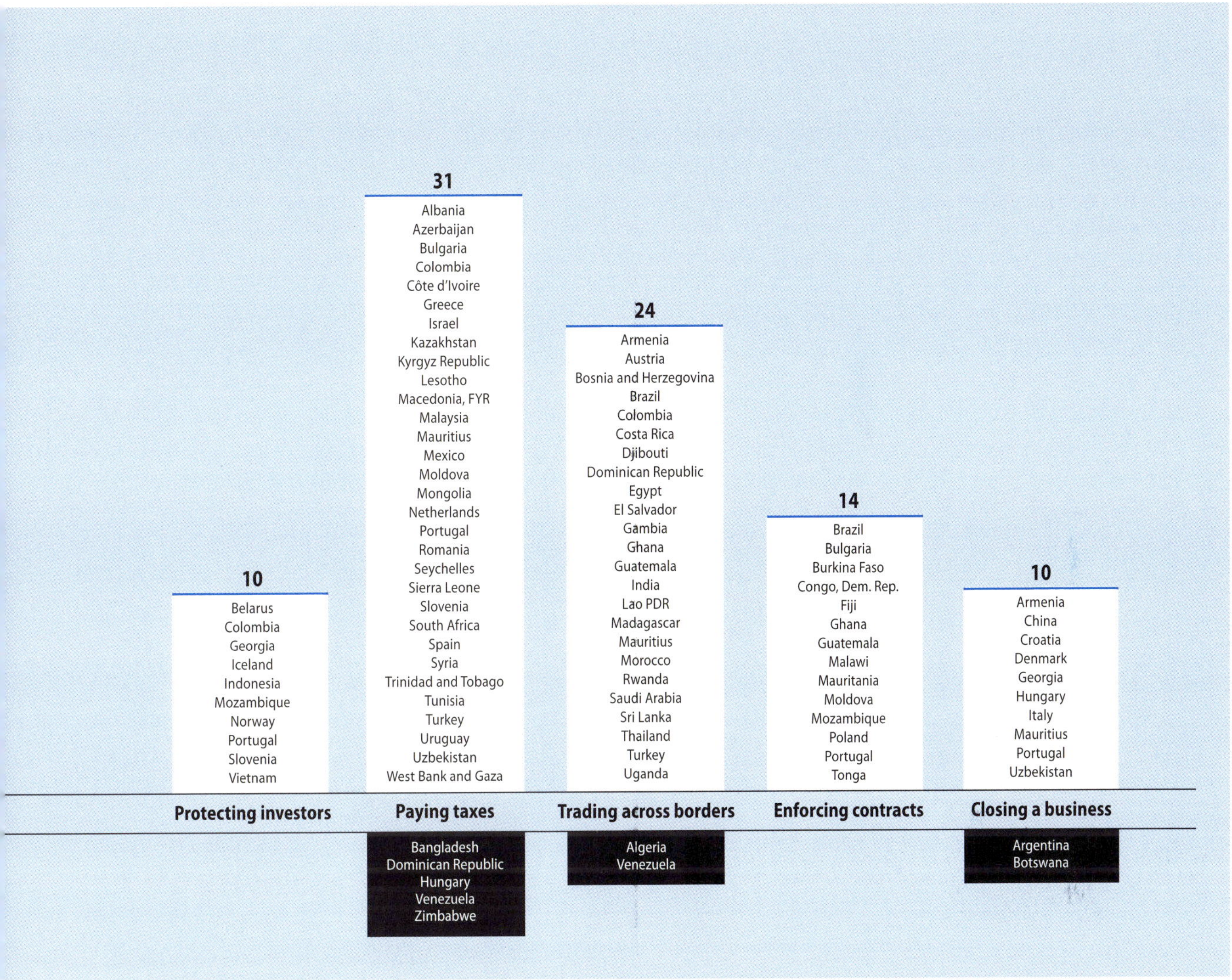

Rankings on the ease of doing business do not tell the whole story. The indicator is limited in scope: it covers only business regulations. It does not account for a country's proximity to large markets, the quality of its infrastructure services (other than those related to trading across borders), the security of property from theft and looting, the transparency of government procurement, macroeconomic conditions or the underlying strength of institutions.

Still, a high ranking on the ease of doing business does mean that the government has created a regulatory environment conducive to operating a business.

Opportunities for women

Payoffs from reform can be large. Higher rankings on the ease of doing business are associated with more growth, more jobs and a smaller share of the economy in the informal sector.[2] Take Mexico, where reforms cut the time to establish a business from 58 days to 27. A recent study reports the payoffs: the number of registered businesses rose by nearly 6%, employment increased by 2.6%, and prices fell by 1% because of the competition from new entrants.[3]

The benefits are especially large for women. Countries with higher scores on the ease of doing business have larger shares of women in the ranks of both entrepreneurs and workers (figure 1.7). Consider Uganda. Complex start-up regulations there allowed more contact between entrepreneurs and public officials—and more chances for bribery. Women were seen as easy targets: 43% of female entrepreneurs reported harassment from government officials, while only 25% of all entrepreneurs did. When reformers simplified business start-up, business registrations shot up. The increase in first-time business owners was 33% higher for women than men.

TABLE 1.2
Rankings on the ease of doing business

2008 rank	Economy	2008 rank	Economy	2008 rank	Economy
1	Singapore	61	Samoa	121	Honduras
2	New Zealand	62	Vanuatu	122	Brazil
3	United States	63	Jamaica	123	Indonesia
4	Hong Kong, China	64	St. Kitts and Nevis	124	Lesotho
5	Denmark	65	Panama	125	Algeria
6	United Kingdom	66	Colombia	126	Egypt
7	Canada	67	Trinidad and Tobago	127	Malawi
8	Ireland	68	United Arab Emirates	128	Ecuador
9	Australia	69	El Salvador	129	Morocco
10	Iceland	70	Grenada	130	Tanzania
11	Norway	71	Kazakhstan	131	Gambia
12	Japan	72	Kenya	132	Cape Verde
13	Finland	73	Kiribati	133	Philippines
14	Sweden	74	Poland	134	Mozambique
15	Thailand	75	Macedonia, FYR	135	Iran
16	Switzerland	76	Pakistan	136	Albania
17	Estonia	77	Dominica	137	Syria
18	Georgia	78	Brunei	138	Uzbekistan
19	Belgium	79	Solomon Islands	139	Ukraine
20	Germany	80	Jordan	140	Bolivia
21	Netherlands	81	Montenegro	141	Iraq
22	Latvia	82	Palau	142	Suriname
23	Saudi Arabia	83	China	143	Sudan
24	Malaysia	84	Papua New Guinea	144	Gabon
25	Austria	85	Lebanon	145	Cambodia
26	Lithuania	86	Serbia	146	Djibouti
27	Mauritius	87	Ghana	147	Comoros
28	Puerto Rico	88	Tunisia	148	Haiti
29	Israel	89	Marshall Islands	149	Madagascar
30	Korea	90	Seychelles	150	Rwanda
31	France	91	Vietnam	151	Benin
32	Slovakia	92	Moldova	152	Zimbabwe
33	Chile	93	Nicaragua	153	Tajikistan
34	St. Lucia	94	Kyrgyz Republic	154	Cameroon
35	South Africa	95	Swaziland	155	Côte d'Ivoire
36	Fiji	96	Azerbaijan	156	Togo
37	Portugal	97	Croatia	157	Mauritania
38	Spain	98	Uruguay	158	Mali
39	Armenia	99	Dominican Republic	159	Afghanistan
40	Kuwait	100	Greece	160	Sierra Leone
41	Antigua and Barbuda	101	Sri Lanka	161	Burkina Faso
42	Luxembourg	102	Ethiopia	162	Senegal
43	Namibia	103	Paraguay	163	São Tomé and Principe
44	Mexico	104	Guyana	164	Lao PDR
45	Hungary	105	Bosnia and Herzegovina	165	Equatorial Guinea
46	Bulgaria	106	Russia	166	Guinea
47	Tonga	107	Bangladesh	167	Angola
48	Romania	108	Nigeria	168	Timor-Leste
49	Oman	109	Argentina	169	Niger
50	Taiwan, China	110	Belarus	170	Liberia
51	Botswana	111	Nepal	171	Eritrea
52	Mongolia	112	Micronesia	172	Venezuela
53	Italy	113	Yemen	173	Chad
54	St. Vincent and the Grenadines	114	Guatemala	174	Burundi
55	Slovenia	115	Costa Rica	175	Congo, Rep.
56	Czech Republic	116	Zambia	176	Guinea-Bissau
57	Turkey	117	West Bank and Gaza	177	Central African Republic
58	Peru	118	Uganda	178	Congo, Dem. Rep.
59	Belize	119	Bhutan		
60	Maldives	120	India		

Note: The rankings for all economies are benchmarked to June 2007 and reported in the Country tables. Rankings on the ease of doing business are the average of the country rankings on the 10 topics covered in *Doing Business 2008*. See Ease of doing business for details.
Source: Doing Business database.

FIGURE 1.7
Greater ease of doing business, more women entrepreneurs and workers

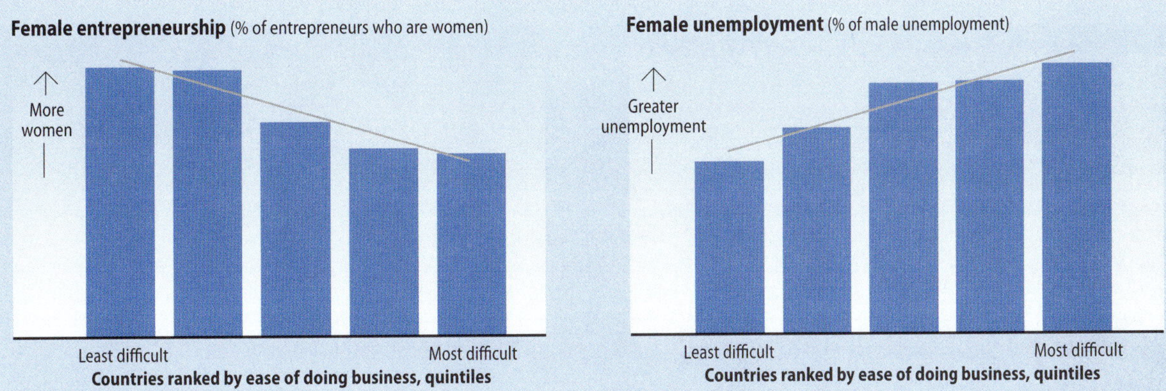

Note: Relationships are significant at the 1% level and remain significant when controlling for income per capita.
Source: Doing Business database; World Bank Enterprise Surveys; World Bank, World Development Indicators database.

In some countries explicit discrimination in laws compounds the effects of complex regulations. Women in the United Arab Emirates and Yemen are forbidden to work at night. And now so are women in Kuwait, thanks to a new law passed in June 2007. In Zimbabwe married women need permission from their husband to register land. In the Democratic Republic of Congo they need their husband's consent to start a business. Women run only 18% of the small businesses there. In neighboring Rwanda, which has no such regulations, women run more than 41% of small businesses.[4]

The idea behind some of these regulations may be to protect women. But they backfire, taking work away from willing workers and business opportunities away from entrepreneurs. Women end up in the informal economy: they are 3 times as likely as men to be hired informally in most developing countries. In these jobs they receive no social benefits. And if they are abused by their employer, they have limited legal recourse.

Some countries are taking action. Lesotho passed a law in November 2006 allowing married women to own and transfer property and engage in legal acts without their husband's signature. Before the reform the law classified women as legal minors.

What gets measured gets done

Publishing comparative data on the ease of doing business inspires governments to reform. Since its start in October 2003 the *Doing Business* project has inspired or informed 113 reforms around the world. In 2006 Georgia targeted the top 25 list and used *Doing Business* indicators as benchmarks of its progress. It now ranks 18 on the ease of doing business, and the government has set an even more ambitious goal. Saudi Arabia and Mauritius have targeted the top 10. Both have made tremendous progress: Saudi Arabia now ranks 23, and Mauritius 27.

Mozambique is reforming several aspects of its business environment, with the goal of reaching the top rank on the ease of doing business in southern Africa. The result: it rose by 6 places in the rankings.

Comparisons among cities within a country are even stronger drivers of reform. The time to obtain a business license in India ranges from 159 days in Bhubaneshwar to 522 in Ranchi. The time to register property, from 35 days in Hyderabad to 155 in Calcutta. A hypothetical Indian city with the country's top performance in each of the *Doing Business* indicators would rank 55 places higher on the ease of doing business than Mumbai. The Indian government is taking action. This year India is the top reformer in trading across borders (table 1.3).

TABLE 1.3
Top reformers in 2006/07 by indicator set

Starting a business	Saudi Arabia
Dealing with licenses	Georgia
Employing workers	Czech Republic
Registering property	Ghana
Getting credit	Croatia
Protecting investors	Georgia
Paying taxes	Bulgaria
Trading across borders	India
Enforcing contracts	Tonga
Closing a business	China

Source: Doing Business database.

Reforms go beyond the fixes that improve the *Doing Business* rankings. When the Philippines issued a decree to lower administrative fees, it covered all types of licenses and permits, not just those measured in *Doing Business.* In Malawi and Rwanda reformers are using the indicators to encourage simplification across all government agencies. Kenya is reforming all business licenses.

To help reformers, this year the *Doing Business* project published a book of 11 case studies of successful reforms.[5] These span the globe—from El Salvador to Serbia, from Egypt to Nigeria—and show what it takes to succeed. In cooperation with the U.S. Agency for International Development, *Doing Business* also created a prize to recognize leading reformers. The first one went to Zurab Nogaideli, the prime minister of Georgia.[6] Since then, several reformist governments—such as those in Azerbaijan, Guatemala and Mozambique—have studied the Georgian reform experience for ideas on how to reform.

Notes

1. World Bank (2006b, p. 5).
2. Djankov, McLiesh and Ramalho (2006) and World Bank (2005a).
3. Bruhn (2007).
4. The percentages of businesses run by women are from the 2006 World Bank Enterprise Surveys, available at http://www.enterprisesurveys.org.
5. World Bank (2007a).
6. For more on those recognized as leading reformers, go to http://www.reformersclub.org.

Starting a business

Starting a business in the Democratic Republic of Congo is not easy. It takes 13 procedures and 155 days—and costs 5 times the annual income per capita. It's worse for women: they need the consent of their husband. If you are a single woman, or if your husband refuses consent or suffers from mental illness, a judge decides whether you can become a businesswoman. The result: only 18% of small businesses are run by women. In neighboring Rwanda, which has no such regulations, more than 41% are.[1]

Thirty-nine countries made it easier for entrepreneurs to start a new business in 2006/07. Eighteen of them reformed for the second year in a row, including Burkina Faso, Egypt, Guatemala and Madagascar. Eastern Europe and Central Asia had 11 reforms. So did Africa, keeping up its growing pace of reform. Mauritius and Georgia entered the top 10 on the ease of starting a business (table 2.1).

Reform pays off. In 2005 Mexico was among the top reformers in simplifying business entry. It cut the time needed to establish a business from 58 days to 27. A recent study reports the results: the number of registered businesses rose by nearly 6%, employment increased by 2.6%, and prices fell by 1% because of the competition from new entrants.[2] Another study estimates that the size of the informal sector in Peru would drop from 60% of the economy to 37% if entry regulations were as simple as those in the United States.[3] Much remains to be done: starting a business takes less than a week in New York, 72 days in Lima.

Cumbersome start-up procedures prevent people from getting out of poverty. Some entrepreneurs still

TABLE 2.1
Where is it easy to start a business—and where not?

Easiest	Rank	Most difficult	Rank
Australia	1	Syria	169
Canada	2	Haiti	170
New Zealand	3	Guinea	171
United States	4	Equatorial Guinea	172
Ireland	5	Angola	173
United Kingdom	6	Eritrea	174
Puerto Rico	7	Yemen	175
Mauritius	8	Togo	176
Singapore	9	Chad	177
Georgia	10	Guinea-Bissau	178

Note: Rankings are the average of the country rankings on the procedures, time, cost and paid-in minimum capital for starting a business. See Data notes for details.
Source: Doing Business database.

FIGURE 2.1
More entry after reform

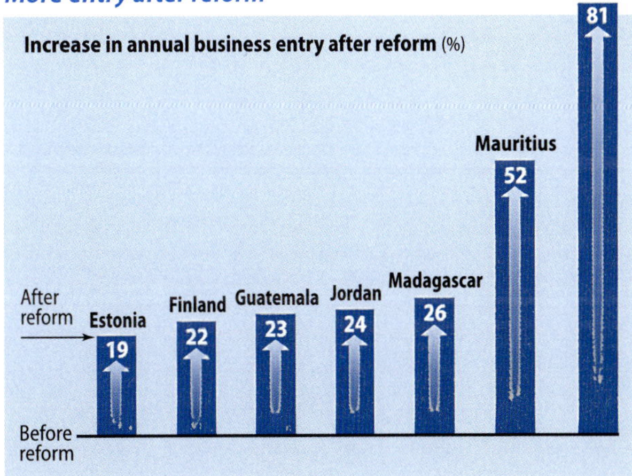

Source: Doing Business database.

start businesses, but only informal ones. Without access to courts and credit, and in constant fear of inspections, informal businesses remain small. A survey in Guinea-Bissau found that, controlling for industry, formal businesses hire 4 times as many workers and produce 4 times as much output as informal ones.[4] That's why many informal businesses are first in the queue when reform makes it easier to legalize operations, resulting in big jumps in registrations (figure 2.1).

And once a large number of informal businesses legalize their operations, staying informal is no longer profitable.[5] Most clients require receipts—because otherwise they'll lose value added tax rebates and other tax benefits. In a short time informality ceases to be an issue. In Slovakia less than 2% of businesses now see informal competition as an issue. In 1999 a third did. Since then Slovakia has slashed the days to start a business from 103 to 25.

Who is reforming?

Saudi Arabia was the top reformer in business start-up in 2006/07 (figure 2.2). Last year it had the fifth largest paid-in minimum capital requirement in the world, at $124,464. In June 2007 the country scrapped that requirement. It also merged publication requirements, combined several procedures at the Ministry of Commerce and launched online social security registration. That reduced the number of procedures from 13 to 7, the time from 39 days to 15, and the cost from 59% of income per capita to 32%.

Four of the top 10 reformers were in Eastern Europe and Central Asia. FYR Macedonia, a repeat top reformer, abolished the paid-in minimum capital requirement. So did Georgia. Belarus launched a one-stop shop that cut 6 procedures and 3 weeks from the start-up process. Estonia cut start-up time from 35 days to 7 by introducing standard articles of association, available on the registry's website. Notaries are now optional, and registration fees are a fixed amount rather than a percentage of capital. These changes cut start-up costs in half.

Another 7 countries in Eastern Europe and Central Asia introduced substantial reforms. Among these, Hungary created standard documents. Croatia streamlined processes at the one-stop shop. Tajikistan simplified licensing requirements, saving entrepreneurs more than 2 weeks. Since the start of *Doing Business* in 2003, 24 of the region's 28 countries have simplified start-up. After 5 years of reform the average time to start a business is now 26 days, approaching that in OECD high-income countries (figure 2.3).

But catching up with rich countries is increasingly tough—they are reforming too. In 2006/07 Portugal eliminated outdated start-up formalities such as registering company books. Belgium—another repeat top 10 reformer—and Germany made registration and publication electronic. Finland reduced its minimum capital requirement by almost 70%. Australia cut registration fees in half. Its start-up process is the least burdensome (table 2.2).

Most African countries focused on improving technology at the business registry. Mauritius launched a virtual one-stop shop linking the commercial registry and tax and local authorities through a central electronic database. Requiring 6 procedures and 7 days, business entry in Mauritius is as easy as in the United Kingdom.

FIGURE 2.2
Top 10 reformers in business start-up

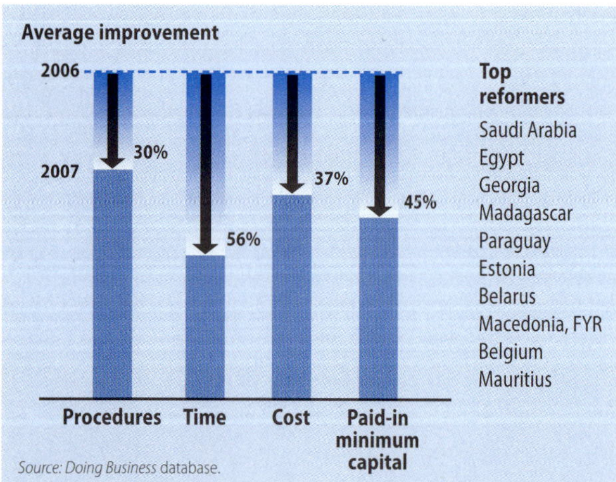

Source: Doing Business database.

FIGURE 2.3
Biggest improvement in Eastern Europe & Central Asia

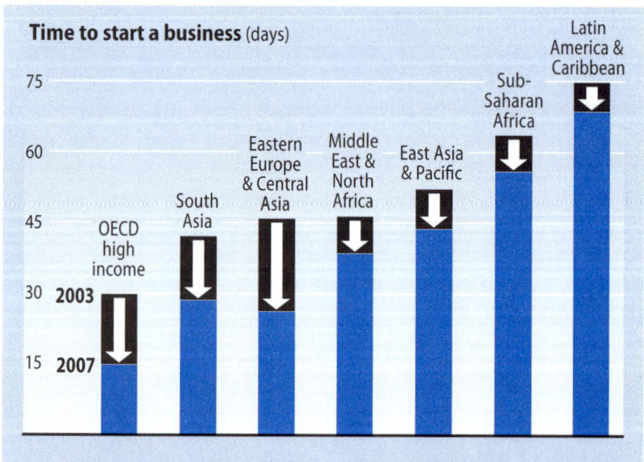

Source: Doing Business database.

TABLE 2.2
Who regulates business start-up the least—and who the most?

Procedures (number)

Fewest		Most	
Australia	2	Bolivia	15
Canada	2	Montenegro	15
New Zealand	2	Philippines	15
Belgium	3	Venezuela	16
Finland	3	Guinea-Bissau	17
Sweden	3	Brazil	18
Afghanistan	4	Brunei	18
Denmark	4	Uganda	18
Ireland	4	Chad	19
Tonga	4	Equatorial Guinea	20

Time (days)

Least		Most	
Australia	2	Brunei	116
Canada	3	Angola	119
Belgium	4	Equatorial Guinea	136
Iceland	5	Venezuela	141
Singapore	5	São Tomé and Principe	144
Denmark	6	Brazil	152
Turkey	6	Congo, Dem. Rep.	155
United States	6	Haiti	202
France	7	Guinea-Bissau	233
Madagascar	7	Suriname	694

Cost (% of income per capita)

Least		Most	
Denmark	0.0	Djibouti	206.6
New Zealand	0.1	Togo	245.7
Ireland	0.3	Burundi	251.0
Sweden	0.6	Guinea-Bissau	255.5
United States	0.7	Gambia	279.0
Puerto Rico	0.8	West Bank and Gaza	280.4
United Kingdom	0.8	Angola	343.7
Singapore	0.8	Congo, Dem. Rep.	487.2
Australia	0.8	Liberia	493.3
Canada	0.9	Sierra Leone	1,075.2

Paid-in minimum capital

Most	% of income per capita	US$
Central African Republic	531	1,912
Oman	542	51,947
Togo	546	1,912
Timor-Leste	595	5,000
Niger	736	1,912
Jordan	795	21,157
Ethiopia	960	1,728
Guinea-Bissau	1,007	1,912
Yemen	2,003	15,225
Syria	3,673	57,670

Note: Sixty-five countries have no paid-in minimum capital requirement.
Source: Doing Business database.

TABLE 2.3
One-stop shops—the most popular reform in 2006/07

Created or improved one-stop shop
Belarus, Burkina Faso, Croatia, Egypt, Guatemala, Jordan, Madagascar, Mauritius, Paraguay, Uzbekistan

Sped registration through administrative reforms
Bhutan, Dominican Republic, Malaysia, Mali, Moldova, Mozambique, Nigeria, Saudi Arabia, Sri Lanka, Timor-Leste

Streamlined or abolished licensing procedures
Bhutan, Ghana, Honduras, Kenya, Lao PDR, Mauritius, Tajikistan, Tanzania

Simplified and standardized document requirements at registry
Burkina Faso, Estonia, Finland, Hungary, Portugal, Uzbekistan

Abolished or reduced paid-in minimum capital requirement
Egypt, Finland, Georgia, FYR Macedonia, Saudi Arabia

Introduced online procedures
Belgium, Estonia, Germany, Hungary, Mauritius

Cut or simplified publication
Egypt, Germany, Mozambique, Portugal, Saudi Arabia

Reduced costs or taxes
Australia, Mauritania, Mozambique, Niger

Reformed company seal requirement
Azerbaijan, Sri Lanka, Tanzania

Introduced statutory time limits on registration
Czech Republic, Uzbekistan

Source: Doing Business database.

Nigeria used computerization to further speed company name verification and registration. Ghana's computerization of its registry is expediting name searches and application processes. Thanks to this as well as licensing reforms, delays fell by 39 days. Tanzania is computerizing its registry too. It also reduced start-up fees from 92% of annual income to 47%. Kenya improved processes at the company registry, saving entrepreneurs 10 days.

Other African countries cut unnecessary procedures (table 2.3). Burkina Faso simplified documentation requirements. Madagascar, again a top reformer, changed publication formalities and dropped the validation of signatures at the mayor's office. It cut 10 procedures to 5, and the time from 3 weeks to 1. Mozambique revised its 1888 commercial code and reformed the business registry. Entrepreneurs no longer have to wait for 3 months to publish their articles of association in the official gazette; the registry publishes extracts online. And the use of notaries is now optional. Start-up cost dropped by two-thirds, and the time from 113 days to 29. Not all news is good for businesses in Mozambique: the minimum capital requirement was raised tenfold and is now equivalent to the average yearly income.

In Latin America and the Caribbean, the Dominican Republic, Guatemala and Honduras reformed for the second year running, joined by Paraguay. More is needed. Latin American entrepreneurs starting a business face 10 procedures on average, compared with 6 in OECD high-income countries. More than half the procedures come after the business is registered, including municipal licenses and inspections. In 2006/07 Honduras reformed municipal licenses and reduced start-up time by 3 weeks. Paraguay took a different approach: it launched a one-stop shop, merging procedures and cutting the time in half—to 35 days.

Egypt was the second biggest reformer in the world. It slashed its minimum capital requirement from 50,000 Egyptian pounds to 1,000. The one-stop shop now processes the tax registration, the publication and the chamber of commerce membership. The reforms cut start-up cost and time by more than half, and reduced 10 procedures to 7. Elsewhere in the Middle East, Jordan improved the operation of its one-stop shop but failed to reduce the minimum capital requirement. At 8 times the annual income, few Jordanians can afford it.

Sri Lanka made the most progress in South Asia. A new companies act eliminated burdensome approvals and introduced a flat registration fee. Company seals and notaries were made optional. Procedures were reduced from 8 to 5, and the time for start-up from 50 days to 39. Bhutan abolished 2 procedures and sped registration. Pakistan simplified tax registration. India is implementing electronic filing.

East Asia made the fewest reforms in 2006/07. Malaysia sped name checking and registration, reducing delays by a week. Timor-Leste eliminated approvals by the Ministry of Land. Indonesia slipped backward, adding a week of delays with additional approvals at the regional level. It now has the longest time for business start-up among Asian economies.

What to reform?

Since 2003, 93 countries have simplified business start-up through 146 reforms. Here are the 5 most successful reforms:

- Cut the minimum capital requirement.
- Introduce a one-stop shop.
- Standardize incorporation documents.
- Cut antiquated formalities.
- Allow online start-up.

Cut the minimum capital requirement

The easiest reform of business entry—one that can be done with the stroke of a pen—is to cut the capital requirement. Some countries justify the capital requirement as protecting creditors, as protecting the company against insolvency and as protecting consumers against bad products. But this makes little sense. Lenders base their decisions on commercial risk, not whether a business meets a government-imposed capital requirement. And in many countries minimum capital can be paid with in-kind contributions or withdrawn immediately after registration—hardly of value in insolvency. Recovery rates in bankruptcy are no higher in countries with capital requirements than in those without.

In about 20 economies the capital requirement is still a major obstacle to starting a business. In these, an entrepreneur needs to put up at least 3 times the average annual income to register—and often much more. Aside from Timor-Leste, all are in Africa and the Middle East. Syria has the highest requirement, with minimum capital equivalent to 37 times the annual income per capita (see table 2.2). Yemen comes next, requiring 20 times the average annual income. Few Yemenis can afford to operate a business legally. The result is widespread informality, the highest in the region.

Here's a question for the governments of Syria, Yemen, Guinea-Bissau, Ethiopia, Jordan, Niger, Timor-Leste, Togo, Oman, the Central African Republic, Djibouti, Mauritania, Eritrea, Guinea, Mali, Burkina Faso, Chad, Benin, Madagascar and the United Arab Emirates: if a high minimum capital requirement is beneficial, why doesn't a single rich country have one?

Introduce a one-stop shop

One-stop shops have been the most common reform in business start-up—24 countries have created one since 2003. On average this has cut 5 procedures from the start-up process and more than halved delays. One-stop shops can show results quickly. Morocco created one in 6 months; Cairo and Alexandria, in Egypt, did so in less than a year.

Reformers have chosen different ways to merge procedures. In Eastern Europe and Central Asia most countries—including Belarus, Georgia, Hungary, Kazakhstan, Lithuania, FYR Macedonia and Russia—have delegated formalities such as tax and statistical registrations to the company registrar. In Latin America one-stop shops bring officials from different agencies together in one location—such as in El Salvador, Guatemala, Nicaragua and Paraguay. This arrangement works when these officials have decision power. That's

FIGURE 2.4
Big gains from standard documents

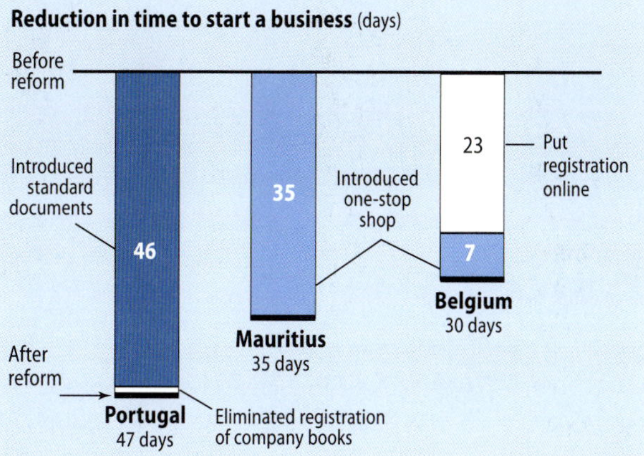

Source: Doing Business database.

not always the case: in Nicaragua the one-stop shop has to forward applications to other agencies and await their approval. Delays have hardly budged.

Reformers may use one-stop shops to create momentum for bigger reforms. Portugal created its first one-stop shop in 1998—but its biggest drop in time came only in 2005, when it introduced standard incorporation documents (figure 2.4). Before, processing start-up applications took 3 weeks.

Standardize incorporation documents

In El Salvador 70% of new business applications are rejected for flawed or insufficient paperwork. In Kazakhstan, 65%. By contrast, the rejection rate is only 3% in Canada, 8% in the United Kingdom and 10% in Mauritius.

Why the difference? Standard incorporation documents. With these, entrepreneurs ensure legality without visiting notaries and lawyers. And the workload eases at the registry, preventing errors and speeding processing. After Estonia introduced standard documents, processing time at the registry fell from 15 days to 1. Entrepreneurs saved another 2 weeks by avoiding the use of notaries. Another 64 countries have standard forms—including China, Egypt, Malaysia, Oman, Slovakia and South Africa.

Cut antiquated formalities

Some requirements are leftovers from a bygone era. These should be cut. One example is the requirement for a company seal or stamp—still on the books in 81 countries. In 7 of these, entrepreneurs have to get official approval to make a seal. In Lao PDR the Ministry of Industry and Commerce designs the seal, while the Ministry of Public Security issues a permit to the entrepreneur to carve and register it.

In earlier centuries a seal symbolized the legal identity of a business and authenticated all its contracts. Now most documents are sent electronically. More than 100 countries have regulations allowing electronic signatures. These cost nothing and are more difficult to forge.

Allow online start-up

In Denmark an entrepreneur can start a business without leaving the house. Using the Internet, the entrepreneur can obtain a digital signature, register with the commercial registry and tax authority and submit the incorporation documents. All data are automatically validated—no public officials are involved. The entrepreneur receives a business identification number online, and the company notice is published on the web.

Making registration electronic is one of the most effective ways to speed start-up. Since 2003, 13 countries have introduced electronic registration, including Belgium, Ireland, Mauritius and Norway. This cut the average time to start a business in those countries from 40 days to 17. And with no contact between the entrepreneur and the public official, no bribes can change hands.

Online start-up works best in countries with high Internet penetration and laws allowing electronic signatures. As a start, countries can introduce online name search and publication or computerize registration records. Since 2005 Germany, FYR Macedonia, Mozambique and Serbia have made the company establishment notice electronic, saving up to 3 months in waiting time. Online name checking is now available in Croatia, Moldova, Nigeria and Vietnam. Such reforms can be cheap. When Guatemala made registry records electronic, it took 5 months to scan nearly 2 million files, all at a cost of $100,000.

Notes

1. The percentages of businesses run by women are from the 2006 World Bank Enterprise Surveys (http://www.enterprisesurveys.org).
2. Bruhn (2007).
3. Antunes and Cavalcanti (2007).
4. These numbers are calculated based on data from the 2006 World Bank Enterprise Surveys for Africa (http://www.enterprisesurveys.org).
5. Masatlioglu and Rigolini (2006).

Dealing with licenses

Sextus Julius Frontinus, water commissioner of Rome in AD 97, wrote the first regulation for the maintenance of the city water system. It starts with this: "Anyone who wishes to draw water for private use must make an official application and deliver in person to the commissioner a written authorization from the emperor."[1] The regulation was prompted by widespread "puncturing" of the aqueducts—illegal water connections. Sadly, it could not be enforced. With more than a million citizens living in ancient Rome, the emperor would have spent most of his time reviewing water applications.

The new inspection rules for construction in Harare would have made Frontinus proud. In an effort to prevent illegal construction, the chief building inspector or his deputy now conducts all building inspections. The downside is a mounting backlog, in a city where it already takes 952 days and $38,347 to obtain all construction approvals. The official construction sector has shrunk to 2% of GDP, and the government periodically bulldozes illegally built houses to show resolve. Zimbabwe ranks 172 on the ease of dealing with licenses (table 3.1).

Georgia used to be like Zimbabwe. Just 3 years ago getting a construction permit for a commercial warehouse in Tbilisi required 29 different procedures. Before even applying for the permit a builder needed permission from agencies as diverse as the Center of Archaeology at the Academy of Science and the Inspector of Sanitary Observation. Illegal construction activity was widespread. In 2004 less than 45% of ongoing construction projects in Tbilisi had permits.

Things have changed. Georgia was one of the top reformers in business licensing in each of the past 3

TABLE 3.1
Where is it easy to deal with licenses—and where not?

Easiest	Rank	Most difficult	Rank
St. Vincent and the Grenadines	1	Burkina Faso	169
New Zealand	2	Tanzania	170
Belize	3	Burundi	171
Marshall Islands	4	Zimbabwe	172
Singapore	5	Kazakhstan	173
Denmark	6	Ukraine	174
St. Kitts and Nevis	7	China	175
Maldives	8	Liberia	176
Kenya	9	Russia	177
Micronesia	10	Eritrea	178

Note: Rankings are the average of the country rankings on the procedures, time and cost to comply with formalities to build a warehouse. See Data notes for details.
Source: Doing Business database.

FIGURE 3.1
More construction permits issued in Georgia since reform

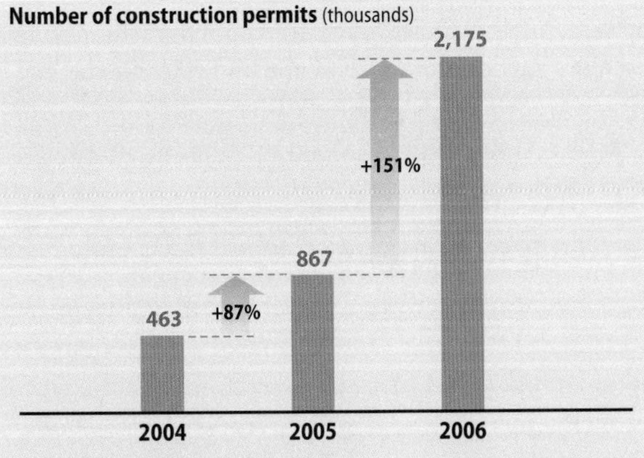

Source: Bagaudinova, Omran and Shavurov (2007).

years, reducing the types of activities subject to licensing from 909 to 159. In the construction industry (which *Doing Business* studies as an example of licensing) Georgia eliminated many of the approvals required to obtain a construction permit and introduced a one-stop shop for licensing, a "silence is consent" rule and statutory time limits—while maintaining procedures necessary for regulating in the public interest. The number of procedures needed to build a warehouse dropped to 12. The time required fell by nearly 3 months. The approval process for building a warehouse in Georgia is now more efficient than in all EU countries except Denmark. The result: in 2006 the number of construction permits issued in Georgia was 151% higher than in 2005 and 370% higher than in 2004 (figure 3.1). Construction grew from 6.4% of the Georgian economy in 2003 to more than 9% in 2006.

The transition to legal construction is not without pain. On July 20, 2007, the residents of downtown Tbilisi woke to the sound of sirens. Fire brigades had begun demolishing a 13-story building that had gone up before the reform and was now in danger of collapsing because of faulty engineering. The building had no project or operating license—and didn't even show up in the city plan. Yet it towered over the surrounding houses, kept from falling over by steel beams. To avoid the many approval procedures, the building company had simply paid off the mayor. Who loses out? The people who bought apartments and now must find a new place to live.[2]

Who is reforming?

Fifteen countries made it easier to comply with building requirements in 2006/07. Eastern Europe had the biggest reforms—in Bulgaria, the Czech Republic, Georgia and FYR Macedonia. Africa followed, with reforms in Kenya, Mauritius, Nigeria and Rwanda. The Middle East and North Africa was next, with reforms in Egypt, Kuwait and Morocco. Three countries—Georgia, Guatemala and Kenya—reformed for the second year in a row.

Some countries reviewed all business licenses required and eliminated unnecessary ones. Kazakhstan cut the number of licensed activities from 426 to 100. Uzbekistan extended the minimum term for a business license from 1 year to 5. And it now allows 13 business activities—including tourism, auditing, brokerage services and securities market operations—to be licensed for life. Kenya eliminated 110 licenses and simplified 8 others. The government plans to cut another 314 licenses and simplify 599 more.

"I recently received a call from the city council to follow up on plans I had submitted—completely unheard of before," comments a Kenyan architect. Such services have become more common since the minister of housing and lands launched a rapid response initiative in November 2006. Getting a building permit used to take 80 days. It required clearances from 6 agencies and review by a ministerial committee. The new initiative removed the committee review, shortening the time to obtain a permit by 30 days (figure 3.2).

Simplifying procedures was the most popular reform in construction licensing in 2006/07 (table 3.2). Mauritius combined its development and building per-

FIGURE 3.2

Cutting time to obtain licenses

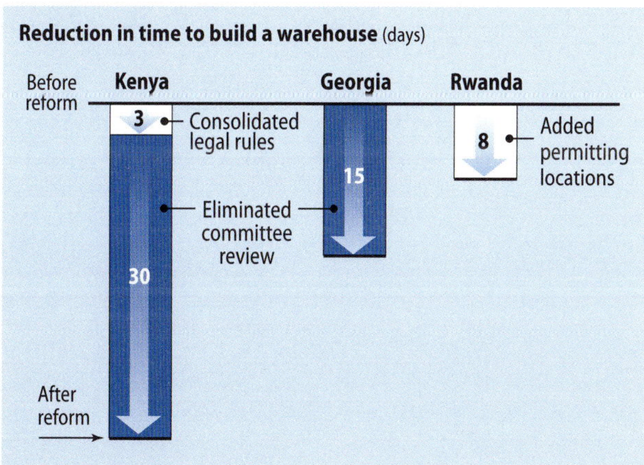

Source: Doing Business database.

TABLE 3.2

Simplifying licensing—the most popular reform in 2006/07

Simplified licensing and inspection procedures
Bulgaria, Czech Republic, Georgia, Guatemala, Indonesia, Kenya, Mauritius, Rwanda

Established statutory time limits for issuing licenses
FYR Macedonia, Mauritius, Nigeria

Introduced electronic processing of applications
China, Honduras, Kuwait, Morocco

Adopted new building code
Czech Republic, Nigeria

Introduced fast-track procedures
Czech Republic, Georgia

Introduced private inspections
Czech Republic

Lowered fees
Egypt

Source: Doing Business database.

TABLE 3.3
Who regulates licensing the least—and who the most?

Procedures (number)

Fewest		Most	
Denmark	6	Brunei	32
New Zealand	7	Burkina Faso	32
Vanuatu	7	Guinea	32
Sweden	8	Tajikistan	32
Chad	9	El Salvador	34
Grenada	9	Czech Republic	36
Maldives	9	China	37
St. Lucia	9	Kazakhstan	38
Jamaica	10	Sierra Leone	47
Kenya	10	Russia	54

Time (days)

Least		Most	
Korea	34	Ukraine	429
Finland	38	Suriname	431
United States	40	Bosnia and Herzegovina	467
Vanuatu	51	Lesotho	601
Marshall Islands	55	Côte d'Ivoire	628
Solomon Islands	62	Iran	670
New Zealand	65	Russia	704
Belize	66	Cambodia	709
Denmark	69	Zimbabwe	952
St. Kitts and Nevis	72	Haiti	1,179

Cost (% of income per capita)

Least		Most	
United Arab Emirates	1.5	Kazakhstan	2,130
Brunei	5.2	Tanzania	2,366
Trinidad and Tobago	5.9	Guinea-Bissau	2,607
Palau	6.1	Serbia	2,713
St. Vincent and the Grenadines	9.2	Niger	2,824
Malaysia	10.0	Russia	3,788
Hungary	10.4	Burundi	9,939
Thailand	10.7	Zimbabwe	11,799
Australia	13.2	Afghanistan	21,231
United States	13.4	Liberia	61,049

Source: Doing Business database.

mits into one. The dual permit is now issued in 2 weeks, reducing the time to complete formalities by 55 days. In Guatemala the Ministry of Environment eliminated duplications in procedures by placing its staff in municipal offices and the Ministry of Healthcare, cutting the time by 60 days. Russia abolished the notification permit required to begin construction (which was separate from the construction permit), saving entrepreneurs 20 days. But more needs to be done in a country where the permitting process still takes almost 2 years.

Other countries focused on cutting delays. The Czech Republic streamlined provisions of its new building code, speeding construction approvals by 50 days. Builders can now apply for 2 permits at the same time, and a simple notification has replaced the occupancy permit. Indonesia introduced a simplified process and new temporary permits that allow construction to begin while the full permit is being approved, cutting the time to obtain a building permit from 49 days to 21. In FYR Macedonia it now takes only 1 day to obtain proof of landownership—59 days less than in 2006. Rwanda sped the issuance of building and occupancy permits by 24 days after transferring authorities from the prefecture to the municipality. Nigeria shifted approval to local authorities and equipped their staff with computers and training, shortening the time for building authorizations from 90 days to 42.

Another popular reform was to make processes electronic. Honduras launched electronic processing of applications for fixed telephone lines, cutting the time for approval from 2 weeks to 1. Kuwait installed a new automated system in all agencies responsible for issuing technical approvals. The time to obtain an approval for a phone line dropped from 30 days to 20, for electricity from 2 weeks to 1, and for a water plan from 14 days to 5. In China, Beijing and Shanghai now process applications for construction permits electronically and allow construction companies to apply for safety certificates online, reducing delays by 2 weeks. But more remains to be done: to complete construction permitting in China still takes 37 procedures and 336 days (table 3.3).

Morocco set up an electronic one-stop shop for construction permits at the end of 2006, reducing the time to obtain a building permit from 30 days to 20. More can be done. The commission that issues approvals reviews projects by neighborhood. Two weeks can pass waiting for your neighborhood's turn in the commission's schedule.

What to reform?

In the past 3 years 42 countries have reformed their construction licensing regulations. Here are the 5 most successful reforms:

- Reduce licensing requirements.
- Make information easily available.
- Introduce online license applications.
- Curb inspections.
- Consolidate project clearances.

Reduce licensing requirements

Reducing business licensing requirements demands action by many ministries. Here are 2 ways to make it happen. First, make the ministry of finance or the prime minister's office responsible for implementation, since other ministries respond best when their budgets depend on it. Second, commit to a target reduction in the administrative costs of issuing and regulating licenses and set up a measuring system to ensure that it is achieved. This holds regulators accountable.

The Netherlands, with the best such reform yet, has done both. The government set a target of reducing the administrative burden by 25% by 2007. The minister of finance was responsible for achieving the target, reporting to parliament every 6 months. Uncooperative ministries could see their budget cut. An independent agency, the Advisory Board on Administrative Burden, was established to monitor progress and publicize its findings. The program aims to save €4 billion. Its savings from streamlining tax requirements alone are estimated at €600 million. And Dutch entrepreneurs have saved €11.3 million from simplifications in construction licensing.[3] The advisory board also vets new regulatory proposals before they reach parliament—to stop creeping reregulation, a common problem.

Other European countries are starting to benefit from this experience, as Dutch reformers are lobbying the European Union to adopt similar targets. Several governments—in the Czech Republic, Denmark and the United Kingdom—have already done so. The European Commission recently announced a target of reducing administrative burdens by 25%—similar to the Dutch approach. Since EU regulations account for about 40% of all business regulations in the 27 member countries, there is a lot to gain.[4] Comprehensive reforms like these are not just for rich countries. With its plan to cut 424 unnecessary licenses well under way, Kenya is the first African country to show how poor ones can gain too.

Make information easily available

In China public utilities are now required to publish online their service fees, time limits for issuing approvals and ways to launch complaints. Another way to save entrepreneurs time: help them navigate the process for a building permit by making all the forms and requirements—including step-by-step charts on procedures—available at municipal offices. When Latvia did this, it cut processing time by 2 months. FYR Macedonia, as part of its recent reforms, distributed an electronic construction permitting package with documents and manuals to all 84 of its municipalities, along with posters and flyers explaining each step for applicants.

Introduce online license applications

In Singapore builders submit all permit applications electronically. Developers in Austria, Denmark, Iceland, Malaysia, Norway and the United States also complete their applications online. Some developing countries with adequate Internet penetration—such as El Salvador, Honduras and Mexico—are introducing online systems too. This reform saves time for both entrepreneurs and government officials. It also removes the contact between them—and the chance for bribe payments along with it.

Curb inspections

In Burkina Faso inspectors visit construction sites every 2 weeks and charge $240 in fees. In Denmark and Singapore there is only one inspection and it's free. But no one would argue that buildings in Copenhagen and Singapore are less safe than those in Ouagadougou.

Inspections are needed to ensure construction quality. But in many countries inspection fees and fines are viewed as an important source of government revenue. That needs to change. Recent studies show that eliminating unnecessary and redundant procedures can increase revenue. Kenya reported a revenue increase of up to 33% after replacing dozens of local permits with a single business permit.[5]

One way to make inspections more efficient is to privatize them. The Czech Republic just did so, by creating a new independent profession—authorized inspectors. By hiring an authorized inspector, an entrepreneur can speed the process of getting a building permit by up to 5 weeks. The inspector issues a certificate confirming that the project documentation is in compliance with the building code and that the building can be constructed.

FIGURE 3.3
Construction licensing in India—fastest in Bhubaneshwar

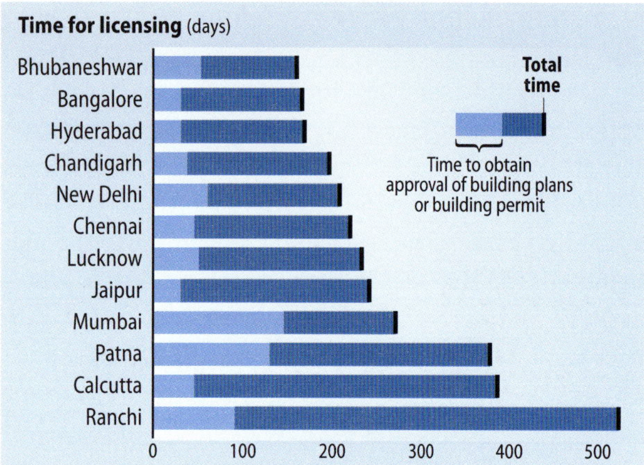

Source: Doing Business database.

FIGURE 3.4
Slow license approvals, high warehouse rents

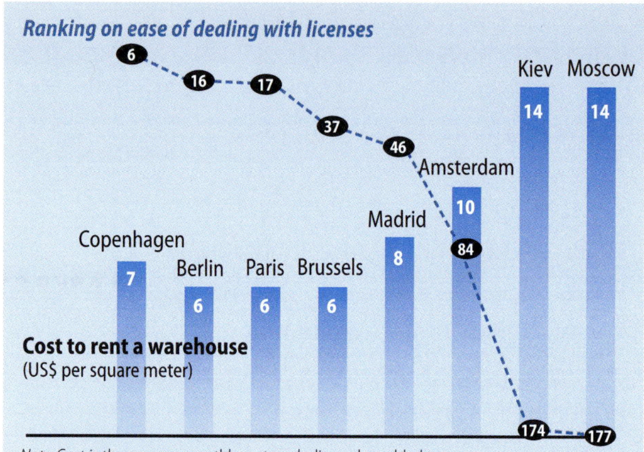

Note: Cost is the average monthly rent, excluding value added tax.
Source: DOEL Partners, *Doing Business* database.

Finland introduced private inspections in 2004. In the United States 25% of inspectors work for private architectural and engineering services firms, conducting inspections for a fee or on a contract basis. One in 10 construction and building inspectors is self-employed.

Consolidate project clearances

In Mauritania applicants for a building permit have to follow up at least twice with each of 7 different departments in the municipality to make sure their application gets processed and approved. Why not centralize all project clearances in a single office at the municipality? That's what Italy did, and the process is much faster now that developers no longer have to make separate trips to the fire, worker safety, water, sanitation, health, project design and tax departments. Another 34 countries—from Armenia to Canada to Panama—have consolidated approvals to simplify the licensing process.

Consolidating project clearances requires reform at the municipal level of government. In India, for example, approving a construction permit takes about 5 months for the municipality of Mumbai—but only 1 month for the municipalities of Hyderabad and Jaipur (figure 3.3). To reduce the delays in Mumbai, the Maharashtra state government is introducing a single window for clearances.

Such reforms encourage investment in property development. That lowers costs for end users. In Kiev, where construction approvals take 429 days, the monthly cost to rent a warehouse averages $14 a square meter. That's twice what an entrepreneur pays in Copenhagen, where licensing takes only 69 days, or Paris, where it takes 137 (figure 3.4). Reforms pay off for governments too. A recent study in the United States showed that a 3-month acceleration in permit approvals on a 22-month project cycle could increase property tax revenue by 16.5% and construction spending for local governments by 5.7%.[6]

Notes

1. Sextus Julius Frontinus, "On the Water Management of the City of Rome," translated by R. H. Rodgers, University of Vermont, Burlington, 2003 (http://www.uvm.edu/~rrodgers/Frontinus.html).
2. The municipality of Tbilisi has offered the residents compensation so they can buy apartments elsewhere.
3. Advisory Board on Administrative Burden (2007).
4. Ladegaard, Djankov and McLiesh (2007).
5. Devas and Kelly (2001).
6. PricewaterhouseCoopers (2005).

Employing workers

In the 1970s symphony orchestras in the United States started using "blind" auditions—where the performer plays behind a screen so the evaluator can hear the music but not see the person. The result: the share of women among new hires shot up by 75%.[1]

Bias against the hiring and promotion of women still exists in some countries. In a few, it is explicit in the regulations. In the Democratic Republic of Congo, the United Arab Emirates and Yemen women are forbidden to work at night. In Lao PDR women are prohibited from performing certain types of manual work. In others, bias is simply the prevailing practice. The example of symphony orchestra hiring is telling—nothing in the rules discriminated against female musicians.

To protect workers from discrimination and other unfair employment practices, countries turn to regulation. The International Labour Organization has established a set of fundamental principles and rights at work covering the right to collective bargaining, the elimination of forced labor, the abolition of child labor and the elimination of discrimination in hiring and work practices.[2]

Beyond these regulations and principles, governments struggle to strike the right balance between labor market flexibility and job stability. Many countries err on the side of excessive rigidity, to the detriment of businesses and workers alike. In Sierra Leone, for example, it costs an employer 189 weeks in severance pay to dismiss a worker. Venezuelan laws ban firing any low-paid workers. These are among the countries with the most rigid employment regulations (table 4.1).

In these and other countries laws created to protect workers often hurt them—especially women, youth and unskilled workers. Their employment opportunities vanish (figure 4.1). They end up in the informal economy. Women are 3 times as likely as men to be hired informally. In these jobs they receive no social benefits. And if they are abused by their employer, they have fewer protections.

More flexible labor regulations boost job creation. And they don't mean giving up protections. Georgia has some of the most flexible labor regulations in the world and it has ratified all the core labor standards of the International Labour Organization. Few can argue that workers are exploited in Denmark, another of the top 10 on the ease of employing workers. Workers in these countries have the best protection—flexible labor regulations that give them the opportunity for a job in the formal sector and easy transitions from one job to another.

TABLE 4.1
Where is it easy to employ workers—and where not?

Easiest	Rank	Most difficult	Rank
United States	1	Sierra Leone	169
Singapore	2	Panama	170
Marshall Islands	3	Congo, Dem. Rep.	171
Georgia	4	Angola	172
Brunei	5	Paraguay	173
Tonga	6	Guinea-Bissau	174
Maldives	7	Equatorial Guinea	175
Australia	8	São Tomé and Principe	176
Palau	9	Bolivia	177
Denmark	10	Venezuela	178

Note: Rankings are the average of the country rankings on the difficulty of hiring, rigidity of hours, difficulty of firing and cost of firing indices. See Data notes for details.
Source: Doing Business database.

FIGURE 4.1
Women and youth lose out from rigid employment laws

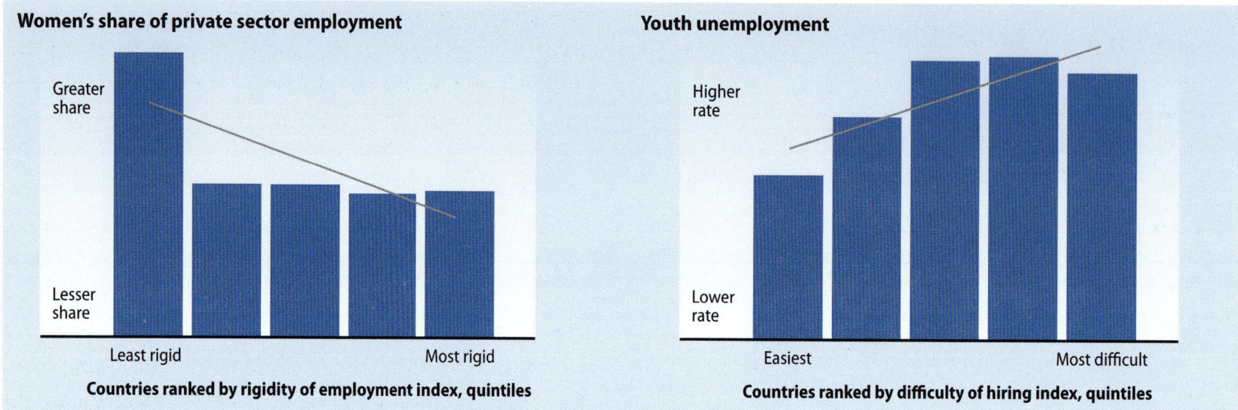

Note: Relationships are significant at the 5% level and remain significant when controlling for income per capita.
Source: Doing Business database; WEF (2006); World Bank, World Development Indicators database.

The collection of data on the flexibility of labor regulations has spurred significant new research: 112 studies have used these *Doing Business* data. One set of studies finds that rigid labor regulation reduces jobs. In the Indian state of Maharashtra, for example, a study finds that rigid labor laws have resulted in 15% fewer jobs being created in the retail sector. Instead, store owners buy expensive computer equipment so they can run their operations with fewer workers.[3]

A second set of studies analyzes the effects of trade openness on the economy in the presence of flexible labor regulations. A study of 90 developing countries finds that exporting businesses grew faster where labor regulations were flexible.[4] Another study shows that this growth is due in part to the ability of these exporters to operate in industries with high volatility in demand. For example, textile exporters, whose business is driven by changes in fashion, thrive in countries with flexible regulation.[5] A third study estimates that in an open economy, flexible labor regulation can increase annual growth by up to 1.5%.[6]

Who is reforming?

Twelve countries made significant changes to their labor regulations in 2006/07. Eight increased flexibility; 4 made regulations more rigid. Eastern Europe and Central Asia had the greatest number of positive reforms, followed by Western Europe and Africa (table 4.2).

The Czech Republic was the top reformer, adopting a new labor code that replaced its 1965 code. The new law provides for more flexible working hours. It also eases restrictions on dismissals. Before the reform an employer could dismiss an employee for economic reasons only if the employee could not be reassigned to another position or retrained. The new law eliminates this requirement. It also reduces notice periods for dismissals from 3 months to 2. Firing costs remain the same, however, because severance pay rose by a month.

Latvia extended the maximum duration of fixed-term contracts from 2 years to 3, making it easier to hire new workers when demand is high without imposing high costs for dismissal if demand declines.

Labor laws in rich countries, already among the most flexible, continued to evolve (table 4.3). Both Switzerland and the Netherlands made working hours more flexible. Switzerland eased restrictions on weekend work. And a new law in the Netherlands increases allowable overtime hours and extends the period for averaging them.

Reforms in Spain made it easier for employers to convert workers' contracts from fixed term to open

TABLE 4.2
More flexible working hours—a popular reform in 2006/07

Made working hours more flexible Czech Republic, Netherlands, Pakistan, Switzerland, Uganda
Extended limits on temporary work Bhutan, Latvia, Togo
Offered incentives to make temporary workers permanent Spain
Made firing more difficult Bhutan, Czech Republic, Latvia, Moldova, Venezuela
Increased restrictions on fixed-term employment Slovenia, Togo

Source: Doing Business database.

TABLE 4.3
Who regulates employment the least—and who the most?

Rigidity of employment index (0–100)

Least		Most	
Hong Kong, China	0	Equatorial Guinea	66
United States	0	Guinea-Bissau	66
Singapore	0	Romania	66
Maldives	0	Angola	69
Marshall Islands	0	Congo, Rep.	69
Australia	3	Panama	69
Uganda	3	Niger	70
Canada	4	Congo, Dem. Rep.	74
Jamaica	4	Bolivia	79
Palau	4	Venezuela	79

Firing cost (weeks of salary)

Least		Most	
Denmark	0	Ecuador	135
New Zealand	0	Argentina	139
United States	0	Mozambique	143
Puerto Rico	0	Sri Lanka	169
Afghanistan	0	Ghana	178
Iraq	0	Zambia	178
Marshall Islands	0	Sierra Leone	189
Micronesia	0	Zimbabwe	446
Palau	0	Bolivia	not possible
Tonga	0	Venezuela	not possible

Nonwage labor cost (% of salary)

Least		Most	
13, including:		Hungary	34
Bangladesh	0	Czech Republic	35
Botswana	0	Slovakia	35
Cambodia	0	Brazil	37
Comoros	0	Italy	37
Eritrea	0	Ukraine	38
Ethiopia	0	Belarus	39
Lesotho	0	China	44
Maldives	0	France	47
West Bank and Gaza	0	Belgium	55

Note: "Not possible" indicates a full ban on firing low-paid workers for economic reasons.
Source: Doing Business database.

ended. The reforms lowered nonwage labor costs and some types of severance payments and offered incentives to make temporary workers permanent. Businesses and workers welcomed the more flexible arrangements: 126,901 conversions took place in July and August 2006, a 204% increase over the same period the previous year.

In Africa, Uganda and Togo adopted new labor laws. Uganda's employment act removed restrictions on weekend work. Employers and employees are free to set the legally required rest day anytime they choose. And there is no required premium for working on a rest day, except for overtime. But the law also requires employers to notify unions and the labor commissioner before dismissing 10 or more redundant workers. Togo's new law extends the maximum duration of fixed-term contracts from 24 months to 48. But it limits fixed-term contracts to temporary tasks, reducing the ease of hiring overall.

In South Asia, Pakistan extended overtime limits for retail workers from 150 hours a year to 624 and made working hours more flexible. Bhutan went much further, implementing its first labor code. The law removes the 12-month limit on fixed-term contracts, eases restrictions on night work and does away with mandatory pay premiums for daytime overtime.

Bhutan's law also prohibits forced labor, discrimination, sexual harassment and child labor. And it replaces protections that hurt workers with ones that make sense. For example, before the reform it was illegal for a pregnant woman to work past 9:00 p.m.—even a woman just 1 month into her pregnancy. Now a pregnant employee can work past 9:00 p.m. if she chooses. More important, the new law prohibits firing a woman on the grounds of pregnancy.

Some countries made their employment regulations more rigid. Venezuela extended its prohibition on redundancy dismissals to workers earning up to 3 times the minimum wage. Moldova increased its severance pay requirements from 20 weeks to 28.7. And Slovenia reduced the maximum duration of fixed-term contracts to 24 months.

What to reform?

Since 2004, 35 countries have made their labor laws more flexible (figure 4.2). Another 15 have made them more rigid. Here are 4 reforms that create job opportunities —especially for women, youth and the unskilled—by making it easier for businesses to operate:

- Allow flexible working hours.
- Introduce apprentice wages.
- Lower dismissal costs.
- Raise and equalize mandatory retirement ages.

Allow flexible working hours

In Ukraine overtime is allowed only under exceptional circumstances—such as to respond to natural disasters or avoid the destruction of property. In Côte d'Ivoire employees cannot work more than 75 hours of overtime a year—even if they want to. In Panama only specially designated businesses can operate on Sundays. In Algeria a woman can work at night only if she has a special exception granted by a labor inspector. These laws were created to protect employees. But they usually backfire—and take work away from willing workers.

Businesses sometimes need longer workweeks to respond to seasonal increases in demand. Reformers in the Czech Republic and Serbia have responded by allowing businesses to shift their work schedules with rising demand. Hours worked can be averaged over a 6-month period—a year in the Czech Republic, if established by collective agreement. Bhutan's new Labor and Employment Act provides for more flexible night work schedules by removing the previous 7-hour cap on night shifts and replacing it with extra pay for overtime at night.

FIGURE 4.2

More labor law reforms in Eastern Europe & Central Asia

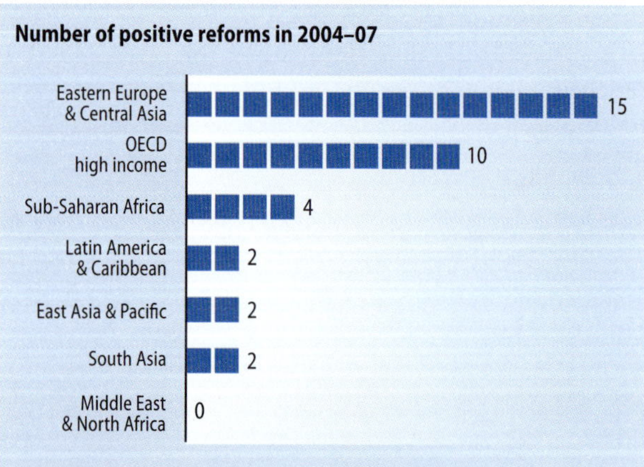

Source: Doing Business database.

Seventy-five countries permit flexible night work and allow employees to work up to 50 hours a week for 2 months a year to respond to a seasonal increase in demand—for example, to serve as a lifeguard at the beach in the summer or to sell Christmas trees in the winter.

Introduce apprentice wages

Apprentice contracts exist in nearly all rich countries along with about 25 others, including Burkina Faso, Chile, Madagascar, Thailand and Tunisia. These allow businesses to hire first-time employees for a portion—typically 75%—of the mandatory wage for a short period. The workers can get training and the opportunity for a job, and the businesses have an incentive to keep the workers once they have invested in their training. This is an easy reform to introduce: beneficiaries are easy to target and political opposition is unlikely, especially in countries with high youth unemployment.

Lower dismissal costs

In the Republic of Congo an employer who wishes to dismiss redundant workers must first write to the workers' representatives, seeking their guidance. Then the employer must obtain the authorization of a commission headed by the labor inspector. If the dismissal is approved, the employer must choose whom to lay off according to the order set out in the law, taking into account seniority and other factors. And the workers can choose to appeal the decision to the minister of labor.

Zambia has no third-party notification requirements. But a worker with 20 years of service is entitled to 40 months' severance pay. In Sri Lanka the law mandates 39 months' severance pay when the layoff is due to economic downturn. These rules hit businesses at the worst possible time—when layoffs are needed because of falling demand for their products.

Some of these requirements were created with good intentions. But high firing costs scare employers away from creating jobs. Women and youth are affected most. One study shows that tougher regulation of dismissals in Chile increased relative employment for middle-aged men at the expense of women, youth and unskilled workers.[7] In Peru reductions in dismissal costs in the 1990s brought more women into the formal sector. And wages for women rose relative to those for men.[8]

Another way to ease dismissal costs is to offer unemployment insurance rather than severance pay. This is a viable reform in middle-income and rich countries.

In Austria employers contribute to a fund from which they may withdraw if a worker is made redundant after 3 years of employment. In St. Kitts and Nevis severance payments are made from a government-administered fund that employers pay into over time. In Italy employers deposit a portion of each employee's salary into a designated fund over the course of the employment relationship. In these countries employers do not have to pay additional severance when dismissing workers because of redundancy.

Raise and equalize mandatory retirement ages

Every country with an aging population faces a choice: raise the mandatory retirement age or face the collapse of the pension system. Pension systems have not kept pace with changing demographics. Most Western European countries introduced their 65-year retirement age before World War II. Life expectancies have risen by a decade, but the retirement age stands unchanged. Requiring more years at work would reduce the burden on social security and make it easier for governments to reduce taxes on business.

When raising retirement ages, reformers can take the opportunity to equalize them. In Russia women live 12 years longer than men on average. But they must retire at age 55, while men retire at 60. Worldwide, women live 4 years longer than men on average. But half of countries force women to retire earlier than men. The retirement age gap is largest in Eastern Europe and Central Asia (figure 4.3). The idea may be to benefit women. Instead, earlier retirement reduces their pension pay and career opportunities.

FIGURE 4.3

Equality in retirement age—lowest in Eastern Europe

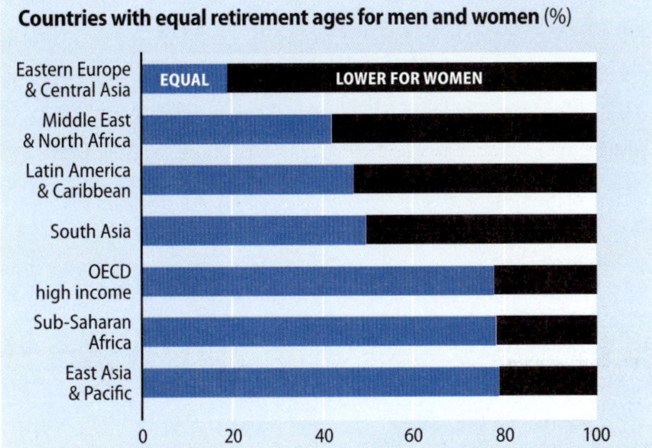

Source: Doing Business database.

The European Union has obliged members to adopt identical retirement ages. Germany just revised its labor law: starting in 2029, both men and women will retire at 67. Other countries should follow. Women will see higher retirement pay. And businesses will be able to keep their productive workers longer.

Notes

1. Goldin and Rouse (2000).
2. ILO (1998).
3. Amin (2007).
4. López-Córdova (2007).
5. Cunat and Melitz (2007).
6. Freund and Bolaky (2007).
7. Montenegro and Pagés (2003).
8. Saavedra (1998).

Registering property

"The process is slow for everyone, but especially for women. I wanted to sell our store last year, but since my husband was abroad, I had to wait 2 months for him to return and sign. When he signed the papers for me, the deal went through—after 3 more months of bureaucracy," says Catherine in Lesotho. This just changed. A law passed in November 2006 allows married women in Lesotho to transfer property without their husband's signature.

Making it easier to transfer property is good for entrepreneurs. Land and buildings account for between half and three-quarters of the wealth in most economies.[1] And with formal property titles, entrepreneurs can obtain mortgages on their land or homes and start businesses. Banks prefer land and buildings as collateral because they are impossible to move or hide. In Zambia 95% of commercial bank loans to businesses are secured by land, in Indonesia 80%, and in Uganda 75%.[2]

But a large share of the property in developing countries is not formally registered. In 2000 Peruvian economist Hernando de Soto estimated the value at $9.3 trillion, calling it "dead capital."[3] Unregistered property limits financing opportunities for new businesses and expansion opportunities for existing ones. In Ethiopia 57% of firms cite access to land as their main obstacle, as do 35% in Bangladesh and 25% in Kenya and Tanzania.[4] Recognizing these bottlenecks, some governments have started extensive property titling programs. Others have focused on making property transfers cheaper and faster.

The 10 countries that make property registration easiest are the same as in last year's report—with New Zealand again at the top (table 5.1). But some at the bottom of the rankings have changed. Uzbekistan moved up 53 places after it cut fees. Guinea-Bissau moved out of the bottom 10 by reducing the property transfer tax by 8 percentage points.

Countries that make property registration simple, fast and cheap have more properties registered formally. That leads to greater access to finance and greater opportunities to invest.[5] Country experience shows the benefits of formalizing title and keeping it that way. Thailand's land reform program has issued more than 8.5 million property titles and created one of the most efficient registration systems in the world. For people who received formal titles, land values and investment almost doubled, and access to credit increased threefold.[6]

TABLE 5.1
Where is registering property easy—and where not?

Easiest	Rank	Most difficult	Rank
New Zealand	1	Afghanistan	169
Armenia	2	Burkina Faso	170
Saudi Arabia	3	Bangladesh	171
Lithuania	4	Sierra Leone	172
Slovakia	5	Nigeria	173
Norway	6	Brunei	174
Sweden	7	Maldives	175
Iceland	8	Marshall Islands	176
United Arab Emirates	9	Micronesia	177
United States	10	Timor-Leste	178

Note: Rankings are the average of the country rankings on the procedures, time and cost to register property. See Data notes for details.
Source: Doing Business database.

Peru's experience is just as striking. Since the late 1990s the time required to formalize property has fallen from 6 years to 33 days. More than 1.3 million titles have been issued, and two-thirds of those issued to individuals have gone to women. The benefits of secure title for women are especially great. Studies in India, Honduras and Nicaragua show that poor women's access to property is associated with more investment in the household, especially in children's health and education.[7]

Who is reforming?

Twenty-seven countries made property registration easier in 2006/07. Most made the process faster through administrative reform. A few simplified it. Some of the biggest gains were in lowering registration costs. On average the top 10 reformers cut the time and cost by a third (figure 5.1).

Ghana made the most progress. A ministerial directive cut the requirement to register deeds of sale with the land commission. Before, entrepreneurs would have to wait 135 days for the commission to issue a registration number. And then they would have to register yet again with the land title registry. With the stroke of a pen the bottleneck is now gone, and the delays with it (figure 5.2).

For the second year running, Africa had the most reforms. Kenya liberalized the profession of land valuers. With more people able to practice, the wait for valuations fell from 34 days to 7. Mali cut delays with quicker services for property registration at the tax authority. But the biggest trend was to slash costs (table 5.2). Burundi abolished its 7% property registration tax. Benin cut registration taxes from 12% of the property value to 8%, Burkina Faso from 15% to 10%, Guinea-Bissau from 10% to 2%, Mauritius and Niger from 10% to 5%.

More is needed. Africa accounts for 9 of the 10 most expensive countries in which to register property. And even with the reforms, costs remain steep. With all costs added in, registration in Burkina Faso still costs 12.2% of the property value. In Burundi the cost is 11.5%—and in Niger, 9%.

Eastern Europe and Central Asia saw 5 reforms. Uzbekistan reduced the notarization fee from 10% of the property value to a fee based on surface area. The cost to register property fell from 10.5% of the property value to 1.4%. Poland converted registration fees from a percentage to a fixed fee, lowering the cost to only 0.5%. In Hungary a second registry operating in Budapest reduced the backlog and cut the time from 78 days to 63. Croatia's computerization of the land registry cut the time from 399 days to 174. Georgia cut the requirement to use notaries in property registration.

In Latin America and the Caribbean reforms targeted delays. The Dominican Republic made the region's biggest reform—passing 6 laws in the past year alone to restructure the registration process—and cut the time from 107 days to 60. Guatemala now allows registrars to sign documents electronically, speeding the process at the registry by a week. Honduras cut delays by imposing time limits and publishing more information online. And Haiti's tax administration hired 60 university interns to reduce the backlog of registrations. The time dropped from 683 days to 405—still a long wait.

FIGURE 5.1

Top 10 reformers in registering property

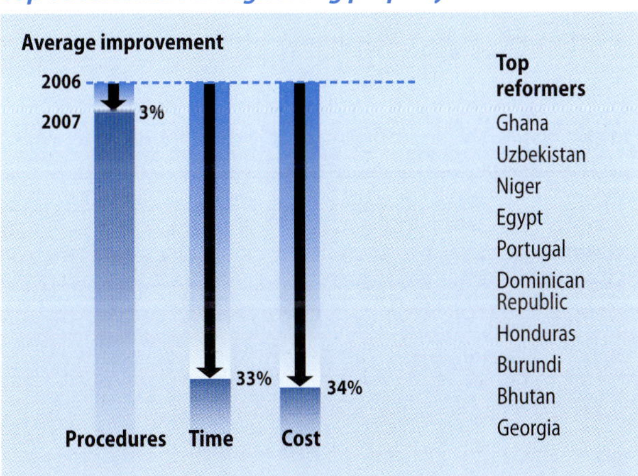

Source: *Doing Business* database.

FIGURE 5.2

Making it easier to register property in Ghana

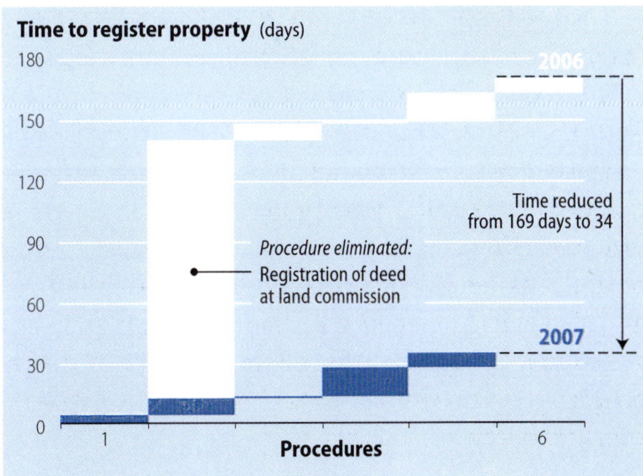

Source: *Doing Business* database.

TABLE 5.2
Lower cost to register—a popular reform in 2006/07

Reduced taxes or fees
Benin, Burkina Faso, Burundi, Egypt, Guinea-Bissau, Mauritius, Mexico, Niger, Poland, Uzbekistan

Sped procedures in the registry
Croatia, Djibouti, Dominican Republic, Haiti, Honduras, Hungary, Lesotho, Mali, Niger, Tunisia

Computerized procedures, put procedures online
France, Guatemala, Portugal

Combined and reduced procedures
Afghanistan, Georgia, Ghana

Sped procedures in the court
Bhutan

Allowed private valuers to complete valuations
Kenya

Source: Doing Business database.

TABLE 5.3
Who regulates property registration the least—and who the most?

Procedures (number)

Fewest		Most	
Norway	1	Swaziland	11
Sweden	1	Eritrea	12
Netherlands	2	Greece	12
New Zealand	2	Uzbekistan	12
Oman	2	Ethiopia	13
Thailand	2	Liberia	13
United Kingdom	2	Uganda	13
Vanuatu	2	Algeria	14
Armenia	3	Brazil	14
Lithuania	3	Nigeria	14

Time (days)

Least		Most	
New Zealand	2	Togo	295
Sweden	2	Solomon Islands	297
Thailand	2	Bosnia and Herzegovina	331
Lithuania	3	Angola	334
Norway	3	Gambia	371
Armenia	4	Rwanda	371
Iceland	4	Slovenia	391
Kyrgyz Republic	4	Haiti	405
Saudi Arabia	4	Bangladesh	425
Netherlands	5	Kiribati	513

Cost (% of property value)

Least		Most	
Saudi Arabia	0.0	Côte d'Ivoire	16.9
Bhutan	0.0	Cameroon	17.8
Belarus	0.1	Senegal	19.5
Kiribati	0.1	Comoros	20.8
Slovakia	0.1	Chad	21.2
New Zealand	0.1	Mali	21.2
Georgia	0.1	Nigeria	22.2
Azerbaijan	0.2	Zimbabwe	25.0
Russia	0.3	Congo, Rep.	27.3
Switzerland	0.4	Syria	28.1

Source: Doing Business database.

Egypt was the top reformer in the Middle East and North Africa. Fees were cut from 3% of the property value to a low fixed fee of 2,000 Egyptian pounds ($350). The total cost to register dropped from 5.9% to 1%. Djibouti reorganized procedures in the registry to cut the time from 49 days to 40. Tunisia digitized property records, allowing notaries to check files more efficiently.

In South Asia, Afghanistan eased registration by eliminating 2 government approvals and simplifying forms. In Bhutan, where registration takes place in the courts, 2 new judges were assigned to deal with cases more promptly. One month was cut from the process.

Rich countries continue to use new technologies to speed property registration. Portugal digitized its registry records, cutting the time from 81 days to 42. France now allows notaries to work online, checking encumbrances, sending property contracts to the registry and receiving confirmation numbers—all electronically.

The countries of East Asia and Pacific distinguished themselves by making no improvements—for the second year running. It was not for lack of need. The region ranks fourth on the ease of registering property, after the OECD high-income countries, Eastern Europe and Central Asia, and the Middle East and North Africa. Several Pacific countries have no functioning property registration. And the only country in the region that reformed in 2006/07 slipped backward. Vanuatu increased the cost of registration from 7% of the property value to 11%.

Another 5 countries made registering property more difficult. The cost to register in the Kyrgyz Republic more than doubled after notary fees rose. With less than half of rural properties registered, the change will increase informality. Morocco now requires entrepreneurs to visit 3 tax agencies to obtain tax clearance. Germany, Paraguay and Zimbabwe increased registration fees. Registering property in Zimbabwe costs 25% of the property's value (table 5.3).

What to reform?

Since 2004 *Doing Business* has recorded 87 reforms in 64 countries that made it easier to register property. Some countries reformed in successive years—Australia, Croatia, the Dominican Republic, Ecuador, Egypt, El Salvador, Georgia, Ghana, Honduras, Mali, Poland and Tanzania. The 5 most effective reforms:

- Simplify and lower fees.
- Introduce fast-track procedures.
- Make the registry electronic.
- Take registration out of the courts.
- Make the use of notaries optional.

Simplify and lower fees

Lowering fees is the simplest way to ease property registration. A more significant reform is to introduce a fixed fee. Seventeen countries have fixed fees, including Armenia, Estonia, Italy and New Zealand as well as reformers such as Egypt, Poland and Uzbekistan. Charging fees on a percentage basis encourages fraudulent declarations of property values. To counter evasion, many governments increase regulation, making the process more complex with physical inspections or record checking at the cadastre. Delays and bribes increase. A fixed fee avoids all this.

Less radical reformers can simply lower percentage fees. Forty-four countries have done so since 2004. This doesn't mean reducing revenues. When India cut its stamp duties from 10% of the property value to 5%, revenue jumped by 20%. In Burkina Faso registrations rose by 27% in the 5 months after this year's reduction in the transfer tax. In Egypt revenue from title registrations increased by 40% between the 6 months before the reform and the 6 months after (figure 5.3). More affordability usually means more registrations and less evasion. Property registries then have better information on property values and who owns what. And that supports the collection of capital gains and property taxes.

FIGURE 5.3

Cutting fees increased revenue in Egypt

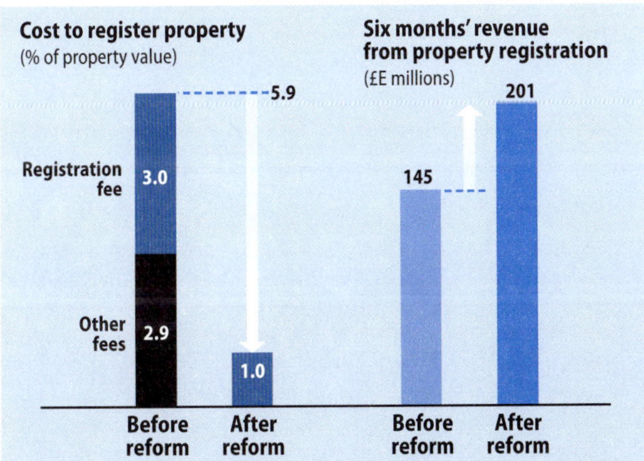

Source: Doing Business database, Egyptian Ministry of State for Administrative Development.

Introduce fast-track procedures

To register property in Lithuania, entrepreneurs must obtain a certificate of execution and a land and building reappraisal. This takes 9 days. Then they apply for transfer of title at the registry, which takes another 20 days. But if they don't want to wait, they can pay a higher official fee and cut delays from 29 days to 3. "I need the title now for collateral to expand my business. If I wait, I lose customers," says one property owner.

Fast-track procedures help prioritize the work of the registry and allow entrepreneurs to focus on their business. Such procedures can save 2 months in Ukraine, 21 days in Argentina, 20 in Russia, 15 in Kazakhstan and Slovakia and 10 in Mongolia.

Another 56 countries try to expedite registration by setting time limits at the registry. This works best when registrars are evaluated on whether they meet the targets. One example is Botswana. The days to register property in Gaborone fell by 25% in 2005 after time limits were imposed and compliance monitored in annual staff performance evaluations. Spain went one step further: if the registrars miss their 15-day deadline, they must cut their fees by 30%.

Make the registry electronic

"It is almost impossible to find records of past land transactions. All records are paper, and the filing system broke down long ago. If there is a fire, we have no records at all," says a public official in Rwanda. It takes 371 days to register property in Kigali.

Countries that transfer records from paper to electronic form always benefit from shorter processing times. Going electronic also makes it easier to identify errors and overlapping titles, improving title security. Croatia digitized land records as part of its far-reaching land reform—and reduced the time for registration by more than 70%. Guatemala has seen the time to register fall from 69 days to 30 since completing its electronic system in 2005. El Salvador, Georgia, Honduras, Poland, Portugal and Tunisia have recorded similar gains.

The next step is to put procedures online. This works when people using the registration services (notaries, lawyers, the public) have Internet access. The Netherlands and New Zealand are leaders in online property registration and, with Internet penetration above 70%, use is brisk.

Other countries can benefit from putting individual procedures rather than the entire system online. Costa Rica allows transfer taxes to be paid online. Brazil has made judicial certificates available over the Internet. Bosnia and Herzegovina recently allowed property records to be checked online. Latvia has done so since 2004.

Take registration out of the courts

In 2004 the Dominican Republic took some property registration procedures out of the courts and made them administrative. The time to register property fell by 44%. El Salvador took registration out of the courts in 1999, cutting several months from the time. Honduras and Serbia are following suit.

In countries where courts are involved in registering property, the process takes 70% longer on average. And judges who deal with property registration have less time for their main work—resolving disputes. Taking registration out of the courts means that it can be more easily linked with the agency responsible for the cadastre, as Norway has done. That makes it easier to detect overlapping and duplicate titles, improving the security of property rights.

Make the use of notaries optional

In Senegal entrepreneurs pay a notary fee of 4.5% of the property value to authenticate a sale deed. Then they pay another 15% when the registry reviews and authenticates it again. In Honduras the notary charges 4% to verify the contract, and the registry costs another 1.6%. Burundi, Costa Rica, Mali and more than 40 other countries require this double verification.

Here are 2 ways to reduce cost and delay. First, provide standard deeds and registration documents. These reduce delays by ensuring fewer mistakes and eliminating the need to scrutinize documents before registration. Registration is just 2 steps in Thailand—pick up standard documents from the Ministry of Commerce, then proceed to the land office to register the transfer. The registration is done in 2 days. Second, in countries where laws require deeds to be notarized, such as Rwanda, reformers can give notary powers to the registrars. When Portugal did this, notary fees fell by between 28% and 60% in less than a year.

Notaries have useful purposes. But their functions in property registration are irrelevant in countries where registry officials perform the same tasks. And in countries where notaries are responsible for registration, costs are 33% higher than average. Three of 4 countries manage property registration without mandating the use of notaries. Property rights are no less secure, and efficiency is greater. Some property owners still use notaries, but they do so by choice.

Notes

1. Fleisig, Safavian and de la Peña (2006).
2. Data are from World Bank Enterprise Surveys conducted in 2006/07 (http://www.enterprisesurveys.org).
3. De Soto (2000).
4. Data are from World Bank Enterprise Surveys conducted in 2006/07 (http://www.enterprisesurveys.org).
5. Field (2006).
6. Feder (2002).
7. Beegle and Strauss (1996) and Katz and Chamorro (2003).

Getting credit

Credit is now more accessible in Panama, thanks to an ambitious reform of the credit bureau law in early 2006. Before the reform many of Panama's 300,000 small and medium-size businesses—employing 68% of the country's workers—were cut off from access to formal credit. So were more than 40% of Panamanian adults, mostly the poorest. They were forced to rely instead on pawnshops and street lenders.

This was despite advanced financial markets. With more than 80 national and foreign banks, Panama has one of the highest ratios of domestic credit to GDP in Latin America. But the 2002 credit bureau law prohibited collecting payment information from utility firms. That made it harder for poor people and small firms without bank loans or credit cards to build a credit history. And the system was opaque for borrowers: they could see the information stored in the credit bureau only by requesting a report in person at its main offices in Panama City or the city of David. "We were seen as the 'bad guy' who was denying credit to people," recalls German Espinosa, an officer at the Panamanian Credit Association.[1]

Lenders look at a borrower's credit history in deciding whether to extend credit and what interest to charge.[2] They also want to know whether they can recover their money if a borrower defaults. The main way to recover bad debt is by taking collateral. By giving creditors the right to an asset on default, collateral also reduces a lender's costs of screening loan applicants.

Where credit registries and effective collateral laws are lacking—as they are in most poor countries—banks make fewer loans.[3] Credit to the private sector averages 8% of GDP in the 10 economies ranking at the bottom on how well credit registries and collateral laws facilitate credit markets (table 6.1). In the top 10 economies it exceeds 130% of GDP.

TABLE 6.1
Where is getting credit easy—and where not?

Easiest	Rank	Most difficult	Rank
United Kingdom	1	Uganda	169
Hong Kong, China	2	Burundi	170
Australia	3	Lao PDR	171
Germany	4	Marshall Islands	172
Malaysia	5	Palau	173
New Zealand	6	Timor-Leste	174
Canada	7	Uzbekistan	175
Israel	8	Madagascar	176
Singapore	9	Afghanistan	177
United States	10	Cambodia	178

Note: Rankings are based on the sum of the strength of legal rights index and the depth of credit information index. See Data notes for details.
Source: Doing Business database.

Who is reforming?

Croatia was the top reformer in 2006/07, improving both its collateral regulations and the availability of credit information. In September 2006 a new collateral registry started operations—and creditors leapt at the opportunity to use this new resource in deciding on loans. In May 2007 a new private credit bureau started distributing information. Coverage of borrowers in credit information systems shot up from 0 to 72%. At that rate it won't be long before Croatia ranks among the economies with the most coverage (table 6.2).

Another 15 economies improved their credit information systems in 2006/07. Armenia and Russia saw new private credit bureaus get off the ground, both providing online access to credit data. The credit bureaus in India and Saudi Arabia now cover information on businesses, not just individuals. Egypt's first private credit bureau will soon start distributing information to clients.

The most popular reform to credit information was to expand the range of data available on borrowers (table 6.3). Georgia added payment information from electricity and telecommunications companies. Kenya incorporated data from retailers and telecommunications companies. Kuwait's credit bureau now includes information from furniture sellers—and those in Saudi Arabia and Trinidad and Tobago information from mobile phone companies. Bosnia and Herzegovina expanded the number of trade creditors providing information on firms, tripling coverage. Colombia's bureau membership jumped from 1,450 to 2,100 in a year after more trade creditors started contributing data. In Brazil credit unions and microfinance institutions started submitting credit information to the public registry. And Honduras tripled its coverage of borrowers by adding new suppliers of information and persuading existing ones to provide all their data.

Some countries revised their credit information regulations. Kenya's central bank issued new regulations requiring banks to report information on defaults to the private credit bureau. In Honduras the National Commission of Banks and Insurance certified the private credit bureau, guaranteeing that borrowers can access their data once a year for free. Serbia now requires lenders to request a credit report before giving a loan. South Africa requires lenders to check their customers' overall debt levels and guarantees borrowers the right to access and challenge their credit records. The public registry in Belarus issued regulations guaranteeing that borrowers can inspect their data.

The biggest pickup in reform was in the Middle East and North Africa (figure 6.1). Tunisia's credit registries now record all loans, expanding coverage of borrowers by 25%. West Bank and Gaza tripled coverage with a similar reform. In Saudi Arabia the public registry closed as the private bureau expanded coverage by 60-fold. Morocco now has legislation in place for a bidding process to establish one or more private bureaus. Egypt's new private bureau will use the data feed between commercial banks and the central bank, avoiding duplicate investments in data transmission technology.

Elsewhere, public registries expanded coverage by lowering or removing the threshold at which loans are included. Indonesia's public registry eliminated its minimum loan cutoff of 50 million rupiah ($5,460), increasing

TABLE 6.2
Who has the most credit information—and who the least?

Borrowers covered as a share of adults

Most	%	Least	%
Argentina	100	Algeria	0.19
Australia	100	Mauritania	0.18
Canada	100	Rwanda	0.17
Iceland	100	Djibouti	0.16
Ireland	100	Chad	0.15
Israel	100	Ethiopia	0.15
New Zealand	100	Madagascar	0.08
Norway	100	Yemen	0.07
Sweden	100	Nigeria	0.04
United States	100	Guinea	0.02

Note: The rankings reflected in the table include only economies with public or private credit registries (122 in total). Another 56 economies have no credit registry and therefore no coverage.
Source: Doing Business database.

TABLE 6.3
More credit information—the most popular reform in 2006/07

Expanded set of information collected in credit registry
Georgia, Honduras, India, Indonesia, Kenya, Kuwait, Pakistan, Saudi Arabia, Trinidad and Tobago, Tunisia, West Bank and Gaza

Established new credit registry or bureau
Armenia, Croatia, Egypt, Russia

Revised credit information regulations
Honduras, Kenya, South Africa

Allowed out-of-court enforcement of collateral
Ghana, Honduras, Romania, Vietnam

Established unified collateral registry
Croatia, France, India, Micronesia

Expanded range of assets that can be used as collateral
China, Croatia, Vietnam

Source: Doing Business database.

FIGURE 6.1

Credit information reform—faster in the Middle East

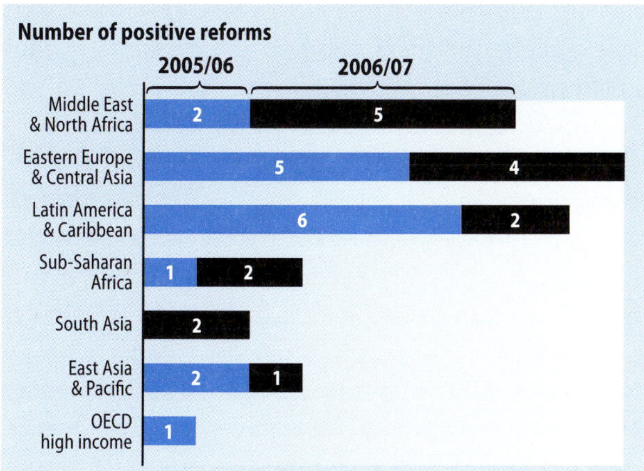

Source: Doing Business database.

TABLE 6.4

Who has the most legal rights for borrowers and lenders —and who the least?

Strength of legal rights index (0–10)

Most		**Least**	
Hong Kong, China	10	Timor-Leste	2
United Kingdom	10	Tunisia	2
Albania	9	Bolivia	1
Australia	9	Burundi	1
New Zealand	9	Ecuador	1
Singapore	9	Egypt	1
Slovakia	9	Madagascar	1
Denmark	8	Rwanda	1
Ireland	8	Afghanistan	0
Malaysia	8	Cambodia	0

Note: See Data notes for details on the index.
Source: Doing Business database.

coverage of loans by 150%. Pakistan eliminated its loan threshold of 500,000 Pakistan rupees ($8,350), boosting coverage by 20 times. Central Africa's monetary union computerized its registry, allowing information to be distributed on all loans above 10,000 CFA francs ($20) rather than 5,000,000 ($10,400) as before.

Sri Lanka slipped backward. It raised its minimum loan cutoff from 100,000 Sri Lanka rupees ($900) to 500,000 ($4,500) and restricted the availability of information on repaid defaults to 1 year.

Reforms also strengthened legal rights for borrowers and lenders. Nine countries made it easier to create and enforce collateral. China made the most progress, exiting the bottom 10 list on the strength of legal rights for borrowers and lenders (table 6.4). A new bankruptcy law gives secured creditors priority in receiving proceeds from their collateral if the borrower becomes insolvent. And a new property law expands the range of assets that can be used as collateral to include inventory and accounts receivable. Before the reform Chinese businesses held more than $2 trillion in "dead capital"—assets that could not be used as collateral because of restrictions in laws. With the new property law, some of these assets can be used for loans to expand businesses.

Two other countries expanded the range of assets that can be used as collateral. Vietnam now allows businesses to use all types of assets and debt. Croatia's new law permits inventory to be used as collateral as long as the location of the goods is specified.

A big trend in collateral reforms was to set up collateral registries. France, the top reformer in getting credit in 2005/06, launched a nationwide online registry of movable collateral. India introduced an electronic registry for security rights granted by companies. Micronesia implemented its first secured transactions law and also launched an online collateral registry. The registry applies to all assets and all types of creditors and debtors.

Making out-of-court enforcement possible was another popular reform to collateral laws. Ghana's new insolvency act allows secured creditors to enforce their security directly rather than waiting for a judge to review their claims and order enforcement. Honduras now permits borrowers to agree with lenders on direct enforcement by notaries. Going through the courts used to take years.

What to reform?

Since 2004 *Doing Business* has recorded 79 reforms to credit information in 56 countries—and 42 reforms to collateral laws in 32 countries (figure 6.2). The experience of these countries points to 5 reforms that help entrepreneurs get loans:

- Expand the range of information available in credit registries.
- Eliminate legal obstacles to sharing credit information.
- Allow all types of assets to be used as collateral.
- Establish registries for all collateral.
- Permit out-of-court enforcement of collateral.

Expand the range of information available in credit registries

Include information on telephone and electricity payments in the credit reporting. That way, people who've never had a bank loan or a credit card can still build a credit history. And avoid limits on this coverage. Panama allows utility information to be included, but only after the consumers give their written permission—making data on such payments expensive to collect.

Credit reporting also is more valuable when it includes both data on defaults over the past 5 years and data on on-time payments. That allows lenders to evaluate the borrowing capacity of clients. And it lets good borrowers benefit from more and cheaper lending. For banks, past payment behavior is the best indicator of future payment behavior.

FIGURE 6.2
Collateral reform—Eastern Europe & Central Asia shows the way

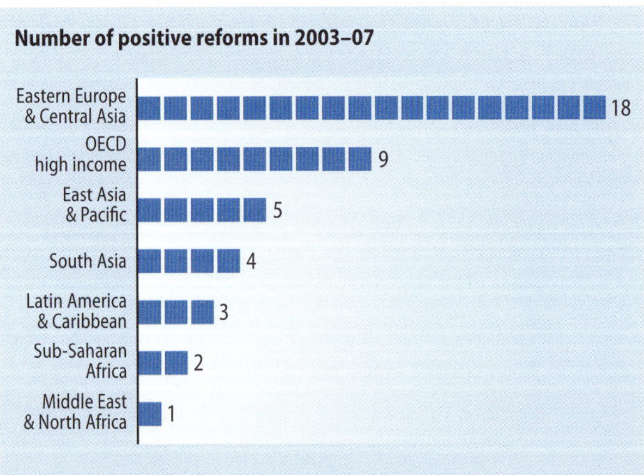

Source: Doing Business database.

Eliminate legal obstacles to sharing credit information

Credit registries store sensitive information, making credit reporting an easy target for critics. The best way to counter their concerns is to introduce laws that safeguard borrowers' privacy and create incentives for registries to maintain high-quality data. Legislation can guarantee borrowers the right to inspect their data, obliging the credit bureau to send them the data for review once a year free of charge. Such legislation is under review in 13 countries.

Many countries—including Bolivia, the Dominican Republic, El Salvador and Honduras—have such regulations in place for private bureaus but not public credit registries. Costa Rica and Malaysia allow borrowers to check their files in public registries but not private bureaus. There is no reason for the different treatment.

Allow all types of assets to be used as collateral

Alejandro, an Internet service provider in Guatemala, describes getting a loan: "I was able to use my business equipment and frequencies as collateral. But they required detailed descriptions in the contract of each of our 6,000-odd units of equipment, including their serial number, brand and model. We hired a technician to help. The contract was 127 pages long! And when we update our equipment in a year, we'll need to renegotiate the loan."

Countries that require specific descriptions of assets in collateral agreements make it impossible for a borrower to use changing pools of assets (such as inventory or receivables), future assets (such as crops) or the entire business as collateral. This is especially costly for small firms, which are less likely to own real property and instead need to rely on receivables and movable property as collateral.

A better way is to permit general descriptions in loan agreements, allowing the use of all types of assets as collateral—present and future, tangible and intangible. Bosnia and Herzegovina, Denmark, France, Peru, Serbia, Ukraine and Vietnam have done so since 2004. When Slovakia allowed general descriptions, credit to the private sector jumped by 10%. More than 70% of the new credit was secured by movables and receivables. Even without such radical change, reformers can ease access to credit by broadening the range of assets that can be used as collateral to include such asset classes as accounts receivable (as China did in 2007), inventory (as Croatia did in 2006) and future assets (as Japan did in 2005).

FIGURE 6.3
Big range in the time and cost to register collateral

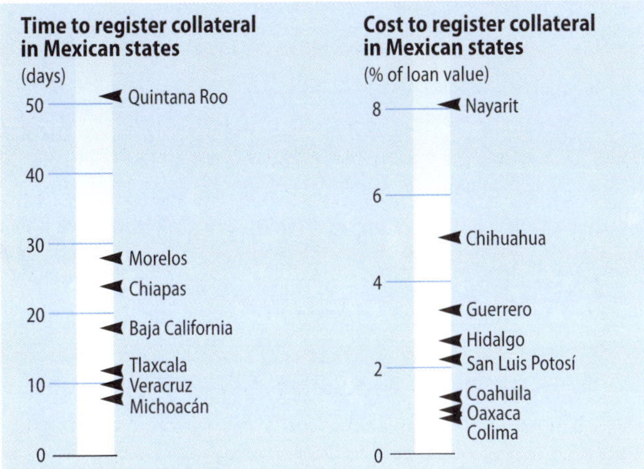

Source: Doing Business database.

FIGURE 6.4
Easier to recover collateral in India

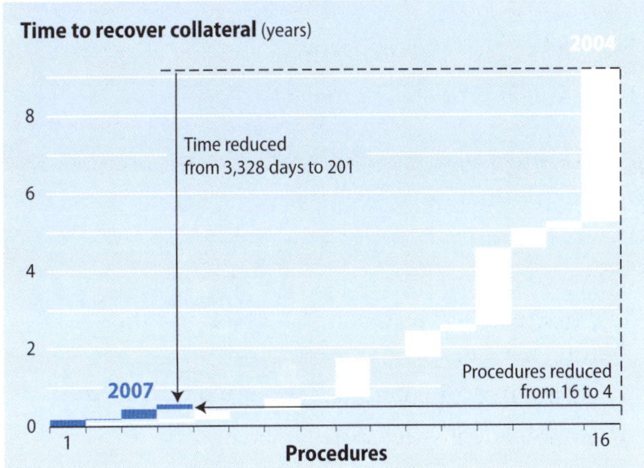

Source: Doing Business database.

Establish registries for all collateral

In Syria charges over movable property are possible only if there is a corresponding registry—now the case only for vehicles, vessels and intellectual property. Turkey has a similar system. The solution: allow all types of assets to be used as collateral and create a unified registry enabling creditors to notify others of their claim. Eastern Europe has led the way in such reforms: in the past decade 12 of the region's 15 countries have created unified registries of charges over movable collateral. Other countries—from Nepal to Vietnam—are in the process of doing so. With the costs of technology falling, establishing a unified registry has never been easier.

Once established, the most efficient registries require only an administrative review for completeness of the application rather than a legal authentication, which stalls the registration process. The time and cost of registering can also be an obstacle. In Mexico, for example, it takes 8 days to register collateral in Michoacán but 51 days in Quintana Roo. And it costs 0.8% of the loan value in Colima but 8.1% in Nayarit (figure 6.3).

Permit out-of-court enforcement of collateral

Allowing creditors to enforce collateral out of court is one of the toughest reforms, opposed by both borrowers and the judiciary. But the benefits can be great. Peru's recent reform to allow out-of-court enforcement reduced enforcement time from more than 2 years (longer than the economic life of many assets) to 3 months. Other reformers—such as Armenia, the Kyrgyz Republic and Slovakia—saw similar gains. Borrowers benefit the most. When creditors know they can enforce their collateral if a borrower defaults, they are more likely to lend in the first place.

Summary proceedings are an important backstop to out-of-court enforcement, which could wind up in the courts if debtors appeal. Only 2 pieces of evidence need to be presented to a court in a summary proceeding: a valid security agreement and proof of default. In the 56 countries with summary proceedings, enforcing collateral takes half as long as in the countries that rely on other judicial measures. When India introduced summary proceedings in 2004, the time to enforce collateral fell from more than 9 years to as little as 6 months (figure 6.4).

Notes

1. Bustelo (2007).
2. Djankov, McLiesh and Shleifer (2007).
3. Sorge and Zhang (2007).

Protecting investors

Mexican investors had a good year in 2006. A new securities law came into effect, replacing outdated regulations with greater investor protections.[1] The stock market soared—equity prices rose by 55% for the year. The good fortune continued into 2007. In June the courts upheld the new law against an appeal by its fiercest opponent, one of the country's richest businessmen. The ruling preserved the law's protections for small shareholders.[2] Stock prices rose even further.

Mexico's reforms helped small investors—by providing for broad disclosure of related-party transactions,[3] clear obligations for company directors and managers and easy access to the courts when investors are harmed. Economies that regulate self-dealing—the use of corporate assets for personal gain—see greater equity investment and lower concentration of ownership.[4] A recent study of Bulgaria found exactly that: tougher investor protections from a 2002 securities law reform stopped a growing flow of delistings from the stock exchange and led to higher equity values.[5]

New Zealand provides the greatest protection against self-dealing (table 7.1). Singapore comes in second. Self-dealing is just one corporate governance failure, but it is the most important. Other investor protections—such as election of directors, disclosure of remuneration or rules on takeover bids—are relevant mostly for richer countries in a position to develop large share markets.

Several developing countries protect investors well. South Africa ranks among the top 10, and Mauritius comes in at 11. But across 178 economies, it is the rich ones that regulate self-dealing the most (figure 7.1). They require greater disclosure for companies, impose stronger duties on directors and make it easier for investors to

TABLE 7.1
Where are investors protected—and where not?

Most protected	Rank	Least protected	Rank
New Zealand	1	Guinea	169
Singapore	2	Micronesia	170
Hong Kong, China	3	Palau	171
Malaysia	4	Venezuela	172
Canada	5	Djibouti	173
Israel	6	Suriname	174
United States	7	Swaziland	175
Ireland	8	Lao PDR	176
South Africa	9	Tajikistan	177
United Kingdom	10	Afghanistan	178

Note: Rankings are on the strength of investor protection index. See Data notes for details.
Source: Doing Business database.

FIGURE 7.1
Fewest investor protections in Africa

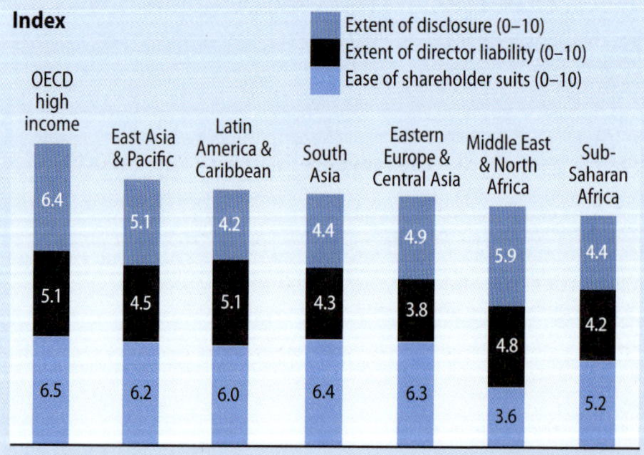

Source: Doing Business database.

FIGURE 7.2
Better investor protection—higher market capitalization and more listed firms

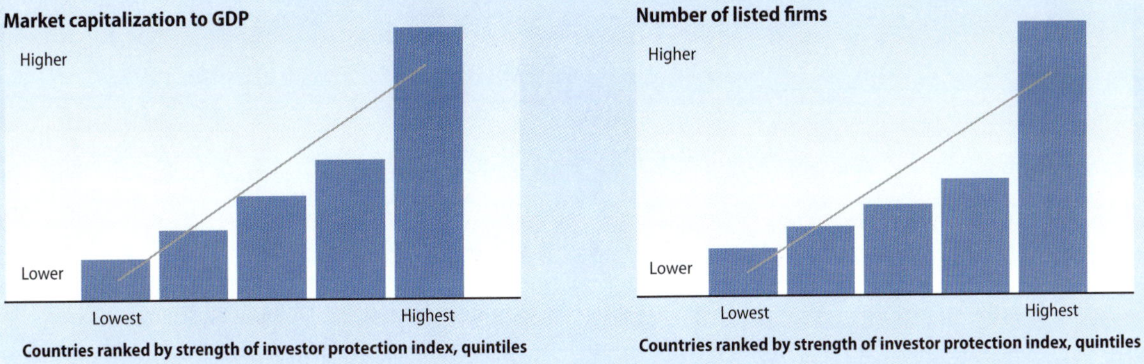

Note: Relationships are significant at the 5% level and remain significant when controlling for income per capita. Higher values on the strength of investor protection index indicate greater protection. See Data notes for details.
Source: Doing Business database, World Bank (2005c).

confront negligent or fraudulent directors in court.

Across regions, Latin America requires the least disclosure of related-party transactions. Countries in Eastern Europe and Central Asia regulate directors' duties only minimally, imposing vague obligations that cannot easily be challenged. And court rules in the Middle East and North Africa make it difficult for small investors to gather evidence. Investors in Syria, for example, have no access to internal company documents when bringing suit. That makes it easy for insiders to hide misconduct.

Both disclosure and extensive approval requirements and private rights of action for minority shareholders are important for developing strong equity markets. Countries that provide both protections have larger and more active stock markets, smaller block premiums and higher rates of new listings (figure 7.2).[6] One example: 2 months after Georgia adopted new securities rules, the country's largest winemaker listed on the Tbilisi stock exchange, and 4 other companies have since started the listing process. In addition, reforms aimed at countering self-dealing are associated with higher equity returns. Investors look for upside potential, and they find it in reforming markets.

Who is reforming?

Ten economies strengthened their investor protections in 2006/07 (table 7.2). Georgia was the top reformer. A revised securities law limits the possibility of self-dealing in several ways. The law defines "interested parties" in a transaction and requires supervisory board or shareholder approval for related-party transactions. It requires companies to immediately notify the securities commission of a related-party transaction and post a notice of the deal, its terms and the conflict of interest on their own website or that of the Georgian stock exchange. Firms must also include such information in their annual report.

TABLE 7.2
Greater disclosure—the most popular reform in 2006/07

Increased disclosure requirements
Belarus, Colombia, Georgia, Iceland, Indonesia, Vietnam
Defined duties for directors and controlling shareholders
Georgia, Mozambique, Portugal
Regulated approval of related-party transactions
Norway, Slovenia
Passed a new securities law
Vietnam

Source: Doing Business database.

The Georgian reforms also allow investors to appeal harmful actions of directors to the court and demand compensation—including a refund of the benefiting director's personal profit. To receive these damages, investors need only prove that the transaction could have had better terms and conditions. "Now directors will think twice before entering into transactions with related parties," says a corporate lawyer in Georgia. All this comes with a clear goal: "We have reformed; we are offering you protections. Now it is your turn to invest in Georgia," says a government official.

Mozambique was the runner-up in reforms, adopting a new commercial code that replaced legislation dating to 1888. The new code makes it easier to hold directors and controlling shareholders liable for misconduct in 4 ways. First, it permits derivative suits—suits by minority investors against company directors in the

TABLE 7.3
Where are investor protections strong—and where not?

Extent of disclosure index (0–10)

Most		Least	
Bulgaria	10	Afghanistan	0
China	10	Albania	0
France	10	Lao PDR	0
Hong Kong, China	10	Maldives	0
Ireland	10	Micronesia	0
Malaysia	10	Palau	0
New Zealand	10	Sudan	0
Singapore	10	Swaziland	0
Thailand	10	Switzerland	0
United Kingdom	10	Tajikistan	0

Extent of director liability index (0–10)

Most		Least	
Cambodia	9	Bulgaria	1
Canada	9	China	1
Israel	9	Afghanistan	0
Malaysia	9	Dominican Republic	0
New Zealand	9	Marshall Islands	0
Singapore	9	Micronesia	0
Trinidad and Tobago	9	Palau	0
United States	9	Suriname	0
Hong Kong, China	8	Tajikistan	0
South Africa	8	Vietnam	0

Ease of shareholder suits index (0–10)

Easiest		Most difficult	
Kenya	10	Afghanistan	2
New Zealand	10	Cambodia	2
Colombia	9	Syria	2
Hong Kong, China	9	Venezuela	2
Ireland	9	Yemen	2
Israel	9	Guinea	1
Mauritius	9	Morocco	1
Mozambique	9	Rwanda	1
Singapore	9	Djibouti	0
United States	9	Iran	0

Source: Doing Business database.

company's name. Second, it provides a detailed list of directors' duties to the company. The previous code assigned directors a vague responsibility to "act in good faith." Third, the code introduced special liability for controlling shareholders, including board approval for decisions that may be harmful to the company. These guidelines for controlling shareholders are demanding—and unique in the world. Finally, the new code gives investors the right to review company documents. If company officials refuse, investors can turn to government inspectors to investigate.

The reform raised Mozambique's score on the extent of director liability index from 2 to 4—and its score on the ease of shareholder suits index from 6 to 9, among the highest in the world (table 7.3). As a local lawyer says, "More information, more chances to win in court."

Vietnam adopted new securities and enterprise laws. The securities law sets up a new securities exchange and trading center. The enterprise law mandates investor involvement in major company actions—for example, transactions exceeding 35% of the assets of the company. The law also increases disclosure for related-party transactions. And it introduces fiduciary duties for directors—but fails to provide a way to enforce those duties. No commercial tribunals in Vietnam have jurisdiction over investor suits against directors.

Last year Belarus ranked among the countries with the least disclosure of corporate dealings. This year it jumped 22 places in the strength of investor protection rankings. A new law requires greater annual disclosure to shareholders and approval of related-party transactions by disinterested shareholders (those without a personal stake in the deal). But shareholder involvement in major decisions comes at a price: directors cannot be held liable for damages if shareholders approve. So if a director persuades the majority of shareholders to support a deal and the deal goes bad, the opposing minority cannot challenge it in court.

Other countries also increased disclosure. Iceland extended requirements for immediate and annual disclosure to all nonlisted public corporations and leapt 17 places in the strength of investor protection rankings. Indonesia now requires more detailed information on companies' activities in their annual report. And Colombia, under its new Decree 3139, requires listed companies to report more information to investors. Before the reform, listed companies had to report any "relevant" or "extraordinary" event—a subjective standard that was open to abuse. The new decree maintains the broad "relevant" requirement but lists specific events that must be disclosed to the financial authorities. It also requires a company to report extensive information before going public.

European countries continued to strengthen protections. Slovenia now requires boards to obtain the prior approval of shareholders in transactions affecting 25% or more of the company's assets. Norway expanded the definition of related-party transactions that shareholders must approve. Portugal made it easier for shareholders to sue by lowering the threshold for derivative suits from 5% of the share capital to 2%. Finland and Ireland implemented a European Union directive to make capital markets more transparent.[7] And the European Commission opened consultations on creating one-stop shops for company information (such as the prospectus, annual report and ownership levels) in member states.

With these, potential investors in Copenhagen, for example, can access information about a company in Greece. Disagreements about harmonizing disclosure forms have delayed implementation.

The most active financial markets reform continually. Japan and the United Kingdom both have company acts that are less than 2 years old. The U.S. Securities and Exchange Commission issued more than 50 rules or amendments in the past 3 years. And Hong Kong (China), now a top destination for new listings, has increased disclosure requirements each of the past 3 years. A note to market regulators: if your country's laws on investor protection haven't changed in the past 5 years, they're out of date.

What to reform?

First, get the basics right. Investor protections are not the first point of reform for many countries. Poor countries would do better to ease business start-up, simplify property registration and strengthen collateral laws first. Too many countries get the order wrong. Take Mozambique. The Maputo stock exchange was established in 1999, before the country had reformed its commercial, investment and trade laws. It lists only 1 domestic company (a brewery, Cervejas de Moçambique), 1 international corporation and 5 government bonds. But a recent overhaul of basic corporate laws will likely attract other listings to the exchange.[8]

Once a country has the basics, it can help protect investors against self-dealing. Since 2005, 43 reforms aimed at this have taken place in 34 economies (table 7.4). Hong Kong (China) is the star reformer, appearing each year among the top 10. Here are the 3 most effective reforms:

- Open company activities to investor scrutiny.
- Require disinterested shareholder approval.
- Where courts are strong, help investors bring suit.

TABLE 7.4
Simple solutions and where they have worked

Reform	Economies
Increased disclosure of related-party transactions	Belarus, Canada, Colombia, Georgia, Iceland, Indonesia, Israel, Italy, Mexico, Pakistan, Peru, Poland, Romania, Spain, Sweden, Thailand, Turkey, United Kingdom, Vietnam
Defined duties for directors and controlling shareholders	Georgia, Jamaica, Mozambique, Namibia, Portugal, Spain
Regulated approval of related-party transactions	Israel, Jamaica, New Zealand, Norway, Thailand
Made it easier to sue directors	Germany, Korea, Mexico, Tanzania
Strengthened audit committees	Costa Rica, India, Indonesia, Thailand
Gave shareholders access to company documents	China, Hong Kong (China), Mozambique
Increased penalties for self-dealing	Malaysia, Pakistan

Source: Doing Business database.

Open company activities to investor scrutiny

Investor protections start with transparency of corporate dealings. Require public reports for large transactions involving directors, as in Poland. Involve shareholders more in corporate decisions, as in South Africa. And open company books for inspection, as in Egypt. Investors need to know what stakes directors have in proposed deals so they can stop harmful activities—or sue for damages.

More disclosure is possible in rich and poor countries alike. The Internet makes distributing financial and ownership information cheap. Malaysia and Thailand, with among the most stringent disclosure rules, require extensive online disclosure on related-party transactions before they go to a vote by the company's disinterested shareholders. Ghana requires directors to disclose any personal interest in a proposed transaction to their fellow board members, detailing both the nature and the extent of that interest. If the transaction is approved, the company's annual report must fully describe the terms of the deal and the director's conflict of interest. In Switzerland, in contrast, no public disclosure is required—not even in the annual report.

Require disinterested shareholder approval

In Colombia and 2 dozen other countries related-party transactions automatically trigger a vote by the company's disinterested shareholders. In 9 of these countries an external auditor does a thorough review of the transaction and reports to the shareholders before the vote takes place. Compare that with Ecuador, where large deals involving company insiders need sign-off by only one person—a manager, director, president or whoever is named in the bylaws. This invites abuse.

Shareholder approval is easily undermined by loopholes, however. Investors in Cameroon vote on related-party transactions months after they have taken place. By then it's too late to undo a bad deal. Lebanese shareholders vote at the annual meeting for all related-party transactions arising during the coming year—turning shareholder involvement into a meaningless rubber stamp. Still other countries, such as Slovakia, exempt related-party transactions from shareholder scrutiny when they occur in the "ordinary course of business." The problem is, Slovak law doesn't say what falls outside the "ordinary course of business." Companies easily bypass shareholder approval.

Where courts are strong, help investors bring suit

Many countries restrict private lawsuits by investors, relying instead on government inspectors to police corporate activities. This has 2 weaknesses. First, no government can investigate every possible crime, especially in poor countries. Second, criminal penalties paid to the state do nothing to repay investors for the loss of their investment. When investors can sue, the damage awards go directly to compensate investors or the company harmed.

Hong Kong (China) does it right. Strict disclosure rules expose company decisions to investors, regulators and the press almost immediately. Unhappy investors can sue directors for multiple misdeeds—including improper personal gains, oppression of minority shareholder interests and negligence in running the company. Once in court, plaintiff investors have full access to company documents to find evidence for proving their case. Cambodia goes only halfway—it permits investors to sue company insiders for a variety of offenses, but court rules block plaintiffs from gathering the evidence needed to prove their case.[9] The result? No cases are brought because proving them is nearly impossible.

FIGURE 7.3

Efficient courts help protect minority shareholders

Note: Relationships are significant at the 1% level and remain significant when controlling for income per capita.
Source: Doing Business database, WEF (2006).

Even the best of rules are useless if courts are weak. Papua New Guinea, Maldives and Slovenia have strong protections on the books allowing investors to bring suit and gather evidence. But even simple commercial disputes take a long time to resolve—591, 665 and 1,350 days, respectively. Less abuse of investors is seen where courts perform well (figure 7.3).

Notes

1. See Johns and Lobet (2007).
2. Jesus Aranda, "Niega la Corte a Tv Azteca amparo contra artículos de la ley del mercado de valores," *La Jornada*, June 28, 2007, http://www.jornada.unam.mx/2007/06/28/index.php?section=economia&article=025n1eco.
3. Transactions between a director or controlling shareholder and the company, such as the example considered by *Doing Business*.
4. Djankov and others (forthcoming).
5. Atanasov, Ciccotello and Gyoshev (2006).
6. See Djankov and others (forthcoming).
7. European Union Directive 2004/109/EC.
8. Moss (2006).
9. Cigna and Enriques (2005).

Paying taxes

"In Sweden we pay taxes online. The corporate income tax, value added tax, labor contributions and property tax are filed on a single form. Doesn't everyone do it that way?" asks Astrid, a Swedish business owner.

Not yet. In Papua New Guinea, Syria and Zimbabwe tax forms are brought in person to the tax office and "discussed" with a tax officer to make sure calculations are correct. To comply with regulations on taxes and contributions[1] in the Republic of Congo, a company must make 89 payments a year, spend 106 days and pay 65.4% of its profits. Meanwhile, the company has to fill out 50 pages of forms for corporate income taxes, 50 for labor taxes and contributions and 36 for consumption taxes. Only Belarus and Ukraine have a more burdensome tax system.

The ease of paying taxes can range from filing a single online form in Sweden to making 124 payments a year in Belarus. Investors make their choices accordingly. Countries with more payments have fewer formal businesses per capita and lower rates of business entry (figure 8.1).[2] In Brazil, for example, the Simples program, which eases tax requirements for small businesses, increased business registrations in the retail sector by 13 percent compared with the year before the program started.[3]

Countries that make it easier to pay taxes and contributions also have higher rates of workforce participation, and lower rates of unemployment, among women.[4] The reason is simple: a burdensome tax system disproportionately hurts smaller businesses, especially in the services sector, and this is where most women work. In Colombia, where women outnumber men almost 2 to 1 among the unemployed, small businesses have to pay 82.4% of their

FIGURE 8.1

More burdensome taxes and contributions, fewer formal businesses

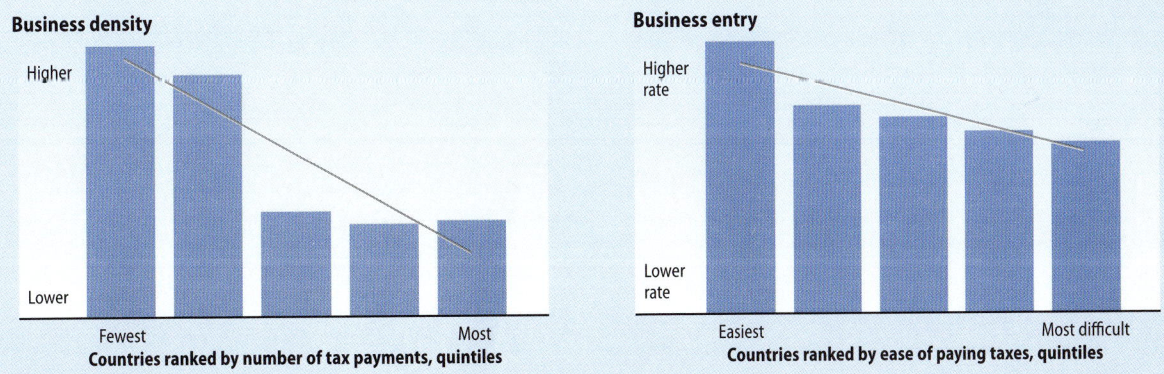

Note: Relationships are significant at the 1% level and remain significant when controlling for income per capita. Business density is the number of formally registered firms per capita. Business entry is the number of firms created in a year as a percentage of all registered firms.
Source: Doing Business database, Djankov and others (2007).

TABLE 8.1
Where is it easy to pay taxes—and where not?

Easiest	Rank	Most difficult	Rank
Maldives	1	Panama	169
Singapore	2	Jamaica	170
Hong Kong, China	3	Mauritania	171
United Arab Emirates	4	Bolivia	172
Oman	5	Gambia	173
Ireland	6	Venezuela	174
Saudi Arabia	7	Central African Republic	175
Kuwait	8	Congo, Rep.	176
New Zealand	9	Ukraine	177
Kiribati	10	Belarus	178

Note: Rankings are the average of the country rankings on the number of payments, time and total tax rate. See Data notes for details.
Source: Doing Business database.

commercial profits, make 69 tax payments a year and spend 47 days to comply with all tax requirements. This is changing, thanks to a new tax law enacted by the congress in late 2006.

There is good news: paying taxes is now easier, especially in Eastern Europe and Central Asia, which had the most reforms in 2006/07. Revenues are growing as well. For example, the Czech Republic saw its tax revenue rise by 2% after reducing the corporate income tax between 2004 and 2005.[5] This is part of a longer global trend—the tax burden on businesses has decreased every year since 1985.[6] A few places—much of Africa, some countries of the former Soviet Union and several Latin American countries—have yet to catch on (table 8.1).

Who is reforming?

Thirty-one economies made it easier to pay taxes in 2006/07. Reducing the corporate income tax rate was the most popular reform, done in 27 economies (table 8.2). Moldova, Mongolia, Sierra Leone, Syria, Turkey and Uruguay made major revisions in their tax codes. Colombia, Israel, the Kyrgyz Republic, South Africa, Uruguay and Uzbekistan reduced the number of taxes paid by businesses by consolidating or eliminating taxes. Azerbaijan, Bulgaria, Colombia, Lesotho, Malaysia, the Netherlands, Turkey and Uzbekistan simplified the process of paying taxes by introducing or expanding electronic filing and reducing the frequency of payments.

Bangladesh, the Dominican Republic, Hungary, Venezuela and Zimbabwe increased the tax burden on businesses. Bangladesh raised its corporate income tax from 37.5% of profits to 40%. Only Comoros and São Tomé and Principe have higher corporate income tax. The Dominican Republic passed a law requiring companies to submit paper receipts every month. Hungary introduced a temporary 4% tax on profits (the solidarity tax) and increased employers' labor contributions by 3.5 percentage points—both with the aim of reducing the budget deficit. Venezuela introduced 3 new taxes. Zimbabwe increased the road tax and the tax on check transactions. It also introduced a new corporate tax form to accompany each quarterly payment. That increased the time for tax compliance by 40 hours a year.

Bulgaria was the top reformer in 2006/07: it reduced the corporate tax from 15% to 10% and employers' labor taxes by 7 percentage points (table 8.3). And online filing is now widely used for corporate income tax and social security contributions.

Turkey was the runner-up in reforms. It reduced the top rate for corporate income tax from 30% in 2005 to 20% in 2006 and introduced a new corporate tax code. Turkey also reduced the tax on interest from 18% to 15% in 2006 and simplified other taxes, such as the property tax and the tax on check transactions. And it improved e-filing, reducing the time businesses need to comply with tax regulations by 31 hours.

Eastern Europe and Central Asia accounted for about a third of the reforms in 2006/07. Besides Bulgaria, 8 countries reduced the corporate income tax and 6 reduced social contributions paid by employers. Uzbekistan reduced the corporate tax from 15% in 2005 to 12% in 2006 and 10% in 2007. It gradually reduced labor contributions from 33% in 2004 to 24% in 2007. And it expanded the single tax payment regime for small

TABLE 8.2
Reducing tax rates—the most common reform in 2006/07

Reduced profit tax
Azerbaijan, Bulgaria, Colombia, Côte d'Ivoire, Greece, Israel, Kazakhstan, Kyrgyz Republic, Lesotho, FYR Macedonia, Malaysia, Mauritius, Mexico, Moldova, Mongolia, Netherlands, Portugal, Slovenia, South Africa, Spain, Syria, Trinidad and Tobago, Tunisia, Turkey, Uruguay, Uzbekistan, West Bank and Gaza

Reduced labor taxes or contributions
Albania, Bulgaria, Israel, Kyrgyz Republic, Mexico, Moldova, Netherlands, Romania, Seychelles, Slovenia, South Africa, Uzbekistan

Simplified process of paying taxes
Azerbaijan, Bulgaria, Colombia, Lesotho, Malaysia, Netherlands, Turkey, Uzbekistan

Revised tax code
Moldova, Mongolia, Sierra Leone, Syria, Turkey, Uruguay

Eliminated taxes
Colombia, Israel, Kyrgyz Republic, South Africa, Uruguay, Uzbekistan

Source: Doing Business database.

TABLE 8.3
Major cuts in corporate income taxes in 2006/07

Region	Changes in corporate income tax rate (%)
Eastern Europe & Central Asia	Azerbaijan 24 to 22
	Bulgaria 15 to 10
	Kyrgyz Republic 20 to 10
	FYR Macedonia 15 to 12
	Moldova 18 to 15
	Slovenia 25 to 23
	Turkey 30 to 20
	Uzbekistan 15 to 12
Sub-Saharan Africa	Côte d'Ivoire 35 to 27
	Lesotho 35 to 25
	Mauritius 25 to 22.5
	South Africa 12.5 to 10[a]
Latin America & Caribbean	Colombia 35 to 34
	Mexico 29 to 28
	Trinidad and Tobago 30 to 25
	Uruguay 30 to 25
OECD high income	Greece 29 to 25
	Netherlands 29.6 to 25.5
	Portugal 27.5 to 26.5
	Spain 35 to 32.5
Middle East & North Africa	Israel 31 to 29
	Syria 35 to 28
	Tunisia 35 to 30
	West Bank and Gaza 16 to 15
East Asia & Pacific	Malaysia 28 to 27
	Mongolia 30 to 25

a. Data are for the secondary company tax, paid on top of the corporate income tax.
Source: Doing Business database.

TABLE 8.4
Who makes paying taxes easy—and who does not?

Payments (number per year)

Fewest		Most	
Maldives	1	Venezuela	70
Sweden	2	Jamaica	72
Hong Kong, China	4	Dominican Republic	74
Norway	4	Kyrgyz Republic	75
Singapore	5	Montenegro	88
Afghanistan	6	Congo, Rep.	89
Kiribati	7	Romania	96
Latvia	7	Ukraine	99
Mauritius	7	Uzbekistan	118
New Zealand	8	Belarus	124

Time (hours per year)

Least		Most	
Maldives	0	Czech Republic	930
United Arab Emirates	12	Azerbaijan	952
Singapore	49	Vietnam	1,050
Luxembourg	58	Bolivia	1,080
Oman	62	Armenia	1,120
Switzerland	63	Nigeria	1,120
New Zealand	70	Belarus	1,188
St. Lucia	71	Cameroon	1,400
Ireland	76	Ukraine	2,085
Seychelles	76	Brazil	2,600

Total tax rate (% of profit)

Lowest		Highest	
Vanuatu	8.4	Eritrea	84.5
Maldives	9.1	Uzbekistan	96.3
United Arab Emirates	14.4	Mauritania	107.5
Kuwait	14.4	Argentina	112.9
Saudi Arabia	14.5	Belarus	144.4
Zambia	16.1	Central African Republic	203.8
West Bank and Gaza	17.1	Congo, Dem. Rep.	229.8
Botswana	17.2	Sierra Leone	233.5
Samoa	19.8	Burundi	278.7
Lesotho	20.8	Gambia	286.7

Source: Doing Business database.

businesses. Moldova is taking the most ambitious step: reducing the corporate income tax from 15% to 0% in 2008 after already lowering it from 18% in 2006. FYR Macedonia committed to reducing the corporate income tax from 15% in 2006 to 12% in 2007 and 10% in 2008.

In Eastern Europe the main motivation for simplifying taxes is joining and being competitive in the European Union. That creates pressure on Western European countries to simplify taxes too. The Netherlands reduced the top rate for corporate income tax from 31.5% in 2005 to 29.6% in 2006 and 25.5% in 2007. It also reduced 3 of the labor contributions. And it introduced e-filing for social security contributions, greatly simplifying the process of paying taxes.

Six countries reformed in Africa. Sierra Leone reduced a cascading sales tax—a sales tax that must be paid on raw materials and cannot be deducted upon sale of the final product—from 15% to 10%. Next year it is likely to complete the process of replacing this tax with a value added tax. Four other African countries lowered their profit tax, and 2 reduced labor contributions. But Africa is still the region with the highest tax rates—with the Central African Republic, the Democratic Republic of Congo, Sierra Leone, Burundi and Gambia each requiring businesses to pay more than 200% of their profits (table 8.4).

In Latin America and the Caribbean, Trinidad and Tobago made the biggest reduction in the total tax rate by cutting the profit tax by 5 percentage points. Uruguay passed a new tax law that eliminates 15 taxes, simplifies the social contributions and reduces the profit, personal income and value added taxes. Colombia eliminated the system of adjustment for inflation, simplifying tax computation.

Four economies in the Middle East and North Africa made their tax law more business friendly. While the main focus of reforms was reducing the profit tax, some countries went beyond that. Israel eliminated the stamp duty. Syria developed a large-taxpayer unit to make it easier for large businesses to pay taxes.

Only 2 countries reformed in East Asia and Pacific, the region with the second lowest tax rate (figure 8.2). Mongolia put in place new laws for the corporate income, value added and personal income taxes, including a new flat tax for individual income. Malaysia reduced the profit tax by 1 percentage point (with another 1 percentage point reduction planned by 2008) and simplified online tax filing.

FIGURE 8.2

Business taxes lowest in Middle East & North Africa

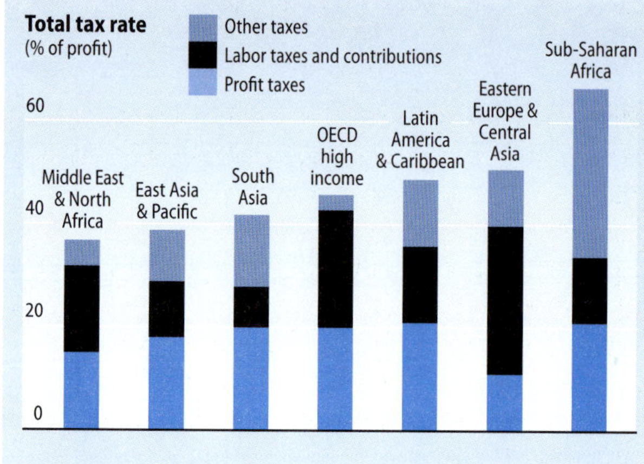

Source: Doing Business database.

What to reform?

Tax reforms are usually controversial, attracting intense political debate. The choice is often perceived as being between lower taxes with more votes but potentially less government revenue—and higher rates with discontented voters but potentially smaller fiscal deficits. In reality there is often no tradeoff between revenues and votes. Since 2005, 90 reforms in 65 economies have pointed to the 4 most successful reforms:

- Introduce online filing.
- Combine taxes.
- Simplify tax administration.
- Reduce tax rates and broaden the base.

Of those 65 economies, 4 improved their tax system every year: Albania, Bulgaria, Mexico and Moldova. Eighteen others reformed twice: the Czech Republic, Estonia, Ghana, Greece, Hungary, India, Israel, Latvia, Lesotho, Lithuania, Morocco, the Netherlands, Pakistan, Senegal, Sierra Leone, Spain, Turkey and Uzbekistan.

Introduce online filing

A quarter of the world's countries have electronic filing and payment of business taxes. That means no need for paper documents—and no need for personal interaction with tax officers. A third of the world's countries now use electronic payment such as bank transfer—and half use payment by check. In Mozambique the tax authority favors check payments by clearing them faster than bank transfers. But this choice has not been incident free: some checks were deposited in accounts belonging to tax officers.

Combine taxes

Almost 50% of countries have more than one labor tax or contribution, 27% more than one tax on profits and 41% more than one tax on property. If the base is the same (salaries, profits or property value), why not just combine these? Having multiple taxes increases the bureaucratic burden for both the taxpayer and the tax administration. Poland has the highest administrative costs of tax collection among OECD countries, at 2.62% of revenue.[7] The reason? A business has to make 41 tax payments a year, including 4 different labor taxes. Many countries in Eastern Europe and Central Asia have a similar burden (figure 8.3). In contrast, tax administration in Sweden costs only 0.59% of revenue, since all business taxes can be paid online.

Several countries have joint tax payments. Bosnia and Herzegovina combines 3 labor contributions—and

FIGURE 8.3

Compliance most burdensome in Eastern Europe & Central Asia

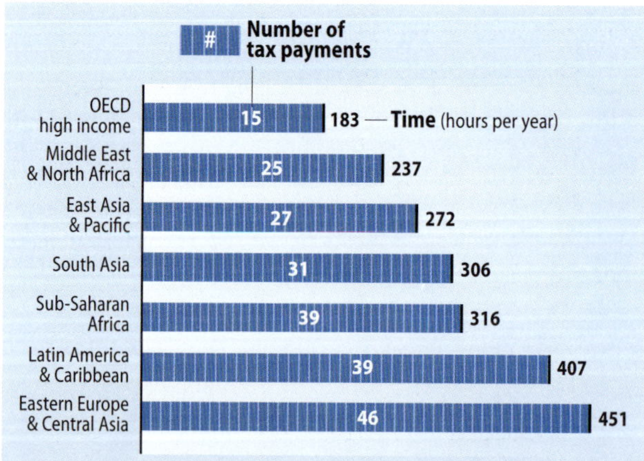

Source: Doing Business database.

Uruguay 4—in one monthly payment. In Portugal companies can pay 2 taxes on profits together.

Simplify tax administration

More than half of countries require special accounting books for tax purposes. Two-fifths have more than one law per type of tax. So businesses spend a lot of time complying with tax regulations (figure 8.4). Making the tax rules for businesses complex is unlikely to bring more revenue—quite the opposite. Countries that don't require special books have 10% more revenue (as a percentage of GDP) on average than countries that do. And having a clear tax law increases tax revenue by 6% on average.[8]

Clarity on audit rules can make a big difference. While the vast majority of countries have a system of self-assessment for calculating taxes, only about 16% use risk analysis as the basis for their tax audits. Yet tax audits are a big opportunity for bribes. Using clear rules (and even statistical analysis) to determine who and how to audit can reduce this opportunity and increase tax revenue. Indeed, countries with audits based on risk analysis have higher tax revenue as a percentage of GDP—18% higher on average—despite having lower tax rates.

The reason is that businesses have fewer incentives to hide revenues. One example: a 2007 study of transition economies finds that businesses that report frequent tax audits are also 17% less likely to borrow from banks. Instead, they resort to informal lenders. That way the borrowed money stays out of the tax records.[9]

FIGURE 8.4

More complexity, more time paying taxes

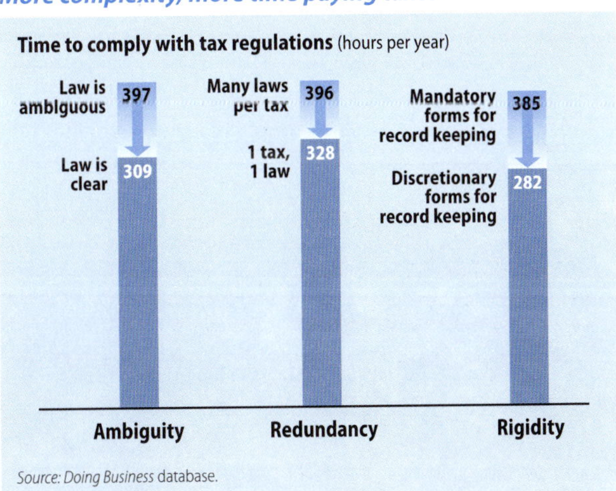

Source: *Doing Business* database.

FIGURE 8.5

Higher tax rate, greater obstacle to business

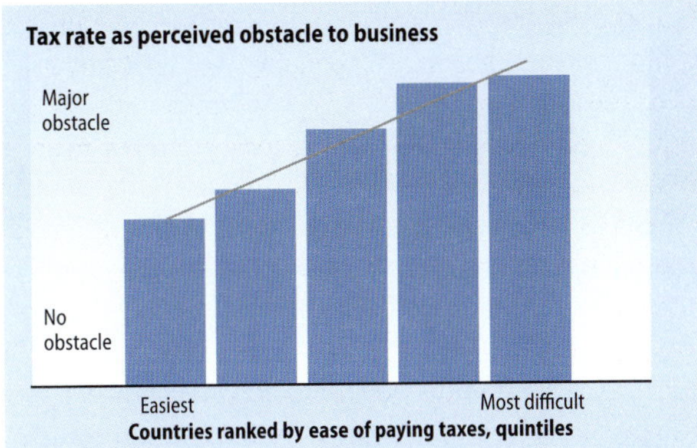

Note: Relationships are significant at the 1% level and remain significant when controlling for income per capita.
Source: Doing Business database, World Bank Enterprise Surveys.

Reduce tax rates and broaden the base

High tax rates can force companies into the informal sector (figure 8.5). In the Democratic Republic of Congo, with taxes as high as twice the commercial profit for a company with a profit margin of 20%, businesses have a strong incentive to evade taxes. Indeed, half the country's manufacturing activity is in the informal sector.[10] Such countries can increase tax revenue by lowering rates and persuading more businesses to comply with the new tax system. Even countries with a smaller informal sector can gain from this strategy. Greece saw its corporate tax revenue grow from 4% of GDP to 5% after reducing the corporate tax rate in 2005.

Notes

1. *Doing Business* measures taxes and contributions paid by a standardized business. The indicator includes taxes as defined by the system of national accounts (compulsory unrequited payments to general government) as well as government-mandated contributions such as compulsory payments to the employee social security where the statutory incidence is on the employer. See Data notes for details.
2. Djankov and others (2007).
3. Monteiro and Assunção (2006).
4. Alesina and Ichino (2007) and Azmat, Guell and Manning (2006).
5. World Bank, World Development Indicators database.
6. Slemrod (2004).
7. OECD (2007).
8. World Bank, World Development Indicators database.
9. Safavian and Wimpey (2007).
10. Schneider (2005).

Trading across borders

Tarik, a fish exporter from Yemen, knows the benefits of reform: "If I export fresh tuna to Germany, I get $5.20 a kilo. If I export frozen tuna to Pakistan, I get $1.10 a kilo. I would like everything to go to Germany. But it takes so long to comply with all the exporting procedures that the fresh tuna frequently goes bad. So only 15% of the fish is sent to Germany. My factory exports 2,000 tons of tuna a year. You make the calculation." Here it is: Tarik loses $7 million a year because exporting from Yemen takes 33 days on average.

Twenty-four countries made it easier to trade in 2006/07. Yemen wasn't one of them. Most countries sped the approvals to import and export. Reforms took place in rich countries like Austria, large emerging markets like Brazil, India and Thailand, and poor countries like Djibouti and Uganda. Africa led, accounting for a third of the reforms. Globally, the time needed to comply with export requirements fell by nearly 1 day (figure 9.1).

Still, in many countries trading across borders is more difficult than it need be. It takes a trader in the Central African Republic 57 days to complete all export formalities. The trader has to submit 8 documents to a range of government agencies, and spend $4,581, before the container leaves the port in Yaoundé, in neighboring Cameroon. That puts the Central African Republic at 172 in the rankings on the ease of trading across borders (table 9.1). In Angola a vessel arriving at the port of Luanda has to wait 8 days before berthing. In the rainy season delays go up to 14 days.

Much is lost from delays in trading. The longest are in Africa (figure 9.2). Each additional day that an export product is delayed reduces exports by more than 1%. For

FIGURE 9.1

Speeding trade—especially in South Asia

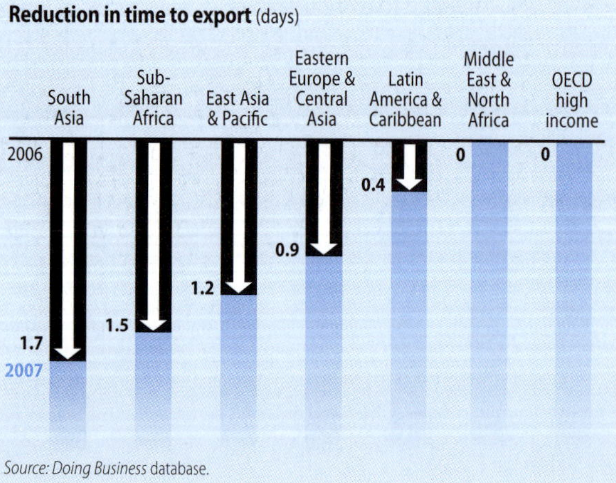

Source: Doing Business database.

TABLE 9.1

Where is trading easy—and where not?

Easiest	Rank	**Most difficult**	Rank
Singapore	1	Zimbabwe	169
Denmark	2	Burkina Faso	170
Hong Kong, China	3	Congo, Rep.	171
Norway	4	Central African Republic	172
Finland	5	Azerbaijan	173
Sweden	6	Afghanistan	174
Estonia	7	Iraq	175
Israel	8	Tajikistan	176
Panama	9	Kyrgyz Republic	177
Germany	10	Kazakhstan	178

Note: Rankings are the average of the country rankings on the documents, time and cost required to import and export. See Data notes for details.
Source: Doing Business database.

FIGURE 9.2
Longest export delays in Africa and South Asia

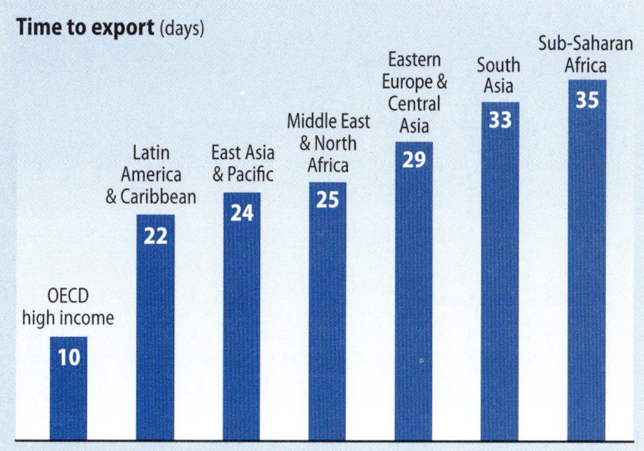

Source: Doing Business database.

time-sensitive agricultural products, reducing delays by 10% increases exports by more than 30%.[1] Often, just a few days less in exporting formalities can bring you into the market. Just ask Tarik.

There are other benefits of reform. In a survey of large multinationals, 65% indicated that they would add new investments in Africa and the Middle East if it were easier to trade.[2] Instead, many prefer to locate in Eastern Europe, closer to home. One example: in 2005 Tunisia lost a bid for a new factory for a German car manufacturer—and the 1,700 jobs it would have created. Romania was chosen instead.[3]

Easier trade across borders can diversify exports and boost employment.[4] In developing countries women benefit the most, because female workers dominate many export-oriented industries. In Kenya, for example, women make up 75% of workers in the cut-flower industry, the country's most successful exporter.[5]

Who is reforming?

India was the top reformer in trading across borders in 2006/07. It introduced online customs declarations for imports and exports. Arriving ships now submit their cargo manifests electronically, allowing the clearance process to begin even before the ship docks. These reforms helped cut delays for exporters and importers by 7 days. On average the top 10 reformers each cut the time to export by 5 days.

In Bosnia and Herzegovina customs clearance sped up sharply, thanks to a new online system. Traders submit their customs declarations electronically and get a response within 30 minutes. Before, this was done face-to-face with customs officials, a long process and a great opportunity to extract bribes. Another 13 reformers set up or improved electronic exchange of information between traders and customs (table 9.2).

Several African countries reformed. Uganda extended online declarations for traders to more border crossings across the country and is linking its new systems with Kenya's. That will speed transit trade through the port of Mombasa to Uganda. In Ghana delays at the Tema port were cut by 2 days with the construction of a new terminal and the creation of a system that allows into the port area only trucks ready to load or unload cargo. The changes also cut trading time for Burkina Faso, a landlocked neighbor.

Mauritius introduced a computerized risk management system for customs clearance. Now less than 30% of cargo undergoes physical inspection. Rwanda partially privatized the customs bonded warehouse, making it cheaper for traders to store goods there. Because of greater competition from newly built warehouses, prices for storage dropped by 40%.

Countries in Eastern Europe and Central Asia continued to reform. Armenia introduced electronic transmission of trading documents, reducing the time to prepare and submit documents to customs by 3 days. FYR Macedonia eliminated duplicate customs procedures at its borders. Waiting time fell by 75%.

Some of the reduction in delays for the region's exporters comes from an unusual source: the entry of foreign banks. "Banking services are improving every day.

TABLE 9.2
Electronic data interchange—the most popular reform in 2006/07

Introduced or improved electronic data interchange system
Armenia, Austria, Bosnia and Herzegovina, Brazil, Costa Rica, Djibouti, Ghana, Guatemala, India, Madagascar, Rwanda, Sri Lanka, Thailand, Turkey, Uganda
Improved customs administration
Colombia, Costa Rica, Dominican Republic, Egypt, El Salvador, Guatemala, India, Mauritius, Morocco, Turkey
Introduced risk-based inspections
Austria, Bosnia and Herzegovina, Brazil, Egypt, Guatemala, India, Uganda
Improved procedures at ports
Colombia, Djibouti, Egypt, Gambia, Ghana, Madagascar, Saudi Arabia
Implemented border cooperation agreements
Bosnia and Herzegovina, Lao PDR, Thailand, Turkey, Uganda

Source: Doing Business database.

FIGURE 9.3

Colombia speeds exports

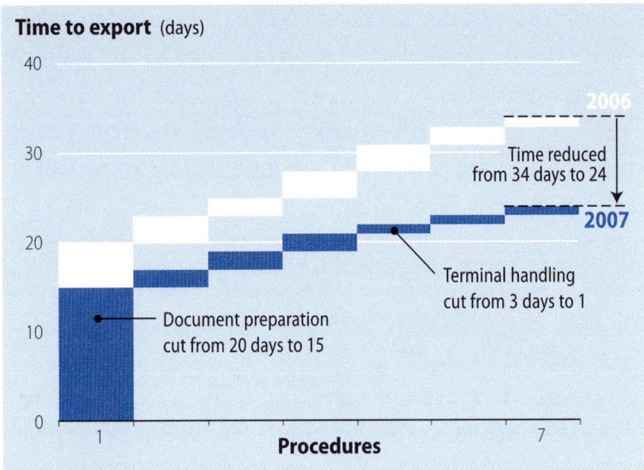

Source: Doing Business database.

Banks from Germany and Greece are opening branches in Albania, and the time to obtain a letter of credit has dropped from 14 days to 7," says Murati, an Albanian exporter. Similar improvements took place in Bulgaria and Croatia.

Customs reforms sped up in Central America, inspired by the recently signed free trade agreements with the United States. Costa Rica cut trading time by more than a week by allowing traders to submit declarations electronically. Guatemala made it easier to pay customs duties by setting up online payment. El Salvador introduced a one-stop shop for importers, bringing together different government ministries and agencies involved in issuing clearances.

The Dominican Republic abolished the requirement for a consular invoice. Before, all trading documents had to be validated at consulates overseas. Brazil upgraded its online declaration system, reducing data requirements by 50%. Colombia expanded operating hours at the ports, improved roads to the ports and introduced selective customs inspections of cargo. All these helped cut the time to export by 10 days (figure 9.3).

In the Middle East and North Africa, Saudi Arabia abolished the requirement for a consular certificate. Much of the information required for customs clearance can now be submitted electronically, reducing trading time by 2 days. Djibouti's customs extended its working hours to weekends and national holidays. And the container terminal, now under new ownership, was refurbished. Morocco applied risk management to customs clearance, halving clearance time. Algeria hastened the approval of licenses for customs brokers. The number of brokers increased, and customs fees dropped by 40%.

In South Asia, Sri Lanka introduced electronic submission of customs declarations, cutting the time for trading by 7 days. Pakistan continued to expand its online declaration system to other parts of the country.

What to reform?

In the past 3 years 55 countries have undertaken 68 reforms to speed trading. Pakistan reformed every year. Austria, China, Egypt, Ghana, Guatemala, India, Jamaica, Mauritius, Pakistan, Rwanda and Yemen reformed twice. Five reforms are most successful in reducing delays and improving export opportunities:

- Limit physical inspections.
- Go online.
- Shorten inland delays in Africa.
- Measure delays at the border.
- Shift from cutting tariffs to cutting delays.

Limit physical inspections

Imports and exports need to undergo several types of inspections—for tax, security, environmental, border control and health and safety reasons. There is no reason these cannot be done at the same time. "At the port there are 5 government agencies that stop your cargo—quality control, port security, police, state security and bomb squad. All of them demand bribes," says Tunde, a freight forwarder in Nigeria. It used to be like that in Pakistan. No more.

Pakistan made risk assessment a priority in its trade reform. "Our studies indicate that up to 80% of trade is by responsible and legitimate businesses and does not pose a threat to the country or its exchequer," writes the customs office.[6] So Pakistan limited physical inspections to the riskiest consignments. These inspections dropped from 100% of cargo before reform to less than 5% today. Now 70% of cargo is cleared in 1 hour, compared with an average of 10 days in 2004. Fewer inspections don't mean less revenue—customs revenue is up by 20%.

Reform wasn't easy. Pakistan had failed earlier.[7] This time customs reforms started with simple administrative improvements. Success in these brought support for further reforms.

Border agencies can combine their teams to reduce the burden on traders. One study estimated that in 2003 exporting from the Kyrgyz Republic to Russia by land took 208 hours and that 60% of this was waiting time at the borders—thanks to multiple inspections by customs, phytosanitary officers, immigration officers and the border police.[8] It used to be like that in Bosnia and Herzegovina. Now there is a single inspection. "The clearance process is very smooth—no delays at all unless you fill in your forms incorrectly," says Sarko, a freight forwarder. Similar reforms have taken place in El Salvador and Georgia.

Go online

In 2005 Kenya set up an electronic system for processing customs declarations. In 2 years clearance times dropped by half. "We have not even started exploiting the potential of our information technology systems," says Buyonge, a Kenyan revenue authority official.

The reforms did not start smoothly. Many traders did not have the Internet access needed to use the new system. At first port congestion worsened. The International Freight and Warehousing Association initiated a court action against the Kenyan revenue authority and won. The court ruled that the old paper-based system had to be restored. The deadlock was broken when the reformers invited the main freight forwarders for consultation. Discussions led to more operational support to make it easier to use the new system. Now nearly all large cross-border trades are submitted online.

Shorten inland delays in Africa

Often goods get delayed because of numerous checks on the roads. Traveling from Lagos to Abidjan (992 kilometers), a trucker faces 69 checkpoints. From Abidjan to Ouagadougou (1,122 kilometers) there are "only" 37. The situation is similar in the Central African Republic and Chad, adding to the already high cost of trading (table 9.3).

Reforms often involve cross-border cooperation—important, because transit regulations often impose restrictions, such as quotas on the number of trucks allowed from neighboring countries. Accords with neighbors can speed the release of transit goods.

Measure delays at the border

In Tanzania the tax authority carries out an annual exercise of random checks across border points. In August 2005 the average time to process documents for imports, from arrival to entry into the country, was 8 days, 23 hours across seaports; 6 days, 15 hours across airports; and 3 days, 9 hours across land crossings. In August 2006 the exercise was repeated to monitor the pace of improvements. In a year, thanks to this and other efforts, delays for importers had been reduced by a quarter on average.

Georgia's customs office is going even further. With the help of the U.S. Agency for International Development, evaluators were posted at random times at the 2 main border crossings (Sarphi and Red Bridge) and the 4 customs terminals (Adlia, Opiza, Lasare and Barvil). Their task was to clock the speed at which inbound cargo is processed. Interesting differences emerged: while processing trucks takes 28 minutes on average at the Red Bridge crossing, it takes 52 minutes at Sarphi. Similar differences were recorded at customs terminals.[9] Customs is now setting up a bonus system to reward teams of customs officials that process goods faster than their colleagues. The bonus is substantial: 2 months' salary for each customs official on a winning team.

Shift from cutting tariffs to cutting delays

Trade reformers still focus too much on cutting tariffs and not enough on cutting delays for exporters and importers. This attention is misplaced: a recent study finds that the cost of import delays exceeds tariff costs in every region, while the cost of export delays exceeds tariff costs in every region but East Asia and Western Europe.[10]

According to the same study, in Africa the cost of delays is 4 times the tariff payments African exporters face. This is corroborated by a striking number: despite the many U.S. trade preferences for African exporters under the African Growth and Opportunity Act, Africa accounts for only 0.23% of U.S. imports.[11] Similarly, only 8.6% of the European Union's imports come from countries in Africa, the Pacific and the Caribbean—all beneficiaries of tariff preferences under the Cotonou agreement.

TABLE 9.3

Who makes exporting easy—and who does not?

Documents (number)

Fewest		Most	
Canada	3	Burkina Faso	11
Estonia	3	Congo, Rep.	11
Micronesia	3	Mauritania	11
Panama	3	Namibia	11
Denmark	4	Afghanistan	12
Finland	4	Angola	12
France	4	Kazakhstan	12
Hong Kong, China	4	Malawi	12
Norway	4	Fiji	13
Singapore	4	Kyrgyz Republic	13

Time (days)

Least		Most	
Denmark	5	Eritrea	59
Estonia	5	Niger	59
Singapore	5	Angola	64
Hong Kong, China	6	Kyrgyz Republic	64
Luxembourg	6	Afghanistan	67
Netherlands	6	Chad	78
United States	6	Uzbekistan	80
Canada	7	Tajikistan	82
Germany	7	Kazakhstan	89
Ireland	7	Iraq	102

Cost (US$ per container)

Least		Most	
China	390	Uzbekistan	2,550
Singapore	416	Azerbaijan	2,715
Finland	420	Kazakhstan	2,730
Malaysia	432	Uganda	2,940
United Arab Emirates	462	Niger	2,945
Iceland	469	Rwanda	2,975
Brunei	515	Tajikistan	3,000
Pakistan	515	Iraq	3,400
Norway	518	Central African Republic	4,581
Hong Kong, China	525	Chad	4,867

Who makes importing easy—and who does not?

Documents (number)

Fewest		Most	
Denmark	3	Tajikistan	11
Sweden	3	Congo, Rep.	12
Canada	4	Eritrea	13
Estonia	4	Fiji	13
Hong Kong, China	4	Kyrgyz Republic	13
Ireland	4	Russia	13
Israel	4	Zimbabwe	13
Norway	4	Azerbaijan	14
Panama	4	Kazakhstan	14
Singapore	4	Central African Republic	18

Time (days)

Least		Most	
Singapore	3	Eritrea	69
Denmark	5	Rwanda	69
Estonia	5	Afghanistan	71
Hong Kong, China	5	Burundi	71
United States	5	Kyrgyz Republic	75
Luxembourg	6	Kazakhstan	76
Netherlands	6	Tajikistan	83
Sweden	6	Iraq	101
Germany	7	Chad	102
Norway	7	Uzbekistan	104

Cost (US$ per container)

Least		Most	
Singapore	367	Uganda	2,990
Malaysia	385	Mongolia	3,197
Finland	420	Iraq	3,400
China	430	Burkina Faso	3,522
Iceland	443	Burundi	3,705
United Arab Emirates	462	Uzbekistan	4,050
Norway	468	Tajikistan	4,500
Hong Kong, China	525	Central African Republic	4,534
Denmark	540	Rwanda	4,970
El Salvador	540	Chad	5,520

Source: Doing Business database.

Notes

1. Djankov, Freund and Pham (2007).
2. ERT (2005).
3. Muller-Jentsch (2005).
4. Dennis and Shepherd (2007).
5. World Bank (2005b).
6. Pakistan Customs Office, "PACCS Salient Features," http://www.paccs.gov.pk/DesktopDefault aspx ?tabindex=0&tabid=8 (accessed May 17, 2007).
7. Dennis (2007).
8. ESCAP (2003).
9. USAID (2006).
10. Hummels (2007).
11. Bureau, Chakir and Gallezot (2006).

Enforcing contracts

Why do many Italians live with their parents? A recent study finds that renting an apartment is difficult in countries where the courts are slow.[1] In Italy resolving disputes in the courts takes 1,210 days on average, so landlords hesitate to rent to young people.

Running efficient courts is a challenge for many governments, even in rich countries such as Italy and Slovenia. In 2006 Slovenia adopted a law obliging the government to pay plaintiffs up to €5,000 per case as a fine for delayed justice. This came after the European Court of Human Rights ruled that the Slovenian government had failed to deliver justice within a reasonable time. Slovenian courts outdo those in Djibouti and Guinea-Bissau in trying the patience of plaintiffs, taking 1,350 days on average to resolve a dispute.

Sometimes governments are to blame for the heavy caseloads in the courts. In Bosnia and Herzegovina state utility companies bring truckloads of claims for unpaid bills to the courthouse. These represented 70% of the court backlog in 2006/07. In India the government is the biggest litigator—mostly on tax matters. That country has one of the least efficient judiciaries in the world (table 10.1).

TABLE 10.1
Where is enforcing contracts easy—and where not?

Easiest	Rank	Most difficult	Rank
Hong Kong, China	1	Central African Republic	169
Luxembourg	2	Belize	170
Latvia	3	Syria	171
Iceland	4	Cameroon	172
Singapore	5	Congo, Dem. Rep.	173
Austria	6	Suriname	174
Finland	7	Bangladesh	175
United States	8	Angola	176
Norway	9	India	177
Korea	10	Timor-Leste	178

Note: Rankings are the average of the country rankings on the procedures, time and cost to resolve a commercial dispute through the courts. See Data notes for details.
Source: Doing Business database.

The primary role of the judiciary is to enhance justice, fairness and equity. But efficient courts do much more—they help the economy grow. A recent study finds that in countries with expedient courts, such as Lithuania, adopting a creditor protection law increases bank lending by 27% on average. But such a law makes little difference in countries with slow courts, such as Serbia, increasing bank lending by only 7%.[2]

In many countries only the rich can afford to resolve disputes through the courts. For the rest, justice is out of reach. In Indonesia recovering an overdue debt of $2,840 (twice the annual income per capita) would often cost more in court and attorney fees than the amount claimed. In Papua New Guinea a creditor might pay as much as $1,700 to recover a debt of $1,540 (again twice the average income). In Mozambique the fees for collecting a debt of $680 can be more than the amount claimed. Businesses have little incentive to use the courts.

Who is reforming?

In 2006/07, 14 countries reformed contract enforcement. Almost half the reforms were in Africa—in Burkina Faso, the Democratic Republic of Congo, Ghana, Malawi, Mauritania and Mozambique. Eastern Europe followed, with reforms in Bulgaria, Moldova and Poland. For the third straight year no major reforms took place in South Asia, the region with the longest court delays (figure 10.1).

Tonga was the top reformer, cutting the time to enforce contracts from 510 days to 350. A newly appointed chief justice introduced case management, transferring 90% of all cases—criminal, commercial and land—from paper to computer. Cases are now monitored daily. If they remain inactive for 3 months, the judge summons the parties and asks whether they plan to pursue the dispute. In this way 472 cases that had been dormant for years were uncovered and dropped. Others were put on a strict timetable.

The reforms also raised the threshold for the magistrates courts fivefold, to 10,000 pa'anga ($5,230), allowing more cases to use a simpler procedure. And new rules of procedure for the supreme court provide for court referral to mediation in civil cases for the first time. Court staff are undergoing training in Australia.

Elsewhere in the Pacific, Fiji reformed. Judges now focus exclusively on deciding legal disputes. A magistrate was appointed to deal with other matters, such as assessing damages after liability has been established.

The big trend in Africa was to introduce specialized commercial courts. All 6 African reformers did so. Since October 2006, 4 judges in Burkina Faso have been dealing exclusively with commercial cases in Bobo-Dioulasso and Ouagadougou. Getting there wasn't easy—the reform had been in the works since 1990. The Democratic Republic of Congo did it faster. Four years after being created on paper, commercial courts in Kinshasa started operating in November 2006. New rules for these courts set strict deadlines, such as 8 days to appeal judgments. Still, the cost of going to court is among the highest in the world (table 10.2).

Ghana's commercial courts, now fully operational, have reduced the time to enforce a contract from 552 days to 487. In Mauritania separate commercial courts

FIGURE 10.1

Longest court delays in South Asia

Source: Doing Business database.

TABLE 10.2

Where is enforcing contracts the most efficient—and where the least?

Procedures (number)

Fewest		Most	
Ireland	20	Guinea	50
Singapore	22	Kuwait	50
Hong Kong, China	24	United Arab Emirates	50
Rwanda	24	Belize	51
Netherlands	25	Iraq	51
Austria	26	Oman	51
Iceland	26	Timor-Leste	51
Luxembourg	26	Sudan	53
Belgium	27	Syria	55
Czech Republic	27	Brunei	58

Time (days)

Fastest		Slowest	
Singapore	120	Sri Lanka	1,318
Kyrgyz Republic	177	Trinidad and Tobago	1,340
Uzbekistan	195	Colombia	1,346
Lithuania	210	Slovenia	1,350
Hong Kong, China	211	India	1,420
New Zealand	216	Bangladesh	1,442
Belarus	225	Guatemala	1,459
Kazakhstan	230	Afghanistan	1,642
Korea	230	Suriname	1,715
Finland	235	Timor-Leste	1,800

Cost (% of claim)

Least		Most	
Bhutan	0.1	Comoros	89.4
Iceland	6.1	Cambodia	102.7
China	8.8	Burkina Faso	107.4
Luxembourg	8.8	Papua New Guinea	110.3
United States	9.4	Indonesia	122.7
Norway	9.9	Malawi	142.4
Poland	10.0	Mozambique	142.5
Korea	10.3	Sierra Leone	149.5
Finland	10.4	Congo, Dem. Rep.	151.8
Germany	11.8	Timor-Leste	163.2

Source: Doing Business database.

have replaced the commercial chambers in the general courts. And in March 2007, 2 commercial judges were added to the 3 judges who had been dealing with all civil matters in Maputo, Mozambique's capital.

More recently, in May 2007, the commercial division of the Blantyre high court in Malawi started hearing cases above 50,000 kwacha ($350). The court had been scheduled to start earlier, but the procurement rules of a major donor delayed the disbursement of money needed to equip the courthouse.

Also in May 2007 Rwanda adopted a law to replace the 12 commercial chambers in the general courts with 3 separate specialized courts, 1 of them in Kigali. The new courts have a separate budget and court rules tailored to resolving commercial disputes. This followed earlier reforms that abolished the requirement for 2 lay judges to assist each professional judge in hearing commercial cases. No one had volunteered to work as a lay judge, as this implied no pay, so no commercial cases were heard between March 2004 and March 2006.

In Eastern Europe reformers in Bulgaria, Moldova and Poland focused on making the enforcement of judgments more efficient and reducing judicial corruption.

Bulgaria introduced private bailiffs in 2006/07, shortening the time to enforce a judgment from 150 days to 125. In Poland judgments are now immediately enforceable, with no need for a separate enforcement procedure. For debt collection, creditors will soon be able to choose the most effective bailiff in each district court, because the restriction of one bailiff per district court was abolished. Poland also changed its procedural code. Now new evidence can be presented for only 2 weeks after the trial starts, and judges can impose fines on parties *and* their attorneys for adjourning cases by relying on false facts. Another common delaying tactic—filing counterclaims—has been restricted. The average time to obtain a judgment fell from 730 days to 580.

TABLE 10.3
Specialized commercial courts—still a popular reform in 2006/07

Introduced specialized commercial courts	Burkina Faso, Democratic Republic of Congo, Ghana, Malawi, Mauritania, Mozambique
Made enforcement of judgments more efficient or cheaper	Brazil, Bulgaria, Burkina Faso, Poland
Expanded scope of small claims courts or introduced simplified rules for small claims	Guatemala, Portugal, Tonga
Established case management	Fiji, Tonga
Made efforts to reduce judicial corruption	Bulgaria, Moldova
Streamlined appeal	Brazil

Source: Doing Business database.

To fight corruption, Bulgaria and Moldova introduced random allocation of court cases to judges and doubled judges' salaries. Bulgaria also made the selection and appointment of judges more transparent.

In Latin America, Brazil continued its efforts to make enforcement easier by allowing assets to be sold through private rather than public sales only. Creditors can often get a higher price that way. Brazil now also obliges debtors to tell their creditors where their goods are. If debtors do not cooperate, they risk a penalty of 20% of the claim. Guatemala focused on expanding its small claims courts; they can now hear cases up to $7,850, rather than $2,000 as before.

Portugal was the only rich country to reform (table 10.3). Since 2006 it has experimented with 4 pilot courts—2 near Lisbon and 2 near Porto. The 4 pilot courts apply simplified rules to debt collection cases below €15,000. If successful by 2008, the reform will be extended to the rest of the country. This reform is based on the model used in the United Kingdom, a country that continues to inspire court reform worldwide.

What to reform?

Doing Business has documented 65 reforms in contract enforcement since 2004. Some countries—Brazil, Burundi, Germany, the Philippines, Poland, Portugal, Rwanda and Serbia—have reformed more than once. Five reforms made the biggest difference:

- Introduce specialized commercial courts.
- Streamline appeals.
- Make the enforcement of judgments faster and cheaper.
- Introduce case management.
- Introduce e-courts.

Introduce specialized commercial courts

Six of the reformers in 2006/07 introduced specialized courts. Other countries, such as Azerbaijan and Egypt, will do so in the coming months. Countries with specialized courts resolve commercial disputes about 30% faster on average than those without them (figure 10.2). And if reforms in the specialized courts yield satisfied users, they embolden governments to try broader reforms.

Success with specialized courts also can bring unreasonable demand. One example is Peru. The Lima commercial courts, in operation since April 2005, made headlines in 2006 for deciding cases in less than a year. In February 2007 the judiciary ordered the transfer to them of 11,000 enforcement cases—about 11 times their caseload—flooding the commercial courts and increasing average delays.

Streamline appeals

A number of countries have reformed their appeals processes, respecting the right to appeal while limiting abuses. A balance can be achieved by excluding only the smallest cases from appeals and by allowing the higher courts to accept only cases that are new and fundamentally important to the country. In Sweden commercial cases can be appealed, but the appeals court now decides which cases to consider.

In Brazil and Denmark the supreme court now determines which cases it will decide. Still, judges are overwhelmed. The supreme court in Brazil issues opinions in 700 times as many cases as that in the United States.

Make the enforcement of judgments faster and cheaper

On average 30% of the total time to resolve a commercial dispute—the number of days from the time a case is filed until payment is made to the winning party—is spent enforcing the judgment. Sometimes enforcement actions take years. In Côte d'Ivoire, for example, enforcing the judgment takes more than half the total time spent to resolve a dispute. Obtaining a written copy of the judgment and resolving disputes over enforcement are the biggest bottlenecks (figure 10.3).

Several countries—Brazil, the Czech Republic, Finland, FYR Macedonia, Poland and Romania—have recently reformed enforcement laws. In Poland creditors can attach debtors' goods while the case is being appealed. If debtors want to keep possession of their goods during appeal, they must give a financial guarantee instead. Since last year courts in the Czech Republic can order all financial institutions in the country to check

FIGURE 10.2
Specialized courts reduce delays

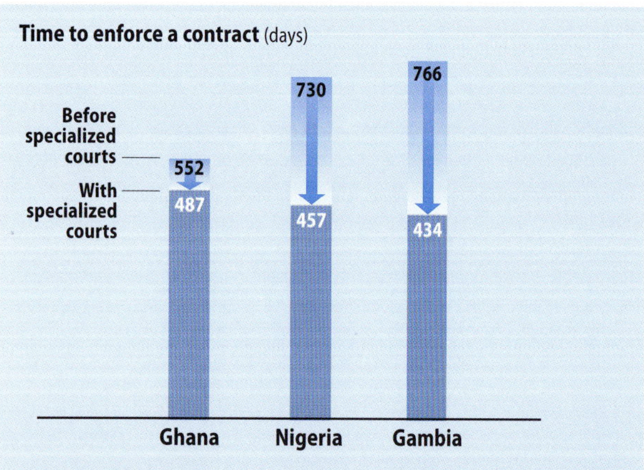

Source: *Doing Business* database.

FIGURE 10.3
Big delays in enforcing judgments in Côte d'Ivoire

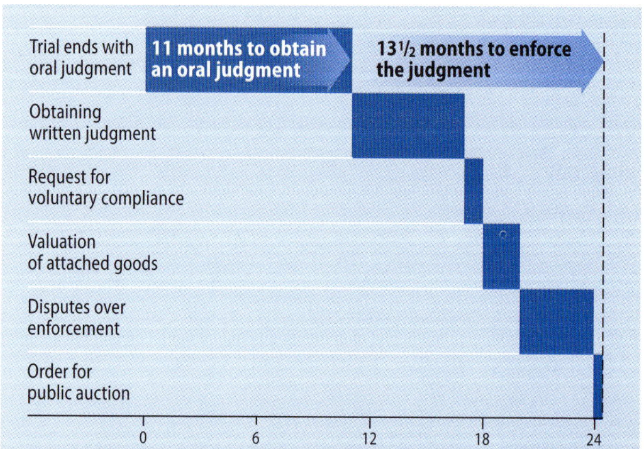

Source: *Doing Business* database.

whether the debtor holds an account with them and, if so, to automatically pay a judgment from that account. Before, creditors themselves had to identify the banks where debtors held an account. In Romania a new law allows creditors to attach credit balances and accounts receivable. In FYR Macedonia private bailiffs have started operating, shortening the average time to enforce a judgment from 90 days to 60.

In some countries creditors pay a registration tax to obtain an original copy of the judgment. Without it, they cannot start enforcement proceedings. In the Central African Republic and the Democratic Republic of Congo creditors pay 6% of the judgment amount as a registration tax. Cameroon, Guinea and Niger impose a 5% tax. In 2006/07 Burkina Faso reduced its registration tax from 4% to 2%. Côte d'Ivoire reduced its tax from 5% to 2.5%.

Introduce case management

Case management involves monitoring and managing cases in the court docket from the moment the action is filed until the moment it is finally decided. Analyzing court workloads can help predict trends and plan strategically.

Case management is successful if court data are simultaneously being computerized and if support functions such as case tracking, document management, deadline reminders and scheduling of hearings are done automatically. In 2006/07 the Philippines introduced such procedures for 60% of all lower courts in Manila.

Case management also makes it possible to measure the performance of judges. And measuring performance enhances performance—even for judges. If lazy judges are not disciplined and hard-working ones not compensated or promoted, performance suffers.

In countries such as Nicaragua judges continue to oppose case management and performance measurement by arguing that they would interfere with their independence. The rationale for this opposition lies elsewhere. Randomly assigning cases to judges, by using case management software, can prevent shopping for the judge most willing to accept bribes. In 2006 FYR Macedonia introduced such software in its effort to fight judicial corruption. By July 2007 the country's judicial council had brought charges of corruption against 10 judges.

Introduce e-courts

Litigants in New York have been able to access case data and documents through the Internet since 2006. Lawyers in Milan can upload case information in a bar code that court staff scan and transfer to a case management database. In 2006 Singapore introduced 3G mobile phones to conduct virtual court hearings and a pilot project allowing pretrial conferences by e-mail. Austria, Finland, Germany, Ireland and the United Kingdom set up online systems with simplified procedures for dealing with small claims. These claims previously took up most of the courts' time.

In rich countries such as Australia, Denmark, Finland, Norway, the Netherlands and Portugal businesses can file court cases electronically. Some middle-income countries, such as Brazil, the Czech Republic, Slovakia and Turkey, made it possible to submit claims by e-mail using electronic signatures.

Courts in some poor countries are going high-tech too. In India, for example, the supreme court, many high courts and even some district courts have their own website where businesses can download forms, look at the court's schedule for the day, check the status of a case or read the judge's orders. The supreme court even allows electronic filing of cases. That saves lawyers time and money, because they no longer need to go to the courthouse to pick up forms or receive the judge's order.

Notes

1. Casas-Arce and Saiz (2006).
2. Safavian and Sharma (forthcoming).

Closing a business

Ahmed, the former owner of a clothing shop in Abu Dhabi, made some bad business decisions that forced him to close shop last year. Hesitant to strike out on his own again, he has been looking for a job—to no avail. "No one wants to hire me," he complains. "There's a stigma to having a business that went bankrupt." It was worse in past centuries. The penalty for declaring bankruptcy in ancient Rome was slavery or being cut to pieces. The choice was left to the creditor. By the Middle Ages the treatment of insolvent debtors had softened. In Northern Italy bankrupt debtors hit their naked backside against a rock 3 times before a jeering crowd and cried out, "I declare bankruptcy." In England bankrupt debtors were often pilloried or thrown into prison and occasionally had an ear cut off.

Attitudes toward bankruptcy are one major obstacle for reformers drafting bankruptcy laws. But there are other good reasons why few bankruptcy reforms take place. First, bankruptcy reforms are complex: they typically involve making changes not only in the bankruptcy code but also in the code of civil procedure and the administration of the judiciary. That may take years. Second, in developing countries a large share of businesses are in the informal sector, and bankruptcy is not a priority reform. Only 10 economies undertook significant bankruptcy reforms in 2006/07.

It's not that reforms are not needed—in many countries creditors recover almost nothing (table 11.1). And everyone agrees on the goals of a good bankruptcy regime. The first goal is to maximize the total value of proceeds received by creditors, shareholders, employees and other stakeholders. Businesses should be rehabilitated, sold as a going concern or liquidated—whichever generates the greatest total value. The second is to rehabilitate viable businesses and liquidate unviable ones. In other words, bankruptcy law should be neither hard on good businesses nor soft on bad ones. The third is to provide for a smooth, predictable transition in the priority of claims as the company moves from a good financial state to a bad one—and thus reduce investors' risk. That goal is achieved by maintaining the absolute priority of claims in bankruptcy.

Why reform bankruptcy? Bankruptcy reform is less glamorous and takes longer than setting up a one-stop business registry. But having laws that deal effectively with troubled businesses helps get entrepreneurs to the one-stop shop in the first place. Easier exit means easier entry. One study shows that reforms to encourage a fresh start

TABLE 11.1
Where is it easy to close a business—and where not?

Easiest	Recovery rate	Most difficult	Recovery rate
Japan	92.6	Liberia	7.8
Singapore	91.3	Mauritania	7.8
Norway	90.7	Suriname	7.4
Canada	88.8	Venezuela	6.6
Finland	88.2	Philippines	4.2
Ireland	87.1	Haiti	3.1
Denmark	87.0	Micronesia	3.1
Netherlands	86.7	Congo, Dem. Rep.	2.9
Belgium	85.5	Zimbabwe	0.1
United Kingdom	84.6	Central African Republic	0.0

Note: Rankings are based on the recovery rate: how many cents on the dollar claimants (creditors, tax authorities and employees) recover from the insolvent firm. See Data notes for details.
Source: Doing Business database.

have raised rates of new business creation by 8–9%.[1] The freedom to fail, and to do so through an efficient process, puts people and capital to their most effective use. The result is more productive businesses and more jobs.

That's not all. A functioning bankruptcy system reassures creditors that if things go wrong, they stand a good chance of getting their money back. So they are more likely to lend, and to require less collateral than they would otherwise.

Who is reforming?

China was the top reformer in bankruptcy in 2006/07. Its Enterprise Bankruptcy Law, 12 years in the making, took effect on June 1, 2007. The law, China's first regulating the bankruptcy of private enterprises since 1949, significantly strengthens creditors' powers. Secured creditors with claims created after the law was passed now rank first in payment priority, even over tax and new wage claims. Another first for China: a reorganization procedure for restructuring insolvent companies. The introduction of creditors' meetings and committees gives creditors more say. Finally, the new law introduces bankruptcy administrators to operate insolvent companies during bankruptcy proceedings.

Five countries in Eastern Europe and Central Asia join China as top reformers this year (figure 11.1). Georgia, the number 2 reformer, passed a new law that maximizes the value of debtors' assets, sets shorter time limits, regulates bankruptcy trustees and strengthens creditors' rights. In place of a liquidation process that takes 3.5 years on average, the law establishes bankruptcy procedures that should take less than 1 year in the event of reorganization and just 6 months if the business is slated for liquidation. That would allow Georgia to enter the top 10 list on the speed of resolving bankruptcy (table 11.2).

Armenia passed a new law that incorporates time limits into the reorganization procedure. Secured creditors no longer vote on a reorganization plan unless the plan involves their pledged property. But the law explicitly prohibits the debtor's owners from voting as well, so creditors will have a greater say. Hungary passed a law that in most cases grants secured creditors absolute priority to the proceeds from the sale of their collateral. Croatia introduced educational and professional requirements for bankruptcy trustees and shortened timelines.

In April 2007 Uzbekistan issued a decree on voluntary winding-up of companies outside regular bankruptcy. The decree simplifies procedures and provides that if the tax authority does not conduct a tax inspection in time, the company pays only its self-assessed taxes. The decree also exempts financial assistance by the company's owners from income taxes and sets out the

FIGURE 11.1
Top 10 reformers in bankruptcy

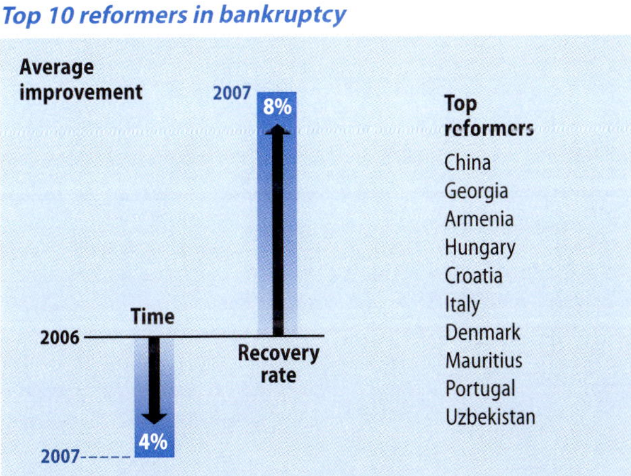

Source: Doing Business database.

TABLE 11.2
Where is bankruptcy the most efficient—and where the least?

Time (years)

Least		Most	
Ireland	0.4	Ecuador	5.3
Japan	0.6	Indonesia	5.5
Canada	0.8	Haiti	5.7
Singapore	0.8	Philippines	5.7
Belgium	0.9	Belarus	5.8
Finland	0.9	Angola	6.2
Norway	0.9	Czech Republic	6.5
Belize	1.0	Maldives	6.7
Iceland	1.0	Mauritania	8.0
Spain	1.0	India	10.0

Cost (% of estate)

Least		Most	
Colombia	1.0	Dominican Republic	38.0
Kuwait	1.0	Marshall Islands	38.0
Norway	1.0	Micronesia	38.0
Singapore	1.0	Philippines	38.0
Brunei	3.5	Solomon Islands	38.0
Finland	3.5	Venezuela	38.0
Georgia	3.5	Sierra Leone	42.0
Japan	3.5	Ukraine	42.0
Korea	3.5	Liberia	42.5
Oman	3.5	Central African Republic	76.0

Source: Doing Business database.

procedure for notifying the company's creditors.

Three rich economies improved their bankruptcy systems. Italy reformed for the second year in a row. Italian trustees now have broader discretion to maximize recovery for creditors in asset sales. This is expected to result in more sales of companies as going concerns. Denmark granted the courts more power to oversee trustees and make sure they act efficiently; this has already shortened bankruptcy proceedings. Portugal created fast-track procedures for the voluntary liquidation of businesses. Now an entrepreneur can wind up a company at the registry office. The changes, similar to the recently adopted fast-track provisions for starting a business, are intended to reduce the administrative burden of voluntary closings.

Mauritius made debt enforcement easier by passing the Borrower Protection Act 2007. Before, asset sales took place through a long "sale by levy" process that failed to realize the assets' market value. The new law allows land and buildings to be sold at private auction (table 11.3). Mauritius was Africa's only reformer. Three regions—Latin America, the Middle East and North Africa and South Asia—saw no reforms.

Two countries made bankruptcy more difficult in 2006/07. Botswana amended its Insolvency Act to give wage claims preference over the claims of secured creditors. This could dampen creditors' interest in extending credit. Meanwhile, Argentina stripped bankruptcy judges of jurisdiction over labor lawsuits and exempted such claims from the automatic stay applicable to claims. Now labor suits are to be concluded at the labor courts before presentation to the bankruptcy court for verification. Argentina also enhanced employees' right to demand payment of wage claims out of a distressed company's assets. A company must set aside 1% of its gross revenue to satisfy labor claims—even if it failed to turn a profit.

TABLE 11.3
Increasing creditors' rights—a popular reform in 2006/07

Reform	Economies
Granted priority to secured creditors	China, Hungary, Uzbekistan
Introduced or shortened time limits on bankruptcy procedures	Armenia, Georgia
Established reorganization procedure	China, Georgia
Set up one-stop shop for voluntary liquidation	Portugal, Uzbekistan
Introduced professional requirements for trustees	Croatia, Georgia
Strengthened trustees' role	Denmark, Italy
Allowed sale at private auction	Mauritius

Source: Doing Business database.

What to reform?

Forty countries have implemented bankruptcy reforms since 2003 (figure 11.2). Many of these reforms were long overdue. That's especially so for poor and middle-income countries, where bankruptcy laws are 40 years old on average. In contrast, rich countries have laws that average 5 years in age. By now the largest emerging economies—such as Brazil, China, India, Indonesia, Thailand and Vietnam—have all introduced significant bankruptcy reforms. Eight types of reform were most effective:

- Minimize dependence on the courts.
- Establish specialized courts.
- Shift power to creditors.
- Limit appeals.
- Introduce time limits.
- Use the Internet to post decisions and publicize auctions.
- Introduce floating charges.
- Develop the trustee profession.

Minimize dependence on the courts

In many countries, improving bankruptcy means improving the courts. The reason is that winding up or reorganizing a company often depends on the judicial system, with courts and court-appointed trustees directing proceedings. Thirteen of the top 25 economies on the ease of closing a business also rank among the top 25 on the ease of enforcing contracts.

One solution is to minimize the involvement of judges. In some economies with efficient bankruptcy, courts play only a limited role, if any. In Australia, Hong Kong (China), Singapore and the United Kingdom secured creditors can appoint a receiver to take control of a distressed company. This happens without any court involvement. The receiver then manages the company in preparation for selling its assets. More often than not the business is sold as a whole unit. The recent reforms in Georgia and Mauritius are based on the same idea. Other countries—such as Portugal and Uzbekistan in 2006/07—have made voluntary liquidation an administrative process.

FIGURE 11.2
Few reforms in South Asia, none in the Middle East

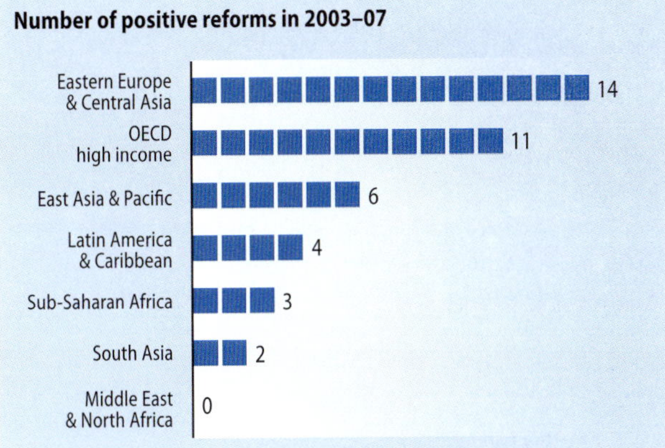

Source: Doing Business database.

Establish specialized courts

Other economies—including the Dominican Republic, Georgia, Moldova, Tanzania, Thailand and Uganda—have made it easier to process bankruptcy cases by creating specialized commercial or even bankruptcy courts. Specialization increases efficiency.[2] Judges can more easily gain expertise in bankruptcy and will be better equipped to deal with issues of insolvent businesses. Bosnia and Herzegovina and Ghana have created bankruptcy sections within commercial courts, with specially trained judges and innovative management systems to deal with court backlogs.

Shift power to creditors

Many economies have altered the roles and responsibilities of stakeholders in bankruptcy proceedings. Those that have strengthened the power of creditors include China, France, Indonesia, Korea, FYR Macedonia, Poland, Puerto Rico, Romania, Serbia, Slovakia, the United States and Vietnam. In Poland the creditors' committee now decides whether a business should be reorganized or liquidated. In France, Korea and Slovakia the creditors' committee votes on reorganization plans. Before, the court made the final decision.

Strengthening creditors' rights—for example, by establishing creditors' committees—increases their confidence in the bankruptcy process. A bankruptcy case is likely to result in the continuation of the underlying business in countries that allow creditors to appoint or replace an administrator and have access to the administrator's report. In contrast, such an outcome occurs in only 34% of countries that do not grant creditors such rights.

Several economies have given priority in bankruptcy claims to creditors. Bosnia and Herzegovina, China, Finland, FYR Macedonia and Vietnam granted a higher priority ranking to secured creditors. France gave a "super secured" position to creditors that lend money to distressed companies, making it easier for such companies to obtain new loans and continue operating.

Limit appeals

Another solution is to limit procedural appeals. In El Salvador the wait for a first-instance court to hand down its decision in a debt enforcement case can last up to 3 years. Appeals may drag the litigation out for another year or more. In both El Salvador and Slovenia, where the initial decision can be appealed to 2 higher levels of courts, restricting appeals to just 1 would speed bankruptcy proceedings. In Spain appeals no longer suspend debt recovery.

Restricting the number of appeals, or allowing debt recovery to proceed even when there is an appeal, is a simple way to make bankruptcy more efficient.[3] When used as a delay tactic, appeals reduce recovery rates, which depend on how quickly the business or its assets are sold.

Introduce time limits

FYR Macedonia, Poland, Portugal, Serbia, Slovakia, Spain and the United States have all either introduced or shortened statutory deadlines for bankruptcy proceedings. Imposing time limits also makes bankruptcy cheaper: reforms in Bulgaria, Estonia and the United Kingdom have halved bankruptcy costs. But some countries have bucked the trend. Thailand abolished a 1999 regulation limiting appeals, making it easier for debtors to abuse the appeals process and prolong bankruptcy.

Use the Internet to post decisions and publicize auctions

Where court reform is difficult, reformers can take advantage of the Internet. Croatia has launched a website, called "Judges Web," where the court posts information on decisions in bankruptcy cases and announcements of asset sales. Assets are more likely to fetch a higher price, because detailed descriptions and even pictures can be posted for long periods. Before, sales would typically draw few buyers because they were advertised only on a certain day and in a certain newspaper. FYR Macedonia and Serbia plan to introduce similar websites.

Introduce floating charges

Reformers need not focus on bankruptcy law alone. Denmark and several Eastern European countries have introduced floating charges (or similar enterprise charges) over the past decade. These are instruments through which companies grant a general security—covering even future assets—over their entire business. With them, viable businesses are more likely to be sold as a going concern in liquidation and foreclosure proceedings, since the charge prevents creditors from laying claim to different assets of the company. Creditors gain maximum flexibility in enforcing their security. They also recover more: countries that allow floating charges have higher recovery rates than countries that don't allow them (figure 11.3).

FIGURE 11.3
Floating charges improve results in bankruptcy

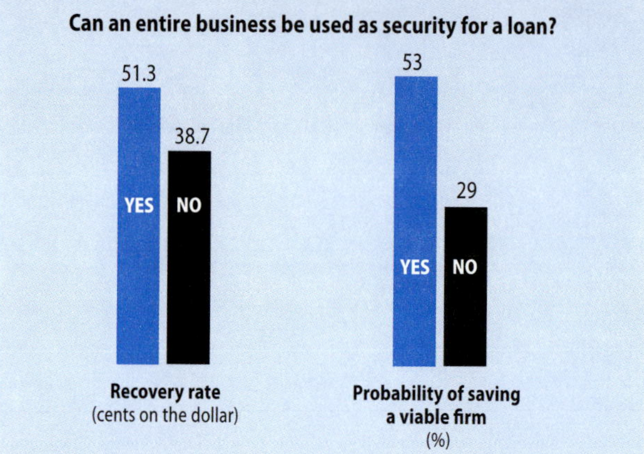

Source: Doing Business database.

Develop the trustee profession

Finally, several middle-income countries have taken steps to develop the profession and role of bankruptcy trustees, who play an important part in reorganization. Argentina, Chile, Serbia and Slovakia require trustees to have certain educational or business qualifications and to pass an exam. Serbia established a special agency to supervise the profession and introduced ethical standards that all administrators must abide by.[4] Chile stopped paying trustees a fixed monthly salary and linked their pay to the proceeds realized from asset sales. That encourages trustees to maximize returns by selling distressed assets quickly and removes any incentive to drag out the bankruptcy process.

Notes

1. Armour and Cumming (2006).
2. World Bank (2005a).
3. Djankov and others (2006).
4. Yap (2007).

What to expect

Doing Business 2009 will bring updates to the 10 sets of indicators reported in this year's edition. It may also incorporate some further improvements in methodology.

Beyond this, *Doing Business 2009* will reflect research on 3 new topics: not paying bribes, opportunities for women and infrastructure (starting with electricity). It will present the findings either as new analysis on the benefits of reforms or as new or developing sets of indicators. Whether the analysis and indicators become a standard part of *Doing Business* depends on the quality of the research and the ability to sustain the new indicators. Quality will be judged by academic peers, through the journal refereeing process. Sustainability will be judged on the basis of the cost of producing these indicators every year.

The choice of these research topics is natural. The research to construct indicators on not paying bribes and on infrastructure is motivated by evidence from the World Bank Enterprise Surveys on the main obstacles businesses face.[1] Corruption and poor access to infrastructure appear among the top constraints to business growth in most African countries, in many Middle Eastern and South Asian countries and in some Central American countries (figure 12.1).

Earlier editions of *Doing Business* have shown that burdensome business regulations hurt women the most. But more analysis is needed on what types of reforms most benefit working women. Expanding job and business opportunities for women is likely to have a large impact on economic growth. Precisely how large can be measured if new data are collected and analyzed. That's what the *Doing Business* team is set to do.

This chapter describes the analysis so far and the work that will take place in the coming year. The research on not paying bribes is most advanced, followed by the analysis on opportunities for women and the preliminary work on infrastructure.

FIGURE 12.1

Top obstacles to enterprises in Africa

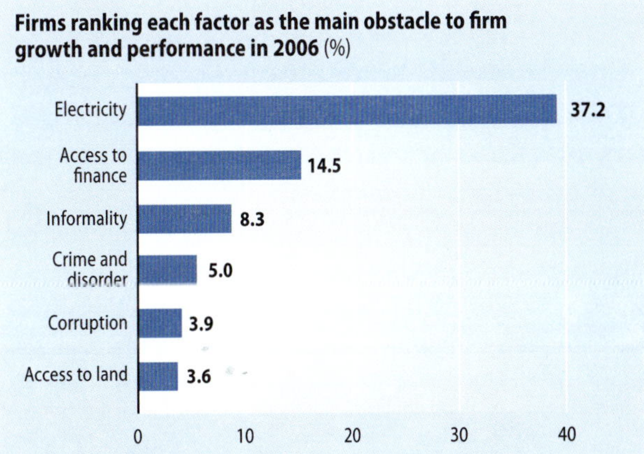

Source: World Bank Enterprise Surveys.

Not paying bribes

In June 2005 the U.S. media reported that the previous year a defense contractor had bought the house of a U.S. congressman, Randy Cunningham, for $1,675,000. A month later the contractor put the property back on the market, where it eventually sold for $975,000. At the time Cunningham was a member of the defense appropriations committee. Soon after purchasing the house, the contractor began to receive tens of millions of dollars in defense and intelligence contracts.

Cunningham resigned in late 2005 after pleading guilty to accepting at least $2.4 million in bribes and underreporting his income the previous year. In March 2006 he received a prison sentence of 8 years and 4 months.

This case would have taken longer to resolve had Cunningham not underreported his income in the disclosure forms that all members of the U.S. Congress file annually. The ability of the media and prosecutors to access these disclosures and point out inconsistencies made all the difference.

That is the focus of ongoing research by the *Doing Business* team: the ability of citizens, the media and prosecutors to monitor whether the actions of government officials are dictated by their private interests.[2] In every country the texts of relevant laws and regulations are collected. As for existing *Doing Business* topics, local partners are identified as contributors, in this case partners knowledgeable about the rules on public procurement and disclosure. Two global partnerships, one with PricewaterhouseCoopers Legal Services and one with Lex Mundi law firms, are also helping verify data.

In 80% of countries that require members of the legislature to disclose their financial or business interests, disclosure requirements also apply to the executive. In countries where there are separate regulations for each branch, both sets are compiled.

Some examples: OECD high-income countries require extensive disclosure on the business interests of public officials. All but one require annual public disclosure on such things as sources of income other than the official's salary, all equity stakes held and all positions held on company boards of directors—as well as disclosure of interests when deciding on laws or contracts that may affect their income (for example, a contract that may be awarded to a business in which a public official has a stake). In South Asia only a third of countries require such disclosure.

Even where public officials are required to make such disclosures, there are differences. In Austria, New Zealand, Switzerland and the United Kingdom legislators are required to disclose the names of all companies in which they have a business interest. In other countries legislators must report only the value of equity holdings and other investments, without naming the companies in which assets are held.

Many countries prohibit legislators from serving on company boards or as company officers. These include the Czech Republic, Georgia, Israel, Russia and Vietnam. Others, such as Lithuania and Slovenia, go even further, prohibiting any employment outside parliament.

Across the current research sample, 79% of countries require disclosure of interests. Among these, more than half mandate that these disclosures be available for public scrutiny. Half a dozen countries, mostly in Latin America and the Caribbean, allow disclosure to the public only when certain conditions are met.

Physical access to disclosures also varies. In the United Kingdom disclosures are available on the House of Commons website. In Pakistan they are published in the official gazette each year. In Moldova the registrar will e-mail you disclosures upon request. In more than a dozen countries you would have to pay the registrar a visit to access disclosures. In some, you would need to submit a request to the chairing committee of the parliament, which decides whether to grant access to disclosures.

In every country where public disclosure is mandated by law, the research team has requested the files of the first 5 members of parliament in alphabetical order. The process of obtaining these disclosures is documented in a time-and-motion study like those done for existing *Doing Business* indicators. The disclosure forms received are then studied to assess the extensiveness and completeness of the information filed.

What remains to be done? The analysis of collected data has started, with a first research paper expected in November 2007. The findings will then be subjected to peer review.

A second area of work is to compare these newly constructed indicators with existing ones. Three previous initiatives have informed the discussion on transparency. The first, conducted by Transparency International, is based on a number of perception surveys. The second, by the World Bank Institute, has similar sources of data but uses a more rigorous methodology for aggregation.

The third is the most recent, conducted by Global Integrity.[3] Like the ongoing *Doing Business* research in this area, it also covers public disclosure. Unlike the *Doing Business* research, its main source of information is local experts on disclosure requirements, not an analysis of the text of the law.

Opportunities for women

The *Doing Business* project commits to a 2-year research program on reforms that improve the job and business opportunities for women. The analysis will be developed in 3 directions.

First, it will identify laws and regulations that discriminate against women. For example, until 2006 Lesotho's law hindered women from becoming landowners and engaging in legal acts such as entering into a contract. Similarly, 2 dozen countries have labor laws that prevent women from having the same freedom to work as men. One example is Kuwait, which in June 2007 passed a law prohibiting women from working between 8 p.m. and 7 a.m., even if they want to. A few countries consider women legal minors and do not allow them standing in court. Instead, a woman must be represented by her husband, father or brother. And several countries do not allow married women to start a business on their own, requiring their husband's consent.

Several other areas of regulation, now beyond the scope of *Doing Business*, also reduce opportunities for women to find a job or start a business. One is inheritance law. In some regions, such as East Africa, women have fewer inheritance rights than men. That makes it harder to show collateral to the bank when starting a business. More important, it sometimes makes it impossible for women to provide for their children if their husband leaves or dies. Other regulatory requirements—such as the need to obtain a husband's consent before getting a passport, or to locate a business in licensed commercial premises—may also indirectly affect women's ability to participate fully in business. The research will study the legal restrictions that women face in such areas.

Second, analyses will identify the traditional reforms—as captured in existing *Doing Business* indicators—that have the biggest benefits for women. Reforms that reduce informality disproportionately benefit women, because they make up a large share of the informal economy. This year's report documents the link between the ease of doing business and the shares of women among workers and among entrepreneurs (see figure 1.7, page 7). In the next 2 years research will focus on reforms that do the most to increase these shares. This work will use the World Bank Enterprise Surveys, which have data on women entrepreneurs and the share of women in total employment since 2005.

Third, the *Doing Business* team will prepare case studies on women entrepreneurs and describe the reasons for their success as well as the main obstacles they face in expanding their business. These case studies may identify additional reforms that the study of laws and regulations might have missed. In particular, even after a government reforms, the prevailing practice takes some time to change.

In areas such as these, the case studies can lead to communication campaigns to promote the benefits of reform. In Uganda, for example, women's groups formed a coalition to lobby for reforms in business law that would especially benefit women. The result: more awareness of the need for reform and new bills drafted by the Ministry of Finance, now awaiting approval by the attorney general. These include the Companies Bill, the Chattels Transfer Act and personal property and securities laws.

Findings in these 3 areas of research will be reported in a stand-alone publication on opportunities for women. Just as for existing *Doing Business* indicators, all research will be subjected to peer review at academic journals.

Infrastructure

A variety of indicators on infrastructure services are available. But these typically measure outcomes: kilometers of paved roads, number of telephone lines, percentage of households connected to running water. Indicators like these have 2 limits. First, since building infrastructure is expensive, the cross-country comparisons show an obvious pattern: rich countries have good infrastructure, and poor countries don't. Second, if a reformist government wants to make its mark by improving infrastructure services, it can do little to change these indicators in a short time. Heavy investment is needed.

What a reformer can do is adopt regulation that facilitates expansion in infrastructure services. A reformer can also simplify the process of hooking up to these services for new businesses. These are the 2 aspects of infrastructure services on which the *Doing Business* team is constructing new indicators.

The first set of indicators builds on a specific case: an unexpected rise in electricity demand in the country has created opportunities for expansion. The case study documents the process that a private or public utility goes through to procure the components needed to extend the electricity distribution grid.

The second set looks at the process of obtaining a power connection, a water connection and a telephone line for a newly constructed building. The number of procedures for getting these services, and the associated time and cost, are recorded. The study does not compare prices of these services after the building is connected. That would involve detailed knowledge of subsidy policies, which is beyond the scope of *Doing Business*.

Notes

1. The World Bank Enterprise Surveys collect information on the main constraints that businesses perceive as well as some hard data on the time and cost of complying with particular regulations. The surveys in Latin America are done in cooperation with the Inter-American Development Bank. Those in Eastern Europe and the former Soviet Union are done in cooperation with the European Bank for Reconstruction and Development. Each year more than 30 surveys are conducted. Data for more than 100 countries are available at http://www.enterprisesurveys.org.
2. The research is done jointly with scholars at Dartmouth College, Harvard University and the University of Nice.
3. For information, go to http://www.globalintegrity.org/ and look for Global Integrity Index 2006.

References

Advisory Board on Administrative Burden. 2007. *Annual Report 2006.* The Hague.

Alesina, Alberto, and Andrea Ichino. 2007. "Gender-Based Taxation." Harvard University, Department of Economics, Cambridge, Mass.

Amin, Mohammad. 2007. "Labor Regulations and Technology in India's Retail Stores." Policy Research Working Paper 4274. World Bank, Washington, D.C.

Antunes, Antonio, and Tiago Cavalcanti. 2007. "Start-Up Costs, Limited Enforcement and the Hidden Economy." *European Economic Review* 51 (1): 203–24.

Armour, John, and Douglas Cumming. 2006. "The Legislative Road to Silicon Valley." *Oxford Economic Papers* 58: 596–635.

Atanasov, Vladimir, Conrad Ciccotello and Stanley Gyoshev. 2006. "How Does Law Affect Finance? An Empirical Examination of Tunneling in an Emerging Market." Babson College, Finance Division, Babson Park, Mass.

Azmat, Ghazala, Maia Guell and Alan Manning. 2006. "Gender Gaps in Unemployment Rates in OECD Countries." *Journal of Labor Economics* 24 (1): 1–38.

Bagaudinova, Svetlana, Dana Omran and Umar Shavurov. 2007. "Licensing 159 Activities—Not 909." In World Bank, *Celebrating Reform.* Washington, D.C.: World Bank Group and U.S. Agency for International Development.

Beegle, Kathleen, and John Strauss. 1996. "Intrahousehold Allocations: A Review of Theories, Empirical Evidence and Policy Issues." Michigan State University, Department of Agricultural Economics, East Lansing.

Botero, Juan C., Simeon Djankov, Rafael La Porta, Florencio López-de-Silanes and Andrei Shleifer. 2004. "The Regulation of Labor." *Quarterly Journal of Economics* 119 (4): 1339–82.

Bruhn, Miriam. 2007. "License to Sell: The Effect of Business Registration Reform on Entrepreneurial Activity in Mexico." Massachusetts Institute of Technology, Department of Economics, Cambridge, Mass.

Bureau, Jean-Cristophe, Raja Chakir and Jacques Gallezot. 2006. "The Utilization of EU and U.S. Trade Preferences for Developing Countries in the Agri-Food Sector." IIIS Discussion Paper 193. Trinity College, Institute for International Integration Studies, Dublin.

Bustelo, Frederic. 2007. "Reforming the Credit Bureau Law." In World Bank, *Celebrating Reform.* Washington, D.C.: World Bank Group and U.S. Agency for International Development.

Casas-Arce, Pablo, and Albert Saiz. 2006. "Do Courts Matter? Rental Markets and the Law." Working Paper Series. University of Pennsylvania, Wharton School, Institute for the Study of Labor (IZA), Philadelphia.

Cigna, Jean Piero, and Luca Enriques. 2005. *Assessing the Effectiveness of Corporate Governance Legislation: Disclosure and Redress in Related-Party Transactions.* EBRD Legal Indicator Survey 2005. London: European Bank for Reconstruction and Development. http://www.ebrd.com/country/sector/law/articles/assess.pdf.

Cunat, Alejandro, and Marc Melitz. 2007. *Volatility, Labor Market Flexibility, and the Pattern of Comparative Advantage.* NBER Working Paper 13062. Cambridge, Mass.: National Bureau of Economic Research.

Dennis, Allen. 2007. "Speeding Trade." In World Bank, *Celebrating Reform.* Washington, D.C.: World Bank Group and U.S. Agency for International Development.

Dennis, Allen, and Ben Shepherd. 2007. "Trade Costs, Barriers to Entry, and Export Diversification in Developing Countries." World Bank, Washington, D.C.

de Soto, Hernando. 2000. *The Mystery of Capital: Why Capitalism Triumphs in the West and Fails Everywhere Else.* New York: Basic Books.

Devas, Nick, and Roy Kelly. 2001. "Regulation or Revenues? An Analysis of Local Business Licences, with a Case Study of the Single Business Permit Reform in Kenya." *Public Administration and Development* 21 (5): 381–91.

Djankov, Simeon, Caroline Freund and Cong Pham. 2007. "Trading on Time." Policy Research Working Paper 3909. World Bank, Washington, D.C.

Djankov, Simeon, Caralee McLiesh and Rita Ramalho. 2006. "Regulation and Growth." *Economics Letters* 92 (3): 395–401.

Djankov, Simeon, Caralee McLiesh and Andrei Shleifer. 2007. "Private Credit in 129 Countries." *Journal of Financial Economics* 84 (2): 299–329.

Djankov, Simeon, Oliver Hart, Caralee McLiesh and Andrei Shleifer. 2006. Debt Enforcement around the World. NBER Working Paper 12807. Cambridge, Mass.: National Bureau of Economic Research.

Djankov, Simeon, Rafael La Porta, Florencio López-de-Silanes and Andrei Shleifer. 2002. "The Regulation of Entry." *Quarterly Journal of Economics* 117 (1): 1–37.

———. 2003. "Courts." *Quarterly Journal of Economics* 118 (2): 453–517.

———. Forthcoming. "The Law and Economics of Self-Dealing." *Journal of Financial Economics.*

Djankov, Simeon, Darshini Manraj, Caralee McLiesh and Rita Ramalho. 2005. "Doing Business Indicators: Why Aggregate, and How to Do It." World Bank, Washington, D.C. http://www.doingbusiness.org/documents/how_to_aggregate.pdf.

Djankov, Simeon, Caralee McLiesh, Rita Ramalho and Andrei Shleifer. 2007. "Taxation, Investment and Entrepreneurship." Harvard University, Department of Economics, Cambridge, Mass.

ERT (European Round Table of Industrialists). 2005. *ERT Survey on Trade Facilitation.* Brussels. http://www.ert.be.

ESCAP (United Nations Economic and Social Commission for Asia and the Pacific). 2003. *Transit Transport Issues in Landlocked and Transit Developing Countries.* Landlocked Developing Countries Series, no. 1. New York: United Nations.

Feder, Gershon. 2002. "The Intricacies of Land Markets: Why the World Bank Succeeds in Economic Reform through Land Registration and Tenure Security." Paper presented at the Conference of the International Federation of Surveyors, Washington, D.C., April 19–26.

Field, Erica. 2006. "Property Rights and Investment in Urban Slums." *Journal of the European Economic Association* 3 (2–3): 279–90.

Fleisig, Heywood, Mehnaz Safavian and Nuria de la Peña. 2006. *Reforming Collateral Laws to Expand Access to Finance.* Washington, D.C.: World Bank.

Freund, Caroline, and Bineswaree Bolaky. 2007. "When Does Trade Promote Growth?" Working paper. International Monetary Fund, Trade Department, Washington, D.C.

Goldin, Claudia, and Cecilia Rouse. 2000. "Orchestrating Impartiality: The Impact of 'Blind' Auditions on Female Musicians." *American Economic Review* 90 (4): 715–41.

Hummels, David. 2007. "Calculating Tariff Equivalents for Time in Trade." Purdue University, Department of Economics, West Lafayette, Ind.

ILO (International Labour Organization). 1998. *ILO Declaration on Fundamental Principles and Rights at Work.* Geneva.

Jacobs, Scott, and César Cordova. 2005. "Good Practices for Regulatory Inspections: Guidelines for Reformers." Report prepared for World Bank Group, Small and Medium Enterprise Department, Washington, D.C.

Johns, Melissa, and Jean Michel Lobet. 2007. "Protecting Investors from Self-Dealing." In World Bank, *Celebrating Reform.* Washington, D.C.: World Bank Group and U.S. Agency for International Development.

Katz, Elizabeth, and Juan Sebastian Chamorro. 2003. "Gender, Land Rights, and the Household Economy in Rural Nicaragua and Honduras." Paper presented at the annual conference of the Latin American and Caribbean Economics Association, Puebla, Mexico, October 9–11.

Ladegaard, Peter, Simeon Djankov and Caralee McLiesh. 2007. "Review of the Dutch Administrative Burden Reduction Programme." World Bank, Investment Climate Department, Washington, D.C.

López-Córdova, Ernesto. 2007. "Labor Regulation and the Allocative Efficiency of International Trade." World Bank, Enterprise Analysis Unit, Washington, D.C.

Masatlioglu, Yusufcan, and Jamele Rigolini. 2006. "Informality Traps." University of Michigan, Department of Economics, Ann Arbor.

Monteiro, Joana C. M., and Juliano J. Assunção. 2005. "Matching e determinação de contratos nas micro empresas no Brasil." Discussion Paper 499. Pontifícia Universidáde Católica, Department of Economics, Rio de Janeiro.

———. 2006. "Outgoing the Shadows: Estimating the Impact of Bureaucracy Simplification and Tax Cut on Formality and Investment." Pontifícia Universidáde Católica, Department of Economics, Rio de Janeiro.

Montenegro, Claudio E., and Carmen Pagés. 2003. *Who Benefits from Labor Market Regulations? Chile 1960–1998.* NBER Working Paper 9850. Cambridge, Mass.: National Bureau of Economic Research. http://www.nber.org/papers/w9850.pdf.

Moss, Todd. 2006. "Why Doesn't Africa Get More Equity Investment?" Center for Global Development, Washington, D.C.

Muller-Jentsch, Daniel. 2005. *Deeper Integration and Trade in Services in the Euro-Mediterranean Region: Southern Dimensions of the European Neighborhood Policy.* Washington, D.C.: World Bank.

OECD (Organisation for Economic Co-operation and Development). 2007. *Tax Administration in OECD and Selected Non-OECD Countries: Comparative Information Series (2006).* Paris.

PricewaterhouseCoopers. 2005. "The Economic Impact of Accelerating Permit Processes on Local Development and Government Revenues." Report prepared for American Institute of Architects, Washington, D.C.

Saavedra, Jaime. 1998. "Crisis Real o Crisis de Expectativas: El Mercado Laboral Peruano Antes y Despues de la Reformas." Working Paper 388. Inter-American Development Bank, Washington, D.C.

Saavedra, Jaime, and Máximo Torero. 2000. "Labor Market Reforms and Their Impact over Formal Labor Demand and Job Market Turnover: The Case of Peru." Research Network Working Paper R-394. Inter-American Development Bank, Washington, D.C.

Safavian, Mehnaz, and Siddharth Sharma. Forthcoming. "When Do Creditor Rights Work?" *Journal of Comparative Economics.*

Safavian, Mehnaz, and Joshua Wimpey. 2007. "When Do Enterprises Prefer Informal Credit?" World Bank, Enterprise Analysis Unit, Washington, D.C.

Schneider, Friedrich. 2005. "Shadow Economies of 145 Countries All Over the World: What Do We Really Know?" CREMA Working Paper 2005-13. Center of Research in Economics, Management and the Arts, Zurich.

Slemrod, Joel. 2004. "Are Corporate Tax Rates, or Countries, Converging?" *Journal of Public Economics* 88 (6): 1169–86.

Sorge, Marco, and Chendi Zhang. 2007. "Credit Information Quality and Corporate Debt Maturity: Theory and Evidence." University of Sheffield, Department of Economics, Sheffield, England.

USAID (U.S. Agency for International Development). 2006. "Time Measurement Related to Customs Clearance and Transit Procedures." Tbilisi.

WEF (World Economic Forum). 2006. *Global Competitiveness Report 2006–2007.* New York: Palgrave Macmillan.

World Bank. 2004. *Doing Business in 2005: Removing Obstacles to Growth.* Washington, D.C.: World Bank Group.

———. 2005a. *Doing Business in 2006: Creating Jobs.* Washington, D.C.: World Bank Group.

———. 2005b. "Kenya: Growth and Competitiveness." Report 31387-KE. Africa Region, Private Sector Unit, Washington, D.C.

———. 2005c. *World Development Indicators 2005.* Washington, D.C.

———. 2006a. *Doing Business in Mexico 2007: Comparing Regulation in the 31 States and Mexico City.* Washington, D.C.: World Bank Group.

———. 2006b. *Doing Business 2007: How to Reform.* Washington, D.C.: World Bank Group.

———. 2007a. *Celebrating Reform.* Washington, D.C.: World Bank Group and U.S. Agency for International Development.

———. 2007b. *World Development Indicators 2007.* Washington, D.C.

Yap, Justin. 2007. "Faster, More Orderly Exit." In World Bank, *Celebrating Reform.* Washington, D.C.: World Bank Group and U.S. Agency for International Development.

Data notes

The indicators presented and analyzed in *Doing Business* measure business regulation and the protection of property rights—and their effect on businesses, especially small and medium-size domestic firms. First, the indicators document the degree of regulation, such as the number of procedures to start a business or register commercial property. Second, they gauge regulatory outcomes, such as the time and cost to enforce a contract, go through bankruptcy or trade across borders. Third, they measure the extent of legal protections of property, for example, the protections of investors against looting by company directors or the range of assets that can be used as collateral according to secured transactions laws. Fourth, they measure the flexibility of employment regulation. Finally, a set of indicators documents the tax burden on businesses. For details on how the rankings on these indicators are constructed, see Ease of doing business, page 82.

The data for all sets of indicators in *Doing Business 2008* are for June 2007. Three new countries—Brunei, Liberia and Luxembourg—were added to the sample, now comprising 178 economies.

Methodology

The *Doing Business* data are collected in a standardized way. To start, the *Doing Business* team, with academic advisers, designs a survey. The survey uses a simple business case to ensure comparability across countries and over time—with assumptions about the legal form of the business, its size, its location and the nature of its operations. Surveys are administered through more than 5,000 local experts, including lawyers, business consultants, accountants, freight forwarders, government officials and other professionals routinely administering or advising on legal and regulatory requirements (table 13.1). These experts have several (typically 4) rounds of interaction with the *Doing Business* team, through conference calls, written correspondence and country visits. For *Doing Business 2008* team members visited 71 countries to verify data and recruit respondents. The data from surveys are subjected to numerous tests for robustness, which lead to revisions or expansions of the information collected.

The *Doing Business* methodology offers several advantages. It is transparent, using factual information about what laws and regulations say and allowing multiple interactions with local respondents to clarify potential misinterpretations of questions. Having representative samples of respondents is not an issue, as the texts of the relevant laws and regulations are collected and answers checked for accuracy. The methodology is inexpensive and easily replicable, so data can be collected in a large sample of economies. Because standard assumptions are used in the data collection, comparisons and benchmarks are valid across countries. And the data not only highlight the extent of obstacles to doing business; they also identify their source and point to the needed reform.

TABLE 13.1
How many experts does *Doing Business* consult?

Indicator set	Number of contributors
Starting a business	970
Dealing with licenses	495
Employing workers	661
Registering property	753
Getting credit	695
Protecting investors	484
Paying taxes	701
Trading across borders	912
Enforcing contracts	676
Closing a business	659

Source: Doing Business database.

FIGURE 13.1

Speed of reform differs across Mexican states

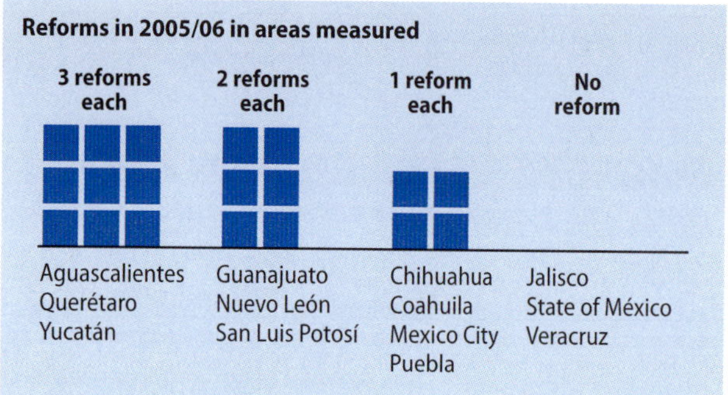

Source: World Bank (2006a).

Limits to what is measured

The *Doing Business* methodology has 5 limitations that should be considered when interpreting the data. First, the collected data refer to businesses in the country's most populous city and may not be representative of regulation in other parts of the country. To address this limitation, subnational *Doing Business* indicators were created for 5 economies in 2006/07: Bangladesh, Brazil, India, Mexico and Pakistan. Eight other subnational studies are under way—for China, Colombia, Egypt, Morocco, Nigeria, the Philippines, Russia and Ukraine. Some of the existing studies are updated annually, such as those in Mexico and the South Asian economies. These subnational studies point to significant differences in the speed of reform and the ease of doing business across cities in the same country (figure 13.1).

Second, the data often focus on a specific business form—a limited liability company of a specified size—and may not be representative of the regulation on other businesses, for example, sole proprietorships. Third, transactions described in a standardized case study refer to a specific set of issues and may not represent the full set of issues a business encounters. Fourth, the measures of time involve an element of judgment by the expert respondents. When sources indicate different estimates, the time indicators reported in *Doing Business* represent the median value of several responses given under the assumptions of the standardized case.

Finally, the methodology assumes that a business has full information on what is required and does not waste time when completing procedures. In practice, completing a procedure may take longer if the business lacks information or is unable to follow up promptly. Alternatively, the business may choose to disregard some burdensome procedures. For both reasons the time delays reported in *Doing Business 2008* would differ from the perceptions of entrepreneurs reported in the World Bank Enterprise Surveys or other perception surveys.

Changes in what is measured

The methodology for 3 of the *Doing Business* topics—dealing with licenses, employing workers and enforcing contracts—improved this year. For dealing with licenses, 3 changes were made. First, the case study now applies to builders that are fully licensed and insured at the start of the project. As a result, procedures that involve insuring or licensing the construction business are no longer counted. Second, inspections are now assumed to take 1 day to complete even where there is a delay between the request for an inspection and its occurrence. This change was made to eliminate discretion in interpreting the time that respondents report for inspections. Third, preconstruction inspections were added to the list of procedures; these affect mainly countries in the former Soviet Union. The first 2 changes reduce the number of procedures and delays associated with the case study; the third increases them.

For employing workers, improvements were made to align the *Doing Business* methodology with International Labour Organization (ILO) conventions. It is now possible for an economy to receive the highest score on the ease of employing workers—indicating the most flexible labor regulations—and comply with all 187 ILO conventions. Two main changes were made. First, the calculation of firing costs was modified so that 8 or fewer weeks of salary now receives a score of 0 for purposes of calculating the rankings on the ease of employing workers. Second, restrictions on night work such as higher overtime premiums or limitations on scheduling work hours are no longer coded as rigidities. Both changes result in more flexibility in employment regulations as coded in *Doing Business*.

For enforcing contracts, the list of procedures was revised to accommodate procedural differences between civil and common law. For example, in civil law countries the judge appoints an independent expert, while in common law countries parties send the court a list of their expert witnesses. Two assumptions were added, on attaching the defendant's goods prior to judgment and on providing expert opinions. To indicate the overall efficiency of court procedures, 1 procedure is now subtracted for countries that have specialized commercial courts and 1 procedure for countries that allow electronic filing of court cases. Finally, the cost indicator now includes all fees for enforcing judgments.

Data corrections

The laws and regulations underlying the *Doing Business* data are available on the *Doing Business* website at http://www.doingbusiness.org. All the sample surveys and the details underlying the indicators are also published on the website. Questions on the methodology and challenges to data can be submitted through the site's "Ask a Question" function.

Doing Business publishes 8,900 indicators each year. To create these indicators, the team measures more than 52,000 data points, each of which is made available on the *Doing Business* website. Since the publication of *Doing Business 2007*, 20 economies have challenged last year's data. In several cases the government reviewed every data point measured. These reviews resulted in corrections to 47 data points. These changes are reflected in the ease of doing business index. They are also reflected in the database on the website.

Economy characteristics

Gross national income (GNI) per capita

Doing Business 2008 reports 2006 income per capita as published in the World Bank's *World Development Indicators 2007*. Income is calculated using the Atlas method (current US$). For cost indicators expressed as a percentage of income per capita, 2006 GNI in local currency units is used as the denominator. GNI data were not available from the World Bank for the Republic of Congo, Iraq, Oman, Puerto Rico, Saudi Arabia, the United Arab Emirates, West Bank and Gaza or Zimbabwe. In these cases GDP or GNP per capita data and growth rates from the Economist Intelligence Unit 2006 country profiles and the U.S. State Department 2007 country profiles were used.

Region and income group

Doing Business uses the World Bank regional and income group classifications, available at http://www.worldbank.org/data/countryclass. Throughout the report the term *rich economies* refers to the high-income group, *middle-income economies* to the upper-middle-income group and *poor economies* to the lower-middle-income and low-income groups.

Population

Doing Business 2008 reports midyear 2006 population statistics as published in *World Development Indicators 2007*.

Starting a business

Doing Business records all procedures that are officially required for an entrepreneur to start up and formally operate an industrial or commercial business. These include obtaining all necessary licenses and permits and completing any required notifications, verifications or inscriptions for the company and employees with relevant authorities.

After a study of laws, regulations and publicly available information on business entry, a detailed list of procedures is developed, along with the time and cost of complying with each procedure under normal circumstances and the paid-in minimum capital requirements. Subsequently, local incorporation lawyers and government officials complete and verify the data.

Information is also collected on the sequence in which procedures are to be completed and whether procedures may be carried out simultaneously. It is assumed that any required information is readily available and that all agencies involved in the start-up process function without corruption. If answers by local experts differ, inquiries continue until the data are reconciled.

To make the data comparable across countries, several assumptions about the business and the procedures are used.

Assumptions about the business

The business:

- Is a limited liability company. If there is more than one type of limited liability company in the country, the limited liability form most popular among domestic firms is chosen. Information on the most popular form is obtained from incorporation lawyers or the statistical office.
- Operates in the country's most populous city.
- Is 100% domestically owned and has 5 owners, none of whom is a legal entity.
- Has start-up capital of 10 times income per capita at the end of 2006, paid in cash.
- Performs general industrial or commercial activities, such as the production or sale of products or services to the public. The business does not perform foreign trade activities and does not handle products subject to a special tax regime, for example, liquor or tobacco. It is not using heavily polluting production processes.
- Leases the commercial plant and offices and is not a proprietor of real estate.
- Does not qualify for investment incentives or any special benefits.
- Has at least 10 and up to 50 employees 1 month after the commencement of operations, all of them nationals.
- Has a turnover of at least 100 times income per capita.
- Has a company deed 10 pages long.

Procedures

A procedure is defined as any interaction of the company founder with external parties (for example, government agencies, lawyers, auditors or notaries). Interactions between company founders or company officers and employees are not counted as procedures. Procedures that must be completed in the same building but in different offices are counted as separate procedures. If founders have to visit the same office several times for different sequential procedures, each is counted separately. The founders are assumed to complete all procedures themselves, without middlemen, facilitators, accountants or lawyers, unless the use of such a third party is mandated by law. If the services of professionals are required, procedures conducted by such professionals on behalf of the company are counted separately.

Both pre- and postincorporation procedures that are officially required for an entrepreneur to formally operate a business are recorded (table 13.2).

Procedures required for official correspondence or transactions with public agencies are also included. For example, if a company seal or stamp is required on official documents, such as tax declarations, obtaining the seal or stamp is counted. Similarly, if a company must open a bank account

TABLE 13.2
What does starting a business measure?

Procedures to legally start and operate a company
- Preregistration (name verification, notarization)
- Registration in the economy's most populous city
- Postregistration (social security registration, company seal)

Time required to complete each procedure
- Does not include time spent gathering information
- Each procedure starts on a separate day
- Procedure completed once final document is received
- No prior contact with officials

Cost required to complete each procedure
- Official costs only, no bribes
- No professional fees unless services required by law

Paid-in minimum capital
- Deposited in a bank or with a notary before registration begins

Source: Doing Business database.

before registering for sales tax or value added tax, this transaction is included as a procedure. Shortcuts are counted only if they fulfill 4 criteria: they are legal, they are available to the general public, they are used by the majority of companies, and avoiding them causes substantial delays.

Only procedures required of all businesses are covered. Industry-specific procedures are excluded. For example, procedures to comply with environmental regulations are included only when they apply to all businesses conducting general commercial or industrial activities. Procedures that the company undergoes to connect to electricity, water, gas and waste disposal services are not included.

Time

Time is recorded in calendar days. The measure captures the median duration that incorporation lawyers indicate is necessary to complete a procedure with minimum follow-up with government agencies and no extra payments. It is assumed that the minimum time required for each procedure is 1 day. Although procedures may take place simultaneously, they cannot start on the same day (that is, simultaneous procedures start on consecutive days). A procedure is considered completed once the company has received the final document, such as the company registration certificate or tax number. If a procedure can be accelerated for an additional cost, the fastest procedure is chosen. It is assumed that the entrepreneur does not waste time and commits to completing each remaining procedure without delay. The time that the entrepreneur spends on gathering information is ignored. It is assumed that the entrepreneur is aware of all entry regulations and their sequence from the beginning but has had no prior contact with any of the officials.

Cost

Cost is recorded as a percentage of the country's income per capita. It includes all official fees and fees for legal or professional services if such services are required by law. Fees for purchasing and legalizing company books are included if these transactions are required by law. The company law, the commercial code and specific regulations and fee schedules are used as sources for calculating costs. In the absence of fee schedules, a government officer's estimate is taken as an official source. In the absence of a government officer's estimate, estimates of incorporation lawyers are used. If several incorporation lawyers provide different estimates, the median reported value is applied. In all cases the cost excludes bribes.

Paid-in minimum capital

The paid-in minimum capital requirement reflects the amount that the entrepreneur needs to deposit in a bank or with a notary before registration and up to 3 months following incorporation and is recorded as a percentage of the country's income per capita. The amount is typically specified in the commercial code or the company law. Many countries have a minimum capital requirement but allow businesses to pay only a part of it before registration, with the rest to be paid after the first year of operation. In Germany in June 2007 the minimum capital requirement for limited liability companies was €25,000, of which at least €12,500 was payable before registration. The paid-in minimum capital recorded for Germany is therefore €12,500, or 42.8% of income per capita. In Serbia the minimum capital requirement was €500, of which only half needed to be paid before registration. The paid-in minimum capital recorded for Serbia is therefore €250, or 8% of income per capita.

This methodology was developed in Djankov and others (2002) and is adopted here with minor changes.

Dealing with licenses

Doing Business records all procedures required for a business in the construction industry to build a standardized warehouse. These procedures include submitting all relevant project-specific documents (for example, building plans and site maps) to the authorities; obtaining all necessary clearances, licenses, permits and certificates; completing all required notifications; and receiving all necessary inspections. *Doing Business* also records procedures for obtaining all utility connections. Procedures necessary to register the property so that it can be used as collateral or transferred are also counted. The survey divides the process of building a warehouse into distinct procedures and calculates the time and cost of completing each procedure in practice under normal circumstances.

Information is collected from experts in construction licensing, including architects, construction lawyers, construction firms, utility service providers and public officials who deal with building regulations, including approvals and inspections. To make the data comparable across countries, several assumptions about the business, the warehouse project and the procedures are used.

Assumptions about the construction company

The business (BuildCo):

- Is a limited liability company.
- Operates in the country's most populous city.
- Is 100% domestically and privately owned.
- Has 5 owners, none of whom is a legal entity.
- Is fully licensed and insured to carry out construction projects, such as building warehouses.
- Has 20 builders and other employees, all of them nationals with the technical expertise and professional experience necessary to obtain construction permits and approvals.
- Has at least 1 employee who is a licensed architect and registered with the local association of architects.
- Has paid all taxes and taken out all necessary insurance applicable to its general business activity (for example, accidental insurance for construction workers and third-person liability insurance).
- Owns the land on which the warehouse is built.

Assumptions about the warehouse project

The warehouse:

- Has 2 stories, both above ground, with a total surface of approximately 14,000 square feet (1,300.6 square meters). Each floor is 9 feet, 10 inches (3 meters) high.
- Has road access and is located in the periurban area of the country's most populous city (that is, is on the fringes of the city but still within its official limits). It is not located in a special economic or industrial zone.
- Is located on a land plot of 10,000 square feet (929 square meters) that is 100% owned by BuildCo and is registered in the cadastre and land registry.
- Is a new construction (there was no previous construction on the land).
- Has complete architectural and technical plans prepared by a licensed architect.
- Will be connected to the following utilities—electricity, water, sewerage (sewage system, septic tank or their equivalent) and one land phone line. The connection to each utility network will be 32 feet, 10 inches (10 meters) long.
- Will require a 10-ampere power connection and 140 kilowatts of electricity.
- Will require up to 100 cubic meters of water daily.
- Will be used for general storage activities, such as storage of books or stationery. The warehouse will not be used for any goods requiring special conditions, such as food, chemicals or pharmaceuticals.
- Will include all technical equipment required to make the warehouse fully operational.
- Will take 30 weeks to construct (excluding all delays due to administrative and regulatory requirements).

Procedures

A procedure is any interaction of the company's employees or managers with external parties, including government agencies, notaries, the land registry, the cadastre, utility companies, public and private inspectors and technical experts apart from in-house architects and engineers. Interactions between company employees, such as development of the warehouse plans and inspections conducted by employees, are not counted as procedures. Procedures that the company undergoes to connect to electricity, water, sewerage and phone services are included. All procedures that are legally or in practice required for building a warehouse are counted, even if they may be avoided in exceptional cases.

Time

Time is recorded in calendar days. The measure captures the median duration that local experts indicate is necessary to complete a procedure in practice. It is assumed that the minimum time required for each procedure is 1 day. If a procedure can be accelerated legally for an additional cost, the fastest procedure is chosen. It is assumed that BuildCo does not waste time and commits to completing each remaining procedure without delay. The time that BuildCo spends on gathering information is ignored. It is assumed that BuildCo is aware of all building requirements and their sequence from the beginning.

Cost

Cost is recorded as a percentage of the country's income per capita. Only official costs are recorded. All the fees associated with completing the procedures to legally build a warehouse are recorded, including those associated with obtaining land use approvals and preconstruction design clearances; receiving inspections before, during and after construction; getting utility connections; and registering the warehouse property. Nonrecurring taxes required for the completion of the warehouse project also are recorded. The building code, information from local experts and specific regulations and fee schedules are used as sources for costs. If several local partners provide different estimates, the median reported value is used.

Employing workers

Doing Business measures the regulation of employment, specifically as it affects the hiring and firing of workers and the rigidity of working hours. The data on employing workers are based on a detailed survey of employment regulations that is completed by local lawyers and public officials. Employment laws and regulations as well as secondary sources are reviewed to ensure accuracy.

To make the data comparable across countries, several assumptions about the worker and the business are used.

Assumptions about the worker

The worker:

- Is a 42-year-old, nonexecutive, full-time, male employee.
- Has worked at the same company for 20 years.
- Earns a salary plus benefits equal to the country's average wage during the entire period of his employment.
- Is a lawful citizen who belongs to the same race and religion as the majority of the country's population.
- Resides in the country's most populous city.
- Is not a member of a labor union, unless membership is mandatory.

Assumptions about the business

The business:

- Is a limited liability company.
- Operates in the country's most populous city.
- Is 100% domestically owned.
- Operates in the manufacturing sector.
- Has 201 employees.
- Is subject to collective bargaining agreements in countries where such agreements cover more than half the manufacturing sector and apply even to firms not party to them.
- Abides by every law and regulation but does not grant workers more benefits than mandated by law, regulation or (if applicable) collective bargaining agreement.

Rigidity of employment index

The rigidity of employment index is the average of 3 subindices: a difficulty of hiring index, a rigidity of hours index and a difficulty of firing index. All the subindices have several components. And all take values between 0 and 100, with higher values indicating more rigid regulation.

The difficulty of hiring index measures (i) whether fixed-term contracts are prohibited for permanent tasks; (ii) the maximum cumulative duration of fixed-term contracts; and (iii) the ratio of the minimum wage for a trainee or first-time employee to the average value added per worker. A country is assigned a score of 1 if fixed-term contracts are prohibited for permanent tasks and a score of 0 if they can be used for any task. A score of 1 is assigned if the maximum cumulative duration of fixed-term contracts is less than 3 years; 0.5 if it is 3 years or more but less than 5 years; and 0 if fixed-term contracts can last 5 years or more. Finally, a score of 1 is assigned if the ratio of the minimum wage to the average value added per worker is 0.75 or more; 0.67 for a ratio of 0.50 or more but less than 0.75; 0.33 for a ratio of 0.25 or more but less than 0.50; and 0 for a ratio of less than 0.25. In the Central African Republic, for example, fixed-term contracts are prohibited for permanent tasks (a score of 1), and they can be used for a maximum of 4 years (a score of 0.5). The ratio of the mandated minimum wage to the value added per worker is 0.64 (a score of 0.67). Averaging the 3 values and scaling the index to 100 gives the Central African Republic a score of 72.

The rigidity of hours index has 5 components: (i) whether night work is unrestricted; (ii) whether weekend work is unrestricted; (iii) whether the workweek can consist of 5.5 days; (iv) whether the workweek can extend to 50 hours or more (including overtime) for 2 months a year to respond to a seasonal increase in production; and (v) whether paid annual vacation is 21 working days or fewer. For each of these questions, if the answer is no, the country is assigned a score of 1; otherwise a score of 0 is assigned. For example, Serbia imposes restrictions on night work (a score of 1) and weekend work (a score of 1), allows 6-day workweeks (a score of 0), permits 50-hour workweeks for 2 months (a score of 0) and requires paid vacation of 20 working days (a score of 0). Averaging the scores and scaling the result to 100 gives a final index of 40 for Serbia.

The difficulty of firing index has 8 components: (i) whether redundancy is disallowed as a basis for terminating workers; (ii) whether the employer needs to notify a third party (such as a government agency) to terminate 1 redundant worker; (iii) whether the employer needs to notify a third party to terminate a group of 25 redundant workers; (iv) whether the employer needs approval from a third party to terminate 1 redundant worker; (v) whether the employer needs approval from a third party to terminate a group of 25 redundant workers; (vi) whether the law requires the employer to consider reassignment or retraining options before redundancy termination; (vii) whether priority rules apply for redundancies; and (viii) whether priority rules apply for reemployment. For the first question an answer of yes for workers of any income level gives a score of 10 and means that the rest of the questions do not apply. An answer of yes to question (iv) gives a score of 2. For every other question, if the answer is yes, a score of 1 is assigned; otherwise a score of 0 is given. Questions (i) and (iv), as the most restrictive regulations, have greater weight in the construction of the index.

In Tunisia, for example, redundancy is allowed as grounds for termination (a score of 0). An employer has to both notify a third party (a score of 1) and obtain its approval (a score of 2) to terminate a single redundant worker, and has to both notify a third party (a score of 1) and obtain its approval (a score of 1) to terminate a group of 25 redundant workers. The law mandates consideration of retraining or alternative placement before termination (a score of 1). There are priority rules for termination (a score of 1) and reemployment (a score of 1). Adding the scores and scaling to 100 gives a final index of 80.

Nonwage labor cost

The nonwage labor cost indicator measures all social security payments (including retirement fund; sickness, maternity and health insurance; workplace injury; family allowance; and other obligatory contributions) and payroll taxes associated with hiring an employee in fiscal 2006. The cost is expressed as a percentage of the worker's salary. In Honduras, for example, the taxes paid by the employer amount to 9.5% of the worker's wages and include 7% for social security, 1% for professional training and 1.5% for the pension contribution.

Firing cost

The firing cost indicator measures the cost of advance notice requirements, severance payments and penalties due when terminating a redundant worker, expressed in weekly wages. If the firing cost adds up to 8 or fewer weeks of salary, a score of 0 is assigned for the purposes of calculating the aggregate ease of doing business ranking. If the cost adds up to more than 8 weeks of salary, the score is the number of weeks. One month is recorded as 4 and 1/3 weeks. In Mozambique, for example, an employer is required to give 90 days' notice before a redundancy termination, and the severance pay for a worker with 20 years of service equals 30 months of wages. No penalty is levied. Altogether, the employer pays the equivalent of 143 weeks of salary to dismiss the worker.

This methodology was developed in Botero and others (2004) and is adopted here with minor changes.

Registering property

Doing Business records the full sequence of procedures necessary when a business purchases land and a building to transfer the property title from another business so that the buyer can use the property for expanding its business, as collateral in taking new loans or, if necessary, to sell to another business. Every procedure required by law or necessary in practice is included, whether it is the responsibility of the seller or the buyer or must be completed by a third party on their behalf. Local property lawyers, notaries and property registries provide information on procedures as well as the time and cost to complete each of them.

To make the data comparable across countries, several assumptions about the parties to the transaction, the property and the procedures are used.

Assumptions about the parties

The parties (buyer and seller):

- Are limited liability companies.
- Are located in the periurban area of the country's most populous city.
- Are 100% domestically and privately owned.
- Have 50 employees each, all of whom are nationals.
- Perform general commercial activities.

Assumptions about the property

The property:

- Has a value of 50 times income per capita. The sale price equals the value.
- Is fully owned by the seller.
- Has no mortgages attached and has been under the same ownership for the past 10 years.
- Is registered in the land registry or cadastre, or both, and is free of title disputes.
- Is located in a periurban commercial zone, and no rezoning is required.
- Consists of land and a building. The land area is 6,000 square feet (557.4 square meters). A 2-story warehouse of 10,000 square feet (929 square meters) is located on the land. The warehouse is 10 years old, is in good condition and complies with all safety standards, building codes and other legal requirements. The property of land and building will be transferred in its entirety.
- Will not be subject to renovations or additional building following the purchase.
- Has no trees, natural water sources, natural reserves or historical monuments of any kind.
- Will not be used for special purposes, and no special permits, such as for residential use, industrial plants, waste storage or certain types of agricultural activities, are required.
- Has no occupants (legal or illegal), and no other party holds a legal interest in it.

Procedures

A procedure is defined as any interaction of the buyer or the seller, their agents (if an agent is legally or in practice required) or the property with external parties, including government agencies, inspectors, notaries and lawyers. Interactions between company officers and employees are not considered. All procedures that are legally or in practice required for registering property are recorded, even if they may be avoided in exceptional cases. It is assumed that the buyer follows the fastest legal option available and used by the majority of property owners. Although the buyer may use lawyers or other professionals where necessary in the registration process, it is assumed that it does not employ an outside facilitator in the registration process unless legally or in practice required to do so (table 13.3).

TABLE 13.3
What does registering property measure?

Procedures to legally transfer title on real property
- Preregistration (checking for liens, notarizing sales agreement)
- Registration in the economy's most populous city
- Postregistration (paying taxes, filing title with municipality)

Time required to complete each procedure
- Does not include time spent gathering information
- Each procedure starts on a separate day
- Procedure completed once final document is received
- No prior contact with officials

Cost required to complete each procedure
- Official costs only, no bribes
- No value added or capital gains taxes included

Source: Doing Business database.

Time

Time is recorded in calendar days. The measure captures the median duration that property lawyers, notaries or registry officials indicate is necessary to complete a procedure. It is assumed that the minimum time required for each procedure is 1 day. Although procedures may take place simultaneously, they cannot start on the same day. It is assumed that the buyer does not waste time and commits to completing each remaining procedure without delay. If a procedure can be accelerated for an additional cost, the fastest legal procedure available and used by the majority of property owners is chosen. If procedures can be undertaken simultaneously, it is assumed that they are. It is assumed that the parties involved are aware of all regulations and their sequence from the beginning. Time spent on gathering information is not considered.

Cost

Cost is recorded as a percentage of the property value, assumed to be equivalent to 50 times income per capita. Only official costs required by law are recorded, including fees, transfer taxes, stamp duties and any other payment to the property registry, notaries, public agencies or lawyers. Other taxes, such as capital gains tax or value added tax, are excluded from the cost measure. Both costs borne by the buyer and those borne by the seller are included. If cost estimates differ among sources, the median reported value is used.

Getting credit

Doing Business constructs measures of the legal rights of borrowers and lenders and the sharing of credit information. The first set of indicators describes how well collateral and bankruptcy laws facilitate lending. The second set measures the coverage, scope, quality and accessibility of credit information available through public and private credit registries.

The data on the legal rights of borrowers and lenders are gathered through a survey of financial lawyers and verified through analysis of laws and regulations as well as public sources of information on collateral and bankruptcy laws. The data on credit information sharing are built in 2 stages. First, banking supervision authorities and public information sources are surveyed to confirm the presence of public credit registries and private credit information bureaus. Second, when applicable, a detailed survey on the public or private credit registry's structure, law and associated rules is administered to the credit registry. Survey responses are verified through several rounds of follow-up communication with respondents as well as by contacting third parties and consulting public sources. The survey data are confirmed through teleconference calls or on-site visits in all countries.

Strength of legal rights index

The strength of legal rights index measures the degree to which collateral and bankruptcy laws protect the rights of borrowers and lenders and thus facilitate lending. The index includes 7 aspects related to legal rights in collateral law and 3 aspects in bankruptcy law. A score of 1 is assigned for each of the following features of the laws:

- General rather than specific description of assets is permitted in collateral agreements.
- General rather than specific description of debt is permitted in collateral agreements.
- Any legal or natural person may grant or take security in the property.
- A unified registry operates that includes charges over movable property.
- Secured creditors have priority outside of bankruptcy.
- Secured creditors, rather than other parties such as government or workers, are paid first out of the proceeds from liquidating a bankrupt firm.
- Secured creditors are able to seize their collateral when a debtor enters reorganization; there is no "automatic stay" or "asset freeze" imposed by the court.
- Management does not stay during reorganization. An administrator is responsible for managing the business during reorganization.
- Parties may agree on out-of-court enforcement by contract.
- By law, and without the need for a contract, creditors may both seize and sell collateral out of court without restriction.

The index ranges from 0 to 10, with higher scores indicating that collateral and bankruptcy laws are better designed to expand access to credit.

Depth of credit information index

The depth of credit information index measures rules affecting the scope, accessibility and quality of credit information available through either public or private credit registries. A score of 1 is assigned for each of the following 6 features of the public registry or the private credit bureau (or both):

- Both positive credit information (for example, loan amounts and pattern of on-time repayments) and negative information (for example, late payments, number and amount of defaults and bankruptcies) are distributed.

- Data on both firms and individuals are distributed.
- Data from retailers, trade creditors or utility companies as well as financial institutions are distributed.
- More than 2 years of historical data are distributed. Registries that erase data on defaults as soon as they are repaid obtain a score of 0 for this indicator.
- Data on loans below 1% of income per capita are distributed. A registry must have a minimum coverage of 1% of the adult population to score a 1 for this indicator.
- By law, borrowers have the right to access their data in the largest registry in the country.

The index ranges from 0 to 6, with higher values indicating the availability of more credit information, from either a public registry or a private bureau, to facilitate lending decisions. If the registry is not operational or has coverage of less than 0.1% of the adult population, the score on the depth of credit index is 0.

In Turkey, for example, both a public and a private registry operate. Both distribute positive and negative information (a score of 1). The private bureau distributes data only on individuals, but the public registry covers firms as well as individuals (a score of 1). The public and private registries share data among financial institutions only; no data are collected from retailers or utilities (a score of 0). The private bureau distributes more than 2 years of historical data (a score of 1). The public registry collects data only on loans of $3,493 (64% of income per capita) or more, but the private bureau collects information on loans of any value (a score of 1). Borrowers have the right to access their data in both the private and the public registry (a score of 1). Summing across the indicators gives Turkey a total score of 5.

Public credit registry coverage

The public credit registry coverage indicator reports the number of individuals and firms listed in a public credit registry with current information on repayment history, unpaid debts or credit outstanding. The number is expressed as a percentage of the adult population. A public credit registry is defined as a database managed by the public sector, usually by the central bank or the superintendent of banks, that collects information on the creditworthiness of borrowers (persons or businesses) in the financial system and makes it available to financial institutions. If no public registry operates, the coverage value is 0.

Private credit bureau coverage

The private credit bureau coverage indicator reports the number of individuals and firms listed by a private credit bureau with current information on repayment history, unpaid debts or credit outstanding. The number is expressed as a percentage of the adult population. A private credit bureau is defined as a private firm or nonprofit organization that maintains a database on the creditworthiness of borrowers (persons or businesses) in the financial system and facilitates the exchange of credit information among banks and financial institutions. Credit investigative bureaus and credit reporting firms that do not directly facilitate information exchange among banks and other financial institutions are not considered. If no private bureau operates, the coverage value is 0.

This methodology was developed in Djankov, McLiesh and Shleifer (2007) and is adopted here with minor changes.

Protecting investors

Doing Business measures the strength of minority shareholder protections against directors' misuse of corporate assets for personal gain. The indicators distinguish 3 dimensions of investor protection: transparency of related-party transactions (extent of disclosure index), liability for self-dealing (extent of director liability index) and shareholders' ability to sue officers and directors for misconduct (ease of shareholder suits index). The data come from a survey of corporate lawyers and are based on securities regulations, company laws and court rules of evidence.

To make the data comparable across countries, several assumptions about the business and the transaction are used.

Assumptions about the business

The business (Buyer):

- Is a publicly traded corporation listed on the country's most important stock exchange. If the number of publicly traded companies listed on that exchange is less than 10, or if there is no stock exchange in the country, it is assumed that Buyer is a large private company with multiple shareholders.
- Has a board of directors and a chief executive officer (CEO) who may legally act on behalf of Buyer where permitted, even if this is not specifically required by law.
- Is a food manufacturer.
- Has its own distribution network.

Assumptions about the transaction

- Mr. James is Buyer's controlling shareholder and a member of Buyer's board of directors. He owns 60% of Buyer and elected 2 directors to Buyer's 5-member board.
- Mr. James also owns 90% of Seller, a company that operates a chain of retail hardware stores. Seller recently closed a large number of its stores.
- Mr. James proposes to Buyer that it purchase Seller's unused fleet of trucks to expand Buyer's distribution of its food products. Buyer agrees. The price is equal to 10% of Buyer's assets and is higher than the market value.

- The proposed transaction is part of the company's ordinary course of business and is not outside the authority of the company.
- Buyer enters into the transaction. All required approvals are obtained, and all required disclosures made (that is, the transaction is not fraudulent).
- The transaction is unfair to Buyer. Shareholders sue Mr. James and the other parties that approved the transaction.

Extent of disclosure index

The extent of disclosure index has 5 components:

- What corporate body can provide legally sufficient approval for the transaction. A score of 0 is assigned if it is the CEO or the managing director alone; 1 if the board of directors or shareholders must vote and Mr. James is permitted to vote; 2 if the board of directors must vote and Mr. James is not permitted to vote; 3 if shareholders must vote and Mr. James is not permitted to vote.
- Whether immediate disclosure of the transaction to the public, the regulator or the shareholders is required. A score of 0 is assigned if no disclosure is required; 1 if disclosure on the terms of the transaction but not Mr. James's conflict of interest is required; 2 if disclosure on both the terms and Mr. James's conflict of interest is required.
- Whether disclosure in the annual report is required. A score of 0 is assigned if no disclosure on the transaction is required; 1 if disclosure on the terms of the transaction but not Mr. James's conflict of interest is required; 2 if disclosure on both the terms and Mr. James's conflict of interest is required.
- Whether disclosure by Mr. James to the board of directors is required. A score of 0 is assigned if no disclosure is required; 1 if a general disclosure of the existence of a conflict of interest is required without any specifics; 2 if full disclosure of all material facts relating to Mr. James's interest in the Buyer-Seller transaction is required.
- Whether it is required that an external body, for example, an external auditor, review the transaction before it takes place. A score of 0 is assigned if no; 1 if yes.

The index ranges from 0 to 10, with higher values indicating greater disclosure. In Poland, for example, the board of directors must approve the transaction and Mr. James is not allowed to vote (a score of 2). Buyer is required to disclose immediately all information affecting the stock price, including the conflict of interest (a score of 2). In its annual report Buyer must also disclose the terms of the transaction and Mr. James's ownership in Buyer and Seller (a score of 2). Before the transaction Mr. James must disclose his conflict of interest to the other directors, but he is not required to provide specific information about it (a score of 1). Poland does not require an external body to review the transaction (a score of 0). Adding these numbers gives Poland a score of 7 on the extent of disclosure index.

Extent of director liability index

The extent of director liability index has 7 components:

- Whether a shareholder plaintiff is able to hold Mr. James liable for damage the Buyer-Seller transaction causes to the company. A score of 0 is assigned if Mr. James cannot be held liable or can be held liable only for fraud or bad faith; 1 if Mr. James can be held liable only if he influenced the approval of the transaction or was negligent; 2 if Mr. James can be held liable when the transaction is unfair or prejudicial to the other shareholders.
- Whether a shareholder plaintiff is able to hold the approving body (the CEO or board of directors) liable for damage the transaction causes to the company. A score of 0 is assigned if the approving body cannot be held liable or can be held liable only for fraud or bad faith; 1 if the approving body can be held liable for negligence; 2 if the approving body can be held liable when the transaction is unfair or prejudicial to the other shareholders.
- Whether a court can void the transaction upon a successful claim by a shareholder plaintiff. A score of 0 is assigned if rescission is unavailable or is available only in case of fraud or bad faith; 1 if rescission is available when the transaction is oppressive or prejudicial to the other shareholders; 2 if rescission is available when the transaction is unfair or entails a conflict of interest.
- Whether Mr. James pays damages for the harm caused to the company upon a successful claim by the shareholder plaintiff. A score of 0 is assigned if no; 1 if yes.
- Whether Mr. James repays profits made from the transaction upon a successful claim by the shareholder plaintiff. A score of 0 is assigned if no; 1 if yes.
- Whether fines and imprisonment can be applied against Mr. James. A score of 0 is assigned if no; 1 if yes.
- Whether shareholder plaintiffs are able to sue directly or derivatively for damage the transaction causes to the company. A score of 0 is assigned if suits are unavailable or are available only for shareholders holding more than 10% of the company's share capital; 1 if direct or derivative suits are available for shareholders holding 10% or less of share capital.

The index ranges from 0 to 10, with higher values indicating greater liability of directors. To hold Mr. James liable in Panama, for example, a plaintiff must prove that Mr. James influenced the approving body or acted negligently (a score of 1). To hold the other directors liable, a plaintiff must prove that they acted negligently (a score of 1). The unfair transaction cannot be voided (a score of 0). If Mr. James is found liable, he must pay damages (a score of 1) but he is not required to disgorge his profits (a score of 0). Mr. James cannot be fined or imprisoned (a score of 0). Direct suits are available for shareholders holding 10% or less of share capital (a score of 1). Adding these numbers gives Panama a score of 4 on the extent of director liability index.

Ease of shareholder suits index

The ease of shareholder suits index has 6 components.

- What range of documents is available to the shareholder plaintiff from the defendant and witnesses during trial. A score of 1 is assigned for each of the following types of documents available: information that the defendant has indicated he intends to rely on for his defense; information that directly proves specific facts in the plaintiff's claim; any information relevant to the subject matter of the claim; and any information that may lead to the discovery of relevant information.
- Whether the plaintiff can directly examine the defendant and witnesses during trial. A score of 0 is assigned if no; 1 if yes, with prior approval of the questions by the judge; 2 if yes, without prior approval.
- Whether the plaintiff can obtain categories of relevant documents from the defendant without identifying each document specifically. A score of 0 is assigned if no; 1 if yes.
- Whether shareholders owning 10% or less of the company's share capital can request that a government inspector investigate the Buyer-Seller transaction without filing suit in court. A score of 0 is assigned if no; 1 if yes.
- Whether shareholders owning 10% or less of the company's share capital have the right to inspect the transaction documents before filing suit. A score of 0 is assigned if no; 1 if yes.
- Whether the standard of proof for civil suits is lower than that for a criminal case. A score of 0 is assigned if no; 1 if yes.

The index ranges from 0 to 10, with higher values indicating greater powers of shareholders to challenge the transaction. In Greece, for example, the plaintiff can access documents that the defendant intends to rely on for his defense and that directly prove facts in the plaintiff's claim (a score of 2). The plaintiff can examine the defendant and witnesses during trial, though only with prior approval of the questions by the court (a score of 1). The plaintiff must specifically identify the documents being sought (for example, the Buyer-Seller purchase agreement of July 15, 2006) and cannot just request categories (for example, all documents related to the transaction) (a score of 0). A shareholder holding 5% of Buyer's shares can request that a government inspector review suspected mismanagement by Mr. James and the CEO without filing suit in court (a score of 1). And any shareholder can inspect the transaction documents before deciding whether to sue (a score of 1). The standard of proof for civil suits is the same as that for a criminal case (a score of 0). Adding these numbers gives Greece a score of 5 on the ease of shareholder suits index.

Strength of investor protection index

The strength of investor protection index is the average of the extent of disclosure index, the extent of director liability index and the ease of shareholder suits index. The index ranges from 0 to 10, with higher values indicating more investor protection.

This methodology was developed in Djankov and others (forthcoming) and is adopted here with minor changes.

Paying taxes

Doing Business records the taxes and mandatory contributions that a medium-size company must pay or withhold in a given year, as well as measures of the administrative burden in paying taxes and contributions. Taxes and contributions measured include the profit or corporate income tax, social contributions and labor taxes paid by the employer, property taxes, property transfer taxes, the dividend tax, the capital gains tax, the financial transactions tax, waste collection taxes and vehicle and road taxes.

Doing Business measures all taxes and contributions that are government mandated (at any level—federal, state or local), apply to the standardized business and have an impact in its income statements. In doing so, *Doing Business* goes beyond the traditional definition of a tax: as defined for the purposes of government national accounts, taxes include only compulsory, unrequited payments to general government. *Doing Business* differs from this definition because it measures imposts that affect business accounts, not government accounts. The main differences are in labor contributions and value added tax. The *Doing Business* measure includes government-mandated contributions paid by the employer to a requited private pension fund or workers' insurance fund. The indicator includes, for example, Australia's compulsory superannuation guarantee and workers' compensation insurance. It excludes value added taxes because they do not affect the accounting profits of the business—that is, they are not reflected in the income statement.

To measure the taxes and contributions paid by a standardized business and the complexity of a country's tax system, a case study is prepared with a set of financial statements and assumptions about transactions made over the year. Experts in each country compute the taxes and contributions owed in their jurisdiction based on the standardized case facts. Information is also compiled on the frequency of filing, audits and other costs of compliance. The project was developed and implemented in cooperation with PricewaterhouseCoopers.

To make the data comparable across countries, several assumptions about the business and the taxes and contributions are used.

Assumptions about the business

The business:

- Is a limited liability, taxable company. If there is more than one type of limited liability company in the country, the limited liability form most popular among domestic firms is chosen. The most popular form is reported by incorporation lawyers or the statistical office.
- Started operations on January 1, 2005. At that time the company purchased all the assets shown in its balance sheet and hired all its workers.
- Operates in the country's most populous city.
- Is 100% domestically owned and has 5 owners, all of whom are natural persons.
- Has a start-up capital of 102 times income per capita at the end of 2005.
- Performs general industrial or commercial activities. Specifically, it produces ceramic flowerpots and sells them at retail. It does not participate in foreign trade (no import or export) and does not handle products subject to a special tax regime, for example, liquor or tobacco.
- Owns 2 plots of land, 1 building, machinery, office equipment, computers and 1 truck and leases 1 truck.
- Does not qualify for investment incentives or any benefits apart from those related to the age or size of the company.
- Has 60 employees—4 managers, 8 assistants and 48 workers. All are nationals, and 1 manager is also an owner.
- Has a turnover of 1,050 times income per capita.
- Makes a loss in the first year of operation.
- Has a gross margin (pretax) of 20% (that is, sales are 120% of the cost of goods sold).
- Distributes 50% of its profits as dividends to the owners at the end of the 2nd year.
- Sells one of its plots of land at a profit during the 2nd year.
- Has annual fuel costs for its trucks equal to twice income per capita.
- Is subject to a series of detailed assumptions on expenses and transactions to further standardize the case. All financial statement variables are proportional to 2005 income per capita. For example, the owner who is also a manager spends 10% of income per capita on traveling for the company (20% of the expenses are purely private, 20% for entertaining customers and 60% for business travel).

Assumptions about the taxes and contributions

- All the taxes and contributions paid or withheld in the second year of operation (fiscal 2006) are recorded. A tax or contribution is considered distinct if it has a different name or is collected by a different agency. Taxes and contributions with the same name and agency, but charged at different rates depending on the business, are counted as the same tax or contribution (table 13.4).
- The number of times the company pays or withholds taxes and contributions in a year is the number of different taxes or contributions multiplied by the frequency of payment (or withholding) for each one. The frequency of payment includes advance payments (or withholding) as well as regular payments (or withholding).

TABLE 13.4
What does paying taxes measure?

Tax payments for a manufacturing company in 2006
- Total number of taxes and contributions paid, including consumption taxes (value added tax)
- Method and frequency of payment

Time required to comply with 3 major taxes
- Collecting information to compute tax payable
- Completing tax forms, filing with proper agencies
- Arranging payment or withholding
- Preparing separate tax accounting books

Total tax rate
- Profit or corporate income tax
- Social contributions and labor taxes paid by the employer
- Property and property transfer taxes
- Dividend, capital gains and financial transactions taxes
- Waste collection, vehicle, road and other taxes

Source: Doing Business database.

Tax payments

The tax payments indicator reflects the total number of taxes and contributions paid, the method of payment, the frequency of payment and the number of agencies involved for this standardized case during the second year of operation. It includes payments made by the company on consumption taxes, such as sales tax or value added tax. These taxes are traditionally withheld on behalf of the consumer. Although they do not affect the income statements of the company, they add to the administrative burden of complying with the tax system and so are included in the tax payments measure.

The number of payments takes into account electronic filing. Where full electronic filing is allowed and it is used by the majority of medium-size businesses, the tax is counted as paid once a year even if the payment is more frequent. For taxes paid through third parties, such as tax on interest paid by a financial institution or fuel tax paid by the fuel distributor, only one payment is included even if payments are more frequent. These are taxes withheld at source where no filing is made by the company.

Where 2 or more taxes or contributions are paid jointly using the same form, each of these joint payments is counted once. For example, if mandatory health insurance contributions and mandatory pension contributions are filed and paid together, only one of these contributions would be included in the number of payments.

Time

Time is recorded in hours per year. The indicator measures the time to prepare, file and pay (or withhold) 3 major types of taxes and contributions: the corporate income tax, value added or sales tax and labor taxes, including payroll taxes and social contributions. Preparation time includes the time to collect all information necessary to compute the tax payable. If separate accounting books must be kept for tax purposes—or separate calculations made—the time associated with these processes is included. This extra time is included only if the regular accounting work is not enough to fulfill the tax accounting requirements. Filing time includes the time to complete all necessary tax forms and make all necessary calculations. Payment time is the hours needed to make the payment online or at the tax office. Where taxes and contributions are paid in person, the time includes delays while waiting.

Total tax rate

The total tax rate measures the amount of taxes and mandatory contributions payable by the business in the second year of operation, expressed as a share of commercial profits. *Doing Business 2008* reports the total tax rate for fiscal 2006. The total amount of taxes is the sum of all the different taxes and contributions payable after accounting for deductions and exemptions. The taxes withheld (such as sales or value added tax or personal income tax) but not paid by the company are excluded. The taxes included can be divided into 5 categories: profit or corporate income tax, social contributions and labor taxes paid by the employer (for which all mandatory contributions are included, even if paid to a private entity such as a requited pension fund), property taxes, turnover taxes and other small taxes (such as municipal fees and vehicle and fuel taxes).

Commercial profits are defined as sales minus cost of goods sold, minus gross salaries, minus administrative expenses, minus other expenses, minus provisions, plus capital gains (from the property sale) minus interest expense, plus interest income and minus commercial depreciation. To compute the commercial depreciation, a straight-line depreciation method is applied with the following rates: 0% for the land, 5% for the building, 10% for the machinery, 33% for the computers, 20% for the office equipment, 20% for the truck and 10% for business development expenses. The assumption on the interest expense was changed this year, reducing the value of this expense. Commercial profits therefore changed from 57.8 times income per capita to 59.4 times.

The methodology is consistent with the calculation of total tax contribution by PricewaterhouseCoopers. The total tax contribution measures the taxes that are borne by companies and affect their income statements, as in *Doing Business*. However, PricewaterhouseCoopers bases its calculation on data from the largest companies in the country, while *Doing Business* focuses on a standardized medium-size company.

This methodology was developed in Djankov and others (2007).

Trading across borders

Doing Business compiles procedural requirements for exporting and importing a standardized cargo of goods by ocean transport. Every official procedure for exporting and importing the goods is recorded—from the contractual agreement between the 2 parties to the delivery of goods—along with the time and cost necessary for completion. All documents required for clearance of the goods across the border are also recorded. For exporting goods, procedures range from packing the goods at the factory to their departure from the port of exit. For importing goods, procedures range from the vessel's arrival at the port of entry to the cargo's delivery at the factory warehouse. Payment is made by letter of credit.

Local freight forwarders, shipping lines, customs brokers and port officials provide information on required documents and cost as well as the time to complete each procedure. To make the data comparable across countries, several assumptions about the business and the traded goods are used.

Assumptions about the business

The business:

- Has 100 or more employees.
- Is located in the country's most populous city.
- Is a private, limited liability company. It does not operate within an export processing zone or an industrial estate with special export or import privileges.
- Is domestically owned with no foreign ownership.
- Exports more than 10% of its sales.

Assumptions about the traded goods

The traded product travels in a dry-cargo, 20-foot, full container load. The product:

- Is not hazardous nor does it include military items.
- Does not require refrigeration or any other special environment.
- Does not require any special phytosanitary or environmental safety standards other than accepted international standards.

Documents

All documents required to export and import the goods are recorded. It is assumed that the contract has already been agreed upon and signed by both parties. Documents include bank documents, customs declaration and clearance documents, port filing documents, import licenses and other official documents exchanged between the concerned parties. Documents filed simultaneously are considered different documents but with the same time frame for completion.

Time

Time is recorded in calendar days. The time calculation for a procedure starts from the moment it is initiated and runs until it is completed. If a procedure can be accelerated for an additional cost, the fastest legal procedure is chosen. It is assumed that neither the exporter nor the importer wastes time and that each commits to completing each remaining procedure without delay. Procedures that can be completed in paral-

TABLE 13.5
What does trading across borders measure?

Documents necessary to import or export
- Bank documents
- Customs clearance documents
- Port and terminal handling documents
- Transport documents

Time required to import or export
- Obtaining all the documents
- Inland transport
- Customs clearance and inspections
- Port and terminal handling
- Does not include ocean transport time

Cost required to import or export
- Obtaining all the documents
- Inland transport
- Customs clearance and inspections
- Port and terminal handling
- Official costs only, no bribes

Source: Doing Business database.

lel are measured as simultaneous. The waiting time between procedures—for example, during unloading of the cargo—is included in the measure (table 13.5).

Cost

Cost measures the fees levied on a 20-foot container in U.S. dollars. All the fees associated with completing the procedures to export or import the goods are included. These include costs for documents, administrative fees for customs clearance and technical control, terminal handling charges and inland transport. The cost measure does not include tariffs or trade taxes. Only official costs are recorded.

This methodology was developed by Djankov, Freund and Pham (2007) and is adopted here with minor changes.

Enforcing contracts

Indicators on enforcing contracts measure the efficiency of the judicial system in resolving a commercial dispute. The data are built by following the step-by-step evolution of a commercial sale dispute before local courts. The data are collected through study of the codes of civil procedure and other court regulations as well as surveys completed by local litigation lawyers (and, in a quarter of the countries, by judges as well).

Assumptions about the case

- The value of the claim equals 200% of the country's income per capita.
- The dispute concerns a lawful transaction between 2 businesses (Seller and Buyer), located in the country's most populous city. Seller sells goods worth 200% of the country's income per capita to Buyer. After Seller delivers the goods to Buyer, Buyer does not pay for the goods on the grounds that the delivered goods were not of adequate quality.
- Seller (the plaintiff) sues Buyer (the defendant) to recover the amount under the sales agreement (that is, 200% of the country's income per capita). Buyer opposes Seller's claim, saying that the quality of the goods is not adequate. The claim is disputed on the merits.
- A court in the country's most populous city with jurisdiction over commercial cases worth 200% of income per capita decides the dispute.
- Seller attaches Buyer's goods prior to obtaining a judgment because Seller fears that Buyer may become insolvent during the lawsuit.
- Expert opinions are given on the quality of the delivered goods. If it is standard practice in the country for parties to call witnesses or expert witnesses to give an opinion on the quality of the goods, the parties each call one witness or expert witness. If it is standard practice for the judge to appoint an independent expert to give an expert opinion on the quality of the goods, the judge does so. In this case the judge does not allow opposing expert testimony.
- The judgment is 100% in favor of Seller: the judge decides that the goods are of adequate quality and that Buyer must pay the agreed price.
- Buyer does not appeal the judgment. The judgment becomes final.
- Seller takes all required steps for prompt enforcement of the judgment. The money is successfully collected through a public sale of Buyer's movable assets (for example, office equipment).

Procedures

A procedure is defined as any interaction between the parties, or between them and the judge or court officer. This includes steps to file the case, steps for trial and judgment and steps necessary to enforce the judgment. This year the survey allowed respondents to record procedures that exist in civil law but not common law jurisdictions, and vice versa. For example, the judge can appoint an independent expert in civil law countries whereas both parties in common law countries send a list of their expert witnesses to the court. To indicate the overall efficiency of court procedures, 1 procedure is now subtracted for countries that have specialized commercial courts and 1 procedure for countries that allow electronic filing of court cases.

Time

Time is recorded in calendar days, counted from the moment the plaintiff files the lawsuit in court until payment. This includes both the days when actions take place and the waiting periods between. The respondents make separate estimates of the average duration of different stages of dispute resolution: the completion of service of process (time to file the case), the issuance of judgment (time for the trial and obtaining the judgment) and the moment of payment (time for enforcement).

Cost

Cost is recorded as a percentage of the claim, assumed to be equivalent to 200% of income per capita. Only official costs required by law are recorded, including court and enforcement costs and average attorney fees where the use of attorneys is mandatory or common.

This methodology was developed in Djankov and others (2003) and is adopted here with minor changes.

Closing a business

Doing Business studies the time, cost and outcomes of bankruptcy proceedings involving domestic entities. The data are derived from survey responses by local insolvency practitioners and verified through a study of laws and regulations as well as public information on bankruptcy systems.

To make the data comparable across countries, several assumptions about the business and the case are used.

Assumptions about the business

The business:

- Is a limited liability company.
- Operates in the country's most populous city.
- Is 100% domestically owned, with the founder, who is also the chairman of the supervisory board, owning 51% (no other shareholder holds more than 5% of shares).
- Has downtown real estate, where it runs a hotel, as its major asset.
- Has a professional general manager.
- Has had average annual revenue of 1,000 times income per capita over the past 3 years.
- Has 201 employees and 50 suppliers, each of which is owed money for the last delivery.
- Borrowed from a domestic bank 5 years ago (the loan has 10 years to full repayment) and bought real estate (the hotel building), using it as security for the bank loan.
- Has observed the payment schedule and all other conditions of the loan up to now.
- Has a mortgage, with the value of the mortgage principal being exactly equal to the market value of the hotel.

Assumptions about the case

The business is experiencing liquidity problems. The company's loss in 2006 reduced its net worth to a negative figure. There is no cash to pay the bank interest or principal in full, due tomorrow. Therefore, the business defaults on its loan. Management believes that losses will be incurred in 2007 and 2008 as well.

The bank holds a floating charge against the hotel in countries where floating charges are possible. If the law does not permit a floating charge but contracts commonly use some other provision to that effect, this provision is specified in the lending contract.

The business has too many creditors to negotiate an informal out-of-court workout. It has the following options: a judicial procedure aimed at the rehabilitation or reorganization of the business to permit its continued operation; a judicial procedure aimed at the liquidation or winding up of the company; or a debt enforcement or foreclosure procedure aimed at selling the hotel either piecemeal or as a going concern, enforced either in court (or through a government authority like a debt collection agency) or out of court (for example, by appointing a receiver).

Time

Time is recorded in calendar years. Information is collected on the sequence of procedures and on whether any procedures can be carried out simultaneously. Potential delay tactics by the parties, such as the filing of dilatory appeals or requests for extension, are taken into consideration.

Cost

The cost of the proceedings is recorded as a percentage of the estate's value. The cost is calculated on the basis of survey responses by insolvency practitioners and includes court fees as well as fees of insolvency practitioners, independent assessors, lawyers and accountants. Respondents provide cost estimates from among the following options: less than 2%, 2–5%, 5–8%, 8–11%, 11–18%, 18–25%, 25–33%, 33–50%, 50–75% and more than 75% of the value of the business estate.

Recovery rate

The recovery rate is recorded as cents on the dollar recouped by creditors through the bankruptcy or insolvency proceedings. The calculation takes into account whether the business emerges from the proceedings as a going concern as well as costs and the loss in value due to the time spent closing down. If the business keeps operating, no value is lost on the initial claim, set at 100 cents on the dollar. If it does not, the initial 100 cents on the dollar are reduced to 70 cents on the dollar. Then the official costs of the insolvency procedure are deducted (1 cent for each percentage of the initial value). Finally, the value lost as a result of the time the money remains tied up in insolvency proceedings is taken into account, including the loss of value due to depreciation of the hotel furniture. Consistent with international accounting practice, the depreciation rate for furniture is taken to be 20%. The furniture is assumed to account for a quarter of the total value of assets. The recovery rate is the present value of the remaining proceeds, based on end-2006 lending rates from the International Monetary Fund's *International Financial Statistics*, supplemented with data from central banks.

This methodology was developed in Djankov and others (2006).

Ease of doing business

The ease of doing business index ranks economies from 1 to 178. The index is calculated as the ranking on the simple average of country percentile rankings on each of the 10 topics covered in *Doing Business 2008*. The ranking on each topic is the simple average of the percentile rankings on its component indicators.

If an economy has no laws or regulations covering a specific area—for example, bankruptcy—it receives a "no practice" or "not possible" mark. Similarly, an economy receives a "no practice" or "not possible" mark if regulation exists but is never used in practice or if a competing regulation prohibits such practice. Either way, such a mark puts the country at the bottom of the rankings on the relevant indicator.

Here is one example of how the ranking on the ease of doing business is constructed. In Iceland it takes 5 procedures, 5 days and 3% of annual income per capita in fees to open a business. The minimum capital required amounts to 14% of income per capita. On these 4 indicators Iceland ranks in the 6th, 2nd, 10th and 55th percentiles. So Iceland ranks in the 18th percentile—the average of the 4 percentiles—on the ease of starting a business. It ranks in the 46th percentile on protecting investors, 11th on trading across borders, 8th on enforcing contracts, 6th on closing a business and so on. Higher rankings indicate simpler regulation and stronger protection of property rights. The simple average of Iceland's percentile rankings on all topics is 19%. When all countries are ordered by their average percentile ranking, Iceland is in 10th place.

More complex aggregation methods—such as principal components and unobserved components—yield nearly identical rankings.[1] The choice of aggregation method has little influence on the rankings because the 10 sets of indicators in *Doing Business* provide sufficiently broad coverage across topics. So *Doing Business* uses the method most likely to lead to reform—the simplest method.

The ease of doing business index is limited in scope. It does not account for a country's proximity to large markets, the quality of its infrastructure services (other than services related to trading across borders), the security of property from theft and looting, macroeconomic conditions or the strength of underlying institutions. There remains a large unfinished agenda for research into what regulation constitutes binding constraints, what package of reforms is most effective and how these issues are shaped by the country context. The *Doing Business* indicators provide a new empirical data set that may improve understanding of these issues.

Doing Business also uses a simple method to determine the top reformers (see table 1.1). First, it selects the economies that reformed in 3 or more of the 10 *Doing Business* topics (table 14.1). This year 21 economies met this criterion: Armenia, Bhutan, Bulgaria, Burkina Faso, China, Colombia, Croatia, the Czech Republic, Egypt, Georgia, Ghana, Guatemala, Honduras, Kenya, FYR Macedonia, Mauritius, Mozambique, Portugal, Saudi Arabia, Tunisia and Uzbekistan. Second, *Doing Business* ranks these economies on the increase in their ranking on the ease of doing business from the previous year. For example, Croatia, Honduras and Kenya each reformed in 4 aspects of business regulation. Croatia's ranking improved from 120 to 97, Honduras's from 126 to 121 and Kenya's from 82 to 72. These changes represent an improvement in the rankings by 23 places, 5 places and 10 places, respectively. Croatia therefore ranks ahead of Kenya in the list of top 10 reformers. Honduras doesn't make the list.

Note

1. See Djankov and others (2005).

TABLE 14.1

✓ Positive reform
✗ Negative reform

Economy	Starting a business	Dealing with licenses	Employing workers	Registering property	Getting credit	Protecting investors	Paying taxes	Trading across borders	Enforcing contracts	Closing a business
	REFORMS IN 2006/07									
Afghanistan				✓						
Albania							✓			
Algeria								✗		
Angola										
Antigua and Barbuda										
Argentina										✗
Armenia					✓			✓		✓
Australia	✓									
Austria								✓		
Azerbaijan	✓						✓			
Bangladesh	✗						✗			
Belarus	✓					✓				
Belgium	✓									
Belize										
Benin				✓						
Bhutan	✓		✓	✓						
Bolivia										
Bosnia and Herzegovina								✓		
Botswana										✗
Brazil								✓	✓	
Brunei										
Bulgaria		✓					✓		✓	
Burkina Faso	✓			✓					✓	
Burundi				✓						
Cambodia										
Cameroon										
Canada										
Cape Verde										
Central African Republic										
Chad										
Chile										
China		✓			✓					✓
Colombia						✓	✓	✓		
Comoros										
Congo, Dem. Rep.									✓	
Congo, Rep.										
Costa Rica								✓		
Côte d'Ivoire							✓			
Croatia	✓			✓	✓					✓
Czech Republic	✓	✓	✓							
Denmark										✓
Djibouti				✓				✓		
Dominica										
Dominican Republic	✓			✓			✗	✓		
Ecuador										
Egypt	✓	✓		✓	✓			✓		
El Salvador								✓		
Equatorial Guinea										
Eritrea										
Estonia	✓									
Ethiopia										
Fiji									✓	
Finland	✓									
France				✓	✓					
Gabon										
Gambia								✓		
Georgia	✓	✓		✓	✓	✓				✓
Germany	✓			✗						
Ghana	✓			✓	✓			✓	✓	

✓ Positive reform
✗ Negative reform

Economy	Starting a business	Dealing with licenses	Employing workers	Registering property	Getting credit	Protecting investors	Paying taxes	Trading across borders	Enforcing contracts	Closing a business
	REFORMS IN 2006/07									
Greece							✓			
Grenada										
Guatemala	✓	✓		✓				✓	✓	
Guinea										
Guinea-Bissau				✓						
Guyana										
Haiti				✓						
Honduras	✓	✓		✓	✓					
Hong Kong, China										
Hungary	✓			✓			✗			✓
Iceland						✓				
India					✓			✓		
Indonesia	✗	✓			✓	✓				
Iran										
Iraq										
Ireland										
Israel							✓			
Italy										✓
Jamaica										
Japan										
Jordan	✓									
Kazakhstan							✓			
Kenya	✓	✓		✓	✓					
Kiribati										
Korea										
Kuwait		✓			✓					
Kyrgyz Republic				✗			✓			
Lao PDR	✓							✓		
Latvia			✓							
Lebanon										
Lesotho				✓			✓			
Liberia										
Lithuania										
Luxembourg										
Macedonia, FYR	✓	✓					✓			
Madagascar	✓							✓		
Malawi									✓	
Malaysia	✓						✓			
Maldives										
Mali	✓			✓						
Marshall Islands										
Mauritania	✓								✓	
Mauritius	✓	✓		✓			✓	✓		✓
Mexico				✓			✓			
Micronesia					✓					
Moldova	✓		✗				✓		✓	
Mongolia							✓			
Montenegro										
Morocco		✓		✗				✓		
Mozambique	✓					✓			✓	
Namibia										
Nepal										
Netherlands			✓				✓			
New Zealand										
Nicaragua										
Niger	✓			✓						
Nigeria	✓	✓								
Norway						✓				
Oman										

✓ Positive reform
✗ Negative reform

Economy	Starting a business	Dealing with licenses	Employing workers	Registering property	Getting credit	Protecting investors	Paying taxes	Trading across borders	Enforcing contracts	Closing a business
	REFORMS IN 2006/07									
Pakistan			✓		✓					
Palau										
Panama										
Papua New Guinea										
Paraguay	✓			✗						
Peru										
Philippines										
Poland				✓					✓	
Portugal	✓			✓		✓	✓		✓	✓
Puerto Rico										
Romania	✗				✓		✓			
Russia		✗			✓					
Rwanda		✓						✓		
Samoa										
São Tomé and Principe										
Saudi Arabia	✓				✓			✓		
Senegal										
Serbia										
Seychelles							✓			
Sierra Leone							✓			
Singapore										
Slovakia										
Slovenia			✗		✗	✓	✓			
Solomon Islands										
South Africa					✓		✓			
Spain			✓				✓			
Sri Lanka	✓				✗			✓		
St. Kitts and Nevis										
St. Lucia										
St. Vincent and the Grenadines										
Sudan										
Suriname										
Swaziland										
Sweden										
Switzerland			✓							
Syria	✗						✓			
Taiwan, China										
Tajikistan	✓									
Tanzania	✓									
Thailand								✓		
Timor-Leste	✓									
Togo			✗							
Tonga									✓	
Trinidad and Tobago					✓		✓			
Tunisia				✓	✓		✓			
Turkey							✓	✓		
Uganda			✓					✓		
Ukraine										
United Arab Emirates										
United Kingdom										
United States										
Uruguay							✓			
Uzbekistan	✓			✓			✓			✓
Vanuatu				✗						
Venezuela			✗				✗	✗		
Vietnam					✓	✓				
West Bank and Gaza					✓		✓			
Yemen										
Zambia										
Zimbabwe		✗		✗			✗			

Indicator tables

Doing business indicators

Country tables

Economy	Starting a business: Procedures (number)	Starting a business: Time (days)	Starting a business: Cost (% of income per capita)	Starting a business: Minimum capital (% of income per capita)	Dealing with licenses: Procedures (number)	Dealing with licenses: Time (days)	Dealing with licenses: Cost (% of income per capita)
Afghanistan	4	9	84.6	0.0	13	340	21,230.8
Albania	10	36	20.9	34.3	24	331	461.0
Algeria	14	24	13.2	45.2	22	240	57.8
Angola	12	119	343.7	50.5	14	337	1,109.7
Antigua and Barbuda	7	21	11.8	0.0	14	157	26.3
Argentina	14	31	9.7	4.8	28	338	234.1
Armenia	9	18	4.8	3.1	19	116	411.3
Australia	2	2	0.8	0.0	16	221	13.2
Austria	8	28	5.4	55.5	13	194	73.7
Azerbaijan	13	30	6.9	0.0	31	207	768.3
Bangladesh	8	74	46.2	0.0	14	252	751.0
Belarus	10	48	8.8	29.7	17	350	60.9
Belgium	3	4	5.3	20.1	14	169	63.7
Belize	9	44	53.1	0.0	11	66	18.5
Benin	7	31	195.0	354.2	15	332	316.6
Bhutan	8	48	10.4	0.0	25	183	195.9
Bolivia	15	50	134.1	3.4	17	249	198.6
Bosnia and Herzegovina	12	54	30.1	43.0	16	467	790.3
Botswana	11	108	9.9	0.0	24	167	322.3
Brazil	18	152	10.4	0.0	18	411	59.4
Brunei	18	116	9.0	0.0	32	167	5.2
Bulgaria	9	32	8.4	56.3	22	131	499.9
Burkina Faso	6	18	82.1	415.7	32	226	701.2
Burundi	11	43	251.0	0.0	20	384	9,939.0
Cambodia	10	86	190.3	50.8	23	709	74.3
Cameroon	13	37	129.2	177.1	15	426	1,202.9
Canada	2	3	0.9	0.0	14	75	125.4
Cape Verde	12	52	40.1	53.4	18	120	718.3
Central African Republic	10	14	205.4	531.2	21	239	288.3
Chad	19	75	188.8	398.4	9	181	1,063.8
Chile	9	27	8.6	0.0	18	155	128.1
China	13	35	8.4	190.2	37	336	840.2
Colombia	11	42	19.3	0.0	14	146	602.8
Comoros	11	23	188.4	280.3	18	164	77.8
Congo, Dem. Rep.	13	155	487.2	0.0	14	322	2,112.6
Congo, Rep.	10	37	150.1	206.3	14	169	565.9
Costa Rica	12	77	21.3	0.0	23	178	244.2
Côte d'Ivoire	10	40	135.8	219.8	21	628	247.7
Croatia	8	40	11.7	18.4	22	255	722.4
Czech Republic	10	17	10.6	34.9	36	180	18.5
Denmark	4	6	0.0	40.7	6	69	61.8
Djibouti	11	37	206.6	530.8	14	195	1,010.6
Dominica	5	19	27.1	0.0	12	219	74.4
Dominican Republic	9	22	31.1	0.0	17	214	116.1
Ecuador	14	65	29.2	7.0	19	148	55.3
Egypt	7	9	28.6	12.9	28	249	474.9
El Salvador	9	26	73.1	112.5	34	155	197.9
Equatorial Guinea	20	136	105.1	23.2	18	201	239.9
Eritrea	13	84	125.8	488.0	no practice	no practice	no practice
Estonia	5	7	2.0	28.1	13	117	28.1
Ethiopia	7	16	41.3	960.0	12	128	1,094.4
Fiji	8	46	25.3	0.0	16	114	40.8
Finland	3	14	1.0	7.7	18	38	122.3
France	5	7	1.1	0.0	13	137	24.9
Gabon	9	58	164.0	38.2	14	210	48.3
Gambia	9	32	279.0	0.0	17	146	363.7
Georgia	5	11	9.5	0.0	12	113	28.9
Germany	9	18	5.7	42.8	12	100	63.1
Ghana	11	42	41.4	20.9	18	220	1,498.3

Economy	Starting a business: Procedures (number)	Starting a business: Time (days)	Starting a business: Cost (% of income per capita)	Starting a business: Minimum capital (% of income per capita)	Dealing with licenses: Procedures (number)	Dealing with licenses: Time (days)	Dealing with licenses: Cost (% of income per capita)
Greece	15	38	23.3	104.1	15	169	61.7
Grenada	6	20	31.7	0.0	9	149	31.0
Guatemala	11	26	47.3	24.9	22	235	1,142.2
Guinea	13	41	138.3	466.5	32	255	237.7
Guinea-Bissau	17	233	255.5	1,006.6	15	167	2,607.0
Guyana	8	44	87.2	0.0	12	222	313.9
Haiti	12	202	133.9	32.2	11	1,179	817.8
Honduras	13	21	59.9	27.4	17	125	634.1
Hong Kong, China	5	11	3.1	0.0	23	155	21.3
Hungary	6	16	17.7	65.1	31	211	10.4
Iceland	5	5	2.7	14.1	18	76	13.9
India	13	33	74.6	0.0	20	224	519.4
Indonesia	12	105	80.0	38.4	19	196	286.8
Iran	8	47	5.3	1.3	19	670	653.4
Iraq	11	77	93.5	65.4	14	215	915.0
Ireland	4	13	0.3	0.0	11	185	19.8
Israel	5	34	4.4	0.0	20	235	115.5
Italy	9	13	18.7	9.8	14	257	138.2
Jamaica	6	8	8.7	0.0	10	236	438.4
Japan	8	23	7.5	0.0	15	177	17.8
Jordan	10	14	66.2	795.4	18	122	486.1
Kazakhstan	8	21	7.6	22.9	38	231	2,129.9
Kenya	12	44	46.1	0.0	10	100	58.8
Kiribati	6	21	56.6	30.6	14	160	629.3
Korea	10	17	16.9	296.0	13	34	170.2
Kuwait	13	35	1.6	99.9	25	104	209.4
Kyrgyz Republic	8	21	8.8	0.5	20	291	555.4
Lao PDR	8	103	16.5	0.0	24	172	202.4
Latvia	5	16	3.0	22.0	26	188	27.5
Lebanon	6	46	94.1	60.4	20	211	229.5
Lesotho	8	73	37.4	14.3	15	601	805.3
Liberia	12	99	493.3	0.0	25	398	61,049.3
Lithuania	7	26	3.0	46.2	17	156	133.1
Luxembourg	6	26	2.3	20.5	13	217	19.4
Macedonia, FYR	9	15	6.6	0.0	19	192	109.3
Madagascar	5	7	22.7	333.4	16	268	880.0
Malawi	10	37	188.7	0.0	21	213	189.2
Malaysia	9	24	18.1	0.0	25	285	10.0
Maldives	5	9	13.4	5.8	9	118	39.9
Mali	11	26	132.1	434.6	14	208	1,320.7
Marshall Islands	5	17	17.7	0.0	10	55	36.8
Mauritania	11	65	56.2	503.1	25	201	565.5
Mauritius	6	7	5.3	0.0	18	107	43.3
Mexico	8	27	13.3	11.6	11	131	103.5
Micronesia	7	16	137.0	0.0	14	73	19.7
Moldova	9	23	11.5	14.6	30	292	154.2
Mongolia	8	20	4.3	96.3	21	126	15.7
Montenegro	15	24	6.2	0.0	19	185	599.6
Morocco	6	12	11.5	59.8	19	163	334.7
Mozambique	10	29	21.6	115.8	17	361	705.0
Namibia	10	99	22.3	0.0	12	139	156.7
Nepal	7	31	73.9	0.0	15	424	304.7
Netherlands	6	10	6.0	52.9	18	230	76.0
New Zealand	2	12	0.1	0.0	7	65	25.0
Nicaragua	6	39	119.1	0.0	17	219	898.6
Niger	11	23	174.8	735.6	16	293	2,823.6
Nigeria	9	34	56.6	0.0	18	350	1,016.0
Norway	6	10	2.3	23.4	14	252	46.2
Oman	9	34	4.3	541.8	16	242	847.6

Economy	Starting a business: Procedures (number)	Starting a business: Time (days)	Starting a business: Cost (% of income per capita)	Starting a business: Minimum capital (% of income per capita)	Dealing with licenses: Procedures (number)	Dealing with licenses: Time (days)	Dealing with licenses: Cost (% of income per capita)
Pakistan	11	24	14.0	0.0	12	223	869.5
Palau	8	28	4.7	12.5	25	118	6.1
Panama	7	19	22.0	0.0	25	149	143.9
Papua New Guinea	8	56	26.4	0.0	24	217	106.3
Paraguay	7	35	77.6	0.0	13	291	439.0
Peru	10	72	29.9	0.0	21	210	165.0
Philippines	15	58	26.8	6.9	21	177	75.9
Poland	10	31	21.2	196.8	30	308	159.8
Portugal	7	7	3.4	34.7	20	327	54.0
Puerto Rico	7	7	0.8	0.0	22	209	550.8
Romania	6	14	4.7	1.5	17	243	124.3
Russia	8	29	3.7	3.2	54	704	3,788.4
Rwanda	9	16	171.5	0.0	16	227	822.1
Samoa	9	35	41.3	0.0	18	88	95.4
São Tomé and Principe	10	144	94.5	0.0	13	255	825.9
Saudi Arabia	7	15	32.3	0.0	18	125	94.5
Senegal	10	58	107.0	255.0	14	217	176.9
Serbia	11	23	8.9	8.0	20	204	2,713.1
Seychelles	9	38	8.7	0.0	19	144	46.5
Sierra Leone	9	26	1,075.2	0.0	47	235	191.7
Singapore	5	5	0.8	0.0	11	102	22.9
Slovakia	9	25	4.2	34.1	13	287	14.9
Slovenia	9	60	8.5	49.8	15	208	113.9
Solomon Islands	7	57	58.9	0.0	12	62	518.0
South Africa	8	31	7.1	0.0	17	174	30.4
Spain	10	47	15.1	13.7	11	233	64.9
Sri Lanka	5	39	8.5	0.0	22	214	1,929.0
St. Kitts and Nevis	9	46	22.9	0.0	14	72	14.0
St. Lucia	6	40	23.7	0.0	9	139	31.9
St. Vincent and the Grenadines	8	12	29.2	0.0	11	74	9.2
Sudan	10	39	57.9	0.0	19	271	296.0
Suriname	13	694	141.8	1.1	14	431	158.0
Swaziland	13	61	38.7	0.6	13	93	94.0
Sweden	3	15	0.6	31.1	8	116	106.4
Switzerland	6	20	2.1	13.9	14	154	52.7
Syria	13	43	55.7	3,673.3	21	128	258.5
Taiwan, China	8	48	4.1	178.4	30	198	206.9
Tajikistan	13	49	39.6	311.0	32	191	1,991.9
Tanzania	12	29	47.1	0.0	21	308	2,365.5
Thailand	8	33	5.6	0.0	11	156	10.7
Timor-Leste	9	82	11.9	595.2	22	208	113.1
Togo	13	53	245.7	546.4	15	277	1,366.3
Tonga	4	32	10.8	0.0	14	88	183.6
Trinidad and Tobago	9	43	0.9	0.0	20	261	5.9
Tunisia	10	11	8.3	25.3	20	93	922.1
Turkey	6	6	20.7	16.2	25	188	369.9
Uganda	18	28	92.0	0.0	16	143	811.8
Ukraine	10	27	7.8	203.1	29	429	668.5
United Arab Emirates	11	62	36.9	312.4	21	125	1.5
United Kingdom	6	13	0.8	0.0	19	144	64.6
United States	6	6	0.7	0.0	19	40	13.4
Uruguay	11	44	46.0	180.6	30	234	135.5
Uzbekistan	7	13	14.2	25.3	26	260	140.7
Vanuatu	8	39	54.9	0.0	7	51	357.7
Venezuela	16	141	28.2	0.0	11	395	326.0
Vietnam	11	50	20.0	0.0	13	194	373.6
West Bank and Gaza	12	92	280.4	9.3	21	199	726.1
Yemen	12	63	178.8	2,003.2	13	107	239.2
Zambia	6	33	30.5	2.2	17	254	1,518.0
Zimbabwe	10	96	21.3	54.6	19	952	11,799.0

Economy	Employing workers						Registering property		
	Difficulty of hiring index (0–100)	Rigidity of hours index (0–100)	Difficulty of firing index (0–100)	Rigidity of employment index (0–100)	Nonwage labor cost (% of salary)	Firing cost (weeks of salary)	Procedures (number)	Time (days)	Cost (% of property value)
Afghanistan	0	40	30	23	0	0	9	250	7.0
Albania	44	40	20	35	22	56	7	47	3.5
Algeria	44	60	40	48	27	17	14	51	7.5
Angola	78	60	70	69	8	58	7	334	11.1
Antigua and Barbuda	11	0	20	10	9	52	5	26	13.0
Argentina	44	60	20	41	26	139	5	65	7.6
Armenia	33	40	20	31	19	13	3	4	0.4
Australia	0	0	10	3	20	4	5	5	4.9
Austria	11	60	40	37	31	2	3	32	4.5
Azerbaijan	33	40	40	38	22	22	7	61	0.2
Bangladesh	44	20	40	35	0	104	8	425	10.3
Belarus	0	40	40	27	39	22	7	231	0.1
Belgium	11	40	10	20	55	16	7	132	12.7
Belize	22	20	0	14	4	24	8	60	4.7
Benin	39	40	40	40	29	36	3	118	11.4
Bhutan	0	0	20	7	1	10	5	64	0.0
Bolivia	78	60	100	79	14	not possible	7	92	4.9
Bosnia and Herzegovina	67	40	30	46	15	31	7	331	5.0
Botswana	0	20	40	20	0	90	4	30	5.0
Brazil	78	60	0	46	37	37	14	45	2.8
Brunei	0	20	0	7	5	4	no practice	no practice	no practice
Bulgaria	17	60	10	29	23	9	9	19	2.3
Burkina Faso	83	60	40	61	20	34	8	182	12.2
Burundi	33	60	30	41	7	26	5	94	11.5
Cambodia	44	60	30	45	0	39	7	56	4.4
Cameroon	28	40	70	46	16	33	5	93	17.8
Canada	11	0	0	4	13	28	6	17	1.8
Cape Verde	33	40	60	44	17	91	6	83	7.8
Central African Republic	72	60	50	61	18	22	3	69	11.7
Chad	39	60	40	46	21	36	6	44	21.2
Chile	33	20	20	24	3	52	6	31	1.3
China	11	20	40	24	44	91	4	29	3.6
Colombia	22	40	20	27	29	59	9	23	2.5
Comoros	39	60	40	46	0	100	5	24	20.8
Congo, Dem. Rep.	72	80	70	74	7	31	8	57	9.4
Congo, Rep.	78	60	70	69	29	33	7	137	27.3
Costa Rica	56	40	0	32	26	35	6	21	3.3
Côte d'Ivoire	33	60	20	38	18	49	7	62	16.9
Croatia	61	40	50	50	17	39	5	174	5.0
Czech Republic	33	40	20	31	35	22	4	123	3.0
Denmark	0	20	10	10	1	0	6	42	0.6
Djibouti	67	40	30	46	16	56	7	40	13.2
Dominica	11	20	20	17	7	58	4	40	13.5
Dominican Republic	56	40	0	32	14	88	7	60	5.1
Ecuador	44	60	50	51	12	135	10	17	3.0
Egypt	0	20	60	27	25	132	7	193	1.0
El Salvador	33	40	0	24	15	86	5	31	3.6
Equatorial Guinea	67	60	70	66	23	133	6	23	6.3
Eritrea	0	40	20	20	0	69	12	101	5.3
Estonia	33	80	60	58	33	35	3	51	0.5
Ethiopia	33	40	30	34	0	40	13	43	7.5
Fiji	22	20	0	14	9	2	3	48	12.0
Finland	44	60	40	48	26	26	3	14	4.0
France	67	60	40	56	47	32	9	123	6.1
Gabon	17	80	80	59	20	43	8	60	10.5
Gambia	0	40	30	23	11	9	5	371	7.6
Georgia	0	20	0	7	20	4	5	5	0.1
Germany	33	60	40	44	19	69	4	40	5.2
Ghana	22	40	50	37	13	178	5	34	1.3

Economy	Employing workers: Difficulty of hiring index (0–100)	Rigidity of hours index (0–100)	Difficulty of firing index (0–100)	Rigidity of employment index (0–100)	Nonwage labor cost (% of salary)	Firing cost (weeks of salary)	Registering property: Procedures (number)	Time (days)	Cost (% of property value)
Greece	44	80	40	55	28	24	12	23	4.0
Grenada	44	20	0	21	5	29	8	77	7.4
Guatemala	44	40	0	28	13	101	5	30	1.0
Guinea	33	60	30	41	27	26	6	104	15.3
Guinea-Bissau	67	60	70	66	22	87	9	211	5.4
Guyana	33	20	20	24	8	56	6	34	4.5
Haiti	22	40	0	21	11	17	5	405	6.5
Honduras	89	40	0	43	10	74	7	24	5.8
Hong Kong, China	0	0	0	0	5	62	5	54	5.0
Hungary	0	80	10	30	34	35	4	63	11.0
Iceland	33	40	10	28	12	13	3	4	2.4
India	0	20	70	30	17	56	6	62	7.7
Indonesia	72	0	60	44	10	108	7	42	10.5
Iran	11	60	50	40	23	91	9	36	10.6
Iraq	33	60	20	38	12	0	5	8	6.3
Ireland	11	20	20	17	11	24	5	38	10.2
Israel	11	60	0	24	6	91	7	144	7.5
Italy	33	40	40	38	37	2	8	27	0.6
Jamaica	11	0	0	4	12	61	5	54	13.5
Japan	0	20	30	17	13	4	6	14	5.0
Jordan	11	20	60	30	11	4	8	22	10.0
Kazakhstan	0	40	20	20	14	9	8	52	0.9
Kenya	33	0	30	21	4	47	8	64	4.2
Kiribati	0	0	50	17	8	4	5	513	0.1
Korea	11	60	40	37	13	91	7	11	6.3
Kuwait	0	40	0	13	11	78	8	55	0.5
Kyrgyz Republic	33	40	40	38	21	17	4	4	4.1
Lao PDR	11	40	60	37	5	19	9	135	4.2
Latvia	50	40	40	43	24	17	8	54	2.0
Lebanon	44	0	30	25	22	17	8	25	5.9
Lesotho	22	40	10	24	0	44	6	101	8.2
Liberia	33	20	40	31	5	84	13	50	14.9
Lithuania	33	80	30	48	31	30	3	3	0.7
Luxembourg	67	80	40	62	13	39	8	29	10.2
Macedonia, FYR	61	60	30	50	33	26	6	98	3.5
Madagascar	89	60	40	63	18	30	8	134	11.6
Malawi	56	0	20	25	1	84	6	88	3.3
Malaysia	0	0	30	10	15	75	5	144	2.4
Maldives	0	0	0	0	0	9	no practice	no practice	no practice
Mali	33	40	40	38	28	31	5	29	21.2
Marshall Islands	0	0	0	0	11	0	no practice	no practice	no practice
Mauritania	56	40	40	45	16	31	4	49	5.2
Mauritius	0	20	50	23	6	35	6	210	10.8
Mexico	33	40	70	48	21	52	5	74	4.7
Micronesia	22	0	0	7	6	0	no practice	no practice	no practice
Moldova	33	40	40	38	28	37	6	48	0.9
Mongolia	22	80	0	34	20	9	5	11	2.2
Montenegro	33	40	40	38	18	39	8	86	2.4
Morocco	100	40	50	63	19	85	8	47	4.9
Mozambique	83	60	20	54	4	143	8	42	8.1
Namibia	0	40	20	20	0	24	9	23	9.9
Nepal	67	20	70	52	10	90	3	5	6.4
Netherlands	17	40	70	42	18	17	2	5	6.2
New Zealand	11	0	10	7	1	0	2	2	0.1
Nicaragua	22	60	0	27	17	24	8	124	3.5
Niger	100	60	50	70	17	31	5	32	9.0
Nigeria	0	0	20	7	9	50	14	82	22.2
Norway	61	40	40	47	14	13	1	3	2.5
Oman	33	40	0	24	11	4	2	16	3.0

Economy	Employing workers: Difficulty of hiring index (0–100)	Rigidity of hours index (0–100)	Difficulty of firing index (0–100)	Rigidity of employment index (0–100)	Nonwage labor cost (% of salary)	Firing cost (weeks of salary)	Registering property: Procedures (number)	Time (days)	Cost (% of property value)
Pakistan	78	20	30	43	11	90	6	50	5.3
Palau	11	0	0	4	6	0	5	14	0.4
Panama	78	60	70	69	19	44	7	44	2.4
Papua New Guinea	11	20	0	10	10	39	4	72	5.1
Paraguay	56	60	60	59	17	113	6	46	3.5
Peru	44	60	60	55	10	52	5	33	3.3
Philippines	56	20	30	35	7	91	8	33	4.2
Poland	11	60	40	37	21	13	6	197	0.5
Portugal	33	60	50	48	24	95	5	42	7.4
Puerto Rico	44	0	20	21	13	0	8	194	1.4
Romania	78	80	40	66	31	8	8	150	2.8
Russia	33	60	40	44	31	17	6	52	0.3
Rwanda	56	40	30	42	5	26	5	371	9.4
Samoa	11	20	0	10	6	9	5	147	1.8
São Tomé and Principe	50	80	60	63	6	91	7	62	12.6
Saudi Arabia	0	40	0	13	11	80	4	4	0.0
Senegal	72	60	50	61	21	38	6	114	19.5
Serbia	67	40	30	46	18	25	6	111	5.4
Seychelles	33	20	50	34	25	39	4	33	7.0
Sierra Leone	44	60	50	51	10	189	8	235	14.9
Singapore	0	0	0	0	13	4	3	9	2.8
Slovakia	17	60	30	36	35	13	3	17	0.1
Slovenia	78	60	50	63	19	40	6	391	2.0
Solomon Islands	11	20	20	17	8	44	10	297	4.9
South Africa	56	40	30	42	4	24	6	24	8.8
Spain	78	60	30	56	33	56	4	18	7.1
Sri Lanka	0	20	60	27	15	169	8	83	5.1
St. Kitts and Nevis	11	20	20	17	10	8	6	81	13.3
St. Lucia	0	20	0	7	5	56	5	20	7.4
St. Vincent and the Grenadines	11	20	20	17	4	54	6	37	11.9
Sudan	39	20	50	36	17	118	6	9	3.2
Suriname	0	20	50	23	0	26	4	193	13.7
Swaziland	11	20	20	17	2	53	11	46	7.1
Sweden	17	60	40	39	32	26	1	2	3.0
Switzerland	0	40	10	17	15	13	4	16	0.4
Syria	22	40	50	37	17	80	4	34	28.1
Taiwan, China	67	40	40	49	13	91	3	5	6.2
Tajikistan	33	80	40	51	25	22	6	37	1.9
Tanzania	89	40	60	63	16	32	10	119	5.3
Thailand	33	20	0	18	6	54	2	2	6.3
Timor-Leste	33	20	50	34	0	17	no practice	no practice	no practice
Togo	61	60	40	54	25	36	5	295	13.9
Tonga	0	20	0	7	0	0	4	108	10.2
Trinidad and Tobago	0	0	20	7	3	67	8	162	7.0
Tunisia	28	40	80	49	22	17	5	49	6.1
Turkey	56	40	30	42	22	95	6	6	3.1
Uganda	0	0	10	3	10	13	13	227	4.6
Ukraine	44	60	30	45	38	13	10	93	3.3
United Arab Emirates	0	60	0	20	13	84	3	6	2.0
United Kingdom	11	0	10	7	11	22	2	21	4.1
United States	0	0	0	0	8	0	4	12	0.5
Uruguay	33	60	0	31	6	31	8	66	7.1
Uzbekistan	33	40	30	34	25	22	12	78	1.4
Vanuatu	22	40	10	24	4	56	2	188	11.0
Venezuela	78	60	100	79	16	not possible	8	47	2.2
Vietnam	0	40	40	27	17	87	4	67	1.2
West Bank and Gaza	33	40	20	31	0	91	10	72	2.2
Yemen	0	60	40	33	9	17	6	21	3.9
Zambia	33	40	30	34	9	178	6	70	9.6
Zimbabwe	0	40	60	33	4	446	4	30	25.0

Economy	Getting credit: Strength of legal rights index (0–10)	Getting credit: Depth of credit information index (0–6)	Getting credit: Public registry coverage (% of adults)	Getting credit: Private bureau coverage (% of adults)	Protecting investors: Extent of disclosure index (0–10)	Protecting investors: Extent of director liability index (0–10)	Protecting investors: Ease of shareholder suits index (0–10)	Protecting investors: Strength of investor protection index (0–10)
Afghanistan	0	0	0.0	0.0	0	0	2	0.7
Albania	9	0	0.0	0.0	0	5	3	2.7
Algeria	3	2	0.2	0.0	6	6	4	5.3
Angola	3	4	2.3	0.0	5	6	6	5.7
Antigua and Barbuda	4	0	0.0	0.0	4	8	7	6.3
Argentina	3	6	25.5	100.0	6	2	6	4.7
Armenia	5	5	2.8	13.5	5	2	8	5.0
Australia	9	5	0.0	100.0	8	2	7	5.7
Austria	5	6	1.3	40.6	3	5	4	4.0
Azerbaijan	7	4	1.4	0.0	4	1	8	4.3
Bangladesh	7	2	0.7	0.0	6	7	7	6.7
Belarus	2	3	..	0.0	5	1	8	4.7
Belgium	5	4	57.2	0.0	8	6	7	7.0
Belize	7	0	0.0	0.0	3	4	6	4.3
Benin	4	1	7.8	0.0	6	1	3	3.3
Bhutan	3	0	0.0	0.0	5	3	4	4.0
Bolivia	1	5	12.1	22.6	1	5	6	4.0
Bosnia and Herzegovina	7	5	0.0	63.7	3	6	6	5.0
Botswana	7	4	0.0	58.3	8	2	3	4.3
Brazil	2	5	17.1	46.4	6	7	3	5.3
Brunei	6	0	0.0	0.0	3	2	8	4.3
Bulgaria	6	6	25.4	3.0	10	1	7	6.0
Burkina Faso	4	1	2.1	0.0	6	1	4	3.7
Burundi	1	1	0.2	0.0	4	1	5	3.3
Cambodia	0	0	0.0	0.0	5	9	2	5.3
Cameroon	3	2	1.0	0.0	6	1	6	4.3
Canada	7	6	0.0	100.0	8	9	8	8.3
Cape Verde	5	3	20.3	0.0	1	5	6	4.0
Central African Republic	3	2	1.4	0.0	6	1	5	4.0
Chad	3	1	0.2	0.0	6	1	5	4.0
Chile	4	5	26.2	33.5	7	6	5	6.0
China	3	4	49.2	0.0	10	1	4	5.0
Colombia	2	5	0.0	39.9	8	2	9	6.3
Comoros	3	0	0.0	0.0	6	1	5	4.0
Congo, Dem. Rep.	3	0	0.0	0.0	3	3	4	3.3
Congo, Rep.	3	2	2.4	0.0	6	1	3	3.3
Costa Rica	4	5	6.1	52.7	2	5	2	3.0
Côte d'Ivoire	3	1	2.8	0.0	6	1	3	3.3
Croatia	6	3	0.0	72.4	1	5	6	4.0
Czech Republic	6	5	4.2	53.0	2	5	8	5.0
Denmark	8	4	0.0	11.5	7	5	7	6.3
Djibouti	3	1	0.2	0.0	5	2	0	2.3
Dominica	6	0	0.0	0.0	4	8	7	6.3
Dominican Republic	4	6	13.3	35.4	5	0	7	4.0
Ecuador	1	5	37.9	44.1	1	5	6	4.0
Egypt	1	4	1.6	..	7	3	5	5.0
El Salvador	3	6	17.2	74.6	5	2	6	4.3
Equatorial Guinea	2	2	1.9	0.0	6	1	4	3.7
Eritrea	3	0	0.0	0.0	4	5	5	4.7
Estonia	4	5	0.0	19.7	8	4	6	6.0
Ethiopia	4	2	0.1	0.0	4	4	5	4.3
Fiji	5	4	0.0	41.2	3	8	7	6.0
Finland	6	5	0.0	14.9	6	4	7	5.7
France	6	4	24.8	0.0	10	1	5	5.3
Gabon	3	2	2.4	0.0	6	1	3	3.3
Gambia	4	0	0.0	0.0	2	1	5	2.7
Georgia	5	4	0.0	0.2	8	6	4	6.0
Germany	8	6	0.7	98.1	5	5	5	5.0
Ghana	5	0	0.0	0.0	7	5	6	6.0

Economy	Getting credit: Strength of legal rights index (0–10)	Getting credit: Depth of credit information index (0–6)	Getting credit: Public registry coverage (% of adults)	Getting credit: Private bureau coverage (% of adults)	Protecting investors: Extent of disclosure index (0–10)	Protecting investors: Extent of director liability index (0–10)	Protecting investors: Ease of shareholder suits index (0–10)	Protecting investors: Strength of investor protection index (0–10)
Greece	3	4	0.0	38.7	1	3	5	3.0
Grenada	6	0	0.0	0.0	4	8	7	6.3
Guatemala	3	5	20.7	13.1	3	3	6	4.0
Guinea	4	0	0.0	0.0	6	1	1	2.7
Guinea-Bissau	3	1	0.9	0.0	6	1	5	4.0
Guyana	3	0	0.0	0.0	5	5	6	5.3
Haiti	3	2	0.7	0.0	2	3	4	3.0
Honduras	6	6	12.7	58.0	1	5	4	3.3
Hong Kong, China	10	5	0.0	64.7	10	8	9	9.0
Hungary	6	5	0.0	6.9	2	4	7	4.3
Iceland	7	5	0.0	100.0	5	5	6	5.3
India	6	4	0.0	10.8	7	4	7	6.0
Indonesia	5	3	20.5	0.2	9	5	3	5.7
Iran	5	3	22.2	0.0	5	4	0	3.0
Iraq	4	0	0.0	0.0	4	5	4	4.3
Ireland	8	5	0.0	100.0	10	6	9	8.3
Israel	8	5	0.0	91.6	7	9	9	8.3
Italy	3	5	11.0	71.5	7	4	6	5.7
Jamaica	5	0	0.0	0.0	4	8	4	5.3
Japan	6	6	0.0	68.3	7	6	8	7.0
Jordan	5	2	0.8	0.0	5	4	4	4.3
Kazakhstan	5	4	0.0	13.7	7	1	9	5.7
Kenya	8	4	0.0	1.5	3	2	10	5.0
Kiribati	3	0	0.0	0.0	6	5	7	6.0
Korea	5	5	0.0	74.2	7	2	7	5.3
Kuwait	4	4	0.0	14.5	7	7	5	6.3
Kyrgyz Republic	5	3	0.0	1.6	8	1	9	6.0
Lao PDR	2	0	0.0	0.0	0	3	2	1.7
Latvia	8	4	2.6	0.0	5	4	8	5.7
Lebanon	4	5	4.7	0.0	9	1	5	5.0
Lesotho	5	0	0.0	0.0	2	1	8	3.7
Liberia	4	0	0.0	0.0	4	1	6	3.7
Lithuania	4	6	6.6	7.3	5	4	6	5.0
Luxembourg	6	0	0.0	0.0	6	4	3	4.3
Macedonia, FYR	6	3	4.0	0.0	5	6	4	5.0
Madagascar	1	0	0.1	0.0	5	6	6	5.7
Malawi	7	0	0.0	0.0	4	7	5	5.3
Malaysia	8	6	44.5	..	10	9	7	8.7
Maldives	4	0	0.0	0.0	0	8	8	5.3
Mali	3	1	2.5	0.0	6	1	3	3.3
Marshall Islands	2	0	0.0	0.0	2	0	8	3.3
Mauritania	4	1	0.2	0.0	5	3	3	3.7
Mauritius	5	1	38.6	0.0	6	8	9	7.7
Mexico	3	6	0.0	61.2	8	5	5	6.0
Micronesia	7	0	0.0	0.0	0	0	8	2.7
Moldova	6	0	0.0	0.0	7	1	6	4.7
Mongolia	5	3	9.5	0.0	5	8	6	6.3
Montenegro	7	0	0.0	0.0	5	8	6	6.3
Morocco	3	1	2.3	0.0	6	2	1	3.0
Mozambique	3	3	0.9	0.0	5	4	9	6.0
Namibia	5	5	0.0	59.9	5	5	6	5.3
Nepal	4	2	0.0	0.2	6	1	9	5.3
Netherlands	7	5	0.0	78.1	4	4	6	4.7
New Zealand	9	5	0.0	100.0	10	9	10	9.7
Nicaragua	3	5	14.8	100.0	4	5	6	5.0
Niger	3	1	1.0	0.0	6	1	3	3.3
Nigeria	7	0	0.0	0.0	5	7	5	5.7
Norway	6	4	0.0	100.0	7	6	7	6.7
Oman	4	2	12.4	0.0	8	5	3	5.3

Economy	Getting credit: Strength of legal rights index (0–10)	Getting credit: Depth of credit information index (0–6)	Getting credit: Public registry coverage (% of adults)	Getting credit: Private bureau coverage (% of adults)	Protecting investors: Extent of disclosure index (0–10)	Protecting investors: Extent of director liability index (0–10)	Protecting investors: Ease of shareholder suits index (0–10)	Protecting investors: Strength of investor protection index (0–10)
Pakistan	4	4	4.6	1.4	6	6	7	6.3
Palau	2	0	0.0	0.0	0	0	8	2.7
Panama	6	6	0.0	41.6	1	4	9	4.7
Papua New Guinea	5	0	0.0	0.0	5	5	8	6.0
Paraguay	3	6	11.0	48.7	6	5	6	5.7
Peru	4	6	20.7	33.0	8	5	7	6.7
Philippines	3	3	0.0	5.5	1	2	8	3.7
Poland	4	4	0.0	51.5	7	2	9	6.0
Portugal	4	4	67.1	11.3	6	5	7	6.0
Puerto Rico	6	5	0.0	62.0	7	6	8	7.0
Romania	7	5	4.1	10.9	9	5	4	6.0
Russia	3	4	0.0	4.4	6	2	7	5.0
Rwanda	1	2	0.2	0.0	2	5	1	2.7
Samoa	4	0	0.0	0.0	5	6	8	6.3
São Tomé and Principe	5	0	0.0	0.0	5	1	6	4.0
Saudi Arabia	3	6	0.0	23.5	7	7	3	5.7
Senegal	3	1	4.0	0.0	6	1	2	3.0
Serbia	7	5	0.1	51.3	7	6	3	5.3
Seychelles	3	0	0.0	0.0	4	8	5	5.7
Sierra Leone	5	0	0.0	0.0	3	6	5	4.7
Singapore	9	4	0.0	42.7	10	9	9	9.3
Slovakia	9	4	1.2	56.0	3	4	7	4.7
Slovenia	6	2	2.5	0.0	3	8	8	6.3
Solomon Islands	4	0	0.0	0.0	3	7	7	5.7
South Africa	5	6	0.0	52.1	8	8	8	8.0
Spain	6	6	44.9	8.3	5	6	4	5.0
Sri Lanka	3	3	0.0	2.9	4	5	7	5.3
St. Kitts and Nevis	5	0	0.0	0.0	4	8	7	6.3
St. Lucia	6	0	0.0	0.0	4	8	7	6.3
St. Vincent and the Grenadines	7	0	0.0	0.0	4	8	7	6.3
Sudan	4	0	0.0	0.0	0	6	5	3.7
Suriname	4	0	0.0	0.0	2	0	5	2.3
Swaziland	5	5	0.0	37.6	0	1	5	2.0
Sweden	6	4	0.0	100.0	6	4	7	5.7
Switzerland	6	5	0.0	24.0	0	5	4	3.0
Syria	3	0	0.0	0.0	6	5	2	4.3
Taiwan, China	4	5	0.0	67.1	7	4	5	5.3
Tajikistan	4	0	0.0	0.0	0	0	5	1.7
Tanzania	5	0	0.0	0.0	3	4	8	5.0
Thailand	5	5	0.0	27.9	10	2	6	6.0
Timor-Leste	2	0	0.0	0.0	3	4	5	4.0
Togo	3	1	2.7	0.0	6	1	4	3.7
Tonga	3	0	0.0	0.0	3	3	8	4.7
Trinidad and Tobago	5	4	0.0	34.4	4	9	7	6.7
Tunisia	2	4	13.7	0.0	0	4	6	3.3
Turkey	3	5	10.3	2.7	8	4	4	5.3
Uganda	3	0	0.0	0.0	2	5	5	4.0
Ukraine	8	0	0.0	0.0	1	3	7	3.7
United Arab Emirates	3	2	1.4	0.0	4	7	2	4.3
United Kingdom	10	6	0.0	84.6	10	7	7	8.0
United States	7	6	0.0	100.0	7	9	9	8.3
Uruguay	5	6	14.1	93.8	3	4	8	5.0
Uzbekistan	2	0	0.0	0.0	4	6	3	4.3
Vanuatu	4	0	0.0	0.0	5	6	5	5.3
Venezuela	4	0	0.0	0.0	3	3	2	2.7
Vietnam	6	3	9.2	0.0	6	0	2	2.7
West Bank and Gaza	5	3	1.8	0.0	6	5	7	6.0
Yemen	3	0	0.0	0.0	6	4	2	4.0
Zambia	6	0	0.0	0.0	3	6	7	5.3
Zimbabwe	6	0	0.0	0.0	8	1	4	4.3

	Paying taxes			Trading across borders					
Economy	**Payments** (number per year)	**Time** (hours per year)	**Total tax rate** (% of profit)	**Documents to export** (number)	**Time to export** (days)	**Cost to export** (US$ per container)	**Documents to import** (number)	**Time to import** (days)	**Cost to import** (US$ per container)
Afghanistan	6	275	35.5	12	67	2,500	11	71	2,100
Albania	44	240	46.8	7	21	745	9	22	750
Algeria	33	451	72.6	8	17	1,198	9	23	1,378
Angola	31	272	53.2	12	64	1,850	9	58	2,325
Antigua and Barbuda	45	184	46.8	5	19	1,107	6	19	1,174
Argentina	19	615	112.9	9	16	1,325	7	20	1,825
Armenia	50	1,120	36.6	7	30	1,165	8	24	1,335
Australia	12	107	50.6	6	9	930	6	12	1,120
Austria	22	170	54.6	4	8	843	5	8	843
Azerbaijan	38	952	40.9	9	56	2,715	14	56	2,945
Bangladesh	17	400	39.5	7	28	844	9	32	1,148
Belarus	124	1,188	144.4	8	24	1,672	8	29	1,672
Belgium	11	156	64.3	4	8	1,600	5	9	1,600
Belize	41	147	30.8	7	23	1,800	6	26	2,130
Benin	55	270	73.3	7	34	1,167	7	41	1,202
Bhutan	19	274	39.8	8	38	1,150	11	38	2,080
Bolivia	41	1,080	78.1	8	24	1,110	7	36	1,230
Bosnia and Herzegovina	51	368	44.1	6	19	1,030	7	18	985
Botswana	19	140	17.2	6	33	2,328	9	43	2,595
Brazil	11	2,600	69.2	8	18	1,090	7	22	1,240
Brunei	15	144	37.4	6	28	515	6	19	590
Bulgaria	17	616	36.7	5	23	1,329	7	21	1,377
Burkina Faso	45	270	48.9	11	45	2,096	11	54	3,522
Burundi	32	140	278.7	9	47	2,147	10	71	3,705
Cambodia	27	137	22.6	11	37	722	11	46	852
Cameroon	41	1,400	51.9	9	27	907	8	33	1,529
Canada	9	119	45.9	3	7	1,385	4	11	1,425
Cape Verde	57	100	54.0	5	21	1,024	5	21	1,024
Central African Republic	54	504	203.8	8	57	4,581	18	66	4,534
Chad	54	122	63.7	6	78	4,867	9	102	5,520
Chile	10	316	25.9	6	21	645	7	21	685
China	35	872	73.9	7	21	390	6	24	430
Colombia	69	268	82.4	6	24	1,440	8	20	1,440
Comoros	20	100	48.8	10	30	971	10	21	974
Congo, Dem. Rep.	32	308	229.8	8	46	2,307	9	66	2,183
Congo, Rep.	89	606	65.4	11	50	2,201	12	62	2,201
Costa Rica	43	402	55.7	7	18	660	8	25	660
Côte d'Ivoire	66	270	45.4	10	23	1,653	8	43	2,457
Croatia	28	196	32.5	7	22	1,200	8	16	1,200
Czech Republic	12	930	48.6	5	16	775	7	18	860
Denmark	9	135	33.3	4	5	540	3	5	540
Djibouti	35	114	38.7	8	22	960	6	18	960
Dominica	38	147	37.1	7	16	1,197	8	18	1,107
Dominican Republic	74	286	40.2	6	12	815	7	13	1,015
Ecuador	8	600	35.3	10	22	1,090	8	44	1,090
Egypt	36	711	47.9	6	15	714	7	18	729
El Salvador	66	224	33.8	8	21	540	11	18	540
Equatorial Guinea	45	212	62.2	7	29	1,403	7	46	1,403
Eritrea	18	216	84.5	9	59	1,331	13	69	1,581
Estonia	10	81	49.2	3	5	675	4	5	675
Ethiopia	20	198	31.1	8	46	1,617	8	42	2,793
Fiji	33	140	38.5	13	25	573	13	25	570
Finland	20	269	47.8	4	8	420	5	8	420
France	23	132	66.3	4	11	1,028	5	12	1,148
Gabon	28	272	44.2	6	19	1,510	7	35	1,600
Gambia	50	376	286.7	7	23	809	8	23	869
Georgia	29	387	38.6	8	12	1,105	7	14	1,105
Germany	16	196	50.8	4	7	740	5	7	765
Ghana	32	304	32.9	6	19	895	7	29	895

Economy	Paying taxes: Payments (number per year)	Paying taxes: Time (hours per year)	Paying taxes: Total tax rate (% of profit)	Trading across borders: Documents to export (number)	Trading across borders: Time to export (days)	Trading across borders: Cost to export (US$ per container)	Trading across borders: Documents to import (number)	Trading across borders: Time to import (days)	Trading across borders: Cost to import (US$ per container)
Greece	21	264	48.6	5	20	998	6	25	1,245
Grenada	30	140	45.3	6	19	820	5	23	1,178
Guatemala	39	344	37.5	11	19	1,052	11	18	1,177
Guinea	56	416	49.9	7	33	570	9	32	995
Guinea-Bissau	46	208	45.9	6	27	1,445	6	26	1,749
Guyana	34	288	39.0	7	30	850	8	35	856
Haiti	53	160	40.0	8	52	1,650	10	53	1,860
Honduras	47	424	51.4	7	20	1,065	11	23	975
Hong Kong, China	4	80	24.4	4	6	525	4	5	525
Hungary	24	340	55.1	5	18	975	7	17	975
Iceland	31	140	27.2	5	15	469	5	14	443
India	60	271	70.6	8	18	820	9	21	910
Indonesia	51	266	37.3	5	21	667	6	27	623
Iran	22	292	47.4	8	26	860	10	42	1,330
Iraq	13	312	24.7	10	102	3,400	10	101	3,400
Ireland	9	76	28.9	4	7	1,090	4	12	1,139
Israel	33	230	36.0	5	12	560	4	12	560
Italy	15	360	76.2	5	20	1,291	5	18	1,291
Jamaica	72	414	51.3	6	21	1,750	6	22	1,350
Japan	13	350	52.0	4	10	989	5	11	1,047
Jordan	26	101	31.1	7	19	680	7	22	1,065
Kazakhstan	9	271	36.7	12	89	2,730	14	76	2,780
Kenya	41	432	50.9	9	29	1,955	8	37	1,995
Kiribati	7	120	31.8	6	21	1,550	7	21	1,550
Korea	48	290	34.9	4	11	745	6	10	745
Kuwait	14	118	14.4	8	20	935	11	20	935
Kyrgyz Republic	75	202	61.4	13	64	2,500	13	75	2,450
Lao PDR	34	672	35.5	9	50	1,750	10	50	1,930
Latvia	7	219	32.6	6	13	800	6	12	800
Lebanon	19	180	35.4	5	27	1,027	7	38	810
Lesotho	22	342	20.8	6	44	1,188	8	49	1,210
Liberia	37	158	81.6	10	20	1,032	9	10	1,032
Lithuania	24	166	48.3	6	10	820	6	13	980
Luxembourg	22	58	35.3	5	6	1,250	4	6	1,250
Macedonia, FYR	52	96	49.8	7	19	1,130	7	17	1,130
Madagascar	26	238	46.5	4	28	1,182	10	49	1,282
Malawi	30	370	32.2	12	45	1,623	10	54	2,500
Malaysia	35	166	36.0	7	18	432	7	14	385
Maldives	1	0	9.1	8	21	1,200	9	20	1,200
Mali	58	270	51.4	9	44	1,752	11	65	2,680
Marshall Islands	21	128	64.9	5	21	765	5	33	765
Mauritania	38	696	107.5	11	35	1,360	11	42	1,363
Mauritius	7	161	21.7	5	17	728	6	16	673
Mexico	27	552	51.2	5	17	1,302	5	23	2,411
Micronesia	21	128	58.7	3	30	1,145	6	30	1,145
Moldova	49	218	44.0	6	32	1,425	7	35	1,545
Mongolia	42	204	38.4	10	58	1,807	10	59	3,197
Montenegro	88	372	31.6	9	18	1,580	7	19	1,780
Morocco	28	358	53.1	8	14	600	11	19	800
Mozambique	37	230	34.3	8	27	1,155	10	38	1,185
Namibia	37	..	26.5	11	29	1,539	9	24	1,550
Nepal	33	408	32.5	9	43	1,600	10	35	1,725
Netherlands	9	180	43.4	4	6	880	5	6	1,005
New Zealand	8	70	35.1	7	10	725	5	9	800
Nicaragua	64	240	63.2	5	36	1,021	5	38	1,054
Niger	42	270	42.4	8	59	2,945	10	68	2,946
Nigeria	35	1,120	29.9	10	26	1,026	9	46	1,047
Norway	4	87	42.0	4	7	518	4	7	468
Oman	14	62	21.6	10	22	665	10	26	824

Economy	Paying taxes: Payments (number per year)	Paying taxes: Time (hours per year)	Paying taxes: Total tax rate (% of profit)	Trading across borders: Documents to export (number)	Time to export (days)	Cost to export (US$ per container)	Documents to import (number)	Time to import (days)	Cost to import (US$ per container)
Pakistan	47	560	40.7	9	24	515	8	19	1,336
Palau	19	128	73.0	6	29	1,160	10	35	1,110
Panama	59	482	50.8	3	9	650	4	9	850
Papua New Guinea	33	206	41.7	7	26	584	9	29	642
Paraguay	35	328	35.3	9	35	720	10	33	900
Peru	9	424	41.5	7	24	590	8	31	670
Philippines	47	195	52.8	8	17	800	8	18	800
Poland	41	418	38.4	5	17	834	5	27	834
Portugal	8	328	44.8	6	16	580	7	16	994
Puerto Rico	16	140	44.3	7	15	1,225	10	16	1,225
Romania	96	202	46.9	5	12	1,075	6	13	1,075
Russia	22	448	51.4	8	36	2,050	13	36	2,050
Rwanda	34	168	33.8	9	47	2,975	9	69	4,970
Samoa	37	224	19.8	7	27	1,010	7	31	1,375
São Tomé and Principe	41	424	51.0	8	27	690	9	29	577
Saudi Arabia	14	79	14.5	5	19	1,008	5	20	758
Senegal	59	696	46.0	11	20	828	11	26	1,720
Serbia	66	279	35.8	6	12	1,240	6	14	1,440
Seychelles	16	76	48.4	6	17	1,839	5	19	1,839
Sierra Leone	22	399	233.5	8	31	1,282	7	34	1,242
Singapore	5	49	23.2	4	5	416	4	3	367
Slovakia	31	344	50.5	6	25	1,015	8	25	1,050
Slovenia	22	260	39.2	6	20	971	8	21	1,019
Solomon Islands	33	80	32.6	7	24	1,056	4	21	1,238
South Africa	11	350	37.1	8	30	1,087	9	35	1,195
Spain	8	298	62.0	6	9	1,000	8	10	1,000
Sri Lanka	62	256	63.7	8	21	810	6	21	844
St. Kitts and Nevis	24	172	52.6	6	15	750	6	17	756
St. Lucia	32	71	36.9	5	18	1,375	8	21	1,420
St. Vincent and the Grenadines	36	76	45.0	6	15	1,770	6	16	1,769
Sudan	42	180	31.6	7	39	1,700	7	54	2,300
Suriname	17	199	27.9	8	25	905	7	25	815
Swaziland	33	104	36.6	9	21	1,798	11	34	1,820
Sweden	2	122	54.5	4	8	561	3	6	619
Switzerland	24	63	29.1	4	8	1,238	5	9	1,333
Syria	21	336	46.7	8	19	1,300	9	23	1,900
Taiwan, China	23	340	40.6	7	13	747	7	12	747
Tajikistan	54	224	82.2	10	82	3,000	11	83	4,500
Tanzania	48	172	44.3	5	24	1,212	7	30	1,425
Thailand	35	264	37.7	7	17	615	9	14	786
Timor-Leste	15	640	28.3	6	25	990	7	26	995
Togo	53	270	48.2	6	24	872	8	29	894
Tonga	23	164	25.0	7	19	545	6	25	620
Trinidad and Tobago	40	114	33.1	5	14	693	7	26	1,100
Tunisia	46	268	61.0	5	17	540	7	22	810
Turkey	15	223	45.1	7	14	865	8	15	1,013
Uganda	33	237	32.3	6	39	2,940	7	37	2,990
Ukraine	99	2,085	57.3	6	31	1,045	10	39	1,065
United Arab Emirates	14	12	14.4	7	13	462	8	13	462
United Kingdom	8	105	35.7	4	13	940	4	13	1,267
United States	10	325	46.2	4	6	960	5	5	1,160
Uruguay	53	304	40.7	10	24	925	10	23	1,180
Uzbekistan	118	196	96.3	7	80	2,550	11	104	4,050
Vanuatu	31	120	8.4	7	26	1,815	9	30	2,225
Venezuela	70	864	53.3	8	45	2,400	9	65	2,400
Vietnam	32	1,050	41.1	6	24	669	8	23	881
West Bank and Gaza	27	154	17.1	6	25	830	6	40	995
Yemen	32	248	41.4	6	33	1,129	9	31	1,475
Zambia	37	132	16.1	8	53	2,098	11	64	2,840
Zimbabwe	52	256	53.0	9	52	1,879	13	67	2,420

Economy	Enforcing contracts: Procedures (number)	Enforcing contracts: Time (days)	Enforcing contracts: Cost (% of claim)	Closing a business: Time (years)	Closing a business: Cost (% of estate)	Closing a business: Recovery rate (cents on the dollar)
Afghanistan	47	1,642	25.0	no practice	no practice	0.0
Albania	39	390	31.8	no practice	no practice	0.0
Algeria	47	630	17.4	2.5	7	41.7
Angola	46	1,011	44.4	6.2	22	10.8
Antigua and Barbuda	45	351	22.7	3.0	7	35.7
Argentina	36	590	16.5	2.8	12	34.4
Armenia	50	285	19.0	1.9	4	42.0
Australia	28	262	20.7	1.0	8	79.2
Austria	26	397	12.7	1.1	18	72.4
Azerbaijan	39	267	18.5	2.7	8	31.5
Bangladesh	41	1,442	63.3	4.0	8	23.2
Belarus	28	225	23.4	5.8	22	33.2
Belgium	27	505	16.6	0.9	4	85.5
Belize	51	892	27.5	1.0	23	63.5
Benin	42	720	58.7	4.0	15	22.6
Bhutan	47	275	0.1	no practice	no practice	0.0
Bolivia	37	591	33.2	1.8	15	38.7
Bosnia and Herzegovina	38	595	38.4	3.3	9	35.0
Botswana	29	987	28.1	1.7	15	59.8
Brazil	45	616	16.5	4.0	12	14.6
Brunei	58	540	36.6	2.5	4	45.3
Bulgaria	40	564	22.2	3.3	9	32.4
Burkina Faso	37	446	107.4	4.0	9	25.6
Burundi	44	558	38.6	no practice	no practice	0.0
Cambodia	44	401	102.7	no practice	no practice	0.0
Cameroon	43	800	46.6	3.2	15	25.5
Canada	36	570	16.2	0.8	4	88.8
Cape Verde	37	465	24.1	no practice	no practice	0.0
Central African Republic	43	660	82.0	4.8	76	0.0
Chad	41	743	77.4	no practice	no practice	0.0
Chile	36	480	28.6	4.5	15	23.8
China	35	406	8.8	1.7	22	35.9
Colombia	34	1,346	52.6	3.0	1	58.3
Comoros	43	506	89.4	no practice	no practice	0.0
Congo, Dem. Rep.	43	685	151.8	5.2	29	2.9
Congo, Rep.	44	560	53.2	3.0	24	20.4
Costa Rica	40	877	24.3	3.5	15	23.1
Côte d'Ivoire	33	770	41.7	2.2	18	33.0
Croatia	38	561	13.8	3.1	15	30.2
Czech Republic	27	820	33.0	6.5	15	21.3
Denmark	34	380	23.3	1.1	4	87.0
Djibouti	40	1,225	34.0	5.0	18	15.9
Dominica	47	681	36.0	no practice	no practice	0.0
Dominican Republic	34	460	40.9	3.5	38	8.4
Ecuador	39	498	20.8	5.3	18	16.9
Egypt	42	1,010	25.3	4.2	22	16.6
El Salvador	30	786	19.2	4.0	9	28.4
Equatorial Guinea	40	553	18.5	no practice	no practice	0.0
Eritrea	39	405	22.6	no practice	no practice	0.0
Estonia	36	425	17.3	3.0	9	39.1
Ethiopia	39	690	15.2	3.0	15	33.1
Fiji	34	397	38.9	1.8	38	20.2
Finland	33	235	10.4	0.9	4	88.2
France	30	331	17.4	1.9	9	47.4
Gabon	38	1,070	34.3	5.0	15	15.2
Gambia	32	434	37.9	3.0	15	19.3
Georgia	36	285	29.9	3.3	4	22.8
Germany	33	394	11.8	1.2	8	53.4
Ghana	36	487	23.0	1.9	22	24.0

Economy	Enforcing contracts: Procedures (number)	Enforcing contracts: Time (days)	Enforcing contracts: Cost (% of claim)	Closing a business: Time (years)	Closing a business: Cost (% of estate)	Closing a business: Recovery rate (cents on the dollar)
Greece	39	819	14.4	2.0	9	44.8
Grenada	47	723	32.6	no practice	no practice	0.0
Guatemala	28	1,459	26.5	3.0	15	28.1
Guinea	50	276	45.0	3.8	8	20.4
Guinea-Bissau	41	1,140	25.0	no practice	no practice	0.0
Guyana	36	581	25.2	3.0	29	17.4
Haiti	35	508	42.6	5.7	30	3.1
Honduras	45	480	30.4	3.8	15	20.3
Hong Kong, China	24	211	14.5	1.1	9	79.0
Hungary	33	335	13.0	2.0	15	38.4
Iceland	26	393	6.1	1.0	4	80.3
India	46	1,420	39.6	10.0	9	11.6
Indonesia	39	570	122.7	5.5	18	12.6
Iran	39	520	17.0	4.5	9	19.0
Iraq	51	520	32.5	no practice	no practice	0.0
Ireland	20	515	26.9	0.4	9	87.1
Israel	35	890	25.3	4.0	23	43.6
Italy	41	1,210	29.9	1.8	22	61.8
Jamaica	34	565	45.6	1.1	18	64.3
Japan	30	316	22.7	0.6	4	92.6
Jordan	39	689	31.2	4.3	9	27.8
Kazakhstan	38	230	22.0	3.3	18	23.4
Kenya	44	465	26.7	4.5	22	31.0
Kiribati	32	660	25.8	no practice	no practice	0.0
Korea	35	230	10.3	1.5	4	81.2
Kuwait	50	566	13.3	4.2	1	33.6
Kyrgyz Republic	39	177	22.0	4.0	15	15.6
Lao PDR	42	443	31.6	no practice	no practice	0.0
Latvia	27	279	12.9	3.0	13	34.6
Lebanon	37	721	30.8	4.0	22	19.1
Lesotho	41	695	16.6	2.6	8	34.9
Liberia	41	1,280	35.0	3.0	43	7.8
Lithuania	30	210	23.6	1.7	7	49.2
Luxembourg	26	321	8.8	2.0	15	41.6
Macedonia, FYR	39	385	33.1	3.7	28	15.8
Madagascar	38	871	42.4	no practice	no practice	0.0
Malawi	42	432	142.4	2.6	30	13.2
Malaysia	30	600	27.5	2.3	15	38.3
Maldives	41	665	16.5	6.7	4	18.2
Mali	39	860	52.0	3.6	18	21.3
Marshall Islands	36	476	27.4	2.0	38	17.9
Mauritania	46	400	23.2	8.0	9	7.8
Mauritius	37	750	17.4	1.7	15	34.3
Mexico	38	415	32.0	1.8	18	63.9
Micronesia	34	965	66.0	5.3	38	3.1
Moldova	31	365	16.6	2.8	9	28.8
Mongolia	32	314	26.1	4.0	8	20.1
Montenegro	49	545	25.7	2.0	8	42.8
Morocco	40	615	25.2	1.8	18	35.3
Mozambique	31	1,010	142.5	5.0	9	13.9
Namibia	33	270	29.9	1.5	15	41.3
Nepal	39	735	26.8	5.0	9	24.5
Netherlands	25	514	24.4	1.1	4	86.7
New Zealand	30	216	22.0	1.3	4	77.1
Nicaragua	35	540	26.8	2.2	15	34.6
Niger	39	545	59.6	5.0	18	14.2
Nigeria	39	457	32.0	2.0	22	27.5
Norway	33	310	9.9	0.9	1	90.7
Oman	51	598	13.5	4.0	4	35.5

Economy	Enforcing contracts: Procedures (number)	Enforcing contracts: Time (days)	Enforcing contracts: Cost (% of claim)	Closing a business: Time (years)	Closing a business: Cost (% of estate)	Closing a business: Recovery rate (cents on the dollar)
Pakistan	47	880	23.8	2.8	4	39.1
Palau	38	885	35.3	1.0	23	38.2
Panama	31	686	50.0	2.5	18	32.3
Papua New Guinea	43	591	110.3	3.0	23	23.9
Paraguay	38	591	30.0	3.9	9	14.6
Peru	41	468	35.7	3.1	7	24.7
Philippines	37	842	26.0	5.7	38	4.2
Poland	38	830	10.0	3.0	22	27.8
Portugal	35	577	17.7	2.0	9	74.0
Puerto Rico	41	620	16.4	3.8	8	54.1
Romania	32	537	19.9	3.3	9	28.9
Russia	37	281	13.4	3.8	9	29.0
Rwanda	24	310	78.7	no practice	no practice	0.0
Samoa	44	455	19.7	2.5	38	15.2
São Tomé and Principe	43	405	34.8	no practice	no practice	0.0
Saudi Arabia	44	635	27.5	2.8	22	29.3
Senegal	44	780	26.5	3.0	7	32.4
Serbia	36	635	28.4	2.7	23	23.1
Seychelles	38	720	14.3	no practice	no practice	0.0
Sierra Leone	40	515	149.5	2.6	42	8.5
Singapore	22	120	17.8	0.8	1	91.3
Slovakia	30	565	25.7	4.0	18	45.2
Slovenia	32	1,350	18.6	2.0	8	46.6
Solomon Islands	37	455	78.9	1.0	38	23.3
South Africa	30	600	33.2	2.0	18	33.2
Spain	39	515	17.2	1.0	15	76.9
Sri Lanka	40	1,318	22.8	1.7	5	44.6
St. Kitts and Nevis	47	578	20.5	no practice	no practice	0.0
St. Lucia	47	635	37.3	2.0	9	41.8
St. Vincent and the Grenadines	45	394	30.3	no practice	no practice	0.0
Sudan	53	810	19.8	no practice	no practice	0.0
Suriname	44	1,715	37.1	5.0	30	7.4
Swaziland	40	972	23.1	2.0	15	36.0
Sweden	30	508	31.3	2.0	9	74.7
Switzerland	32	417	21.2	3.0	4	47.1
Syria	55	872	29.3	4.1	9	30.8
Taiwan, China	47	510	17.4	1.9	4	80.2
Tajikistan	34	295	20.5	3.0	9	23.6
Tanzania	38	462	14.3	3.0	22	20.5
Thailand	35	479	14.3	2.7	36	41.8
Timor-Leste	51	1,800	163.2	no practice	no practice	0.0
Togo	41	588	47.5	3.0	15	26.3
Tonga	37	350	30.5	2.7	22	25.3
Trinidad and Tobago	42	1,340	33.5	no practice	no practice	0.0
Tunisia	39	565	21.8	1.3	7	51.5
Turkey	36	420	18.8	3.3	15	20.3
Uganda	38	535	44.9	2.2	30	41.0
Ukraine	30	354	41.5	2.9	42	9.1
United Arab Emirates	50	607	26.2	5.1	30	10.1
United Kingdom	30	404	23.4	1.0	6	84.6
United States	32	300	9.4	1.5	7	75.9
Uruguay	40	720	16.2	2.1	7	44.8
Uzbekistan	42	195	22.2	4.0	10	18.7
Vanuatu	30	430	74.7	2.6	38	39.3
Venezuela	29	510	43.7	4.0	38	6.6
Vietnam	34	295	31.0	5.0	15	18.0
West Bank and Gaza	44	700	21.2	no practice	no practice	0.0
Yemen	37	520	16.5	3.0	8	28.6
Zambia	35	471	38.7	2.7	9	28.4
Zimbabwe	38	410	32.0	3.3	22	0.1

AFGHANISTAN

Ease of doing business (rank)	159
South Asia	
Low income	
GNI per capita (US$)	260
Population (m)	30.9

Starting a business (rank)	24
Procedures (number)	4
Time (days)	9
Cost (% of income per capita)	84.6
Minimum capital (% of income per capita)	0.0
Dealing with licenses (rank)	141
Procedures (number)	13
Time (days)	340
Cost (% of income per capita)	21,230.8
Employing workers (rank)	24
Difficulty of hiring index (0–100)	0
Rigidity of hours index (0–100)	40
Difficulty of firing index (0–100)	30
Rigidity of employment index (0–100)	23
Nonwage labor cost (% of salary)	0
Firing cost (weeks of salary)	0

Registering property (rank)	169
Procedures (number)	9
Time (days)	250
Cost (% of property value)	7.0
Getting credit (rank)	177
Strength of legal rights index (0–10)	0
Depth of credit information index (0–6)	0
Public registry coverage (% of adults)	0.0
Private bureau coverage (% of adults)	0.0
Protecting investors (rank)	178
Extent of disclosure index (0–10)	0
Extent of director liability index (0–10)	0
Ease of shareholder suits index (0–10)	2
Strength of investor protection index (0–10)	0.7
Paying taxes (rank)	38
Payments (number per year)	6
Time (hours per year)	275
Total tax rate (% of profit)	35.5

Trading across borders (rank)	174
Documents to export (number)	12
Time to export (days)	67
Cost to export (US$ per container)	2,500
Documents to import (number)	11
Time to import (days)	71
Cost to import (US$ per container)	2,100
Enforcing contracts (rank)	160
Procedures (number)	47
Time (days)	1,642
Cost (% of claim)	25.0
Closing a business (rank)	178
Time (years)	NO PRACTICE
Cost (% of estate)	NO PRACTICE
Recovery rate (cents on the dollar)	0.0

ALBANIA

Ease of doing business (rank)	136
Eastern Europe & Central Asia	
Lower middle income	
GNI per capita (US$)	2,960
Population (m)	3.1

Starting a business (rank)	123
Procedures (number)	10
Time (days)	36
Cost (% of income per capita)	20.9
Minimum capital (% of income per capita)	34.3
Dealing with licenses (rank)	168
Procedures (number)	24
Time (days)	331
Cost (% of income per capita)	461.0
Employing workers (rank)	109
Difficulty of hiring index (0–100)	44
Rigidity of hours index (0–100)	40
Difficulty of firing index (0–100)	20
Rigidity of employment index (0–100)	35
Nonwage labor cost (% of salary)	22
Firing cost (weeks of salary)	56

Registering property (rank)	82
Procedures (number)	7
Time (days)	47
Cost (% of property value)	3.5
Getting credit (rank)	48
Strength of legal rights index (0–10)	9
Depth of credit information index (0–6)	0
Public registry coverage (% of adults)	0.0
Private bureau coverage (% of adults)	0.0
Protecting investors (rank)	165
Extent of disclosure index (0–10)	0
Extent of director liability index (0–10)	5
Ease of shareholder suits index (0–10)	3
Strength of investor protection index (0–10)	2.7
Paying taxes (rank)	118
Payments (number per year)	44
Time (hours per year)	240
Total tax rate (% of profit)	46.8

Trading across borders (rank)	70
Documents to export (number)	7
Time to export (days)	21
Cost to export (US$ per container)	745
Documents to import (number)	9
Time to import (days)	22
Cost to import (US$ per container)	750
Enforcing contracts (rank)	74
Procedures (number)	39
Time (days)	390
Cost (% of claim)	31.8
Closing a business (rank)	178
Time (years)	NO PRACTICE
Cost (% of estate)	NO PRACTICE
Recovery rate (cents on the dollar)	0.0

ALGERIA

Ease of doing business (rank)	125
Middle East & North Africa	
Lower middle income	
GNI per capita (US$)	3,030
Population (m)	33.3

Starting a business (rank)	131
Procedures (number)	14
Time (days)	24
Cost (% of income per capita)	13.2
Minimum capital (% of income per capita)	45.2
Dealing with licenses (rank)	108
Procedures (number)	22
Time (days)	240
Cost (% of income per capita)	57.8
Employing workers (rank)	118
Difficulty of hiring index (0–100)	44
Rigidity of hours index (0–100)	60
Difficulty of firing index (0–100)	40
Rigidity of employment index (0–100)	48
Nonwage labor cost (% of salary)	27
Firing cost (weeks of salary)	17

Registering property (rank)	156
Procedures (number)	14
Time (days)	51
Cost (% of property value)	7.5
Getting credit (rank)	115
Strength of legal rights index (0–10)	3
Depth of credit information index (0–6)	2
Public registry coverage (% of adults)	0.2
Private bureau coverage (% of adults)	0.0
Protecting investors (rank)	64
Extent of disclosure index (0–10)	6
Extent of director liability index (0–10)	6
Ease of shareholder suits index (0–10)	4
Strength of investor protection index (0–10)	5.3
Paying taxes (rank)	157
Payments (number per year)	33
Time (hours per year)	451
Total tax rate (% of profit)	72.6

Trading across borders (rank)	114
Documents to export (number)	8
Time to export (days)	17
Cost to export (US$ per container)	1,198
Documents to import (number)	9
Time to import (days)	23
Cost to import (US$ per container)	1,378
Enforcing contracts (rank)	117
Procedures (number)	47
Time (days)	630
Cost (% of claim)	17.4
Closing a business (rank)	45
Time (years)	2.5
Cost (% of estate)	7
Recovery rate (cents on the dollar)	41.7

ANGOLA

Ease of doing business (rank)	167	Sub-Saharan Africa		GNI per capita (US$)	1,980
		Lower middle income		Population (m)	16.4
Starting a business (rank)	173	**Registering property** (rank)	166	**Trading across borders** (rank)	164
Procedures (number)	12	Procedures (number)	7	Documents to export (number)	12
Time (days)	119	Time (days)	334	Time to export (days)	64
Cost (% of income per capita)	343.7	Cost (% of property value)	11.1	Cost to export (US$ per container)	1,850
Minimum capital (% of income per capita)	50.5			Documents to import (number)	9
		Getting credit (rank)	84	Time to import (days)	58
Dealing with licenses (rank)	136	Strength of legal rights index (0–10)	3	Cost to import (US$ per container)	2,325
Procedures (number)	14	Depth of credit information index (0–6)	4		
Time (days)	337	Public registry coverage (% of adults)	2.3	**Enforcing contracts** (rank)	176
Cost (% of income per capita)	1,109.7	Private bureau coverage (% of adults)	0.0	Procedures (number)	46
				Time (days)	1,011
Employing workers (rank)	172	**Protecting investors** (rank)	51	Cost (% of claim)	44.4
Difficulty of hiring index (0–100)	78	Extent of disclosure index (0–10)	5		
Rigidity of hours index (0–100)	60	Extent of director liability index (0–10)	6	**Closing a business** (rank)	138
Difficulty of firing index (0–100)	70	Ease of shareholder suits index (0–10)	6	Time (years)	6.2
Rigidity of employment index (0–100)	69	Strength of investor protection index (0–10)	5.7	Cost (% of estate)	22
Nonwage labor cost (% of salary)	8			Recovery rate (cents on the dollar)	10.8
Firing cost (weeks of salary)	58	**Paying taxes** (rank)	120		
		Payments (number per year)	31		
		Time (hours per year)	272		
		Total tax rate (% of profit)	53.2		

ANTIGUA AND BARBUDA

Ease of doing business (rank)	41	Latin America & Caribbean		GNI per capita (US$)	11,210
		High income		Population (m)	0.1
Starting a business (rank)	27	**Registering property** (rank)	75	**Trading across borders** (rank)	55
Procedures (number)	7	Procedures (number)	5	Documents to export (number)	5
Time (days)	21	Time (days)	26	Time to export (days)	19
Cost (% of income per capita)	11.8	Cost (% of property value)	13.0	Cost to export (US$ per container)	1,107
Minimum capital (% of income per capita)	0.0			Documents to import (number)	6
		Getting credit (rank)	135	Time to import (days)	19
Dealing with licenses (rank)	26	Strength of legal rights index (0–10)	4	Cost to import (US$ per container)	1,174
Procedures (number)	14	Depth of credit information index (0–6)	0		
Time (days)	157	Public registry coverage (% of adults)	0.0	**Enforcing contracts** (rank)	74
Cost (% of income per capita)	26.3	Private bureau coverage (% of adults)	0.0	Procedures (number)	45
				Time (days)	351
Employing workers (rank)	41	**Protecting investors** (rank)	19	Cost (% of claim)	22.7
Difficulty of hiring index (0–100)	11	Extent of disclosure index (0–10)	4		
Rigidity of hours index (0–100)	0	Extent of director liability index (0–10)	8	**Closing a business** (rank)	58
Difficulty of firing index (0–100)	20	Ease of shareholder suits index (0–10)	7	Time (years)	3.0
Rigidity of employment index (0–100)	10	Strength of investor protection index (0–10)	6.3	Cost (% of estate)	7
Nonwage labor cost (% of salary)	9			Recovery rate (cents on the dollar)	35.7
Firing cost (weeks of salary)	52	**Paying taxes** (rank)	108		
		Payments (number per year)	45		
		Time (hours per year)	184		
		Total tax rate (% of profit)	46.8		

ARGENTINA

Ease of doing business (rank)	109	Latin America & Caribbean		GNI per capita (US$)	5,150
		Upper middle income		Population (m)	39.1
Starting a business (rank)	114	**Registering property** (rank)	96	**Trading across borders** (rank)	107
Procedures (number)	14	Procedures (number)	5	Documents to export (number)	9
Time (days)	31	Time (days)	65	Time to export (days)	16
Cost (% of income per capita)	9.7	Cost (% of property value)	7.6	Cost to export (US$ per container)	1,325
Minimum capital (% of income per capita)	4.8			Documents to import (number)	7
		Getting credit (rank)	48	Time to import (days)	20
Dealing with licenses (rank)	165	Strength of legal rights index (0–10)	3	Cost to import (US$ per container)	1,825
Procedures (number)	28	Depth of credit information index (0–6)	6		
Time (days)	338	Public registry coverage (% of adults)	25.5	**Enforcing contracts** (rank)	47
Cost (% of income per capita)	234.1	Private bureau coverage (% of adults)	100.0	Procedures (number)	36
				Time (days)	590
Employing workers (rank)	147	**Protecting investors** (rank)	98	Cost (% of claim)	16.5
Difficulty of hiring index (0–100)	44	Extent of disclosure index (0–10)	6		
Rigidity of hours index (0–100)	60	Extent of director liability index (0–10)	2	**Closing a business** (rank)	65
Difficulty of firing index (0–100)	20	Ease of shareholder suits index (0–10)	6	Time (years)	2.8
Rigidity of employment index (0–100)	41	Strength of investor protection index (0–10)	4.7	Cost (% of estate)	12
Nonwage labor cost (% of salary)	26			Recovery rate (cents on the dollar)	34.4
Firing cost (weeks of salary)	139	**Paying taxes** (rank)	147		
		Payments (number per year)	19		
		Time (hours per year)	615		
		Total tax rate (% of profit)	112.9		

ARMENIA

Ease of doing business (rank)	39	Eastern Europe & Central Asia		GNI per capita (US$)	1,930
		Lower middle income		Population (m)	3.0
Starting a business (rank)	47	**Registering property** (rank)	2	**Trading across borders** (rank)	118
Procedures (number)	9	Procedures (number)	3	Documents to export (number)	7
Time (days)	18	Time (days)	4	Time to export (days)	30
Cost (% of income per capita)	4.8	Cost (% of property value)	0.4	Cost to export (US$ per container)	1,165
Minimum capital (% of income per capita)	3.1			Documents to import (number)	8
		Getting credit (rank)	36	Time to import (days)	24
Dealing with licenses (rank)	73	Strength of legal rights index (0–10)	5	Cost to import (US$ per container)	1,335
Procedures (number)	19	Depth of credit information index (0–6)	5		
Time (days)	116	Public registry coverage (% of adults)	2.8	**Enforcing contracts** (rank)	64
Cost (% of income per capita)	411.3	Private bureau coverage (% of adults)	13.5	Procedures (number)	50
				Time (days)	285
Employing workers (rank)	48	**Protecting investors** (rank)	83	Cost (% of claim)	19.0
Difficulty of hiring index (0–100)	33	Extent of disclosure index (0–10)	5		
Rigidity of hours index (0–100)	40	Extent of director liability index (0–10)	2	**Closing a business** (rank)	42
Difficulty of firing index (0–100)	20	Ease of shareholder suits index (0–10)	8	Time (years)	1.9
Rigidity of employment index (0–100)	31	Strength of investor protection index (0–10)	5.0	Cost (% of estate)	4
Nonwage labor cost (% of salary)	19			Recovery rate (cents on the dollar)	42.0
Firing cost (weeks of salary)	13	**Paying taxes** (rank)	143		
		Payments (number per year)	50		
		Time (hours per year)	1,120		
		Total tax rate (% of profit)	36.6		

AUSTRALIA

Ease of doing business (rank)	9	OECD: High Income		GNI per capita (US$)	35,990
		High income		Population (m)	20.5
Starting a business (rank)	1	**Registering property** (rank)	27	**Trading across borders** (rank)	34
Procedures (number)	2	Procedures (number)	5	Documents to export (number)	6
Time (days)	2	Time (days)	5	Time to export (days)	9
Cost (% of income per capita)	0.8	Cost (% of property value)	4.9	Cost to export (US$ per container)	930
Minimum capital (% of income per capita)	0.0			Documents to import (number)	6
		Getting credit (rank)	3	Time to import (days)	12
Dealing with licenses (rank)	52	Strength of legal rights index (0–10)	9	Cost to import (US$ per container)	1,120
Procedures (number)	16	Depth of credit information index (0–6)	5		
Time (days)	221	Public registry coverage (% of adults)	0.0	**Enforcing contracts** (rank)	11
Cost (% of income per capita)	13.2	Private bureau coverage (% of adults)	100.0	Procedures (number)	28
				Time (days)	262
Employing workers (rank)	8	**Protecting investors** (rank)	51	Cost (% of claim)	20.7
Difficulty of hiring index (0–100)	0	Extent of disclosure index (0–10)	8		
Rigidity of hours index (0–100)	0	Extent of director liability index (0–10)	2	**Closing a business** (rank)	14
Difficulty of firing index (0–100)	10	Ease of shareholder suits index (0–10)	7	Time (years)	1.0
Rigidity of employment index (0–100)	3	Strength of investor protection index (0–10)	5.7	Cost (% of estate)	8
Nonwage labor cost (% of salary)	20			Recovery rate (cents on the dollar)	79.2
Firing cost (weeks of salary)	4	**Paying taxes** (rank)	41		
		Payments (number per year)	12		
		Time (hours per year)	107		
		Total tax rate (% of profit)	50.6		

AUSTRIA

Ease of doing business (rank)	25	OECD: High Income		GNI per capita (US$)	39,590
		High income		Population (m)	8.2
Starting a business (rank)	83	**Registering property** (rank)	30	**Trading across borders** (rank)	12
Procedures (number)	8	Procedures (number)	3	Documents to export (number)	4
Time (days)	28	Time (days)	32	Time to export (days)	8
Cost (% of income per capita)	5.4	Cost (% of property value)	4.5	Cost to export (US$ per container)	843
Minimum capital (% of income per capita)	55.5			Documents to import (number)	5
		Getting credit (rank)	26	Time to import (days)	8
Dealing with licenses (rank)	40	Strength of legal rights index (0–10)	5	Cost to import (US$ per container)	843
Procedures (number)	13	Depth of credit information index (0–6)	6		
Time (days)	194	Public registry coverage (% of adults)	1.3	**Enforcing contracts** (rank)	6
Cost (% of income per capita)	73.7	Private bureau coverage (% of adults)	40.6	Procedures (number)	26
				Time (days)	397
Employing workers (rank)	62	**Protecting investors** (rank)	122	Cost (% of claim)	12.7
Difficulty of hiring index (0–100)	11	Extent of disclosure index (0–10)	3		
Rigidity of hours index (0–100)	60	Extent of director liability index (0–10)	5	**Closing a business** (rank)	21
Difficulty of firing index (0–100)	40	Ease of shareholder suits index (0–10)	4	Time (years)	1.1
Rigidity of employment index (0–100)	37	Strength of investor protection index (0–10)	4.0	Cost (% of estate)	18
Nonwage labor cost (% of salary)	31			Recovery rate (cents on the dollar)	72.4
Firing cost (weeks of salary)	2	**Paying taxes** (rank)	80		
		Payments (number per year)	22		
		Time (hours per year)	170		
		Total tax rate (% of profit)	54.6		

AZERBAIJAN

Ease of doing business (rank)	96
Eastern Europe & Central Asia	
Lower middle income	
GNI per capita (US$)	1,850
Population (m)	8.5

Starting a business (rank)	64
Procedures (number)	13
Time (days)	30
Cost (% of income per capita)	6.9
Minimum capital (% of income per capita)	0.0
Dealing with licenses (rank)	159
Procedures (number)	31
Time (days)	207
Cost (% of income per capita)	768.3
Employing workers (rank)	80
Difficulty of hiring index (0–100)	33
Rigidity of hours index (0–100)	40
Difficulty of firing index (0–100)	40
Rigidity of employment index (0–100)	38
Nonwage labor cost (% of salary)	22
Firing cost (weeks of salary)	22
Registering property (rank)	56
Procedures (number)	7
Time (days)	61
Cost (% of property value)	0.2
Getting credit (rank)	26
Strength of legal rights index (0–10)	7
Depth of credit information index (0–6)	4
Public registry coverage (% of adults)	1.4
Private bureau coverage (% of adults)	0.0
Protecting investors (rank)	107
Extent of disclosure index (0–10)	4
Extent of director liability index (0–10)	1
Ease of shareholder suits index (0–10)	8
Strength of investor protection index (0–10)	4.3
Paying taxes (rank)	141
Payments (number per year)	38
Time (hours per year)	952
Total tax rate (% of profit)	40.9
Trading across borders (rank)	173
Documents to export (number)	9
Time to export (days)	56
Cost to export (US$ per container)	2,715
Documents to import (number)	14
Time to import (days)	56
Cost to import (US$ per container)	2,945
Enforcing contracts (rank)	30
Procedures (number)	39
Time (days)	267
Cost (% of claim)	18.5
Closing a business (rank)	75
Time (years)	2.7
Cost (% of estate)	8
Recovery rate (cents on the dollar)	31.5

BANGLADESH

Ease of doing business (rank)	107
South Asia	
Low income	
GNI per capita (US$)	480
Population (m)	144.3

Starting a business (rank)	92
Procedures (number)	8
Time (days)	74
Cost (% of income per capita)	46.2
Minimum capital (% of income per capita)	0.0
Dealing with licenses (rank)	116
Procedures (number)	14
Time (days)	252
Cost (% of income per capita)	751.0
Employing workers (rank)	129
Difficulty of hiring index (0–100)	44
Rigidity of hours index (0–100)	20
Difficulty of firing index (0–100)	40
Rigidity of employment index (0–100)	35
Nonwage labor cost (% of salary)	0
Firing cost (weeks of salary)	104
Registering property (rank)	171
Procedures (number)	8
Time (days)	425
Cost (% of property value)	10.3
Getting credit (rank)	48
Strength of legal rights index (0–10)	7
Depth of credit information index (0–6)	2
Public registry coverage (% of adults)	0.7
Private bureau coverage (% of adults)	0.0
Protecting investors (rank)	15
Extent of disclosure index (0–10)	6
Extent of director liability index (0–10)	7
Ease of shareholder suits index (0–10)	7
Strength of investor protection index (0–10)	6.7
Paying taxes (rank)	81
Payments (number per year)	17
Time (hours per year)	400
Total tax rate (% of profit)	39.5
Trading across borders (rank)	112
Documents to export (number)	7
Time to export (days)	28
Cost to export (US$ per container)	844
Documents to import (number)	9
Time to import (days)	32
Cost to import (US$ per container)	1,148
Enforcing contracts (rank)	175
Procedures (number)	41
Time (days)	1,442
Cost (% of claim)	63.3
Closing a business (rank)	102
Time (years)	4.0
Cost (% of estate)	8
Recovery rate (cents on the dollar)	23.2

BELARUS

Ease of doing business (rank)	110
Eastern Europe & Central Asia	
Lower middle income	
GNI per capita (US$)	3,380
Population (m)	9.7

Starting a business (rank)	119
Procedures (number)	10
Time (days)	48
Cost (% of income per capita)	8.8
Minimum capital (% of income per capita)	29.7
Dealing with licenses (rank)	94
Procedures (number)	17
Time (days)	350
Cost (% of income per capita)	60.9
Employing workers (rank)	43
Difficulty of hiring index (0–100)	0
Rigidity of hours index (0–100)	40
Difficulty of firing index (0–100)	40
Rigidity of employment index (0–100)	27
Nonwage labor cost (% of salary)	39
Firing cost (weeks of salary)	22
Registering property (rank)	94
Procedures (number)	7
Time (days)	231
Cost (% of property value)	0.1
Getting credit (rank)	115
Strength of legal rights index (0–10)	2
Depth of credit information index (0–6)	3
Public registry coverage (% of adults)	..
Private bureau coverage (% of adults)	0.0
Protecting investors (rank)	98
Extent of disclosure index (0–10)	5
Extent of director liability index (0–10)	1
Ease of shareholder suits index (0–10)	8
Strength of investor protection index (0–10)	4.7
Paying taxes (rank)	178
Payments (number per year)	124
Time (hours per year)	1,188
Total tax rate (% of profit)	144.4
Trading across borders (rank)	137
Documents to export (number)	8
Time to export (days)	24
Cost to export (US$ per container)	1,672
Documents to import (number)	8
Time to import (days)	29
Cost to import (US$ per container)	1,672
Enforcing contracts (rank)	16
Procedures (number)	28
Time (days)	225
Cost (% of claim)	23.4
Closing a business (rank)	69
Time (years)	5.8
Cost (% of estate)	22
Recovery rate (cents on the dollar)	33.2

BELGIUM

BELGIUM		OECD: High Income		GNI per capita (US$)	38,600
Ease of doing business (rank)	19	High income		Population (m)	10.5
Starting a business (rank)	19	**Registering property** (rank)	161	**Trading across borders** (rank)	48
Procedures (number)	3	Procedures (number)	7	Documents to export (number)	4
Time (days)	4	Time (days)	132	Time to export (days)	8
Cost (% of income per capita)	5.3	Cost (% of property value)	12.7	Cost to export (US$ per container)	1,600
Minimum capital (% of income per capita)	20.1			Documents to import (number)	5
		Getting credit (rank)	48	Time to import (days)	9
Dealing with licenses (rank)	37	Strength of legal rights index (0–10)	5	Cost to import (US$ per container)	1,600
Procedures (number)	14	Depth of credit information index (0–6)	4		
Time (days)	169	Public registry coverage (% of adults)	57.2	**Enforcing contracts** (rank)	22
Cost (% of income per capita)	63.7	Private bureau coverage (% of adults)	0.0	Procedures (number)	27
				Time (days)	505
Employing workers (rank)	36	**Protecting investors** (rank)	12	Cost (% of claim)	16.6
Difficulty of hiring index (0–100)	11	Extent of disclosure index (0–10)	8		
Rigidity of hours index (0–100)	40	Extent of director liability index (0–10)	6	**Closing a business** (rank)	9
Difficulty of firing index (0–100)	10	Ease of shareholder suits index (0–10)	7	Time (years)	0.9
Rigidity of employment index (0–100)	20	Strength of investor protection index (0–10)	7.0	Cost (% of estate)	4
Nonwage labor cost (% of salary)	55			Recovery rate (cents on the dollar)	85.5
Firing cost (weeks of salary)	16	**Paying taxes** (rank)	65		
		Payments (number per year)	11		
		Time (hours per year)	156		
		Total tax rate (% of profit)	64.3		

BELIZE

BELIZE		Latin America & Caribbean		GNI per capita (US$)	3,650
Ease of doing business (rank)	59	Upper middle income		Population (m)	0.3
Starting a business (rank)	116	**Registering property** (rank)	113	**Trading across borders** (rank)	116
Procedures (number)	9	Procedures (number)	8	Documents to export (number)	7
Time (days)	44	Time (days)	60	Time to export (days)	23
Cost (% of income per capita)	53.1	Cost (% of property value)	4.7	Cost to export (US$ per container)	1,800
Minimum capital (% of income per capita)	0.0			Documents to import (number)	6
		Getting credit (rank)	84	Time to import (days)	26
Dealing with licenses (rank)	3	Strength of legal rights index (0–10)	7	Cost to import (US$ per container)	2,130
Procedures (number)	11	Depth of credit information index (0–6)	0		
Time (days)	66	Public registry coverage (% of adults)	0.0	**Enforcing contracts** (rank)	170
Cost (% of income per capita)	18.5	Private bureau coverage (% of adults)	0.0	Procedures (number)	51
				Time (days)	892
Employing workers (rank)	28	**Protecting investors** (rank)	107	Cost (% of claim)	27.5
Difficulty of hiring index (0–100)	22	Extent of disclosure index (0–10)	3		
Rigidity of hours index (0–100)	20	Extent of director liability index (0–10)	4	**Closing a business** (rank)	24
Difficulty of firing index (0–100)	0	Ease of shareholder suits index (0–10)	6	Time (years)	1.0
Rigidity of employment index (0–100)	14	Strength of investor protection index (0–10)	4.3	Cost (% of estate)	23
Nonwage labor cost (% of salary)	4			Recovery rate (cents on the dollar)	63.5
Firing cost (weeks of salary)	24	**Paying taxes** (rank)	47		
		Payments (number per year)	41		
		Time (hours per year)	147		
		Total tax rate (% of profit)	30.8		

BENIN

BENIN		Sub-Saharan Africa		GNI per capita (US$)	540
Ease of doing business (rank)	151	Low income		Population (m)	8.7
Starting a business (rank)	137	**Registering property** (rank)	105	**Trading across borders** (rank)	124
Procedures (number)	7	Procedures (number)	3	Documents to export (number)	7
Time (days)	31	Time (days)	118	Time to export (days)	34
Cost (% of income per capita)	195.0	Cost (% of property value)	11.4	Cost to export (US$ per container)	1,167
Minimum capital (% of income per capita)	354.2			Documents to import (number)	7
		Getting credit (rank)	115	Time to import (days)	41
Dealing with licenses (rank)	123	Strength of legal rights index (0–10)	4	Cost to import (US$ per container)	1,202
Procedures (number)	15	Depth of credit information index (0–6)	1		
Time (days)	332	Public registry coverage (% of adults)	7.8	**Enforcing contracts** (rank)	166
Cost (% of income per capita)	316.6	Private bureau coverage (% of adults)	0.0	Procedures (number)	42
				Time (days)	720
Employing workers (rank)	115	**Protecting investors** (rank)	147	Cost (% of claim)	58.7
Difficulty of hiring index (0–100)	39	Extent of disclosure index (0–10)	6		
Rigidity of hours index (0–100)	40	Extent of director liability index (0–10)	1	**Closing a business** (rank)	106
Difficulty of firing index (0–100)	40	Ease of shareholder suits index (0–10)	3	Time (years)	4.0
Rigidity of employment index (0–100)	40	Strength of investor protection index (0–10)	3.3	Cost (% of estate)	15
Nonwage labor cost (% of salary)	29			Recovery rate (cents on the dollar)	22.6
Firing cost (weeks of salary)	36	**Paying taxes** (rank)	161		
		Payments (number per year)	55		
		Time (hours per year)	270		
		Total tax rate (% of profit)	73.3		

BHUTAN

Ease of doing business (rank)	119
South Asia	
Low income	
GNI per capita (US$)	1,410
Population (m)	0.6
Starting a business (rank)	52
Procedures (number)	8
Time (days)	48
Cost (% of income per capita)	10.4
Minimum capital (% of income per capita)	0.0
Dealing with licenses (rank)	119
Procedures (number)	25
Time (days)	183
Cost (% of income per capita)	195.9
Employing workers (rank)	14
Difficulty of hiring index (0–100)	0
Rigidity of hours index (0–100)	0
Difficulty of firing index (0–100)	20
Rigidity of employment index (0–100)	7
Nonwage labor cost (% of salary)	1
Firing cost (weeks of salary)	10
Registering property (rank)	33
Procedures (number)	5
Time (days)	64
Cost (% of property value)	0.0
Getting credit (rank)	158
Strength of legal rights index (0–10)	3
Depth of credit information index (0–6)	0
Public registry coverage (% of adults)	0.0
Private bureau coverage (% of adults)	0.0
Protecting investors (rank)	122
Extent of disclosure index (0–10)	5
Extent of director liability index (0–10)	3
Ease of shareholder suits index (0–10)	4
Strength of investor protection index (0–10)	4.0
Paying taxes (rank)	68
Payments (number per year)	19
Time (hours per year)	274
Total tax rate (% of profit)	39.8
Trading across borders (rank)	149
Documents to export (number)	8
Time to export (days)	38
Cost to export (US$ per container)	1,150
Documents to import (number)	11
Time to import (days)	38
Cost to import (US$ per container)	2,080
Enforcing contracts (rank)	38
Procedures (number)	47
Time (days)	275
Cost (% of claim)	0.1
Closing a business (rank)	178
Time (years)	NO PRACTICE
Cost (% of estate)	NO PRACTICE
Recovery rate (cents on the dollar)	0.0

BOLIVIA

Ease of doing business (rank)	140
Latin America & Caribbean	
Lower middle income	
GNI per capita (US$)	1,100
Population (m)	9.3
Starting a business (rank)	157
Procedures (number)	15
Time (days)	50
Cost (% of income per capita)	134.1
Minimum capital (% of income per capita)	3.4
Dealing with licenses (rank)	106
Procedures (number)	17
Time (days)	249
Cost (% of income per capita)	198.6
Employing workers (rank)	177
Difficulty of hiring index (0–100)	78
Rigidity of hours index (0–100)	60
Difficulty of firing index (0–100)	100
Rigidity of employment index (0–100)	79
Nonwage labor cost (% of salary)	14
Firing cost (weeks of salary)	NOT POSSIBLE
Registering property (rank)	120
Procedures (number)	7
Time (days)	92
Cost (% of property value)	4.9
Getting credit (rank)	97
Strength of legal rights index (0–10)	1
Depth of credit information index (0–6)	5
Public registry coverage (% of adults)	12.1
Private bureau coverage (% of adults)	22.6
Protecting investors (rank)	122
Extent of disclosure index (0–10)	1
Extent of director liability index (0–10)	5
Ease of shareholder suits index (0–10)	6
Strength of investor protection index (0–10)	4.0
Paying taxes (rank)	172
Payments (number per year)	41
Time (hours per year)	1,080
Total tax rate (% of profit)	78.1
Trading across borders (rank)	115
Documents to export (number)	8
Time to export (days)	24
Cost to export (US$ per container)	1,110
Documents to import (number)	7
Time to import (days)	36
Cost to import (US$ per container)	1,230
Enforcing contracts (rank)	112
Procedures (number)	37
Time (days)	591
Cost (% of claim)	33.2
Closing a business (rank)	52
Time (years)	1.8
Cost (% of estate)	15
Recovery rate (cents on the dollar)	38.7

BOSNIA AND HERZEGOVINA

Ease of doing business (rank)	105
Eastern Europe & Central Asia	
Lower middle income	
GNI per capita (US$)	2,980
Population (m)	3.9
Starting a business (rank)	150
Procedures (number)	12
Time (days)	54
Cost (% of income per capita)	30.1
Minimum capital (% of income per capita)	43.0
Dealing with licenses (rank)	150
Procedures (number)	16
Time (days)	467
Cost (% of income per capita)	790.3
Employing workers (rank)	114
Difficulty of hiring index (0–100)	67
Rigidity of hours index (0–100)	40
Difficulty of firing index (0–100)	30
Rigidity of employment index (0–100)	46
Nonwage labor cost (% of salary)	15
Firing cost (weeks of salary)	31
Registering property (rank)	144
Procedures (number)	7
Time (days)	331
Cost (% of property value)	5.0
Getting credit (rank)	13
Strength of legal rights index (0–10)	7
Depth of credit information index (0–6)	5
Public registry coverage (% of adults)	0.0
Private bureau coverage (% of adults)	63.7
Protecting investors (rank)	83
Extent of disclosure index (0–10)	3
Extent of director liability index (0–10)	6
Ease of shareholder suits index (0–10)	6
Strength of investor protection index (0–10)	5.0
Paying taxes (rank)	142
Payments (number per year)	51
Time (hours per year)	368
Total tax rate (% of profit)	44.1
Trading across borders (rank)	53
Documents to export (number)	6
Time to export (days)	19
Cost to export (US$ per container)	1,030
Documents to import (number)	7
Time to import (days)	18
Cost to import (US$ per container)	985
Enforcing contracts (rank)	126
Procedures (number)	38
Time (days)	595
Cost (% of claim)	38.4
Closing a business (rank)	61
Time (years)	3.3
Cost (% of estate)	9
Recovery rate (cents on the dollar)	35.0

BOTSWANA

Ease of doing business (rank)	51
Sub-Saharan Africa	
Upper middle income	
GNI per capita (US$)	5,900
Population (m)	1.8

Starting a business (rank)	99
Procedures (number)	11
Time (days)	108
Cost (% of income per capita)	9.9
Minimum capital (% of income per capita)	0.0
Dealing with licenses (rank)	122
Procedures (number)	24
Time (days)	167
Cost (% of income per capita)	322.3
Employing workers (rank)	70
Difficulty of hiring index (0–100)	0
Rigidity of hours index (0–100)	20
Difficulty of firing index (0–100)	40
Rigidity of employment index (0–100)	20
Nonwage labor cost (% of salary)	0
Firing cost (weeks of salary)	90
Registering property (rank)	36
Procedures (number)	4
Time (days)	30
Cost (% of property value)	5.0
Getting credit (rank)	26
Strength of legal rights index (0–10)	7
Depth of credit information index (0–6)	4
Public registry coverage (% of adults)	0.0
Private bureau coverage (% of adults)	58.3
Protecting investors (rank)	107
Extent of disclosure index (0–10)	8
Extent of director liability index (0–10)	2
Ease of shareholder suits index (0–10)	3
Strength of investor protection index (0–10)	4.3
Paying taxes (rank)	14
Payments (number per year)	19
Time (hours per year)	140
Total tax rate (% of profit)	17.2
Trading across borders (rank)	145
Documents to export (number)	6
Time to export (days)	33
Cost to export (US$ per container)	2,328
Documents to import (number)	9
Time to import (days)	43
Cost to import (US$ per container)	2,595
Enforcing contracts (rank)	95
Procedures (number)	29
Time (days)	987
Cost (% of claim)	28.1
Closing a business (rank)	26
Time (years)	1.7
Cost (% of estate)	15
Recovery rate (cents on the dollar)	59.8

BRAZIL

Ease of doing business (rank)	122
Latin America & Caribbean	
Lower middle income	
GNI per capita (US$)	4,730
Population (m)	188.7

Starting a business (rank)	122
Procedures (number)	18
Time (days)	152
Cost (% of income per capita)	10.4
Minimum capital (% of income per capita)	0.0
Dealing with licenses (rank)	107
Procedures (number)	18
Time (days)	411
Cost (% of income per capita)	59.4
Employing workers (rank)	119
Difficulty of hiring index (0–100)	78
Rigidity of hours index (0–100)	60
Difficulty of firing index (0–100)	0
Rigidity of employment index (0–100)	46
Nonwage labor cost (% of salary)	37
Firing cost (weeks of salary)	37
Registering property (rank)	110
Procedures (number)	14
Time (days)	45
Cost (% of property value)	2.8
Getting credit (rank)	84
Strength of legal rights index (0–10)	2
Depth of credit information index (0–6)	5
Public registry coverage (% of adults)	17.1
Private bureau coverage (% of adults)	46.4
Protecting investors (rank)	64
Extent of disclosure index (0–10)	6
Extent of director liability index (0–10)	7
Ease of shareholder suits index (0–10)	3
Strength of investor protection index (0–10)	5.3
Paying taxes (rank)	137
Payments (number per year)	11
Time (hours per year)	2,600
Total tax rate (% of profit)	69.2
Trading across borders (rank)	93
Documents to export (number)	8
Time to export (days)	18
Cost to export (US$ per container)	1,090
Documents to import (number)	7
Time to import (days)	22
Cost to import (US$ per container)	1,240
Enforcing contracts (rank)	106
Procedures (number)	45
Time (days)	616
Cost (% of claim)	16.5
Closing a business (rank)	131
Time (years)	4.0
Cost (% of estate)	12
Recovery rate (cents on the dollar)	14.6

BRUNEI

Ease of doing business (rank)	78
East Asia & Pacific	
High income	
GNI per capita (US$)	36,216
Population (m)	0.4

Starting a business (rank)	117
Procedures (number)	18
Time (days)	116
Cost (% of income per capita)	9.0
Minimum capital (% of income per capita)	0.0
Dealing with licenses (rank)	66
Procedures (number)	32
Time (days)	167
Cost (% of income per capita)	5.2
Employing workers (rank)	4
Difficulty of hiring index (0–100)	0
Rigidity of hours index (0–100)	20
Difficulty of firing index (0–100)	0
Rigidity of employment index (0–100)	7
Nonwage labor cost (% of salary)	5
Firing cost (weeks of salary)	4
Registering property (rank)	178
Procedures (number)	NO PRACTICE
Time (days)	NO PRACTICE
Cost (% of property value)	NO PRACTICE
Getting credit (rank)	97
Strength of legal rights index (0–10)	6
Depth of credit information index (0–6)	0
Public registry coverage (% of adults)	0.0
Private bureau coverage (% of adults)	0.0
Protecting investors (rank)	121
Extent of disclosure index (0–10)	3
Extent of director liability index (0–10)	2
Ease of shareholder suits index (0–10)	8
Strength of investor protection index (0–10)	4.3
Paying taxes (rank)	28
Payments (number per year)	15
Time (hours per year)	144
Total tax rate (% of profit)	37.4
Trading across borders (rank)	36
Documents to export (number)	6
Time to export (days)	28
Cost to export (US$ per container)	515
Documents to import (number)	6
Time to import (days)	19
Cost to import (US$ per container)	590
Enforcing contracts (rank)	158
Procedures (number)	58
Time (days)	540
Cost (% of claim)	36.6
Closing a business (rank)	35
Time (years)	2.5
Cost (% of estate)	4
Recovery rate (cents on the dollar)	45.3

BULGARIA

Ease of doing business (rank)	46
Eastern Europe & Central Asia	
Lower middle income	
GNI per capita (US$)	3,990
Population (m)	7.7

Starting a business (rank)	100
Procedures (number)	9
Time (days)	32
Cost (% of income per capita)	8.4
Minimum capital (% of income per capita)	56.3
Dealing with licenses (rank)	103
Procedures (number)	22
Time (days)	131
Cost (% of income per capita)	499.9
Employing workers (rank)	57
Difficulty of hiring index (0–100)	17
Rigidity of hours index (0–100)	60
Difficulty of firing index (0–100)	10
Rigidity of employment index (0–100)	29
Nonwage labor cost (% of salary)	23
Firing cost (weeks of salary)	9
Registering property (rank)	62
Procedures (number)	9
Time (days)	19
Cost (% of property value)	2.3
Getting credit (rank)	13
Strength of legal rights index (0–10)	6
Depth of credit information index (0–6)	6
Public registry coverage (% of adults)	25.4
Private bureau coverage (% of adults)	3.0
Protecting investors (rank)	33
Extent of disclosure index (0–10)	10
Extent of director liability index (0–10)	1
Ease of shareholder suits index (0–10)	7
Strength of investor protection index (0–10)	6.0
Paying taxes (rank)	88
Payments (number per year)	17
Time (hours per year)	616
Total tax rate (% of profit)	36.7
Trading across borders (rank)	89
Documents to export (number)	5
Time to export (days)	23
Cost to export (US$ per container)	1,329
Documents to import (number)	7
Time to import (days)	21
Cost to import (US$ per container)	1,377
Enforcing contracts (rank)	90
Procedures (number)	40
Time (days)	564
Cost (% of claim)	22.2
Closing a business (rank)	72
Time (years)	3.3
Cost (% of estate)	9
Recovery rate (cents on the dollar)	32.4

BURKINA FASO

Ease of doing business (rank)	161
Sub-Saharan Africa	
Low income	
GNI per capita (US$)	460
Population (m)	13.6

Starting a business (rank)	105
Procedures (number)	6
Time (days)	18
Cost (% of income per capita)	82.1
Minimum capital (% of income per capita)	415.7
Dealing with licenses (rank)	169
Procedures (number)	32
Time (days)	226
Cost (% of income per capita)	701.2
Employing workers (rank)	152
Difficulty of hiring index (0–100)	83
Rigidity of hours index (0–100)	60
Difficulty of firing index (0–100)	40
Rigidity of employment index (0–100)	61
Nonwage labor cost (% of salary)	20
Firing cost (weeks of salary)	34
Registering property (rank)	170
Procedures (number)	8
Time (days)	182
Cost (% of property value)	12.2
Getting credit (rank)	115
Strength of legal rights index (0–10)	4
Depth of credit information index (0–6)	1
Public registry coverage (% of adults)	2.1
Private bureau coverage (% of adults)	0.0
Protecting investors (rank)	138
Extent of disclosure index (0–10)	6
Extent of director liability index (0–10)	1
Ease of shareholder suits index (0–10)	4
Strength of investor protection index (0–10)	3.7
Paying taxes (rank)	133
Payments (number per year)	45
Time (hours per year)	270
Total tax rate (% of profit)	48.9
Trading across borders (rank)	170
Documents to export (number)	11
Time to export (days)	45
Cost to export (US$ per container)	2,096
Documents to import (number)	11
Time to import (days)	54
Cost to import (US$ per container)	3,522
Enforcing contracts (rank)	109
Procedures (number)	37
Time (days)	446
Cost (% of claim)	107.4
Closing a business (rank)	91
Time (years)	4.0
Cost (% of estate)	9
Recovery rate (cents on the dollar)	25.6

BURUNDI

Ease of doing business (rank)	174
Sub-Saharan Africa	
Low income	
GNI per capita (US$)	100
Population (m)	7.8

Starting a business (rank)	124
Procedures (number)	11
Time (days)	43
Cost (% of income per capita)	251.0
Minimum capital (% of income per capita)	0.0
Dealing with licenses (rank)	171
Procedures (number)	20
Time (days)	384
Cost (% of income per capita)	9,939.0
Employing workers (rank)	99
Difficulty of hiring index (0–100)	33
Rigidity of hours index (0–100)	60
Difficulty of firing index (0–100)	30
Rigidity of employment index (0–100)	41
Nonwage labor cost (% of salary)	7
Firing cost (weeks of salary)	26
Registering property (rank)	122
Procedures (number)	5
Time (days)	94
Cost (% of property value)	11.5
Getting credit (rank)	170
Strength of legal rights index (0–10)	1
Depth of credit information index (0–6)	1
Public registry coverage (% of adults)	0.2
Private bureau coverage (% of adults)	0.0
Protecting investors (rank)	147
Extent of disclosure index (0–10)	4
Extent of director liability index (0–10)	1
Ease of shareholder suits index (0–10)	5
Strength of investor protection index (0–10)	3.3
Paying taxes (rank)	109
Payments (number per year)	32
Time (hours per year)	140
Total tax rate (% of profit)	278.7
Trading across borders (rank)	167
Documents to export (number)	9
Time to export (days)	47
Cost to export (US$ per container)	2,147
Documents to import (number)	10
Time to import (days)	71
Cost to import (US$ per container)	3,705
Enforcing contracts (rank)	148
Procedures (number)	44
Time (days)	558
Cost (% of claim)	38.6
Closing a business (rank)	178
Time (years)	NO PRACTICE
Cost (% of estate)	NO PRACTICE
Recovery rate (cents on the dollar)	0.0

CAMBODIA

Ease of doing business (rank)	145	East Asia & Pacific		GNI per capita (US$)	480
		Low income		Population (m)	14.4

Starting a business (rank)	162	**Registering property** (rank)	98	**Trading across borders** (rank)	139
Procedures (number)	10	Procedures (number)	7	Documents to export (number)	11
Time (days)	86	Time (days)	56	Time to export (days)	37
Cost (% of income per capita)	190.3	Cost (% of property value)	4.4	Cost to export (US$ per container)	722
Minimum capital (% of income per capita)	50.8			Documents to import (number)	11
		Getting credit (rank)	177	Time to import (days)	46
Dealing with licenses (rank)	144	Strength of legal rights index (0–10)	0	Cost to import (US$ per container)	852
Procedures (number)	23	Depth of credit information index (0–6)	0		
Time (days)	709	Public registry coverage (% of adults)	0.0	**Enforcing contracts** (rank)	134
Cost (% of income per capita)	74.3	Private bureau coverage (% of adults)	0.0	Procedures (number)	44
				Time (days)	401
Employing workers (rank)	133	**Protecting investors** (rank)	64	Cost (% of claim)	102.7
Difficulty of hiring index (0–100)	44	Extent of disclosure index (0–10)	5		
Rigidity of hours index (0–100)	60	Extent of director liability index (0–10)	9	**Closing a business** (rank)	178
Difficulty of firing index (0–100)	30	Ease of shareholder suits index (0–10)	2	Time (years)	NO PRACTICE
Rigidity of employment index (0–100)	45	Strength of investor protection index (0–10)	5.3	Cost (% of estate)	NO PRACTICE
Nonwage labor cost (% of salary)	0			Recovery rate (cents on the dollar)	0.0
Firing cost (weeks of salary)	39	**Paying taxes** (rank)	21		
		Payments (number per year)	27		
		Time (hours per year)	137		
		Total tax rate (% of profit)	22.6		

CAMEROON

Ease of doing business (rank)	154	Sub-Saharan Africa		GNI per capita (US$)	1,080
		Lower middle income		Population (m)	16.7

Starting a business (rank)	160	**Registering property** (rank)	134	**Trading across borders** (rank)	132
Procedures (number)	13	Procedures (number)	5	Documents to export (number)	9
Time (days)	37	Time (days)	93	Time to export (days)	27
Cost (% of income per capita)	129.2	Cost (% of property value)	17.8	Cost to export (US$ per container)	907
Minimum capital (% of income per capita)	177.1			Documents to import (number)	8
		Getting credit (rank)	115	Time to import (days)	33
Dealing with licenses (rank)	154	Strength of legal rights index (0–10)	3	Cost to import (US$ per container)	1,529
Procedures (number)	15	Depth of credit information index (0–6)	2		
Time (days)	426	Public registry coverage (% of adults)	1.0	**Enforcing contracts** (rank)	172
Cost (% of income per capita)	1,202.9	Private bureau coverage (% of adults)	0.0	Procedures (number)	43
				Time (days)	800
Employing workers (rank)	120	**Protecting investors** (rank)	107	Cost (% of claim)	46.6
Difficulty of hiring index (0–100)	28	Extent of disclosure index (0–10)	6		
Rigidity of hours index (0–100)	40	Extent of director liability index (0–10)	1	**Closing a business** (rank)	92
Difficulty of firing index (0–100)	70	Ease of shareholder suits index (0–10)	6	Time (years)	3.2
Rigidity of employment index (0–100)	46	Strength of investor protection index (0–10)	4.3	Cost (% of estate)	15
Nonwage labor cost (% of salary)	16			Recovery rate (cents on the dollar)	25.5
Firing cost (weeks of salary)	33	**Paying taxes** (rank)	166		
		Payments (number per year)	41		
		Time (hours per year)	1,400		
		Total tax rate (% of profit)	51.9		

CANADA

Ease of doing business (rank)	7	OECD: High Income		GNI per capita (US$)	36,170
		High income		Population (m)	32.6

Starting a business (rank)	2	**Registering property** (rank)	28	**Trading across borders** (rank)	39
Procedures (number)	2	Procedures (number)	6	Documents to export (number)	3
Time (days)	3	Time (days)	17	Time to export (days)	7
Cost (% of income per capita)	0.9	Cost (% of property value)	1.8	Cost to export (US$ per container)	1,385
Minimum capital (% of income per capita)	0.0			Documents to import (number)	4
		Getting credit (rank)	7	Time to import (days)	11
Dealing with licenses (rank)	26	Strength of legal rights index (0–10)	7	Cost to import (US$ per container)	1,425
Procedures (number)	14	Depth of credit information index (0–6)	6		
Time (days)	75	Public registry coverage (% of adults)	0.0	**Enforcing contracts** (rank)	43
Cost (% of income per capita)	125.4	Private bureau coverage (% of adults)	100.0	Procedures (number)	36
				Time (days)	570
Employing workers (rank)	19	**Protecting investors** (rank)	5	Cost (% of claim)	16.2
Difficulty of hiring index (0–100)	11	Extent of disclosure index (0–10)	8		
Rigidity of hours index (0–100)	0	Extent of director liability index (0–10)	9	**Closing a business** (rank)	4
Difficulty of firing index (0–100)	0	Ease of shareholder suits index (0–10)	8	Time (years)	0.8
Rigidity of employment index (0–100)	4	Strength of investor protection index (0–10)	8.3	Cost (% of estate)	4
Nonwage labor cost (% of salary)	13			Recovery rate (cents on the dollar)	88.8
Firing cost (weeks of salary)	28	**Paying taxes** (rank)	25		
		Payments (number per year)	9		
		Time (hours per year)	119		
		Total tax rate (% of profit)	45.9		

CAPE VERDE

Ease of doing business (rank)	132	Sub-Saharan Africa		GNI per capita (US$)	2,130
		Lower middle income		Population (m)	0.5
Starting a business (rank)	156	**Registering property** (rank)	127	**Trading across borders** (rank)	51
Procedures (number)	12	Procedures (number)	6	Documents to export (number)	5
Time (days)	52	Time (days)	83	Time to export (days)	21
Cost (% of income per capita)	40.1	Cost (% of property value)	7.8	Cost to export (US$ per container)	1,024
Minimum capital (% of income per capita)	53.4			Documents to import (number)	5
		Getting credit (rank)	68	Time to import (days)	21
Dealing with licenses (rank)	79	Strength of legal rights index (0–10)	5	Cost to import (US$ per container)	1,024
Procedures (number)	18	Depth of credit information index (0–6)	3		
Time (days)	120	Public registry coverage (% of adults)	20.3	**Enforcing contracts** (rank)	56
Cost (% of income per capita)	718.3	Private bureau coverage (% of adults)	0.0	Procedures (number)	37
				Time (days)	465
Employing workers (rank)	143	**Protecting investors** (rank)	122	Cost (% of claim)	24.1
Difficulty of hiring index (0–100)	33	Extent of disclosure index (0–10)	1		
Rigidity of hours index (0–100)	40	Extent of director liability index (0–10)	5	**Closing a business** (rank)	178
Difficulty of firing index (0–100)	60	Ease of shareholder suits index (0–10)	6	Time (years)	NO PRACTICE
Rigidity of employment index (0–100)	44	Strength of investor protection index (0–10)	4.0	Cost (% of estate)	NO PRACTICE
Nonwage labor cost (% of salary)	17			Recovery rate (cents on the dollar)	0.0
Firing cost (weeks of salary)	91	**Paying taxes** (rank)	117		
		Payments (number per year)	57		
		Time (hours per year)	100		
		Total tax rate (% of profit)	54.0		

CENTRAL AFRICAN REPUBLIC

Ease of doing business (rank)	177	Sub-Saharan Africa		GNI per capita (US$)	360
		Low income		Population (m)	4.1
Starting a business (rank)	139	**Registering property** (rank)	95	**Trading across borders** (rank)	172
Procedures (number)	10	Procedures (number)	3	Documents to export (number)	8
Time (days)	14	Time (days)	69	Time to export (days)	57
Cost (% of income per capita)	205.4	Cost (% of property value)	11.7	Cost to export (US$ per container)	4,581
Minimum capital (% of income per capita)	531.2			Documents to import (number)	18
		Getting credit (rank)	115	Time to import (days)	66
Dealing with licenses (rank)	133	Strength of legal rights index (0–10)	3	Cost to import (US$ per container)	4,534
Procedures (number)	21	Depth of credit information index (0–6)	2		
Time (days)	239	Public registry coverage (% of adults)	1.4	**Enforcing contracts** (rank)	169
Cost (% of income per capita)	288.3	Private bureau coverage (% of adults)	0.0	Procedures (number)	43
				Time (days)	660
Employing workers (rank)	149	**Protecting investors** (rank)	122	Cost (% of claim)	82.0
Difficulty of hiring index (0–100)	72	Extent of disclosure index (0–10)	6		
Rigidity of hours index (0–100)	60	Extent of director liability index (0–10)	1	**Closing a business** (rank)	178
Difficulty of firing index (0–100)	50	Ease of shareholder suits index (0–10)	5	Time (years)	4.8
Rigidity of employment index (0–100)	61	Strength of investor protection index (0–10)	4.0	Cost (% of estate)	76
Nonwage labor cost (% of salary)	18			Recovery rate (cents on the dollar)	0.0
Firing cost (weeks of salary)	22	**Paying taxes** (rank)	175		
		Payments (number per year)	54		
		Time (hours per year)	504		
		Total tax rate (% of profit)	203.8		

CHAD

Ease of doing business (rank)	173	Sub-Saharan Africa		GNI per capita (US$)	480
		Low income		Population (m)	10.0
Starting a business (rank)	177	**Registering property** (rank)	123	**Trading across borders** (rank)	157
Procedures (number)	19	Procedures (number)	6	Documents to export (number)	6
Time (days)	75	Time (days)	44	Time to export (days)	78
Cost (% of income per capita)	188.8	Cost (% of property value)	21.2	Cost to export (US$ per container)	4,867
Minimum capital (% of income per capita)	398.4			Documents to import (number)	9
		Getting credit (rank)	135	Time to import (days)	102
Dealing with licenses (rank)	68	Strength of legal rights index (0–10)	3	Cost to import (US$ per container)	5,520
Procedures (number)	9	Depth of credit information index (0–6)	1		
Time (days)	181	Public registry coverage (% of adults)	0.2	**Enforcing contracts** (rank)	167
Cost (% of income per capita)	1,063.8	Private bureau coverage (% of adults)	0.0	Procedures (number)	41
				Time (days)	743
Employing workers (rank)	135	**Protecting investors** (rank)	122	Cost (% of claim)	77.4
Difficulty of hiring index (0–100)	39	Extent of disclosure index (0–10)	6		
Rigidity of hours index (0–100)	60	Extent of director liability index (0–10)	1	**Closing a business** (rank)	178
Difficulty of firing index (0–100)	40	Ease of shareholder suits index (0–10)	5	Time (years)	NO PRACTICE
Rigidity of employment index (0–100)	46	Strength of investor protection index (0–10)	4.0	Cost (% of estate)	NO PRACTICE
Nonwage labor cost (% of salary)	21			Recovery rate (cents on the dollar)	0.0
Firing cost (weeks of salary)	36	**Paying taxes** (rank)	124		
		Payments (number per year)	54		
		Time (hours per year)	122		
		Total tax rate (% of profit)	63.7		

CHILE

CHILE		Latin America & Caribbean		GNI per capita (US$)	6,980
Ease of doing business (rank)	33	Upper middle income		Population (m)	16.5
Starting a business (rank)	39	**Registering property** (rank)	34	**Trading across borders** (rank)	43
Procedures (number)	9	Procedures (number)	6	Documents to export (number)	6
Time (days)	27	Time (days)	31	Time to export (days)	21
Cost (% of income per capita)	8.6	Cost (% of property value)	1.3	Cost to export (US$ per container)	645
Minimum capital (% of income per capita)	0.0			Documents to import (number)	7
		Getting credit (rank)	48	Time to import (days)	21
Dealing with licenses (rank)	58	Strength of legal rights index (0–10)	4	Cost to import (US$ per container)	685
Procedures (number)	18	Depth of credit information index (0–6)	5		
Time (days)	155	Public registry coverage (% of adults)	26.2	**Enforcing contracts** (rank)	64
Cost (% of income per capita)	128.1	Private bureau coverage (% of adults)	33.5	Procedures (number)	36
				Time (days)	480
Employing workers (rank)	68	**Protecting investors** (rank)	33	Cost (% of claim)	28.6
Difficulty of hiring index (0–100)	33	Extent of disclosure index (0–10)	7		
Rigidity of hours index (0–100)	20	Extent of director liability index (0–10)	6	**Closing a business** (rank)	98
Difficulty of firing index (0–100)	20	Ease of shareholder suits index (0–10)	5	Time (years)	4.5
Rigidity of employment index (0–100)	24	Strength of investor protection index (0–10)	6.0	Cost (% of estate)	15
Nonwage labor cost (% of salary)	3			Recovery rate (cents on the dollar)	23.8
Firing cost (weeks of salary)	52	**Paying taxes** (rank)	34		
		Payments (number per year)	10		
		Time (hours per year)	316		
		Total tax rate (% of profit)	25.9		

CHINA

CHINA		East Asia & Pacific		GNI per capita (US$)	2,010
Ease of doing business (rank)	83	Lower middle income		Population (m)	1,311.8
Starting a business (rank)	135	**Registering property** (rank)	29	**Trading across borders** (rank)	42
Procedures (number)	13	Procedures (number)	4	Documents to export (number)	7
Time (days)	35	Time (days)	29	Time to export (days)	21
Cost (% of income per capita)	8.4	Cost (% of property value)	3.6	Cost to export (US$ per container)	390
Minimum capital (% of income per capita)	190.2			Documents to import (number)	6
		Getting credit (rank)	84	Time to import (days)	24
Dealing with licenses (rank)	175	Strength of legal rights index (0–10)	3	Cost to import (US$ per container)	430
Procedures (number)	37	Depth of credit information index (0–6)	4		
Time (days)	336	Public registry coverage (% of adults)	49.2	**Enforcing contracts** (rank)	20
Cost (% of income per capita)	840.2	Private bureau coverage (% of adults)	0.0	Procedures (number)	35
				Time (days)	406
Employing workers (rank)	86	**Protecting investors** (rank)	83	Cost (% of claim)	8.8
Difficulty of hiring index (0–100)	11	Extent of disclosure index (0–10)	10		
Rigidity of hours index (0–100)	20	Extent of director liability index (0–10)	1	**Closing a business** (rank)	57
Difficulty of firing index (0–100)	40	Ease of shareholder suits index (0–10)	4	Time (years)	1.7
Rigidity of employment index (0–100)	24	Strength of investor protection index (0–10)	5.0	Cost (% of estate)	22
Nonwage labor cost (% of salary)	44			Recovery rate (cents on the dollar)	35.9
Firing cost (weeks of salary)	91	**Paying taxes** (rank)	168		
		Payments (number per year)	35		
		Time (hours per year)	872		
		Total tax rate (% of profit)	73.9		

COLOMBIA

COLOMBIA		Latin America & Caribbean		GNI per capita (US$)	2,740
Ease of doing business (rank)	66	Lower middle income		Population (m)	45.6
Starting a business (rank)	88	**Registering property** (rank)	69	**Trading across borders** (rank)	105
Procedures (number)	11	Procedures (number)	9	Documents to export (number)	6
Time (days)	42	Time (days)	23	Time to export (days)	24
Cost (% of income per capita)	19.3	Cost (% of property value)	2.5	Cost to export (US$ per container)	1,440
Minimum capital (% of income per capita)	0.0			Documents to import (number)	8
		Getting credit (rank)	84	Time to import (days)	20
Dealing with licenses (rank)	61	Strength of legal rights index (0–10)	2	Cost to import (US$ per container)	1,440
Procedures (number)	14	Depth of credit information index (0–6)	5		
Time (days)	146	Public registry coverage (% of adults)	0.0	**Enforcing contracts** (rank)	147
Cost (% of income per capita)	602.8	Private bureau coverage (% of adults)	39.9	Procedures (number)	34
				Time (days)	1,346
Employing workers (rank)	83	**Protecting investors** (rank)	19	Cost (% of claim)	52.6
Difficulty of hiring index (0–100)	22	Extent of disclosure index (0–10)	8		
Rigidity of hours index (0–100)	40	Extent of director liability index (0–10)	2	**Closing a business** (rank)	27
Difficulty of firing index (0–100)	20	Ease of shareholder suits index (0–10)	9	Time (years)	3.0
Rigidity of employment index (0–100)	27	Strength of investor protection index (0–10)	6.3	Cost (% of estate)	1
Nonwage labor cost (% of salary)	29			Recovery rate (cents on the dollar)	58.3
Firing cost (weeks of salary)	59	**Paying taxes** (rank)	167		
		Payments (number per year)	69		
		Time (hours per year)	268		
		Total tax rate (% of profit)	82.4		

COMOROS

Ease of doing business (rank)	147	Sub-Saharan Africa		GNI per capita (US$)	660
		Low income		Population (m)	0.6
Starting a business (rank)	145	**Registering property** (rank)	84	**Trading across borders** (rank)	119
Procedures (number)	11	Procedures (number)	5	Documents to export (number)	10
Time (days)	23	Time (days)	24	Time to export (days)	30
Cost (% of income per capita)	188.4	Cost (% of property value)	20.8	Cost to export (US$ per container)	971
Minimum capital (% of income per capita)	280.3			Documents to import (number)	10
		Getting credit (rank)	158	Time to import (days)	21
Dealing with licenses (rank)	56	Strength of legal rights index (0–10)	3	Cost to import (US$ per container)	974
Procedures (number)	18	Depth of credit information index (0–6)	0		
Time (days)	164	Public registry coverage (% of adults)	0.0	**Enforcing contracts** (rank)	152
Cost (% of income per capita)	77.8	Private bureau coverage (% of adults)	0.0	Procedures (number)	43
				Time (days)	506
Employing workers (rank)	158	**Protecting investors** (rank)	122	Cost (% of claim)	89.4
Difficulty of hiring index (0–100)	39	Extent of disclosure index (0–10)	6		
Rigidity of hours index (0–100)	60	Extent of director liability index (0–10)	1	**Closing a business** (rank)	178
Difficulty of firing index (0–100)	40	Ease of shareholder suits index (0–10)	5	Time (years)	NO PRACTICE
Rigidity of employment index (0–100)	46	Strength of investor protection index (0–10)	4.0	Cost (% of estate)	NO PRACTICE
Nonwage labor cost (% of salary)	0			Recovery rate (cents on the dollar)	0.0
Firing cost (weeks of salary)	100	**Paying taxes** (rank)	46		
		Payments (number per year)	20		
		Time (hours per year)	100		
		Total tax rate (% of profit)	48.8		

CONGO, DEM. REP.

Ease of doing business (rank)	178	Sub-Saharan Africa		GNI per capita (US$)	130
		Low income		Population (m)	59.3
Starting a business (rank)	146	**Registering property** (rank)	141	**Trading across borders** (rank)	154
Procedures (number)	13	Procedures (number)	8	Documents to export (number)	8
Time (days)	155	Time (days)	57	Time to export (days)	46
Cost (% of income per capita)	487.2	Cost (% of property value)	9.4	Cost to export (US$ per container)	2,307
Minimum capital (% of income per capita)	0.0			Documents to import (number)	9
		Getting credit (rank)	158	Time to import (days)	66
Dealing with licenses (rank)	138	Strength of legal rights index (0–10)	3	Cost to import (US$ per container)	2,183
Procedures (number)	14	Depth of credit information index (0–6)	0		
Time (days)	322	Public registry coverage (% of adults)	0.0	**Enforcing contracts** (rank)	173
Cost (% of income per capita)	2,112.6	Private bureau coverage (% of adults)	0.0	Procedures (number)	43
				Time (days)	685
Employing workers (rank)	171	**Protecting investors** (rank)	147	Cost (% of claim)	151.8
Difficulty of hiring index (0–100)	72	Extent of disclosure index (0–10)	3		
Rigidity of hours index (0–100)	80	Extent of director liability index (0–10)	3	**Closing a business** (rank)	150
Difficulty of firing index (0–100)	70	Ease of shareholder suits index (0–10)	4	Time (years)	5.2
Rigidity of employment index (0–100)	74	Strength of investor protection index (0–10)	3.3	Cost (% of estate)	29
Nonwage labor cost (% of salary)	7			Recovery rate (cents on the dollar)	2.9
Firing cost (weeks of salary)	31	**Paying taxes** (rank)	149		
		Payments (number per year)	32		
		Time (hours per year)	308		
		Total tax rate (% of profit)	229.8		

CONGO, REP.

Ease of doing business (rank)	175	Sub-Saharan Africa		GNI per capita (US$)	927
		Lower middle income		Population (m)	4.1
Starting a business (rank)	154	**Registering property** (rank)	168	**Trading across borders** (rank)	171
Procedures (number)	10	Procedures (number)	7	Documents to export (number)	11
Time (days)	37	Time (days)	137	Time to export (days)	50
Cost (% of income per capita)	150.1	Cost (% of property value)	27.3	Cost to export (US$ per container)	2,201
Minimum capital (% of income per capita)	206.3			Documents to import (number)	12
		Getting credit (rank)	115	Time to import (days)	62
Dealing with licenses (rank)	67	Strength of legal rights index (0–10)	3	Cost to import (US$ per container)	2,201
Procedures (number)	14	Depth of credit information index (0–6)	2		
Time (days)	169	Public registry coverage (% of adults)	2.4	**Enforcing contracts** (rank)	156
Cost (% of income per capita)	565.9	Private bureau coverage (% of adults)	0.0	Procedures (number)	44
				Time (days)	560
Employing workers (rank)	167	**Protecting investors** (rank)	147	Cost (% of claim)	53.2
Difficulty of hiring index (0–100)	78	Extent of disclosure index (0–10)	6		
Rigidity of hours index (0–100)	60	Extent of director liability index (0–10)	1	**Closing a business** (rank)	110
Difficulty of firing index (0–100)	70	Ease of shareholder suits index (0–10)	3	Time (years)	3.0
Rigidity of employment index (0–100)	69	Strength of investor protection index (0–10)	3.3	Cost (% of estate)	24
Nonwage labor cost (% of salary)	29			Recovery rate (cents on the dollar)	20.4
Firing cost (weeks of salary)	33	**Paying taxes** (rank)	176		
		Payments (number per year)	89		
		Time (hours per year)	606		
		Total tax rate (% of profit)	65.4		

COSTA RICA

Ease of doing business (rank)	115	Latin America & Caribbean Upper middle income		GNI per capita (US$) Population (m)	4,980 4.4
Starting a business (rank)	113	**Registering property** (rank)	41	**Trading across borders** (rank)	54
Procedures (number)	12	Procedures (number)	6	Documents to export (number)	7
Time (days)	77	Time (days)	21	Time to export (days)	18
Cost (% of income per capita)	21.3	Cost (% of property value)	3.3	Cost to export (US$ per container)	660
Minimum capital (% of income per capita)	0.0			Documents to import (number)	8
		Getting credit (rank)	48	Time to import (days)	25
Dealing with licenses (rank)	120	Strength of legal rights index (0–10)	4	Cost to import (US$ per container)	660
Procedures (number)	23	Depth of credit information index (0–6)	5		
Time (days)	178	Public registry coverage (% of adults)	6.1	**Enforcing contracts** (rank)	130
Cost (% of income per capita)	244.2	Private bureau coverage (% of adults)	52.7	Procedures (number)	40
				Time (days)	877
Employing workers (rank)	79	**Protecting investors** (rank)	158	Cost (% of claim)	24.3
Difficulty of hiring index (0–100)	56	Extent of disclosure index (0–10)	2		
Rigidity of hours index (0–100)	40	Extent of director liability index (0–10)	5	**Closing a business** (rank)	104
Difficulty of firing index (0–100)	0	Ease of shareholder suits index (0–10)	2	Time (years)	3.5
Rigidity of employment index (0–100)	32	Strength of investor protection index (0–10)	3.0	Cost (% of estate)	15
Nonwage labor cost (% of salary)	26			Recovery rate (cents on the dollar)	23.1
Firing cost (weeks of salary)	35	**Paying taxes** (rank)	162		
		Payments (number per year)	43		
		Time (hours per year)	402		
		Total tax rate (% of profit)	55.7		

COTE D'IVOIRE

Ease of doing business (rank)	155	Sub-Saharan Africa Low income		GNI per capita (US$) Population (m)	870 18.5
Starting a business (rank)	155	**Registering property** (rank)	153	**Trading across borders** (rank)	147
Procedures (number)	10	Procedures (number)	7	Documents to export (number)	10
Time (days)	40	Time (days)	62	Time to export (days)	23
Cost (% of income per capita)	135.8	Cost (% of property value)	16.9	Cost to export (US$ per container)	1,653
Minimum capital (% of income per capita)	219.8			Documents to import (number)	8
		Getting credit (rank)	135	Time to import (days)	43
Dealing with licenses (rank)	157	Strength of legal rights index (0–10)	3	Cost to import (US$ per container)	2,457
Procedures (number)	21	Depth of credit information index (0–6)	1		
Time (days)	628	Public registry coverage (% of adults)	2.8	**Enforcing contracts** (rank)	122
Cost (% of income per capita)	247.7	Private bureau coverage (% of adults)	0.0	Procedures (number)	33
				Time (days)	770
Employing workers (rank)	112	**Protecting investors** (rank)	147	Cost (% of claim)	41.7
Difficulty of hiring index (0–100)	33	Extent of disclosure index (0–10)	6		
Rigidity of hours index (0–100)	60	Extent of director liability index (0–10)	1	**Closing a business** (rank)	71
Difficulty of firing index (0–100)	20	Ease of shareholder suits index (0–10)	3	Time (years)	2.2
Rigidity of employment index (0–100)	38	Strength of investor protection index (0–10)	3.3	Cost (% of estate)	18
Nonwage labor cost (% of salary)	18			Recovery rate (cents on the dollar)	33.0
Firing cost (weeks of salary)	49	**Paying taxes** (rank)	140		
		Payments (number per year)	66		
		Time (hours per year)	270		
		Total tax rate (% of profit)	45.4		

CROATIA

Ease of doing business (rank)	97	Eastern Europe & Central Asia Upper middle income		GNI per capita (US$) Population (m)	9,330 4.4
Starting a business (rank)	93	**Registering property** (rank)	99	**Trading across borders** (rank)	96
Procedures (number)	8	Procedures (number)	5	Documents to export (number)	7
Time (days)	40	Time (days)	174	Time to export (days)	22
Cost (% of income per capita)	11.7	Cost (% of property value)	5.0	Cost to export (US$ per container)	1,200
Minimum capital (% of income per capita)	18.4			Documents to import (number)	8
		Getting credit (rank)	48	Time to import (days)	16
Dealing with licenses (rank)	162	Strength of legal rights index (0–10)	6	Cost to import (US$ per container)	1,200
Procedures (number)	22	Depth of credit information index (0–6)	3		
Time (days)	255	Public registry coverage (% of adults)	0.0	**Enforcing contracts** (rank)	45
Cost (% of income per capita)	722.4	Private bureau coverage (% of adults)	72.4	Procedures (number)	38
				Time (days)	561
Employing workers (rank)	139	**Protecting investors** (rank)	122	Cost (% of claim)	13.8
Difficulty of hiring index (0–100)	61	Extent of disclosure index (0–10)	1		
Rigidity of hours index (0–100)	40	Extent of director liability index (0–10)	5	**Closing a business** (rank)	78
Difficulty of firing index (0–100)	50	Ease of shareholder suits index (0–10)	6	Time (years)	3.1
Rigidity of employment index (0–100)	50	Strength of investor protection index (0–10)	4.0	Cost (% of estate)	15
Nonwage labor cost (% of salary)	17			Recovery rate (cents on the dollar)	30.2
Firing cost (weeks of salary)	39	**Paying taxes** (rank)	43		
		Payments (number per year)	28		
		Time (hours per year)	196		
		Total tax rate (% of profit)	32.5		

CZECH REPUBLIC

Ease of doing business (rank)	56	Eastern Europe & Central Asia		GNI per capita (US$)	12,680
		Upper middle income		Population (m)	10.2
Starting a business (rank)	91	**Registering property** (rank)	54	**Trading across borders** (rank)	30
Procedures (number)	10	Procedures (number)	4	Documents to export (number)	5
Time (days)	17	Time (days)	123	Time to export (days)	16
Cost (% of income per capita)	10.6	Cost (% of property value)	3.0	Cost to export (US$ per container)	775
Minimum capital (% of income per capita)	34.9			Documents to import (number)	7
		Getting credit (rank)	26	Time to import (days)	18
Dealing with licenses (rank)	83	Strength of legal rights index (0–10)	6	Cost to import (US$ per container)	860
Procedures (number)	36	Depth of credit information index (0–6)	5		
Time (days)	180	Public registry coverage (% of adults)	4.2	**Enforcing contracts** (rank)	97
Cost (% of income per capita)	18.5	Private bureau coverage (% of adults)	53.0	Procedures (number)	27
				Time (days)	820
Employing workers (rank)	55	**Protecting investors** (rank)	83	Cost (% of claim)	33.0
Difficulty of hiring index (0–100)	33	Extent of disclosure index (0–10)	2		
Rigidity of hours index (0–100)	40	Extent of director liability index (0–10)	5	**Closing a business** (rank)	108
Difficulty of firing index (0–100)	20	Ease of shareholder suits index (0–10)	8	Time (years)	6.5
Rigidity of employment index (0–100)	31	Strength of investor protection index (0–10)	5.0	Cost (% of estate)	15
Nonwage labor cost (% of salary)	35			Recovery rate (cents on the dollar)	21.3
Firing cost (weeks of salary)	22	**Paying taxes** (rank)	113		
		Payments (number per year)	12		
		Time (hours per year)	930		
		Total tax rate (% of profit)	48.6		

DENMARK

Ease of doing business (rank)	5	OECD: High Income		GNI per capita (US$)	51,700
		High income		Population (m)	5.4
Starting a business (rank)	18	**Registering property** (rank)	39	**Trading across borders** (rank)	2
Procedures (number)	4	Procedures (number)	6	Documents to export (number)	4
Time (days)	6	Time (days)	42	Time to export (days)	5
Cost (% of income per capita)	0.0	Cost (% of property value)	0.6	Cost to export (US$ per container)	540
Minimum capital (% of income per capita)	40.7			Documents to import (number)	3
		Getting credit (rank)	13	Time to import (days)	5
Dealing with licenses (rank)	6	Strength of legal rights index (0–10)	8	Cost to import (US$ per container)	540
Procedures (number)	6	Depth of credit information index (0–6)	4		
Time (days)	69	Public registry coverage (% of adults)	0.0	**Enforcing contracts** (rank)	30
Cost (% of income per capita)	61.8	Private bureau coverage (% of adults)	11.5	Procedures (number)	34
				Time (days)	380
Employing workers (rank)	10	**Protecting investors** (rank)	19	Cost (% of claim)	23.3
Difficulty of hiring index (0–100)	0	Extent of disclosure index (0–10)	7		
Rigidity of hours index (0–100)	20	Extent of director liability index (0–10)	5	**Closing a business** (rank)	7
Difficulty of firing index (0–100)	10	Ease of shareholder suits index (0–10)	7	Time (years)	1.1
Rigidity of employment index (0–100)	10	Strength of investor protection index (0–10)	6.3	Cost (% of estate)	4
Nonwage labor cost (% of salary)	1			Recovery rate (cents on the dollar)	87.0
Firing cost (weeks of salary)	0	**Paying taxes** (rank)	13		
		Payments (number per year)	9		
		Time (hours per year)	135		
		Total tax rate (% of profit)	33.3		

DJIBOUTI

Ease of doing business (rank)	146	Middle East & North Africa		GNI per capita (US$)	1,060
		Lower middle income		Population (m)	0.8
Starting a business (rank)	165	**Registering property** (rank)	131	**Trading across borders** (rank)	66
Procedures (number)	11	Procedures (number)	7	Documents to export (number)	8
Time (days)	37	Time (days)	40	Time to export (days)	22
Cost (% of income per capita)	206.6	Cost (% of property value)	13.2	Cost to export (US$ per container)	960
Minimum capital (% of income per capita)	530.8			Documents to import (number)	6
		Getting credit (rank)	135	Time to import (days)	18
Dealing with licenses (rank)	92	Strength of legal rights index (0–10)	3	Cost to import (US$ per container)	960
Procedures (number)	14	Depth of credit information index (0–6)	1		
Time (days)	195	Public registry coverage (% of adults)	0.2	**Enforcing contracts** (rank)	159
Cost (% of income per capita)	1,010.6	Private bureau coverage (% of adults)	0.0	Procedures (number)	40
				Time (days)	1,225
Employing workers (rank)	130	**Protecting investors** (rank)	173	Cost (% of claim)	34.0
Difficulty of hiring index (0–100)	67	Extent of disclosure index (0–10)	5		
Rigidity of hours index (0–100)	40	Extent of director liability index (0–10)	2	**Closing a business** (rank)	126
Difficulty of firing index (0–100)	30	Ease of shareholder suits index (0–10)	0	Time (years)	5.0
Rigidity of employment index (0–100)	46	Strength of investor protection index (0–10)	2.3	Cost (% of estate)	18
Nonwage labor cost (% of salary)	16			Recovery rate (cents on the dollar)	15.9
Firing cost (weeks of salary)	56	**Paying taxes** (rank)	51		
		Payments (number per year)	35		
		Time (hours per year)	114		
		Total tax rate (% of profit)	38.7		

DOMINICA

Ease of doing business (rank)	77
Latin America & Caribbean	
Upper middle income	
GNI per capita (US$)	3,960
Population (m)	0.1
Starting a business (rank)	23
Procedures (number)	5
Time (days)	19
Cost (% of income per capita)	27.1
Minimum capital (% of income per capita)	0.0
Dealing with licenses (rank)	47
Procedures (number)	12
Time (days)	219
Cost (% of income per capita)	74.4
Employing workers (rank)	54
Difficulty of hiring index (0–100)	11
Rigidity of hours index (0–100)	20
Difficulty of firing index (0–100)	20
Rigidity of employment index (0–100)	17
Nonwage labor cost (% of salary)	7
Firing cost (weeks of salary)	58
Registering property (rank)	83
Procedures (number)	4
Time (days)	40
Cost (% of property value)	13.5
Getting credit (rank)	97
Strength of legal rights index (0–10)	6
Depth of credit information index (0–6)	0
Public registry coverage (% of adults)	0.0
Private bureau coverage (% of adults)	0.0
Protecting investors (rank)	19
Extent of disclosure index (0–10)	4
Extent of director liability index (0–10)	8
Ease of shareholder suits index (0–10)	7
Strength of investor protection index (0–10)	6.3
Paying taxes (rank)	64
Payments (number per year)	38
Time (hours per year)	147
Total tax rate (% of profit)	37.1
Trading across borders (rank)	80
Documents to export (number)	7
Time to export (days)	16
Cost to export (US$ per container)	1,197
Documents to import (number)	8
Time to import (days)	18
Cost to import (US$ per container)	1,107
Enforcing contracts (rank)	164
Procedures (number)	47
Time (days)	681
Cost (% of claim)	36.0
Closing a business (rank)	178
Time (years)	NO PRACTICE
Cost (% of estate)	NO PRACTICE
Recovery rate (cents on the dollar)	0.0

DOMINICAN REPUBLIC

Ease of doing business (rank)	99
Latin America & Caribbean	
Lower middle income	
GNI per capita (US$)	2,850
Population (m)	9.6
Starting a business (rank)	84
Procedures (number)	9
Time (days)	22
Cost (% of income per capita)	31.1
Minimum capital (% of income per capita)	0.0
Dealing with licenses (rank)	74
Procedures (number)	17
Time (days)	214
Cost (% of income per capita)	116.1
Employing workers (rank)	106
Difficulty of hiring index (0–100)	56
Rigidity of hours index (0–100)	40
Difficulty of firing index (0–100)	0
Rigidity of employment index (0–100)	32
Nonwage labor cost (% of salary)	14
Firing cost (weeks of salary)	88
Registering property (rank)	106
Procedures (number)	7
Time (days)	60
Cost (% of property value)	5.1
Getting credit (rank)	36
Strength of legal rights index (0–10)	4
Depth of credit information index (0–6)	6
Public registry coverage (% of adults)	13.3
Private bureau coverage (% of adults)	35.4
Protecting investors (rank)	122
Extent of disclosure index (0–10)	5
Extent of director liability index (0–10)	0
Ease of shareholder suits index (0–10)	7
Strength of investor protection index (0–10)	4.0
Paying taxes (rank)	139
Payments (number per year)	74
Time (hours per year)	286
Total tax rate (% of profit)	40.2
Trading across borders (rank)	35
Documents to export (number)	6
Time to export (days)	12
Cost to export (US$ per container)	815
Documents to import (number)	7
Time to import (days)	13
Cost to import (US$ per container)	1,015
Enforcing contracts (rank)	82
Procedures (number)	34
Time (days)	460
Cost (% of claim)	40.9
Closing a business (rank)	142
Time (years)	3.5
Cost (% of estate)	38
Recovery rate (cents on the dollar)	8.4

ECUADOR

Ease of doing business (rank)	128
Latin America & Caribbean	
Lower middle income	
GNI per capita (US$)	2,840
Population (m)	13.4
Starting a business (rank)	148
Procedures (number)	14
Time (days)	65
Cost (% of income per capita)	29.2
Minimum capital (% of income per capita)	7.0
Dealing with licenses (rank)	53
Procedures (number)	19
Time (days)	148
Cost (% of income per capita)	55.3
Employing workers (rank)	168
Difficulty of hiring index (0–100)	44
Rigidity of hours index (0–100)	60
Difficulty of firing index (0–100)	50
Rigidity of employment index (0–100)	51
Nonwage labor cost (% of salary)	12
Firing cost (weeks of salary)	135
Registering property (rank)	70
Procedures (number)	10
Time (days)	17
Cost (% of property value)	3.0
Getting credit (rank)	97
Strength of legal rights index (0–10)	1
Depth of credit information index (0–6)	5
Public registry coverage (% of adults)	37.9
Private bureau coverage (% of adults)	44.1
Protecting investors (rank)	122
Extent of disclosure index (0–10)	1
Extent of director liability index (0–10)	5
Ease of shareholder suits index (0–10)	6
Strength of investor protection index (0–10)	4.0
Paying taxes (rank)	57
Payments (number per year)	8
Time (hours per year)	600
Total tax rate (% of profit)	35.3
Trading across borders (rank)	131
Documents to export (number)	10
Time to export (days)	22
Cost to export (US$ per container)	1,090
Documents to import (number)	8
Time to import (days)	44
Cost to import (US$ per container)	1,090
Enforcing contracts (rank)	59
Procedures (number)	39
Time (days)	498
Cost (% of claim)	20.8
Closing a business (rank)	124
Time (years)	5.3
Cost (% of estate)	18
Recovery rate (cents on the dollar)	16.9

EGYPT

Ease of doing business (rank)	126	Middle East & North Africa Lower middle income		GNI per capita (US$) Population (m)	1,350 75.4
Starting a business (rank)	55	**Registering property** (rank)	101	**Trading across borders** (rank)	26
Procedures (number)	7	Procedures (number)	7	Documents to export (number)	6
Time (days)	9	Time (days)	193	Time to export (days)	15
Cost (% of income per capita)	28.6	Cost (% of property value)	1.0	Cost to export (US$ per container)	714
Minimum capital (% of income per capita)	12.9			Documents to import (number)	7
		Getting credit (rank)	115	Time to import (days)	18
Dealing with licenses (rank)	163	Strength of legal rights index (0–10)	1	Cost to import (US$ per container)	729
Procedures (number)	28	Depth of credit information index (0–6)	4		
Time (days)	249	Public registry coverage (% of adults)	1.6	**Enforcing contracts** (rank)	145
Cost (% of income per capita)	474.9	Private bureau coverage (% of adults)	..	Procedures (number)	42
				Time (days)	1,010
Employing workers (rank)	108	**Protecting investors** (rank)	83	Cost (% of claim)	25.3
Difficulty of hiring index (0–100)	0	Extent of disclosure index (0–10)	7		
Rigidity of hours index (0–100)	20	Extent of director liability index (0–10)	3	**Closing a business** (rank)	125
Difficulty of firing index (0–100)	60	Ease of shareholder suits index (0–10)	5	Time (years)	4.2
Rigidity of employment index (0–100)	27	Strength of investor protection index (0–10)	5.0	Cost (% of estate)	22
Nonwage labor cost (% of salary)	25			Recovery rate (cents on the dollar)	16.6
Firing cost (weeks of salary)	132	**Paying taxes** (rank)	150		
		Payments (number per year)	36		
		Time (hours per year)	711		
		Total tax rate (% of profit)	47.9		

EL SALVADOR

Ease of doing business (rank)	69	Latin America & Caribbean Lower middle income		GNI per capita (US$) Population (m)	2,540 7.0
Starting a business (rank)	130	**Registering property** (rank)	37	**Trading across borders** (rank)	68
Procedures (number)	9	Procedures (number)	5	Documents to export (number)	8
Time (days)	26	Time (days)	31	Time to export (days)	21
Cost (% of income per capita)	73.1	Cost (% of property value)	3.6	Cost to export (US$ per container)	540
Minimum capital (% of income per capita)	112.5			Documents to import (number)	11
		Getting credit (rank)	48	Time to import (days)	18
Dealing with licenses (rank)	121	Strength of legal rights index (0–10)	3	Cost to import (US$ per container)	540
Procedures (number)	34	Depth of credit information index (0–6)	6		
Time (days)	155	Public registry coverage (% of adults)	17.2	**Enforcing contracts** (rank)	54
Cost (% of income per capita)	197.9	Private bureau coverage (% of adults)	74.6	Procedures (number)	30
				Time (days)	786
Employing workers (rank)	76	**Protecting investors** (rank)	107	Cost (% of claim)	19.2
Difficulty of hiring index (0–100)	33	Extent of disclosure index (0–10)	5		
Rigidity of hours index (0–100)	40	Extent of director liability index (0–10)	2	**Closing a business** (rank)	85
Difficulty of firing index (0–100)	0	Ease of shareholder suits index (0–10)	6	Time (years)	4.0
Rigidity of employment index (0–100)	24	Strength of investor protection index (0–10)	4.3	Cost (% of estate)	9
Nonwage labor cost (% of salary)	15			Recovery rate (cents on the dollar)	28.4
Firing cost (weeks of salary)	86	**Paying taxes** (rank)	101		
		Payments (number per year)	66		
		Time (hours per year)	224		
		Total tax rate (% of profit)	33.8		

EQUATORIAL GUINEA

Ease of doing business (rank)	165	Sub-Saharan Africa Upper middle income		GNI per capita (US$) Population (m)	8,250 0.5
Starting a business (rank)	172	**Registering property** (rank)	56	**Trading across borders** (rank)	133
Procedures (number)	20	Procedures (number)	6	Documents to export (number)	7
Time (days)	136	Time (days)	23	Time to export (days)	29
Cost (% of income per capita)	105.1	Cost (% of property value)	6.3	Cost to export (US$ per container)	1,403
Minimum capital (% of income per capita)	23.2			Documents to import (number)	7
		Getting credit (rank)	135	Time to import (days)	46
Dealing with licenses (rank)	90	Strength of legal rights index (0–10)	2	Cost to import (US$ per container)	1,403
Procedures (number)	18	Depth of credit information index (0–6)	2		
Time (days)	201	Public registry coverage (% of adults)	1.9	**Enforcing contracts** (rank)	72
Cost (% of income per capita)	239.9	Private bureau coverage (% of adults)	0.0	Procedures (number)	40
				Time (days)	553
Employing workers (rank)	175	**Protecting investors** (rank)	141	Cost (% of claim)	18.5
Difficulty of hiring index (0–100)	67	Extent of disclosure index (0–10)	6		
Rigidity of hours index (0–100)	60	Extent of director liability index (0–10)	1	**Closing a business** (rank)	178
Difficulty of firing index (0–100)	70	Ease of shareholder suits index (0–10)	4	Time (years)	NO PRACTICE
Rigidity of employment index (0–100)	66	Strength of investor protection index (0–10)	3.7	Cost (% of estate)	NO PRACTICE
Nonwage labor cost (% of salary)	23			Recovery rate (cents on the dollar)	0.0
Firing cost (weeks of salary)	133	**Paying taxes** (rank)	136		
		Payments (number per year)	45		
		Time (hours per year)	212		
		Total tax rate (% of profit)	62.2		

ERITREA

ERITREA		Sub-Saharan Africa		GNI per capita (US$)	200
Ease of doing business (rank)	171	Low income		Population (m)	4.5
Starting a business (rank)	174	**Registering property** (rank)	158	**Trading across borders** (rank)	159
Procedures (number)	13	Procedures (number)	12	Documents to export (number)	9
Time (days)	84	Time (days)	101	Time to export (days)	59
Cost (% of income per capita)	125.8	Cost (% of property value)	5.3	Cost to export (US$ per container)	1,331
Minimum capital (% of income per capita)	488.0			Documents to import (number)	13
		Getting credit (rank)	158	Time to import (days)	69
Dealing with licenses (rank)	178	Strength of legal rights index (0–10)	3	Cost to import (US$ per container)	1,581
Procedures (number)	NO PRACTICE	Depth of credit information index (0–6)	0		
Time (days)	NO PRACTICE	Public registry coverage (% of adults)	0.0	**Enforcing contracts** (rank)	52
Cost (% of income per capita)	NO PRACTICE	Private bureau coverage (% of adults)	0.0	Procedures (number)	39
				Time (days)	405
Employing workers (rank)	58	**Protecting investors** (rank)	98	Cost (% of claim)	22.6
Difficulty of hiring index (0–100)	0	Extent of disclosure index (0–10)	4		
Rigidity of hours index (0–100)	40	Extent of director liability index (0–10)	5	**Closing a business** (rank)	178
Difficulty of firing index (0–100)	20	Ease of shareholder suits index (0–10)	5	Time (years)	NO PRACTICE
Rigidity of employment index (0–100)	20	Strength of investor protection index (0–10)	4.7	Cost (% of estate)	NO PRACTICE
Nonwage labor cost (% of salary)	0			Recovery rate (cents on the dollar)	0.0
Firing cost (weeks of salary)	69	**Paying taxes** (rank)	103		
		Payments (number per year)	18		
		Time (hours per year)	216		
		Total tax rate (% of profit)	84.5		

ESTONIA

ESTONIA		Eastern Europe & Central Asia		GNI per capita (US$)	11,410
Ease of doing business (rank)	17	Upper middle income		Population (m)	1.3
Starting a business (rank)	20	**Registering property** (rank)	21	**Trading across borders** (rank)	7
Procedures (number)	5	Procedures (number)	3	Documents to export (number)	3
Time (days)	7	Time (days)	51	Time to export (days)	5
Cost (% of income per capita)	2.0	Cost (% of property value)	0.5	Cost to export (US$ per container)	675
Minimum capital (% of income per capita)	28.1			Documents to import (number)	4
		Getting credit (rank)	48	Time to import (days)	5
Dealing with licenses (rank)	14	Strength of legal rights index (0–10)	4	Cost to import (US$ per container)	675
Procedures (number)	13	Depth of credit information index (0–6)	5		
Time (days)	117	Public registry coverage (% of adults)	0.0	**Enforcing contracts** (rank)	29
Cost (% of income per capita)	28.1	Private bureau coverage (% of adults)	19.7	Procedures (number)	36
				Time (days)	425
Employing workers (rank)	156	**Protecting investors** (rank)	33	Cost (% of claim)	17.3
Difficulty of hiring index (0–100)	33	Extent of disclosure index (0–10)	8		
Rigidity of hours index (0–100)	80	Extent of director liability index (0–10)	4	**Closing a business** (rank)	50
Difficulty of firing index (0–100)	60	Ease of shareholder suits index (0–10)	6	Time (years)	3.0
Rigidity of employment index (0–100)	58	Strength of investor protection index (0–10)	6.0	Cost (% of estate)	9
Nonwage labor cost (% of salary)	33			Recovery rate (cents on the dollar)	39.1
Firing cost (weeks of salary)	35	**Paying taxes** (rank)	31		
		Payments (number per year)	10		
		Time (hours per year)	81		
		Total tax rate (% of profit)	49.2		

ETHIOPIA

ETHIOPIA		Sub-Saharan Africa		GNI per capita (US$)	180
Ease of doing business (rank)	102	Low income		Population (m)	72.7
Starting a business (rank)	106	**Registering property** (rank)	147	**Trading across borders** (rank)	150
Procedures (number)	7	Procedures (number)	13	Documents to export (number)	8
Time (days)	16	Time (days)	43	Time to export (days)	46
Cost (% of income per capita)	41.3	Cost (% of property value)	7.5	Cost to export (US$ per container)	1,617
Minimum capital (% of income per capita)	960.0			Documents to import (number)	8
		Getting credit (rank)	97	Time to import (days)	42
Dealing with licenses (rank)	58	Strength of legal rights index (0–10)	4	Cost to import (US$ per container)	2,793
Procedures (number)	12	Depth of credit information index (0–6)	2		
Time (days)	128	Public registry coverage (% of adults)	0.1	**Enforcing contracts** (rank)	77
Cost (% of income per capita)	1,094.4	Private bureau coverage (% of adults)	0.0	Procedures (number)	39
				Time (days)	690
Employing workers (rank)	89	**Protecting investors** (rank)	107	Cost (% of claim)	15.2
Difficulty of hiring index (0–100)	33	Extent of disclosure index (0–10)	4		
Rigidity of hours index (0–100)	40	Extent of director liability index (0–10)	4	**Closing a business** (rank)	70
Difficulty of firing index (0–100)	30	Ease of shareholder suits index (0–10)	5	Time (years)	3.0
Rigidity of employment index (0–100)	34	Strength of investor protection index (0–10)	4.3	Cost (% of estate)	15
Nonwage labor cost (% of salary)	0			Recovery rate (cents on the dollar)	33.1
Firing cost (weeks of salary)	40	**Paying taxes** (rank)	29		
		Payments (number per year)	20		
		Time (hours per year)	198		
		Total tax rate (% of profit)	31.1		

FIJI

Ease of doing business (rank)	36	East Asia & Pacific Lower middle income		GNI per capita (US$) Population (m)	3,300 0.9
Starting a business (rank)	69	**Registering property** (rank)	77	**Trading across borders** (rank)	111
Procedures (number)	8	Procedures (number)	3	Documents to export (number)	13
Time (days)	46	Time (days)	48	Time to export (days)	25
Cost (% of income per capita)	25.3	Cost (% of property value)	12.0	Cost to export (US$ per container)	573
Minimum capital (% of income per capita)	0.0			Documents to import (number)	13
		Getting credit (rank)	48	Time to import (days)	25
Dealing with licenses (rank)	28	Strength of legal rights index (0–10)	5	Cost to import (US$ per container)	570
Procedures (number)	16	Depth of credit information index (0–6)	4		
Time (days)	114	Public registry coverage (% of adults)	0.0	**Enforcing contracts** (rank)	62
Cost (% of income per capita)	40.8	Private bureau coverage (% of adults)	41.2	Procedures (number)	34
				Time (days)	397
Employing workers (rank)	16	**Protecting investors** (rank)	33	Cost (% of claim)	38.9
Difficulty of hiring index (0–100)	22	Extent of disclosure index (0–10)	3		
Rigidity of hours index (0–100)	20	Extent of director liability index (0–10)	8	**Closing a business** (rank)	114
Difficulty of firing index (0–100)	0	Ease of shareholder suits index (0–10)	7	Time (years)	1.8
Rigidity of employment index (0–100)	14	Strength of investor protection index (0–10)	6.0	Cost (% of estate)	38
Nonwage labor cost (% of salary)	9			Recovery rate (cents on the dollar)	20.2
Firing cost (weeks of salary)	2	**Paying taxes** (rank)	52		
		Payments (number per year)	33		
		Time (hours per year)	140		
		Total tax rate (% of profit)	38.5		

FINLAND

Ease of doing business (rank)	13	OECD: High Income High income		GNI per capita (US$) Population (m)	40,650 5.3
Starting a business (rank)	16	**Registering property** (rank)	17	**Trading across borders** (rank)	5
Procedures (number)	3	Procedures (number)	3	Documents to export (number)	4
Time (days)	14	Time (days)	14	Time to export (days)	8
Cost (% of income per capita)	1.0	Cost (% of property value)	4.0	Cost to export (US$ per container)	420
Minimum capital (% of income per capita)	7.7			Documents to import (number)	5
		Getting credit (rank)	26	Time to import (days)	8
Dealing with licenses (rank)	39	Strength of legal rights index (0–10)	6	Cost to import (US$ per container)	420
Procedures (number)	18	Depth of credit information index (0–6)	5		
Time (days)	38	Public registry coverage (% of adults)	0.0	**Enforcing contracts** (rank)	7
Cost (% of income per capita)	122.3	Private bureau coverage (% of adults)	14.9	Procedures (number)	33
				Time (days)	235
Employing workers (rank)	127	**Protecting investors** (rank)	51	Cost (% of claim)	10.4
Difficulty of hiring index (0–100)	44	Extent of disclosure index (0–10)	6		
Rigidity of hours index (0–100)	60	Extent of director liability index (0–10)	4	**Closing a business** (rank)	5
Difficulty of firing index (0–100)	40	Ease of shareholder suits index (0–10)	7	Time (years)	0.9
Rigidity of employment index (0–100)	48	Strength of investor protection index (0–10)	5.7	Cost (% of estate)	4
Nonwage labor cost (% of salary)	26			Recovery rate (cents on the dollar)	88.2
Firing cost (weeks of salary)	26	**Paying taxes** (rank)	83		
		Payments (number per year)	20		
		Time (hours per year)	269		
		Total tax rate (% of profit)	47.8		

FRANCE

Ease of doing business (rank)	31	OECD: High Income High income		GNI per capita (US$) Population (m)	36,550 61.0
Starting a business (rank)	12	**Registering property** (rank)	159	**Trading across borders** (rank)	25
Procedures (number)	5	Procedures (number)	9	Documents to export (number)	4
Time (days)	7	Time (days)	123	Time to export (days)	11
Cost (% of income per capita)	1.1	Cost (% of property value)	6.1	Cost to export (US$ per container)	1,028
Minimum capital (% of income per capita)	0.0			Documents to import (number)	5
		Getting credit (rank)	36	Time to import (days)	12
Dealing with licenses (rank)	17	Strength of legal rights index (0–10)	6	Cost to import (US$ per container)	1,148
Procedures (number)	13	Depth of credit information index (0–6)	4		
Time (days)	137	Public registry coverage (% of adults)	24.8	**Enforcing contracts** (rank)	14
Cost (% of income per capita)	24.9	Private bureau coverage (% of adults)	0.0	Procedures (number)	30
				Time (days)	331
Employing workers (rank)	144	**Protecting investors** (rank)	64	Cost (% of claim)	17.4
Difficulty of hiring index (0–100)	67	Extent of disclosure index (0–10)	10		
Rigidity of hours index (0–100)	60	Extent of director liability index (0–10)	1	**Closing a business** (rank)	32
Difficulty of firing index (0–100)	40	Ease of shareholder suits index (0–10)	5	Time (years)	1.9
Rigidity of employment index (0–100)	56	Strength of investor protection index (0–10)	5.3	Cost (% of estate)	9
Nonwage labor cost (% of salary)	47			Recovery rate (cents on the dollar)	47.4
Firing cost (weeks of salary)	32	**Paying taxes** (rank)	82		
		Payments (number per year)	23		
		Time (hours per year)	132		
		Total tax rate (% of profit)	66.3		

GABON

Ease of doing business (rank)	144	Sub-Saharan Africa Upper middle income		GNI per capita (US$) Population (m)	5,000 1.4
Starting a business (rank)	147	**Registering property** (rank)	148	**Trading across borders** (rank)	106
Procedures (number)	9	Procedures (number)	8	Documents to export (number)	6
Time (days)	58	Time (days)	60	Time to export (days)	19
Cost (% of income per capita)	164.0	Cost (% of property value)	10.5	Cost to export (US$ per container)	1,510
Minimum capital (% of income per capita)	38.2			Documents to import (number)	7
		Getting credit (rank)	115	Time to import (days)	35
Dealing with licenses (rank)	44	Strength of legal rights index (0–10)	3	Cost to import (US$ per container)	1,600
Procedures (number)	14	Depth of credit information index (0–6)	2		
Time (days)	210	Public registry coverage (% of adults)	2.4	**Enforcing contracts** (rank)	145
Cost (% of income per capita)	48.3	Private bureau coverage (% of adults)	0.0	Procedures (number)	38
				Time (days)	1,070
Employing workers (rank)	163	**Protecting investors** (rank)	147	Cost (% of claim)	34.3
Difficulty of hiring index (0–100)	17	Extent of disclosure index (0–10)	6		
Rigidity of hours index (0–100)	80	Extent of director liability index (0–10)	1	**Closing a business** (rank)	130
Difficulty of firing index (0–100)	80	Ease of shareholder suits index (0–10)	3	Time (years)	5.0
Rigidity of employment index (0–100)	59	Strength of investor protection index (0–10)	3.3	Cost (% of estate)	15
Nonwage labor cost (% of salary)	20			Recovery rate (cents on the dollar)	15.2
Firing cost (weeks of salary)	43	**Paying taxes** (rank)	93		
		Payments (number per year)	28		
		Time (hours per year)	272		
		Total tax rate (% of profit)	44.2		

GAMBIA

Ease of doing business (rank)	131	Sub-Saharan Africa Low income		GNI per capita (US$) Population (m)	310 1.6
Starting a business (rank)	94	**Registering property** (rank)	133	**Trading across borders** (rank)	73
Procedures (number)	9	Procedures (number)	5	Documents to export (number)	7
Time (days)	32	Time (days)	371	Time to export (days)	23
Cost (% of income per capita)	279.0	Cost (% of property value)	7.6	Cost to export (US$ per container)	809
Minimum capital (% of income per capita)	0.0			Documents to import (number)	8
		Getting credit (rank)	135	Time to import (days)	23
Dealing with licenses (rank)	70	Strength of legal rights index (0–10)	4	Cost to import (US$ per container)	869
Procedures (number)	17	Depth of credit information index (0–6)	0		
Time (days)	146	Public registry coverage (% of adults)	0.0	**Enforcing contracts** (rank)	61
Cost (% of income per capita)	363.7	Private bureau coverage (% of adults)	0.0	Procedures (number)	32
				Time (days)	434
Employing workers (rank)	29	**Protecting investors** (rank)	165	Cost (% of claim)	37.9
Difficulty of hiring index (0–100)	0	Extent of disclosure index (0–10)	2		
Rigidity of hours index (0–100)	40	Extent of director liability index (0–10)	1	**Closing a business** (rank)	116
Difficulty of firing index (0–100)	30	Ease of shareholder suits index (0–10)	5	Time (years)	3.0
Rigidity of employment index (0–100)	23	Strength of investor protection index (0–10)	2.7	Cost (% of estate)	15
Nonwage labor cost (% of salary)	11			Recovery rate (cents on the dollar)	19.3
Firing cost (weeks of salary)	9	**Paying taxes** (rank)	173		
		Payments (number per year)	50		
		Time (hours per year)	376		
		Total tax rate (% of profit)	286.7		

GEORGIA

Ease of doing business (rank)	18	Eastern Europe & Central Asia Lower middle income		GNI per capita (US$) Population (m)	1,560 4.4
Starting a business (rank)	10	**Registering property** (rank)	11	**Trading across borders** (rank)	64
Procedures (number)	5	Procedures (number)	5	Documents to export (number)	8
Time (days)	11	Time (days)	5	Time to export (days)	12
Cost (% of income per capita)	9.5	Cost (% of property value)	0.1	Cost to export (US$ per container)	1,105
Minimum capital (% of income per capita)	0.0			Documents to import (number)	7
		Getting credit (rank)	48	Time to import (days)	14
Dealing with licenses (rank)	11	Strength of legal rights index (0–10)	5	Cost to import (US$ per container)	1,105
Procedures (number)	12	Depth of credit information index (0–6)	4		
Time (days)	113	Public registry coverage (% of adults)	0.0	**Enforcing contracts** (rank)	42
Cost (% of income per capita)	28.9	Private bureau coverage (% of adults)	0.2	Procedures (number)	36
				Time (days)	285
Employing workers (rank)	4	**Protecting investors** (rank)	33	Cost (% of claim)	29.9
Difficulty of hiring index (0–100)	0	Extent of disclosure index (0–10)	8		
Rigidity of hours index (0–100)	20	Extent of director liability index (0–10)	6	**Closing a business** (rank)	105
Difficulty of firing index (0–100)	0	Ease of shareholder suits index (0–10)	4	Time (years)	3.3
Rigidity of employment index (0–100)	7	Strength of investor protection index (0–10)	6.0	Cost (% of estate)	4
Nonwage labor cost (% of salary)	20			Recovery rate (cents on the dollar)	22.8
Firing cost (weeks of salary)	4	**Paying taxes** (rank)	102		
		Payments (number per year)	29		
		Time (hours per year)	387		
		Total tax rate (% of profit)	38.6		

GERMANY

Ease of doing business (rank)	20	OECD: High Income		GNI per capita (US$)	36,620
		High income		Population (m)	82.4
Starting a business (rank)	71	**Registering property** (rank)	47	**Trading across borders** (rank)	10
Procedures (number)	9	Procedures (number)	4	Documents to export (number)	4
Time (days)	18	Time (days)	40	Time to export (days)	7
Cost (% of income per capita)	5.7	Cost (% of property value)	5.2	Cost to export (US$ per container)	740
Minimum capital (% of income per capita)	42.8			Documents to import (number)	5
		Getting credit (rank)	3	Time to import (days)	7
Dealing with licenses (rank)	16	Strength of legal rights index (0–10)	8	Cost to import (US$ per container)	765
Procedures (number)	12	Depth of credit information index (0–6)	6		
Time (days)	100	Public registry coverage (% of adults)	0.7	**Enforcing contracts** (rank)	15
Cost (% of income per capita)	63.1	Private bureau coverage (% of adults)	98.1	Procedures (number)	33
				Time (days)	394
Employing workers (rank)	137	**Protecting investors** (rank)	83	Cost (% of claim)	11.8
Difficulty of hiring index (0–100)	33	Extent of disclosure index (0–10)	5		
Rigidity of hours index (0–100)	60	Extent of director liability index (0–10)	5	**Closing a business** (rank)	29
Difficulty of firing index (0–100)	40	Ease of shareholder suits index (0–10)	5	Time (years)	1.2
Rigidity of employment index (0–100)	44	Strength of investor protection index (0–10)	5.0	Cost (% of estate)	8
Nonwage labor cost (% of salary)	19			Recovery rate (cents on the dollar)	53.4
Firing cost (weeks of salary)	69	**Paying taxes** (rank)	67		
		Payments (number per year)	16		
		Time (hours per year)	196		
		Total tax rate (% of profit)	50.8		

GHANA

Ease of doing business (rank)	87	Sub-Saharan Africa		GNI per capita (US$)	520
		Low income		Population (m)	22.5
Starting a business (rank)	138	**Registering property** (rank)	26	**Trading across borders** (rank)	61
Procedures (number)	11	Procedures (number)	5	Documents to export (number)	6
Time (days)	42	Time (days)	34	Time to export (days)	19
Cost (% of income per capita)	41.4	Cost (% of property value)	1.3	Cost to export (US$ per container)	895
Minimum capital (% of income per capita)	20.9			Documents to import (number)	7
		Getting credit (rank)	115	Time to import (days)	29
Dealing with licenses (rank)	140	Strength of legal rights index (0–10)	5	Cost to import (US$ per container)	895
Procedures (number)	18	Depth of credit information index (0–6)	0		
Time (days)	220	Public registry coverage (% of adults)	0.0	**Enforcing contracts** (rank)	51
Cost (% of income per capita)	1,498.3	Private bureau coverage (% of adults)	0.0	Procedures (number)	36
				Time (days)	487
Employing workers (rank)	138	**Protecting investors** (rank)	33	Cost (% of claim)	23.0
Difficulty of hiring index (0–100)	22	Extent of disclosure index (0–10)	7		
Rigidity of hours index (0–100)	40	Extent of director liability index (0–10)	5	**Closing a business** (rank)	96
Difficulty of firing index (0–100)	50	Ease of shareholder suits index (0–10)	6	Time (years)	1.9
Rigidity of employment index (0–100)	37	Strength of investor protection index (0–10)	6.0	Cost (% of estate)	22
Nonwage labor cost (% of salary)	13			Recovery rate (cents on the dollar)	24.0
Firing cost (weeks of salary)	178	**Paying taxes** (rank)	75		
		Payments (number per year)	32		
		Time (hours per year)	304		
		Total tax rate (% of profit)	32.9		

GREECE

Ease of doing business (rank)	100	OECD: High Income		GNI per capita (US$)	21,690
		High income		Population (m)	11.1
Starting a business (rank)	152	**Registering property** (rank)	93	**Trading across borders** (rank)	65
Procedures (number)	15	Procedures (number)	12	Documents to export (number)	5
Time (days)	38	Time (days)	23	Time to export (days)	20
Cost (% of income per capita)	23.3	Cost (% of property value)	4.0	Cost to export (US$ per container)	998
Minimum capital (% of income per capita)	104.1			Documents to import (number)	6
		Getting credit (rank)	84	Time to import (days)	25
Dealing with licenses (rank)	42	Strength of legal rights index (0–10)	3	Cost to import (US$ per container)	1,245
Procedures (number)	15	Depth of credit information index (0–6)	4		
Time (days)	169	Public registry coverage (% of adults)	0.0	**Enforcing contracts** (rank)	87
Cost (% of income per capita)	61.7	Private bureau coverage (% of adults)	38.7	Procedures (number)	39
				Time (days)	819
Employing workers (rank)	142	**Protecting investors** (rank)	158	Cost (% of claim)	14.4
Difficulty of hiring index (0–100)	44	Extent of disclosure index (0–10)	1		
Rigidity of hours index (0–100)	80	Extent of director liability index (0–10)	3	**Closing a business** (rank)	38
Difficulty of firing index (0–100)	40	Ease of shareholder suits index (0–10)	5	Time (years)	2.0
Rigidity of employment index (0–100)	55	Strength of investor protection index (0–10)	3.0	Cost (% of estate)	9
Nonwage labor cost (% of salary)	28			Recovery rate (cents on the dollar)	44.8
Firing cost (weeks of salary)	24	**Paying taxes** (rank)	86		
		Payments (number per year)	21		
		Time (hours per year)	264		
		Total tax rate (% of profit)	48.6		

GRENADA

Ease of doing business (rank)	70	Latin America & Caribbean		GNI per capita (US$)	4,420
		Upper middle income		Population (m)	0.1
Starting a business (rank)	32	**Registering property** (rank)	145	**Trading across borders** (rank)	52
Procedures (number)	6	Procedures (number)	8	Documents to export (number)	6
Time (days)	20	Time (days)	77	Time to export (days)	19
Cost (% of income per capita)	31.7	Cost (% of property value)	7.4	Cost to export (US$ per container)	820
Minimum capital (% of income per capita)	0.0			Documents to import (number)	5
		Getting credit (rank)	97	Time to import (days)	23
Dealing with licenses (rank)	15	Strength of legal rights index (0–10)	6	Cost to import (US$ per container)	1,178
Procedures (number)	9	Depth of credit information index (0–6)	0		
Time (days)	149	Public registry coverage (% of adults)	0.0	**Enforcing contracts** (rank)	163
Cost (% of income per capita)	31.0	Private bureau coverage (% of adults)	0.0	Procedures (number)	47
				Time (days)	723
Employing workers (rank)	46	**Protecting investors** (rank)	19	Cost (% of claim)	32.6
Difficulty of hiring index (0–100)	44	Extent of disclosure index (0–10)	4		
Rigidity of hours index (0–100)	20	Extent of director liability index (0–10)	8	**Closing a business** (rank)	178
Difficulty of firing index (0–100)	0	Ease of shareholder suits index (0–10)	7	Time (years)	NO PRACTICE
Rigidity of employment index (0–100)	21	Strength of investor protection index (0–10)	6.3	Cost (% of estate)	NO PRACTICE
Nonwage labor cost (% of salary)	5			Recovery rate (cents on the dollar)	0.0
Firing cost (weeks of salary)	29	**Paying taxes** (rank)	59		
		Payments (number per year)	30		
		Time (hours per year)	140		
		Total tax rate (% of profit)	45.3		

GUATEMALA

Ease of doing business (rank)	114	Latin America & Caribbean		GNI per capita (US$)	2,640
		Lower middle income		Population (m)	12.9
Starting a business (rank)	128	**Registering property** (rank)	23	**Trading across borders** (rank)	116
Procedures (number)	11	Procedures (number)	5	Documents to export (number)	11
Time (days)	26	Time (days)	30	Time to export (days)	19
Cost (% of income per capita)	47.3	Cost (% of property value)	1.0	Cost to export (US$ per container)	1,052
Minimum capital (% of income per capita)	24.9			Documents to import (number)	11
		Getting credit (rank)	68	Time to import (days)	18
Dealing with licenses (rank)	167	Strength of legal rights index (0–10)	3	Cost to import (US$ per container)	1,177
Procedures (number)	22	Depth of credit information index (0–6)	5		
Time (days)	235	Public registry coverage (% of adults)	20.7	**Enforcing contracts** (rank)	98
Cost (% of income per capita)	1,142.2	Private bureau coverage (% of adults)	13.1	Procedures (number)	28
				Time (days)	1,459
Employing workers (rank)	105	**Protecting investors** (rank)	122	Cost (% of claim)	26.5
Difficulty of hiring index (0–100)	44	Extent of disclosure index (0–10)	3		
Rigidity of hours index (0–100)	40	Extent of director liability index (0–10)	3	**Closing a business** (rank)	86
Difficulty of firing index (0–100)	0	Ease of shareholder suits index (0–10)	6	Time (years)	3.0
Rigidity of employment index (0–100)	28	Strength of investor protection index (0–10)	4.0	Cost (% of estate)	15
Nonwage labor cost (% of salary)	13			Recovery rate (cents on the dollar)	28.1
Firing cost (weeks of salary)	101	**Paying taxes** (rank)	116		
		Payments (number per year)	39		
		Time (hours per year)	344		
		Total tax rate (% of profit)	37.5		

GUINEA

Ease of doing business (rank)	166	Sub-Saharan Africa		GNI per capita (US$)	410
		Low income		Population (m)	9.2
Starting a business (rank)	171	**Registering property** (rank)	151	**Trading across borders** (rank)	102
Procedures (number)	13	Procedures (number)	6	Documents to export (number)	7
Time (days)	41	Time (days)	104	Time to export (days)	33
Cost (% of income per capita)	138.3	Cost (% of property value)	15.3	Cost to export (US$ per container)	570
Minimum capital (% of income per capita)	466.5			Documents to import (number)	9
		Getting credit (rank)	135	Time to import (days)	32
Dealing with licenses (rank)	158	Strength of legal rights index (0–10)	4	Cost to import (US$ per container)	995
Procedures (number)	32	Depth of credit information index (0–6)	0		
Time (days)	255	Public registry coverage (% of adults)	0.0	**Enforcing contracts** (rank)	127
Cost (% of income per capita)	237.7	Private bureau coverage (% of adults)	0.0	Procedures (number)	50
				Time (days)	276
Employing workers (rank)	99	**Protecting investors** (rank)	165	Cost (% of claim)	45.0
Difficulty of hiring index (0–100)	33	Extent of disclosure index (0–10)	6		
Rigidity of hours index (0–100)	60	Extent of director liability index (0–10)	1	**Closing a business** (rank)	111
Difficulty of firing index (0–100)	30	Ease of shareholder suits index (0–10)	1	Time (years)	3.8
Rigidity of employment index (0–100)	41	Strength of investor protection index (0–10)	2.7	Cost (% of estate)	8
Nonwage labor cost (% of salary)	27			Recovery rate (cents on the dollar)	20.4
Firing cost (weeks of salary)	26	**Paying taxes** (rank)	163		
		Payments (number per year)	56		
		Time (hours per year)	416		
		Total tax rate (% of profit)	49.9		

GUINEA-BISSAU

Ease of doing business (rank)	176	Sub-Saharan Africa Low income		GNI per capita (US$)	190
				Population (m)	1.6
Starting a business (rank)	178	**Registering property** (rank)	164	**Trading across borders** (rank)	109
Procedures (number)	17	Procedures (number)	9	Documents to export (number)	6
Time (days)	233	Time (days)	211	Time to export (days)	27
Cost (% of income per capita)	255.5	Cost (% of property value)	5.4	Cost to export (US$ per container)	1,445
Minimum capital (% of income per capita)	1,006.6			Documents to import (number)	6
		Getting credit (rank)	135	Time to import (days)	26
Dealing with licenses (rank)	101	Strength of legal rights index (0–10)	3	Cost to import (US$ per container)	1,749
Procedures (number)	15	Depth of credit information index (0–6)	1		
Time (days)	167	Public registry coverage (% of adults)	0.9	**Enforcing contracts** (rank)	137
Cost (% of income per capita)	2,607.0	Private bureau coverage (% of adults)	0.0	Procedures (number)	41
				Time (days)	1,140
Employing workers (rank)	174	**Protecting investors** (rank)	122	Cost (% of claim)	25.0
Difficulty of hiring index (0–100)	67	Extent of disclosure index (0–10)	6		
Rigidity of hours index (0–100)	60	Extent of director liability index (0–10)	1	**Closing a business** (rank)	178
Difficulty of firing index (0–100)	70	Ease of shareholder suits index (0–10)	5	Time (years)	NO PRACTICE
Rigidity of employment index (0–100)	66	Strength of investor protection index (0–10)	4.0	Cost (% of estate)	NO PRACTICE
Nonwage labor cost (% of salary)	22			Recovery rate (cents on the dollar)	0.0
Firing cost (weeks of salary)	87	**Paying taxes** (rank)	112		
		Payments (number per year)	46		
		Time (hours per year)	208		
		Total tax rate (% of profit)	45.9		

GUYANA

Ease of doing business (rank)	104	Latin America & Caribbean Lower middle income		GNI per capita (US$)	1,130
				Population (m)	0.8
Starting a business (rank)	86	**Registering property** (rank)	53	**Trading across borders** (rank)	101
Procedures (number)	8	Procedures (number)	6	Documents to export (number)	7
Time (days)	44	Time (days)	34	Time to export (days)	30
Cost (% of income per capita)	87.2	Cost (% of property value)	4.5	Cost to export (US$ per container)	850
Minimum capital (% of income per capita)	0.0			Documents to import (number)	8
		Getting credit (rank)	158	Time to import (days)	35
Dealing with licenses (rank)	69	Strength of legal rights index (0–10)	3	Cost to import (US$ per container)	856
Procedures (number)	12	Depth of credit information index (0–6)	0		
Time (days)	222	Public registry coverage (% of adults)	0.0	**Enforcing contracts** (rank)	73
Cost (% of income per capita)	313.9	Private bureau coverage (% of adults)	0.0	Procedures (number)	36
				Time (days)	581
Employing workers (rank)	71	**Protecting investors** (rank)	64	Cost (% of claim)	25.2
Difficulty of hiring index (0–100)	33	Extent of disclosure index (0–10)	5		
Rigidity of hours index (0–100)	20	Extent of director liability index (0–10)	5	**Closing a business** (rank)	123
Difficulty of firing index (0–100)	20	Ease of shareholder suits index (0–10)	6	Time (years)	3.0
Rigidity of employment index (0–100)	24	Strength of investor protection index (0–10)	5.3	Cost (% of estate)	29
Nonwage labor cost (% of salary)	8			Recovery rate (cents on the dollar)	17.4
Firing cost (weeks of salary)	56	**Paying taxes** (rank)	100		
		Payments (number per year)	34		
		Time (hours per year)	288		
		Total tax rate (% of profit)	39.0		

HAITI

Ease of doing business (rank)	148	Latin America & Caribbean Low income		GNI per capita (US$)	480
				Population (m)	8.6
Starting a business (rank)	170	**Registering property** (rank)	128	**Trading across borders** (rank)	153
Procedures (number)	12	Procedures (number)	5	Documents to export (number)	8
Time (days)	202	Time (days)	405	Time to export (days)	52
Cost (% of income per capita)	133.9	Cost (% of property value)	6.5	Cost to export (US$ per container)	1,650
Minimum capital (% of income per capita)	32.2			Documents to import (number)	10
		Getting credit (rank)	115	Time to import (days)	53
Dealing with licenses (rank)	126	Strength of legal rights index (0–10)	3	Cost to import (US$ per container)	1,860
Procedures (number)	11	Depth of credit information index (0–6)	2		
Time (days)	1,179	Public registry coverage (% of adults)	0.7	**Enforcing contracts** (rank)	95
Cost (% of income per capita)	817.8	Private bureau coverage (% of adults)	0.0	Procedures (number)	35
				Time (days)	508
Employing workers (rank)	35	**Protecting investors** (rank)	158	Cost (% of claim)	42.6
Difficulty of hiring index (0–100)	22	Extent of disclosure index (0–10)	2		
Rigidity of hours index (0–100)	40	Extent of director liability index (0–10)	3	**Closing a business** (rank)	148
Difficulty of firing index (0–100)	0	Ease of shareholder suits index (0–10)	4	Time (years)	5.7
Rigidity of employment index (0–100)	21	Strength of investor protection index (0–10)	3.0	Cost (% of estate)	30
Nonwage labor cost (% of salary)	11			Recovery rate (cents on the dollar)	3.1
Firing cost (weeks of salary)	17	**Paying taxes** (rank)	96		
		Payments (number per year)	53		
		Time (hours per year)	160		
		Total tax rate (% of profit)	40.0		

HONDURAS

HONDURAS		Latin America & Caribbean		GNI per capita (US$)	1,200
Ease of doing business (rank)	121	Lower middle income		Population (m)	7.4
Starting a business (rank)	135	**Registering property** (rank)	78	**Trading across borders** (rank)	103
Procedures (number)	13	Procedures (number)	7	Documents to export (number)	7
Time (days)	21	Time (days)	24	Time to export (days)	20
Cost (% of income per capita)	59.9	Cost (% of property value)	5.8	Cost to export (US$ per container)	1,065
Minimum capital (% of income per capita)	27.4			Documents to import (number)	11
		Getting credit (rank)	13	Time to import (days)	23
Dealing with licenses (rank)	72	Strength of legal rights index (0–10)	6	Cost to import (US$ per container)	975
Procedures (number)	17	Depth of credit information index (0–6)	6		
Time (days)	125	Public registry coverage (% of adults)	12.7	**Enforcing contracts** (rank)	124
Cost (% of income per capita)	634.1	Private bureau coverage (% of adults)	58.0	Procedures (number)	45
				Time (days)	480
Employing workers (rank)	116	**Protecting investors** (rank)	147	Cost (% of claim)	30.4
Difficulty of hiring index (0–100)	89	Extent of disclosure index (0–10)	1		
Rigidity of hours index (0–100)	40	Extent of director liability index (0–10)	5	**Closing a business** (rank)	113
Difficulty of firing index (0–100)	0	Ease of shareholder suits index (0–10)	4	Time (years)	3.8
Rigidity of employment index (0–100)	43	Strength of investor protection index (0–10)	3.3	Cost (% of estate)	15
Nonwage labor cost (% of salary)	10			Recovery rate (cents on the dollar)	20.3
Firing cost (weeks of salary)	74	**Paying taxes** (rank)	160		
		Payments (number per year)	47		
		Time (hours per year)	424		
		Total tax rate (% of profit)	51.4		

HONG KONG, CHINA

HONG KONG, CHINA		East Asia & Pacific		GNI per capita (US$)	28,460
Ease of doing business (rank)	4	High income		Population (m)	7.0
Starting a business (rank)	13	**Registering property** (rank)	58	**Trading across borders** (rank)	3
Procedures (number)	5	Procedures (number)	5	Documents to export (number)	4
Time (days)	11	Time (days)	54	Time to export (days)	6
Cost (% of income per capita)	3.1	Cost (% of property value)	5.0	Cost to export (US$ per container)	525
Minimum capital (% of income per capita)	0.0			Documents to import (number)	4
		Getting credit (rank)	2	Time to import (days)	5
Dealing with licenses (rank)	60	Strength of legal rights index (0–10)	10	Cost to import (US$ per container)	525
Procedures (number)	23	Depth of credit information index (0–6)	5		
Time (days)	155	Public registry coverage (% of adults)	0.0	**Enforcing contracts** (rank)	1
Cost (% of income per capita)	21.3	Private bureau coverage (% of adults)	64.7	Procedures (number)	24
				Time (days)	211
Employing workers (rank)	23	**Protecting investors** (rank)	3	Cost (% of claim)	14.5
Difficulty of hiring index (0–100)	0	Extent of disclosure index (0–10)	10		
Rigidity of hours index (0–100)	0	Extent of director liability index (0–10)	8	**Closing a business** (rank)	15
Difficulty of firing index (0–100)	0	Ease of shareholder suits index (0–10)	9	Time (years)	1.1
Rigidity of employment index (0–100)	0	Strength of investor protection index (0–10)	9.0	Cost (% of estate)	9
Nonwage labor cost (% of salary)	5			Recovery rate (cents on the dollar)	79.0
Firing cost (weeks of salary)	62	**Paying taxes** (rank)	3		
		Payments (number per year)	4		
		Time (hours per year)	80		
		Total tax rate (% of profit)	24.4		

HUNGARY

HUNGARY		Eastern Europe & Central Asia		GNI per capita (US$)	10,950
Ease of doing business (rank)	45	Upper middle income		Population (m)	10.1
Starting a business (rank)	67	**Registering property** (rank)	96	**Trading across borders** (rank)	45
Procedures (number)	6	Procedures (number)	4	Documents to export (number)	5
Time (days)	16	Time (days)	63	Time to export (days)	18
Cost (% of income per capita)	17.7	Cost (% of property value)	11.0	Cost to export (US$ per container)	975
Minimum capital (% of income per capita)	65.1			Documents to import (number)	7
		Getting credit (rank)	26	Time to import (days)	17
Dealing with licenses (rank)	87	Strength of legal rights index (0–10)	6	Cost to import (US$ per container)	975
Procedures (number)	31	Depth of credit information index (0–6)	5		
Time (days)	211	Public registry coverage (% of adults)	0.0	**Enforcing contracts** (rank)	12
Cost (% of income per capita)	10.4	Private bureau coverage (% of adults)	6.9	Procedures (number)	33
				Time (days)	335
Employing workers (rank)	81	**Protecting investors** (rank)	107	Cost (% of claim)	13.0
Difficulty of hiring index (0–100)	0	Extent of disclosure index (0–10)	2		
Rigidity of hours index (0–100)	80	Extent of director liability index (0–10)	4	**Closing a business** (rank)	53
Difficulty of firing index (0–100)	10	Ease of shareholder suits index (0–10)	7	Time (years)	2.0
Rigidity of employment index (0–100)	30	Strength of investor protection index (0–10)	4.3	Cost (% of estate)	15
Nonwage labor cost (% of salary)	34			Recovery rate (cents on the dollar)	38.4
Firing cost (weeks of salary)	35	**Paying taxes** (rank)	127		
		Payments (number per year)	24		
		Time (hours per year)	340		
		Total tax rate (% of profit)	55.1		

ICELAND

Ease of doing business (rank)	10	OECD: High Income		GNI per capita (US$)	50,580
		High income		Population (m)	0.3
Starting a business (rank)	14	**Registering property** (rank)	8	**Trading across borders** (rank)	11
Procedures (number)	5	Procedures (number)	3	Documents to export (number)	5
Time (days)	5	Time (days)	4	Time to export (days)	15
Cost (% of income per capita)	2.7	Cost (% of property value)	2.4	Cost to export (US$ per container)	469
Minimum capital (% of income per capita)	14.1			Documents to import (number)	5
		Getting credit (rank)	13	Time to import (days)	14
Dealing with licenses (rank)	23	Strength of legal rights index (0–10)	7	Cost to import (US$ per container)	443
Procedures (number)	18	Depth of credit information index (0–6)	5		
Time (days)	76	Public registry coverage (% of adults)	0.0	**Enforcing contracts** (rank)	4
Cost (% of income per capita)	13.9	Private bureau coverage (% of adults)	100.0	Procedures (number)	26
				Time (days)	393
Employing workers (rank)	42	**Protecting investors** (rank)	64	Cost (% of claim)	6.1
Difficulty of hiring index (0–100)	33	Extent of disclosure index (0–10)	5		
Rigidity of hours index (0–100)	40	Extent of director liability index (0–10)	5	**Closing a business** (rank)	12
Difficulty of firing index (0–100)	10	Ease of shareholder suits index (0–10)	6	Time (years)	1.0
Rigidity of employment index (0–100)	28	Strength of investor protection index (0–10)	5.3	Cost (% of estate)	4
Nonwage labor cost (% of salary)	12			Recovery rate (cents on the dollar)	80.3
Firing cost (weeks of salary)	13	**Paying taxes** (rank)	27		
		Payments (number per year)	31		
		Time (hours per year)	140		
		Total tax rate (% of profit)	27.2		

INDIA

Ease of doing business (rank)	120	South Asia		GNI per capita (US$)	820
		Low income		Population (m)	1,109.8
Starting a business (rank)	111	**Registering property** (rank)	112	**Trading across borders** (rank)	79
Procedures (number)	13	Procedures (number)	6	Documents to export (number)	8
Time (days)	33	Time (days)	62	Time to export (days)	18
Cost (% of income per capita)	74.6	Cost (% of property value)	7.7	Cost to export (US$ per container)	820
Minimum capital (% of income per capita)	0.0			Documents to import (number)	9
		Getting credit (rank)	36	Time to import (days)	21
Dealing with licenses (rank)	134	Strength of legal rights index (0–10)	6	Cost to import (US$ per container)	910
Procedures (number)	20	Depth of credit information index (0–6)	4		
Time (days)	224	Public registry coverage (% of adults)	0.0	**Enforcing contracts** (rank)	177
Cost (% of income per capita)	519.4	Private bureau coverage (% of adults)	10.8	Procedures (number)	46
				Time (days)	1,420
Employing workers (rank)	85	**Protecting investors** (rank)	33	Cost (% of claim)	39.6
Difficulty of hiring index (0–100)	0	Extent of disclosure index (0–10)	7		
Rigidity of hours index (0–100)	20	Extent of director liability index (0–10)	4	**Closing a business** (rank)	137
Difficulty of firing index (0–100)	70	Ease of shareholder suits index (0–10)	7	Time (years)	10.0
Rigidity of employment index (0–100)	30	Strength of investor protection index (0–10)	6.0	Cost (% of estate)	9
Nonwage labor cost (% of salary)	17			Recovery rate (cents on the dollar)	11.6
Firing cost (weeks of salary)	56	**Paying taxes** (rank)	165		
		Payments (number per year)	60		
		Time (hours per year)	271		
		Total tax rate (% of profit)	70.6		

INDONESIA

Ease of doing business (rank)	123	East Asia & Pacific		GNI per capita (US$)	1,420
		Lower middle income		Population (m)	223.0
Starting a business (rank)	168	**Registering property** (rank)	121	**Trading across borders** (rank)	41
Procedures (number)	12	Procedures (number)	7	Documents to export (number)	5
Time (days)	105	Time (days)	42	Time to export (days)	21
Cost (% of income per capita)	80.0	Cost (% of property value)	10.5	Cost to export (US$ per container)	667
Minimum capital (% of income per capita)	38.4			Documents to import (number)	6
		Getting credit (rank)	68	Time to import (days)	27
Dealing with licenses (rank)	99	Strength of legal rights index (0–10)	5	Cost to import (US$ per container)	623
Procedures (number)	19	Depth of credit information index (0–6)	3		
Time (days)	196	Public registry coverage (% of adults)	20.5	**Enforcing contracts** (rank)	141
Cost (% of income per capita)	286.8	Private bureau coverage (% of adults)	0.2	Procedures (number)	39
				Time (days)	570
Employing workers (rank)	153	**Protecting investors** (rank)	51	Cost (% of claim)	122.7
Difficulty of hiring index (0–100)	72	Extent of disclosure index (0–10)	9		
Rigidity of hours index (0–100)	0	Extent of director liability index (0–10)	5	**Closing a business** (rank)	136
Difficulty of firing index (0–100)	60	Ease of shareholder suits index (0–10)	3	Time (years)	5.5
Rigidity of employment index (0–100)	44	Strength of investor protection index (0–10)	5.7	Cost (% of estate)	18
Nonwage labor cost (% of salary)	10			Recovery rate (cents on the dollar)	12.6
Firing cost (weeks of salary)	108	**Paying taxes** (rank)	110		
		Payments (number per year)	51		
		Time (hours per year)	266		
		Total tax rate (% of profit)	37.3		

IRAN

Ease of doing business (rank)	135
Starting a business (rank)	77
Procedures (number)	8
Time (days)	47
Cost (% of income per capita)	5.3
Minimum capital (% of income per capita)	1.3
Dealing with licenses (rank)	164
Procedures (number)	19
Time (days)	670
Cost (% of income per capita)	653.4
Employing workers (rank)	141
Difficulty of hiring index (0–100)	11
Rigidity of hours index (0–100)	60
Difficulty of firing index (0–100)	50
Rigidity of employment index (0–100)	40
Nonwage labor cost (% of salary)	23
Firing cost (weeks of salary)	91

Middle East & North Africa	
Lower middle income	
Registering property (rank)	143
Procedures (number)	9
Time (days)	36
Cost (% of property value)	10.6
Getting credit (rank)	68
Strength of legal rights index (0–10)	5
Depth of credit information index (0–6)	3
Public registry coverage (% of adults)	22.2
Private bureau coverage (% of adults)	0.0
Protecting investors (rank)	158
Extent of disclosure index (0–10)	5
Extent of director liability index (0–10)	4
Ease of shareholder suits index (0–10)	0
Strength of investor protection index (0–10)	3.0
Paying taxes (rank)	97
Payments (number per year)	22
Time (hours per year)	292
Total tax rate (% of profit)	47.4

GNI per capita (US$)	3,000
Population (m)	69.2
Trading across borders (rank)	135
Documents to export (number)	8
Time to export (days)	26
Cost to export (US$ per container)	860
Documents to import (number)	10
Time to import (days)	42
Cost to import (US$ per container)	1,330
Enforcing contracts (rank)	57
Procedures (number)	39
Time (days)	520
Cost (% of claim)	17.0
Closing a business (rank)	118
Time (years)	4.5
Cost (% of estate)	9
Recovery rate (cents on the dollar)	19.0

IRAQ

Ease of doing business (rank)	141
Starting a business (rank)	164
Procedures (number)	11
Time (days)	77
Cost (% of income per capita)	93.5
Minimum capital (% of income per capita)	65.4
Dealing with licenses (rank)	104
Procedures (number)	14
Time (days)	215
Cost (% of income per capita)	915.0
Employing workers (rank)	60
Difficulty of hiring index (0–100)	33
Rigidity of hours index (0–100)	60
Difficulty of firing index (0–100)	20
Rigidity of employment index (0–100)	38
Nonwage labor cost (% of salary)	12
Firing cost (weeks of salary)	0

Middle East & North Africa	
Lower middle income	
Registering property (rank)	40
Procedures (number)	5
Time (days)	8
Cost (% of property value)	6.3
Getting credit (rank)	135
Strength of legal rights index (0–10)	4
Depth of credit information index (0–6)	0
Public registry coverage (% of adults)	0.0
Private bureau coverage (% of adults)	0.0
Protecting investors (rank)	107
Extent of disclosure index (0–10)	4
Extent of director liability index (0–10)	5
Ease of shareholder suits index (0–10)	4
Strength of investor protection index (0–10)	4.3
Paying taxes (rank)	37
Payments (number per year)	13
Time (hours per year)	312
Total tax rate (% of profit)	24.7

GNI per capita (US$)	1,224
Population (m)	28.5
Trading across borders (rank)	175
Documents to export (number)	10
Time to export (days)	102
Cost to export (US$ per container)	3,400
Documents to import (number)	10
Time to import (days)	101
Cost to import (US$ per container)	3,400
Enforcing contracts (rank)	150
Procedures (number)	51
Time (days)	520
Cost (% of claim)	32.5
Closing a business (rank)	178
Time (years)	NO PRACTICE
Cost (% of estate)	NO PRACTICE
Recovery rate (cents on the dollar)	0.0

IRELAND

Ease of doing business (rank)	8
Starting a business (rank)	5
Procedures (number)	4
Time (days)	13
Cost (% of income per capita)	0.3
Minimum capital (% of income per capita)	0.0
Dealing with licenses (rank)	20
Procedures (number)	11
Time (days)	185
Cost (% of income per capita)	19.8
Employing workers (rank)	37
Difficulty of hiring index (0–100)	11
Rigidity of hours index (0–100)	20
Difficulty of firing index (0–100)	20
Rigidity of employment index (0–100)	17
Nonwage labor cost (% of salary)	11
Firing cost (weeks of salary)	24

OECD: High Income	
High income	
Registering property (rank)	79
Procedures (number)	5
Time (days)	38
Cost (% of property value)	10.2
Getting credit (rank)	7
Strength of legal rights index (0–10)	8
Depth of credit information index (0–6)	5
Public registry coverage (% of adults)	0.0
Private bureau coverage (% of adults)	100.0
Protecting investors (rank)	5
Extent of disclosure index (0–10)	10
Extent of director liability index (0–10)	6
Ease of shareholder suits index (0–10)	9
Strength of investor protection index (0–10)	8.3
Paying taxes (rank)	6
Payments (number per year)	9
Time (hours per year)	76
Total tax rate (% of profit)	28.9

GNI per capita (US$)	45,580
Population (m)	4.2
Trading across borders (rank)	20
Documents to export (number)	4
Time to export (days)	7
Cost to export (US$ per container)	1,090
Documents to import (number)	4
Time to import (days)	12
Cost to import (US$ per container)	1,139
Enforcing contracts (rank)	39
Procedures (number)	20
Time (days)	515
Cost (% of claim)	26.9
Closing a business (rank)	6
Time (years)	0.4
Cost (% of estate)	9
Recovery rate (cents on the dollar)	87.1

ISRAEL

Ease of doing business (rank)	29	Middle East & North Africa High income		GNI per capita (US$) Population (m)	18,280 7.0
Starting a business (rank)	17	**Registering property** (rank)	152	**Trading across borders** (rank)	8
Procedures (number)	5	Procedures (number)	7	Documents to export (number)	5
Time (days)	34	Time (days)	144	Time to export (days)	12
Cost (% of income per capita)	4.4	Cost (% of property value)	7.5	Cost to export (US$ per container)	560
Minimum capital (% of income per capita)	0.0			Documents to import (number)	4
		Getting credit (rank)	7	Time to import (days)	12
Dealing with licenses (rank)	109	Strength of legal rights index (0–10)	8	Cost to import (US$ per container)	560
Procedures (number)	20	Depth of credit information index (0–6)	5		
Time (days)	235	Public registry coverage (% of adults)	0.0	**Enforcing contracts** (rank)	102
Cost (% of income per capita)	115.5	Private bureau coverage (% of adults)	91.6	Procedures (number)	35
				Time (days)	890
Employing workers (rank)	87	**Protecting investors** (rank)	5	Cost (% of claim)	25.3
Difficulty of hiring index (0–100)	11	Extent of disclosure index (0–10)	7		
Rigidity of hours index (0–100)	60	Extent of director liability index (0–10)	9	**Closing a business** (rank)	40
Difficulty of firing index (0–100)	0	Ease of shareholder suits index (0–10)	9	Time (years)	4.0
Rigidity of employment index (0–100)	24	Strength of investor protection index (0–10)	8.3	Cost (% of estate)	23
Nonwage labor cost (% of salary)	6			Recovery rate (cents on the dollar)	43.6
Firing cost (weeks of salary)	91	**Paying taxes** (rank)	69		
		Payments (number per year)	33		
		Time (hours per year)	230		
		Total tax rate (% of profit)	36.0		

ITALY

Ease of doing business (rank)	53	OECD: High Income High income		GNI per capita (US$) Population (m)	32,020 58.6
Starting a business (rank)	65	**Registering property** (rank)	49	**Trading across borders** (rank)	62
Procedures (number)	9	Procedures (number)	8	Documents to export (number)	5
Time (days)	13	Time (days)	27	Time to export (days)	20
Cost (% of income per capita)	18.7	Cost (% of property value)	0.6	Cost to export (US$ per container)	1,291
Minimum capital (% of income per capita)	9.8			Documents to import (number)	5
		Getting credit (rank)	68	Time to import (days)	18
Dealing with licenses (rank)	78	Strength of legal rights index (0–10)	3	Cost to import (US$ per container)	1,291
Procedures (number)	14	Depth of credit information index (0–6)	5		
Time (days)	257	Public registry coverage (% of adults)	11.0	**Enforcing contracts** (rank)	155
Cost (% of income per capita)	138.2	Private bureau coverage (% of adults)	71.5	Procedures (number)	41
				Time (days)	1,210
Employing workers (rank)	56	**Protecting investors** (rank)	51	Cost (% of claim)	29.9
Difficulty of hiring index (0–100)	33	Extent of disclosure index (0–10)	7		
Rigidity of hours index (0–100)	40	Extent of director liability index (0–10)	4	**Closing a business** (rank)	25
Difficulty of firing index (0–100)	40	Ease of shareholder suits index (0–10)	6	Time (years)	1.8
Rigidity of employment index (0–100)	38	Strength of investor protection index (0–10)	5.7	Cost (% of estate)	22
Nonwage labor cost (% of salary)	37			Recovery rate (cents on the dollar)	61.8
Firing cost (weeks of salary)	2	**Paying taxes** (rank)	122		
		Payments (number per year)	15		
		Time (hours per year)	360		
		Total tax rate (% of profit)	76.2		

JAMAICA

Ease of doing business (rank)	63	Latin America & Caribbean Lower middle income		GNI per capita (US$) Population (m)	3,480 2.7
Starting a business (rank)	11	**Registering property** (rank)	108	**Trading across borders** (rank)	92
Procedures (number)	6	Procedures (number)	5	Documents to export (number)	6
Time (days)	8	Time (days)	54	Time to export (days)	21
Cost (% of income per capita)	8.7	Cost (% of property value)	13.5	Cost to export (US$ per container)	1,750
Minimum capital (% of income per capita)	0.0			Documents to import (number)	6
		Getting credit (rank)	115	Time to import (days)	22
Dealing with licenses (rank)	74	Strength of legal rights index (0–10)	5	Cost to import (US$ per container)	1,350
Procedures (number)	10	Depth of credit information index (0–6)	0		
Time (days)	236	Public registry coverage (% of adults)	0.0	**Enforcing contracts** (rank)	103
Cost (% of income per capita)	438.4	Private bureau coverage (% of adults)	0.0	Procedures (number)	34
				Time (days)	565
Employing workers (rank)	33	**Protecting investors** (rank)	64	Cost (% of claim)	45.6
Difficulty of hiring index (0–100)	11	Extent of disclosure index (0–10)	4		
Rigidity of hours index (0–100)	0	Extent of director liability index (0–10)	8	**Closing a business** (rank)	22
Difficulty of firing index (0–100)	0	Ease of shareholder suits index (0–10)	4	Time (years)	1.1
Rigidity of employment index (0–100)	4	Strength of investor protection index (0–10)	5.3	Cost (% of estate)	18
Nonwage labor cost (% of salary)	12			Recovery rate (cents on the dollar)	64.3
Firing cost (weeks of salary)	61	**Paying taxes** (rank)	170		
		Payments (number per year)	72		
		Time (hours per year)	414		
		Total tax rate (% of profit)	51.3		

JAPAN

Ease of doing business (rank)	12
OECD: High Income	
High income	
GNI per capita (US$)	38,410
Population (m)	127.6
Starting a business (rank)	44
Procedures (number)	8
Time (days)	23
Cost (% of income per capita)	7.5
Minimum capital (% of income per capita)	0.0
Dealing with licenses (rank)	32
Procedures (number)	15
Time (days)	177
Cost (% of income per capita)	17.8
Employing workers (rank)	17
Difficulty of hiring index (0–100)	0
Rigidity of hours index (0–100)	20
Difficulty of firing index (0–100)	30
Rigidity of employment index (0–100)	17
Nonwage labor cost (% of salary)	13
Firing cost (weeks of salary)	4
Registering property (rank)	48
Procedures (number)	6
Time (days)	14
Cost (% of property value)	5.0
Getting credit (rank)	13
Strength of legal rights index (0–10)	6
Depth of credit information index (0–6)	6
Public registry coverage (% of adults)	0.0
Private bureau coverage (% of adults)	68.3
Protecting investors (rank)	12
Extent of disclosure index (0–10)	7
Extent of director liability index (0–10)	6
Ease of shareholder suits index (0–10)	8
Strength of investor protection index (0–10)	7.0
Paying taxes (rank)	105
Payments (number per year)	13
Time (hours per year)	350
Total tax rate (% of profit)	52.0
Trading across borders (rank)	18
Documents to export (number)	4
Time to export (days)	10
Cost to export (US$ per container)	989
Documents to import (number)	5
Time to import (days)	11
Cost to import (US$ per container)	1,047
Enforcing contracts (rank)	21
Procedures (number)	30
Time (days)	316
Cost (% of claim)	22.7
Closing a business (rank)	1
Time (years)	0.6
Cost (% of estate)	4
Recovery rate (cents on the dollar)	92.6

JORDAN

Ease of doing business (rank)	80
Middle East & North Africa	
Lower middle income	
GNI per capita (US$)	2,660
Population (m)	5.5
Starting a business (rank)	133
Procedures (number)	10
Time (days)	14
Cost (% of income per capita)	66.2
Minimum capital (% of income per capita)	795.4
Dealing with licenses (rank)	71
Procedures (number)	18
Time (days)	122
Cost (% of income per capita)	486.1
Employing workers (rank)	45
Difficulty of hiring index (0–100)	11
Rigidity of hours index (0–100)	20
Difficulty of firing index (0–100)	60
Rigidity of employment index (0–100)	30
Nonwage labor cost (% of salary)	11
Firing cost (weeks of salary)	4
Registering property (rank)	109
Procedures (number)	8
Time (days)	22
Cost (% of property value)	10.0
Getting credit (rank)	84
Strength of legal rights index (0–10)	5
Depth of credit information index (0–6)	2
Public registry coverage (% of adults)	0.8
Private bureau coverage (% of adults)	0.0
Protecting investors (rank)	107
Extent of disclosure index (0–10)	5
Extent of director liability index (0–10)	4
Ease of shareholder suits index (0–10)	4
Strength of investor protection index (0–10)	4.3
Paying taxes (rank)	19
Payments (number per year)	26
Time (hours per year)	101
Total tax rate (% of profit)	31.1
Trading across borders (rank)	59
Documents to export (number)	7
Time to export (days)	19
Cost to export (US$ per container)	680
Documents to import (number)	7
Time to import (days)	22
Cost to import (US$ per container)	1,065
Enforcing contracts (rank)	128
Procedures (number)	39
Time (days)	689
Cost (% of claim)	31.2
Closing a business (rank)	87
Time (years)	4.3
Cost (% of estate)	9
Recovery rate (cents on the dollar)	27.8

KAZAKHSTAN

Ease of doing business (rank)	71
Eastern Europe & Central Asia	
Lower middle income	
GNI per capita (US$)	3,790
Population (m)	15.3
Starting a business (rank)	57
Procedures (number)	8
Time (days)	21
Cost (% of income per capita)	7.6
Minimum capital (% of income per capita)	22.9
Dealing with licenses (rank)	173
Procedures (number)	38
Time (days)	231
Cost (% of income per capita)	2,129.9
Employing workers (rank)	22
Difficulty of hiring index (0–100)	0
Rigidity of hours index (0–100)	40
Difficulty of firing index (0–100)	20
Rigidity of employment index (0–100)	20
Nonwage labor cost (% of salary)	14
Firing cost (weeks of salary)	9
Registering property (rank)	72
Procedures (number)	8
Time (days)	52
Cost (% of property value)	0.9
Getting credit (rank)	48
Strength of legal rights index (0–10)	5
Depth of credit information index (0–6)	4
Public registry coverage (% of adults)	0.0
Private bureau coverage (% of adults)	13.7
Protecting investors (rank)	51
Extent of disclosure index (0–10)	7
Extent of director liability index (0–10)	1
Ease of shareholder suits index (0–10)	9
Strength of investor protection index (0–10)	5.7
Paying taxes (rank)	44
Payments (number per year)	9
Time (hours per year)	271
Total tax rate (% of profit)	36.7
Trading across borders (rank)	178
Documents to export (number)	12
Time to export (days)	89
Cost to export (US$ per container)	2,730
Documents to import (number)	14
Time to import (days)	76
Cost to import (US$ per container)	2,780
Enforcing contracts (rank)	28
Procedures (number)	38
Time (days)	230
Cost (% of claim)	22.0
Closing a business (rank)	100
Time (years)	3.3
Cost (% of estate)	18
Recovery rate (cents on the dollar)	23.4

KENYA

Ease of doing business (rank)	72	Sub-Saharan Africa Low income		GNI per capita (US$) Population (m)	580 35.1
Starting a business (rank)	112	**Registering property** (rank)	114	**Trading across borders** (rank)	148
Procedures (number)	12	Procedures (number)	8	Documents to export (number)	9
Time (days)	44	Time (days)	64	Time to export (days)	29
Cost (% of income per capita)	46.1	Cost (% of property value)	4.2	Cost to export (US$ per container)	1,955
Minimum capital (% of income per capita)	0.0			Documents to import (number)	8
		Getting credit (rank)	13	Time to import (days)	37
Dealing with licenses (rank)	9	Strength of legal rights index (0–10)	8	Cost to import (US$ per container)	1,995
Procedures (number)	10	Depth of credit information index (0–6)	4		
Time (days)	100	Public registry coverage (% of adults)	0.0	**Enforcing contracts** (rank)	107
Cost (% of income per capita)	58.8	Private bureau coverage (% of adults)	1.5	Procedures (number)	44
				Time (days)	465
Employing workers (rank)	66	**Protecting investors** (rank)	83	Cost (% of claim)	26.7
Difficulty of hiring index (0–100)	33	Extent of disclosure index (0–10)	3		
Rigidity of hours index (0–100)	0	Extent of director liability index (0–10)	2	**Closing a business** (rank)	76
Difficulty of firing index (0–100)	30	Ease of shareholder suits index (0–10)	10	Time (years)	4.5
Rigidity of employment index (0–100)	21	Strength of investor protection index (0–10)	5.0	Cost (% of estate)	22
Nonwage labor cost (% of salary)	4			Recovery rate (cents on the dollar)	31.0
Firing cost (weeks of salary)	47	**Paying taxes** (rank)	154		
		Payments (number per year)	41		
		Time (hours per year)	432		
		Total tax rate (% of profit)	50.9		

KIRIBATI

Ease of doing business (rank)	73	East Asia & Pacific Lower middle income		GNI per capita (US$) Population (m)	1,230 0.1
Starting a business (rank)	86	**Registering property** (rank)	60	**Trading across borders** (rank)	97
Procedures (number)	6	Procedures (number)	5	Documents to export (number)	6
Time (days)	21	Time (days)	513	Time to export (days)	21
Cost (% of income per capita)	56.6	Cost (% of property value)	0.1	Cost to export (US$ per container)	1,550
Minimum capital (% of income per capita)	30.6			Documents to import (number)	7
		Getting credit (rank)	158	Time to import (days)	21
Dealing with licenses (rank)	65	Strength of legal rights index (0–10)	3	Cost to import (US$ per container)	1,550
Procedures (number)	14	Depth of credit information index (0–6)	0		
Time (days)	160	Public registry coverage (% of adults)	0.0	**Enforcing contracts** (rank)	71
Cost (% of income per capita)	629.3	Private bureau coverage (% of adults)	0.0	Procedures (number)	32
				Time (days)	660
Employing workers (rank)	25	**Protecting investors** (rank)	33	Cost (% of claim)	25.8
Difficulty of hiring index (0–100)	0	Extent of disclosure index (0–10)	6		
Rigidity of hours index (0–100)	0	Extent of director liability index (0–10)	5	**Closing a business** (rank)	178
Difficulty of firing index (0–100)	50	Ease of shareholder suits index (0–10)	7	Time (years)	NO PRACTICE
Rigidity of employment index (0–100)	17	Strength of investor protection index (0–10)	6.0	Cost (% of estate)	NO PRACTICE
Nonwage labor cost (% of salary)	8			Recovery rate (cents on the dollar)	0.0
Firing cost (weeks of salary)	4	**Paying taxes** (rank)	10		
		Payments (number per year)	7		
		Time (hours per year)	120		
		Total tax rate (% of profit)	31.8		

KOREA

Ease of doing business (rank)	30	OECD: High Income High income		GNI per capita (US$) Population (m)	17,690 48.4
Starting a business (rank)	110	**Registering property** (rank)	68	**Trading across borders** (rank)	13
Procedures (number)	10	Procedures (number)	7	Documents to export (number)	4
Time (days)	17	Time (days)	11	Time to export (days)	11
Cost (% of income per capita)	16.9	Cost (% of property value)	6.3	Cost to export (US$ per container)	745
Minimum capital (% of income per capita)	296.0			Documents to import (number)	6
		Getting credit (rank)	36	Time to import (days)	10
Dealing with licenses (rank)	22	Strength of legal rights index (0–10)	5	Cost to import (US$ per container)	745
Procedures (number)	13	Depth of credit information index (0–6)	5		
Time (days)	34	Public registry coverage (% of adults)	0.0	**Enforcing contracts** (rank)	10
Cost (% of income per capita)	170.2	Private bureau coverage (% of adults)	74.2	Procedures (number)	35
				Time (days)	230
Employing workers (rank)	131	**Protecting investors** (rank)	64	Cost (% of claim)	10.3
Difficulty of hiring index (0–100)	11	Extent of disclosure index (0–10)	7		
Rigidity of hours index (0–100)	60	Extent of director liability index (0–10)	2	**Closing a business** (rank)	11
Difficulty of firing index (0–100)	40	Ease of shareholder suits index (0–10)	7	Time (years)	1.5
Rigidity of employment index (0–100)	37	Strength of investor protection index (0–10)	5.3	Cost (% of estate)	4
Nonwage labor cost (% of salary)	13			Recovery rate (cents on the dollar)	81.2
Firing cost (weeks of salary)	91	**Paying taxes** (rank)	106		
		Payments (number per year)	48		
		Time (hours per year)	290		
		Total tax rate (% of profit)	34.9		

KUWAIT

Ease of doing business (rank)	40	Middle East & North Africa High income		GNI per capita (US$) Population (m)	25,963 2.6
Starting a business (rank)	121	**Registering property** (rank)	72	**Trading across borders** (rank)	99
Procedures (number)	13	Procedures (number)	8	Documents to export (number)	8
Time (days)	35	Time (days)	55	Time to export (days)	20
Cost (% of income per capita)	1.6	Cost (% of property value)	0.5	Cost to export (US$ per container)	935
Minimum capital (% of income per capita)	99.9			Documents to import (number)	11
		Getting credit (rank)	68	Time to import (days)	20
Dealing with licenses (rank)	85	Strength of legal rights index (0–10)	4	Cost to import (US$ per container)	935
Procedures (number)	25	Depth of credit information index (0–6)	4		
Time (days)	104	Public registry coverage (% of adults)	0.0	**Enforcing contracts** (rank)	99
Cost (% of income per capita)	209.4	Private bureau coverage (% of adults)	14.5	Procedures (number)	50
				Time (days)	566
Employing workers (rank)	39	**Protecting investors** (rank)	19	Cost (% of claim)	13.3
Difficulty of hiring index (0–100)	0	Extent of disclosure index (0–10)	7		
Rigidity of hours index (0–100)	40	Extent of director liability index (0–10)	7	**Closing a business** (rank)	67
Difficulty of firing index (0–100)	0	Ease of shareholder suits index (0–10)	5	Time (years)	4.2
Rigidity of employment index (0–100)	13	Strength of investor protection index (0–10)	6.3	Cost (% of estate)	1
Nonwage labor cost (% of salary)	11			Recovery rate (cents on the dollar)	33.6
Firing cost (weeks of salary)	78	**Paying taxes** (rank)	8		
		Payments (number per year)	14		
		Time (hours per year)	118		
		Total tax rate (% of profit)	14.4		

KYRGYZ REPUBLIC

Ease of doing business (rank)	94	Eastern Europe & Central Asia Low income		GNI per capita (US$) Population (m)	490 5.2
Starting a business (rank)	49	**Registering property** (rank)	16	**Trading across borders** (rank)	177
Procedures (number)	8	Procedures (number)	4	Documents to export (number)	13
Time (days)	21	Time (days)	4	Time to export (days)	64
Cost (% of income per capita)	8.8	Cost (% of property value)	4.1	Cost to export (US$ per container)	2,500
Minimum capital (% of income per capita)	0.5			Documents to import (number)	13
		Getting credit (rank)	68	Time to import (days)	75
Dealing with licenses (rank)	152	Strength of legal rights index (0–10)	5	Cost to import (US$ per container)	2,450
Procedures (number)	20	Depth of credit information index (0–6)	3		
Time (days)	291	Public registry coverage (% of adults)	0.0	**Enforcing contracts** (rank)	32
Cost (% of income per capita)	555.4	Private bureau coverage (% of adults)	1.6	Procedures (number)	39
				Time (days)	177
Employing workers (rank)	74	**Protecting investors** (rank)	33	Cost (% of claim)	22.0
Difficulty of hiring index (0–100)	33	Extent of disclosure index (0–10)	8		
Rigidity of hours index (0–100)	40	Extent of director liability index (0–10)	1	**Closing a business** (rank)	128
Difficulty of firing index (0–100)	40	Ease of shareholder suits index (0–10)	9	Time (years)	4.0
Rigidity of employment index (0–100)	38	Strength of investor protection index (0–10)	6.0	Cost (% of estate)	15
Nonwage labor cost (% of salary)	21			Recovery rate (cents on the dollar)	15.6
Firing cost (weeks of salary)	17	**Paying taxes** (rank)	152		
		Payments (number per year)	75		
		Time (hours per year)	202		
		Total tax rate (% of profit)	61.4		

LAO PDR

Ease of doing business (rank)	164	East Asia & Pacific Low income		GNI per capita (US$) Population (m)	500 5.8
Starting a business (rank)	78	**Registering property** (rank)	149	**Trading across borders** (rank)	158
Procedures (number)	8	Procedures (number)	9	Documents to export (number)	9
Time (days)	103	Time (days)	135	Time to export (days)	50
Cost (% of income per capita)	16.5	Cost (% of property value)	4.2	Cost to export (US$ per container)	1,750
Minimum capital (% of income per capita)	0.0			Documents to import (number)	10
		Getting credit (rank)	170	Time to import (days)	50
Dealing with licenses (rank)	111	Strength of legal rights index (0–10)	2	Cost to import (US$ per container)	1,930
Procedures (number)	24	Depth of credit information index (0–6)	0		
Time (days)	172	Public registry coverage (% of adults)	0.0	**Enforcing contracts** (rank)	111
Cost (% of income per capita)	202.4	Private bureau coverage (% of adults)	0.0	Procedures (number)	42
				Time (days)	443
Employing workers (rank)	82	**Protecting investors** (rank)	176	Cost (% of claim)	31.6
Difficulty of hiring index (0–100)	11	Extent of disclosure index (0–10)	0		
Rigidity of hours index (0–100)	40	Extent of director liability index (0–10)	3	**Closing a business** (rank)	178
Difficulty of firing index (0–100)	60	Ease of shareholder suits index (0–10)	2	Time (years)	NO PRACTICE
Rigidity of employment index (0–100)	37	Strength of investor protection index (0–10)	1.7	Cost (% of estate)	NO PRACTICE
Nonwage labor cost (% of salary)	5			Recovery rate (cents on the dollar)	0.0
Firing cost (weeks of salary)	19	**Paying taxes** (rank)	114		
		Payments (number per year)	34		
		Time (hours per year)	672		
		Total tax rate (% of profit)	35.5		

LATVIA

Ease of doing business (rank)	22
Starting a business (rank)	30
Procedures (number)	5
Time (days)	16
Cost (% of income per capita)	3.0
Minimum capital (% of income per capita)	22.0
Dealing with licenses (rank)	82
Procedures (number)	26
Time (days)	188
Cost (% of income per capita)	27.5
Employing workers (rank)	96
Difficulty of hiring index (0–100)	50
Rigidity of hours index (0–100)	40
Difficulty of firing index (0–100)	40
Rigidity of employment index (0–100)	43
Nonwage labor cost (% of salary)	24
Firing cost (weeks of salary)	17

Eastern Europe & Central Asia	
Upper middle income	
Registering property (rank)	85
Procedures (number)	8
Time (days)	54
Cost (% of property value)	2.0
Getting credit (rank)	13
Strength of legal rights index (0–10)	8
Depth of credit information index (0–6)	4
Public registry coverage (% of adults)	2.6
Private bureau coverage (% of adults)	0.0
Protecting investors (rank)	51
Extent of disclosure index (0–10)	5
Extent of director liability index (0–10)	4
Ease of shareholder suits index (0–10)	8
Strength of investor protection index (0–10)	5.7
Paying taxes (rank)	20
Payments (number per year)	7
Time (hours per year)	219
Total tax rate (% of profit)	32.6

GNI per capita (US$)	8,100
Population (m)	2.3
Trading across borders (rank)	19
Documents to export (number)	6
Time to export (days)	13
Cost to export (US$ per container)	800
Documents to import (number)	6
Time to import (days)	12
Cost to import (US$ per container)	800
Enforcing contracts (rank)	3
Procedures (number)	27
Time (days)	279
Cost (% of claim)	12.9
Closing a business (rank)	64
Time (years)	3.0
Cost (% of estate)	13
Recovery rate (cents on the dollar)	34.6

LEBANON

Ease of doing business (rank)	85
Starting a business (rank)	132
Procedures (number)	6
Time (days)	46
Cost (% of income per capita)	94.1
Minimum capital (% of income per capita)	60.4
Dealing with licenses (rank)	113
Procedures (number)	20
Time (days)	211
Cost (% of income per capita)	229.5
Employing workers (rank)	53
Difficulty of hiring index (0–100)	44
Rigidity of hours index (0–100)	0
Difficulty of firing index (0–100)	30
Rigidity of employment index (0–100)	25
Nonwage labor cost (% of salary)	22
Firing cost (weeks of salary)	17

Middle East & North Africa	
Upper middle income	
Registering property (rank)	92
Procedures (number)	8
Time (days)	25
Cost (% of property value)	5.9
Getting credit (rank)	48
Strength of legal rights index (0–10)	4
Depth of credit information index (0–6)	5
Public registry coverage (% of adults)	4.7
Private bureau coverage (% of adults)	0.0
Protecting investors (rank)	83
Extent of disclosure index (0–10)	9
Extent of director liability index (0–10)	1
Ease of shareholder suits index (0–10)	5
Strength of investor protection index (0–10)	5.0
Paying taxes (rank)	33
Payments (number per year)	19
Time (hours per year)	180
Total tax rate (% of profit)	35.4

GNI per capita (US$)	5,490
Population (m)	4.1
Trading across borders (rank)	83
Documents to export (number)	5
Time to export (days)	27
Cost to export (US$ per container)	1,027
Documents to import (number)	7
Time to import (days)	38
Cost to import (US$ per container)	810
Enforcing contracts (rank)	121
Procedures (number)	37
Time (days)	721
Cost (% of claim)	30.8
Closing a business (rank)	117
Time (years)	4.0
Cost (% of estate)	22
Recovery rate (cents on the dollar)	19.1

LESOTHO

Ease of doing business (rank)	124
Starting a business (rank)	126
Procedures (number)	8
Time (days)	73
Cost (% of income per capita)	37.4
Minimum capital (% of income per capita)	14.3
Dealing with licenses (rank)	146
Procedures (number)	15
Time (days)	601
Cost (% of income per capita)	805.3
Employing workers (rank)	69
Difficulty of hiring index (0–100)	22
Rigidity of hours index (0–100)	40
Difficulty of firing index (0–100)	10
Rigidity of employment index (0–100)	24
Nonwage labor cost (% of salary)	0
Firing cost (weeks of salary)	44

Sub-Saharan Africa	
Lower middle income	
Registering property (rank)	132
Procedures (number)	6
Time (days)	101
Cost (% of property value)	8.2
Getting credit (rank)	115
Strength of legal rights index (0–10)	5
Depth of credit information index (0–6)	0
Public registry coverage (% of adults)	0.0
Private bureau coverage (% of adults)	0.0
Protecting investors (rank)	141
Extent of disclosure index (0–10)	2
Extent of director liability index (0–10)	1
Ease of shareholder suits index (0–10)	8
Strength of investor protection index (0–10)	3.7
Paying taxes (rank)	49
Payments (number per year)	22
Time (hours per year)	342
Total tax rate (% of profit)	20.8

GNI per capita (US$)	1,030
Population (m)	1.8
Trading across borders (rank)	129
Documents to export (number)	6
Time to export (days)	44
Cost to export (US$ per container)	1,188
Documents to import (number)	8
Time to import (days)	49
Cost to import (US$ per container)	1,210
Enforcing contracts (rank)	99
Procedures (number)	41
Time (days)	695
Cost (% of claim)	16.6
Closing a business (rank)	62
Time (years)	2.6
Cost (% of estate)	8
Recovery rate (cents on the dollar)	34.9

LIBERIA

Ease of doing business (rank)	170
Sub-Saharan Africa	
Low income	
GNI per capita (US$)	140
Population (m)	3.4

Starting a business (rank)	141
Procedures (number)	12
Time (days)	99
Cost (% of income per capita)	493.3
Minimum capital (% of income per capita)	0.0

Dealing with licenses (rank)	176
Procedures (number)	25
Time (days)	398
Cost (% of income per capita)	61,049.3

Employing workers (rank)	103
Difficulty of hiring index (0–100)	33
Rigidity of hours index (0–100)	20
Difficulty of firing index (0–100)	40
Rigidity of employment index (0–100)	31
Nonwage labor cost (% of salary)	5
Firing cost (weeks of salary)	84

Registering property (rank)	167
Procedures (number)	13
Time (days)	50
Cost (% of property value)	14.9

Getting credit (rank)	135
Strength of legal rights index (0–10)	4
Depth of credit information index (0–6)	0
Public registry coverage (% of adults)	0.0
Private bureau coverage (% of adults)	0.0

Protecting investors (rank)	138
Extent of disclosure index (0–10)	4
Extent of director liability index (0–10)	1
Ease of shareholder suits index (0–10)	6
Strength of investor protection index (0–10)	3.7

Paying taxes (rank)	119
Payments (number per year)	37
Time (hours per year)	158
Total tax rate (% of profit)	81.6

Trading across borders (rank)	98
Documents to export (number)	10
Time to export (days)	20
Cost to export (US$ per container)	1,032
Documents to import (number)	9
Time to import (days)	10
Cost to import (US$ per container)	1,032

Enforcing contracts (rank)	165
Procedures (number)	41
Time (days)	1,280
Cost (% of claim)	35.0

Closing a business (rank)	144
Time (years)	3.0
Cost (% of estate)	43
Recovery rate (cents on the dollar)	7.8

LITHUANIA

Ease of doing business (rank)	26
Eastern Europe & Central Asia	
Upper middle income	
GNI per capita (US$)	7,870
Population (m)	3.4

Starting a business (rank)	57
Procedures (number)	7
Time (days)	26
Cost (% of income per capita)	3.0
Minimum capital (% of income per capita)	46.2

Dealing with licenses (rank)	57
Procedures (number)	17
Time (days)	156
Cost (% of income per capita)	133.1

Employing workers (rank)	124
Difficulty of hiring index (0–100)	33
Rigidity of hours index (0–100)	80
Difficulty of firing index (0–100)	30
Rigidity of employment index (0–100)	48
Nonwage labor cost (% of salary)	31
Firing cost (weeks of salary)	30

Registering property (rank)	4
Procedures (number)	3
Time (days)	3
Cost (% of property value)	0.7

Getting credit (rank)	36
Strength of legal rights index (0–10)	4
Depth of credit information index (0–6)	6
Public registry coverage (% of adults)	6.6
Private bureau coverage (% of adults)	7.3

Protecting investors (rank)	83
Extent of disclosure index (0–10)	5
Extent of director liability index (0–10)	4
Ease of shareholder suits index (0–10)	6
Strength of investor protection index (0–10)	5.0

Paying taxes (rank)	71
Payments (number per year)	24
Time (hours per year)	166
Total tax rate (% of profit)	48.3

Trading across borders (rank)	23
Documents to export (number)	6
Time to export (days)	10
Cost to export (US$ per container)	820
Documents to import (number)	6
Time to import (days)	13
Cost to import (US$ per container)	980

Enforcing contracts (rank)	18
Procedures (number)	30
Time (days)	210
Cost (% of claim)	23.6

Closing a business (rank)	31
Time (years)	1.7
Cost (% of estate)	7
Recovery rate (cents on the dollar)	49.2

LUXEMBOURG

Ease of doing business (rank)	42
OECD: High Income	
High income	
GNI per capita (US$)	76,040
Population (m)	0.5

Starting a business (rank)	41
Procedures (number)	6
Time (days)	26
Cost (% of income per capita)	2.3
Minimum capital (% of income per capita)	20.5

Dealing with licenses (rank)	36
Procedures (number)	13
Time (days)	217
Cost (% of income per capita)	19.4

Employing workers (rank)	164
Difficulty of hiring index (0–100)	67
Rigidity of hours index (0–100)	80
Difficulty of firing index (0–100)	40
Rigidity of employment index (0–100)	62
Nonwage labor cost (% of salary)	13
Firing cost (weeks of salary)	39

Registering property (rank)	116
Procedures (number)	8
Time (days)	29
Cost (% of property value)	10.2

Getting credit (rank)	97
Strength of legal rights index (0–10)	6
Depth of credit information index (0–6)	0
Public registry coverage (% of adults)	0.0
Private bureau coverage (% of adults)	0.0

Protecting investors (rank)	107
Extent of disclosure index (0–10)	6
Extent of director liability index (0–10)	4
Ease of shareholder suits index (0–10)	3
Strength of investor protection index (0–10)	4.3

Paying taxes (rank)	17
Payments (number per year)	22
Time (hours per year)	58
Total tax rate (% of profit)	35.3

Trading across borders (rank)	32
Documents to export (number)	5
Time to export (days)	6
Cost to export (US$ per container)	1,250
Documents to import (number)	4
Time to import (days)	6
Cost to import (US$ per container)	1,250

Enforcing contracts (rank)	2
Procedures (number)	26
Time (days)	321
Cost (% of claim)	8.8

Closing a business (rank)	46
Time (years)	2.0
Cost (% of estate)	15
Recovery rate (cents on the dollar)	41.6

MACEDONIA, FYR

Ease of doing business (rank)	75	Eastern Europe & Central Asia		GNI per capita (US$)	3,060
		Lower middle income		Population (m)	2.0
Starting a business (rank)	21	**Registering property** (rank)	91	**Trading across borders** (rank)	72
Procedures (number)	9	Procedures (number)	6	Documents to export (number)	7
Time (days)	15	Time (days)	98	Time to export (days)	19
Cost (% of income per capita)	6.6	Cost (% of property value)	3.5	Cost to export (US$ per container)	1,130
Minimum capital (% of income per capita)	0.0			Documents to import (number)	7
		Getting credit (rank)	48	Time to import (days)	17
Dealing with licenses (rank)	76	Strength of legal rights index (0–10)	6	Cost to import (US$ per container)	1,130
Procedures (number)	19	Depth of credit information index (0–6)	3		
Time (days)	192	Public registry coverage (% of adults)	4.0	**Enforcing contracts** (rank)	84
Cost (% of income per capita)	109.3	Private bureau coverage (% of adults)	0.0	Procedures (number)	39
				Time (days)	385
Employing workers (rank)	128	**Protecting investors** (rank)	83	Cost (% of claim)	33.1
Difficulty of hiring index (0–100)	61	Extent of disclosure index (0–10)	5		
Rigidity of hours index (0–100)	60	Extent of director liability index (0–10)	6	**Closing a business** (rank)	127
Difficulty of firing index (0–100)	30	Ease of shareholder suits index (0–10)	4	Time (years)	3.7
Rigidity of employment index (0–100)	50	Strength of investor protection index (0–10)	5.0	Cost (% of estate)	28
Nonwage labor cost (% of salary)	33			Recovery rate (cents on the dollar)	15.8
Firing cost (weeks of salary)	26	**Paying taxes** (rank)	99		
		Payments (number per year)	52		
		Time (hours per year)	96		
		Total tax rate (% of profit)	49.8		

MADAGASCAR

Ease of doing business (rank)	149	Sub-Saharan Africa		GNI per capita (US$)	280
		Low income		Population (m)	19.1
Starting a business (rank)	61	**Registering property** (rank)	165	**Trading across borders** (rank)	126
Procedures (number)	5	Procedures (number)	8	Documents to export (number)	4
Time (days)	7	Time (days)	134	Time to export (days)	28
Cost (% of income per capita)	22.7	Cost (% of property value)	11.6	Cost to export (US$ per container)	1,182
Minimum capital (% of income per capita)	333.4			Documents to import (number)	10
		Getting credit (rank)	176	Time to import (days)	49
Dealing with licenses (rank)	139	Strength of legal rights index (0–10)	1	Cost to import (US$ per container)	1,282
Procedures (number)	16	Depth of credit information index (0–6)	0		
Time (days)	268	Public registry coverage (% of adults)	0.1	**Enforcing contracts** (rank)	151
Cost (% of income per capita)	880.0	Private bureau coverage (% of adults)	0.0	Procedures (number)	38
				Time (days)	871
Employing workers (rank)	150	**Protecting investors** (rank)	51	Cost (% of claim)	42.4
Difficulty of hiring index (0–100)	89	Extent of disclosure index (0–10)	5		
Rigidity of hours index (0–100)	60	Extent of director liability index (0–10)	6	**Closing a business** (rank)	178
Difficulty of firing index (0–100)	40	Ease of shareholder suits index (0–10)	6	Time (years)	NO PRACTICE
Rigidity of employment index (0–100)	63	Strength of investor protection index (0–10)	5.7	Cost (% of estate)	NO PRACTICE
Nonwage labor cost (% of salary)	18			Recovery rate (cents on the dollar)	0.0
Firing cost (weeks of salary)	30	**Paying taxes** (rank)	86		
		Payments (number per year)	26		
		Time (hours per year)	238		
		Total tax rate (% of profit)	46.5		

MALAWI

Ease of doing business (rank)	127	Sub-Saharan Africa		GNI per capita (US$)	170
		Low income		Population (m)	13.2
Starting a business (rank)	108	**Registering property** (rank)	87	**Trading across borders** (rank)	161
Procedures (number)	10	Procedures (number)	6	Documents to export (number)	12
Time (days)	37	Time (days)	88	Time to export (days)	45
Cost (% of income per capita)	188.7	Cost (% of property value)	3.3	Cost to export (US$ per container)	1,623
Minimum capital (% of income per capita)	0.0			Documents to import (number)	10
		Getting credit (rank)	84	Time to import (days)	54
Dealing with licenses (rank)	117	Strength of legal rights index (0–10)	7	Cost to import (US$ per container)	2,500
Procedures (number)	21	Depth of credit information index (0–6)	0		
Time (days)	213	Public registry coverage (% of adults)	0.0	**Enforcing contracts** (rank)	135
Cost (% of income per capita)	189.2	Private bureau coverage (% of adults)	0.0	Procedures (number)	42
				Time (days)	432
Employing workers (rank)	90	**Protecting investors** (rank)	64	Cost (% of claim)	142.4
Difficulty of hiring index (0–100)	56	Extent of disclosure index (0–10)	4		
Rigidity of hours index (0–100)	0	Extent of director liability index (0–10)	7	**Closing a business** (rank)	135
Difficulty of firing index (0–100)	20	Ease of shareholder suits index (0–10)	5	Time (years)	2.6
Rigidity of employment index (0–100)	25	Strength of investor protection index (0–10)	5.3	Cost (% of estate)	30
Nonwage labor cost (% of salary)	1			Recovery rate (cents on the dollar)	13.2
Firing cost (weeks of salary)	84	**Paying taxes** (rank)	78		
		Payments (number per year)	30		
		Time (hours per year)	370		
		Total tax rate (% of profit)	32.2		

MALAYSIA

MALAYSIA		East Asia & Pacific		GNI per capita (US$)	5,490
Ease of doing business (rank)	24	Upper middle income		Population (m)	25.8
Starting a business (rank)	74	**Registering property** (rank)	67	**Trading across borders** (rank)	21
Procedures (number)	9	Procedures (number)	5	Documents to export (number)	7
Time (days)	24	Time (days)	144	Time to export (days)	18
Cost (% of income per capita)	18.1	Cost (% of property value)	2.4	Cost to export (US$ per container)	432
Minimum capital (% of income per capita)	0.0			Documents to import (number)	7
		Getting credit (rank)	3	Time to import (days)	14
Dealing with licenses (rank)	105	Strength of legal rights index (0–10)	8	Cost to import (US$ per container)	385
Procedures (number)	25	Depth of credit information index (0–6)	6		
Time (days)	285	Public registry coverage (% of adults)	44.5	**Enforcing contracts** (rank)	63
Cost (% of income per capita)	10.0	Private bureau coverage (% of adults)	..	Procedures (number)	30
				Time (days)	600
Employing workers (rank)	43	**Protecting investors** (rank)	4	Cost (% of claim)	27.5
Difficulty of hiring index (0–100)	0	Extent of disclosure index (0–10)	10		
Rigidity of hours index (0–100)	0	Extent of director liability index (0–10)	9	**Closing a business** (rank)	54
Difficulty of firing index (0–100)	30	Ease of shareholder suits index (0–10)	7	Time (years)	2.3
Rigidity of employment index (0–100)	10	Strength of investor protection index (0–10)	8.7	Cost (% of estate)	15
Nonwage labor cost (% of salary)	15			Recovery rate (cents on the dollar)	38.3
Firing cost (weeks of salary)	75	**Paying taxes** (rank)	56		
		Payments (number per year)	35		
		Time (hours per year)	166		
		Total tax rate (% of profit)	36.0		

MALDIVES

MALDIVES		South Asia		GNI per capita (US$)	2,680
Ease of doing business (rank)	60	Lower middle income		Population (m)	0.3
Starting a business (rank)	34	**Registering property** (rank)	178	**Trading across borders** (rank)	110
Procedures (number)	5	Procedures (number)	NO PRACTICE	Documents to export (number)	8
Time (days)	9	Time (days)	NO PRACTICE	Time to export (days)	21
Cost (% of income per capita)	13.4	Cost (% of property value)	NO PRACTICE	Cost to export (US$ per container)	1,200
Minimum capital (% of income per capita)	5.8			Documents to import (number)	9
		Getting credit (rank)	135	Time to import (days)	20
Dealing with licenses (rank)	8	Strength of legal rights index (0–10)	4	Cost to import (US$ per container)	1,200
Procedures (number)	9	Depth of credit information index (0–6)	0		
Time (days)	118	Public registry coverage (% of adults)	0.0	**Enforcing contracts** (rank)	94
Cost (% of income per capita)	39.9	Private bureau coverage (% of adults)	0.0	Procedures (number)	41
				Time (days)	665
Employing workers (rank)	7	**Protecting investors** (rank)	64	Cost (% of claim)	16.5
Difficulty of hiring index (0–100)	0	Extent of disclosure index (0–10)	0		
Rigidity of hours index (0–100)	0	Extent of director liability index (0–10)	8	**Closing a business** (rank)	120
Difficulty of firing index (0–100)	0	Ease of shareholder suits index (0–10)	8	Time (years)	6.7
Rigidity of employment index (0–100)	0	Strength of investor protection index (0–10)	5.3	Cost (% of estate)	4
Nonwage labor cost (% of salary)	0			Recovery rate (cents on the dollar)	18.2
Firing cost (weeks of salary)	9	**Paying taxes** (rank)	1		
		Payments (number per year)	1		
		Time (hours per year)	-		
		Total tax rate (% of profit)	9.1		

MALI

MALI		Sub-Saharan Africa		GNI per capita (US$)	440
Ease of doing business (rank)	158	Low income		Population (m)	13.9
Starting a business (rank)	149	**Registering property** (rank)	90	**Trading across borders** (rank)	162
Procedures (number)	11	Procedures (number)	5	Documents to export (number)	9
Time (days)	26	Time (days)	29	Time to export (days)	44
Cost (% of income per capita)	132.1	Cost (% of property value)	21.2	Cost to export (US$ per container)	1,752
Minimum capital (% of income per capita)	434.6			Documents to import (number)	11
		Getting credit (rank)	135	Time to import (days)	65
Dealing with licenses (rank)	101	Strength of legal rights index (0–10)	3	Cost to import (US$ per container)	2,680
Procedures (number)	14	Depth of credit information index (0–6)	1		
Time (days)	208	Public registry coverage (% of adults)	2.5	**Enforcing contracts** (rank)	157
Cost (% of income per capita)	1,320.7	Private bureau coverage (% of adults)	0.0	Procedures (number)	39
				Time (days)	860
Employing workers (rank)	88	**Protecting investors** (rank)	147	Cost (% of claim)	52.0
Difficulty of hiring index (0–100)	33	Extent of disclosure index (0–10)	6		
Rigidity of hours index (0–100)	40	Extent of director liability index (0–10)	1	**Closing a business** (rank)	107
Difficulty of firing index (0–100)	40	Ease of shareholder suits index (0–10)	3	Time (years)	3.6
Rigidity of employment index (0–100)	38	Strength of investor protection index (0–10)	3.3	Cost (% of estate)	18
Nonwage labor cost (% of salary)	28			Recovery rate (cents on the dollar)	21.3
Firing cost (weeks of salary)	31	**Paying taxes** (rank)	151		
		Payments (number per year)	58		
		Time (hours per year)	270		
		Total tax rate (% of profit)	51.4		

MARSHALL ISLANDS

Ease of doing business (rank)	89
Starting a business (rank)	15
Procedures (number)	5
Time (days)	17
Cost (% of income per capita)	17.7
Minimum capital (% of income per capita)	0.0
Dealing with licenses (rank)	4
Procedures (number)	10
Time (days)	55
Cost (% of income per capita)	36.8
Employing workers (rank)	1
Difficulty of hiring index (0–100)	0
Rigidity of hours index (0–100)	0
Difficulty of firing index (0–100)	0
Rigidity of employment index (0–100)	0
Nonwage labor cost (% of salary)	11
Firing cost (weeks of salary)	0

East Asia & Pacific	
Lower middle income	
Registering property (rank)	178
Procedures (number)	NO PRACTICE
Time (days)	NO PRACTICE
Cost (% of property value)	NO PRACTICE
Getting credit (rank)	170
Strength of legal rights index (0–10)	2
Depth of credit information index (0–6)	0
Public registry coverage (% of adults)	0.0
Private bureau coverage (% of adults)	0.0
Protecting investors (rank)	147
Extent of disclosure index (0–10)	2
Extent of director liability index (0–10)	0
Ease of shareholder suits index (0–10)	8
Strength of investor protection index (0–10)	3.3
Paying taxes (rank)	74
Payments (number per year)	21
Time (hours per year)	128
Total tax rate (% of profit)	64.9

GNI per capita (US$)	3,000
Population (m)	0.1
Trading across borders (rank)	46
Documents to export (number)	5
Time to export (days)	21
Cost to export (US$ per container)	765
Documents to import (number)	5
Time to import (days)	33
Cost to import (US$ per container)	765
Enforcing contracts (rank)	60
Procedures (number)	36
Time (days)	476
Cost (% of claim)	27.4
Closing a business (rank)	122
Time (years)	2.0
Cost (% of estate)	38
Recovery rate (cents on the dollar)	17.9

MAURITANIA

Ease of doing business (rank)	157
Starting a business (rank)	167
Procedures (number)	11
Time (days)	65
Cost (% of income per capita)	56.2
Minimum capital (% of income per capita)	503.1
Dealing with licenses (rank)	142
Procedures (number)	25
Time (days)	201
Cost (% of income per capita)	565.5
Employing workers (rank)	117
Difficulty of hiring index (0–100)	56
Rigidity of hours index (0–100)	40
Difficulty of firing index (0–100)	40
Rigidity of employment index (0–100)	45
Nonwage labor cost (% of salary)	16
Firing cost (weeks of salary)	31

Sub-Saharan Africa	
Low income	
Registering property (rank)	52
Procedures (number)	4
Time (days)	49
Cost (% of property value)	5.2
Getting credit (rank)	115
Strength of legal rights index (0–10)	4
Depth of credit information index (0–6)	1
Public registry coverage (% of adults)	0.2
Private bureau coverage (% of adults)	0.0
Protecting investors (rank)	141
Extent of disclosure index (0–10)	5
Extent of director liability index (0–10)	3
Ease of shareholder suits index (0–10)	3
Strength of investor protection index (0–10)	3.7
Paying taxes (rank)	171
Payments (number per year)	38
Time (hours per year)	696
Total tax rate (% of profit)	107.5

GNI per capita (US$)	740
Population (m)	3.2
Trading across borders (rank)	152
Documents to export (number)	11
Time to export (days)	35
Cost to export (US$ per container)	1,360
Documents to import (number)	11
Time to import (days)	42
Cost to import (US$ per container)	1,363
Enforcing contracts (rank)	89
Procedures (number)	46
Time (days)	400
Cost (% of claim)	23.2
Closing a business (rank)	143
Time (years)	8.0
Cost (% of estate)	9
Recovery rate (cents on the dollar)	7.8

MAURITIUS

Ease of doing business (rank)	27
Starting a business (rank)	8
Procedures (number)	6
Time (days)	7
Cost (% of income per capita)	5.3
Minimum capital (% of income per capita)	0.0
Dealing with licenses (rank)	33
Procedures (number)	18
Time (days)	107
Cost (% of income per capita)	43.3
Employing workers (rank)	61
Difficulty of hiring index (0–100)	0
Rigidity of hours index (0–100)	20
Difficulty of firing index (0–100)	50
Rigidity of employment index (0–100)	23
Nonwage labor cost (% of salary)	6
Firing cost (weeks of salary)	35

Sub-Saharan Africa	
Upper middle income	
Registering property (rank)	153
Procedures (number)	6
Time (days)	210
Cost (% of property value)	10.8
Getting credit (rank)	97
Strength of legal rights index (0–10)	5
Depth of credit information index (0–6)	1
Public registry coverage (% of adults)	38.6
Private bureau coverage (% of adults)	0.0
Protecting investors (rank)	11
Extent of disclosure index (0–10)	6
Extent of director liability index (0–10)	8
Ease of shareholder suits index (0–10)	9
Strength of investor protection index (0–10)	7.7
Paying taxes (rank)	11
Payments (number per year)	7
Time (hours per year)	161
Total tax rate (% of profit)	21.7

GNI per capita (US$)	5,450
Population (m)	1.3
Trading across borders (rank)	17
Documents to export (number)	5
Time to export (days)	17
Cost to export (US$ per container)	728
Documents to import (number)	6
Time to import (days)	16
Cost to import (US$ per container)	673
Enforcing contracts (rank)	78
Procedures (number)	37
Time (days)	750
Cost (% of claim)	17.4
Closing a business (rank)	66
Time (years)	1.7
Cost (% of estate)	15
Recovery rate (cents on the dollar)	34.3

MEXICO

MEXICO		Latin America & Caribbean		GNI per capita (US$)	7,870
Ease of doing business (rank)	44	Upper middle income		Population (m)	104.2
Starting a business (rank)	75	**Registering property** (rank)	71	**Trading across borders** (rank)	76
Procedures (number)	8	Procedures (number)	5	Documents to export (number)	5
Time (days)	27	Time (days)	74	Time to export (days)	17
Cost (% of income per capita)	13.3	Cost (% of property value)	4.7	Cost to export (US$ per container)	1,302
Minimum capital (% of income per capita)	11.6			Documents to import (number)	5
		Getting credit (rank)	48	Time to import (days)	23
Dealing with licenses (rank)	21	Strength of legal rights index (0–10)	3	Cost to import (US$ per container)	2,411
Procedures (number)	11	Depth of credit information index (0–6)	6		
Time (days)	131	Public registry coverage (% of adults)	0.0	**Enforcing contracts** (rank)	83
Cost (% of income per capita)	103.5	Private bureau coverage (% of adults)	61.2	Procedures (number)	38
				Time (days)	415
Employing workers (rank)	134	**Protecting investors** (rank)	33	Cost (% of claim)	32.0
Difficulty of hiring index (0–100)	33	Extent of disclosure index (0–10)	8		
Rigidity of hours index (0–100)	40	Extent of director liability index (0–10)	5	**Closing a business** (rank)	23
Difficulty of firing index (0–100)	70	Ease of shareholder suits index (0–10)	5	Time (years)	1.8
Rigidity of employment index (0–100)	48	Strength of investor protection index (0–10)	6.0	Cost (% of estate)	18
Nonwage labor cost (% of salary)	21			Recovery rate (cents on the dollar)	63.9
Firing cost (weeks of salary)	52	**Paying taxes** (rank)	135		
		Payments (number per year)	27		
		Time (hours per year)	552		
		Total tax rate (% of profit)	51.2		

MICRONESIA

MICRONESIA		East Asia & Pacific		GNI per capita (US$)	2,380
Ease of doing business (rank)	112	Lower middle income		Population (m)	0.1
Starting a business (rank)	46	**Registering property** (rank)	178	**Trading across borders** (rank)	85
Procedures (number)	7	Procedures (number)	NO PRACTICE	Documents to export (number)	3
Time (days)	16	Time (days)	NO PRACTICE	Time to export (days)	30
Cost (% of income per capita)	137.0	Cost (% of property value)	NO PRACTICE	Cost to export (US$ per container)	1,145
Minimum capital (% of income per capita)	0.0			Documents to import (number)	6
		Getting credit (rank)	84	Time to import (days)	30
Dealing with licenses (rank)	9	Strength of legal rights index (0–10)	7	Cost to import (US$ per container)	1,145
Procedures (number)	14	Depth of credit information index (0–6)	0		
Time (days)	73	Public registry coverage (% of adults)	0.0	**Enforcing contracts** (rank)	139
Cost (% of income per capita)	19.7	Private bureau coverage (% of adults)	0.0	Procedures (number)	34
				Time (days)	965
Employing workers (rank)	12	**Protecting investors** (rank)	165	Cost (% of claim)	66.0
Difficulty of hiring index (0–100)	22	Extent of disclosure index (0–10)	0		
Rigidity of hours index (0–100)	0	Extent of director liability index (0–10)	0	**Closing a business** (rank)	149
Difficulty of firing index (0–100)	0	Ease of shareholder suits index (0–10)	8	Time (years)	5.3
Rigidity of employment index (0–100)	7	Strength of investor protection index (0–10)	2.7	Cost (% of estate)	38
Nonwage labor cost (% of salary)	6			Recovery rate (cents on the dollar)	3.1
Firing cost (weeks of salary)	0	**Paying taxes** (rank)	70		
		Payments (number per year)	21		
		Time (hours per year)	128		
		Total tax rate (% of profit)	58.7		

MOLDOVA

MOLDOVA		Eastern Europe & Central Asia		GNI per capita (US$)	1,100
Ease of doing business (rank)	92	Lower middle income		Population (m)	3.8
Starting a business (rank)	81	**Registering property** (rank)	46	**Trading across borders** (rank)	122
Procedures (number)	9	Procedures (number)	6	Documents to export (number)	6
Time (days)	23	Time (days)	48	Time to export (days)	32
Cost (% of income per capita)	11.5	Cost (% of property value)	0.9	Cost to export (US$ per container)	1,425
Minimum capital (% of income per capita)	14.6			Documents to import (number)	7
		Getting credit (rank)	97	Time to import (days)	35
Dealing with licenses (rank)	153	Strength of legal rights index (0–10)	6	Cost to import (US$ per container)	1,545
Procedures (number)	30	Depth of credit information index (0–6)	0		
Time (days)	292	Public registry coverage (% of adults)	0.0	**Enforcing contracts** (rank)	17
Cost (% of income per capita)	154.2	Private bureau coverage (% of adults)	0.0	Procedures (number)	31
				Time (days)	365
Employing workers (rank)	93	**Protecting investors** (rank)	98	Cost (% of claim)	16.6
Difficulty of hiring index (0–100)	33	Extent of disclosure index (0–10)	7		
Rigidity of hours index (0–100)	40	Extent of director liability index (0–10)	1	**Closing a business** (rank)	82
Difficulty of firing index (0–100)	40	Ease of shareholder suits index (0–10)	6	Time (years)	2.8
Rigidity of employment index (0–100)	38	Strength of investor protection index (0–10)	4.7	Cost (% of estate)	9
Nonwage labor cost (% of salary)	28			Recovery rate (cents on the dollar)	28.8
Firing cost (weeks of salary)	37	**Paying taxes** (rank)	111		
		Payments (number per year)	49		
		Time (hours per year)	218		
		Total tax rate (% of profit)	44.0		

MONGOLIA

Ease of doing business (rank)	52	East Asia & Pacific		GNI per capita (US$)	880
		Low income		Population (m)	2.6
Starting a business (rank)	62	**Registering property** (rank)	18	**Trading across borders** (rank)	168
Procedures (number)	8	Procedures (number)	5	Documents to export (number)	10
Time (days)	20	Time (days)	11	Time to export (days)	58
Cost (% of income per capita)	4.3	Cost (% of property value)	2.2	Cost to export (US$ per container)	1,807
Minimum capital (% of income per capita)	96.3			Documents to import (number)	10
		Getting credit (rank)	68	Time to import (days)	59
Dealing with licenses (rank)	43	Strength of legal rights index (0–10)	5	Cost to import (US$ per container)	3,197
Procedures (number)	21	Depth of credit information index (0–6)	3		
Time (days)	126	Public registry coverage (% of adults)	9.5	**Enforcing contracts** (rank)	27
Cost (% of income per capita)	15.7	Private bureau coverage (% of adults)	0.0	Procedures (number)	32
				Time (days)	314
Employing workers (rank)	64	**Protecting investors** (rank)	19	Cost (% of claim)	26.1
Difficulty of hiring index (0–100)	22	Extent of disclosure index (0–10)	5		
Rigidity of hours index (0–100)	80	Extent of director liability index (0–10)	8	**Closing a business** (rank)	115
Difficulty of firing index (0–100)	0	Ease of shareholder suits index (0–10)	6	Time (years)	4.0
Rigidity of employment index (0–100)	34	Strength of investor protection index (0–10)	6.3	Cost (% of estate)	8
Nonwage labor cost (% of salary)	20			Recovery rate (cents on the dollar)	20.1
Firing cost (weeks of salary)	9	**Paying taxes** (rank)	90		
		Payments (number per year)	42		
		Time (hours per year)	204		
		Total tax rate (% of profit)	38.4		

MONTENEGRO

Ease of doing business (rank)	81	Eastern Europe & Central Asia		GNI per capita (US$)	3,860
		Lower middle income		Population (m)	0.6
Starting a business (rank)	98	**Registering property** (rank)	103	**Trading across borders** (rank)	113
Procedures (number)	15	Procedures (number)	8	Documents to export (number)	9
Time (days)	24	Time (days)	86	Time to export (days)	18
Cost (% of income per capita)	6.2	Cost (% of property value)	2.4	Cost to export (US$ per container)	1,580
Minimum capital (% of income per capita)	0.0			Documents to import (number)	7
		Getting credit (rank)	84	Time to import (days)	19
Dealing with licenses (rank)	113	Strength of legal rights index (0–10)	7	Cost to import (US$ per container)	1,780
Procedures (number)	19	Depth of credit information index (0–6)	0		
Time (days)	185	Public registry coverage (% of adults)	0.0	**Enforcing contracts** (rank)	131
Cost (% of income per capita)	599.6	Private bureau coverage (% of adults)	0.0	Procedures (number)	49
				Time (days)	545
Employing workers (rank)	98	**Protecting investors** (rank)	19	Cost (% of claim)	25.7
Difficulty of hiring index (0–100)	33	Extent of disclosure index (0–10)	5		
Rigidity of hours index (0–100)	40	Extent of director liability index (0–10)	8	**Closing a business** (rank)	41
Difficulty of firing index (0–100)	40	Ease of shareholder suits index (0–10)	6	Time (years)	2.0
Rigidity of employment index (0–100)	38	Strength of investor protection index (0–10)	6.3	Cost (% of estate)	8
Nonwage labor cost (% of salary)	18			Recovery rate (cents on the dollar)	42.8
Firing cost (weeks of salary)	39	**Paying taxes** (rank)	129		
		Payments (number per year)	88		
		Time (hours per year)	372		
		Total tax rate (% of profit)	31.6		

MOROCCO

Ease of doing business (rank)	129	Middle East & North Africa		GNI per capita (US$)	1,900
		Lower middle income		Population (m)	30.5
Starting a business (rank)	51	**Registering property** (rank)	102	**Trading across borders** (rank)	67
Procedures (number)	6	Procedures (number)	8	Documents to export (number)	8
Time (days)	12	Time (days)	47	Time to export (days)	14
Cost (% of income per capita)	11.5	Cost (% of property value)	4.9	Cost to export (US$ per container)	600
Minimum capital (% of income per capita)	59.8			Documents to import (number)	11
		Getting credit (rank)	135	Time to import (days)	19
Dealing with licenses (rank)	88	Strength of legal rights index (0–10)	3	Cost to import (US$ per container)	800
Procedures (number)	19	Depth of credit information index (0–6)	1		
Time (days)	163	Public registry coverage (% of adults)	2.3	**Enforcing contracts** (rank)	114
Cost (% of income per capita)	334.7	Private bureau coverage (% of adults)	0.0	Procedures (number)	40
				Time (days)	615
Employing workers (rank)	165	**Protecting investors** (rank)	158	Cost (% of claim)	25.2
Difficulty of hiring index (0–100)	100	Extent of disclosure index (0–10)	6		
Rigidity of hours index (0–100)	40	Extent of director liability index (0–10)	2	**Closing a business** (rank)	60
Difficulty of firing index (0–100)	50	Ease of shareholder suits index (0–10)	1	Time (years)	1.8
Rigidity of employment index (0–100)	63	Strength of investor protection index (0–10)	3.0	Cost (% of estate)	18
Nonwage labor cost (% of salary)	19			Recovery rate (cents on the dollar)	35.3
Firing cost (weeks of salary)	85	**Paying taxes** (rank)	132		
		Payments (number per year)	28		
		Time (hours per year)	358		
		Total tax rate (% of profit)	53.1		

MOZAMBIQUE

Ease of doing business (rank)	134
Sub-Saharan Africa	
Low income	
GNI per capita (US$)	340
Population (m)	20.1

Starting a business (rank)	125
Procedures (number)	10
Time (days)	29
Cost (% of income per capita)	21.6
Minimum capital (% of income per capita)	115.8
Dealing with licenses (rank)	147
Procedures (number)	17
Time (days)	361
Cost (% of income per capita)	705.0
Employing workers (rank)	162
Difficulty of hiring index (0–100)	83
Rigidity of hours index (0–100)	60
Difficulty of firing index (0–100)	20
Rigidity of employment index (0–100)	54
Nonwage labor cost (% of salary)	4
Firing cost (weeks of salary)	143

Registering property (rank)	126
Procedures (number)	8
Time (days)	42
Cost (% of property value)	8.1
Getting credit (rank)	97
Strength of legal rights index (0–10)	3
Depth of credit information index (0–6)	3
Public registry coverage (% of adults)	0.9
Private bureau coverage (% of adults)	0.0
Protecting investors (rank)	33
Extent of disclosure index (0–10)	5
Extent of director liability index (0–10)	4
Ease of shareholder suits index (0–10)	9
Strength of investor protection index (0–10)	6.0
Paying taxes (rank)	72
Payments (number per year)	37
Time (hours per year)	230
Total tax rate (% of profit)	34.3

Trading across borders (rank)	140
Documents to export (number)	8
Time to export (days)	27
Cost to export (US$ per container)	1,155
Documents to import (number)	10
Time to import (days)	38
Cost to import (US$ per container)	1,185
Enforcing contracts (rank)	138
Procedures (number)	31
Time (days)	1,010
Cost (% of claim)	142.5
Closing a business (rank)	134
Time (years)	5.0
Cost (% of estate)	9
Recovery rate (cents on the dollar)	13.9

NAMIBIA

Ease of doing business (rank)	43
Sub-Saharan Africa	
Lower middle income	
GNI per capita (US$)	3,230
Population (m)	2.1

Starting a business (rank)	101
Procedures (number)	10
Time (days)	99
Cost (% of income per capita)	22.3
Minimum capital (% of income per capita)	0.0
Dealing with licenses (rank)	31
Procedures (number)	12
Time (days)	139
Cost (% of income per capita)	156.7
Employing workers (rank)	33
Difficulty of hiring index (0–100)	0
Rigidity of hours index (0–100)	40
Difficulty of firing index (0–100)	20
Rigidity of employment index (0–100)	20
Nonwage labor cost (% of salary)	0
Firing cost (weeks of salary)	24

Registering property (rank)	128
Procedures (number)	9
Time (days)	23
Cost (% of property value)	9.9
Getting credit (rank)	36
Strength of legal rights index (0–10)	5
Depth of credit information index (0–6)	5
Public registry coverage (% of adults)	0.0
Private bureau coverage (% of adults)	59.9
Protecting investors (rank)	64
Extent of disclosure index (0–10)	5
Extent of director liability index (0–10)	5
Ease of shareholder suits index (0–10)	6
Strength of investor protection index (0–10)	5.3
Paying taxes (rank)	48
Payments (number per year)	37
Time (hours per year)	..
Total tax rate (% of profit)	26.5

Trading across borders (rank)	144
Documents to export (number)	11
Time to export (days)	29
Cost to export (US$ per container)	1,539
Documents to import (number)	9
Time to import (days)	24
Cost to import (US$ per container)	1,550
Enforcing contracts (rank)	33
Procedures (number)	33
Time (days)	270
Cost (% of claim)	29.9
Closing a business (rank)	47
Time (years)	1.5
Cost (% of estate)	15
Recovery rate (cents on the dollar)	41.3

NEPAL

Ease of doing business (rank)	111
South Asia	
Low income	
GNI per capita (US$)	290
Population (m)	27.7

Starting a business (rank)	60
Procedures (number)	7
Time (days)	31
Cost (% of income per capita)	73.9
Minimum capital (% of income per capita)	0.0
Dealing with licenses (rank)	125
Procedures (number)	15
Time (days)	424
Cost (% of income per capita)	304.7
Employing workers (rank)	155
Difficulty of hiring index (0–100)	67
Rigidity of hours index (0–100)	20
Difficulty of firing index (0–100)	70
Rigidity of employment index (0–100)	52
Nonwage labor cost (% of salary)	10
Firing cost (weeks of salary)	90

Registering property (rank)	25
Procedures (number)	3
Time (days)	5
Cost (% of property value)	6.4
Getting credit (rank)	97
Strength of legal rights index (0–10)	4
Depth of credit information index (0–6)	2
Public registry coverage (% of adults)	0.0
Private bureau coverage (% of adults)	0.2
Protecting investors (rank)	64
Extent of disclosure index (0–10)	6
Extent of director liability index (0–10)	1
Ease of shareholder suits index (0–10)	9
Strength of investor protection index (0–10)	5.3
Paying taxes (rank)	92
Payments (number per year)	33
Time (hours per year)	408
Total tax rate (% of profit)	32.5

Trading across borders (rank)	151
Documents to export (number)	9
Time to export (days)	43
Cost to export (US$ per container)	1,600
Documents to import (number)	10
Time to import (days)	35
Cost to import (US$ per container)	1,725
Enforcing contracts (rank)	123
Procedures (number)	39
Time (days)	735
Cost (% of claim)	26.8
Closing a business (rank)	95
Time (years)	5.0
Cost (% of estate)	9
Recovery rate (cents on the dollar)	24.5

NETHERLANDS

Ease of doing business (rank)	21	OECD: High Income High income		GNI per capita (US$) Population (m)	42,670 16.4
Starting a business (rank)	41	**Registering property** (rank)	22	**Trading across borders** (rank)	14
Procedures (number)	6	Procedures (number)	2	Documents to export (number)	4
Time (days)	10	Time (days)	5	Time to export (days)	6
Cost (% of income per capita)	6.0	Cost (% of property value)	6.2	Cost to export (US$ per container)	880
Minimum capital (% of income per capita)	52.9			Documents to import (number)	5
		Getting credit (rank)	13	Time to import (days)	6
Dealing with licenses (rank)	84	Strength of legal rights index (0–10)	7	Cost to import (US$ per container)	1,005
Procedures (number)	18	Depth of credit information index (0–6)	5		
Time (days)	230	Public registry coverage (% of adults)	0.0	**Enforcing contracts** (rank)	36
Cost (% of income per capita)	76.0	Private bureau coverage (% of adults)	78.1	Procedures (number)	25
				Time (days)	514
Employing workers (rank)	92	**Protecting investors** (rank)	98	Cost (% of claim)	24.4
Difficulty of hiring index (0–100)	17	Extent of disclosure index (0–10)	4		
Rigidity of hours index (0–100)	40	Extent of director liability index (0–10)	4	**Closing a business** (rank)	8
Difficulty of firing index (0–100)	70	Ease of shareholder suits index (0–10)	6	Time (years)	1.1
Rigidity of employment index (0–100)	42	Strength of investor protection index (0–10)	4.7	Cost (% of estate)	4
Nonwage labor cost (% of salary)	18			Recovery rate (cents on the dollar)	86.7
Firing cost (weeks of salary)	17	**Paying taxes** (rank)	36		
		Payments (number per year)	9		
		Time (hours per year)	180		
		Total tax rate (% of profit)	43.4		

NEW ZEALAND

Ease of doing business (rank)	2	OECD: High Income High income		GNI per capita (US$) Population (m)	27,250 4.1
Starting a business (rank)	3	**Registering property** (rank)	1	**Trading across borders** (rank)	16
Procedures (number)	2	Procedures (number)	2	Documents to export (number)	7
Time (days)	12	Time (days)	2	Time to export (days)	10
Cost (% of income per capita)	0.1	Cost (% of property value)	0.1	Cost to export (US$ per container)	725
Minimum capital (% of income per capita)	0.0			Documents to import (number)	5
		Getting credit (rank)	3	Time to import (days)	9
Dealing with licenses (rank)	2	Strength of legal rights index (0–10)	9	Cost to import (US$ per container)	800
Procedures (number)	7	Depth of credit information index (0–6)	5		
Time (days)	65	Public registry coverage (% of adults)	0.0	**Enforcing contracts** (rank)	13
Cost (% of income per capita)	25.0	Private bureau coverage (% of adults)	100.0	Procedures (number)	30
				Time (days)	216
Employing workers (rank)	13	**Protecting investors** (rank)	1	Cost (% of claim)	22.0
Difficulty of hiring index (0–100)	11	Extent of disclosure index (0–10)	10		
Rigidity of hours index (0–100)	0	Extent of director liability index (0–10)	9	**Closing a business** (rank)	16
Difficulty of firing index (0–100)	10	Ease of shareholder suits index (0–10)	10	Time (years)	1.3
Rigidity of employment index (0–100)	7	Strength of investor protection index (0–10)	9.7	Cost (% of estate)	4
Nonwage labor cost (% of salary)	1			Recovery rate (cents on the dollar)	77.1
Firing cost (weeks of salary)	0	**Paying taxes** (rank)	9		
		Payments (number per year)	8		
		Time (hours per year)	70		
		Total tax rate (% of profit)	35.1		

NICARAGUA

Ease of doing business (rank)	93	Latin America & Caribbean Lower middle income		GNI per capita (US$) Population (m)	1,000 5.2
Starting a business (rank)	70	**Registering property** (rank)	130	**Trading across borders** (rank)	87
Procedures (number)	6	Procedures (number)	8	Documents to export (number)	5
Time (days)	39	Time (days)	124	Time to export (days)	36
Cost (% of income per capita)	119.1	Cost (% of property value)	3.5	Cost to export (US$ per container)	1,021
Minimum capital (% of income per capita)	0.0			Documents to import (number)	5
		Getting credit (rank)	68	Time to import (days)	38
Dealing with licenses (rank)	127	Strength of legal rights index (0–10)	3	Cost to import (US$ per container)	1,054
Procedures (number)	17	Depth of credit information index (0–6)	5		
Time (days)	219	Public registry coverage (% of adults)	14.8	**Enforcing contracts** (rank)	69
Cost (% of income per capita)	898.6	Private bureau coverage (% of adults)	100.0	Procedures (number)	35
				Time (days)	540
Employing workers (rank)	59	**Protecting investors** (rank)	83	Cost (% of claim)	26.8
Difficulty of hiring index (0–100)	22	Extent of disclosure index (0–10)	4		
Rigidity of hours index (0–100)	60	Extent of director liability index (0–10)	5	**Closing a business** (rank)	63
Difficulty of firing index (0–100)	0	Ease of shareholder suits index (0–10)	6	Time (years)	2.2
Rigidity of employment index (0–100)	27	Strength of investor protection index (0–10)	5.0	Cost (% of estate)	15
Nonwage labor cost (% of salary)	17			Recovery rate (cents on the dollar)	34.6
Firing cost (weeks of salary)	24	**Paying taxes** (rank)	156		
		Payments (number per year)	64		
		Time (hours per year)	240		
		Total tax rate (% of profit)	63.2		

NIGER

Ease of doing business (rank)	169	Sub-Saharan Africa		GNI per capita (US$)	260
		Low income		Population (m)	14.4
Starting a business (rank)	153	**Registering property** (rank)	63	**Trading across borders** (rank)	163
Procedures (number)	11	Procedures (number)	5	Documents to export (number)	8
Time (days)	23	Time (days)	32	Time to export (days)	59
Cost (% of income per capita)	174.8	Cost (% of property value)	9.0	Cost to export (US$ per container)	2,945
Minimum capital (% of income per capita)	735.6			Documents to import (number)	10
		Getting credit (rank)	135	Time to import (days)	68
Dealing with licenses (rank)	155	Strength of legal rights index (0–10)	3	Cost to import (US$ per container)	2,946
Procedures (number)	16	Depth of credit information index (0–6)	1		
Time (days)	293	Public registry coverage (% of adults)	1.0	**Enforcing contracts** (rank)	132
Cost (% of income per capita)	2,823.6	Private bureau coverage (% of adults)	0.0	Procedures (number)	39
				Time (days)	545
Employing workers (rank)	161	**Protecting investors** (rank)	147	Cost (% of claim)	59.6
Difficulty of hiring index (0–100)	100	Extent of disclosure index (0–10)	6		
Rigidity of hours index (0–100)	60	Extent of director liability index (0–10)	1	**Closing a business** (rank)	133
Difficulty of firing index (0–100)	50	Ease of shareholder suits index (0–10)	3	Time (years)	5.0
Rigidity of employment index (0–100)	70	Strength of investor protection index (0–10)	3.3	Cost (% of estate)	18
Nonwage labor cost (% of salary)	17			Recovery rate (cents on the dollar)	14.2
Firing cost (weeks of salary)	31	**Paying taxes** (rank)	115		
		Payments (number per year)	42		
		Time (hours per year)	270		
		Total tax rate (% of profit)	42.4		

NIGERIA

Ease of doing business (rank)	108	Sub-Saharan Africa		GNI per capita (US$)	640
		Low income		Population (m)	144.7
Starting a business (rank)	80	**Registering property** (rank)	173	**Trading across borders** (rank)	138
Procedures (number)	9	Procedures (number)	14	Documents to export (number)	10
Time (days)	34	Time (days)	82	Time to export (days)	26
Cost (% of income per capita)	56.6	Cost (% of property value)	22.2	Cost to export (US$ per container)	1,026
Minimum capital (% of income per capita)	0.0			Documents to import (number)	9
		Getting credit (rank)	84	Time to import (days)	46
Dealing with licenses (rank)	161	Strength of legal rights index (0–10)	7	Cost to import (US$ per container)	1,047
Procedures (number)	18	Depth of credit information index (0–6)	0		
Time (days)	350	Public registry coverage (% of adults)	0.0	**Enforcing contracts** (rank)	93
Cost (% of income per capita)	1,016.0	Private bureau coverage (% of adults)	0.0	Procedures (number)	39
				Time (days)	457
Employing workers (rank)	30	**Protecting investors** (rank)	51	Cost (% of claim)	32.0
Difficulty of hiring index (0–100)	0	Extent of disclosure index (0–10)	5		
Rigidity of hours index (0–100)	0	Extent of director liability index (0–10)	7	**Closing a business** (rank)	89
Difficulty of firing index (0–100)	20	Ease of shareholder suits index (0–10)	5	Time (years)	2.0
Rigidity of employment index (0–100)	7	Strength of investor protection index (0–10)	5.7	Cost (% of estate)	22
Nonwage labor cost (% of salary)	9			Recovery rate (cents on the dollar)	27.5
Firing cost (weeks of salary)	50	**Paying taxes** (rank)	107		
		Payments (number per year)	35		
		Time (hours per year)	1,120		
		Total tax rate (% of profit)	29.9		

NORWAY

Ease of doing business (rank)	11	OECD: High Income		GNI per capita (US$)	66,530
		High income		Population (m)	4.6
Starting a business (rank)	28	**Registering property** (rank)	6	**Trading across borders** (rank)	4
Procedures (number)	6	Procedures (number)	1	Documents to export (number)	4
Time (days)	10	Time (days)	3	Time to export (days)	7
Cost (% of income per capita)	2.3	Cost (% of property value)	2.5	Cost to export (US$ per container)	518
Minimum capital (% of income per capita)	23.4			Documents to import (number)	4
		Getting credit (rank)	36	Time to import (days)	7
Dealing with licenses (rank)	55	Strength of legal rights index (0–10)	6	Cost to import (US$ per container)	468
Procedures (number)	14	Depth of credit information index (0–6)	4		
Time (days)	252	Public registry coverage (% of adults)	0.0	**Enforcing contracts** (rank)	9
Cost (% of income per capita)	46.2	Private bureau coverage (% of adults)	100.0	Procedures (number)	33
				Time (days)	310
Employing workers (rank)	94	**Protecting investors** (rank)	15	Cost (% of claim)	9.9
Difficulty of hiring index (0–100)	61	Extent of disclosure index (0–10)	7		
Rigidity of hours index (0–100)	40	Extent of director liability index (0–10)	6	**Closing a business** (rank)	3
Difficulty of firing index (0–100)	40	Ease of shareholder suits index (0–10)	7	Time (years)	0.9
Rigidity of employment index (0–100)	47	Strength of investor protection index (0–10)	6.7	Cost (% of estate)	1
Nonwage labor cost (% of salary)	14			Recovery rate (cents on the dollar)	90.7
Firing cost (weeks of salary)	13	**Paying taxes** (rank)	16		
		Payments (number per year)	4		
		Time (hours per year)	87		
		Total tax rate (% of profit)	42.0		

OMAN

Ease of doing business (rank)	49	Middle East & North Africa Upper middle income		GNI per capita (US$) Population (m)	9,587 2.6
Starting a business (rank)	107	**Registering property** (rank)	15	**Trading across borders** (rank)	104
Procedures (number)	9	Procedures (number)	2	Documents to export (number)	10
Time (days)	34	Time (days)	16	Time to export (days)	22
Cost (% of income per capita)	4.3	Cost (% of property value)	3.0	Cost to export (US$ per container)	665
Minimum capital (% of income per capita)	541.8			Documents to import (number)	10
		Getting credit (rank)	97	Time to import (days)	26
Dealing with licenses (rank)	130	Strength of legal rights index (0–10)	4	Cost to import (US$ per container)	824
Procedures (number)	16	Depth of credit information index (0–6)	2		
Time (days)	242	Public registry coverage (% of adults)	12.4	**Enforcing contracts** (rank)	110
Cost (% of income per capita)	847.6	Private bureau coverage (% of adults)	0.0	Procedures (number)	51
				Time (days)	598
Employing workers (rank)	26	**Protecting investors** (rank)	64	Cost (% of claim)	13.5
Difficulty of hiring index (0–100)	33	Extent of disclosure index (0–10)	8		
Rigidity of hours index (0–100)	40	Extent of director liability index (0–10)	5	**Closing a business** (rank)	59
Difficulty of firing index (0–100)	0	Ease of shareholder suits index (0–10)	3	Time (years)	4.0
Rigidity of employment index (0–100)	24	Strength of investor protection index (0–10)	5.3	Cost (% of estate)	4
Nonwage labor cost (% of salary)	11			Recovery rate (cents on the dollar)	35.5
Firing cost (weeks of salary)	4	**Paying taxes** (rank)	5		
		Payments (number per year)	14		
		Time (hours per year)	62		
		Total tax rate (% of profit)	21.6		

PAKISTAN

Ease of doing business (rank)	76	South Asia Low income		GNI per capita (US$) Population (m)	770 159.0
Starting a business (rank)	59	**Registering property** (rank)	88	**Trading across borders** (rank)	94
Procedures (number)	11	Procedures (number)	6	Documents to export (number)	9
Time (days)	24	Time (days)	50	Time to export (days)	24
Cost (% of income per capita)	14.0	Cost (% of property value)	5.3	Cost to export (US$ per container)	515
Minimum capital (% of income per capita)	0.0			Documents to import (number)	8
		Getting credit (rank)	68	Time to import (days)	19
Dealing with licenses (rank)	93	Strength of legal rights index (0–10)	4	Cost to import (US$ per container)	1,336
Procedures (number)	12	Depth of credit information index (0–6)	4		
Time (days)	223	Public registry coverage (% of adults)	4.6	**Enforcing contracts** (rank)	154
Cost (% of income per capita)	869.5	Private bureau coverage (% of adults)	1.4	Procedures (number)	47
				Time (days)	880
Employing workers (rank)	132	**Protecting investors** (rank)	19	Cost (% of claim)	23.8
Difficulty of hiring index (0–100)	78	Extent of disclosure index (0–10)	6		
Rigidity of hours index (0–100)	20	Extent of director liability index (0–10)	6	**Closing a business** (rank)	51
Difficulty of firing index (0–100)	30	Ease of shareholder suits index (0–10)	7	Time (years)	2.8
Rigidity of employment index (0–100)	43	Strength of investor protection index (0–10)	6.3	Cost (% of estate)	4
Nonwage labor cost (% of salary)	11			Recovery rate (cents on the dollar)	39.1
Firing cost (weeks of salary)	90	**Paying taxes** (rank)	146		
		Payments (number per year)	47		
		Time (hours per year)	560		
		Total tax rate (% of profit)	40.7		

PALAU

Ease of doing business (rank)	82	East Asia & Pacific Upper middle income		GNI per capita (US$) Population (m)	7,990 0.0
Starting a business (rank)	56	**Registering property** (rank)	14	**Trading across borders** (rank)	121
Procedures (number)	8	Procedures (number)	5	Documents to export (number)	6
Time (days)	28	Time (days)	14	Time to export (days)	29
Cost (% of income per capita)	4.7	Cost (% of property value)	0.4	Cost to export (US$ per container)	1,160
Minimum capital (% of income per capita)	12.5			Documents to import (number)	10
		Getting credit (rank)	170	Time to import (days)	35
Dealing with licenses (rank)	47	Strength of legal rights index (0–10)	2	Cost to import (US$ per container)	1,110
Procedures (number)	25	Depth of credit information index (0–6)	0		
Time (days)	118	Public registry coverage (% of adults)	0.0	**Enforcing contracts** (rank)	142
Cost (% of income per capita)	6.1	Private bureau coverage (% of adults)	0.0	Procedures (number)	38
				Time (days)	885
Employing workers (rank)	9	**Protecting investors** (rank)	165	Cost (% of claim)	35.3
Difficulty of hiring index (0–100)	11	Extent of disclosure index (0–10)	0		
Rigidity of hours index (0–100)	0	Extent of director liability index (0–10)	0	**Closing a business** (rank)	55
Difficulty of firing index (0–100)	0	Ease of shareholder suits index (0–10)	8	Time (years)	1.0
Rigidity of employment index (0–100)	4	Strength of investor protection index (0–10)	2.7	Cost (% of estate)	23
Nonwage labor cost (% of salary)	6			Recovery rate (cents on the dollar)	38.2
Firing cost (weeks of salary)	0	**Paying taxes** (rank)	73		
		Payments (number per year)	19		
		Time (hours per year)	128		
		Total tax rate (% of profit)	73.0		

PANAMA

Ease of doing business (rank)	65	Latin America & Caribbean		GNI per capita (US$)	4,890
		Upper middle income		Population (m)	3.3
Starting a business (rank)	31	**Registering property** (rank)	61	**Trading across borders** (rank)	9
Procedures (number)	7	Procedures (number)	7	Documents to export (number)	3
Time (days)	19	Time (days)	44	Time to export (days)	9
Cost (% of income per capita)	22.0	Cost (% of property value)	2.4	Cost to export (US$ per container)	650
Minimum capital (% of income per capita)	0.0			Documents to import (number)	4
		Getting credit (rank)	13	Time to import (days)	9
Dealing with licenses (rank)	89	Strength of legal rights index (0–10)	6	Cost to import (US$ per container)	850
Procedures (number)	25	Depth of credit information index (0–6)	6		
Time (days)	149	Public registry coverage (% of adults)	0.0	**Enforcing contracts** (rank)	116
Cost (% of income per capita)	143.9	Private bureau coverage (% of adults)	41.6	Procedures (number)	31
				Time (days)	686
Employing workers (rank)	170	**Protecting investors** (rank)	98	Cost (% of claim)	50.0
Difficulty of hiring index (0–100)	78	Extent of disclosure index (0–10)	1		
Rigidity of hours index (0–100)	60	Extent of director liability index (0–10)	4	**Closing a business** (rank)	74
Difficulty of firing index (0–100)	70	Ease of shareholder suits index (0–10)	9	Time (years)	2.5
Rigidity of employment index (0–100)	69	Strength of investor protection index (0–10)	4.7	Cost (% of estate)	18
Nonwage labor cost (% of salary)	19			Recovery rate (cents on the dollar)	32.3
Firing cost (weeks of salary)	44	**Paying taxes** (rank)	169		
		Payments (number per year)	59		
		Time (hours per year)	482		
		Total tax rate (% of profit)	50.8		

PAPUA NEW GUINEA

Ease of doing business (rank)	84	East Asia & Pacific		GNI per capita (US$)	770
		Low income		Population (m)	6.0
Starting a business (rank)	76	**Registering property** (rank)	64	**Trading across borders** (rank)	82
Procedures (number)	8	Procedures (number)	4	Documents to export (number)	7
Time (days)	56	Time (days)	72	Time to export (days)	26
Cost (% of income per capita)	26.4	Cost (% of property value)	5.1	Cost to export (US$ per container)	584
Minimum capital (% of income per capita)	0.0			Documents to import (number)	9
		Getting credit (rank)	115	Time to import (days)	29
Dealing with licenses (rank)	118	Strength of legal rights index (0–10)	5	Cost to import (US$ per container)	642
Procedures (number)	24	Depth of credit information index (0–6)	0		
Time (days)	217	Public registry coverage (% of adults)	0.0	**Enforcing contracts** (rank)	162
Cost (% of income per capita)	106.3	Private bureau coverage (% of adults)	0.0	Procedures (number)	43
				Time (days)	591
Employing workers (rank)	31	**Protecting investors** (rank)	33	Cost (% of claim)	110.3
Difficulty of hiring index (0–100)	11	Extent of disclosure index (0–10)	5		
Rigidity of hours index (0–100)	20	Extent of director liability index (0–10)	5	**Closing a business** (rank)	97
Difficulty of firing index (0–100)	0	Ease of shareholder suits index (0–10)	8	Time (years)	3.0
Rigidity of employment index (0–100)	10	Strength of investor protection index (0–10)	6.0	Cost (% of estate)	23
Nonwage labor cost (% of salary)	10			Recovery rate (cents on the dollar)	23.9
Firing cost (weeks of salary)	39	**Paying taxes** (rank)	79		
		Payments (number per year)	33		
		Time (hours per year)	206		
		Total tax rate (% of profit)	41.7		

PARAGUAY

Ease of doing business (rank)	103	Latin America & Caribbean		GNI per capita (US$)	1,400
		Lower middle income		Population (m)	6.0
Starting a business (rank)	66	**Registering property** (rank)	55	**Trading across borders** (rank)	123
Procedures (number)	7	Procedures (number)	6	Documents to export (number)	9
Time (days)	35	Time (days)	46	Time to export (days)	35
Cost (% of income per capita)	77.6	Cost (% of property value)	3.5	Cost to export (US$ per container)	720
Minimum capital (% of income per capita)	0.0			Documents to import (number)	10
		Getting credit (rank)	48	Time to import (days)	33
Dealing with licenses (rank)	98	Strength of legal rights index (0–10)	3	Cost to import (US$ per container)	900
Procedures (number)	13	Depth of credit information index (0–6)	6		
Time (days)	291	Public registry coverage (% of adults)	11.0	**Enforcing contracts** (rank)	105
Cost (% of income per capita)	439.0	Private bureau coverage (% of adults)	48.7	Procedures (number)	38
				Time (days)	591
Employing workers (rank)	173	**Protecting investors** (rank)	51	Cost (% of claim)	30.0
Difficulty of hiring index (0–100)	56	Extent of disclosure index (0–10)	6		
Rigidity of hours index (0–100)	60	Extent of director liability index (0–10)	5	**Closing a business** (rank)	132
Difficulty of firing index (0–100)	60	Ease of shareholder suits index (0–10)	6	Time (years)	3.9
Rigidity of employment index (0–100)	59	Strength of investor protection index (0–10)	5.7	Cost (% of estate)	9
Nonwage labor cost (% of salary)	17			Recovery rate (cents on the dollar)	14.6
Firing cost (weeks of salary)	113	**Paying taxes** (rank)	93		
		Payments (number per year)	35		
		Time (hours per year)	328		
		Total tax rate (% of profit)	35.3		

PERU

Ease of doing business (rank)	58	Latin America & Caribbean		GNI per capita (US$)	2,920
		Lower middle income		Population (m)	28.4
Starting a business (rank)	102	**Registering property** (rank)	35	**Trading across borders** (rank)	71
Procedures (number)	10	Procedures (number)	5	Documents to export (number)	7
Time (days)	72	Time (days)	33	Time to export (days)	24
Cost (% of income per capita)	29.9	Cost (% of property value)	3.3	Cost to export (US$ per container)	590
Minimum capital (% of income per capita)	0.0			Documents to import (number)	8
		Getting credit (rank)	36	Time to import (days)	31
Dealing with licenses (rank)	109	Strength of legal rights index (0–10)	4	Cost to import (US$ per container)	670
Procedures (number)	21	Depth of credit information index (0–6)	6		
Time (days)	210	Public registry coverage (% of adults)	20.7	**Enforcing contracts** (rank)	119
Cost (% of income per capita)	165.0	Private bureau coverage (% of adults)	33.0	Procedures (number)	41
				Time (days)	468
Employing workers (rank)	159	**Protecting investors** (rank)	15	Cost (% of claim)	35.7
Difficulty of hiring index (0–100)	44	Extent of disclosure index (0–10)	8		
Rigidity of hours index (0–100)	60	Extent of director liability index (0–10)	5	**Closing a business** (rank)	94
Difficulty of firing index (0–100)	60	Ease of shareholder suits index (0–10)	7	Time (years)	3.1
Rigidity of employment index (0–100)	55	Strength of investor protection index (0–10)	6.7	Cost (% of estate)	7
Nonwage labor cost (% of salary)	10			Recovery rate (cents on the dollar)	24.7
Firing cost (weeks of salary)	52	**Paying taxes** (rank)	77		
		Payments (number per year)	9		
		Time (hours per year)	424		
		Total tax rate (% of profit)	41.5		

PHILIPPINES

Ease of doing business (rank)	133	East Asia & Pacific		GNI per capita (US$)	1,420
		Lower middle income		Population (m)	84.6
Starting a business (rank)	144	**Registering property** (rank)	86	**Trading across borders** (rank)	57
Procedures (number)	15	Procedures (number)	8	Documents to export (number)	8
Time (days)	58	Time (days)	33	Time to export (days)	17
Cost (% of income per capita)	26.8	Cost (% of property value)	4.2	Cost to export (US$ per container)	800
Minimum capital (% of income per capita)	6.9			Documents to import (number)	8
		Getting credit (rank)	97	Time to import (days)	18
Dealing with licenses (rank)	77	Strength of legal rights index (0–10)	3	Cost to import (US$ per container)	800
Procedures (number)	21	Depth of credit information index (0–6)	3		
Time (days)	177	Public registry coverage (% of adults)	0.0	**Enforcing contracts** (rank)	113
Cost (% of income per capita)	75.9	Private bureau coverage (% of adults)	5.5	Procedures (number)	37
				Time (days)	842
Employing workers (rank)	122	**Protecting investors** (rank)	141	Cost (% of claim)	26.0
Difficulty of hiring index (0–100)	56	Extent of disclosure index (0–10)	1		
Rigidity of hours index (0–100)	20	Extent of director liability index (0–10)	2	**Closing a business** (rank)	147
Difficulty of firing index (0–100)	30	Ease of shareholder suits index (0–10)	8	Time (years)	5.7
Rigidity of employment index (0–100)	35	Strength of investor protection index (0–10)	3.7	Cost (% of estate)	38
Nonwage labor cost (% of salary)	7			Recovery rate (cents on the dollar)	4.2
Firing cost (weeks of salary)	91	**Paying taxes** (rank)	126		
		Payments (number per year)	47		
		Time (hours per year)	195		
		Total tax rate (% of profit)	52.8		

POLAND

Ease of doing business (rank)	74	Eastern Europe & Central Asia		GNI per capita (US$)	8,190
		Upper middle income		Population (m)	38.1
Starting a business (rank)	129	**Registering property** (rank)	81	**Trading across borders** (rank)	40
Procedures (number)	10	Procedures (number)	6	Documents to export (number)	5
Time (days)	31	Time (days)	197	Time to export (days)	17
Cost (% of income per capita)	21.2	Cost (% of property value)	0.5	Cost to export (US$ per container)	834
Minimum capital (% of income per capita)	196.8			Documents to import (number)	5
		Getting credit (rank)	68	Time to import (days)	27
Dealing with licenses (rank)	156	Strength of legal rights index (0–10)	4	Cost to import (US$ per container)	834
Procedures (number)	30	Depth of credit information index (0–6)	4		
Time (days)	308	Public registry coverage (% of adults)	0.0	**Enforcing contracts** (rank)	68
Cost (% of income per capita)	159.8	Private bureau coverage (% of adults)	51.5	Procedures (number)	38
				Time (days)	830
Employing workers (rank)	78	**Protecting investors** (rank)	33	Cost (% of claim)	10.0
Difficulty of hiring index (0–100)	11	Extent of disclosure index (0–10)	7		
Rigidity of hours index (0–100)	60	Extent of director liability index (0–10)	2	**Closing a business** (rank)	88
Difficulty of firing index (0–100)	40	Ease of shareholder suits index (0–10)	9	Time (years)	3.0
Rigidity of employment index (0–100)	37	Strength of investor protection index (0–10)	6.0	Cost (% of estate)	22
Nonwage labor cost (% of salary)	21			Recovery rate (cents on the dollar)	27.8
Firing cost (weeks of salary)	13	**Paying taxes** (rank)	125		
		Payments (number per year)	41		
		Time (hours per year)	418		
		Total tax rate (% of profit)	38.4		

PORTUGAL

Ease of doing business (rank)	37
OECD: High Income	
High income	
GNI per capita (US$)	18,100
Population (m)	10.6
Starting a business (rank)	38
Procedures (number)	7
Time (days)	7
Cost (% of income per capita)	3.4
Minimum capital (% of income per capita)	34.7
Dealing with licenses (rank)	112
Procedures (number)	20
Time (days)	327
Cost (% of income per capita)	54.0
Employing workers (rank)	157
Difficulty of hiring index (0–100)	33
Rigidity of hours index (0–100)	60
Difficulty of firing index (0–100)	50
Rigidity of employment index (0–100)	48
Nonwage labor cost (% of salary)	24
Firing cost (weeks of salary)	95
Registering property (rank)	65
Procedures (number)	5
Time (days)	42
Cost (% of property value)	7.4
Getting credit (rank)	68
Strength of legal rights index (0–10)	4
Depth of credit information index (0–6)	4
Public registry coverage (% of adults)	67.1
Private bureau coverage (% of adults)	11.3
Protecting investors (rank)	33
Extent of disclosure index (0–10)	6
Extent of director liability index (0–10)	5
Ease of shareholder suits index (0–10)	7
Strength of investor protection index (0–10)	6.0
Paying taxes (rank)	66
Payments (number per year)	8
Time (hours per year)	328
Total tax rate (% of profit)	44.8
Trading across borders (rank)	31
Documents to export (number)	6
Time to export (days)	16
Cost to export (US$ per container)	580
Documents to import (number)	7
Time to import (days)	16
Cost to import (US$ per container)	994
Enforcing contracts (rank)	49
Procedures (number)	35
Time (days)	577
Cost (% of claim)	17.7
Closing a business (rank)	20
Time (years)	2.0
Cost (% of estate)	9
Recovery rate (cents on the dollar)	74.0

PUERTO RICO

Ease of doing business (rank)	28
Latin America & Caribbean	
High income	
GNI per capita (US$)	14,371
Population (m)	3.9
Starting a business (rank)	7
Procedures (number)	7
Time (days)	7
Cost (% of income per capita)	0.8
Minimum capital (% of income per capita)	0.0
Dealing with licenses (rank)	135
Procedures (number)	22
Time (days)	209
Cost (% of income per capita)	550.8
Employing workers (rank)	32
Difficulty of hiring index (0–100)	44
Rigidity of hours index (0–100)	0
Difficulty of firing index (0–100)	20
Rigidity of employment index (0–100)	21
Nonwage labor cost (% of salary)	13
Firing cost (weeks of salary)	0
Registering property (rank)	117
Procedures (number)	8
Time (days)	194
Cost (% of property value)	1.4
Getting credit (rank)	26
Strength of legal rights index (0–10)	6
Depth of credit information index (0–6)	5
Public registry coverage (% of adults)	0.0
Private bureau coverage (% of adults)	62.0
Protecting investors (rank)	12
Extent of disclosure index (0–10)	7
Extent of director liability index (0–10)	6
Ease of shareholder suits index (0–10)	8
Strength of investor protection index (0–10)	7.0
Paying taxes (rank)	39
Payments (number per year)	16
Time (hours per year)	140
Total tax rate (% of profit)	44.3
Trading across borders (rank)	95
Documents to export (number)	7
Time to export (days)	15
Cost to export (US$ per container)	1,225
Documents to import (number)	10
Time to import (days)	16
Cost to import (US$ per container)	1,225
Enforcing contracts (rank)	88
Procedures (number)	41
Time (days)	620
Cost (% of claim)	16.4
Closing a business (rank)	28
Time (years)	3.8
Cost (% of estate)	8
Recovery rate (cents on the dollar)	54.1

ROMANIA

Ease of doing business (rank)	48
Eastern Europe & Central Asia	
Upper middle income	
GNI per capita (US$)	4,850
Population (m)	21.5
Starting a business (rank)	26
Procedures (number)	6
Time (days)	14
Cost (% of income per capita)	4.7
Minimum capital (% of income per capita)	1.5
Dealing with licenses (rank)	90
Procedures (number)	17
Time (days)	243
Cost (% of income per capita)	124.3
Employing workers (rank)	145
Difficulty of hiring index (0–100)	78
Rigidity of hours index (0–100)	80
Difficulty of firing index (0–100)	40
Rigidity of employment index (0–100)	66
Nonwage labor cost (% of salary)	31
Firing cost (weeks of salary)	8
Registering property (rank)	123
Procedures (number)	8
Time (days)	150
Cost (% of property value)	2.8
Getting credit (rank)	13
Strength of legal rights index (0–10)	7
Depth of credit information index (0–6)	5
Public registry coverage (% of adults)	4.1
Private bureau coverage (% of adults)	10.9
Protecting investors (rank)	33
Extent of disclosure index (0–10)	9
Extent of director liability index (0–10)	5
Ease of shareholder suits index (0–10)	4
Strength of investor protection index (0–10)	6.0
Paying taxes (rank)	134
Payments (number per year)	96
Time (hours per year)	202
Total tax rate (% of profit)	46.9
Trading across borders (rank)	38
Documents to export (number)	5
Time to export (days)	12
Cost to export (US$ per container)	1,075
Documents to import (number)	6
Time to import (days)	13
Cost to import (US$ per container)	1,075
Enforcing contracts (rank)	37
Procedures (number)	32
Time (days)	537
Cost (% of claim)	19.9
Closing a business (rank)	81
Time (years)	3.3
Cost (% of estate)	9
Recovery rate (cents on the dollar)	28.9

RUSSIA

Ease of doing business (rank)	106	Eastern Europe & Central Asia		GNI per capita (US$)	5,780
		Upper middle income		Population (m)	142.4
Starting a business (rank)	50	**Registering property** (rank)	45	**Trading across borders** (rank)	155
Procedures (number)	8	Procedures (number)	6	Documents to export (number)	8
Time (days)	29	Time (days)	52	Time to export (days)	36
Cost (% of income per capita)	3.7	Cost (% of property value)	0.3	Cost to export (US$ per container)	2,050
Minimum capital (% of income per capita)	3.2			Documents to import (number)	13
		Getting credit (rank)	84	Time to import (days)	36
Dealing with licenses (rank)	177	Strength of legal rights index (0–10)	3	Cost to import (US$ per container)	2,050
Procedures (number)	54	Depth of credit information index (0–6)	4		
Time (days)	704	Public registry coverage (% of adults)	0.0	**Enforcing contracts** (rank)	19
Cost (% of income per capita)	3,788.4	Private bureau coverage (% of adults)	4.4	Procedures (number)	37
				Time (days)	281
Employing workers (rank)	101	**Protecting investors** (rank)	83	Cost (% of claim)	13.4
Difficulty of hiring index (0–100)	33	Extent of disclosure index (0–10)	6		
Rigidity of hours index (0–100)	60	Extent of director liability index (0–10)	2	**Closing a business** (rank)	80
Difficulty of firing index (0–100)	40	Ease of shareholder suits index (0–10)	7	Time (years)	3.8
Rigidity of employment index (0–100)	44	Strength of investor protection index (0–10)	5.0	Cost (% of estate)	9
Nonwage labor cost (% of salary)	31			Recovery rate (cents on the dollar)	29.0
Firing cost (weeks of salary)	17	**Paying taxes** (rank)	130		
		Payments (number per year)	22		
		Time (hours per year)	448		
		Total tax rate (% of profit)	51.4		

RWANDA

Ease of doing business (rank)	150	Sub-Saharan Africa		GNI per capita (US$)	250
		Low income		Population (m)	9.2
Starting a business (rank)	63	**Registering property** (rank)	137	**Trading across borders** (rank)	166
Procedures (number)	9	Procedures (number)	5	Documents to export (number)	9
Time (days)	16	Time (days)	371	Time to export (days)	47
Cost (% of income per capita)	171.5	Cost (% of property value)	9.4	Cost to export (US$ per container)	2,975
Minimum capital (% of income per capita)	0.0			Documents to import (number)	9
		Getting credit (rank)	158	Time to import (days)	69
Dealing with licenses (rank)	124	Strength of legal rights index (0–10)	1	Cost to import (US$ per container)	4,970
Procedures (number)	16	Depth of credit information index (0–6)	2		
Time (days)	227	Public registry coverage (% of adults)	0.2	**Enforcing contracts** (rank)	44
Cost (% of income per capita)	822.1	Private bureau coverage (% of adults)	0.0	Procedures (number)	24
				Time (days)	310
Employing workers (rank)	95	**Protecting investors** (rank)	165	Cost (% of claim)	78.7
Difficulty of hiring index (0–100)	56	Extent of disclosure index (0–10)	2		
Rigidity of hours index (0–100)	40	Extent of director liability index (0–10)	5	**Closing a business** (rank)	178
Difficulty of firing index (0–100)	30	Ease of shareholder suits index (0–10)	1	Time (years)	NO PRACTICE
Rigidity of employment index (0–100)	42	Strength of investor protection index (0–10)	2.7	Cost (% of estate)	NO PRACTICE
Nonwage labor cost (% of salary)	5			Recovery rate (cents on the dollar)	0.0
Firing cost (weeks of salary)	26	**Paying taxes** (rank)	50		
		Payments (number per year)	34		
		Time (hours per year)	168		
		Total tax rate (% of profit)	33.8		

SAMOA

Ease of doing business (rank)	61	East Asia & Pacific		GNI per capita (US$)	2,270
		Lower middle income		Population (m)	0.2
Starting a business (rank)	104	**Registering property** (rank)	58	**Trading across borders** (rank)	108
Procedures (number)	9	Procedures (number)	5	Documents to export (number)	7
Time (days)	35	Time (days)	147	Time to export (days)	27
Cost (% of income per capita)	41.3	Cost (% of property value)	1.8	Cost to export (US$ per container)	1,010
Minimum capital (% of income per capita)	0.0			Documents to import (number)	7
		Getting credit (rank)	135	Time to import (days)	31
Dealing with licenses (rank)	41	Strength of legal rights index (0–10)	4	Cost to import (US$ per container)	1,375
Procedures (number)	18	Depth of credit information index (0–6)	0		
Time (days)	88	Public registry coverage (% of adults)	0.0	**Enforcing contracts** (rank)	80
Cost (% of income per capita)	95.4	Private bureau coverage (% of adults)	0.0	Procedures (number)	44
				Time (days)	455
Employing workers (rank)	15	**Protecting investors** (rank)	19	Cost (% of claim)	19.7
Difficulty of hiring index (0–100)	11	Extent of disclosure index (0–10)	5		
Rigidity of hours index (0–100)	20	Extent of director liability index (0–10)	6	**Closing a business** (rank)	129
Difficulty of firing index (0–100)	0	Ease of shareholder suits index (0–10)	8	Time (years)	2.5
Rigidity of employment index (0–100)	10	Strength of investor protection index (0–10)	6.3	Cost (% of estate)	38
Nonwage labor cost (% of salary)	6			Recovery rate (cents on the dollar)	15.2
Firing cost (weeks of salary)	9	**Paying taxes** (rank)	53		
		Payments (number per year)	37		
		Time (hours per year)	224		
		Total tax rate (% of profit)	19.8		

SAO TOME AND PRINCIPE

Ease of doing business (rank)	163	Sub-Saharan Africa		GNI per capita (US$)	780
		Low income		Population (m)	0.2
Starting a business (rank)	126	**Registering property** (rank)	146	**Trading across borders** (rank)	91
Procedures (number)	10	Procedures (number)	7	Documents to export (number)	8
Time (days)	144	Time (days)	62	Time to export (days)	27
Cost (% of income per capita)	94.5	Cost (% of property value)	12.6	Cost to export (US$ per container)	690
Minimum capital (% of income per capita)	0.0			Documents to import (number)	9
		Getting credit (rank)	115	Time to import (days)	29
Dealing with licenses (rank)	113	Strength of legal rights index (0–10)	5	Cost to import (US$ per container)	577
Procedures (number)	13	Depth of credit information index (0–6)	0		
Time (days)	255	Public registry coverage (% of adults)	0.0	**Enforcing contracts** (rank)	115
Cost (% of income per capita)	825.9	Private bureau coverage (% of adults)	0.0	Procedures (number)	43
				Time (days)	405
Employing workers (rank)	176	**Protecting investors** (rank)	122	Cost (% of claim)	34.8
Difficulty of hiring index (0–100)	50	Extent of disclosure index (0–10)	5		
Rigidity of hours index (0–100)	80	Extent of director liability index (0–10)	1	**Closing a business** (rank)	178
Difficulty of firing index (0–100)	60	Ease of shareholder suits index (0–10)	6	Time (years)	NO PRACTICE
Rigidity of employment index (0–100)	63	Strength of investor protection index (0–10)	4.0	Cost (% of estate)	NO PRACTICE
Nonwage labor cost (% of salary)	6			Recovery rate (cents on the dollar)	0.0
Firing cost (weeks of salary)	91	**Paying taxes** (rank)	153		
		Payments (number per year)	41		
		Time (hours per year)	424		
		Total tax rate (% of profit)	51.0		

SAUDI ARABIA

Ease of doing business (rank)	23	Middle East & North Africa		GNI per capita (US$)	12,464
		High income		Population (m)	23.7
Starting a business (rank)	36	**Registering property** (rank)	3	**Trading across borders** (rank)	33
Procedures (number)	7	Procedures (number)	4	Documents to export (number)	5
Time (days)	15	Time (days)	4	Time to export (days)	19
Cost (% of income per capita)	32.3	Cost (% of property value)	0.0	Cost to export (US$ per container)	1,008
Minimum capital (% of income per capita)	0.0			Documents to import (number)	5
		Getting credit (rank)	48	Time to import (days)	20
Dealing with licenses (rank)	47	Strength of legal rights index (0–10)	3	Cost to import (US$ per container)	758
Procedures (number)	18	Depth of credit information index (0–6)	6		
Time (days)	125	Public registry coverage (% of adults)	0.0	**Enforcing contracts** (rank)	136
Cost (% of income per capita)	94.5	Private bureau coverage (% of adults)	23.5	Procedures (number)	44
				Time (days)	635
Employing workers (rank)	40	**Protecting investors** (rank)	50	Cost (% of claim)	27.5
Difficulty of hiring index (0–100)	0	Extent of disclosure index (0–10)	7		
Rigidity of hours index (0–100)	40	Extent of director liability index (0–10)	7	**Closing a business** (rank)	79
Difficulty of firing index (0–100)	0	Ease of shareholder suits index (0–10)	3	Time (years)	2.8
Rigidity of employment index (0–100)	13	Strength of investor protection index (0–10)	5.7	Cost (% of estate)	22
Nonwage labor cost (% of salary)	11			Recovery rate (cents on the dollar)	29.3
Firing cost (weeks of salary)	80	**Paying taxes** (rank)	7		
		Payments (number per year)	14		
		Time (hours per year)	79		
		Total tax rate (% of profit)	14.5		

SENEGAL

Ease of doing business (rank)	162	Sub-Saharan Africa		GNI per capita (US$)	750
		Low income		Population (m)	11.9
Starting a business (rank)	159	**Registering property** (rank)	155	**Trading across borders** (rank)	136
Procedures (number)	10	Procedures (number)	6	Documents to export (number)	11
Time (days)	58	Time (days)	114	Time to export (days)	20
Cost (% of income per capita)	107.0	Cost (% of property value)	19.5	Cost to export (US$ per container)	828
Minimum capital (% of income per capita)	255.0			Documents to import (number)	11
		Getting credit (rank)	135	Time to import (days)	26
Dealing with licenses (rank)	64	Strength of legal rights index (0–10)	3	Cost to import (US$ per container)	1,720
Procedures (number)	14	Depth of credit information index (0–6)	1		
Time (days)	217	Public registry coverage (% of adults)	4.0	**Enforcing contracts** (rank)	148
Cost (% of income per capita)	176.9	Private bureau coverage (% of adults)	0.0	Procedures (number)	44
				Time (days)	780
Employing workers (rank)	160	**Protecting investors** (rank)	158	Cost (% of claim)	26.5
Difficulty of hiring index (0–100)	72	Extent of disclosure index (0–10)	6		
Rigidity of hours index (0–100)	60	Extent of director liability index (0–10)	1	**Closing a business** (rank)	73
Difficulty of firing index (0–100)	50	Ease of shareholder suits index (0–10)	2	Time (years)	3.0
Rigidity of employment index (0–100)	61	Strength of investor protection index (0–10)	3.0	Cost (% of estate)	7
Nonwage labor cost (% of salary)	21			Recovery rate (cents on the dollar)	32.4
Firing cost (weeks of salary)	38	**Paying taxes** (rank)	164		
		Payments (number per year)	59		
		Time (hours per year)	696		
		Total tax rate (% of profit)	46.0		

SERBIA

Ease of doing business (rank)	86	Eastern Europe & Central Asia		GNI per capita (US$)	3,910
		Lower middle income		Population (m)	10.2
Starting a business (rank)	90	**Registering property** (rank)	115	**Trading across borders** (rank)	58
Procedures (number)	11	Procedures (number)	6	Documents to export (number)	6
Time (days)	23	Time (days)	111	Time to export (days)	12
Cost (% of income per capita)	8.9	Cost (% of property value)	5.4	Cost to export (US$ per container)	1,240
Minimum capital (% of income per capita)	8.0			Documents to import (number)	6
		Getting credit (rank)	13	Time to import (days)	14
Dealing with licenses (rank)	149	Strength of legal rights index (0–10)	7	Cost to import (US$ per container)	1,440
Procedures (number)	20	Depth of credit information index (0–6)	5		
Time (days)	204	Public registry coverage (% of adults)	0.1	**Enforcing contracts** (rank)	101
Cost (% of income per capita)	2,713.1	Private bureau coverage (% of adults)	51.3	Procedures (number)	36
				Time (days)	635
Employing workers (rank)	110	**Protecting investors** (rank)	64	Cost (% of claim)	28.4
Difficulty of hiring index (0–100)	67	Extent of disclosure index (0–10)	7		
Rigidity of hours index (0–100)	40	Extent of director liability index (0–10)	6	**Closing a business** (rank)	103
Difficulty of firing index (0–100)	30	Ease of shareholder suits index (0–10)	3	Time (years)	2.7
Rigidity of employment index (0–100)	46	Strength of investor protection index (0–10)	5.3	Cost (% of estate)	23
Nonwage labor cost (% of salary)	18			Recovery rate (cents on the dollar)	23.1
Firing cost (weeks of salary)	25	**Paying taxes** (rank)	121		
		Payments (number per year)	66		
		Time (hours per year)	279		
		Total tax rate (% of profit)	35.8		

SEYCHELLES

Ease of doing business (rank)	90	Sub-Saharan Africa		GNI per capita (US$)	8,650
		Upper middle income		Population (m)	0.1
Starting a business (rank)	48	**Registering property** (rank)	50	**Trading across borders** (rank)	84
Procedures (number)	9	Procedures (number)	4	Documents to export (number)	6
Time (days)	38	Time (days)	33	Time to export (days)	17
Cost (% of income per capita)	8.7	Cost (% of property value)	7.0	Cost to export (US$ per container)	1,839
Minimum capital (% of income per capita)	0.0			Documents to import (number)	5
		Getting credit (rank)	158	Time to import (days)	19
Dealing with licenses (rank)	51	Strength of legal rights index (0–10)	3	Cost to import (US$ per container)	1,839
Procedures (number)	19	Depth of credit information index (0–6)	0		
Time (days)	144	Public registry coverage (% of adults)	0.0	**Enforcing contracts** (rank)	66
Cost (% of income per capita)	46.5	Private bureau coverage (% of adults)	0.0	Procedures (number)	38
				Time (days)	720
Employing workers (rank)	97	**Protecting investors** (rank)	51	Cost (% of claim)	14.3
Difficulty of hiring index (0–100)	33	Extent of disclosure index (0–10)	4		
Rigidity of hours index (0–100)	20	Extent of director liability index (0–10)	8	**Closing a business** (rank)	178
Difficulty of firing index (0–100)	50	Ease of shareholder suits index (0–10)	5	Time (years)	NO PRACTICE
Rigidity of employment index (0–100)	34	Strength of investor protection index (0–10)	5.7	Cost (% of estate)	NO PRACTICE
Nonwage labor cost (% of salary)	25			Recovery rate (cents on the dollar)	0.0
Firing cost (weeks of salary)	39	**Paying taxes** (rank)	35		
		Payments (number per year)	16		
		Time (hours per year)	76		
		Total tax rate (% of profit)	48.4		

SIERRA LEONE

Ease of doing business (rank)	160	Sub-Saharan Africa		GNI per capita (US$)	240
		Low income		Population (m)	5.6
Starting a business (rank)	89	**Registering property** (rank)	172	**Trading across borders** (rank)	130
Procedures (number)	9	Procedures (number)	8	Documents to export (number)	8
Time (days)	26	Time (days)	235	Time to export (days)	31
Cost (% of income per capita)	1,075.2	Cost (% of property value)	14.9	Cost to export (US$ per container)	1,282
Minimum capital (% of income per capita)	0.0			Documents to import (number)	7
		Getting credit (rank)	115	Time to import (days)	34
Dealing with licenses (rank)	151	Strength of legal rights index (0–10)	5	Cost to import (US$ per container)	1,242
Procedures (number)	47	Depth of credit information index (0–6)	0		
Time (days)	235	Public registry coverage (% of adults)	0.0	**Enforcing contracts** (rank)	140
Cost (% of income per capita)	191.7	Private bureau coverage (% of adults)	0.0	Procedures (number)	40
				Time (days)	515
Employing workers (rank)	169	**Protecting investors** (rank)	98	Cost (% of claim)	149.5
Difficulty of hiring index (0–100)	44	Extent of disclosure index (0–10)	3		
Rigidity of hours index (0–100)	60	Extent of director liability index (0–10)	6	**Closing a business** (rank)	141
Difficulty of firing index (0–100)	50	Ease of shareholder suits index (0–10)	5	Time (years)	2.6
Rigidity of employment index (0–100)	51	Strength of investor protection index (0–10)	4.7	Cost (% of estate)	42
Nonwage labor cost (% of salary)	10			Recovery rate (cents on the dollar)	8.5
Firing cost (weeks of salary)	189	**Paying taxes** (rank)	145		
		Payments (number per year)	22		
		Time (hours per year)	399		
		Total tax rate (% of profit)	233.5		

SINGAPORE

Ease of doing business (rank)	1	East Asia & Pacific		GNI per capita (US$)	29,320
		High income		Population (m)	4.4
Starting a business (rank)	9	**Registering property** (rank)	13	**Trading across borders** (rank)	1
Procedures (number)	5	Procedures (number)	3	Documents to export (number)	4
Time (days)	5	Time (days)	9	Time to export (days)	5
Cost (% of income per capita)	0.8	Cost (% of property value)	2.8	Cost to export (US$ per container)	416
Minimum capital (% of income per capita)	0.0			Documents to import (number)	4
		Getting credit (rank)	7	Time to import (days)	3
Dealing with licenses (rank)	5	Strength of legal rights index (0–10)	9	Cost to import (US$ per container)	367
Procedures (number)	11	Depth of credit information index (0–6)	4		
Time (days)	102	Public registry coverage (% of adults)	0.0	**Enforcing contracts** (rank)	4
Cost (% of income per capita)	22.9	Private bureau coverage (% of adults)	42.7	Procedures (number)	22
				Time (days)	120
Employing workers (rank)	1	**Protecting investors** (rank)	2	Cost (% of claim)	17.8
Difficulty of hiring index (0–100)	0	Extent of disclosure index (0–10)	10		
Rigidity of hours index (0–100)	0	Extent of director liability index (0–10)	9	**Closing a business** (rank)	2
Difficulty of firing index (0–100)	0	Ease of shareholder suits index (0–10)	9	Time (years)	0.8
Rigidity of employment index (0–100)	0	Strength of investor protection index (0–10)	9.3	Cost (% of estate)	1
Nonwage labor cost (% of salary)	13			Recovery rate (cents on the dollar)	91.3
Firing cost (weeks of salary)	4	**Paying taxes** (rank)	2		
		Payments (number per year)	5		
		Time (hours per year)	49		
		Total tax rate (% of profit)	23.2		

SLOVAKIA

Ease of doing business (rank)	32	Eastern Europe & Central Asia		GNI per capita (US$)	9,870
		Upper middle income		Population (m)	5.4
Starting a business (rank)	72	**Registering property** (rank)	5	**Trading across borders** (rank)	90
Procedures (number)	9	Procedures (number)	3	Documents to export (number)	6
Time (days)	25	Time (days)	17	Time to export (days)	25
Cost (% of income per capita)	4.2	Cost (% of property value)	0.1	Cost to export (US$ per container)	1,015
Minimum capital (% of income per capita)	34.1			Documents to import (number)	8
		Getting credit (rank)	7	Time to import (days)	25
Dealing with licenses (rank)	50	Strength of legal rights index (0–10)	9	Cost to import (US$ per container)	1,050
Procedures (number)	13	Depth of credit information index (0–6)	4		
Time (days)	287	Public registry coverage (% of adults)	1.2	**Enforcing contracts** (rank)	50
Cost (% of income per capita)	14.9	Private bureau coverage (% of adults)	56.0	Procedures (number)	30
				Time (days)	565
Employing workers (rank)	75	**Protecting investors** (rank)	98	Cost (% of claim)	25.7
Difficulty of hiring index (0–100)	17	Extent of disclosure index (0–10)	3		
Rigidity of hours index (0–100)	60	Extent of director liability index (0–10)	4	**Closing a business** (rank)	36
Difficulty of firing index (0–100)	30	Ease of shareholder suits index (0–10)	7	Time (years)	4.0
Rigidity of employment index (0–100)	36	Strength of investor protection index (0–10)	4.7	Cost (% of estate)	18
Nonwage labor cost (% of salary)	35			Recovery rate (cents on the dollar)	45.2
Firing cost (weeks of salary)	13	**Paying taxes** (rank)	122		
		Payments (number per year)	31		
		Time (hours per year)	344		
		Total tax rate (% of profit)	50.5		

SLOVENIA

Ease of doing business (rank)	55	Eastern Europe & Central Asia		GNI per capita (US$)	18,890
		High income		Population (m)	2.0
Starting a business (rank)	120	**Registering property** (rank)	99	**Trading across borders** (rank)	69
Procedures (number)	9	Procedures (number)	6	Documents to export (number)	6
Time (days)	60	Time (days)	391	Time to export (days)	20
Cost (% of income per capita)	8.5	Cost (% of property value)	2.0	Cost to export (US$ per container)	971
Minimum capital (% of income per capita)	49.8			Documents to import (number)	8
		Getting credit (rank)	68	Time to import (days)	21
Dealing with licenses (rank)	62	Strength of legal rights index (0–10)	6	Cost to import (US$ per container)	1,019
Procedures (number)	15	Depth of credit information index (0–6)	2		
Time (days)	208	Public registry coverage (% of adults)	2.5	**Enforcing contracts** (rank)	79
Cost (% of income per capita)	113.9	Private bureau coverage (% of adults)	0.0	Procedures (number)	32
				Time (days)	1,350
Employing workers (rank)	166	**Protecting investors** (rank)	19	Cost (% of claim)	18.6
Difficulty of hiring index (0–100)	78	Extent of disclosure index (0–10)	3		
Rigidity of hours index (0–100)	60	Extent of director liability index (0–10)	8	**Closing a business** (rank)	34
Difficulty of firing index (0–100)	50	Ease of shareholder suits index (0–10)	8	Time (years)	2.0
Rigidity of employment index (0–100)	63	Strength of investor protection index (0–10)	6.3	Cost (% of estate)	8
Nonwage labor cost (% of salary)	19			Recovery rate (cents on the dollar)	46.6
Firing cost (weeks of salary)	40	**Paying taxes** (rank)	63		
		Payments (number per year)	22		
		Time (hours per year)	260		
		Total tax rate (% of profit)	39.2		

SOLOMON ISLANDS

Ease of doing business (rank)	79	East Asia & Pacific		GNI per capita (US$)	680
		Low income		Population (m)	0.5
Starting a business (rank)	85	**Registering property** (rank)	162	**Trading across borders** (rank)	74
Procedures (number)	7	Procedures (number)	10	Documents to export (number)	7
Time (days)	57	Time (days)	297	Time to export (days)	24
Cost (% of income per capita)	58.9	Cost (% of property value)	4.9	Cost to export (US$ per container)	1,056
Minimum capital (% of income per capita)	0.0			Documents to import (number)	4
		Getting credit (rank)	135	Time to import (days)	21
Dealing with licenses (rank)	34	Strength of legal rights index (0–10)	4	Cost to import (US$ per container)	1,238
Procedures (number)	12	Depth of credit information index (0–6)	0		
Time (days)	62	Public registry coverage (% of adults)	0.0	**Enforcing contracts** (rank)	104
Cost (% of income per capita)	518.0	Private bureau coverage (% of adults)	0.0	Procedures (number)	37
				Time (days)	455
Employing workers (rank)	47	**Protecting investors** (rank)	51	Cost (% of claim)	78.9
Difficulty of hiring index (0–100)	11	Extent of disclosure index (0–10)	3		
Rigidity of hours index (0–100)	20	Extent of director liability index (0–10)	7	**Closing a business** (rank)	101
Difficulty of firing index (0–100)	20	Ease of shareholder suits index (0–10)	7	Time (years)	1.0
Rigidity of employment index (0–100)	17	Strength of investor protection index (0–10)	5.7	Cost (% of estate)	38
Nonwage labor cost (% of salary)	8			Recovery rate (cents on the dollar)	23.3
Firing cost (weeks of salary)	44	**Paying taxes** (rank)	26		
		Payments (number per year)	33		
		Time (hours per year)	80		
		Total tax rate (% of profit)	32.6		

SOUTH AFRICA

Ease of doing business (rank)	35	Sub-Saharan Africa		GNI per capita (US$)	5,390
		Upper middle income		Population (m)	47.4
Starting a business (rank)	53	**Registering property** (rank)	76	**Trading across borders** (rank)	134
Procedures (number)	8	Procedures (number)	6	Documents to export (number)	8
Time (days)	31	Time (days)	24	Time to export (days)	30
Cost (% of income per capita)	7.1	Cost (% of property value)	8.8	Cost to export (US$ per container)	1,087
Minimum capital (% of income per capita)	0.0			Documents to import (number)	9
		Getting credit (rank)	26	Time to import (days)	35
Dealing with licenses (rank)	45	Strength of legal rights index (0–10)	5	Cost to import (US$ per container)	1,195
Procedures (number)	17	Depth of credit information index (0–6)	6		
Time (days)	174	Public registry coverage (% of adults)	0.0	**Enforcing contracts** (rank)	85
Cost (% of income per capita)	30.4	Private bureau coverage (% of adults)	52.1	Procedures (number)	30
				Time (days)	600
Employing workers (rank)	91	**Protecting investors** (rank)	9	Cost (% of claim)	33.2
Difficulty of hiring index (0–100)	56	Extent of disclosure index (0–10)	8		
Rigidity of hours index (0–100)	40	Extent of director liability index (0–10)	8	**Closing a business** (rank)	68
Difficulty of firing index (0–100)	30	Ease of shareholder suits index (0–10)	8	Time (years)	2.0
Rigidity of employment index (0–100)	42	Strength of investor protection index (0–10)	8.0	Cost (% of estate)	18
Nonwage labor cost (% of salary)	4			Recovery rate (cents on the dollar)	33.2
Firing cost (weeks of salary)	24	**Paying taxes** (rank)	61		
		Payments (number per year)	11		
		Time (hours per year)	350		
		Total tax rate (% of profit)	37.1		

SPAIN

Ease of doing business (rank)	38	OECD: High Income		GNI per capita (US$)	27,570
		High income		Population (m)	43.5
Starting a business (rank)	118	**Registering property** (rank)	42	**Trading across borders** (rank)	47
Procedures (number)	10	Procedures (number)	4	Documents to export (number)	6
Time (days)	47	Time (days)	18	Time to export (days)	9
Cost (% of income per capita)	15.1	Cost (% of property value)	7.1	Cost to export (US$ per container)	1,000
Minimum capital (% of income per capita)	13.7			Documents to import (number)	8
		Getting credit (rank)	13	Time to import (days)	10
Dealing with licenses (rank)	46	Strength of legal rights index (0–10)	6	Cost to import (US$ per container)	1,000
Procedures (number)	11	Depth of credit information index (0–6)	6		
Time (days)	233	Public registry coverage (% of adults)	44.9	**Enforcing contracts** (rank)	55
Cost (% of income per capita)	64.9	Private bureau coverage (% of adults)	8.3	Procedures (number)	39
				Time (days)	515
Employing workers (rank)	154	**Protecting investors** (rank)	83	Cost (% of claim)	17.2
Difficulty of hiring index (0–100)	78	Extent of disclosure index (0–10)	5		
Rigidity of hours index (0–100)	60	Extent of director liability index (0–10)	6	**Closing a business** (rank)	17
Difficulty of firing index (0–100)	30	Ease of shareholder suits index (0–10)	4	Time (years)	1.0
Rigidity of employment index (0–100)	56	Strength of investor protection index (0–10)	5.0	Cost (% of estate)	15
Nonwage labor cost (% of salary)	33			Recovery rate (cents on the dollar)	76.9
Firing cost (weeks of salary)	56	**Paying taxes** (rank)	93		
		Payments (number per year)	8		
		Time (hours per year)	298		
		Total tax rate (% of profit)	62.0		

SRI LANKA

Ease of doing business (rank)	101	South Asia		GNI per capita (US$)	1,300
		Lower middle income		Population (m)	19.8
Starting a business (rank)	29	**Registering property** (rank)	134	**Trading across borders** (rank)	60
Procedures (number)	5	Procedures (number)	8	Documents to export (number)	8
Time (days)	39	Time (days)	83	Time to export (days)	21
Cost (% of income per capita)	8.5	Cost (% of property value)	5.1	Cost to export (US$ per container)	810
Minimum capital (% of income per capita)	0.0			Documents to import (number)	6
		Getting credit (rank)	97	Time to import (days)	21
Dealing with licenses (rank)	160	Strength of legal rights index (0–10)	3	Cost to import (US$ per container)	844
Procedures (number)	22	Depth of credit information index (0–6)	3		
Time (days)	214	Public registry coverage (% of adults)	0.0	**Enforcing contracts** (rank)	133
Cost (% of income per capita)	1,929.0	Private bureau coverage (% of adults)	2.9	Procedures (number)	40
				Time (days)	1,318
Employing workers (rank)	111	**Protecting investors** (rank)	64	Cost (% of claim)	22.8
Difficulty of hiring index (0–100)	0	Extent of disclosure index (0–10)	4		
Rigidity of hours index (0–100)	20	Extent of director liability index (0–10)	5	**Closing a business** (rank)	39
Difficulty of firing index (0–100)	60	Ease of shareholder suits index (0–10)	7	Time (years)	1.7
Rigidity of employment index (0–100)	27	Strength of investor protection index (0–10)	5.3	Cost (% of estate)	5
Nonwage labor cost (% of salary)	15			Recovery rate (cents on the dollar)	44.6
Firing cost (weeks of salary)	169	**Paying taxes** (rank)	158		
		Payments (number per year)	62		
		Time (hours per year)	256		
		Total tax rate (% of profit)	63.7		

ST. KITTS AND NEVIS

Ease of doing business (rank)	64	Latin America & Caribbean		GNI per capita (US$)	8,840
		Upper middle income		Population (m)	0.0
Starting a business (rank)	79	**Registering property** (rank)	140	**Trading across borders** (rank)	22
Procedures (number)	9	Procedures (number)	6	Documents to export (number)	6
Time (days)	46	Time (days)	81	Time to export (days)	15
Cost (% of income per capita)	22.9	Cost (% of property value)	13.3	Cost to export (US$ per container)	750
Minimum capital (% of income per capita)	0.0			Documents to import (number)	6
		Getting credit (rank)	115	Time to import (days)	17
Dealing with licenses (rank)	7	Strength of legal rights index (0–10)	5	Cost to import (US$ per container)	756
Procedures (number)	14	Depth of credit information index (0–6)	0		
Time (days)	72	Public registry coverage (% of adults)	0.0	**Enforcing contracts** (rank)	117
Cost (% of income per capita)	14.0	Private bureau coverage (% of adults)	0.0	Procedures (number)	47
				Time (days)	578
Employing workers (rank)	18	**Protecting investors** (rank)	19	Cost (% of claim)	20.5
Difficulty of hiring index (0–100)	11	Extent of disclosure index (0–10)	4		
Rigidity of hours index (0–100)	20	Extent of director liability index (0–10)	8	**Closing a business** (rank)	178
Difficulty of firing index (0–100)	20	Ease of shareholder suits index (0–10)	7	Time (years)	NO PRACTICE
Rigidity of employment index (0–100)	17	Strength of investor protection index (0–10)	6.3	Cost (% of estate)	NO PRACTICE
Nonwage labor cost (% of salary)	10			Recovery rate (cents on the dollar)	0.0
Firing cost (weeks of salary)	8	**Paying taxes** (rank)	85		
		Payments (number per year)	24		
		Time (hours per year)	172		
		Total tax rate (% of profit)	52.6		

ST. LUCIA

Ease of doing business (rank)	34	Latin America & Caribbean		GNI per capita (US$)	5,110
		Upper middle income		Population (m)	0.2
Starting a business (rank)	45	**Registering property** (rank)	51	**Trading across borders** (rank)	88
Procedures (number)	6	Procedures (number)	5	Documents to export (number)	5
Time (days)	40	Time (days)	20	Time to export (days)	18
Cost (% of income per capita)	23.7	Cost (% of property value)	7.4	Cost to export (US$ per container)	1,375
Minimum capital (% of income per capita)	0.0			Documents to import (number)	8
		Getting credit (rank)	97	Time to import (days)	21
Dealing with licenses (rank)	13	Strength of legal rights index (0–10)	6	Cost to import (US$ per container)	1,420
Procedures (number)	9	Depth of credit information index (0–6)	0		
Time (days)	139	Public registry coverage (% of adults)	0.0	**Enforcing contracts** (rank)	161
Cost (% of income per capita)	31.9	Private bureau coverage (% of adults)	0.0	Procedures (number)	47
				Time (days)	635
Employing workers (rank)	27	**Protecting investors** (rank)	19	Cost (% of claim)	37.3
Difficulty of hiring index (0–100)	0	Extent of disclosure index (0–10)	4		
Rigidity of hours index (0–100)	20	Extent of director liability index (0–10)	8	**Closing a business** (rank)	43
Difficulty of firing index (0–100)	0	Ease of shareholder suits index (0–10)	7	Time (years)	2.0
Rigidity of employment index (0–100)	7	Strength of investor protection index (0–10)	6.3	Cost (% of estate)	9
Nonwage labor cost (% of salary)	5			Recovery rate (cents on the dollar)	41.8
Firing cost (weeks of salary)	56	**Paying taxes** (rank)	32		
		Payments (number per year)	32		
		Time (hours per year)	71		
		Total tax rate (% of profit)	36.9		

ST. VINCENT AND THE GRENADINES

Ease of doing business (rank)	54
Latin America & Caribbean	
Upper middle income	
GNI per capita (US$)	3,930
Population (m)	0.1

Starting a business (rank)	32
Procedures (number)	8
Time (days)	12
Cost (% of income per capita)	29.2
Minimum capital (% of income per capita)	0.0
Dealing with licenses (rank)	1
Procedures (number)	11
Time (days)	74
Cost (% of income per capita)	9.2
Employing workers (rank)	52
Difficulty of hiring index (0–100)	11
Rigidity of hours index (0–100)	20
Difficulty of firing index (0–100)	20
Rigidity of employment index (0–100)	17
Nonwage labor cost (% of salary)	4
Firing cost (weeks of salary)	54
Registering property (rank)	104
Procedures (number)	6
Time (days)	37
Cost (% of property value)	11.9
Getting credit (rank)	84
Strength of legal rights index (0–10)	7
Depth of credit information index (0–6)	0
Public registry coverage (% of adults)	0.0
Private bureau coverage (% of adults)	0.0
Protecting investors (rank)	19
Extent of disclosure index (0–10)	4
Extent of director liability index (0–10)	8
Ease of shareholder suits index (0–10)	7
Strength of investor protection index (0–10)	6.3
Paying taxes (rank)	58
Payments (number per year)	36
Time (hours per year)	76
Total tax rate (% of profit)	45.0
Trading across borders (rank)	75
Documents to export (number)	6
Time to export (days)	15
Cost to export (US$ per container)	1,770
Documents to import (number)	6
Time to import (days)	16
Cost to import (US$ per container)	1,769
Enforcing contracts (rank)	108
Procedures (number)	45
Time (days)	394
Cost (% of claim)	30.3
Closing a business (rank)	178
Time (years)	NO PRACTICE
Cost (% of estate)	NO PRACTICE
Recovery rate (cents on the dollar)	0.0

SUDAN

Ease of doing business (rank)	143
Sub-Saharan Africa	
Low income	
GNI per capita (US$)	810
Population (m)	37.0

Starting a business (rank)	95
Procedures (number)	10
Time (days)	39
Cost (% of income per capita)	57.9
Minimum capital (% of income per capita)	0.0
Dealing with licenses (rank)	131
Procedures (number)	19
Time (days)	271
Cost (% of income per capita)	296.0
Employing workers (rank)	140
Difficulty of hiring index (0–100)	39
Rigidity of hours index (0–100)	20
Difficulty of firing index (0–100)	50
Rigidity of employment index (0–100)	36
Nonwage labor cost (% of salary)	17
Firing cost (weeks of salary)	118
Registering property (rank)	32
Procedures (number)	6
Time (days)	9
Cost (% of property value)	3.2
Getting credit (rank)	135
Strength of legal rights index (0–10)	4
Depth of credit information index (0–6)	0
Public registry coverage (% of adults)	0.0
Private bureau coverage (% of adults)	0.0
Protecting investors (rank)	141
Extent of disclosure index (0–10)	0
Extent of director liability index (0–10)	6
Ease of shareholder suits index (0–10)	5
Strength of investor protection index (0–10)	3.7
Paying taxes (rank)	60
Payments (number per year)	42
Time (hours per year)	180
Total tax rate (% of profit)	31.6
Trading across borders (rank)	143
Documents to export (number)	7
Time to export (days)	39
Cost to export (US$ per container)	1,700
Documents to import (number)	7
Time to import (days)	54
Cost to import (US$ per container)	2,300
Enforcing contracts (rank)	143
Procedures (number)	53
Time (days)	810
Cost (% of claim)	19.8
Closing a business (rank)	178
Time (years)	NO PRACTICE
Cost (% of estate)	NO PRACTICE
Recovery rate (cents on the dollar)	0.0

SURINAME

Ease of doing business (rank)	142
Latin America & Caribbean	
Lower middle income	
GNI per capita (US$)	3,200
Population (m)	0.5

Starting a business (rank)	163
Procedures (number)	13
Time (days)	694
Cost (% of income per capita)	141.8
Minimum capital (% of income per capita)	1.1
Dealing with licenses (rank)	97
Procedures (number)	14
Time (days)	431
Cost (% of income per capita)	158.0
Employing workers (rank)	50
Difficulty of hiring index (0–100)	0
Rigidity of hours index (0–100)	20
Difficulty of firing index (0–100)	50
Rigidity of employment index (0–100)	23
Nonwage labor cost (% of salary)	0
Firing cost (weeks of salary)	26
Registering property (rank)	136
Procedures (number)	4
Time (days)	193
Cost (% of property value)	13.7
Getting credit (rank)	135
Strength of legal rights index (0–10)	4
Depth of credit information index (0–6)	0
Public registry coverage (% of adults)	0.0
Private bureau coverage (% of adults)	0.0
Protecting investors (rank)	174
Extent of disclosure index (0–10)	2
Extent of director liability index (0–10)	0
Ease of shareholder suits index (0–10)	5
Strength of investor protection index (0–10)	2.3
Paying taxes (rank)	23
Payments (number per year)	17
Time (hours per year)	199
Total tax rate (% of profit)	27.9
Trading across borders (rank)	86
Documents to export (number)	8
Time to export (days)	25
Cost to export (US$ per container)	905
Documents to import (number)	7
Time to import (days)	25
Cost to import (US$ per container)	815
Enforcing contracts (rank)	174
Procedures (number)	44
Time (days)	1,715
Cost (% of claim)	37.1
Closing a business (rank)	145
Time (years)	5.0
Cost (% of estate)	30
Recovery rate (cents on the dollar)	7.4

SWAZILAND

Ease of doing business (rank)	95	Sub-Saharan Africa		GNI per capita (US$)	2,430
		Lower middle income		Population (m)	1.1
Starting a business (rank)	142	**Registering property** (rank)	142	**Trading across borders** (rank)	146
Procedures (number)	13	Procedures (number)	11	Documents to export (number)	9
Time (days)	61	Time (days)	46	Time to export (days)	21
Cost (% of income per capita)	38.7	Cost (% of property value)	7.1	Cost to export (US$ per container)	1,798
Minimum capital (% of income per capita)	0.6			Documents to import (number)	11
		Getting credit (rank)	36	Time to import (days)	34
Dealing with licenses (rank)	19	Strength of legal rights index (0–10)	5	Cost to import (US$ per container)	1,820
Procedures (number)	13	Depth of credit information index (0–6)	5		
Time (days)	93	Public registry coverage (% of adults)	0.0	**Enforcing contracts** (rank)	129
Cost (% of income per capita)	94.0	Private bureau coverage (% of adults)	37.6	Procedures (number)	40
				Time (days)	972
Employing workers (rank)	51	**Protecting investors** (rank)	175	Cost (% of claim)	23.1
Difficulty of hiring index (0–100)	11	Extent of disclosure index (0–10)	0		
Rigidity of hours index (0–100)	20	Extent of director liability index (0–10)	1	**Closing a business** (rank)	56
Difficulty of firing index (0–100)	20	Ease of shareholder suits index (0–10)	5	Time (years)	2.0
Rigidity of employment index (0–100)	17	Strength of investor protection index (0–10)	2.0	Cost (% of estate)	15
Nonwage labor cost (% of salary)	2			Recovery rate (cents on the dollar)	36.0
Firing cost (weeks of salary)	53	**Paying taxes** (rank)	40		
		Payments (number per year)	33		
		Time (hours per year)	104		
		Total tax rate (% of profit)	36.6		

SWEDEN

Ease of doing business (rank)	14	OECD: High Income		GNI per capita (US$)	43,580
		High income		Population (m)	9.0
Starting a business (rank)	22	**Registering property** (rank)	7	**Trading across borders** (rank)	6
Procedures (number)	3	Procedures (number)	1	Documents to export (number)	4
Time (days)	15	Time (days)	2	Time to export (days)	8
Cost (% of income per capita)	0.6	Cost (% of property value)	3.0	Cost to export (US$ per container)	561
Minimum capital (% of income per capita)	31.1			Documents to import (number)	3
		Getting credit (rank)	36	Time to import (days)	6
Dealing with licenses (rank)	17	Strength of legal rights index (0–10)	6	Cost to import (US$ per container)	619
Procedures (number)	8	Depth of credit information index (0–6)	4		
Time (days)	116	Public registry coverage (% of adults)	0.0	**Enforcing contracts** (rank)	53
Cost (% of income per capita)	106.4	Private bureau coverage (% of adults)	100.0	Procedures (number)	30
				Time (days)	508
Employing workers (rank)	107	**Protecting investors** (rank)	51	Cost (% of claim)	31.3
Difficulty of hiring index (0–100)	17	Extent of disclosure index (0–10)	6		
Rigidity of hours index (0–100)	60	Extent of director liability index (0–10)	4	**Closing a business** (rank)	19
Difficulty of firing index (0–100)	40	Ease of shareholder suits index (0–10)	7	Time (years)	2.0
Rigidity of employment index (0–100)	39	Strength of investor protection index (0–10)	5.7	Cost (% of estate)	9
Nonwage labor cost (% of salary)	32			Recovery rate (cents on the dollar)	74.7
Firing cost (weeks of salary)	26	**Paying taxes** (rank)	42		
		Payments (number per year)	2		
		Time (hours per year)	122		
		Total tax rate (% of profit)	54.5		

SWITZERLAND

Ease of doing business (rank)	16	OECD: High Income		GNI per capita (US$)	57,230
		High income		Population (m)	7.4
Starting a business (rank)	35	**Registering property** (rank)	12	**Trading across borders** (rank)	37
Procedures (number)	6	Procedures (number)	4	Documents to export (number)	4
Time (days)	20	Time (days)	16	Time to export (days)	8
Cost (% of income per capita)	2.1	Cost (% of property value)	0.4	Cost to export (US$ per container)	1,238
Minimum capital (% of income per capita)	13.9			Documents to import (number)	5
		Getting credit (rank)	26	Time to import (days)	9
Dealing with licenses (rank)	29	Strength of legal rights index (0–10)	6	Cost to import (US$ per container)	1,333
Procedures (number)	14	Depth of credit information index (0–6)	5		
Time (days)	154	Public registry coverage (% of adults)	0.0	**Enforcing contracts** (rank)	25
Cost (% of income per capita)	52.7	Private bureau coverage (% of adults)	24.0	Procedures (number)	32
				Time (days)	417
Employing workers (rank)	20	**Protecting investors** (rank)	158	Cost (% of claim)	21.2
Difficulty of hiring index (0–100)	0	Extent of disclosure index (0–10)	0		
Rigidity of hours index (0–100)	40	Extent of director liability index (0–10)	5	**Closing a business** (rank)	33
Difficulty of firing index (0–100)	10	Ease of shareholder suits index (0–10)	4	Time (years)	3.0
Rigidity of employment index (0–100)	17	Strength of investor protection index (0–10)	3.0	Cost (% of estate)	4
Nonwage labor cost (% of salary)	15			Recovery rate (cents on the dollar)	47.1
Firing cost (weeks of salary)	13	**Paying taxes** (rank)	15		
		Payments (number per year)	24		
		Time (hours per year)	63		
		Total tax rate (% of profit)	29.1		

SYRIA

Ease of doing business (rank)	137	Middle East & North Africa		GNI per capita (US$)	1,570
		Lower middle income		Population (m)	19.5
Starting a business (rank)	169	**Registering property** (rank)	89	**Trading across borders** (rank)	127
Procedures (number)	13	Procedures (number)	4	Documents to export (number)	8
Time (days)	43	Time (days)	34	Time to export (days)	19
Cost (% of income per capita)	55.7	Cost (% of property value)	28.1	Cost to export (US$ per container)	1,300
Minimum capital (% of income per capita)	3,673.3			Documents to import (number)	9
		Getting credit (rank)	158	Time to import (days)	23
Dealing with licenses (rank)	86	Strength of legal rights index (0–10)	3	Cost to import (US$ per container)	1,900
Procedures (number)	21	Depth of credit information index (0–6)	0		
Time (days)	128	Public registry coverage (% of adults)	0.0	**Enforcing contracts** (rank)	171
Cost (% of income per capita)	258.5	Private bureau coverage (% of adults)	0.0	Procedures (number)	55
				Time (days)	872
Employing workers (rank)	126	**Protecting investors** (rank)	107	Cost (% of claim)	29.3
Difficulty of hiring index (0–100)	22	Extent of disclosure index (0–10)	6		
Rigidity of hours index (0–100)	40	Extent of director liability index (0–10)	5	**Closing a business** (rank)	77
Difficulty of firing index (0–100)	50	Ease of shareholder suits index (0–10)	2	Time (years)	4.1
Rigidity of employment index (0–100)	37	Strength of investor protection index (0–10)	4.3	Cost (% of estate)	9
Nonwage labor cost (% of salary)	17			Recovery rate (cents on the dollar)	30.8
Firing cost (weeks of salary)	80	**Paying taxes** (rank)	98		
		Payments (number per year)	21		
		Time (hours per year)	336		
		Total tax rate (% of profit)	46.7		

TAIWAN, CHINA

Ease of doing business (rank)	50	East Asia & Pacific		GNI per capita (US$)	17,230
		High income		Population (m)	22.8
Starting a business (rank)	103	**Registering property** (rank)	24	**Trading across borders** (rank)	29
Procedures (number)	8	Procedures (number)	3	Documents to export (number)	7
Time (days)	48	Time (days)	5	Time to export (days)	13
Cost (% of income per capita)	4.1	Cost (% of property value)	6.2	Cost to export (US$ per container)	747
Minimum capital (% of income per capita)	178.4			Documents to import (number)	7
		Getting credit (rank)	48	Time to import (days)	12
Dealing with licenses (rank)	128	Strength of legal rights index (0–10)	4	Cost to import (US$ per container)	747
Procedures (number)	30	Depth of credit information index (0–6)	5		
Time (days)	198	Public registry coverage (% of adults)	0.0	**Enforcing contracts** (rank)	92
Cost (% of income per capita)	206.9	Private bureau coverage (% of adults)	67.1	Procedures (number)	47
				Time (days)	510
Employing workers (rank)	148	**Protecting investors** (rank)	64	Cost (% of claim)	17.4
Difficulty of hiring index (0–100)	67	Extent of disclosure index (0–10)	7		
Rigidity of hours index (0–100)	40	Extent of director liability index (0–10)	4	**Closing a business** (rank)	13
Difficulty of firing index (0–100)	40	Ease of shareholder suits index (0–10)	5	Time (years)	1.9
Rigidity of employment index (0–100)	49	Strength of investor protection index (0–10)	5.3	Cost (% of estate)	4
Nonwage labor cost (% of salary)	13			Recovery rate (cents on the dollar)	80.2
Firing cost (weeks of salary)	91	**Paying taxes** (rank)	91		
		Payments (number per year)	23		
		Time (hours per year)	340		
		Total tax rate (% of profit)	40.6		

TAJIKISTAN

Ease of doing business (rank)	153	Eastern Europe & Central Asia		GNI per capita (US$)	390
		Low income		Population (m)	6.6
Starting a business (rank)	161	**Registering property** (rank)	43	**Trading across borders** (rank)	176
Procedures (number)	13	Procedures (number)	6	Documents to export (number)	10
Time (days)	49	Time (days)	37	Time to export (days)	82
Cost (% of income per capita)	39.6	Cost (% of property value)	1.9	Cost to export (US$ per container)	3,000
Minimum capital (% of income per capita)	311.0			Documents to import (number)	11
		Getting credit (rank)	135	Time to import (days)	83
Dealing with licenses (rank)	166	Strength of legal rights index (0–10)	4	Cost to import (US$ per container)	4,500
Procedures (number)	32	Depth of credit information index (0–6)	0		
Time (days)	191	Public registry coverage (% of adults)	0.0	**Enforcing contracts** (rank)	23
Cost (% of income per capita)	1,991.9	Private bureau coverage (% of adults)	0.0	Procedures (number)	34
				Time (days)	295
Employing workers (rank)	125	**Protecting investors** (rank)	176	Cost (% of claim)	20.5
Difficulty of hiring index (0–100)	33	Extent of disclosure index (0–10)	0		
Rigidity of hours index (0–100)	80	Extent of director liability index (0–10)	0	**Closing a business** (rank)	99
Difficulty of firing index (0–100)	40	Ease of shareholder suits index (0–10)	5	Time (years)	3.0
Rigidity of employment index (0–100)	51	Strength of investor protection index (0–10)	1.7	Cost (% of estate)	9
Nonwage labor cost (% of salary)	25			Recovery rate (cents on the dollar)	23.6
Firing cost (weeks of salary)	22	**Paying taxes** (rank)	155		
		Payments (number per year)	54		
		Time (hours per year)	224		
		Total tax rate (% of profit)	82.2		

TANZANIA

Ease of doing business (rank)	130	Sub-Saharan Africa		GNI per capita (US$)	350
		Low income		Population (m)	39.5
Starting a business (rank)	95	**Registering property** (rank)	160	**Trading across borders** (rank)	100
Procedures (number)	12	Procedures (number)	10	Documents to export (number)	5
Time (days)	29	Time (days)	119	Time to export (days)	24
Cost (% of income per capita)	47.1	Cost (% of property value)	5.3	Cost to export (US$ per container)	1,212
Minimum capital (% of income per capita)	0.0			Documents to import (number)	7
		Getting credit (rank)	115	Time to import (days)	30
Dealing with licenses (rank)	170	Strength of legal rights index (0–10)	5	Cost to import (US$ per container)	1,425
Procedures (number)	21	Depth of credit information index (0–6)	0		
Time (days)	308	Public registry coverage (% of adults)	0.0	**Enforcing contracts** (rank)	35
Cost (% of income per capita)	2,365.5	Private bureau coverage (% of adults)	0.0	Procedures (number)	38
				Time (days)	462
Employing workers (rank)	151	**Protecting investors** (rank)	83	Cost (% of claim)	14.3
Difficulty of hiring index (0–100)	89	Extent of disclosure index (0–10)	3		
Rigidity of hours index (0–100)	40	Extent of director liability index (0–10)	4	**Closing a business** (rank)	109
Difficulty of firing index (0–100)	60	Ease of shareholder suits index (0–10)	8	Time (years)	3.0
Rigidity of employment index (0–100)	63	Strength of investor protection index (0–10)	5.0	Cost (% of estate)	22
Nonwage labor cost (% of salary)	16			Recovery rate (cents on the dollar)	20.5
Firing cost (weeks of salary)	32	**Paying taxes** (rank)	104		
		Payments (number per year)	48		
		Time (hours per year)	172		
		Total tax rate (% of profit)	44.3		

THAILAND

Ease of doing business (rank)	15	East Asia & Pacific		GNI per capita (US$)	2,990
		Lower middle income		Population (m)	64.7
Starting a business (rank)	36	**Registering property** (rank)	20	**Trading across borders** (rank)	50
Procedures (number)	8	Procedures (number)	2	Documents to export (number)	7
Time (days)	33	Time (days)	2	Time to export (days)	17
Cost (% of income per capita)	5.6	Cost (% of property value)	6.3	Cost to export (US$ per container)	615
Minimum capital (% of income per capita)	0.0			Documents to import (number)	9
		Getting credit (rank)	36	Time to import (days)	14
Dealing with licenses (rank)	12	Strength of legal rights index (0–10)	5	Cost to import (US$ per container)	786
Procedures (number)	11	Depth of credit information index (0–6)	5		
Time (days)	156	Public registry coverage (% of adults)	0.0	**Enforcing contracts** (rank)	26
Cost (% of income per capita)	10.7	Private bureau coverage (% of adults)	27.9	Procedures (number)	35
				Time (days)	479
Employing workers (rank)	49	**Protecting investors** (rank)	33	Cost (% of claim)	14.3
Difficulty of hiring index (0–100)	33	Extent of disclosure index (0–10)	10		
Rigidity of hours index (0–100)	20	Extent of director liability index (0–10)	2	**Closing a business** (rank)	44
Difficulty of firing index (0–100)	0	Ease of shareholder suits index (0–10)	6	Time (years)	2.7
Rigidity of employment index (0–100)	18	Strength of investor protection index (0–10)	6.0	Cost (% of estate)	36
Nonwage labor cost (% of salary)	6			Recovery rate (cents on the dollar)	41.8
Firing cost (weeks of salary)	54	**Paying taxes** (rank)	89		
		Payments (number per year)	35		
		Time (hours per year)	264		
		Total tax rate (% of profit)	37.7		

TIMOR-LESTE

Ease of doing business (rank)	168	East Asia & Pacific		GNI per capita (US$)	840
		Low income		Population (m)	1.0
Starting a business (rank)	140	**Registering property** (rank)	178	**Trading across borders** (rank)	78
Procedures (number)	9	Procedures (number)	NO PRACTICE	Documents to export (number)	6
Time (days)	82	Time (days)	NO PRACTICE	Time to export (days)	25
Cost (% of income per capita)	11.9	Cost (% of property value)	NO PRACTICE	Cost to export (US$ per container)	990
Minimum capital (% of income per capita)	595.2			Documents to import (number)	7
		Getting credit (rank)	170	Time to import (days)	26
Dealing with licenses (rank)	100	Strength of legal rights index (0–10)	2	Cost to import (US$ per container)	995
Procedures (number)	22	Depth of credit information index (0–6)	0		
Time (days)	208	Public registry coverage (% of adults)	0.0	**Enforcing contracts** (rank)	178
Cost (% of income per capita)	113.1	Private bureau coverage (% of adults)	0.0	Procedures (number)	51
				Time (days)	1,800
Employing workers (rank)	73	**Protecting investors** (rank)	122	Cost (% of claim)	163.2
Difficulty of hiring index (0–100)	33	Extent of disclosure index (0–10)	3		
Rigidity of hours index (0–100)	20	Extent of director liability index (0–10)	4	**Closing a business** (rank)	178
Difficulty of firing index (0–100)	50	Ease of shareholder suits index (0–10)	5	Time (years)	NO PRACTICE
Rigidity of employment index (0–100)	34	Strength of investor protection index (0–10)	4.0	Cost (% of estate)	NO PRACTICE
Nonwage labor cost (% of salary)	0			Recovery rate (cents on the dollar)	0.0
Firing cost (weeks of salary)	17	**Paying taxes** (rank)	62		
		Payments (number per year)	15		
		Time (hours per year)	640		
		Total tax rate (% of profit)	28.3		

TOGO

Ease of doing business (rank)	156	Sub-Saharan Africa Low income		GNI per capita (US$) Population (m)	350 6.3
Starting a business (rank)	176	**Registering property** (rank)	150	**Trading across borders** (rank)	81
Procedures (number)	13	Procedures (number)	5	Documents to export (number)	6
Time (days)	53	Time (days)	295	Time to export (days)	24
Cost (% of income per capita)	245.7	Cost (% of property value)	13.9	Cost to export (US$ per container)	872
Minimum capital (% of income per capita)	546.4			Documents to import (number)	8
		Getting credit (rank)	135	Time to import (days)	29
Dealing with licenses (rank)	143	Strength of legal rights index (0–10)	3	Cost to import (US$ per container)	894
Procedures (number)	15	Depth of credit information index (0–6)	1		
Time (days)	277	Public registry coverage (% of adults)	2.7	**Enforcing contracts** (rank)	153
Cost (% of income per capita)	1,366.3	Private bureau coverage (% of adults)	0.0	Procedures (number)	41
				Time (days)	588
Employing workers (rank)	146	**Protecting investors** (rank)	138	Cost (% of claim)	47.5
Difficulty of hiring index (0–100)	61	Extent of disclosure index (0–10)	6		
Rigidity of hours index (0–100)	60	Extent of director liability index (0–10)	1	**Closing a business** (rank)	90
Difficulty of firing index (0–100)	40	Ease of shareholder suits index (0–10)	4	Time (years)	3.0
Rigidity of employment index (0–100)	54	Strength of investor protection index (0–10)	3.7	Cost (% of estate)	15
Nonwage labor cost (% of salary)	25			Recovery rate (cents on the dollar)	26.3
Firing cost (weeks of salary)	36	**Paying taxes** (rank)	138		
		Payments (number per year)	53		
		Time (hours per year)	270		
		Total tax rate (% of profit)	48.2		

TONGA

Ease of doing business (rank)	47	East Asia & Pacific Lower middle income		GNI per capita (US$) Population (m)	2,170 0.1
Starting a business (rank)	24	**Registering property** (rank)	106	**Trading across borders** (rank)	44
Procedures (number)	4	Procedures (number)	4	Documents to export (number)	7
Time (days)	32	Time (days)	108	Time to export (days)	19
Cost (% of income per capita)	10.8	Cost (% of property value)	10.2	Cost to export (US$ per container)	545
Minimum capital (% of income per capita)	0.0			Documents to import (number)	6
		Getting credit (rank)	158	Time to import (days)	25
Dealing with licenses (rank)	30	Strength of legal rights index (0–10)	3	Cost to import (US$ per container)	620
Procedures (number)	14	Depth of credit information index (0–6)	0		
Time (days)	88	Public registry coverage (% of adults)	0.0	**Enforcing contracts** (rank)	58
Cost (% of income per capita)	183.6	Private bureau coverage (% of adults)	0.0	Procedures (number)	37
				Time (days)	350
Employing workers (rank)	4	**Protecting investors** (rank)	98	Cost (% of claim)	30.5
Difficulty of hiring index (0–100)	0	Extent of disclosure index (0–10)	3		
Rigidity of hours index (0–100)	20	Extent of director liability index (0–10)	3	**Closing a business** (rank)	93
Difficulty of firing index (0–100)	0	Ease of shareholder suits index (0–10)	8	Time (years)	2.7
Rigidity of employment index (0–100)	7	Strength of investor protection index (0–10)	4.7	Cost (% of estate)	22
Nonwage labor cost (% of salary)	0			Recovery rate (cents on the dollar)	25.3
Firing cost (weeks of salary)	0	**Paying taxes** (rank)	24		
		Payments (number per year)	23		
		Time (hours per year)	164		
		Total tax rate (% of profit)	25.0		

TRINIDAD AND TOBAGO

Ease of doing business (rank)	67	Latin America & Caribbean Upper middle income		GNI per capita (US$) Population (m)	13,340 1.3
Starting a business (rank)	40	**Registering property** (rank)	157	**Trading across borders** (rank)	49
Procedures (number)	9	Procedures (number)	8	Documents to export (number)	5
Time (days)	43	Time (days)	162	Time to export (days)	14
Cost (% of income per capita)	0.9	Cost (% of property value)	7.0	Cost to export (US$ per container)	693
Minimum capital (% of income per capita)	0.0			Documents to import (number)	7
		Getting credit (rank)	48	Time to import (days)	26
Dealing with licenses (rank)	79	Strength of legal rights index (0–10)	5	Cost to import (US$ per container)	1,100
Procedures (number)	20	Depth of credit information index (0–6)	4		
Time (days)	261	Public registry coverage (% of adults)	0.0	**Enforcing contracts** (rank)	168
Cost (% of income per capita)	5.9	Private bureau coverage (% of adults)	34.4	Procedures (number)	42
				Time (days)	1,340
Employing workers (rank)	38	**Protecting investors** (rank)	15	Cost (% of claim)	33.5
Difficulty of hiring index (0–100)	0	Extent of disclosure index (0–10)	4		
Rigidity of hours index (0–100)	0	Extent of director liability index (0–10)	9	**Closing a business** (rank)	178
Difficulty of firing index (0–100)	20	Ease of shareholder suits index (0–10)	7	Time (years)	NO PRACTICE
Rigidity of employment index (0–100)	7	Strength of investor protection index (0–10)	6.7	Cost (% of estate)	NO PRACTICE
Nonwage labor cost (% of salary)	3			Recovery rate (cents on the dollar)	0.0
Firing cost (weeks of salary)	67	**Paying taxes** (rank)	45		
		Payments (number per year)	40		
		Time (hours per year)	114		
		Total tax rate (% of profit)	33.1		

TUNISIA

Ease of doing business (rank)	88	Middle East & North Africa		GNI per capita (US$)	2,970
		Lower middle income		Population (m)	10.1
Starting a business (rank)	68	**Registering property** (rank)	66	**Trading across borders** (rank)	28
Procedures (number)	10	Procedures (number)	5	Documents to export (number)	5
Time (days)	11	Time (days)	49	Time to export (days)	17
Cost (% of income per capita)	8.3	Cost (% of property value)	6.1	Cost to export (US$ per container)	540
Minimum capital (% of income per capita)	25.3			Documents to import (number)	7
		Getting credit (rank)	97	Time to import (days)	22
Dealing with licenses (rank)	96	Strength of legal rights index (0–10)	2	Cost to import (US$ per container)	810
Procedures (number)	20	Depth of credit information index (0–6)	4		
Time (days)	93	Public registry coverage (% of adults)	13.7	**Enforcing contracts** (rank)	80
Cost (% of income per capita)	922.1	Private bureau coverage (% of adults)	0.0	Procedures (number)	39
				Time (days)	565
Employing workers (rank)	113	**Protecting investors** (rank)	147	Cost (% of claim)	21.8
Difficulty of hiring index (0–100)	28	Extent of disclosure index (0–10)	0		
Rigidity of hours index (0–100)	40	Extent of director liability index (0–10)	4	**Closing a business** (rank)	30
Difficulty of firing index (0–100)	80	Ease of shareholder suits index (0–10)	6	Time (years)	1.3
Rigidity of employment index (0–100)	49	Strength of investor protection index (0–10)	3.3	Cost (% of estate)	7
Nonwage labor cost (% of salary)	22			Recovery rate (cents on the dollar)	51.5
Firing cost (weeks of salary)	17	**Paying taxes** (rank)	148		
		Payments (number per year)	46		
		Time (hours per year)	268		
		Total tax rate (% of profit)	61.0		

TURKEY

Ease of doing business (rank)	57	Eastern Europe & Central Asia		GNI per capita (US$)	5,400
		Upper middle income		Population (m)	72.9
Starting a business (rank)	43	**Registering property** (rank)	31	**Trading across borders** (rank)	56
Procedures (number)	6	Procedures (number)	6	Documents to export (number)	7
Time (days)	6	Time (days)	6	Time to export (days)	14
Cost (% of income per capita)	20.7	Cost (% of property value)	3.1	Cost to export (US$ per container)	865
Minimum capital (% of income per capita)	16.2			Documents to import (number)	8
		Getting credit (rank)	68	Time to import (days)	15
Dealing with licenses (rank)	128	Strength of legal rights index (0–10)	3	Cost to import (US$ per container)	1,013
Procedures (number)	25	Depth of credit information index (0–6)	5		
Time (days)	188	Public registry coverage (% of adults)	10.3	**Enforcing contracts** (rank)	34
Cost (% of income per capita)	369.9	Private bureau coverage (% of adults)	2.7	Procedures (number)	36
				Time (days)	420
Employing workers (rank)	136	**Protecting investors** (rank)	64	Cost (% of claim)	18.8
Difficulty of hiring index (0–100)	56	Extent of disclosure index (0–10)	8		
Rigidity of hours index (0–100)	40	Extent of director liability index (0–10)	4	**Closing a business** (rank)	112
Difficulty of firing index (0–100)	30	Ease of shareholder suits index (0–10)	4	Time (years)	3.3
Rigidity of employment index (0–100)	42	Strength of investor protection index (0–10)	5.3	Cost (% of estate)	15
Nonwage labor cost (% of salary)	22			Recovery rate (cents on the dollar)	20.3
Firing cost (weeks of salary)	95	**Paying taxes** (rank)	54		
		Payments (number per year)	15		
		Time (hours per year)	223		
		Total tax rate (% of profit)	45.1		

UGANDA

Ease of doing business (rank)	118	Sub-Saharan Africa		GNI per capita (US$)	300
		Low income		Population (m)	29.9
Starting a business (rank)	114	**Registering property** (rank)	163	**Trading across borders** (rank)	141
Procedures (number)	18	Procedures (number)	13	Documents to export (number)	6
Time (days)	28	Time (days)	227	Time to export (days)	39
Cost (% of income per capita)	92.0	Cost (% of property value)	4.6	Cost to export (US$ per container)	2,940
Minimum capital (% of income per capita)	0.0			Documents to import (number)	7
		Getting credit (rank)	158	Time to import (days)	37
Dealing with licenses (rank)	81	Strength of legal rights index (0–10)	3	Cost to import (US$ per container)	2,990
Procedures (number)	16	Depth of credit information index (0–6)	0		
Time (days)	143	Public registry coverage (% of adults)	0.0	**Enforcing contracts** (rank)	119
Cost (% of income per capita)	811.8	Private bureau coverage (% of adults)	0.0	Procedures (number)	38
				Time (days)	535
Employing workers (rank)	11	**Protecting investors** (rank)	122	Cost (% of claim)	44.9
Difficulty of hiring index (0–100)	0	Extent of disclosure index (0–10)	2		
Rigidity of hours index (0–100)	0	Extent of director liability index (0–10)	5	**Closing a business** (rank)	48
Difficulty of firing index (0–100)	10	Ease of shareholder suits index (0–10)	5	Time (years)	2.2
Rigidity of employment index (0–100)	3	Strength of investor protection index (0–10)	4.0	Cost (% of estate)	30
Nonwage labor cost (% of salary)	10			Recovery rate (cents on the dollar)	41.0
Firing cost (weeks of salary)	13	**Paying taxes** (rank)	55		
		Payments (number per year)	33		
		Time (hours per year)	237		
		Total tax rate (% of profit)	32.3		

UKRAINE

Ease of doing business (rank)	139	Eastern Europe & Central Asia		GNI per capita (US$)	1,950
		Lower middle income		Population (m)	46.6
Starting a business (rank)	109	**Registering property** (rank)	138	**Trading across borders** (rank)	120
Procedures (number)	10	Procedures (number)	10	Documents to export (number)	6
Time (days)	27	Time (days)	93	Time to export (days)	31
Cost (% of income per capita)	7.8	Cost (% of property value)	3.3	Cost to export (US$ per container)	1,045
Minimum capital (% of income per capita)	203.1			Documents to import (number)	10
		Getting credit (rank)	68	Time to import (days)	39
Dealing with licenses (rank)	174	Strength of legal rights index (0–10)	8	Cost to import (US$ per container)	1,065
Procedures (number)	29	Depth of credit information index (0–6)	0		
Time (days)	429	Public registry coverage (% of adults)	0.0	**Enforcing contracts** (rank)	46
Cost (% of income per capita)	668.5	Private bureau coverage (% of adults)	0.0	Procedures (number)	30
				Time (days)	354
Employing workers (rank)	102	**Protecting investors** (rank)	141	Cost (% of claim)	41.5
Difficulty of hiring index (0–100)	44	Extent of disclosure index (0–10)	1		
Rigidity of hours index (0–100)	60	Extent of director liability index (0–10)	3	**Closing a business** (rank)	140
Difficulty of firing index (0–100)	30	Ease of shareholder suits index (0–10)	7	Time (years)	2.9
Rigidity of employment index (0–100)	45	Strength of investor protection index (0–10)	3.7	Cost (% of estate)	42
Nonwage labor cost (% of salary)	38			Recovery rate (cents on the dollar)	9.1
Firing cost (weeks of salary)	13	**Paying taxes** (rank)	177		
		Payments (number per year)	99		
		Time (hours per year)	2,085		
		Total tax rate (% of profit)	57.3		

UNITED ARAB EMIRATES

Ease of doing business (rank)	68	Middle East & North Africa		GNI per capita (US$)	26,147
		High income		Population (m)	4.6
Starting a business (rank)	158	**Registering property** (rank)	8	**Trading across borders** (rank)	24
Procedures (number)	11	Procedures (number)	3	Documents to export (number)	7
Time (days)	62	Time (days)	6	Time to export (days)	13
Cost (% of income per capita)	36.9	Cost (% of property value)	2.0	Cost to export (US$ per container)	462
Minimum capital (% of income per capita)	312.4			Documents to import (number)	8
		Getting credit (rank)	115	Time to import (days)	13
Dealing with licenses (rank)	38	Strength of legal rights index (0–10)	3	Cost to import (US$ per container)	462
Procedures (number)	21	Depth of credit information index (0–6)	2		
Time (days)	125	Public registry coverage (% of adults)	1.4	**Enforcing contracts** (rank)	144
Cost (% of income per capita)	1.5	Private bureau coverage (% of adults)	0.0	Procedures (number)	50
				Time (days)	607
Employing workers (rank)	65	**Protecting investors** (rank)	107	Cost (% of claim)	26.2
Difficulty of hiring index (0–100)	0	Extent of disclosure index (0–10)	4		
Rigidity of hours index (0–100)	60	Extent of director liability index (0–10)	7	**Closing a business** (rank)	139
Difficulty of firing index (0–100)	0	Ease of shareholder suits index (0–10)	2	Time (years)	5.1
Rigidity of employment index (0–100)	20	Strength of investor protection index (0–10)	4.3	Cost (% of estate)	30
Nonwage labor cost (% of salary)	13			Recovery rate (cents on the dollar)	10.1
Firing cost (weeks of salary)	84	**Paying taxes** (rank)	4		
		Payments (number per year)	14		
		Time (hours per year)	12		
		Total tax rate (% of profit)	14.4		

UNITED KINGDOM

Ease of doing business (rank)	6	OECD: High Income		GNI per capita (US$)	40,180
		High income		Population (m)	60.4
Starting a business (rank)	6	**Registering property** (rank)	19	**Trading across borders** (rank)	27
Procedures (number)	6	Procedures (number)	2	Documents to export (number)	4
Time (days)	13	Time (days)	21	Time to export (days)	13
Cost (% of income per capita)	0.8	Cost (% of property value)	4.1	Cost to export (US$ per container)	940
Minimum capital (% of income per capita)	0.0			Documents to import (number)	4
		Getting credit (rank)	1	Time to import (days)	13
Dealing with licenses (rank)	54	Strength of legal rights index (0–10)	10	Cost to import (US$ per container)	1,267
Procedures (number)	19	Depth of credit information index (0–6)	6		
Time (days)	144	Public registry coverage (% of adults)	0.0	**Enforcing contracts** (rank)	24
Cost (% of income per capita)	64.6	Private bureau coverage (% of adults)	84.6	Procedures (number)	30
				Time (days)	404
Employing workers (rank)	21	**Protecting investors** (rank)	9	Cost (% of claim)	23.4
Difficulty of hiring index (0–100)	11	Extent of disclosure index (0–10)	10		
Rigidity of hours index (0–100)	0	Extent of director liability index (0–10)	7	**Closing a business** (rank)	10
Difficulty of firing index (0–100)	10	Ease of shareholder suits index (0–10)	7	Time (years)	1.0
Rigidity of employment index (0–100)	7	Strength of investor protection index (0–10)	8.0	Cost (% of estate)	6
Nonwage labor cost (% of salary)	11			Recovery rate (cents on the dollar)	84.6
Firing cost (weeks of salary)	22	**Paying taxes** (rank)	12		
		Payments (number per year)	8		
		Time (hours per year)	105		
		Total tax rate (% of profit)	35.7		

UNITED STATES

Ease of doing business (rank)	3	OECD: High Income		GNI per capita (US$)	44,970
		High income		Population (m)	299.0
Starting a business (rank)	4	**Registering property** (rank)	10	**Trading across borders** (rank)	15
Procedures (number)	6	Procedures (number)	4	Documents to export (number)	4
Time (days)	6	Time (days)	12	Time to export (days)	6
Cost (% of income per capita)	0.7	Cost (% of property value)	0.5	Cost to export (US$ per container)	960
Minimum capital (% of income per capita)	0.0			Documents to import (number)	5
		Getting credit (rank)	7	Time to import (days)	5
Dealing with licenses (rank)	24	Strength of legal rights index (0–10)	7	Cost to import (US$ per container)	1,160
Procedures (number)	19	Depth of credit information index (0–6)	6		
Time (days)	40	Public registry coverage (% of adults)	0.0	**Enforcing contracts** (rank)	8
Cost (% of income per capita)	13.4	Private bureau coverage (% of adults)	100.0	Procedures (number)	32
				Time (days)	300
Employing workers (rank)	1	**Protecting investors** (rank)	5	Cost (% of claim)	9.4
Difficulty of hiring index (0–100)	0	Extent of disclosure index (0–10)	7		
Rigidity of hours index (0–100)	0	Extent of director liability index (0–10)	9	**Closing a business** (rank)	18
Difficulty of firing index (0–100)	0	Ease of shareholder suits index (0–10)	9	Time (years)	1.5
Rigidity of employment index (0–100)	0	Strength of investor protection index (0–10)	8.3	Cost (% of estate)	7
Nonwage labor cost (% of salary)	8			Recovery rate (cents on the dollar)	75.9
Firing cost (weeks of salary)	0	**Paying taxes** (rank)	76		
		Payments (number per year)	10		
		Time (hours per year)	325		
		Total tax rate (% of profit)	46.2		

URUGUAY

Ease of doing business (rank)	98	Latin America & Caribbean		GNI per capita (US$)	5,310
		Upper middle income		Population (m)	3.3
Starting a business (rank)	151	**Registering property** (rank)	139	**Trading across borders** (rank)	125
Procedures (number)	11	Procedures (number)	8	Documents to export (number)	10
Time (days)	44	Time (days)	66	Time to export (days)	24
Cost (% of income per capita)	46.0	Cost (% of property value)	7.1	Cost to export (US$ per container)	925
Minimum capital (% of income per capita)	180.6			Documents to import (number)	10
		Getting credit (rank)	26	Time to import (days)	23
Dealing with licenses (rank)	137	Strength of legal rights index (0–10)	5	Cost to import (US$ per container)	1,180
Procedures (number)	30	Depth of credit information index (0–6)	6		
Time (days)	234	Public registry coverage (% of adults)	14.1	**Enforcing contracts** (rank)	91
Cost (% of income per capita)	135.5	Private bureau coverage (% of adults)	93.8	Procedures (number)	40
				Time (days)	720
Employing workers (rank)	72	**Protecting investors** (rank)	83	Cost (% of claim)	16.2
Difficulty of hiring index (0–100)	33	Extent of disclosure index (0–10)	3		
Rigidity of hours index (0–100)	60	Extent of director liability index (0–10)	4	**Closing a business** (rank)	37
Difficulty of firing index (0–100)	0	Ease of shareholder suits index (0–10)	8	Time (years)	2.1
Rigidity of employment index (0–100)	31	Strength of investor protection index (0–10)	5.0	Cost (% of estate)	7
Nonwage labor cost (% of salary)	6			Recovery rate (cents on the dollar)	44.8
Firing cost (weeks of salary)	31	**Paying taxes** (rank)	131		
		Payments (number per year)	53		
		Time (hours per year)	304		
		Total tax rate (% of profit)	40.7		

UZBEKISTAN

Ease of doing business (rank)	138	Eastern Europe & Central Asia		GNI per capita (US$)	610
		Low income		Population (m)	26.5
Starting a business (rank)	54	**Registering property** (rank)	119	**Trading across borders** (rank)	165
Procedures (number)	7	Procedures (number)	12	Documents to export (number)	7
Time (days)	13	Time (days)	78	Time to export (days)	80
Cost (% of income per capita)	14.2	Cost (% of property value)	1.4	Cost to export (US$ per container)	2,550
Minimum capital (% of income per capita)	25.3			Documents to import (number)	11
		Getting credit (rank)	170	Time to import (days)	104
Dealing with licenses (rank)	145	Strength of legal rights index (0–10)	2	Cost to import (US$ per container)	4,050
Procedures (number)	26	Depth of credit information index (0–6)	0		
Time (days)	260	Public registry coverage (% of adults)	0.0	**Enforcing contracts** (rank)	48
Cost (% of income per capita)	140.7	Private bureau coverage (% of adults)	0.0	Procedures (number)	42
				Time (days)	195
Employing workers (rank)	67	**Protecting investors** (rank)	107	Cost (% of claim)	22.2
Difficulty of hiring index (0–100)	33	Extent of disclosure index (0–10)	4		
Rigidity of hours index (0–100)	40	Extent of director liability index (0–10)	6	**Closing a business** (rank)	119
Difficulty of firing index (0–100)	30	Ease of shareholder suits index (0–10)	3	Time (years)	4.0
Rigidity of employment index (0–100)	34	Strength of investor protection index (0–10)	4.3	Cost (% of estate)	10
Nonwage labor cost (% of salary)	25			Recovery rate (cents on the dollar)	18.7
Firing cost (weeks of salary)	22	**Paying taxes** (rank)	159		
		Payments (number per year)	118		
		Time (hours per year)	196		
		Total tax rate (% of profit)	96.3		

VANUATU

Ease of doing business (rank)	62	East Asia & Pacific Lower middle income		GNI per capita (US$) Population (m)	1,710 0.2
Starting a business (rank)	73	**Registering property** (rank)	111	**Trading across borders** (rank)	142
Procedures (number)	8	Procedures (number)	2	Documents to export (number)	7
Time (days)	39	Time (days)	188	Time to export (days)	26
Cost (% of income per capita)	54.9	Cost (% of property value)	11.0	Cost to export (US$ per container)	1,815
Minimum capital (% of income per capita)	0.0			Documents to import (number)	9
		Getting credit (rank)	135	Time to import (days)	30
Dealing with licenses (rank)	24	Strength of legal rights index (0–10)	4	Cost to import (US$ per container)	2,225
Procedures (number)	7	Depth of credit information index (0–6)	0		
Time (days)	51	Public registry coverage (% of adults)	0.0	**Enforcing contracts** (rank)	66
Cost (% of income per capita)	357.7	Private bureau coverage (% of adults)	0.0	Procedures (number)	30
				Time (days)	430
Employing workers (rank)	77	**Protecting investors** (rank)	64	Cost (% of claim)	74.7
Difficulty of hiring index (0–100)	22	Extent of disclosure index (0–10)	5		
Rigidity of hours index (0–100)	40	Extent of director liability index (0–10)	6	**Closing a business** (rank)	49
Difficulty of firing index (0–100)	10	Ease of shareholder suits index (0–10)	5	Time (years)	2.6
Rigidity of employment index (0–100)	24	Strength of investor protection index (0–10)	5.3	Cost (% of estate)	38
Nonwage labor cost (% of salary)	4			Recovery rate (cents on the dollar)	39.3
Firing cost (weeks of salary)	56	**Paying taxes** (rank)	18		
		Payments (number per year)	31		
		Time (hours per year)	120		
		Total tax rate (% of profit)	8.4		

VENEZUELA

Ease of doing business (rank)	172	Latin America & Caribbean Upper middle income		GNI per capita (US$) Population (m)	6,070 27.0
Starting a business (rank)	134	**Registering property** (rank)	74	**Trading across borders** (rank)	156
Procedures (number)	16	Procedures (number)	8	Documents to export (number)	8
Time (days)	141	Time (days)	47	Time to export (days)	45
Cost (% of income per capita)	28.2	Cost (% of property value)	2.2	Cost to export (US$ per container)	2,400
Minimum capital (% of income per capita)	0.0			Documents to import (number)	9
		Getting credit (rank)	135	Time to import (days)	65
Dealing with licenses (rank)	95	Strength of legal rights index (0–10)	4	Cost to import (US$ per container)	2,400
Procedures (number)	11	Depth of credit information index (0–6)	0		
Time (days)	395	Public registry coverage (% of adults)	0.0	**Enforcing contracts** (rank)	70
Cost (% of income per capita)	326.0	Private bureau coverage (% of adults)	0.0	Procedures (number)	29
				Time (days)	510
Employing workers (rank)	177	**Protecting investors** (rank)	165	Cost (% of claim)	43.7
Difficulty of hiring index (0–100)	78	Extent of disclosure index (0–10)	3		
Rigidity of hours index (0–100)	60	Extent of director liability index (0–10)	3	**Closing a business** (rank)	146
Difficulty of firing index (0–100)	100	Ease of shareholder suits index (0–10)	2	Time (years)	4.0
Rigidity of employment index (0–100)	79	Strength of investor protection index (0–10)	2.7	Cost (% of estate)	38
Nonwage labor cost (% of salary)	16			Recovery rate (cents on the dollar)	6.6
Firing cost (weeks of salary)	NOT POSSIBLE	**Paying taxes** (rank)	174		
		Payments (number per year)	70		
		Time (hours per year)	864		
		Total tax rate (% of profit)	53.3		

VIETNAM

Ease of doing business (rank)	91	East Asia & Pacific Low income		GNI per capita (US$) Population (m)	690 84.1
Starting a business (rank)	97	**Registering property** (rank)	38	**Trading across borders** (rank)	63
Procedures (number)	11	Procedures (number)	4	Documents to export (number)	6
Time (days)	50	Time (days)	67	Time to export (days)	24
Cost (% of income per capita)	20.0	Cost (% of property value)	1.2	Cost to export (US$ per container)	669
Minimum capital (% of income per capita)	0.0			Documents to import (number)	8
		Getting credit (rank)	48	Time to import (days)	23
Dealing with licenses (rank)	63	Strength of legal rights index (0–10)	6	Cost to import (US$ per container)	881
Procedures (number)	13	Depth of credit information index (0–6)	3		
Time (days)	194	Public registry coverage (% of adults)	9.2	**Enforcing contracts** (rank)	40
Cost (% of income per capita)	373.6	Private bureau coverage (% of adults)	0.0	Procedures (number)	34
				Time (days)	295
Employing workers (rank)	84	**Protecting investors** (rank)	165	Cost (% of claim)	31.0
Difficulty of hiring index (0–100)	0	Extent of disclosure index (0–10)	6		
Rigidity of hours index (0–100)	40	Extent of director liability index (0–10)	0	**Closing a business** (rank)	121
Difficulty of firing index (0–100)	40	Ease of shareholder suits index (0–10)	2	Time (years)	5.0
Rigidity of employment index (0–100)	27	Strength of investor protection index (0–10)	2.7	Cost (% of estate)	15
Nonwage labor cost (% of salary)	17			Recovery rate (cents on the dollar)	18.0
Firing cost (weeks of salary)	87	**Paying taxes** (rank)	128		
		Payments (number per year)	32		
		Time (hours per year)	1,050		
		Total tax rate (% of profit)	41.1		

WEST BANK AND GAZA

Ease of doing business (rank)	117	Middle East & North Africa Lower middle income		GNI per capita (US$) Population (m)	1,120 3.7
Starting a business (rank)	166	**Registering property** (rank)	118	**Trading across borders** (rank)	77
Procedures (number)	12	Procedures (number)	10	Documents to export (number)	6
Time (days)	92	Time (days)	72	Time to export (days)	25
Cost (% of income per capita)	280.4	Cost (% of property value)	2.2	Cost to export (US$ per container)	830
Minimum capital (% of income per capita)	9.3			Documents to import (number)	6
		Getting credit (rank)	68	Time to import (days)	40
Dealing with licenses (rank)	132	Strength of legal rights index (0–10)	5	Cost to import (US$ per container)	995
Procedures (number)	21	Depth of credit information index (0–6)	3		
Time (days)	199	Public registry coverage (% of adults)	1.8	**Enforcing contracts** (rank)	125
Cost (% of income per capita)	726.1	Private bureau coverage (% of adults)	0.0	Procedures (number)	44
				Time (days)	700
Employing workers (rank)	103	**Protecting investors** (rank)	33	Cost (% of claim)	21.2
Difficulty of hiring index (0–100)	33	Extent of disclosure index (0–10)	6		
Rigidity of hours index (0–100)	40	Extent of director liability index (0–10)	5	**Closing a business** (rank)	178
Difficulty of firing index (0–100)	20	Ease of shareholder suits index (0–10)	7	Time (years)	NO PRACTICE
Rigidity of employment index (0–100)	31	Strength of investor protection index (0–10)	6.0	Cost (% of estate)	NO PRACTICE
Nonwage labor cost (% of salary)	0			Recovery rate (cents on the dollar)	0.0
Firing cost (weeks of salary)	91	**Paying taxes** (rank)	22		
		Payments (number per year)	27		
		Time (hours per year)	154		
		Total tax rate (% of profit)	17.1		

YEMEN

Ease of doing business (rank)	113	Middle East & North Africa Low income		GNI per capita (US$) Population (m)	760 21.6
Starting a business (rank)	175	**Registering property** (rank)	44	**Trading across borders** (rank)	128
Procedures (number)	12	Procedures (number)	6	Documents to export (number)	6
Time (days)	63	Time (days)	21	Time to export (days)	33
Cost (% of income per capita)	178.8	Cost (% of property value)	3.9	Cost to export (US$ per container)	1,129
Minimum capital (% of income per capita)	2,003.2			Documents to import (number)	9
		Getting credit (rank)	158	Time to import (days)	31
Dealing with licenses (rank)	35	Strength of legal rights index (0–10)	3	Cost to import (US$ per container)	1,475
Procedures (number)	13	Depth of credit information index (0–6)	0		
Time (days)	107	Public registry coverage (% of adults)	0.1	**Enforcing contracts** (rank)	41
Cost (% of income per capita)	239.2	Private bureau coverage (% of adults)	0.0	Procedures (number)	37
				Time (days)	520
Employing workers (rank)	63	**Protecting investors** (rank)	122	Cost (% of claim)	16.5
Difficulty of hiring index (0–100)	0	Extent of disclosure index (0–10)	6		
Rigidity of hours index (0–100)	60	Extent of director liability index (0–10)	4	**Closing a business** (rank)	83
Difficulty of firing index (0–100)	40	Ease of shareholder suits index (0–10)	2	Time (years)	3.0
Rigidity of employment index (0–100)	33	Strength of investor protection index (0–10)	4.0	Cost (% of estate)	8
Nonwage labor cost (% of salary)	9			Recovery rate (cents on the dollar)	28.6
Firing cost (weeks of salary)	17	**Paying taxes** (rank)	84		
		Payments (number per year)	32		
		Time (hours per year)	248		
		Total tax rate (% of profit)	41.4		

ZAMBIA

Ease of doing business (rank)	116	Sub-Saharan Africa Low income		GNI per capita (US$) Population (m)	630 11.9
Starting a business (rank)	82	**Registering property** (rank)	125	**Trading across borders** (rank)	160
Procedures (number)	6	Procedures (number)	6	Documents to export (number)	8
Time (days)	33	Time (days)	70	Time to export (days)	53
Cost (% of income per capita)	30.5	Cost (% of property value)	9.6	Cost to export (US$ per container)	2,098
Minimum capital (% of income per capita)	2.2			Documents to import (number)	11
		Getting credit (rank)	97	Time to import (days)	64
Dealing with licenses (rank)	148	Strength of legal rights index (0–10)	6	Cost to import (US$ per container)	2,840
Procedures (number)	17	Depth of credit information index (0–6)	0		
Time (days)	254	Public registry coverage (% of adults)	0.0	**Enforcing contracts** (rank)	86
Cost (% of income per capita)	1,518.0	Private bureau coverage (% of adults)	0.0	Procedures (number)	35
				Time (days)	471
Employing workers (rank)	121	**Protecting investors** (rank)	64	Cost (% of claim)	38.7
Difficulty of hiring index (0–100)	33	Extent of disclosure index (0–10)	3		
Rigidity of hours index (0–100)	40	Extent of director liability index (0–10)	6	**Closing a business** (rank)	84
Difficulty of firing index (0–100)	30	Ease of shareholder suits index (0–10)	7	Time (years)	2.7
Rigidity of employment index (0–100)	34	Strength of investor protection index (0–10)	5.3	Cost (% of estate)	9
Nonwage labor cost (% of salary)	9			Recovery rate (cents on the dollar)	28.4
Firing cost (weeks of salary)	178	**Paying taxes** (rank)	30		
		Payments (number per year)	37		
		Time (hours per year)	132		
		Total tax rate (% of profit)	16.1		

ZIMBABWE

Ease of doing business (rank)	152
Sub-Saharan Africa	
Low income	
GNI per capita (US$)	325
Population (m)	13.1

Starting a business (rank)	143
Procedures (number)	10
Time (days)	96
Cost (% of income per capita)	21.3
Minimum capital (% of income per capita)	54.6
Dealing with licenses (rank)	172
Procedures (number)	19
Time (days)	952
Cost (% of income per capita)	11,799.0
Employing workers (rank)	123
Difficulty of hiring index (0–100)	0
Rigidity of hours index (0–100)	40
Difficulty of firing index (0–100)	60
Rigidity of employment index (0–100)	33
Nonwage labor cost (% of salary)	4
Firing cost (weeks of salary)	446
Registering property (rank)	79
Procedures (number)	4
Time (days)	30
Cost (% of property value)	25.0
Getting credit (rank)	97
Strength of legal rights index (0–10)	6
Depth of credit information index (0–6)	0
Public registry coverage (% of adults)	0.0
Private bureau coverage (% of adults)	0.0
Protecting investors (rank)	107
Extent of disclosure index (0–10)	8
Extent of director liability index (0–10)	1
Ease of shareholder suits index (0–10)	4
Strength of investor protection index (0–10)	4.3
Paying taxes (rank)	144
Payments (number per year)	52
Time (hours per year)	256
Total tax rate (% of profit)	53.0
Trading across borders (rank)	169
Documents to export (number)	9
Time to export (days)	52
Cost to export (US$ per container)	1,879
Documents to import (number)	13
Time to import (days)	67
Cost to import (US$ per container)	2,420
Enforcing contracts (rank)	74
Procedures (number)	38
Time (days)	410
Cost (% of claim)	32.0
Closing a business (rank)	151
Time (years)	3.3
Cost (% of estate)	22
Recovery rate (cents on the dollar)	0.1

Acknowledgments

Contact details for local partners are available on the *Doing Business* website at http://www.doingbusiness.org

Doing Business 2008 was prepared by a team led by Simeon Djankov and Caralee McLiesh under the general direction of Michael Klein. Svetlana Bagaudinova, Frederic Bustelo, Allen Dennis, Penelope Fidas, Elena Gasol Ramos, Carolin Geginat, Sabine Hertveldt, Melissa Johns, Julien Levis, Janet Morris, Rita Ramalho, Sylvia Solf and Justin Yap led sets of indicators. The team also included Mema Beye, Doina Cebotari, César Chaparro Yedro, Hania Dawood, Marie Delion, Jacqueline den Otter, Cemile Hacibeyoglu, Jamal Ibrahim Haidar, Benjamin Horne, Dahlia Khalifa, Adam Larson, Jean Michel Lobet, Oliver Lorenz, Dana Omran, Camille Ramos, Ivana Rossi, Rachel Shahidsaless, Umar Shavurov, Tea Trumbic, Caroline van Coppenolle, Adriana Vicentini, Maria-Eleni Vlachakou and Bryan Welsh. Karim Belayachi, Maya Choueiri, Alejandro Espinosa-Wang, Kjartan Fjeldsted, Palarp Jumpasut, Jana Matesova, Caroline Otonglo, Djasurbek Teshaev and Lior Ziv assisted in the months prior to publication.

Oliver Hart, Rafael La Porta and Andrei Shleifer provided academic advice on the project. The paying taxes project was conducted in partnership with PricewaterhouseCoopers, led by Robert Morris. The protecting investors, enforcing contracts and not paying bribes projects are conducted in partnership with the Lex Mundi association, led by Carl Anduri and Sam Nolen. The IFC gender team, led by Amanda Ellis, advised on analysis of women and business regulations.

Alison Strong edited the manuscript. Gerry Quinn designed the report and the graphs. Kim Bieler assisted in the report layout. The online service of the *Doing Business* database is managed by Graeme Littler, Felipe Escudero and Ramin Aliyev under the direction of Suzanne Smith.

We are grateful for valuable comments and review provided by the World Bank Group's country and network teams as well as World Bank Group Executive Directors.

The report was made possible by the generous contribution of more than 5,000 lawyers, accountants, judges, businesspeople and public officials in 178 economies. Quotations in this report are from *Doing Business* local partners unless otherwise indicated. The names of those wishing to be acknowledged individually are listed below. Contact details are posted on the *Doing Business* website at http://www.doingbusiness.org.

GLOBAL CONTRIBUTORS

Allen & Overy LLP
APL Ltd.
Baker & McKenzie
Cleary Gottlieb Steen & Hamilton LLP
Hawkamah - The Institute for Corporate Governance
Ius Laboris, Alliance of Labor, Employment, Benefits and Pensions Law Firms
Lawyers Without Borders
Lex Mundi, Association of Independent Law Firms
Lovells LLP
PricewaterhouseCoopers
PricewaterhouseCoopers Legal Services
SDV International Logistics
The Adora Group Ltd (Freightnet)
TOBOC Inc.

REGIONAL CONTRIBUTORS

Abu-Ghazaleh Legal
EcoBank
Federación Interamericana de la Industria de la Construcción
Globalink Transportation & Logistics Worldwide LLP
IKRP Rokas & Partners
University of South Pacific
TransUnion International

AFGHANISTAN

Rashid Ibrahim
A. F. Ferguson & Co.

T. Ud-Din A. Mirza
A. F. Ferguson & Co.

Habibullah Peerzada
ACCL International

Sargon Heinrich
ACCL International

Ehsan Sahar
Afghan Container Transport Co.

M. Azam Kargar
Afghan Transit Company

Muslimul Haq
Afghanistan Banks Association

Najibullah Amiri
Afghanistan Banks Association

Ben Turnbull
Afghanistan International Bank

Saduddin Haziq
Afghanistan International Bank

Shahzad Haider
Afghanistan International Bank

Ellaha Salimi
Afghanistan International Chamber of Commerce

Hamidullah Farooqi
Afghanistan International Chamber of Commerce

Farzana Rashid Rahimi
Afghanistan National Development Strategy

Ziauddin Zia
Afghanistan National Development Strategy

Abdul Salam Zahed
AISA

Naseem Akbar
AISA

Said Mubin Shah
AISA

Simran Kaur Lohnes
AISA

Khwaga Kakar
Asian Development Bank

BearingPoint

Tim Bisbee
Center for International Private Enterprise

Khalid Sekander
Consultant

Khan Afzal
Da Afghanistan Bank

Naser Shahalemi
Gilbert Real Estate

Zahoor Malla
Globalink Transportation & Logistics Worldwide LLP

Hosam Helal
IDLO

Wadir Safi
IDLO

Lorenzo Delesgues
Integrity Watch Afghanistan

Muhamed Jafar Khohistany
Kabul University Faculty of Law and Political Sciences

Shahla Farid
Kabul University Faculty of Law and Political Sciences

M. Wisal Khan
Mandviwalla & Zafar

Mehmood Y. Mandviwalla
Mandviwalla & Zafar

Abdul Rahman Watanwal
MBC Construction

Abdul Rahim Saeedi
Ministry of Commerce

Zarmeena Njeem
Parliament

Kalimuddin Ghauri
PricewaterhouseCoopers

Mirza Taqi Ud-Din Ahmad
PricewaterhouseCoopers

Richard Scarth
Property Consulting Afghanistan

Inayetullah Zare
Pyramid Geo-Engineering & Construction Co.

Samir Satchu
Roshan

Bahauddin Baha
Supreme Court

A. Farid Barakzai
TNT Global Express

Gregory Hicks
US Embassy

John F. Ewald III
USAID/Bearing Point

Kevin O'Brien
USAID/Bearing Point

Martin Dinning
USAID/Bearing Point

Megan Asdorian
USAID/Bearing Point

William E. Kosar
USAID/Bearing Point

Andre Hernandez
USAID/Emerging Markets Group

Gregory F. Maassen
USAID/Emerging Markets Group

Habib Zikria
USAID/Emerging Markets Group

Naeem Yassin
Yassin Construction Co., Afghan Builders Association

ALBANIA

Fiorilda Bregu
Boga & Associates

Renata Leka
Boga & Associates

Sokol Elmazaj
Boga & Associates

Andi Memi
Hoxha, Memi & Hoxha

Shpati Hoxha
Hoxha, Memi & Hoxha

Georgios K. Lemonis
IKRP Rokas & Partners

Sonila Dheri
IKRP Rokas & Partners

Genci Krasniqi
Kalo & Associates

Jola Gjuzi
Kalo & Associates

Perparim Kalo
Kalo & Associates

Vilma Gjyshi
Kalo & Associates

Jean-Pierre Vigroux
PricewaterhouseCoopers

Laura Qorlaze
PricewaterhouseCoopers

Loreta Peci
PricewaterhouseCoopers

Albert Murati
Shega Group

Ilir Bejleri
Son - Group Ltd.

Olsi Ibro
TBI Law Firm

Artur Asllani
Tonucci & Partners

ALGERIA

Africa Multiple

Mourad Dubert
Architect

Mourad Terbaoui
Architect

Djilali Hadjadj
Association Algerienne de lutte contre la Corruption

Nabil Belloula

Tayeb Belloula
Attorney-at-Law

Badredine Saadi
AX - Consult, Agence d'Architecture et d'Urbanisme

Branka Achari-Djokic
Bank of Algeria

Fares Ouzegdouh
Béjaia Mediterranean Terminal

Fériel Oulounis
Cabinet d'Avocats Samir Hamouda

Nabiha Zerigui
Cabinet d'Avocats Samir Hamouda

Samir Hamouda
Cabinet d'Avocats Samir Hamouda

Ali Ait Amar
Cabinet Sator

Maya Sator
Cabinet Sator

Malik Elkettas
Elkettas International

Tarik Zahzah
Ghellal & Mekerba

Arezki Djadour
Gide Loyrette Nouel, member of Lex Mundi

Samy Laghouati
Gide Loyrette Nouel, member of Lex Mundi

Rdha Halit
Hadj Ali Audit Practice

Gerard Morin
Landwell & Associés - PricewaterhouseCoopers

Jérôme Le Hec
Landwell & Associés - PricewaterhouseCoopers

Marc Veuillot
Landwell & Associés - PricewaterhouseCoopers

Michel Lecerf
Landwell & Associés - PricewaterhouseCoopers

Nora Djadoun
Landwell & Associés - PricewaterhouseCoopers

Khaled Goussanem
Law Firm Goussanem & Aloui

Salima Aloui
Law Firm Goussanem & Aloui

Ryad Chabouni
NSC

Hassan Yassine
Thompson & Knight LLP

ANGOLA

Guilherme Santos Silva
Abreu Advogados

Miguel de Avillez Pereira
Abreu Advogados

Rita Maltez
Abreu Advogados

Alexandre Do Rêgo Pegado
Alexandre Pegado - Escritório de Advogados

Paulo Muginga
Alexandre Pegado - Escritório de Advogados

Ana Fernandes

Laurinda Prazeres
Faria de Bastos, Sebastião e Lopes - Advogados Associados

Teresinha Lopes
Faria de Bastos, Sebastião e Lopes - Advogados Associados

Fernando Barros

Sika Awoonor
GoodWorks International Angola, Lda.

Lourdes Caposso Fernandes

Judith De Fatima Dos Santos Lima
National Bank of Angola

Pedro Calixto

Elisa Rangel Nunes
Rangel, Nunes & Teresa

Alain Brachet
SDV AMI International Logistics

Aymeric Frisch
SDV AMI International Logistics

Guirec Malfait
SDV AMI International Logistics

Tropicos e Servicos, Lda.

ANTIGUA AND BARBUDA

Eleanor R. Clark
Clarke & Clarke

Carden Conliffe Clarke
Commodore & Associates

Vernon Edwards
Freight Forwarding & Deconsolidating

Ann Henry
Henry & Burnette

Hesketh Williams
Ministry of Labor

Phillip Jr. Isaacs
OBM International, Antigua Ltd.

Charles Walwyn
PricewaterhouseCoopers

Neil Coates
PricewaterhouseCoopers

Stacy Richards-Anjo
Richards & Co.

Clare Roberts
Roberts & Co.

ARGENTINA

Julian A. Collados
Accountant

Agustín Marra
Alfaro Abogados

Ana Candelaria Alonso Negre
Alfaro Abogados

Carlos Alfaro
Alfaro Abogados

Gisela Candurra
Alfaro Abogados

Sebastián Rodrigo
Alfaro Abogados

Soledad Matteozzi
Alfaro Abogados

Teresa Noceto
Alfaro Abogados

Federico Villarino
Álvarez Prado & Asociados

Octavio Miguel Zenarruza
Álvarez Prado & Asociados

C. Gustavo Ferrante
Brons & Salas Abogados

Guillermo Pavan
Brons & Salas Abogados

Lisandro A. Allende
Brons & Salas Abogados

Pablo Grillo Ciocchini
Brons & Salas Abogados

Carlos María Rotman
Bruchou, Fernandez Madero, Lombardi & Mitrani

Oscar Alberto del Río
Central Bank of Argentina

Enrique Monsegur
Clippers S.A.

Jorge Miranda
Clippers S.A.

Comercial del Oeste

Eduardo Corso

Pablo L. Cavallaro
Estudio Cavallaro Abogados

Mariano Carricart
Fornieles Law Firm

Eduardo J. Viñales
Funes de Rioja & Asociados, member of Ius Laboris

Ignacio Funes de Rioja
Funes de Rioja & Asociados, member of Ius Laboris

Gonzalo Carlos Ballester
J.P.O'Farrell Abogados

Joaquín Emilio Zappa
J.P.O'Farrell Abogados

Santiago Varela
J.P.O'Farrell Abogados

Nicolás Dassen
Jorge & Dassen Abogados - Consultores

Alfredo Miguel O'Farrell
Marval, O'Farrell & Mairal, member of Lex Mundi

Patricia Ruhman Seggiaro
Marval, O'Farrell & Mairal, member of Lex Mundi

Santiago Laclau
Marval, O'Farrell & Mairal, member of Lex Mundi

Sonia F. Salvatierra
Marval, O'Farrell & Mairal, member of Lex Mundi

Materiales Benavidez s.r.l.

MissionLine Logistics S.A.

Agata Mendoza
Mollard, Mendoza & Asociados

Miguel P. Murray
Murray, d'André, Isasmendi & Sirito de Zavalía

Pablo Murray
Murray, d'André, Isasmendi & Sirito de Zavalía

Enrique Pugliano
Organización Veraz S.A., in affiliation with Equifax Inc.

Abraham Viera
Planosnet.com Consultoria Municipal

Andrés M. Edelstein
PricewaterhouseCoopers

Carlos D. Zima
PricewaterhouseCoopers

Ignacio E. Rodriguez
PricewaterhouseCoopers

Juan Manuel Magadan
PricewaterhouseCoopers

Alejandro Vidal
PricewaterhouseCoopers Legal Services

Azul García Duffy
PricewaterhouseCoopers Legal Services

Hernán Gonzalo Cuenca Martínez
PricewaterhouseCoopers Legal Services

Julio Alberto Pueyrredon
PricewaterhouseCoopers Legal Services

Monserrat García
PricewaterhouseCoopers Legal Services

Pablo González del Solar
PricewaterhouseCoopers Legal Services

Liliana Cecilia Segade
Quattrini, Laprida & Asociados

Adolfo Rouillon
The World Bank Group

Vanesa Balda
Vitale, Manoff & Feilbogen

ARMENIA

Artak Arzoyan
ACRA Credit Reporting CJSC

David Sargsyan
Ameria CJSC

Karine Khachatryan
BearingPoint

Central bank of Armenia

Shushan Doydoyan
Freedom of Information, Center of Armenia

Rajiv Nagri
Globalink Transportation & Logistics Worldwide LLP

Aram Poghosyan
Grant Thornton Amyot

Hakob Tadevosyan
Grant Thornton Amyot

Hakob Bagdasaryan

Gagik Galstyan
Horizon 95

Mher Grigoryan
Inecoabnk CJSC

Vardan Bezhanyan
Inecobank CJSC

Karen Petrosyan
Investment Law Group LLC

Vahe Kakoyan
Investment Law Group LLC

Eduard Mesropyan
JINJ Ltd.

Artur Tunyan
Judicial Reform Project

Hayk Ghazazyan
KPMG

Tigran Sukiasyan
OSCE

Bela Gutidze
PricewaterhouseCoopers

Jorge Intriago
PricewaterhouseCoopers

Matthew Tallarovic
PricewaterhouseCoopers

Rusa Sreseli
PricewaterhouseCoopers

Sergi Kobakhidze
PricewaterhouseCoopers

Hayk Sahakyan
State Committee of the Real Property Cadastre

AUSTRALIA

Georgia Price
Allens Arthur Robinson

Michael Quinlan
Allens Arthur Robinson

Steven Fleming
Allens Arthur Robinson

Leon Zwier
Arnold Bloch Leibler

AussieROO

Matthew Allison
Baycorp Advantage

Ian Humphreys
Blake Dawson Waldron

John Lobban
Blake Dawson Waldron

Mark Grdovich
Blake Dawson Waldron

Marcus Connor
Chang, Pistilli & Simmons

Mark Pistilli
Chang, Pistilli & Simmons

Doug Jones
Clayton Utz, member of Lex Mundi

Lucy Adamson
Clayton Utz, member of Lex Mundi

Nick Thomas
Clayton Utz, member of Lex Mundi

Owen Hayford
Clayton Utz, member of Lex Mundi

Paul James
Clayton Utz, member of Lex Mundi

Penny Grau
Clayton Utz, member of Lex Mundi

Ron Schaffer
Clayton Utz, member of Lex Mundi

Mitchell Mathas
Deacons

Dean Schiller

Greg Channell
Department of Lands

Morgan Kelly
Ferrier Hodgson

Peter Walker
Ferrier Hodgson

Import-Export Services Pty. Ltd.

Moving Imports and Exports

Ann Previtera
PricewaterhouseCoopers

Luke Sayers
PricewaterhouseCoopers

Lynda Brumm
PricewaterhouseCoopers

Tim Cox
PricewaterhouseCoopers

Aaron Goonrey
PricewaterhouseCoopers Legal Services

Andrew Wheeler
PricewaterhouseCoopers Legal Services

Anna Dileo
PricewaterhouseCoopers Legal Services

Mark Swan
PricewaterhouseCoopers Legal Services

David Buda
RBHM Commercial Lawyers

SDV Pty. Ltd.

Swire Shipping Ltd.

David Zwi
Thomson Playford

John Martin
Thomson Playford

Daniel Clough
Victorian Bar

AUSTRIA

Irene Mandl
Austrian Institute for SME Research

Andreas Hable
Binder Grösswang Rechtsanwälte

Doris Buxbaum
Binder Grösswang Rechtsanwälte

Tibor Fabian
Binder Grösswang Rechtsanwälte

BIO-4 Umwelttechnik GmbH

Alexander Klauser
Brauneis Klauser Prändl Rechtsanwälte GmbH

Gregor Maderbacher
Brauneis Klauser Prändl Rechtsanwälte GmbH

Angela Zaffalon
Cerha Hempel & Spiegelfeld Hlawati, member of Lex Mundi

Benedikt Spiegelfeld
Cerha Hempel & Spiegelfeld Hlawati, member of Lex Mundi

Hans Kristoferitsch
Cerha Hempel & Spiegelfeld Hlawati, member of Lex Mundi

Julian Feichtinger
Cerha Hempel & Spiegelfeld Hlawati, member of Lex Mundi

Harald E. Heschl
Consumer Credit Information

Martin Eckel
e|n|w|c Eiselsberg Natlacen Walderdorff Cancola Rechtsanwälte GmbH

Alexander Isola
Graf & Pitkowitz Rechtsanwälte GMBH

Ferdinand Graf
Graf & Pitkowitz Rechtsanwälte GMBH

Ruth Rosenkranz
Graf & Pitkowitz Rechtsanwälte GMBH

Rudolf Kaindl
Koehler, Kaindl, Duerr & Partner, Civil Law Notaries

Kraus & Co Warenhandelsgesellschaft mbH

Andrea Schwartz
Kunz Schima Wallentin Rechtsanwälte KEG, member of Ius Laboris

Birgit Vogt-Majarek
Kunz Schima Wallentin Rechtsanwälte KEG, member of Ius Laboris

Georg Schima
Kunz Schima Wallentin Rechtsanwälte KEG, member of Ius Laboris

Alfred Nepf
Ministry of Finance

Wolfgang Messeritsch
National Bank of Austria

Gerhard Antenreiter
Notariat Dr. Gerhard Antenreiter

Klaus Woschnak
Notary Office Dr. Woschnak

Ernst Biebl
PricewaterhouseCoopers

Friedrich Roedler
PricewaterhouseCoopers

Michael Podesser
PricewaterhouseCoopers

Rudolf Krickl
PricewaterhouseCoopers

Peter Madl
Schönherr Rechtsanwälte GmbH / Attorneys-at-Law

Ulrike Langwallner
Schönherr Rechtsanwälte GmbH / Attorneys-at-Law

Birgit Schneider
Urbanek Lind Schmied Reisch Rechtsanwälte OG

Ulla Reisch
Urbanek Lind Schmied Reisch Rechtsanwälte OG

Stephan Schmalzl
WallnöferSchmalzl-Rechtsanwälte

Lothar A. Wachter
Wolf Theiss

AZERBAIJAN

John Quinn
ACE Forwarding Caspian

Zohrad Ismayilov
Association for Assistance to Free Economy

Azad Aliyev
Association of Social Economic Researches

Abbas Guliyev
Baker & McKenzie - CIS, Ltd.

Aykhan Asadov
Baker & McKenzie - CIS, Ltd.

Gunduz Karimov
Baker & McKenzie - CIS, Ltd.

Farhad Mirzayev
BM International LLC

Sahib Mammadov
Citizens' Labour Rights Protection League

Sabit A. Bagirov
Entrepreneurship Development Foundation

Anar Aliyev
IFC Corporate Governance Project

Eldar Adilzade
IFC Corporate Governance Projectf

Kamil Valiyev

Kamil Mammadov
Mammadov & Partners Law Firm

Maksud Mirzoyev
McDonald's Azerbaijan LLC

Benjamin Paine
McGrigors Baku Ltd.

Sabina Gulmaliyeva
McGrigors Baku Ltd.

Mehriban Efendiyeva
Michael Wilson & Partners Ltd.

Aiyar Mammadyarov
National Bank of Azerbaijan

Emin Huseynov
National Bank of Azerbaijan

Rufat Aslanli
National Bank of Azerbaijan

Roman Alloyarov
OMNI Law Firm

Arif Guliyev
PricewaterhouseCoopers

Jeyhun Huseynzada
PricewaterhouseCoopers

Movlan Pashayev
PricewaterhouseCoopers

Vugar Mammadov
PricewaterhouseCoopers

Ingilab Ahmadov
Public Finance Monitoring Center

Emma Silyayeva
Salans

Vagif Ahmadov
Salans

Yusif Aghayev
Transparency International

Faig Huseynov
Unibank

Samir Balayev
Unibank

BANGLADESH

Badrul Ahsan
A. Qasem & Co. / PricewaterhouseCoopers

Sohel Kasem
A. Qasem & Co. / PricewaterhouseCoopers

Zainul Abedin
A. Qasem & Co. / PricewaterhouseCoopers

ABM Dress

Mirza Quamrul Hasan
Adviser's Legal Alliance

Banasree Barua
Air Link Ltd.

Clifford Gonsalves
Air Link Ltd.

M. Iqbal Ali
Air Link Ltd.

Monoranjan Guha
Air Link Ltd.

Md. Ayub Chowdhury
Ayub & Mahmood Chartered Accountants

Md. Abdullah
Bangladesh Bank, Head Office Dhaka

Ariful Islam
Bhuiyan Islam & Zaidi

Bin Ali Trading Est.

Q.M. Mahtab-Uz Zaman
BRAC University

Mahfuz-ul-Haque Seleym
Contemplus Real Estate

MD. Nurul Amin
Development Constructions Ltd.

Saady Amin
Development Constructions Ltd.

Ferdaus Ara Begum
Dhaka Chamber of Commerce and Industry (DCCI)

Badrud Doulah
Doulah & Doulah Advocates

Nasirud Doulah
Doulah & Doulah Advocates

Shamsud Doulah
Doulah & Doulah Advocates

Karishma Jahan
Dr. Kamal Hossain & Associates

Sharif Bhuiyan
Dr. Kamal Hossain & Associates

Quazi Reza-Ul Hoque
ERGO Legal Counsels

Md. Halim Bepari
Halim Law Associate

Aneek Haque
Haque & Associates

Huatex Import Export Co. Ltd.

Khairul Alam Chowdhury
Huq and Co.

Margub Kabir
Huq and Co.

Rabeya Jamali
Huq and Co.

Rafique-ul Huq
Huq and Co.

Index Corporation Ltd.

Munir Uddin Ahamed
Integrated Transportation Services Ltd., Agent of Panalpina

Rezaur Rahman Rizon
Integrated Transportation Services Ltd., Agent of Panalpina

Asm Abdur Razzaque
Lee, Khan & Partners

Mohammad Zeeshan Hyder
Lee, Khan & Partners

Moksadul Islam
Legal Steps

Md. Mehedi Hasan
MGH Group

Abdul Mannan
Ministry of Commerce

Proactive

Quazi Reza-Ul Hoque

Omar Sadat
Sadat Sarwat and Associates

C.R. Mazumder
Saha Mazumder & Co. Chartered Accountants

Sikder Buying Ltd.

Mirza Quamrul Hasan
Square Pharmaceuticals Ltd.

Tareq Hasan Siddiqui
Square Pharmaceuticals Ltd.

Syed Associates

Mohammed Asaduzzaman
Syed Ishtiaq Ahmed & Associates

Syed Afzal Hasan Uddin
Syed Ishtiaq Ahmed & Associates

Md. Shafiul Alam
The Hongkong and Shanghai Banking Corporation Ltd.

Sheher Imam Chowdhury
The Hongkong and Shanghai Banking Corporation Ltd.

Amir-Ul Islam
The Law Associates, member of Lex Mundi

Shamsul Hasan
The Law Associates, member of Lex Mundi

Habibur Rahman
The Law Counsel

Imran Siddiq
The Law Counsel

Ratnadwip Foods Limited

V-Teac Garments Pvt. Ltd.

BELARUS

AsstrA

Alexander Botian
Borovtsov & Salei Law Offices

Marina Dymovich
Borovtsov & Salei Law Offices

Vladimir G. Biruk
Capital Ltd.

Aliaksandr Danilevich
Danilevich

Antonina Ivanova
DICSA International Group of Lawyers

Olga Polozova
DICSA International Group of Lawyers

Oleg Gvozd
Gvozd, Lakizo & Partners LLC

Sergei Oditsov
Gvozd, Lakizo & Partners LLC

Ivan Alievich
Mikhel & Partners

Konstantin Mikhel
Mikhel & Partners

Alexandr Ignatov
National Bank of the Republic of Belarus

Igor Dankov
PricewaterhouseCoopers

Jorge Intriago
PricewaterhouseCoopers

Maxim Korsheniuk
PricewaterhouseCoopers

Ron J. Barden
PricewaterhouseCoopers

Evgeniya Motina
The Institute of State and Law of the National Academy of Science of Belarus

Alexander Vasilevsky
Valex Consult

Sergey Strelchik
Valex Consult

BELGIUM

Allen & Overy LLP

Almalux S. A.

Fannia Polet
Altius

Kurt Grillet
Altius

Tom Vantroyen
Altius

William Timmermans
Altius

Carl Meyntjens
Ashurst

David Du Pont
Ashurst

Alexis Lemmerling
Berquin Notaires

Dominique Mougenot
Commercial Court Mons

Cour de Cassation

Conny Grenson
Eubelius Attorneys

Stephan Legein
Federal Public Service Finance

Dirt Lindemans
Liedekerke Wolters Waelbroeck Kirkpatrick, member of Lex Mundi

Frank Judo
Liedekerke Wolters Waelbroeck Kirkpatrick, member of Lex Mundi

Christian Willems
Loyens

Suzy Vande Wiele
Loyens

Hubert André-Dumont
McGuire Woods Kazakhstan LLP, member of Lex Mundi

MedicCleanAir

Didier Muraille
National Bank of Belgium

Thomas Hürner
National Bank of Belgium

Robert Meunier
Notary

Poligoods International S.A.

Amaury Della Faille
PricewaterhouseCoopers

Bart Vanham
PricewaterhouseCoopers

Frank Dierckx
PricewaterhouseCoopers

Frédéric Souchon
PricewaterhouseCoopers

Katrien Schillemans
PricewaterhouseCoopers

Koen Cooreman
PricewaterhouseCoopers

Luc Legon
PricewaterhouseCoopers

Roel Verhulst
PricewaterhouseCoopers

Sabrina Otten
PricewaterhouseCoopers

Sibylle Vandenberghe
PricewaterhouseCoopers

Yves Voeten
PricewaterhouseCoopers

Bart Vanstaen
PricewaterhouseCoopers Legal Services

Dirk Van Strijthem
PricewaterhouseCoopers Legal Services

Karin Winters
PricewaterhouseCoopers Legal Services

Axel Maeterlinck
Simont Braun

Sandrine Hirsch
Simont Braun

Pierrette Fraisse
SPF Finances - AGDP

Steven de Schrijver
Van Bael & Bellis

Thierry Bosly
White & Case

BELIZE

Emil Arguelles
Arguelles & Co.

Saidi M. Vaccaro
Arguelles & Co.

Tania Moody
Barrow & Williams

Patricia Rodriguez
Belize Companies and Corporate Affairs Registry

Fred Lumor
Fred Lumor & Co.

Reynaldo F. Magana
Frontier International Business Services Ltd.

Gian C. Gandhi
International Financial Services Commission

C. Phillip Waight
Waight & Associates

Carlton Young
Young's Engineering Consultancy Ltd.

BENIN

Philippe Nadaud
Banque de l'Habitat du Bénin

Charles Ki-Zerbo
BCEAO

Alice Codjia-Sohouenou
Cabinet Agbantou Saidou

Saïdou Agbantou
Cabinet Agbantou Saidou

Victoire Agbanrin-Elisha
Cabinet d'Avocat Agbanrin-Elisha

Rafikou Alabi
Cabinet Me Alabi

Agnès A. Campbell
Campbell & Associés

Eurydice Adjovi
Continental Bank - Bénin

Cyrille Laleye
EcoBank - Benin

Veronique Akankossi Deguenon
Etude Me Veronique Akankossi Deguenon

Adeline Messou
FIDAFRICA / PricewaterhouseCoopers

Dominique Taty
FIDAFRICA / PricewaterhouseCoopers

Evelyne M'Bassidgé
FIDAFRICA / PricewaterhouseCoopers

Fousséni Traoré
FIDAFRICA / PricewaterhouseCoopers

Jean Claude Gnamien
FIDAFRICA / PricewaterhouseCoopers

Luc-M. C. Gnacadja
Imoteph

Didier Sterlingot
SDV - SAGA

Zakari Djibril Sambaou

BHUTAN

Karma Thinlay
Anti-Corruption Commission, Royal Government of Bhutan

Neten Zangmo
Anti-Corruption Commission, Royal Government of Bhutan

Phub Tshering
Bhutan Chamber of Commerce & Industry

Namgay Dorji
Bhutan Development Finance Corporation Ltd.

Ugyen Namgyal
Bhutan Development Finance Corporation Ltd.

Leki Dorji Norbu
Bhutan Engineering Company Pvt. Ltd.

Sonam Penjore
Bhutan National Bank

Prakash Rasaily
City Legal Unit

N.B. Gurung
DHL

Lhundub Dorji
East - West Construction

S.N. Muruli
Gyelsa -Tewa Real Estate Developer (GRED)

Tshering Tobgey
Gyelsa -Tewa Real Estate Developer (GRED)

Kincho Dorjee
Leko Packers

Ugen Takchhu
Ministry of Agriculture

Sonam Tshering
Ministry of Finance

Sonam Wangchuk
Ministry of Finance

Tashi Wangmo
Ministry of Labor & Human Resources

Karma Tshering
Ministry of Trade & Industry

Kiazang Tahgyal
Ministry of Trade & Industry

Rinzin Dorji
Ministry of Trade & Industry

Ugyen Dorji
Ministry of Trade & Industry

Susan Collier
Orrick, Herrington & Sutcliffe (Lawyers without Borders)

Tshering Wangchuk
Royal Court of Justice

Damcho Dorji
Royal Government of Bhutan

Eden Dema
Royal Monetary Authority of Bhutan

Dophu Dorji
Royal Securities Exchange of Bhutan Ltd.

Tashi Yezer
Royal Securities Exchange of Bhutan Ltd.

Ugyen Dorji
Thimphu City Co.

Pema Tashi
XPS

Karma Lotey
Yangphel Adventure Travel

BOLIVIA

Carolina Aguirre Urioste
Bufete Aguirre Soc. Civ.

Fernando Aguirre
Bufete Aguirre Soc. Civ.

Carola Ayaroa Mantilla

Ariel Morales Vasquez
C.R. & F. Rojas, member of Lex Mundi

Carlos Ferreira
C.R. & F. Rojas, member of Lex Mundi

Diego Rojas
C.R. & F. Rojas, member of Lex Mundi

Fernando Rojas
C.R. & F. Rojas, member of Lex Mundi

Manfredo Kempff
C.R. & F. Rojas, member of Lex Mundi

Sandra Salinas
C.R. & F. Rojas, member of Lex Mundi

Edith Loza
College of Architects

Jose Gamboa
College of Architects

Adrián Barrenechea Bazoberry
Criales, Urcullo & Antezana

Oscar Antonio Plaza Ponte
Entidad De Servicios De Información Enserbic S.A.

Gonzalo Mendieta Romero
Estudio de Abogados Mendieta Romero & Asociados

Francisco Bollini Roca
Guevara & Gutiérrez S.C.

Jorge Luis Inchauste
Guevara & Gutiérrez S.C.

Primitivo Gutiérrez
Guevara & Gutiérrez S.C.

Alejandro Peláez Kay
Indacochea & Asociados

Mariana Pereira Nava
Indacochea & Asociados

Carlos Alberto Iacia
PricewaterhouseCoopers

Evany Oliveira
PricewaterhouseCoopers

Roberto Viscafé Ureña
PricewaterhouseCoopers

A. Mauricio Torrico Galindo
Quintanilla & Soria, Soc. Civ.

Julio Quintanilla Quiroga
Quintanilla & Soria, Soc. Civ.

Ramiro Guevara

Ana Carola Guzman Gonzales
Salazar, Salazar & Asociados

Sergio Salazar-Machicado
Salazar, Salazar & Asociados

Enrique F. Hurtado
Superintendencia De Bancos y Entidades Financieras

Soraya Quiroga Berazain
Superintendencia De Bancos y Entidades Financieras

BOSNIA AND HERZEGOVINA

Adnan Kulenović

Branko Marić
Branko Marić Law Office

Nusmir Huskic
Branko Marić Law Office

Daniela Terzic
DLA Piper Weiss -Tessbach

Edisa Peštek
DLA Piper Weiss -Tessbach

Nedzida Salihovic-Whalen
DLA Piper Weiss -Tessbach

Emmanuel Koenig

Mira Todorovic-Symeonidis
IKRP Rokas & Partners

Petros Doukas
IKRP Rokas & Partners

Vildana Mandalovic
IKRP Rokas & Partners

Hasib Salkić
Interšped

Nikola M. Janković
Lansky, Ganzger & Partner d.o.o.

Emir Kovačević
Law Office of Emir Kovačević

Muhidin Karšić
Law Office of Emir Kovačević

Mehmed Spaho
Law Office Spaho

Bojana Tkalcic-Djulic
Lawyers' Office Bojana Tkalcic-Djulic & Olodar Prebanic

Senada Havic
LRC Credit Bureau

Mark Davidson

Sabina Buco
PricewaterhouseCoopers

Sandra Djuragic
PricewaterhouseCoopers

Boris Divjak
TI-Bosnia and Herzegovina

BOTSWANA

Akheel Jinabhai

Chazha Kgalemang
Armstrongs Attorneys, member of Lex Mundi

Sipho Ziga
Armstrongs Attorneys, member of Lex Mundi

Wandipa Tshambani
Armstrongs Attorneys, member of Lex Mundi

Edward W. Fashole-Luke II
Luke & Associates

Mmatshipi Motsepe
Manica Africa Pty. Ltd.

Diba M. Diba
Minchin & Kelly

Kwadwo Osei-Ofei
Osei-Ofei Swabi & Co.

Anura Suren Perera
PricewaterhouseCoopers

Uttum Corea
PricewaterhouseCoopers

Vincent Galeromeloe
TransUnion ITC

Alfred Ngowi
University of Botswana

BRAZIL

Camilla Sisti
Araújo e Policastro Advogados

Esther Jerussalmy
Araújo e Policastro Advogados

Biroex Export Import Ltda

Rodrigo Matos
Cargo Logistics

Andréa Pitthan Françolin
De Vivo Whitaker e Castro Advogados

Walter Abrahão Nimir Junior
De Vivo Whitaker e Castro Advogados

Daniel Valle
Demarest e Almeida, member of Lex Mundi

Thiago Giantomassi
Demarest e Almeida, member of Lex Mundi

Eliane Ribeiro Gago
Duarte Garcia, Caselli Guimarães e Terra Advogados

José Ricardo dos Santos Luz Júnior
Duarte Garcia, Caselli Guimarães e Terra Advogados

Fernanda Cirne Montorfano
Escritorio de Advocacia Gouvêa Vieira

Pedro Vitor Araujo da Costa
Escritorio de Advocacia Gouvêa Vieira

Rafael Frota Indio do Brasil Ferraz
Escritorio de Advocacia Gouvêa Vieira

Andrea Acerbi
Felsberg, Pedretti, Mannrich e Aidar Advogados e Consultores Legais

Thomas Benes Felsberg
Felsberg, Pedretti, Mannrich e Aidar Advogados e Consultores Legais

Beatriz Ryoko Yamashita
Fischer & Forster Advogados

Susan Christina Forster
Fischer & Forster Advogados

Gilberto Beleza
IAB

Claúdia Iaconelli Alves da Silva
IFC

Alessandra Souza
Loeser e Portela Advogados, PricewaterhouseCoopers Legal Services

Durval Portela
Loeser e Portela Advogados, PricewaterhouseCoopers Legal Services

Enrique Tello Hadad
Loeser e Portela Advogados, PricewaterhouseCoopers Legal Services

Fernando Loeser
Loeser e Portela Advogados, PricewaterhouseCoopers Legal Services

Richard Blanchet
Loeser e Portela Advogados, PricewaterhouseCoopers Legal Services

Rita Nader
Loeser e Portela Advogados, PricewaterhouseCoopers Legal Services

Samira Gouvea
Loeser e Portela Advogados, PricewaterhouseCoopers Legal Services

Thelma Eliza Gatuzzo
Loeser e Portela Advogados, PricewaterhouseCoopers Legal Services

Manoel I. T. Monteiro

Cássio Mesquita Barros
Mesquita Barros Advogados, member of Ius Laboris

Nadia Demoliner Lacerda
Mesquita Barros Advogados, member of Ius Laboris

Eduardo Augusto Mattar
Pinheiro Guimarães - Advogados

Adriana Grizante de Almeida
PricewaterhouseCoopers

Carlos Alberto Iacia
PricewaterhouseCoopers

Elidie P. Bifano
PricewaterhouseCoopers

Evany Oliveira
PricewaterhouseCoopers

Michelle Giraldi Lacerda
PricewaterhouseCoopers

R. Mola Comercio e Servicos Ltda.

Ricardo Loureiro
Serasa S.A.

Renato Berger
Tozzini Freire Advogados

Rodrigo Souza Mendes de Araujo
Tozzini Freire Advogados

Ana Beatriz Fett Dixon
Veirano Advogados

Diogo Fries
Veirano Advogados

Eduardo Guimarães Wanderley
Veirano Advogados

Gabriela Weirich Mottin
Veirano Advogados

Gilberto Deon Corrêa Junior
Veirano Advogados

Guilherme Rizzo Amaral
Veirano Advogados

Itiberê de Oliveira Castellano Rodrigues
Veirano Advogados

José Wahle
Veirano Advogados

Lúcia Carvalhal Sica
Veirano Advogados

Marcos Tiraboschi
Veirano Advogados

Maria Fernanda Pecora
Veirano Advogados

Pedro Maciel
Veirano Advogados

Roberta Feiten Silva
Veirano Advogados

Sergio Bronstein
Veirano Advogados

Vanessa Felício
Veirano Advogados

Flavia Bailone Marcilio
Veirano Advogados Associados

Andrea Oricchio Kirsh
Viseu Cunha Oricchio Advogados

Verônica Madureira Pereira
Viseu Cunha Oricchio Advogados

World Line Freight Forwarder Ltda

BRUNEI

Arkitek Ibrahim

Attorney General's Chambers

Nuralia Abdul Rahim
Brunei International Financial Centre, Ministry of Finance

Danny Chua
Brunei Transporting Company

Colin Ong
Dr. Colin Ong Legal Services

Teck Guan Lim
Ernst & Young

Kelvin Lim
K. Lim & Co.

Alimin Hj Kalong
Lands Department, Ministry of Development

Michael Guan
Lee Corporatehouse Associates

Nancy Lai
Lee Corporatehouse Associates

Norman Jalil
Municipal Department, Bandar Seri Begawan

Caroline Chong
The Hongkong and Shanghai Banking Corporation Ltd.

Rosdi Amin Yaakub
The Hongkong and Shanghai Banking Corporation Ltd.

Syed Alwi Alkaff
The Hongkong and Shanghai Banking Corporation Ltd.

Yu Kwang Lim
The Hongkong and Shanghai Banking Corporation Ltd.

Yew Choh Lee
Y.C. Lee & Lee Advocates & Solicitors

BULGARIA

A.M.G - Anna Faklieva

Darina Palova
Access to Information Programme

Gergana Jouleva
Access to Information Programme

Ralitza Katzarska
Access to Information Programme

Dessislava Loukarova
Arsov, Natchev, Ganeva

Vladimir Natchev
Arsov, Natchev, Ganeva

Jordan Manahilov
Bulgarian National Bank

Kalina Tchakarova
Djingov, Gouginski, Kyutchukov & Velichkov

Lilia Kisseva
Djingov, Gouginski, Kyutchukov & Velichkov

Ralitsa Gougleva
Djingov, Gouginski, Kyutchukov & Velichkov

Alexander Georgiev
Dobrev, Kinkin & Lyutskanov

Iassen Hristev
Dobrev, Kinkin & Lyutskanov

Katerina Gramatikova
Dobrev, Kinkin & Lyutskanov

Plamen Georgiev
Economou International Shipping Agency

Darina Oresharova
Experian-Scorex Bulgaria

FreshUP Cosmetics

Georgi Stoilov

Bogdan Drenski
Georgiev, Todorov & Co.

Dimitar Danailov
Georgiev, Todorov & Co.

Gerdana Popova
Georgiev, Todorov & Co.

Yordanka Panchovska
Georgiev, Todorov & Co.

Daniela Dzabarova
IKRP Rokas & Partners

Emil Enev
IKRP Rokas & Partners

Angel Kalaidjiev
Kalaidjiev, Georgiev & Minchev

Hristina Kirilova
Kambourov & Partners

Margarita Stoyanova
Kambourov & Partners

Nikolay Bandakov
Kambourov & Partners

Stefan Tzakov
Kambourov & Partners

Albena Grozeva
Landwell, PricewaterhouseCoopers Legal Services

Angel Panayotov
Landwell, PricewaterhouseCoopers Legal Services

Borislav Dimitrov
Landwell, PricewaterhouseCoopers Legal Services

Galina Bunkova
Landwell, PricewaterhouseCoopers Legal Services

Georgy Georgiev
Landwell, PricewaterhouseCoopers Legal Services

Ilya Komarevski
Landwell, PricewaterhouseCoopers Legal Services

Lora Kapelovska
Landwell, PricewaterhouseCoopers Legal Services

Maria Urmanova
Landwell, PricewaterhouseCoopers Legal Services

Peter Takov
Landwell, PricewaterhouseCoopers Legal Services

Vesselin Dinkov
Landwell, PricewaterhouseCoopers Legal Services

Dimitar Ivanov
Landwell, PricewaterhouseCoopers Legal Servicess

Ivan Markov
LIC - Penkov, Markov & Partners

Svetlin Adrianov
LIC - Penkov, Markov & Partners

Vladimir Penkov
LIC - Penkov, Markov & Partners

Laura Thomas
LM Legal Services Ltd.

Julian Spassov
McGregor & Partners

Totyu Mladenov
Ministry of Labor & Social Policy

Nikolay Kiskinov

Anelia Tatarova
PricewaterhouseCoopers

Ginka Iskrova
PricewaterhouseCoopers

Irina Tsvetkova
PricewaterhouseCoopers

Marieta Getcheva
PricewaterhouseCoopers

Mina Kapsazova
PricewaterhouseCoopers

Stephan Z. Kyutchukov

Anastassia Dyulgerova
Stoeva, Kuyumdjieva & Vitliemov

Borislava Pokrass
Stoeva, Kuyumdjieva & Vitliemov

Irina Stoeva
Stoeva, Kuyumdjieva & Vitliemov

Nevena Radlova
Stoeva, Kuyumdjieva & Vitliemov

Pavel Vitliemov
Stoeva, Kuyumdjieva & Vitliemov

Stella Bozova
Stoeva, Kuyumdjieva & Vitliemov

Svilen Todorov
Todorov & Doykova Law Firm

Miroslav Varnaliev
Unimasters Logistics Plc.

Nikolai Bozhilov
Unimasters Logistics Plc.

Yabor Kambourov

BURKINA FASO

Wango Pieree Sawadogo
AAED - Agence d'architecture, d'engineering et de design

Serge Damiba
Archi Consult

Vincent Armand Kobiane
ARDI – Architectes Conseils

Alphonse K. Nombre
Assemblee Nationale

Barterlé Mathieu Some

Gilles Corneille Yaméogo
Barreau du Burkina Faso

Marie Ouedraogo
Barreau du Burkina Faso

Hamadé Ouedraogo
Bâtir S.A.R.L.

Charles Ki-Zerbo
BCEAO

Birika Jean Claude Bonzi

Bouba Yaguibou

Bernardin Dabire
Cabinet Bernardin Dabire

Barthélémy Kere
Cabinet d'Avocats Barthélemy Kere

Benewende S. Sankara
Cabinet Maitre Sankara

Seydou Roger Yamba
Cabinet Maitre Sankara

Anna T. Ouattara-Sory
Cabinet Me Paulin Salambéré

Evelyne Mandessi Bell
Cabinet Ouedraogo & Bonkoungou

Bernardin M. T. Sagnon
Cabinet Sagnon-Zagre

Dieudonne Bonkoungou

Eddie Koimboiko

Farima Diarra

Adeline Messou
FIDAFRICA / PricewaterhouseCoopers

Dominique Taty
FIDAFRICA / PricewaterhouseCoopers

Evelyne M'Bassidgé
FIDAFRICA / PricewaterhouseCoopers

Fousséni Traoré
FIDAFRICA / PricewaterhouseCoopers

Jean Claude Gnamien
FIDAFRICA / PricewaterhouseCoopers

Fortune Bicaba

Colette Lefebvre
Inspection du travail

Fati Balma Congo
Ministere des Finances et du Budget

N. Henri Ouedraogo
Ministere des Finances et du Budget

Ministère de l'Habitat

Messan Lawson

Moussa Sogodogo

Denis Dawende
Office Notarial Me Jean Celestin Zoure

Jean Celestin Zoure
Office Notarial Me Jean Celestin Zoure

Theophane Noel Zoure
Office Notarial Me Jean Celestin Zoure

Oumarou Ouedraogo

Ousmane Prosper Zoungrana

Blaise Sondo
Reseau National de Lutte Anti-Corruption (RENLAC)

Yemdaogo Maxime Nikiema
Reseau National de Lutte Anti-Corruption (RENLAC)

Rene Bonou
SAFTRANS (Societe d'Affretement et de Transit)

Hamidou Savadogo
SCM - Justice & Liberte Cabinet d'Avocats

Jean de Dieu Some
SDV

Sibila Francois Yameogo
Bureau d'Etudes l'Espace

Yaguibou & Yanogo

BURUNDI

Audace Bireha
APF Conseils

Déogratias Nzemba
Attorney-at-Law

Emmanuel Niyonkuru
Banque de la République du Burundi

Tharcisse Ntakiyica
Barreau du Burundi

Anatole Miburo
Cabinet Anatole Miburo

Gabriel Sinarinzi
Cabinet MeGabriel Sinarinzi

Gaspard Rwasoni
Cabinet Rwasoni

Willy Rubeya
Cabinet Willy Rubeya

Benjamin Rufagari
Deloitte & Touche

Jean De Dieu Basabakwinshi
IMATCO

Bonaventure Nicimpaye
Intercontact Services, S.A.

Rodrigue Majambere
Intercontact Services, S.A.

Clémence Rwamo
Ministère de la Justice

Laurent Nzeyimana
President du Conseil d'Arbitrage CEBAC

Jean Anastase Hicuburundi
President du Tribunal de Commerce

Prosper Niyoyankana

Salvatore Sindayihebura

CAMBODIA

Hans Hwang
Arbitration Council Foundation

Megan Reeve
Arbitration Council Foundation

Nimmith Men
Arbitration Council Foundation

Sok Lor
Arbitration Council Foundation

Naryth H. Hem
B.N.G. - Advocates & Solicitors

Socheata Seng
B.N.G. - Advocates & Solicitors

Vannarith Siv
B.N.G. - Advocates & Solicitors

Brennan Coleman
DFDL Mekong Law Group

Louis-Martin Desautels
DFDL Mekong Law Group

Tayseng Ly
DFDL Mekong Law Group

Chhung Kong
Dirksen Flipse Doran & Le

Samvutheary Mao
Dirksen Flipse Doran & Le

Ham Phea
Ever Peace Consultant

Pises Mao
HR Inc.

Samyith Seng
HR Inc.

Chee Cheong Low
KPMG Cambodia Ltd.

Sovann Bun
KPMG Cambodia Ltd.

Jean Loi
PricewaterhouseCoopers

Ngov Chong
PricewaterhouseCoopers

Michael Tan
RAF International Forwarding Inc.

Song Khun
RAF International Forwarding Inc.

Denora Sarin
Sarin & Associates

Sorya Sin
SHA Transport Express Co. Ltd.

CAMEROON

Jean Aimet Kounga
Abeng Law Firm

Julius Ngu Tabe Achu
Achu and Fon-Ndikum Law Firm

Augustin Mbami

Achu Julius
Avocat

Caroline Idrissou-Belingar
BEAC - Headquarters

Paul Marie Djamen
BICEC

Pierre Bertin Simbafo
BICEC

Henri Pierre Job
Cabinet d'Avocats Henri Job

Emmanuel Ekobo
Cabinet Ekobo

Lucas Florent Essomba
Cabinet Essomba & Associés

Isabelle Fomukong
Cabinet Fomukong

Ariane Marceau-Cotte
Cabinet Maître Marie Andrée NGWE

Marie-Andrée Ngwe
Cabinet Maître Marie Andrée NGWE

Patrice Guy Njoya
Cabinet Maître Marie Andrée NGWE

Serge Jokung
Cabinet Maître Marie Andrée NGWE

Simon Pierre Nemba
Cabinet Maître Marie Andrée NGWE

Charles Tchuente
Cabinet Nyemb

Jacques Nyem
Cabinet Nyemb

Laurent Dongmo
Cabinet Paul Jing

Daniel Fourier

EcoBank - Cameroon

D. Etah Akoh
Etah-Nan & C Société d'Avocats, Barristers & Solicitors

Berangere Monin
FIDAFRICA / PricewaterhouseCoopers

Dominique Taty
FIDAFRICA / PricewaterhouseCoopers

Isidore Baudouin Ndzana
FIDAFRICA / PricewaterhouseCoopers

Jacques Chareyre
FIDAFRICA / PricewaterhouseCoopers

Nadine Tinen Tchangoum
FIDAFRICA / PricewaterhouseCoopers

Pierre Roger Ngangwou
FIDAFRICA / PricewaterhouseCoopers

Henry Feh

Ivo Dogo Tamfu
Henry, Samuelson & Co.

Jacqueline Moussinga

David Boyo
Jing & Partners

Paul Jing
Jing & Partners

Kumfa Jude Kwenyui
Juris Consul Law Firm

Marceau Cotte

Aimé Ndock Len
M & N Law Firm, cabinet d'avocats

Hermine Fréderique Mbendang Essanguy
M & N Law Firm, cabinet d'avocats

Jean Michel Mbock Biumla
M & N Law Firm, cabinet d'avocats

Angoh Angoh Jacob
Nico Halle & Co. Law Firm

Rebecca Enonchong

Jean Paul Ngalle Miano
SCP Ngalle-Miano, Bekima-Ndjam & Ekane

Roland Abeng
The ABENG Law Firm

Unique Investment Ltd.

CANADA

ABH Importers

Bennett Fleet Inc.

Anne Glover
Blake, Cassels & Graydon, member of Lex Mundi

Pamela S. Hughes
Blake, Cassels & Graydon, member of Lex Mundi

Paul Schabas
Blake, Cassels & Graydon, member of Lex Mundi

Pierre Gemson
Blake, Cassels & Graydon, member of Lex Mundi

Tony Wong
Blake, Cassels & Graydon, member of Lex Mundi

Alfred Page
Borden Ladner Gervais LLP

Francis Allen
Borden Ladner Gervais LLP

Caravan Trade

David G. Ellis
CB Richard Ellis

Bhavin Ganatra
Comage Container Lines

Joshua Kochath
Comage Container Lines

Harris M. Rosen
Fogler Rubinoff

Fraser Export

FreightPlus Group of Companies

David Bish
Goodmans LLP

Jay A. Carfagnini
Goodmans LLP

Groupe Rousseau Construction Inc.

John Craig
Heenan Blaikie LLP, member of Ius Laboris

Jonathan Rabinovitch
Heenan Blaikie LLP, member of Ius Laboris

Vittorio Maio
Industry Canada

Gian Fortuna
Kenaidan Contracting Ltd.

Wayne W. Fedun
MacLeod Dixon

Andrew Kent
McMillan Binch Mendelsohn

MLG Enterprises Ltd.

Allan Coleman
Osler, Hoskin & Harcourt LLP

Damian Rigolo
Osler, Hoskin & Harcourt LLP

Marc Wasserman
Osler, Hoskin & Harcourt LLP

Rod Davidge
Osler, Hoskin & Harcourt LLP

Susan Clifford
Osler, Hoskin & Harcourt LLP

Matthew Marcus
PricewaterhouseCoopers

Michael S. Bondy
PricewaterhouseCoopers

SDV

Shoppers WebMart

Spirits of the Creek Ltd.

Steven Golick

Colin L. Campbell
Superior Court of Justice of Ontario

Velmo International Inc.

CAPE VERDE

José Manuel Pinto Monteiro
Advogados & Jurisconsultos

Eldetrudes Pires Neves
Araújo, Neves, Santos & Miranda, Advogados Associados

Joao M. A. Mendes
Auditec

Ricardo G. Pereira
BDO Capeaudit

Ana Denise Lima Barber
CWV & Advogados

Carlos Veiga
CWV & Advogados

Elsa Tavares
CWV & Advogados

Vera Andrade
CWV & Advogados

Vasco Carvalho Oliveira Ramos
Engic

Ilídio Cruz
Gabinete de Advocacia Consultoria e Procuradoria Juridica

Jorge Teixeira

Maria de Fatima Lopes Varela

João Dono
Maria João de Novais Advogados - Miranda Alliance

Armando J.F. Rodrigues
PricewaterhouseCoopers

Herminio Afonso
PricewaterhouseCoopers

Tito Lívio Santos Oliveira Ramos

CENTRAL AFRICAN REPUBLIC

Caroline Idrissou-Belingar
BEAC - Headquarters

Jean Baptiste Nouganga
Bureau Comptable Fiscal - Cabinet Nouganga

Marie-Edith Douzima-Lawson
Cabinet Douzima & Ministère de la fonction publique

Gabriel Houndoni
Club OHADA

Symphorien Bandiba
Club OHADA

Serge Médard Missamou
Club OHADA

Jean Noel Bangue
Cour d'Appel de Bangui

Jean-Noël Bangue
Cour d'Appel de Bangui

Maurice Dibert- Dollet
Ministère de la Justice

CHAD

Caroline Idrissou-Belingar
BEAC - Headquarters

Thomas Dingamgoto
Cabinet Thomas Dingamgoto

Naramadji Mekonné
Clerc d'Huissier de Justice

N'Doningar Djimasna
Faculté de Droit, Université de N'Djamena

Dominique Taty
FIDAFRICA / PricewaterhouseCoopers

Karine Lasne
FIDAFRICA / PricewaterhouseCoopers

Nadine Tinen Tchangoum
FIDAFRICA / PricewaterhouseCoopers

Nicolas Ronzié
FIDAFRICA / PricewaterhouseCoopers

Gérard Leclaire
Ingénierie & Architecture

Sobdibé Zoua
Law Firm SCPP

Narcisse Madjiyore Dongar

Béchir Madet
Office Notarial

Abdelkerim Ahmat
SDV

CHILE

Adriana Salias

Alvaro Rosenblut
Albagli Zaliasnik Abogados

Camilo Cortés
Alessandri & Compañía

Fernando Jamarne
Alessandri & Compañía

León Larrain
Baker & McKenzie (Cruzat, Ortúzar y Mackenna Ltda.)

Miguel Capo Valdez
Besalco S.A.

Cristian Garcia-Huidobro
Boletin Comercial

Carlos Torres

Claudio Rivera
Carey y Cía Ltda.

María Agnes Salah
Carey y Cía Ltda.

Mariana Castro
Carey y Cía Ltda.

Pedro Pablo Gutierrez
Carey y Cía Ltda.

Alfonso Reymond Larrain
Chadwick & Aldunate Abogados

Aldo Molinari
Claro &Ciá., Abogados, member of Lex Mundi

Alex van Weezel
Claro & Ciá., Abogados, member of Lex Mundi

Felipe Ossa
Claro & Ciá., Abogados, member of Lex Mundi

Nicolás Luco
Claro & Ciá., Abogados, member of Lex Mundi

Edmundo Rojas García
Conservador de Bienes Raíces de Santiago

Luis Maldonado Croquevielle
Conservador de Bienes Raíces de Santiago

Luis Felipe Vergara Maldonado
Conservador de Bienes Raíces de Santiago

Silvio Figari Napoli
Databusiness

Cristián S. Eyzaguirre
Eyzaguirre & Cía.

Ricardo Riesco
Eyzaguirre & Cía.

Jimena Bronfman
Guerrero, Olivos, Novoa y Errázuriz

Juan Pablo Gonzalez M.
Guerrero, Olivos, Novoa y Errázuriz

Sebastián Yunge
Guerrero, Olivos, Novoa y Errázuriz

Didier Lara
PricewaterhouseCoopers

Miguel Massone
PricewaterhouseCoopers

Myriam Retamal
PricewaterhouseCoopers

Osvaldo Villagra
PricewaterhouseCoopers

Juan Mesías
PricewaterhouseCoopers Legal Services

Leticia Acosta Aguirre
Redlines Group

Sofia Dias
SDV S.A.

Héctor Carrasco Reyes
Superintendencia de Bancos e Instituciones Financieras

Enrique Benitez Urrutia
Urrutia & Cía

Jorge Benitez Urrutia
Urrutia & Cía

Xavier Guijón

CHINA

Add Xd Imp & Exp Co., Ltd.

Amico Pipeline Co., Ltd.

Amoy Paintings International

Anwan International Trade Co., Ltd.

Crystal Zang
Asia Connect Consultants

Asia Imp & Exp Co., Ltd.

Alexander Gong
Baker & McKenzie

Rico Chan
Baker & McKenzie

Beijing Dongxing Kaiyuan Textile Co., Ltd.

Fengli Zhang
Beijing Huanzhong & Partners

Xuehua Wang
Beijing Huanzhong & Partners

Beijing Shunxing Trademark Co., Ltd.

Bekoh Technologies Ltd.

Candas Lee
Burke, Fung & Li Solicitors

Tommy Li
Burke, Fung & Li Solicitors

Canadian Exhibitions Group Co.,Ltd.

Chengdu Share Building Material Co., Ltd.

China Net Communication Shanghai Branch

China Tycentre Vehicles Ltd.

Chongqing Youbang Gifts Co. Ltd.

ChunXiao Toy Factory

Cixi Huaheng Rubber & Plastic Factory

Cixi Wolee Bearing Co., Ltd.

Eu Jin Chua
Clifford Chance

Dalian Sparkin Apparel Inc.

Danya Optoelectronic Tech., Ltd.

Beiheng Ren
DeHeng Law Offices

He Jun
DeHeng Law Offices

Kejun Guo
DeHeng Law Offices

Li Wang
DeHeng Law Offices

Rue Qiu
DeHeng Law Offices

Yichi Zhang
DeHeng Law Offices

Dniya Ornaments Co., Ltd.

Dongguan Asny Craft Factory

Dongguan Litong Hardware Manufactory

Dongguan Webber Furniture Co., Ltd.

Easy Count Electronic Co., Ltd.

EnerSine High Technology Ltd.

Enxun Digital Technology Co., Ltd.

Fit Precision Mold Co., Ltd.

Foresight Technology (Shenzhen) Co., Ltd.

Fortuna Technology Co., Ltd.

Foshan Yinggelong Sanitary Ware Co., Ltd.

Fuan City Longhe Electrical Machinery Co., Ltd.

Fujian Haiding Global Foods Industry Co., Ltd.

Fujian Western Gulf Seafood Co., Ltd.

Futon (Shenzhen) Adhesive Products Co., Ltd.

Fuyilai Hardware Furniture Factory

Gaoyao Rongxing Hardware Manufactory Co., Ltd.

Jessie Tang
Global Star Logistics Co. Ltd.

Leo Ge
Global Star Logistics Co. Ltd.

Globiz Corporation

Gobery Trading Co., Ltd.

Guangbo Handcrafts Co., Ltd.

Guangzhou Yufa Carpet Co., Ltd.

Hainan Howard Town Export & Import Trading Co., Ltd.

Haining XinGuangYuan Lighting Co., Ltd.

Haiyan Puguang Lighting Co., Ltd.

Hanzhong Industrial Ltd.

Harvest International Group Co., Ltd.

Hebei Anping Hengmao Metal Products Wire Mesh Factory

Hebei Rising Chemical Co., Ltd.

Hebei Seawell Import & Export Co., Ltd.

Hebei Xingshuo Saw Co., Ltd.

Henan Harvest Chem Co., Ltd.

Hongkong Huike Technology Ltd.

Hunan O.E.D Casting & Forging Co., Ltd.

Hunan O.E.D. Co., Ltd.

Hunbear Industry Trade Co., Ltd.

Lihong Wang
IFC

Innovation Medical Instrument Co., Ltd.

Jiangsu Feichi Co., Ltd.

Jiangyin Mingzhu Export & Import Co., Ltd.

Jie Chen
Jun He Law Office, member of Lex Mundi

Linfei Liu
Jun He Law Office, member of Lex Mundi

Shyian Zhang
Jun He Law Office, member of Lex Mundi

Yan Guo
Jun He Law Office, member of Lex Mundi

Yu Qin
Junyi Law Office

Kaier Investment Ltd.

Kangzhou Arts & Crafts

Raymond Ng
Kenneth C C Man & Co.

Kestar Electronic Co., Ltd.

Kinder Industry & Trade Co., Ltd.

Yi Zhang
King & Wood PRC Lawyers

Barry Cheung
KPMG Huazhen

Bolivia Cheung
KPMG Huazhen

Chris Long
KPMG Huazhen

Kui Lu

Lifecare Instruments Co., Ltd.

Lovells

Luquan Supply and Marketing Co., Ltd.

Merlin Consumable Co. Ltd.

Nanjing Baiguan Glass Handiwork Co., Ltd.

Nanjing Textile Co.

Nantong Xinbang Chemical Co., Ltd.

Neumek Shanghai Corporation

New Benefit Hardware Co., Ltd.

New Olympic Trading Co.

Han Shen
New York University

Ningbo C&T Tek Co., Ltd.

Ningbo Flight Rigging & Tool Co., Ltd.

Ningbo Liftstar Material Transport Equipment Factory

Ningbo New Century Import & Export Co., Ltd. Six Operation Dept.

Ningbo NGYC (Ninggang Permanent Magnetic) Material Co., Ltd.

Ningbo Zhongbin Fastener MFG.Co., Ltd.

Cevela Zhou
O'Melveny & Myers LLP

Lawrence Sussman
O'Melveny & Myers LLP

Randolph Perry
Orrick, Herrington & Sutcliffe LLP

Zhang Hongsheng
People's Bank of China

Philip Gilligan

Piko Leather Goods Co., Ltd.

Kian Heong Hew
Pinsent Masons

Lin Luo
Pinsent Masons

Cassie Wong
PricewaterhouseCoopers

Celia Wang
PricewaterhouseCoopers

Rex Chan
PricewaterhouseCoopers

Pujiang Jiamei Crafts & Textiles Co., Ltd.

Puyang Isaac Group

Shoulong Mao
Renmin University of China

Rising Auto Parts

Runhong Enterprise Co., Ltd.

Sansen Technology Co., Ltd.

SDA

Berry Lin
SDV Ltd.

Shanghai Electrical Power Co. Ltd.

Shanghai Greenland International Trade Co., Ltd.

Shanghai Hai Cheng Economy & Trade Development Co., Ltd.

Shanghai Municipal Government

Jammy Qian
Shanghai S&J Forwarding Co. Ltd.

Shenyang Sanyuan Oil-filler Manufacturing Co., Ltd.

Shenzhen Bosston Manufacturer Co., Ltd.

Shenzhen Fanvil Electronics Co., Ltd.

Shenzhen Lahoode Business Co., Ltd.

Shenzhen Shengcheng Industrial Co., Ltd.

Shenzhen Solartycoon Technology Co., Ltd.

Shenzhen Subor Electric Technology Co., Ltd.

Shenzhen Wenkui Stationery Corporation

Shenzhen Zhuangzheng Electronic Technology Co., Ltd.

Sichuan Metals & Minerals Import & Export Corp.

Sincoheren

Stone Industrial Co., Ltd.

Tigerdog Trading

TW Furniture

Umedisc

Venus Holdings HK Co., Ltd.

Henry Tsang
Vinner Health Products Co., Ltd.

Vogue Industries Co., Ltd.

Wafangdian Yushi Energy Co., Ltd.

Waynex International Trade Co., Ltd.

Weihai Jucheng Textile Co., Ltd.

Wuhan Fiberpon Technology Co., Ltd.

Xiamen All Carbon Corporation

Xiamen Ningsheng Industry & Trade Co., Ltd.

Xiamen Zhanlu Industry & Trade Co., Ltd.

Xinghua Hongtai Stainless Steel Wire Rope Co., Ltd.

Xinzheng Chengxin Carbon Co., Ltd.

Yanzhou Xi'er Kangtai Pharmaceutical Co., Ltd.

Yi Fu Ltd.

Yiwu Dannasi Trade Co., Ltd.

Yiwu Fengcheng Commodity Co., Ltd.

Yiwu Gaoge Arts & Crafts Co., Ltd.

Yiwu Hollytown Import & Export Co., Ltd.

Yiwu Hollytown Printer Consumables Co., Ltd.

Yuanfeng Textiles Co., Ltd.

Zhejiang Maigela Accessory Co., Ltd.

Zhejiang Ruipu Titanium Industry Co., Ltd.

Zhejiang Wuyi Zongheng Tools Co., Ltd.

Zhengzhou Ancai Refractory Co., Ltd.

Zhengzhou Great Wall Heavy Industry Machinery Co., Ltd.

Zhengzhou Sanhui Trading Co., Ltd.

ZhongYi International Trade Information Ltd.Co.

Zhuji Junma Import & Export Co., Ltd.

Zibo Sanfeng Chemical Industry Co., Ltd.

COLOMBIA

Jorge Lara Urbaneja
Baker & McKenzie (Raisbeck, Lara, Rodriguez & Rueda)

Carlos Fradique-Méndez
Brigard & Urrutia, member of Lex Mundi

Carolina Arciniegas Parga
Brigard & Urrutia, member of Lex Mundi

Cristina Lloreda
Brigard & Urrutia, member of Lex Mundi

Juan Carlos Perez
Brigard & Urrutia, member of Lex Mundi

Pablo Barraquer-Uprimny
Brigard & Urrutia, member of Lex Mundi

Ana Maria Quintero
Cámara Colombiana de la Construcción

Beatriz Uribe Botero
Cámara Colombiana de la Construcción

Viviana Hernández Grajales
Cámara Colombiana de la Construcción

Darío Cárdenas
Cárdenas & Cárdenas

Gabriela Mancero
Cavelier Abogados

Julia Uribe
Cavelier Abogados

Claudia Vargas

Mauricio Angulo
Computec - DataCrédito

Alessandra Laureiro
Gómez-Pinzón Abogados

Felipe Sandoval Villamil
Gómez-Pinzón Abogados

Juan Manuel Ruiz
Gómez-Pinzón Abogados

Juan Sebastian Torres
Gómez-Pinzón Abogados

Patricia Arrázola Bustillo
Gómez-Pinzón Abogados

Paula Samper Salazar
Gómez-Pinzón Abogados

Guillermo Bayona

Clara Inés Gómez
José Lloreda Camacho & Co.

Felipe Valencia
José Lloreda Camacho & Co.

Gustavo Tamayo
José Lloreda Camacho & Co.

Jinna Pastrana
José Lloreda Camacho & Co.

Juan Carlos Ruiz
José Lloreda Camacho & Co.

Juliana Bazzani Botero
José Lloreda Camacho & Co.

Lorena Diaz
José Lloreda Camacho & Co.

Manuel Muñoz
José Lloreda Camacho & Co.

Santiago Gutiérrez
José Lloreda Camacho & Co.

Latintradex, Inc.

María Helena Díaz Méndez

Mario Ramirez Lozano

Nacira Lamprea

Luis E. Nieto
Nieto & Chalela

Felipe Arbouin Gómez
Pinilla González & Prieto Abogados

Eliana Bernal Castro
PricewaterhouseCoopers

Adriana Hincapié
PricewaterhouseCoopers Legal Services

Andrés Millán Pineda
PricewaterhouseCoopers Legal Services

Daniel Cardoso
PricewaterhouseCoopers Legal Services

Diego Vega
PricewaterhouseCoopers Legal Services

Juan Becerra
PricewaterhouseCoopers Legal Services

Santiago Lopez
PricewaterhouseCoopers Legal Services

Wilson Herrera
PricewaterhouseCoopers Legal Services

Ana Giraldo
Prieto & Carrizosa S.A.

Felipe Cuberos
Prieto & Carrizosa S.A.

Margarita María Núñez
Prieto & Carrizosa S.A.

Quasar Sucesores & Ltda.

Raul Alberto Suarez

Representaciones GC & LS C.I. Colombia Ltda.

Carlos Umaña
Rigard & Urrutia, member of Lex Mundi

Carlos Urrutia
Rigard & Urrutia, member of Lex Mundi

José Francisco Mafla Ruiz
Rigard & Urrutia, member of Lex Mundi

Julio Ortiz
Rigard & Urrutia, member of Lex Mundi

Grace Sandoval
Sociedad Portuaria Regional de Cartagena

Gustavo Florez
Sociedad Portuaria Regional de Cartagena

Termocuplas S.A.

COMOROS

Said Ibrahim Mourad
Ancien Magistrat

Ahamada Mahamoudou
Avocat à la Cour

Hassani Assoumani
C.V.P. - Biocom

Zainaba Mohamed
Fonds d'Appui au Développement Communautaire

Mohamed Abdallah Halifa
Groupe Hassanati Soilihi - Groupe Hasoil

Youssouf Yahaya
Impots de la Grande Comore

Ali Mohamed Choybou
Palais de la Justice

Aboubakar Abdou
President de l'Ile Autonome de la Grande Comore

Haroussi Idrissa
Tribunal de premiere instance de Moroni

Mohamed Salipi
Tribunal de premiere instance de Moroni

CONGO, DEM. REP

Louman Mpoy
Cabinet Mpoy - Louman & Associés

Regis De Oliveira
Agetraf s.a.r.l.

Yves Debiesme
Agetraf s.a.r.l.

Amisi Herady
ANAPI

Thierry Mutombo Kalonji
ANAPI

Roger Masamba Makela
Avocat, Doyen de Faculté

Caroline Idrissou-Belingar
BEAC - Headquarters

Victor Créspel Musafiri
Cabinet d'avocat JCC & A

Andre Malangu Muabila
Cabinet Famille

Christie Madudu Sulubika
Cabinet G.B. Moka Ngolo & Associés

Francis Lugunda Lubamba
Cabinet Lugunda Lubamba

Siku Beya
Cabinet Lugunda Lubamba

Marius Tshieuy
Cabinet Mbaki et Associés

Tanayi Mbuy-Mbiye
Cabinet Mbuy-Mbiye & Associés

Louman Mpoy
Cabinet Mpoy - Louman & Associés

Jacques Munday
Cabinet Ntoto et Nswal

Toto Wa Kinkela
Cabinet Toto

EcoBank - Congo, Dem. Rep.

Dominique Taty
FIDAFRICA / PricewaterhouseCoopers

Jolivet Thomas
FIDAFRICA / PricewaterhouseCoopers

G. Le Dourain

Gaston Kalambay Lumpungu

David Guarnieri
PricewaterhouseCoopers Legal Services

Léon wa Kinkela
Toto & Associés Cabinet d'Avocats

Mukoko Aloni
Université de Kinshasa

CONGO, REP.

Daniel Bolletot
Bureau Veritas

Jean-Claude Marc
Bureau Veritas

Claude Coelho
Cabinet d'Avocats Claude Coelho

Mathias Essereke
Cabinet d'Avocats Claude Coelho

Muzembe Mpungu Marius
Cabinet d'Avocats Claude Coelho

Francis Sassa
Cabinet d'Avocats Jean Petro

Jean Petro
Cabinet d'Avocats Jean Petro

Thierry Mamimoue
Cabinet d'Avocats Jean Petro

Jean-Philippe Esseau
Cabinet Esseau

Ludovic Désiré Essou
Cabinet Essou

Françoise Mbongo
Cabinet Mbongo

David Bourion
FIDAFRICA / PricewaterhouseCoopers

Dominique Taty
FIDAFRICA / PricewaterhouseCoopers

Emmanuel Le Bras
FIDAFRICA / PricewaterhouseCoopers

Moise Kokolo
FIDAFRICA / PricewaterhouseCoopers

Prosper Bizitou
FIDAFRICA / PricewaterhouseCoopers

COSTA RICA

Andrea Saenz
Aguilar Castillo Love

John Aguilar
Aguilar Castillo Love

Silvia Chacon
Alfredo Fournier & Asociados

Roger Petersen
Alliance Law Group, SRL

Vicente Lines
Arias & Muñoz

Gastón Certad
Batalla & Asociados

Luis Manuel Castro
BLP Abogados

Neftali Garro
BLP Abogados

Eduardo Calderón-Odio
Bufete Facio & Cañas, member of Ius Laboris & Lex Mundi

Federico Solís
Bufete Facio & Cañas, member of Ius Laboris & Lex Mundi

Giselle Solís
Bufete Facio & Cañas, member of Ius Laboris & Lex Mundi

Jaime Molina
Cámara Costarricense de la Construcción

Stanley Villegas
Decisa

Alejandro Bettoni Traube
Doninelli & Doninelli - Asesores Jurídicos Asociados

Jaime Ordoñez
Estudios para el Futuro

Facio & Cañas, member of Lex Mundi

Daniel de LaGarza
J. de Cano Estudio Legal

Felix Pecou
Japdeva

Carlos Arrea
LEX Counsel

Cecilia Naranjo
LEX Counsel

Luis Sibaja
LEX Counsel

Miguel Ruiz Herrera
LEX Counsel

Rodrigo Zapata
LEX Counsel

Ivannia Méndez Rodríguez
Oller Abogados

Pedro Oller
Oller Abogados

Alejandro Antillon
Pacheco Coto

Carlos Barrantes
PricewaterhouseCoopers

Katherine Monge
PricewaterhouseCoopers

Marianela Vargas
PricewaterhouseCoopers

Ramon Ortega
PricewaterhouseCoopers

V. Andrés Gómez
PricewaterhouseCoopers

Adriana Calero
PricewaterhouseCoopers Legal Services

Ingrid Jiménez Godoy
PricewaterhouseCoopers Legal Services

Luis Diego Barahona
PricewaterhouseCoopers Legal Services

Carmen Gamboa
Quiros & Asociados, Abogados y Notarios

Jose Luis Salinas
SCGMT Arquitectura y Diseño

Rosemary Escalante
Scotiabank

Eduardo Montoya Solano
Superintendencia General de Entidades Financieras

CÔTE D'IVOIRE

Charles Ki-Zerbo
BCEAO

Hawa Kone
BCEAO

Yaya Sissoko
BCEAO

BNETD

Kouame Klemet
Cabinet Jean-François Chauveau

Seyanne Groga
Cabinet Jean-François Chauveau

Zinda Sawadogo
Cabinet Jean-François Chauveau

Cabinet Kouassi et Associés

César Asman
Cabinet N'Goan, Asman & Associés

Georges N'Goan
Cabinet N'Goan, Asman & Associés

Jacques Raphaël Kouassi
Cabinet N'Goan, Asman & Associés

Nadia Vanie
Cabinet N'Goan, Asman & Associés

Athanase Raux
Cabinet Raux et Associés

Antoine Niamien
Chambre des Notaires de Cote d'Ivoire

Guillaume Koffi
Conseil National de l'Ordre des Architectes

Jacque Otro
Conseil National de l'Ordre des Architectes

COTAM

Jean-Pierre Elisha
Elisha & Associés

Nathalie Assou
Elisha & Associés

Dorothée K. Dreesen
Etude Maitre Dreesen

Serge Roux
Etude Maitre Roux

Adeline Messou
FIDAFRICA / PricewaterhouseCoopers

Dominique Taty
FIDAFRICA / PricewaterhouseCoopers

Evelyne M'Bassidgé
FIDAFRICA / PricewaterhouseCoopers

Fousséni Traoré
FIDAFRICA / PricewaterhouseCoopers

Jean Claude Gnamien
FIDAFRICA / PricewaterhouseCoopers

Herman Kouao

Joachim Bile-Aka

Landry Baguy

SABKA

Abbé Yao
SCPA Dogué-Abbé Yao & Associés

Arsène Dable
SCPA Dogué-Abbé Yao & Associés

Seydou Zerbo
SCPA Dogué-Abbé Yao & Associés

Dogbémin Gérard Kone
SCPA Nambeya - Dogbemin & Associés

Guillaume Dufaux
SDV

Jerome Beseme
SDV

Bertrand Fleury
SDV - SAGA CI

SIMAT

CROATIA

Ludovic Coquillet
AGS d.o.o.

Luka Tadić-Čolić
Babić & Partners

Tin Dolički
Bogdanović, Dolički & Partneri

Belinda Čačić
Čačić & Partners

Hrvoje Čipčić-Bragadin
Čipčić-Bragadin

Gregor Famira
CMS Zagreb

Ivana Mucić
CMS Zagreb

Jasmina Crnalić
CMS Zagreb

Marija Mušec
CMS Zagreb

Zoran Tasić
CMS Zagreb

Djuro Sessa
County Court in Zagreb

Zoran Bohaček
Croatian Banking Association

Dean Balint

Emir Bahtijarević
Divjak, Topić & Bahtijarević, member of SEE Legal

Ivana Zovko
Divjak, Topić & Bahtijarević, member of SEE Legal

Saša Divjak
Divjak, Topić & Bahtijarević, member of SEE Legal

Eugen Zadravec
Eugen Zadravec Law Firm

Irina Jelčić
Hanžeković, Radaković & Partners, member of Lex Mundi

Marijan Hanžeković
Hanžeković, Radaković & Partners, member of Lex Mundi

Andrea August
HITRO.HR

Lidija Hanžek
HROK

Branimir Iveković
Iveković & Vidan

Hrvoje Vidan
Iveković & Vidan

Stefanija Čukman
Jurić Law Offices

Nikola Klaić
Klaić & Klaić

Marija Haramija
Korper & Haramija

Goranka Šumonja Laktić
Laktić & Partners

Mate Lovrić
Laktić & Partners

Mladen Dragičević
Law Office Dragičević

Snježana Premus Baltić
Law Office Dragičević

Zvonko Nogolica
Law Offices Nogolica

Andrej Bolfek
Leko & Partners

Krešimir Ljubić
Leko & Partners

Manuela Špoljarić
Leko & Partners

Miroslav Leko
Leko & Partners

Martina Mladina Kavurić
Mamić Reberski & Partners

Vladimir Mamić
Mamić Reberski & Partners

Gordan Marović
Marović & Partners

Andrej Matijevich
Matijevich Law Office

Tamiko R. Franklin
Matijevich Law offices

Miroljub Macesic

Dragomir Modrušan
Modrušan & Filipčić

Željka Filipčić
Modrušan & Filipčić

Martina Kalamiza
Odvjetničko društvo Laktić & Partneri

Nataša Owens
Owens and Houška

Petar Petrić
Petrić Law Office

Ivan Gjurgjan
Porobija & Porobija Law Firm

Margita Kiš-Kapetanović
Porobija & Porobija Law Firm

Sanja Porobija
Porobija & Porobija Law Firm

Don Markušić
PricewaterhouseCoopers

Gordan Rotkvić
PricewaterhouseCoopers

Iain McGuire
PricewaterhouseCoopers

Ivo Bijelić
PricewaterhouseCoopers

Lana Brlek
PricewaterhouseCoopers

Ronald Pusić
PricewaterhouseCoopers

Sanja Jurković
PricewaterhouseCoopers

Filip Sulić
PricewaterhouseCoopers Legal Services

Jelena Madir
Privredna Banka Zagreb

Gordon Kunštek
Šavorić & Partners

Marijana Jelić
Šavorić & Partners

Ana Sihtar
Sihtar Attorneys at Law

Natko Bilić
Studio 3LHD

Zorislav Petrović
TI-Croatia

Tin Matić
Tin Matić Law Office

Transadria

Mario Stefanić
Transadria

Irena Tušak-Miletić
Tušak-Miletić & Partners

Zoran Vujasin
Vujasin Law Office

Tomislava Furčić
Vukić, Jelusić, Šulima, Stanković, Jurcan & Jabuka

Mladen Vukmir
Vukmir Law Office

Tomislav Nagy
Vukmir Law Office

Bojan Fras
Žurić i Partneri

CZECH REPUBLIC

Allen & Overy, Praha Advokátní kancelář

Jan Spáčil
Ambruz & Dark advokáti, v.o.s. PricewaterhouseCoopers Legal Services

Jiří Markvart
Ambruz & Dark advokáti, v.o.s. PricewaterhouseCoopers Legal Services

Kateřina Vysloužilová
Ambruz & Dark advokáti, v.o.s. PricewaterhouseCoopers Legal Services

Klara Valentova
Ambruz & Dark advokáti, v.o.s. PricewaterhouseCoopers Legal Services

Ludvik Juricka
Ambruz & Dark advokáti, v.o.s. PricewaterhouseCoopers Legal Services

Marketa Penazova
Ambruz & Dark advokáti, v.o.s. PricewaterhouseCoopers Legal Services

Martin Bohuslav
Ambruz & Dark advokáti, v.o.s. PricewaterhouseCoopers Legal Services

Michal Hrncir
Ambruz & Dark advokáti, v.o.s. PricewaterhouseCoopers Legal Services

Vladimír Ambruz
Ambruz & Dark advokáti, v.o.s. PricewaterhouseCoopers Legal Services

Tomáš Zlámal
Ateliér Zlámal

Cosmin Anghel
Badea Asociatii in Association with Clifford Chance

Petr Kucera
CCB - Czech Banking Credit Bureau

Stanislav Myslil
Cermak Horejs Myslil a spol.

Tomas Richter
Clifford Chance LLP/ Institute of Economic Studies, Faculty of Social Sciences, Charles University

Jarmila Musilova

Jörg Nürnberger
DLA Piper

Exim Consulting

Vít Horáček
Glatzová & Co. Law Offices Prague

Roman Grones
Gleiss Lutz

Athanassios Pantazopoulos
IKRP Rokas & Partners & Dr. A. Pantazopoulos

Jan Slaby
Karl Heinz Dietrich s.r.o.

Ludìk Vrána
Linklaters

Petr Mestanek
Linklaters

Růžena Trojánková
Linklaters

Lenka Petráková
Ozivení

Robert Sgariboldi
Panalpina s.r.o.

Gabriela Hájková
Peterka & Partners

Jiří Černý
Peterka & Partners

Martin Sip
Peterka & Partners

Pavla Prikrylova
Peterka & Partners

David Musil
PricewaterhouseCoopers

Lenka Mrazova
PricewaterhouseCoopers

Stephen B. Booth
PricewaterhouseCoopers

Irena Dolezelova
Procházka Randl Kubr, member of Ius Laboris & Lex Mundi

Jarmila Hanzalova
Procházka Randl Kubr, member of Ius Laboris & Lex Mundi

Natasa Randlová
Procházka Randl Kubr, member of Ius Laboris & Lex Mundi

Sarka Jandova
Procházka Randl Kubr, member of Ius Laboris & Lex Mundi

Tereza Řihošková
Procházka Randl Kubr, member of Ius Laboris & Lex Mundi

Jana Pavlasova
Squire, Sanders & Dempsey, v.o.s. advokátní kancelář

Zdenek Rosicky
Squire, Sanders & Dempsey, v.o.s. advokátní kancelář

Markéta Zachová
Vejmelka & Wünsch v.o.s.

DENMARK

Jeppe Jørgensen
Bech-Bruun Law Firm

Ole Borch
Bech-Bruun Law Firm

Pia Justesen
Bech-Bruun Law Firm

Heidi Hoelgaard
Experian Northern Europe

Jan Hoej Soerensen
Experian Northern Europe

Alice Folker
Gorrissen Federspiel Kierkegaard

Jonas Bøgelund
Gorrissen Federspiel Kierkegaard

Niels Bang Sørensen
Gorrissen Federspiel Kierkegaard

Jesper Trommer Volf

Mogens Ebeling
Jonas Bruun

Soren Plomgaard
Jonas Bruun

Jens Steen Jensen
Kromann Reumert, member of Lex Mundi

Jørgen B. Jepsen
Kromann Reumert, member of Lex Mundi

Kim Trenskow
Kromann Reumert, member of Lex Mundi

Peter Honoré
Kromann Reumert, member of Lex Mundi

Susanne Madsen
Kromann Reumert, member of Lex Mundi

Susanne Schjølin Larsen
Kromann Reumert, member of Lex Mundi

Knud Villemoes Hansen
National Survey and Cadastre - Denmark/Kort & Matrikelstyrelsen

Elsebeth Aaes-Jørgensen
Norrbom Vinding, member of Ius Laboris

Thomas Bech Olsen
Panalpina World Transport

Peter Bang

Claus Kaare Pedersen
Philip & Partnere

Eivind Einersen
Philip & Partnere

Jens Hjortskov
Philip & Partnere

Ann Kell
PricewaterhouseCoopers

Arne J. Gehring
PricewaterhouseCoopers

Jan Huusmann Christensen
PricewaterhouseCoopers

Karin L. Nielsen
PricewaterhouseCoopers

Mona Lorentsen
PricewaterhouseCoopers

Torben Wolsted
PricewaterhouseCoopers

DJIBOUTI

Wabat Daoud
Avocat à la Cour

Rahma Abdi Abdillahi
Banque Centrale de Djibouti

Ibrahim Mohamed Omar
Cabinet d'Expertise Comptable et d'Audit

Félix Emok N'Dolo
CHD Group

Koran Ahmed Aouled
Conseil Superieur de la Magistrature

Abdallah Mohamed Kamil
Etude Notariale

Lantosoa Hurfin Ralaiarinosy
Groupement Cosmezz Djibouti S. A.

Mohamed Omar Mohamed

Mourad Farah

Jean Phillipe Delarue
Société Maritime L. Savon & Ries

Jerome Passicos
Société Maritime L. Savon & Ries

Luc Deruyer
Société Maritime L. Savon & Ries

Oubah Mohamed Omar
Société Maritime L. Savon & Ries

DOMINICA

Kathy Buffong
Attorney General's Chambers

Mrs. Carrette

Kerry George
C I S Enterprises Ltd.

Linda Singletary
C I S Enterprises Ltd.

Francine Royr
De Freitas de Freitas & Baron

Leah Shillingford
Dominica Amalgamated Workers Union

Caryl Paul
Dominica Coconut Products Ltd.

Alex Phillip
House of Assembly

Issa Trading Ltd.

J. Gildon Richards
J. Gildon Richards Chambers

Alick C. Lawrence
Lawrence Alick C. Chambers

Laurina Vidal
Lawrence Alick C. Chambers

Severin McKenzie
McKenzie Architectural & Construction Services Inc.

Richard Peterkin
PricewaterhouseCoopers

Singoalla Blomqvist-Williams

Ruby Joseph

Kirtiste Augustus
Waterfront and Alied Workers Union

DOMINICAN REPUBLIC

Raúl De Moya
Arquitectura & Planificación

Pablo Gonzalez Tapia
Biaggi & Messina

Maria Portes
Castillo y Castillo

Xavier Marra Martínez
Dhimes & Marra

Fabio Guzmán-Ariza
Guzmán Ariza

Claudia Roca
Headrick Rizik Alvarez & Fernandez

Claudia Taveras
Headrick Rizik Alvarez & Fernandez

Mary Fernández Rodríguez
Headrick Rizik Alvarez & Fernandez

Sarah de León
Headrick Rizik Alvarez & Fernandez

Wilfredo Senior
Headrick Rizik Alvarez & Fernandez

Carlos Hernández
Instituto de Estudios del Trabajo

Philippe Lescuras
Panalpina

Luis R. Pellerano
Pellerano & Herrera, member of Lex Mundi

Alejandro Fernandez de Castro
PricewaterhouseCoopers

Andrea Paniagua
PricewaterhouseCoopers

Caroline Bono
PricewaterhouseCoopers

Juan Tejada
PricewaterhouseCoopers

Julio Pinedo
PricewaterhouseCoopers

Ramon Ortega
PricewaterhouseCoopers

Superintendencia de Bancos

Wendy Sánchez
TransUnion

Ana Isabel Caceres
Troncoso y Caceres

Juan Manuel Caceres
Troncoso y Caceres

ECUADOR

Jorge Eduardo Fernández Perdomo
Acredita Buró de información crediticia S.A

Alprojansa

Patricia Ponce
Bustamante y Bustamante

Patricio Carrion
Constructora Naranjo & Ordoñez

Andrés Tobar
Corporación Latinoamericana para el Desarrollo

Daniel Pino Arroba

Xavier Amador Pino
Estudio Juridico Amador

Lucía Cordero-Ledergerber
Falconi Puig Abogados

Fernando Del Pozo Contreras
Gallegos, Valarezo & Neira

Juan Carlos Gallegos Happle
Gallegos, Valarezo & Niera

Macias Hurtado & Macias

Fernando Redin
Notaria Vigesimo Cuarta

Diego Cabezas-Klaere
Ortega Moreira & Ortega Trujillo

Fernando Coral
Panalpina

Jorge Paz
Paz Horowitz

Leopoldo González R.
Paz Horowitz

Xavier Sisa
Paz Horowitz

Juan Manuel Marchán
Pérez, Bustamante y Ponce, member of Lex Mundi

Sandra Reed
Pérez, Bustamante y Ponce, member of Lex Mundi

Christof Baer
PricewaterhouseCoopers

Luciano Almeida
PricewaterhouseCoopers

Pablo Aguirre
PricewaterhouseCoopers

Rodrigo Jijón

Myriam Rosales
Superintendencia de Bancos y Seguros del Ecuador

EGYPT

Ahmed Abdel Warith
AAW Consulting Engineers

Nahed Saad
AAW Consulting Engineers

Badr Abd El Khalek
Abu-Ghazaleh Legal

Mohamed Elwany
Abu-Ghazaleh Legal

Mohamed Hussien
Abu-Ghazaleh Legal

Yasser Yousry
Abu-Ghazaleh Legal

Tarek El-Marsafawy
Adel Kamel & Associates

Greiss Youssef
Afifi Air Cargo

Abdel Aal Aly
Afifi World Transport

Mostafa Mostafa
Al Kamel Law Office

Cairo International Trade Co.

Zeinab Saieed Gohar
Central Bank of Egypt

Ashraf Gamal El-Din
Egyptian Institute of Directors

El Bahrain Tours

Elkarnak for Export & Trading

Elsewedy United Industries Co.

Hassan Fahmy
General Authority for Investment "GAFI"

Ibrahim Mustafa Ibrahim Abdel Khalek
General Authority for Investment "GAFI"

Mustafa Ali
General Authority for Investment "GAFI"

Salama Fares
General Authority for Investment "GAFI"

Ahmed Abou Ali
Hassouna & Abou Ali Law Firm

Hatco

Ashraf Elibrachy
Ibrachy Law Firm

Infocast ME

Island Group

Amr Mohamed Hosny
Karim Adel Law Office

Ibrahim Daker
Karim Adel Law Office

Karim Adel Kamel Ghobrial
Karim Adel Law Office

Ramez Mounir Abdel-Nour
Karim Adel Law Office

Kenouz El Sharek

Keshawy Export & Marketing

Hend Abdel Ghany
Mena Associates, member of Amereller Rechtsanwälte

Ingy Rasekh
Mena Associates, member of Amereller Rechtsanwälte

Amr Elmonayer
Ministry of Finance

Ashraf El Arabi
Ministry of Finance

Hussein Mahmoud Gaafar El Gebaly
Ministry of Housing, Utilities & Urban Development

Mona Zobaa
Ministry of Investment

Mohamed El Homosany
Ministry of Justice

Eman Zakaria
Ministry of Manpower & Migration

Emad Hassan
Ministry of State for Administrative Development

Modern Agricultural Est.

Ashraf Nadhoury
Nadoury & Nahas Law Offices

George Samy
Nadoury & Nahas Law Offices

Intsar Khairy
Nadoury & Nahas Law Offices

Mohamed El-Labboudy
Nadoury & Nahas Law Offices

Samir Gharib
Office of the Minister of State for Local Development

Port Said Star

Mohamed Fahim
PricewaterhouseCoopers / Mansour & Co.

Sherif Mansour
PricewaterhouseCoopers / Mansour & Co.

Girgis Abd El-Shahid
Sarwat A. Shahid Law Firm

Sarwat Group

Mohamed Serry
Serry Law Office

Adel Hanna
Shalakany Law Office, member of Lex Mundi

Dina Salah
Shalakany Law Office, member of Lex Mundi

Emad El Shalakany
Shalakany Law Office, member of Lex Mundi

Mona Zulficar
Shalakany Law Office, member of Lex Mundi

Shereen Zaky
Shalakany Law Office, member of Lex Mundi

Tegara Net

Omneia Helmy
The Egyptian Center for Economic Studies

Yaser Gamaluddin Hamam
The Egyptian Law Firm

Ahmed Ibrahim
Trowers & Hamlins

Tim Armsby
Trowers & Hamlins

United for Export

EL SALVADOR

Mónica Guadalupe Pineda Machuca
ACZALAW

Francisco José Barrientos
Aguilar Castillo Love

Miguel Angel
ALE Cargo S.A. de C.V.

Roberta Gallardo de Cromeyer
Arias & Muñoz

Irene Arrieta de Díaz Nuila
Arrieta Bustamante

Karla Maley Guzmán Martinez
Arrieta Bustamante

Lilliam Arrieta Carsana
Arrieta Bustamante

Monica Hernandez
Arrieta Bustamante

Giovanni Rosales
Bendek & Asociados

Carlos Oviedo
Consortium Centro América Abogados

Ricardo Cevallos
Consortium Centro América Abogados

Porfirio Diaz Fuentes
DLM & Asociados

Maria Martha Delgado Molina
Espino Nieto & Asociados, member of Ius Laboris

Pedro Alejandro Mendoza
Espino Nieto & Asociados, member of Ius Laboris

Francisco Armando Arias Rivera
F.A. Arias & Muñoz

Juan Carlos Herrera
F.A. Arias & Muñoz

Walter Chávez Velasco
Gold Service / MSI

Mauricio Melhado
Gold Service / MSI

Ana Patricia Portillo Reyes
Guandique Segovia Quintanilla

Manuel Telles Suvillaga
Lexincorp

Luis Ninez

Ramon Ortega
PricewaterhouseCoopers, S.A. de C.V.

Adonay Rosales
PricewaterhouseCoopers, S.A. de C.V.

Carlos Roberto Alfaro
PricewaterhouseCoopers, S.A. de C.V.

Ernesto Hempe
PricewaterhouseCoopers, S.A. de C.V.

Laura Duran De Jimenez
Procredito - Transunion Central America

Antonio R. Mendez Llort
Romero Pineda & Asociados, member of Lex Mundi

Luis Medina
Rusconi, Valdez, Medina & Asociados

Mario Enrique Sáenz
Sáenz & Asociados

Thelma Dino Lizama de Osorio
Superintendencia del Sistema Financiero

Mauricio Antonio Urrutia
Superintendencia del Sistema Financiero

EQUATORIAL GUINEA

Mariam Laine
Airfreight

Antonio-Pascual Oko Ebobo
Attorney-at-Law

Francisco Javier Mbe Ngomo
Attorney-at-Law

Honorio Ndong Obama
Attorney-at-Law

Jose-Antonio Lluch Ondo Matojo
Attorney-at-Law

Solvador-Ondo Ncume Oye
Attorney-at-Law

Caroline Idrissou-Belingar
BEAC - Headquarters

Benoit Kanyandekme
BK Architects SL

Diosdado Nchama
C/O Ministerio de Minas, Industria y Energia

Vicente-Nse Ondo-Mitogo
Corte Suprema de Justicia

Augustin Chicampo Barila
District Judge

Dominique Taty
FIDAFRICA / PricewaterhouseCoopers

Jacques Chareyre
FIDAFRICA / PricewaterhouseCoopers

Sébastien Lechêne
FIDAFRICA / PricewaterhouseCoopers

Ponciano Mbomio Nvo
Gabinete Juridico

Heidi Johansen
Globaltrans

Jenaro Obuno Ela
Ministerio de Hacienda y Presupuesto

Reginaldo Egido Panades
Ministerio de Justicia, Culto e Instituciones Penitenciaras

Pedro Nsue Ela Eyang
Notary

Paulino Mbo Obama
Oficina de Estudieos - ATEG

Franck Mamelin
Panalpina Transportes - Mundiales Guinea Ecuatorial S. A. R. L.

ERITREA

Akberom Tedla

Ataklti H. Mariam

Fessahaie Habte
Attorney-at-Law and Legal Consultant

Berhane Gila-Michael
Berhane Gila-Michael Law Firm

Michael Joseph
Ernst & Young East Africa

Isac Tesfazion

Kebreab Habte Michael

Tekeste Mesghenna
MTD Enterprises PLC

Tadesse Beraki

ESTONIA

Maris Tudre
Centre of Registers & Information Systems

Sirje Rogova
Centre of Registers & Information Systems

Ants Ratas
CF & S Agentide AS

Andres Juss
Estonian Land Board

Andres Vinkel
Hansa Law Offices

Igor Kostjuk
Hough, Hübner, Hütt & Partners

Indrek Link
Hough, Hübner, Hütt & Partners

Veiko Meos
Krediidiinfo A.S.

Aet Bergmann
Law Office Luiga Mody Hääl Borenius

Jaan Lindmäe
Law Office Tark & Co.

Olger Marjak
Law Office Tark & Co.

Ermo Kosk
Lepik & Luhaäär LAWIN, member of Lex Mundi

Maarja Torga
Lepik & Luhaäär LAWIN, member of Lex Mundi

Marko Mehilane
Lepik & Luhaäär LAWIN, member of Lex Mundi

Rajar Miller
Lextal Law Office

Karolina Ullman
MAQS Law Firm

Veikko Toomere
MAQS Law Firm

Metaprint Ltd.

Aare Kurist
PricewaterhouseCoopers

Villi Tõntson
PricewaterhouseCoopers

Cameron Greaves
PricewaterhouseCoopers

Heili Haabu
Raidla & Partners, member of Ius Laboris

Karin Madisson
Sorainen Law Offices

Statistical Office of Estonia

Kilvar Kessler
Tark & Co.

Risto Hübner
Tark & Co.

Vesse Võhma

ETHIOPIA

Amsale Tsehaye
Amsale Tsehaye & Associates Law Office

Bekure Assefa
Bekure Assefa Law Office

Berhane Ghebray
Berhane Ghebray & Associates

Nega Getahun
City Administration of Addis Ababa

Jennifer Gohlke
GE Foundation

Solomon Gizaw
HST & Co.

Woldegabriel Naizghi
HST & Co.

Shimelise Eshete
MIDROC Construction PLC

Wondimeneh Asrat
National Bank of Ethiopia

Getachew Kebede
Packford International

Andrew Giddings
Shearman & Sterling LLP

Tadesse Kiros
Tadesse, Getachew & Abate Law Office

Teshome G.M. Bokan
TGMB law office

FIJI

Ramesh Prasad Lal
Carpenters Shipping

Paul McDonnell
Cromptons Solicitors

Delores Elliott
Databureau, Baycorp Advantage

Litiana Morris
Howards Lawyers

William Wylie Clarke
Howards Lawyers

Fapna Vithal
Lateef & Lateef

John Apted
Munro Leys Notaries Public

Nehla Basawaiya
Munro Leys Notaries Public

Richard Naidu
Munro Leys Notaries Public

Shelvin Singh
Parshotam & Co.

Chirk Yam
PricewaterhouseCoopers

Eddielin Almonte
PricewaterhouseCoopers

Jenny Seeto
PricewaterhouseCoopers

Narotam Solanki
PricewaterhouseCoopers

FINLAND

Claudio Busi
Castrén & Snellman Attorneys Ltd.

Jenni Hupli
Castrén & Snellman Attorneys Ltd.

Lasse Luukkainen
Castrén & Snellman Attorneys Ltd.

Pekka Jaatinen
Castrén & Snellman Attorneys Ltd.

Sami Rautiainen
Castrén & Snellman Attorneys Ltd.

Johanna Haltia-Tapio
Hannes Snellman, Attorneys-at-Law Ltd.

Patrik Lindfors
Hannes Snellman, Attorneys-at-Law Ltd.

Saini Siitarinen
Hannes Snellman, Attorneys-at-Law Ltd.

Sarah Tähkälä
Hannes Snellman, Attorneys-at-Law Ltd.

Jyrki Mustonen
Hedman Osborne Clarke

Timo Tammelin
Mega Trend Nordica Oy

Mikko Mali

Sakari Kauppinen
National Board of Patents & Registration

Tuomas Lukkarinen
National Land Survey of Finland

Mikko Reinikainen
PricewaterhouseCoopers Legal Services

Minna Oksa
PricewaterhouseCoopers Legal Services

Sannna Väänänen
PricewaterhouseCoopers Legal Services

Tero Malmivaara
PricewaterhouseCoopers Legal Services

Tuija Hartikainen
PricewaterhouseCoopers Legal Services

Ilkka Kajas
PricewaterhouseCoopers Oy - SVH

Jetta Hyvärinen-Kari
PricewaterhouseCoopers Oy - SVH

Maarit Pokkinen
PricewaterhouseCoopers Oy - SVH

Risto Löf
PricewaterhouseCoopers Oy - SVH

Vesa-Pekka Nuotio
PricewaterhouseCoopers Oy - SVH

Bernt Juthstrom
Roschier Attorneys Ltd., member of Ius Laboris & Lex Mundi

Carita Wallgren
Roschier Attorneys Ltd., member of Ius Laboris & Lex Mundi

Gunnar Westerlund
Roschier Attorneys Ltd., member of Ius Laboris & Lex Mundi

Johannes Frände
Roschier Attorneys Ltd., member of Ius Laboris & Lex Mundi

Manne Airaksinen
Roschier Attorneys Ltd., member of Ius Laboris & Lex Mundi

Micaela Thorström
Roschier Attorneys Ltd., member of Ius Laboris & Lex Mundi

Olav Hermanson
Roschier Attorneys Ltd., member of Ius Laboris & Lex Mundi

Sini Soini
Roschier Attorneys Ltd., member of Ius Laboris & Lex Mundi

Tiina Hakri
Roschier Attorneys Ltd., member of Ius Laboris & Lex Mundi

Wilhelm Guthwert
Roschier Attorneys Ltd., member of Ius Laboris & Lex Mundi

Timo Laukkanen
Statistics Finland

Juuso Jokela
Suomen Asiakastieto Oy - Finska

Ari Eklund
Transcontainer

Leila Mustanoja
Transparency International Suomi - Finland

FRANCE

Alain Moreau

Allen & Overy LLP

Andrew Booth
Andrew Booth Architect

Annie Sauve
Banque de France

Benoit Fauvelet
Banque de France

Sylvie Ghesquiere
Banque de France

Frédérique Chifflot Bourgeois
Bar of Paris

Daniel Arthur Laprès
Cabinet d'Avocats

Gerard Kaeufling
Cabinet de Notaire

Florence Grillier
Cabinet TAJ

Chambre Syndicale des Importateurs Francais de Fruits et Legumes (CSIF)

Hugues Pouzin
Confédération Française du Commerce Interentreprises (CGI)

Raymond Gianno
Curtis, Mallet-Prevost, Colt & Mosle LLP

Frédéric Roussel
Fontaine, Roussel & Associés

Bertrand Barrier
Gide Loyrette Nouel, member of Lex Mundi

Philippe Xavier-Bender
Gide Loyrette Nouel, member of Lex Mundi

Ludovic Couturier
Institut de Droit International des Transports (IDIT)

Michel Gout
Institut de Droit International des Transports (IDIT)

Jacques Pourciel

Marc Jobert
Jobert & Associés

Carol Khoury
Jones Day

Jean-Louis Martin
Jones Day

Nicolas de Germay
Kroll Talbot Hughes

Arnaud Chastel
Landwell & Associés - PricewaterhouseCoopers

Aurelie Ange
Landwell & Associés - PricewaterhouseCoopers

Jennifer Juvénal
Landwell & Associés - PricewaterhouseCoopers

Laure Poindessault-Bernard
Landwell & Associés - PricewaterhouseCoopers

Renaud Jouffroy
Landwell & Associés - PricewaterhouseCoopers

Benoît Le Bars
Landwell & Associés - PricewaterhouseCoopers Legal Services

Bruno Thomas
Landwell & Associés - PricewaterhouseCoopers Legal Services

Jean-Philippe Dom
Landwell & Associés - PricewaterhouseCoopers Legal Services

Olivier Gorand

Xavier-Philippe Gruwez
Saint Georges Avocats

Ann Creelman
Vatier & Associés

Isabelle Smith Monnerville
Vaughan Avocats

Jean Gerard Eveillard
Cabinet Eveillard

GABON

Thierry Ngomo
ArchiPro International

Celestin Mba Ndong
Attorney-at-Law

Jean Raymond Zassi-Mikala
Avocat à la Cour

Itchola Mano Alade
Avocate

Ntoutoume Lubin
Avocate

Caroline Idrissou-Belingar
BEAC - Headquarters

François Nguema Ebane
Cabinet Atelier 5A

Y.A. Adetona
Cabinet Fidexce S. A. R. L.

Ruben Mindonga
Cabinet Me Anguiler

Josette Olendo
Cabinet Olendo

Cherif Agbanrin

César Apollinaire Ondo Mve
Cour d'Appel Judiciaire de Libreville

Charles Adenet
FIDAFRICA / PricewaterhouseCoopers

Pélagie Massamba Mouckocko
FIDAFRICA / PricewaterhouseCoopers

Christophe A Relongoue
FIDAFRICA / PricewaterhouseCoopers Legal Services

Hugues Boguikouma

Marcel Owono

Marie Clarisse Avore Bekale

Mirielle Moundakou Mapicka

Olivier N'zahou

François Coron
Panalpina S.A.

Gianni Ardizzone
Panalpina S.A.

Pierre-flavien Mendoume-Ba-N'nanng

Reine Sylvie Tsonga

Roland Matsiendi

Zita Eurydice Ndogui

GAMBIA

Amie Bensouda
Amie Bensouda & Co.

Victoria Andrews
Amie Bensouda & Co.

Emmanuel E. Chime
Chime Chambers

Alpha Amadou Barry
Deloitte, member of Deloitte Touche Tohmatsu

Cherno Alieu Jallow
Deloitte, member of Deloitte Touche Tohmatsu

Jatta Lamin
Deloitte, member of Deloitte Touche Tohmatsu

Joseph Sarre
Gambia Architectural and Planning Consultants

Hawa Sisay-Sabally
Hawa Sisay-Sabally

Ida Denise Drameh
Ida D. Drameh & Associates

Amie Joof-Conteh
Kunni Boy Chambers

Mary Abdoulie Samba-Christensen
Legal Practitioner

Rodolphe K. Akoto
Maersk Ltd.

Darcy White
PricewaterhouseCoopers

Gideon Ayi-owoo
PricewaterhouseCoopers

Thomas Murega
PricewaterhouseCoopers

Soul Joof

Pa MM Njie
Trust Bank Ltd.

GEORGIA

Aieti Kukava
Alliance Group Holding

David Giorgadze
Association for Protection of Landowners Rights (APLR)

Avto Namicheishvili
Begiashvili & Co.

Giorgi Begiashvili
Begiashvili & Co.

Jaba Mamulashvili
Begiashvili & Co.

Zaza Bibilashvili
BGI Legal

Booz Allen Hamilton

Joseph Salukvadze
Cadastre and Land Register Project

Sandro Amashukeli
Chemonics

Maka Khitsishvili
D & G Holding Ltd.

Avto Svadnize
DLA Piper Gvinadze & Partners LP

Ted Jonas
DLA Piper Gvinadze & Partners LP

David Kakabadze
Georgian Legal Partnership

Gia Kurtskalia

Vazha Chopikashvili
IPRSC Immovable Property Registration Service Center

Ivan Khokhlov

Mariam Gabunia

Merab Barbakadze

Natalia Babakishvili
Mgaloblishvili, Kipiani, Dzidziguri (MKD) Law Firm

Lika Chanturia
National Agency of Public Registry

Bela Gutidze
PricewaterhouseCoopers

Courtney Fowler
PricewaterhouseCoopers

Matthew Tallarovic
PricewaterhouseCoopers

Sergi Kobakhidze
PricewaterhouseCoopers

David Arsenashvili
Tbilisi Title Company Ltd.

Lela Shatirishvili
Tbilisi Title Company Ltd.

Levan Gotua
The Office of the State Minister on Reforms Coordination

D. Lelashvili
USAID Business Climate Reform Project

Olin McGill
USAID Business Climate Reform Project

Tato Urjumelashvili
USAID Business Climate Reform Project

Temur Bolotashvili
USAID Business Climate Reform Project

Vakhtang Lejava

GERMANY

Allen & Overy LLP

Werner M. Mues
C· B· H Rechtsanwälte

Christoph Schauenburg
Cleary Gottlieb Steen & Hamilton LLP

Daniel Panajotow
Cleary Gottlieb Steen & Hamilton LLP

Frank Lohrmann
Cleary Gottlieb Steen & Hamilton LLP

Gabriele Apfelbacher
Cleary Gottlieb Steen & Hamilton LLP

Hanno Sperlich
Cleary Gottlieb Steen & Hamilton LLP

Klaus Riehmer
Cleary Gottlieb Steen & Hamilton LLP

Peter Polke
Cleary Gottlieb Steen & Hamilton LLP

Robert Gutte
Cleary Gottlieb Steen & Hamilton LLP

Tobias Tillmann
Cleary Gottlieb Steen & Hamilton LLP

Werner Meier
Cleary Gottlieb Steen & Hamilton LLP

Wiebke Holzapfel
Cleary Gottlieb Steen & Hamilton LLP

Malte Hansen
Cleary Gottlieb Steen & Hamilton LLP

Björn Gaul
CMS Hasche Sigle

Dieter Straub
CMS Hasche Sigle

Gerlind Wisskirchen
CMS Hasche Sigle

Manfred Heinrich
Deutsche Bundesbank

Andre Jahn
Dr. Hök Stieglmeier & Partner

Götz-Sebastian Hök
Dr. Hök Stieglmeier & Partner

Jennifer Bierly
Gassner Stockmann & Kollegen

Werner Geue
G-Loxx

Friedrich Tobias Schoene
Hogan & Hartson LLP

Klaus Günther
Linklaters Oppenhoff & Rädler

Silvanne Helle
Linklaters Oppenhoff & Rädler

Christian Pelz
Nörr Stiefenhofer Lutz, member of Lex Mundi

Klaus Berner
Nörr Stiefenhofer Lutz, member of Lex Mundi

Cornelia Marquardt
Norton Rose

Dirk Otto
Norton Rose

Peter Limmer
Notare Dr. Limmer & Dr. Friederich

Sigrun Erber-Faller
Notare Erber-Faller und Voran

Dieter Endres
PricewaterhouseCoopers AG

Dirk Baumgardt
PricewaterhouseCoopers AG

Pia Dorfmueller
PricewaterhouseCoopers AG

Andreas Eckhardt
PricewaterhouseCoopers Legal Services

Annekatren Werthmann-Feldhues
PricewaterhouseCoopers Legal Services

Carsten Witter
PricewaterhouseCoopers Legal Services

Christoph Torwegge
PricewaterhouseCoopers Legal Services

Dirk Stiller
PricewaterhouseCoopers Legal Services

Isabella Niklas
PricewaterhouseCoopers Legal Services

Kai Bandilla
PricewaterhouseCoopers Legal Services

Kai Christian Jaenecke
PricewaterhouseCoopers Legal Services

Malte Passarge
PricewaterhouseCoopers Legal Services

Oliver Kunert
PricewaterhouseCoopers Legal Services

Wulf Bach
Schufa

Holger Thomas
SJ Berwin LLP

Wilhelm Zeddies
Surveying Authorities - AdV c/o LGN

Henning Berger
White & Case

Wimexas Ltd.

GHANA

Kojo Bentsi-Enchill
Bentsi-Enchill & Letsa, member of Lex Mundi

Rosa Kudoadzi
Bentsi-Enchill & Letsa, member of Lex Mundi

Reginald Bannerman
Bruce-Lyle Bannerman & Thompson

Dorothy Kingsley Nyinah
Commercial Division, High Court

Eric Wiafe
Dony Engineering

Kwasi Poku
Dony Engineering

Morgan Asiedu
EcoBank - Ghana

Adwoah Asamoah Addo
Fugar & Co.

Seth Agyapong-Mensah
Fugar & Co.

William Edem Fugar
Fugar & Co.

Fredrick Koranteng Ohene
Ghana Audit Service

John Robert Jenkins
Golden Jubilee Terminal

Kingsford Otoo
Golden Jubilee Terminal

Benjamin
H & G Architects and Consultants

Alfred Walter Addy
H & G Architects and Consultants

C.N.K Boateng
H & G Architects and Consultants

David A. Hesse
Hesse & Hesse

Wilfred Anim-Odame
Land Valuation Board

Kenneth D. Laryea
Laryea, Laryea & Co. P. C.

Larry Adjetey
Law Trust Company

Lackson Agbeko Legah
Logistics @ Legacy Ltd.

Woodsworth Odame Larbi
Ministry of Lands, Forestry & Mines

N. O. Odotei

Darcy White
PricewaterhouseCoopers

Gideon Ayi-owoo
PricewaterhouseCoopers

Kelvin Abdallah
PricewaterhouseCoopers

Thomas Murega
PricewaterhouseCoopers

Robert Agbozo
Reindorf Chambers

Adwoa Yarney
Saah & Co.

Cynthia Jumu
Saah & Co.

Jacob Saah
Saah & Co.

Nene Amegatcher
Sam Okudzeto & Associates

Sam Okudzeto
Sam Okudzeto & Associates

Emmanuel Dorsu
Town and Country Planning Dept

GREECE

Constantinos Klissouras
Anagnostopoulos Bazinas Fifis

Georgios B. Bazinas
Anagnostopoulos Bazinas Fifis

Panos Koromantzos
Bahas, Gramatidis & Partners

Charalampos Skordakis

Margarita Flerianou
Economou International Shipping Agencies

Dimitris E. Paraskevas
Elias Paraskevas Attorneys 1933

Antonios Tsavdaridis
IKRP Rokas & Partners

Dimitra Rachouti
IKRP Rokas & Partners

Evi Martinovits
IKRP Rokas & Partners

Veronica Deleti
Karatzas & Partners

Andreas Bagias
Kelemenis & Co.

Athanassia Papantoniou
Kelemenis & Co.

Polykarpos Adamidis
Kelemenis & Co.

Yannis Kelemenis
Kelemenis & Co.

Dimitrios Kremalis
Kremalis Law Firm, member of Ius Laboris

Chryssiis Poulakou
Kyriakides Georgopoulos & Daniolos Issaias, member of SEE Legal

Effie G. Mitsopoulou
Kyriakides Georgopoulos & Daniolos Issaias, member of SEE Legal

Ioanna Argyraki
Kyriakides Georgopoulos & Daniolos Issaias, member of SEE Legal

Leonidas Georgopoulos
Kyriakides Georgopoulos & Daniolos Issaias, member of SEE Legal

Vicky Xourafa
Kyriakides Georgopoulos & Daniolos Issaias, member of SEE Legal

Antigoni Tsirou
M & P Bernitsas Law Offices

Christina Vlachtsis
M & P Bernitsas Law Offices

Katia Papantonopoulou
M & P Bernitsas Law Offices

Yannis Kourniotis
M & P Bernitsas Law Offices

M. B. D. A. (Mediterranean Business Development Agency)

Alexandros Sakipis
PricewaterhouseCoopers

Antigoni Gkarla
PricewaterhouseCoopers

Freddy Yatracou
PricewaterhouseCoopers

Mary Psylla
PricewaterhouseCoopers

Olga Koromilia
PricewaterhouseCoopers Legal Services

Stella Danelaki
PricewaterhouseCoopers Legal Services

Vassiliki Tsigarida
PricewaterhouseCoopers Legal Services

Ennie Dodou
Sarantitis Law Firm

Theodora D. Karagiorgou
T.J.Koutalidis Law Office

Helen Dikonimaki
Teiresias S. A. Interbanking Information Systems

Nicholas Kontizas
Zepos & Yannopoulos, member of Lex Mundi

Vassiliki G. Lazarakou
Zepos & Yannopoulos, member of Lex Mundi

GRENADA

C/O Supreme Court Registry

Dickon Mitchell
Grant Joseph & Co., member of Lex Mundi

Niel Noel
Henry Hudson - Phillips & Co.

Thaddus Charles
Inland Revenue Department

Andrew DeBourg
Labour Department

Cyrus Griffith
Labour Department

Trevor St. Bernard
Lewis & Renwick

Claudia Francis
PricewaterhouseCoopers

Yvonne Gellineau
PricewaterhouseCoopers

David Sinclaire
Sinclair Enterprises Ltd.

Phinsley St. Louis
St. Louis Service

Roselyn Wilkinson
Wilkinson, Wilkinson & Wilkinson

GUATEMALA

Ruby María Asturias Castillo
ACZALAW

Juan Gilberto Ortega Cifuentes
Agencia de Aduanas Logistics

Luis Enrique Gaytán Menéndez
Agencia de Aduanas Logistics

Juan Carlos Castillo Chacón
Aguilar Castillo Love

Agustín Buezo
Arrow Cargo

Julio Artemio Juárez Moran
Asociación de Transportistas Internacionales (ATI)

Maria del Pilar Bonilla
Bonilla, Montano, Toriello & Barrios

Guillermo Lopez-Cordero
Bufete Lopez Cordero

Enrique Maldonado
Cámara Guatemalteca de la Construcción

Marco Tulio Reyna
Cámara Guatemalteca de la Construcción

Paola van der Beek de Andrino
Cámara Guatemalteca de la Construcción

Alfonso Carrillo
Carrillo & Asociados

Isabel Coma Martin de Samayoa
Carrillo & Asociados

Rodrigo Callejas Aquino
Carrillo & Asociados

Carlos Neftali Mendez Ramirez
Central Almacenadores S.A.

Juan Francisco Toruño Rodriguez
Consolidados 807 S.A.

Karla de Mata
CPS Logistics

Marco Antonio Martinez
CPS Logistics

Allan F. Unfried
DHL

Mario Adolfo Búcaro Flores
Díaz - Duran & Asociados

Jorge Mario Mendoza Sandoval
FedEx

Jaime Godinez
Intercapitales, S.A.

Ana Alfaro
Mayora & Mayora, member of Lex Mundi

Sandra Castillo
Mayora & Mayora, member of Lex Mundi

Michael Daniels Toriello

Luis Pedro Cazali Leal
Palacios & Asociados

Roberto Ozaeta
Pricewaterhouse Coopers Legal Services

Alejandro Fernandez de Castro
PricewaterhouseCoopers

Edgar Mendoza
PricewaterhouseCoopers

Erik Coy
PricewaterhouseCoopers

Samuel Elías
PricewaterhouseCoopers

Walter Saldana
PricewaterhouseCoopers

Ramon Ortega
PricewaterhouseCoopers

José Cerezo
PricewaterhouseCoopers Legal Services

Rodolfo Fuentes
Protectora de Crèdito Comercial

Arabella Castro Quiñones
Registradora General de la Propiedad

Ricardo Lopez Reina

Alfredo Rodríguez Mahuad
Rodriguez, Castellanos, Solares & Aguilar, S.C. -Consortium legal-

Elias Arriaza
Rodriguez, Castellanos, Solares & Aguilar, S.C. -Consortium legal-

Jorge Martínez Sanche
Rodriguez, Castellanos, Solares & Aguilar, S.C. -Consortium legal-

Mario R. Archila
Rodriguez, Castellanos, Solares & Aguilar, S.C. -Consortium legal-

Juan Jegerlehner
Saravia & Muñoz

María de los Angeles Barillas Buchhalter
Saravia & Muñoz

Salvador A. Saravia Castillo
Saravia & Muñoz

José Rubén Castaneda Romero
Servicios Urgentes S.A.

Ana Lucía Alvarado Kepfler
Solosa - UPS Express

Andres Porras Castillo
TransUnion Guatemala, S.A.

Estuardo Enrique Echeverria Nova
Unidad de CDR y Control de la Calidad, Superintendencia de Bancos

GUINEA

Ahmadou Diallo

Oumar Dabo
ARCHI

Bajirt Berete
Banque Centrale - B.C.R.G.

Cheick Mohamed Tidjane Sylla
Banque Centrale - B.C.R.G.

Ibrahima Sory Sow
Banque Centrale - B.C.R.G.

Alpha Bakar Barry
Cabinet Karamoko Alpha Barry

Raffi Raja
Cabinet Koûmy

Alpha Camara
Cabinet Ousmane Camara

Christian Sow
Cabinet Sow

Lansana Kaba
CARID

EcoBank - Guinea

Dominique Taty
FIDAFRICA / PricewaterhouseCoopers

Famourou Kourouma
Hyperdynamics Corp

Mountaga Sylla
IFES

Djibril Kouyate
Jurifis Consult Guinee

Ibrahima Diakite
LandNet

Yansane Soumah
Manquapas

Guy Piam
Nimba Conseil

Raoul Mouthe
Nimba Conseil

Office de Promotion des Investissements Privés

Alpha Sampil
PricewaterhouseCoopers

Mohamed Lahlou
PricewaterhouseCoopers

Safiatou Kalissa
PricewaterhouseCoopers

Boubacar Barry
SCP d'Avocats "Jurifis Consult Guinee"

Mohamed Camara
SOCOPAO

Olivier Buquet
SOCOPAO

Aliou Barry
STATView International

Gerard Coker
UNDP

GUINEA-BISSAU

Adelaida Mesa D'Almeida
Attorney-at-Law

Miguel Mango
Audi - Conta Lda

Charles Ki-Zerbo
BCEAO

Jaló Pires
Ministerio da Justica

Octavio Gomez
Octávio Lopes Advogados - Miranda Alliance

Octávio Lopes
Octávio Lopes Advogados - Miranda Alliance

João Daniel Vaz Jr.
TransVaz, Lda

GUYANA

Cliffton Mortimer Llewelyn John
Attorney-at-Law

Mark Waldron
Attorney-at-Law

Roger Yearwood
Britton, Hamilton & Adams

Josephine Whitehead
Cameron & Shepherd

Germene Stewart
Central Housing & Planning Authority

Raphael Trotman
Chapman & Trotman

Colin Murray
Coastal Construction Services

Desmond Correia
Correia & Correia Ltd.

Carol Paul
Deeds registry, Law Courts

Garry Ramlochan

Godwin F. McPherson

K.A. Juman-Yessi
Guyana Olympic Association

C.A. Nigel Hughes
Hughes, Fields & Stoby

Harinarine Singh
Integrity Commission

Chris Fernandes
John Fernandes Ltd.

Juman Yessi

Kashir Khan

Ashton Chase
Law office of Ashton Chase

William Sampson
Lincoln Chambers & Associates

Leslie Sobers

Lucia Loretta Desir

Edward Luckhoo
Luckhoo & Luckhoo

Gidel Thomside
National Shipping Corporation Ltd.

Gary Holder
Orin Hinds & Assoclates Arch. Ltd.

Christopher Ram
Ram & McRae

Rakesh Latchana
Ram & McRae

Troy Williams
Ram & McRae

Narendra Singh
Registrar

Nigel Niles
Robin M.S. Stoby, S.C.

Robin Stoby
Robin M.S. Stoby, S.C.

R.N. Poonai

Rexford Jackson
Singh, Doodnauth Law Firm

HAITI

Marc Kinson Antoine
A.I. Shipping International

Hamelkart Ataya
Abu-Ghazaleh Legal

Leon Saint -Louis
Avocat

Margarette Sanon
Banque de la Republique d'Haiti

Jean Erick Alexis
Banque de la République d'Haiti

Marc Hebert Ignace
Banque de la République d'Haiti

Robinson Charles
Banque de la République d'Haiti

Adele Decastro
Brown Legal Group

Gemma Anglade
Brown Legal Group

Jean Baptiste Brown
Brown Legal Group

Steve Christian Brown
Brown Legal Group

Christian De Lespinasse
Cabinet de Lespinasse

Jean Gerard Eveillard
Cabinet Eveillard

Enerlio Gassant
Cabinet Gassant

Eneland Jabouin
Cabinet Jabouin Regis Descardes

Robert Laforest
Cabinet LaForest

Louis Gary Lissade
Cabinet Lissade

Salim Succar
Cabinet Lissade

Claudette Belfont
Cabinet Pierre Delva

Jean Frederic Sales
Cabinet Sales

Pierre Brierre
Comptable

Diggan d'Adesky
D'Adesky Import Export S.A.

Emile Giordani

Garry Lhérisson

Gilbert Giordani

Raoul Celestin
Les Entreprises Commerciales Joseph Nadal S.A.

Martine Chevalier

Joseph Palliant
Ordre des Comptables Professionels Agrees d'Haiti

Edmonde Suplice Beauzile
Parliament

Youri Latortue
Parliament

Paul Emile Simon

Rigaud Duplan

Amos Durosier
ULLC

Kareen T. Laplanche
UN Habitat

Jean Vandal
Vandal & Vandal

HONDURAS

Adolfo Pineda Padilla

Enrique Rodriguez Burchard
Aguilar Castillo Love

Dino Rietti
Arquitecnic

Carmen Chevez
Comision Nacional de Bancos y Seguros

Janeth Castañeda
Cropa Panalpina Tegucigalpa

Jose Conrado Osorio McCormick
Grupo McCOS

Juan Carlos Mejía Cotto
Instituto de la Propiedad

Jose Ramon Paz
J.R. Paz & Asociados

José Rafael Rivera Ferrari

Allan Elvir
Lexincorp

Maria del Carmen Jovel
PricewaterhouseCoopers

Ramón E. Morales
PricewaterhouseCoopers

Ramon Ortega
PricewaterhouseCoopers

Marysabel Maldonado
Pricewaterhousecoopers Legal Services

Milton Rivera
PricewaterhouseCoopers Legal Services

Victor Garcia
PricewaterhouseCoopers Legal Services

Ramon Discua

Stephen Daniels

Roberto Manuel Zacarías Urrutia
Zacarías & Asociados

HONG KONG, CHINA

Simon Smith
Allens Arthur Robinson

Tommy Li
Burke, Fung & Li Solicitors

Andrew Dale
Coudert Brothers in association with Orrick, Herrington & Sutcliffe

Billy Wong
Coudert Brothers in association with Orrick, Herrington & Sutcliffe

David Lawrence
Deacons

Excellence International

Philip Smart
Faculty of Law - University of Hong Kong

Roderick John Sutton
Ferrier Hodgson Limited

David Hooi
Financial Secretary's Office

Matthew Mui
Financial Secretary's Office

Garment

Richard Tollan
Johnson Stokes & Master, member of Lex Mundi

Patrick Fontaine
Linklaters

Martinal Quan
Metopro Associates Limited

Leonard Ng
Orrick, Herrington & Sutcliffe LLP

Mimi Sze
Orrick, Herrington & Sutcliffe LLP

Agatha Chan
PricewaterhouseCoopers

Rod Houng-Lee
PricewaterhouseCoopers

Raymond Wong
PricewaterhouseCoopers Legal Services

Raymond Wong
Johnson, Stokes & Master, member of Lex Mundi

Rich Tiem Enterprise Ltd.

Bertrand Gruez
SDV Ltd.

Simon Kai
SDV Ltd.

Thomas Duplan
SDV Ltd.

William Chong
SDV Ltd.

Chi May Kwok
Squire, Sanders & Dempsey

Nicholas Chan
Squire, Sanders & Dempsey

Sara Tong
Temple Chambers

Stephen Briscoe

Albert P.C. Chan
The Hong Kong Polytechnic University

Alex Chan
The Land Registry of Hong Kong

Lawrence Tsong Tsong
Transunion Ltd.

Charles D. Booth
University of Hawaii

Keith Man Kei Ho
Wilkinson & Grist

HUNGARY

Zsuzsanna Cseri
Bárd, Cseri & Partners Law Firm

György Fehér
Bellák & Partners Law Office, member of Ius Laboris

Judit Nagy
Bellák & Partners Law Office, member of Ius Laboris

Zoltán Gvenge
Bellák & Partners Law Office, member of Ius Laboris

Beringer Allen & Overy Iroda

Pethő Ádám
BISZ Central Credit Information Ltd.

Anna Gáspár
Build-Econ Ltd.

Tamás Saád
Build-Econ Ltd.

Zoltan Krausz
Build-Econ Ltd.

Judit Bókai
Dr Bókai Notary Office

Ádám Tóth
Dr. Tóth & Dr. Gáspár Közjegyzői Iroda

Mark Balastyai
Futureal Holding Co.

IFS Ltd.

Péter Bárdos
Law Firm Dr. Péter and Rita Bárdos

Rita Bárdos
Law Firm Dr. Péter and Rita Bárdos

Csaba Pigler
Nagy és Trócsányi Law Office, member of Lex Mundi

Péter Berethalmi
Nagy és Trócsányi Law Office, member of Lex Mundi

Viktória Szilágyi
Nagy és Trócsányi Law Office, member of Lex Mundi

Christopher Noblet
Partos & Noblet Lovells

Andrea Kocziha
PricewaterhouseCoopers Kft

Dora Mathe
PricewaterhouseCoopers Kft

Gabriella Erdos
PricewaterhouseCoopers Kft

Norbert Izer
PricewaterhouseCoopers Kft

Russell Lambert
PricewaterhouseCoopers Kft

Tibor Torok
PricewaterhouseCoopers Kft

Dóra Horváth
Réti, Antall & Madl Landwell, PricewaterhouseCoopers Legal Services

Gabor Eisenbacher
Réti, Antall & Madl Landwell, PricewaterhouseCoopers Legal Services

László Réti
Réti, Antall & Madl Landwell, PricewaterhouseCoopers Legal Services

László Szűcs
Réti, Antall & Madl Landwell, PricewaterhouseCoopers Legal Services

Péter Mezei
Réti, Antall & Madl Landwell, PricewaterhouseCoopers Legal Services

Zoltán Várszegi
Réti, Antall & Madl Landwell, PricewaterhouseCoopers Legal Services

Ágnes Szent-Ivány
Sándor Szegedi Szent-Ivány & Komáromi

Szarvasi Altalanos Informatikai KFT

András Szecskay
Szecskay - Attorneys-at-Law

Hedi Bozsonyik
Szecskay - Attorneys-at-Law

Sándor Németh
Szecskay - Attorneys-at-Law

Vera Várkonyi

ICELAND

BBA Legal

Eyvindur Sólnes

Skuli Th. Fjeldsted
Fjeldsted, Blöndal & Fjeldsted

Fridgeir Sigurdsson

Sigrun Helga Johannsdottir
Fulltingi Legal Services

Bergþór Þormóðsson
ISTAK

Erlingur E. Jónasson
ISTAK

Ragna Matthíasdóttir
ISTAK

Johanna A. Jonsdottir

Kristján Pálsson
Jónar Transport

Reynir Haraldsson
Jónar Transport

Edda Andradóttir
JURIS Law office

Jóhannes R. Jóhannsson
JURIS Law office

Stefán A. Svensson
JURIS Law office

Björg Arnardóttir
Lánstraust ltd/ Creditinfo Group

Erlendur Gíslason
LOGOS, member of Lex Mundi

Gunnar Sturluson
LOGOS, member of Lex Mundi

Elin Arnadottir
PricewaterhouseCoopers hf.

Ásta Kristjánsdóttir
PricewaterhouseCoopers Legal Services

Elísabet Guðbjörnsdóttir
PricewaterhouseCoopers Legal Services

Steinthor Haraldsson
Ríkisskattstjóri

Vala Valtýsdóttir
Taxis Attorneys

Margrét Hauksdóttir
The Land Registry of Iceland

INDIA

3 Global Services

A - 1 Electricals

A K Exports

Aar Pee Industries

AdWorks

Ajay Enterprises

Ally Exim

Amarchand & Mangaldas & Suresh A. Shroff & Co., member of Lex Mundi

Amees Trading & Services Pvt. Ltd.

Amman Entrprises

Am-Tech Engineering Services

Anant Industries

Anuj Woollens Pvt. Ltd.

Arcata Trade-Links Pvt. Ltd.

Asiatic Colourchem Industries Ltd.

B&G Combines

Baby Boom

Bartronics India Ltd.

Basundhara Overseas

Bhasin International

Blue Blends India Ltd.

Bohra Rubber Pvt. Ltd.

Boksi International

Canar Exports

Harminder Chawla
Chawla & Co.

Neti Paul
Chawla & Co.

Rudra Srivastava
Chawla & Co.

Chonar Enterprises

Cloriwat Water Purifier Pvt. Ltd.

Rajendranath Bharati
Concorde Zoom

Harshala Chandorkar
Credit Information Bureau Ltd.

Dakshin Kreations Pvt. Ltd.

Derika International

Vijay G. Kalantri
Dighi Port Ltd.

Doss Traders

Anand Nivas
Dragon Express Freight Pvt. Ltd.

Vijayadas Saji
Dragon Express Freight Pvt. Ltd.

Eastern Medikit Ltd.

Elam Stones

Emerald International

Eshyl Services

Excel Enterprises

Vinod T
Expeditors International Pvt. Ltd.

Ferrocrafts

Flex Industries Ltd.

Ajay Khatlawala
Fox Mandal

Anuja Trivedi
Fox Mandal

Radhika Sankaran
Fox Mandal

Santanu Roy
Fox Mandal

Shreyas Patel
Fox Mandal

Siddharth Seshan
Fox Mandal

Som Mandal
Fox Mandal

G.P. Systems

Gafoor Exports

Gamzen Plast Pvt. Ltd.

Ganapati Udyog

Gayatri International Trading Co.

Gayatri Polymers & Geosynthetics.

Gfive Impex

GNA Udyog Ltd.

Grorich Horivert Pvt. Ltd.

Harsh Impex

Indusinoimpex

Abhishek Saket
Infini Juridique

Aparna Tripathy
Infini Juridique

Manish Madhukar
Infini Juridique

Innovative Eco-Care Pvt Ltd.

J. J. Exports

Nitin Potdar
J. Sagar Associates, Advocates & Solicitors

Dheep Kumar
JBS Shipping & Marine Consultants

JKG Services

John Fabrix

Anuradha Sharma
Kachwaha & Partners

Sumeet Kachwaha
Kachwaha & Partners

Vasanth Rajasekaran
Kachwaha & Partners

Kalki International

C.V. Ganesh
Karthik Diesel Sales & Service

Koshy G. George
Karthik Diesel Sales & Service

Kavjess Export Import Trading Company

Aashii Yadav
Kesar Dass B & Associates

Sumant Batra
Kesar Dass B & Associates

Nitin Sharma
Kesar Dass B. & Associates

Khyati Enterprises

Kissan Iron Works

Knight Trading Co.

Mukesh Kumar
KNM & Partners, Law Offices

Vijay Nair
KNM & Partners, Law Offices

Vipender Mann
KNM & Partners, Law Offices

Kunal Exports

Laxmi Compugraphics Pvt. Ltd.

Leelaram Exports Pvt. Ltd.

Ramesh K.K.
Leemik Logistics Pvt. Ltd.

Shrishail Kittad
Legasis Services Pvt. Ltd.

Suhas Tuljapurkar
Legasis Services Pvt. Ltd.

Leo Circuit Boards Pvt. Ltd.

Mangesh Jadhav
LG Electronics I P Ltd.

Dara Mehta
Little & Co.

Rajas Kasbekar
Little & Co.

M/s Angel Creations Inc.

M/s Globe Exports

M/s P.C. Merchandise

M/s Rahul Crafts

M/s Regency Exports

M/s Sushrut Molds & Dies

M/s Vishal Woollen Mills

M/s Vivy Fashions

M/s Weldone Textiles

Maersk Pvt. Ltd.

Magnus Speranza

Malani Gems & Jewels

Mangal Exports

Marian Marketing

Maztech International

Mekatronics Products Pvt. Ltd.

Mesha Paradise

Satish Murti
Murti & Murti Interlational Law Firm

Naren Electronics and Services

Neo Multimedian

Nevitad Distillers Pvt. Ltd.

New Fibre Glass Industries

Newrama

Nine International

Oasis Enterprises

Murli Nagrani
Pan Liner Clearing & Forwarding Agency

Paragon Industries

Param Overseas

Parveen Kumar
Parnami Overseas Logistics Pvt. Ltd.

Partnership

Patsons India

Ponmani Knitting Co.

Portoworld

Preeti Woollens

Premaa Textiles

Amit Agarwal
PricewaterhouseCoopers

Nityanand Gupta
PricewaterhouseCoopers

R. Muralidharan
PricewaterhouseCoopers

Rahul Garg
PricewaterhouseCoopers

Ravi Prakash
PricewaterhouseCoopers

Richa Agarwal
PricewaterhouseCoopers

Rohini Aggarawal
PricewaterhouseCoopers

Sandhya Vishal
PricewaterhouseCoopers

Jawahar Kothari
Profound Outsourcing Solutions Pvt. Ltd.

Vir Gandhi
Profound Outsourcing Solutions Pvt. Ltd.

Promax Corporation

QG Exports

R. K. Industries

Rahul Exports

Raj Gharana Gems

Raja Exports

Reliable Textile

Reliable Trans & Impex Services Pvt. Ltd.

RSN Consultancy & Exports

Saalvi Agro Mushrooms

Sarit Exports Consortium

Saurashtra Solid Industries Pvt. Ltd.

Seven Stars Sanspareil

Oommen George
SGSL Shipping & Logistics Pvt. Ltd.

Shachi Engineering Pvt. Ltd.

Shree Matha Exports

Shri Abinaya Mercantiles Pvt. Ltd.

Shri Ramdev Exports

Shri Sai Exports

Dipak Rao
Singhania & Partners, Solicitors & Advocates

Manju Mohotra
Singhania & Partners, Solicitors & Advocates

Ravinder Singhania
Singhania & Partners, Solicitors & Advocates

SMGL Corporation

Soundharya Enterprises

Space Granite and Marbles

Anant Jhunjhunwala
Space International

Spark Peripheral Technologies

Spartan Trends Inc.

Srinarayanas Garments Pvt. Ltd.

SSGrandson Group Co.

SSKS Infotech

Sukirti Overseas

Suraj Enterprises

T.S. Classique

Textile Machinery Mfg Co.

TMG Agro Solutions Pvt. Ltd.

Anand Prasad
Trilegal

Kaviraj Singh
Trustman & Co.

Tulja International

Uniworld Trading Co.

Vaibrant Biofuels

Balanchandran I
Varunapriya

Vetri International

Vinay Gupta
Vinay K Gupta & Co.

VSS Associates

Zedd Trade

Zeebra Hosieries

Zeus Exim

INDONESIA

Andre Panggabean
Ali Budiardjo, Nugroho, Reksodiputro, member of Lex Mundi

Ayik Gunadi
Ali Budiardjo, Nugroho, Reksodiputro, member of Lex Mundi

Ernst G. Tehuteru
Ali Budiardjo, Nugroho, Reksodiputro, member of Lex Mundi

Ferry P. Madian
Ali Budiardjo, Nugroho, Reksodiputro, member of Lex Mundi

Hamud M. Balfas
Ali Budiardjo, Nugroho, Reksodiputro, member of Lex Mundi

Indra Setiawan
Ali Budiardjo, Nugroho, Reksodiputro, member of Lex Mundi

Kevin Omar Sidharta
Ali Budiardjo, Nugroho, Reksodiputro, member of Lex Mundi

Nafis Adwani
Ali Budiardjo, Nugroho, Reksodiputro, member of Lex Mundi

Bakrie Niaga Tehnik

Bank of Indonesia

Hartono Parbudi
Biro Kredit

Ahmad Fadli
Brigitta I. Rahayoe & Syamsuddin

Brigitta I. Rahayoe
Brigitta I. Rahayoe & Syamsuddin

Rick Beckmann
Brigitta I. Rahayoe & Syamsuddin

Buana Elektronik

CV. Javanusa Furni

Elha Interior

Fortune Enterprise

Alexander Nainggolan
Hadromi & Partners

Iqbal Hadromi
Hadromi & Partners

Andre Rahadian
Hanafiah Ponggawa & Partners

Fabian Buddy Pascoal
Hanafiah Ponggawa & Partners

Iswahjudi A. Karim
KarimSyah Law Firm

Karen Mills
KarimSyah Law Firm

Gatot Sanyoto
Kusnandar & Co.

Winita E. Kusnandar
Kusnandar & Co.

Galinar Kartakusuma
Makarim & Taira S.

Jenny Budiman
Makarim & Taira S.

Rika Hardaini
Makarim & Taira S.

Mine and Hers International

Almer Apon
PT Buana Mas Citra Lestari

PT Karya Mulia

PT Nominasi Chandra Wisata

Ray Headifen
PT Prima Wahana Caraka / PricewaterhouseCoopers

Robertus Winarto
PT Prima Wahana Caraka / PricewaterhouseCoopers

Yuni Triuningsih
PT Prima Wahana Caraka / PricewaterhouseCoopers

PT Ruby Privatindo

PT Tempo Inti Media Tbk.

Arfidea Dwi Saraswati
SSEK Indonesian Legal Consultants

Darrell R. Johnson
SSEK Indonesian Legal Consultants

Ira A. Eddymurthy
SSEK Indonesian Legal Consultants

Tagaya Florindo International

Bambang Soelaksono
The SMERU Research Institute

Gatot Triprasetio
Widyawan & Partners

Yicheng International

IRAN

Behzad Feizi
Agahan & Co.

Alvand Sayan International Trading Co, Ltd.

Babak Namazi
Atieh Associates

Faraz Naji
Atieh Associates

Parisa Mazaheri
Atieh Associates

Atieh International Transport Co.

Jamal Seifi
Dr. Jamal Seifi & Associates

Mir Shahbiz Shafe'e
Dr. Jamal Seifi & Associates

FGR Co.

Reza Askari
Foreign Legal Affairs Group

Behrooz Akhlaghi
International Law Office of Dr.Behrooz Akhlaghi & Associates

Akbar Hendizadeh
Iran Counselors

Pejman Eshtehardi
Iran Counselors

Rouzbeh Hazrati
Iran Counselors

KTSCO

Mahmoud Ebadi Tabrizi
M. Ebadi Tabrizi & Associates

Yahya Rayegani
MBSR Law Office

Nejat Steel Co.

Nader Sheybani
Sheybani & Associates

Cyrus Shafizadeh
Tavakoli & Shahabi

Mostafa Shahabi
Tavakoli & Shahabi

Mozaffar Mohammadian
Teema Bar International Transport

IRAQ

Ahmad Al Jannabi

Husam Addin Hatim
Al Fadhaa Co. Ltd.

Florian Amereller
Amereller Rechtsanwälte

Stephan Jäger
Amereller Rechtsanwälte

Farquad Al-Salman
F. H. Al-Salman & Co.

Ahmed Abboud Al-Janabi
Mena Associates

Hadeel Al Janabi

Hadeel Salih Abboud Al-Janabi
Mena Associates

Hussein A. H. Damirji
The New Iraq Law Firm

IRELAND

Niav Ohiggins
Arthur Cox, member of Lex Mundi

John Doyle
Dillon Eustace

Niamh Loughran
Dillon Eustace

Barry O'Neill
Eugene F. Collins Solicitors

Gavin Doherty
Eugene F. Collins Solicitors

Gavin Simons
Eugene F. Collins Solicitors

Sinead Power
Irish Credit Bureau

Colm Walsh
Irish International Freight Association

Garrett Breen
Landwell, PricewaterhouseCoopers Legal Services

Alan Browning
LK Shields Solicitors, member of Ius Laboris

Eoin Cunneen
LK Shields Solicitors, member of Ius Laboris

Fiona Thornton
LK Shields Solicitors, member of Ius Laboris

Gillian Dully
LK Shields Solicitors, member of Ius Laboris

Ian Lavelle
LK Shields Solicitors, member of Ius Laboris

Jonathan Cullen
LK Shields Solicitors, member of Ius Laboris

Richard Curran
LK Shields Solicitors, member of Ius Laboris

Judith Riordan
Mason Hayes & Curran

Maurice Phelan
Mason Hayes & Curran

Micheál Grace
Mason Hayes & Curran

Will Carmody
Mason Hayes & Curran

Georgina Kabemba
Matheson Ormsby Prentice

Paul Glenfeld
Matheson Ormsby Prentice

Colm Kelly
PricewaterhouseCoopers

Gavan Neary
PricewaterhouseCoopers

Margaret Masterson
PricewaterhouseCoopers

Brendan Sharkey
Reddy Charlton McKnight

Elaine McGrath
Reddy Charlton McKnight

Maeve Valsh
Reddy Charlton McKnight

ISRAEL

A. Moskovits & Sons Ltd.

Gideon Koren
Ben Zvi Koren & Co. Law Offices

Daniel Singerman
Business Data Israel + Personal Check

Jakob Melcer Adv.
E. S. Shimron, I. Molho, Persky & Co.

Dina Brown
Elchanan Landau Law Offices

June Dilevsky
Israel Securities Authority

Gerry Seligman
Kesselman & Kesselman

Koby Cohen
Kesselman & Kesselman

Lior Crystal
Kesselman & Kesselman

Vered Kirshner
Kesselman & Kesselman

Zeev Katz
Kesselman & Kesselman

Clifford Davis
S. Horowitz & Co., member of Lex Mundi

Michelle Liberman
S. Horowitz & Co., member of Lex Mundi

Ofer Bar-On
Shavit Bar-On Gal-On Tzin Nov Yagur, Law Offices

Ron Ben-Menachem
Weil, Gotshal & Manges LLP

Aaron Jaffe
Yigal Arnon & Co.

Paul Baris
Yigal Arnon & Co.

Ronen Bar-Even
Zeev Weiss Law Offices

ITALY

Giovanni Izzo
Abbatescianni Studio Legale e Tributario

Alessandro Caridi

Gennaro Cassiani
Architect

Carlo Bruno
Ashurst

Paola Flora
Ashurst

Vincenzo Giannantonio
Ashurst

Maria Pia Ascenzo
Bank of Italy

Bill Harrison-Cripps

Fabrizio Colonna
Camozzi Bonissoni Varrenti & Associati

Marco Ettorre
Camozzi Bonissoni Varrenti & Associati

Pier Andrea Fré Torelli Massini
Carabba & Partners

Alessandra Palladini
Cleary Gottlieb Steen & Hamilton LLP

Alessandro Pellegrini
Cleary Gottlieb Steen & Hamilton LLP

Benedetta Vannini
Cleary Gottlieb Steen & Hamilton LLP

Claudio Di Falco
Cleary Gottlieb Steen & Hamilton LLP

Giovanni B. Sandicchi
Cleary Gottlieb Steen & Hamilton LLP

Patrizia Masselli
Cleary Gottlieb Steen & Hamilton LLP

Roberto Bonsignore
Cleary Gottlieb Steen & Hamilton LLP

Tommaso Ariani
Cleary Gottlieb Steen & Hamilton LLP

CRIF S. p.A.

Giuseppe Antonio Recchia
Faculty of Law - University of Foggia

Madia D'Onghia
Faculty of Law - University of Foggia

Valentina Pasquarella
Faculty of Law - University of Foggia

Francesco Nuzzolo

Mattia Colonnelli de Gasperis
Freshfields Bruckhaus Deringer

Stefano Macchi di Cellere
Jones Day

Klamflexeurope s.r.l.

Angelo Zambelli
LabLaw Studio legale - Failla, Rotondi & Zambelli

Vincenzo Fabrizio Giglio
LabLaw Studio legale - Failla, Rotondi & Zambelli

Loran Ltd.

Silvio Tersilla
Lovells

Marco Vozzi

Giancarlo Laurini
Notaio Giancarlo Laurini

Mario Miccoli
Notaio Miccoli

Paolo Pasqualis
Notary

Sergio Calderara
Nunziante Magrone

Giorgio Cherubini
Pirola Pennuto Zei Associati

Chiara Tufarelli
Ristuccia & Tufarelli

Gaia Silvi
Ristuccia & Tufarelli

Luca Tufarelli
Ristuccia & Tufarelli

Marianna Ristuccia
Ristuccia & Tufarelli

Luigi Brunetti
SDV

Piervincenzo Spasaro
Spasaro De Martinis Law Firm

Fabrizio Mariotti
Studio Legale Beltramo

Susanna Beltramo
Studio Legale Beltramo

Federico Guasti
Studio Legale Guasti

Giuseppe Ramondelli
Studio Legale Notarile Di Fabio Ramondelli Cantamagli

Lamberto Schiona
Studio legale Schiona

Paolo Pedrazzoli
Studio Notaio Pedrazzoli

Emanuele Ferrari
Studio Notarile Ferrari

Fabrizio Acerbis
TLS / PricewaterhouseCoopers

Filippo Zucchinelli
TLS / PricewaterhouseCoopers Legal Services

Gaetano Arnò
TLS / PricewaterhouseCoopers Legal Services

Paola Barazzetta
TLS / PricewaterhouseCoopers Legal Services

Salvatore Cuzzocrea
TLS / PricewaterhouseCoopers Legal Services

Valeria Morossini
Toffoletto e Soci Law Firm, member of Ius Laboris

Paolo Fergola
University of Turin

Maria Grazia Medici
Verusio e Cosmelli Studio Legale

JAMAICA

Nicole Foga
Foga Daley & Co.

Global Trading

Herbert Winston Grant
Grant, Stewart, Phillips & Co.

Karen Wilson

Noel Mcken
Kier Construction Ltd.

Alicia P. Hussey
Myers, Fletcher & Gordon, member of Lex Mundi

Corrine N. Henry
Myers, Fletcher & Gordon, member of Lex Mundi

Dave García
Myers, Fletcher & Gordon, member of Lex Mundi

Hilary Reid
Myers, Fletcher & Gordon, member of Lex Mundi

Lisa Russell
Myers, Fletcher & Gordon, member of Lex Mundi

Malaica Wong
Myers, Fletcher & Gordon, member of Lex Mundi

Sandra Minott-Phillips
Myers, Fletcher & Gordon, member of Lex Mundi

Lorna Phillips
Nicholson Phillips, Attorneys-at-Law

Arlene Burton
PricewaterhouseCoopers

Eric Crawford
PricewaterhouseCoopers

Michael Hall
PricewaterhouseCoopers

Viveen Morrison
PricewaterhouseCoopers

Sekeywi Carruthers
Sekeywi Carruthers & Associates

Humprey Taylor
Taylor Construction Ltd.

JAPAN

Mijo Fujita
Adachi, Henderson, Miyatake & Fujita

Toshio Miyatake
Adachi, Henderson, Miyatake & Fujita

Hideki Thurgood Kano
Anderson Mori & Tomotsune

Michi Yamagami
Anderson Mori & Tomotsune

Yoshimasa Furuta
Anderson Mori & Tomotsune

Shinichiro Abe
Bingham McCutchen Murase, Sakai & Mimura Foreign Law Joint Enterprise

Yoshihito Shibata
Bingham McCutchen Murase, Sakai & Mimura Foreign Law Joint Enterprise

Credit Information Center Corp.

Tamotsu Hatasawa
Hatasawa & Wakai Law Firm

Health Food

Heartland Company Ltd.

Toshio Taikoji
Kajima Corporation

Soichiro Fujiwara
Mori Hamada & Matsumoto

Tohru Motobayashi
Mori Hamada & Matsumoto

Kenji Utsumi
Nagashima Ohno & Tsunematsu

Eri Sugihara
Nishimura & Partners

Kazuhiro Yanagida
Nishimura & Partners

Michihiro Mori
Nishimura & Partners

Takafumi Nihei
Nishimura & Partners

Takanobu Takehara
Nishimura & Partners

Yutaro Kawabata
Nishimura & Partners

Susumi Kawaguchi
Obayashi Corporation

Kosei Watanabe
O'Melveny & Myers Gaikokuho Kyodojigyo Horitsujimusho

Azniv Ksachikyan
Orrick, Herrington & Sutcliffe LLP

Laurent Develle
Orrick, Herrington & Sutcliffe LLP

Naomasa Nakagawa
Orrick, Herrington & Sutcliffe LLP

Shuhei Tsudo
Orrick, Herrington & Sutcliffe LLP

Nobuaki Matsuoka
Osaka International Law Offices

Hiroyuki Suzuki
PricewaterhouseCoopers / Zeirishi-Hojin ChuoAoyama

Kotaku Kimu
PricewaterhouseCoopers / Zeirishi-Hojin ChuoAoyama

Shigeru Hasegawa
PricewaterhouseCoopers / Zeirishi-Hojin ChuoAoyama

Tokyo Trading Co. Ltd.

Kenichi Kojima
Ushijima & Partners

JORDAN

Maher Melhem
Abu-Ghazaleh Professional Consulting (AGPC)

Mohammed Quttaineh
Abu-Ghazaleh Professional Consulting (AGPC)

Bassam Abu-Rumman
Ali Sharif Zu'bi, Advocates & Legal Consultants, member of Lex Mundi

Iyad Zawaideh
Ali Sharif Zu'bi, Advocates & Legal Consultants, member of Lex Mundi

Saleh Abdelati
Ali Sharif Zu'bi, Advocates & Legal Consultants, member of Lex Mundi

Omar Aljazy
Aljazy& Co. Advocates & Legal Consultants

Sabri Al Khassib
Amman Chamber of Commerce

Chaled Abu-Gharbieh
Arch EPE, Enterprise Business Solutions

Francis Bawab
Bawab & Co. / PricewaterhouseCoopers

Stephan Stephan
Bawab & Co. / PricewaterhouseCoopers

Zeina Jaradat
Bawab & Co. / PricewaterhouseCoopers

Arafat Alfayoumi
Central Bank of Jordan

George Hazboun

Tariq Hammouri
Hammouri & Partners

Waddah Rawashdeh
Hammouri & Partners

Wafa Aranki
IFC

Eman M. Al-Dabbas
International Business Legal Associates

Firas Malhas
International Business Legal Associates

Basel Kawar
Kawar Transport & Transit Kargo

Akram Obeidat
Khalifeh & Partners

Khaldoun Nazer
Khalifeh & Partners

Tamara Al-Banna
Khalifeh & Partners

Ibrahim Abunameh
Law & Arbitration Centre

Michael Dabit
Michael T. Dabit & Associates

Mufida Art Mosaic

Omq Al Bihar Est.

Azzam Zalloum
Zalloum & Laswi Law Firm

Rasha Laswi
Zalloum & Laswi Law Firm

KAZAKHSTAN

Semion Issyk
Aequitas Law Firm

Nursultan Kassenov
Aristan Property Advisers

Amy Clark
Assistance, LLC Law Firm

Maria Lensky
Assistance, LLC Law Firm

Tair Kulteleev
Assistance, LLC Law Firm

Zhaniya Ussen
Assistance, LLC Law Firm

Anara Shaikenova
Business Environment Improvement Project (by Pragma Corporation)

Kelly Seibold
Business Environment Improvement Project (by Pragma Corporation)

Almaz Dosserbekov
Denton Wilde Sapte

Thomas Johnson
Denton Wilde Sapte

Timur Khasanov-Batirov
Derbes Brewery, Subsidiary of BBH

Anvar Akhmedov
First Credit Bureau

Pasha Karim
Globalink Transportation & Logistics Worldwide LLP

Sabina Barayeva
JS Venture investment fund JSC

Elvis Roberts
M & M Logistics

Irina Chen
M & M Logistics

Oleg Gnoev
M & M Logistics

Ruslan Murzashev
McGuire Woods Kazakhstan LLP, member of Lex Mundi

Vsevolod Markov
McGuire Woods Kazakhstan LLP, member of Lex Mundi

Asel Umysheva
Michael Wilson & Partners Ltd.

Michael S. Dark
Michael Wilson & Partners Ltd.

Yekaterina V. Kim
Michael Wilson & Partners Ltd.

Abdulkhamid Muminov
PricewaterhouseCoopers

Aliya Utegaliyeva
PricewaterhouseCoopers

Bakhytzhan Kadyrov
PricewaterhouseCoopers

Bob Jurik
PricewaterhouseCoopers

Courtney Fowler
PricewaterhouseCoopers

Elena Kaeva
PricewaterhouseCoopers

Ilyas Jumambaev
PricewaterhouseCoopers

Natalya Revenko
PricewaterhouseCoopers

Dina Kali
PricewaterhouseCoopers Legal Services

Karina Iliusizova
PricewaterhouseCoopers Legal Services

Sergey Kalashnikov
PricewaterhouseCoopers Legal Services

Dina Khakimzhanova
Salans

Kanat Skakov
Salans

Yuliya Mitrofanskaya
Salans

KENYA

George Akoto
Akoto & Company Advocates

Washington Muthamia
Alexandria Freight Forwarders Ltd.

Sonal Sejpal
Anjarwalla & Khanna Advocates

Andrew Mwaura
B. M. Musau & Co. Advocates

Benjamin Musau
B. M. Musau & Co. Advocates

Micky Matheka
B. M. Musau & Co. Advocates

Morris Kimuli
B. M. Musau & Co. Advocates

Muthoni Murage
B. M. Musau & Co. Advocates

Onesmus Nzuki
B. M. Musau & Co. Advocates

Victor Ayieko
B. M. Musau & Co. Advocates

Bobcare Medical Systems Ltd.

Fiona Fox
Chunga Associates

Judy Mwangi
Chunga Associates

Wachira Ndege
Credit Reference Bureau Africa Ltd.

Martin Simiyu
InterAfrika Consult

William Maema
Iseme, Kamau & Maema Advocates

Peter Gachuhi
Kaplan & Stratton

Kazuri Treasures Ltd.

Jacqueline Wanjiku
Kenya Revenue Authority

George Kigathi
Kigathi & Associates

Jinaro Kibet
Ochieng, Onyango, Kibet & Ohaga

Tom Onyango
Ochieng, Onyango, Kibet & Ohaga

Daniel Ngumy
PricewaterhouseCoopers

David Tarimo
PricewaterhouseCoopers

Dipak Shah
PricewaterhouseCoopers

Gavin McEwen
PricewaterhouseCoopers

Meenal Shah
PricewaterhouseCoopers

Rishit Shah
PricewaterhouseCoopers

Adrian Dearing
PricewaterhouseCoopers Legal Services

Russell Eastaugh
PricewaterhouseCoopers Legal Services

Francis Gichuhi
Prism Designs Africa

Luke Kenei
Siginon Freight Ltd.

Meshack Kipturgo
Siginon Freight Ltd.

voIPKenya International

Deepen Shah
Walker Kontos Advocates

KIRIBATI

Batira Tekanito

Lawrence Muller
Betio City Council

Batira Tekarmito
Development Bank of Kiribati

Romano Reo
Land Management Division

Kenneth Barden
Ministry of Finance

Matereta Raiman
Ministry of Finance & Economic Development

Office of the People's Lawyer

Aomoro Amten
Taoaba & Amten

KOREA

Hye Jeong Lee
Ahnse Law Offices

Sung Whan Lee
Ahnse Law Offices

Eui Jong Chung
Bae, Kim & Lee

Jeong Seo
Daejeon District Court

Eun Joo Shin

EVT (Eastern Video Tech.) Co., Ltd.

Jung Myung Lee
Hwang Mok Park P.C., member of Lex Mundi

Sang Il Park
Hwang Mok Park P.C., member of Lex Mundi

Ae-Ryun Rho
Kim & Chang

C.W. Hyun
Kim & Chang

Hi-Taek Shin
Kim & Chang

J.T. Park
Kim & Chang

Jin-Ho Song
Kim & Chang

Mia Kim
Kim & Chang

KT & C Co., Ltd.

Hyun Tae Kim
Lee & Ko

Kyu Wha Lee
Lee & Ko

Yong Seok An
Lee & Ko

MJ Co., Ltd.

Office of the Peoples Lawyer

Cheol Kim
Samil PricewaterhouseCoopers

Han-Jun Chon
Samil PricewaterhouseCoopers

Jin-Young Lee
Samil PricewaterhouseCoopers

Lionel Darrieutort
SDV

B.H. Nam
Seohan Industries Co.

Wonhyung Kim
Yoon Yang Kim Shin & Yu

Young Su Shin
Yoon Yang Kim Shin & Yu

Sung Jin Kim
Yulchon

Won-Il Sohn
Yulchon

Young-Cheol Jeong
Yulchon

KUWAIT

Abdullah Al-Ayoub
Abdullah Kh. Al-Ayoub & Associates, member of Lex Mundi

Jasmin Paurus Kohina
Abdullah Kh. Al-Ayoub & Associates, member of Lex Mundi

Sunil Jose
Abu-Ghazaleh Legal

Ghina W. Malek
Al Khebra Legal Consultants & Lawyers

Mohammed H. Al-Dallal
Al Khebra Legal Consultants & Lawyers

Mary Carmel Byrne
Al Markaz Law Firm

Roupen Avsharian
Al Markaz Law Firm

Hossam Abdullah
Al Sarraf & Al Ruwayeh

Sam Habbas
Al Sarraf & Al Ruwayeh

Ihab Abbas
Al-Fahad & Co, Deloitte & Touche

Tim Bullock
Al-Fahad & Co, Deloitte & Touche

Reema Ali
Ali & Partners

Amal Abdallah
Al-Saleh & Partners

Nazih Abdul Hameed
Al-Saleh & Partners

Credit Information Network

Khaled F. Al Hendi
Justice Palace - Court of Appeal

Rola A. Dashti
Kuwait Economic Society

Salah Al-Shammari
Kuwait Oil Co.

Wayne Fidyk
Mashor Advocates & Legal Consultants

Ahmad A.T. Al-Melaifi
National Assembly

Packaging and Plastic Industries Co. (KSC)

Mazen A. Khoursheed
PPIC

Labeed Abdal
The Law Firm of Labeed Abdal

Lina A. Adlouni
The Law office of Al-Essa & Partners

Omar Hamad Yousuf Al-Essa
The Law office of Al-Essa & Partners

Mishari M. Al-Ghazali
The Law Offices of Mishari Al-Ghazali

Rawan M. Al-Ghazali
The Law Offices of Mishari Al-Ghazali

Yousof M. Al-Ali
The Law Offices of Mishari Al-Ghazali

Union International Cargo Group

KYRGYZ REPUBLIC

Kamila Mateeva
American University - Central Asia

Larisa Janibekova
Anel Company Ltd.

Asel Kenenbaeva
Attorney-at-Law

Barno Marazykova
Attorney-at-Law

Meerim Nurkamilova
Attorney-at-Law

Akjoltoy Elebesova
Credit Information Bureau Ishenim

Galina Kucherayvaya
Demir Kyrgyz International Bank

Anastasiya Shloeva
Globalink Transportation & Logistics Worldwide LLP

Azim Usmanov
Grata Law Firm

Bakay Junushov
iCAP Investment

Gulnara Ahmatova
International Business Council

Natalia Dolinskaya
International Business Council

Talay Asylbekov
International Business Council

Aijana Bekkulieva
Kalikova & Associates Law Firm

Gulnara Kalikova
Kalikova & Associates Law Firm

Marina Lim
Kalikova & Associates Law Firm

Nurbek Chonbashev
Kalikova & Associates Law Firm

Ulan Tilenbaev
Kalikova & Associates Law Firm

Rakhman Asylbekov
Kyrgyz Gripro Stroi

Kwang Young Choi
Kyrgyz Investment and Credit Bank

Shabdan Tagaev
Kyrgyz Investment and Credit Bank

Mirulan Jamshitov

Abdulkhamid Muminov
PricewaterhouseCoopers

Almas Nakipov
PricewaterhouseCoopers

Bakhytzhan Kadyrov
PricewaterhouseCoopers

Bob Jurik
PricewaterhouseCoopers

Courtney Fowler
PricewaterhouseCoopers

Elena Kaeva
PricewaterhouseCoopers

Saltanat Ismailova
PricewaterhouseCoopers

LAO PDR

Nokeo Mounivong
Bank of the Lao PDR, Banks and Financial Institutions Supervision Department

Phonxay Southiphong
Design Group Co Ltd.

Maligna Saignavongs
Lao Bar Association

One-Sy Boutsivongsakd
Lao National Chamber of Commerce and Industry

Grant Follet
DFDL Mekong Law Group

Ketsana Phommachanh
Ministry of Justice, Law Research and International Cooperation Institute

Janist Aphornratana
PricewaterhouseCoopers

Pradthanaadt Ratanatanungpong
PricewaterhouseCoopers

Richard Irwin
PricewaterhouseCoopers

Supanan Promphiphat
PricewaterhouseCoopers

Thavorn Rujivanarom
PricewaterhouseCoopers

Xaynari Chanthala
PricewaterhouseCoopers

Daodeuane Duangdara
PricewaterhouseCoopers Legal Services

Intong Oudom
Seneoudom Trading Co. Ltd.

Khampheng Vongkhanty
Société Mixte de Transport Co., Ltd.

Vasco Ltd.

LATVIA

Edijs Poga
Baltmane & Bitāns - Attorneys-at-Law

Maris Vainovskis
Baltmane & Bitāns - Attorneys-at-Law

Ludmila Kornijenko
Blueger & Plaude

Andris Ignatenko
Estma SIA

Zane Stalberga - Markvarte
Hansa Law Offices

Janis Loze

Daiga Zivtiņa
Klavins & Slaidins, member of Lex Mundi

Filip Klavins
Klavins & Slaidins, member of Lex Mundi

Mikus Buls
Klavins & Slaidins, member of Lex Mundi

Sarmis Spilbergs
Klavins & Slaidins, member of Lex Mundi

Andis Čonka
Latvijas Banka

Law Offices Blueger & Plaude

Aigars Gozitis
Lejins, Torgans & Partners, member of Ius Laboris

Aldis Gobzems
Lejins, Torgans & Partners, member of Ius Laboris

Dace Silava-Tomsone
Lejins, Torgans & Partners, member of Ius Laboris

Elina Bedanova
Lejins, Torgans & Partners, member of Ius Laboris

Maija Volkova
Lejins, Torgans & Partners, member of Ius Laboris

Ilze Bukaldere
Liepa, Skopiņa/ Borenius

Indrikis Liepa
Liepa, Skopiņa/ Borenius

Inese Rendeniece
Loze, Grunte & Cers

Aija Klavinska
PricewaterhouseCoopers

Gunita Puzule
PricewaterhouseCoopers

Zlata Elksnina-Zascirinska
PricewaterhouseCoopers

Cameron Greaves
PricewaterhouseCoopers

Ilze Abika
Skudra & Udris Law Offices

Agris Repss
Sorainen Law Offices

Andis Burkevics
Sorainen Law Offices

Brigita Terauda
Sorainen Law Offices

Ilmars Naglis
Sorainen Law Offices

Vilmars Vanags

LEBANON

Samir Ali Ahmad
AA Architects

Hamelkart Ataya
Abu-Ghazaleh Legal

Albert Laham

Chadia El Meouchi
Badri and Salim El Meouchi Law Firm, member of Interleges

Christel Salem
Badri and Salim El Meouchi Law Firm, member of Interleges

Fady Ghanem
Badri and Salim El Meouchi Law Firm, member of Interleges

Greta Habib
Badri and Salim El Meouchi Law Firm, member of Interleges

Jihad Rizkallah
Badri and Salim El Meouchi Law Firm, member of Interleges

Mazen Rasamny
Badri and Salim El Meouchi Law Firm, member of Interleges

Theodore De Mar Youssef
Badri and Salim El Meouchi Law Firm, member of Interleges

Jean Baroudi
Baroudi & Associates

Najib Choucair
Central Bank of Lebanon

Albert Nasr
Chamber of Commerce, Industry & Agriculture of Beirut

Aline Dantziguian
Chamber of Commerce, Industry & Agriculture of Beirut

Chez Pierre

Georges Jureidini
Coserv SARL - Panalpina Agents

Rachad Medawar
El Khoury Law Firm

Electricité du Liban

George Jabre
George Jabre & Associates

Joseph Safar
Hayek Group

Eddy Maghariki
Hyam G. Mallat Law Firm

Georges Mallat
Hyam G. Mallat Law Firm

Nabil Mallat
Hyam G. Mallat Law Firm

Fady Jamaleddine
Jamaleddine Law Firm

Georges Kadige
Kadige & Kadige Law Firm

Librex Group

Bernard Choueiri
Ministry of Justice

Fadi Moghaizel
Moghaizel Law Firm, member of Lex Mundi

Zeina Abi Chahine
Nabil Abdel-Malek Law Offices

Mario Mohanna
Patrimoine Conseil SARL

Bassel Habiby
PricewaterhouseCoopers

Camille C. Sifri
PricewaterhouseCoopers

Ramzi George
PricewaterhouseCoopers

Wadih Abounasr
PricewaterhouseCoopers

Toufic Nehme

Nady Tyan
Tyan & Zgheib Law Firm

LESOTHO

Lindiwe Sephomolo
Association of Lesotho Employers and Business

Theodore Ntlatlapa
DNT Architects

Harley & Morris

Mei & Mei Attorneys Inc.

Peter Sands
SDV

Thuso Green
Sechaba Consultants

Tiisetso Sello-Mafatle
Sello - Mafatle Chambers

Duduzile Seamatha
Sheeran & Associates

Marorisang Thekiso
Sheeran & Associates

Mathias Matshe
Sheeran & Associates

Molunngoa Lekhotsa
Sheeran & Associates

Denis Molyneaux
Webber Newdigate

LIBERIA

Jane B. Barker
Center For National Documents & Records (National Archives)

Christine Sonpon Freeman
Cooper & Togbah Law Firm

Henry Reed Cooper
Cooper & Togbah Law Firm

David A.B. Jallah
David A.B. Jallah Law Firm

Frank Musah Dean
Dean & Associates

Charles Gongar
Debt Court

Amos P. Andrews
EcoBank - Liberia

Patrick S. Fallah
EcoBank - Liberia

Patricia Clark
Female Lawyers Association of Liberia

Joseph N. Blidi
J. Nagbe Blidi Law firm & Consultancy, Inc.

Cyril Jones
Jones & Jones

Barbu
Liberia Bar Association

Kolubahzizi T. Howard
Liberia Telecommunications Corporation

Joseph N. Siaway
Maersk Ltd.

Henry B. Freeman, Jr.
Milton & Richards, Inc.

Lawrence Y. Paye
Ministry of Public Works

James E. Pierre
Pierre, Tweh & Associates

Miatta Korpo
Pierre, Tweh & Associates

Oswald Tweh
Pierre, Tweh & Associates

T. Negbalee Warner
Pierre, Tweh & Associates

Darcy White
PricewaterhouseCoopers

George Kwatia
PricewaterhouseCoopers

Gideon Ayi-owoo
PricewaterhouseCoopers

Thomas Murega
PricewaterhouseCoopers

Siata Lyonel Freeman
Safmarine, Maersk Ltd.

Betty Lamin Blamol
Sherman & Sherman

Chan-Chan A. Paegar
Sherman & Sherman

G. Moses Paegar
Sherman & Sherman

Golda A. Bonah
Sherman & Sherman

J. Johnny Momoh
Sherman & Sherman

Roy Chalkley
Umarco

Powo Hilton
Verdier and Associates

Wilkins Wright
Wright & Associates Law Firm

LITHUANIA

AsstrA UAB

Kazimieras Ramonas
Bank of Lithuania

Audrius Žvybas
Bernotas & Dominas Glimstedt

Kim Bartholdy
DSV Transport UAB

Petras Baltusevicius
DSV Transport UAB

Sergej Markevic
DSV Transport UAB

Jonas Kiauleikis
Foigt & Partners / Regija Borenius

Andrius Bogdanovicius
Infobankas UAB

Giedre Domkute - Lukauskiene
Law Firm AAA Baltic Service Company

Asta Rušinskaitė
Law Firm Bernotas & Dominas Glimstedt

Ernesta Zutautaite
Law firm Foresta

Tomas Mieliauskas
Law firm Foresta

Dovilė Burgienė
Law Firm Lideika, Petrauskas, Valiūnas ir partneriai LAWIN, member of Lex Mundi

Ieva Buteniene
Law Firm Lideika, Petrauskas, Valiūnas ir partneriai LAWIN, member of Lex Mundi

Indrė Jonaitytė
Law Firm Lideika, Petrauskas, Valiūnas ir partneriai LAWIN, member of Lex Mundi

Laimonas Skibarka
Law Firm Lideika, Petrauskas, Valiūnas ir partneriai LAWIN, member of Lex Mundi

Mindaugas Kiškis
Law Firm Lideika, Petrauskas, Valiūnas ir partneriai LAWIN, member of Lex Mundi

Ramūnas Petravičius
Law Firm Lideika, Petrauskas, Valiūnas ir partneriai LAWIN, member of Lex Mundi

Rolandas Galvėnas
Law Firm Lideika, Petrauskas, Valiūnas ir partneriai LAWIN, member of Lex Mundi

Rolandas Valiunas
Law Firm Lideika, Petrauskas, Valiūnas ir partneriai LAWIN, member of Lex Mundi

Darius Zabiela
Law Firm Zabiela, Zabielaite & Partners

Linas Margevicius

Dmitrij Dolgin
Norcous & Partners, member of Ius Laboris

Leva Dosinaite
Norcous & Partners, member of Ius Laboris

Rimantas Simaitis
Norcous & Partners, member of Ius Laboris

Žilvinas Kvietkus
Norcous & Partners, member of Ius Laboris

Cameron Greaves
PricewaterhouseCoopers
Kristina Bartuseviciene
PricewaterhouseCoopers

Robert Rajpold
PricewaterhouseCoopers

Vilius Kolelis
PricewaterhouseCoopers

Renata Beržanskiene
Sorainen Law Offices

Tomas Davidonis
Sorainen Law Offices

Viktorija Kapustinskaja
Sorainen Law Offices

Aidas Petrosius
State Enterprise Centre of Registers

LUXEMBOURG

Allen & Overy Luxembourg

Claude Kremer
Arendt & Medernach

Paul Mousel
Arendt & Medernach

Alain GrosJean
Bonn Schmitt Steichen, Member of Lex Mundi

Alex Schmitt
Bonn Schmitt Steichen, Member of Lex Mundi

Elisabeth Omes
Bonn Schmitt Steichen, Member of Lex Mundi

Guy Castegnaro
Castegnaro Cabinet d'avocats, member of Ius Laboris

Gérard Eischen
Chamber of Commerce

Patricia Dillas
Chamber of Commerce

Groupe AOH S.A.

Anne Singer
Loyens Winandy

Françoise Pfeiffer
Loyens Winandy

Geoffrey Scardoni
Loyens Winandy

Jean-Luc Schaus
Loyens Winandy

Nuria Martin
Loyens Winandy

Simon Paul
Loyens Winandy

Paul Wurth S.A. Engineering & Project Management

A. Murrath
PricewaterhouseCoopers SàRL

Anabela Fernandes Goncalves
PricewaterhouseCoopers SàRL

Dominique Robinet
PricewaterhouseCoopers SàRL

Isabel Lapietra
PricewaterhouseCoopers SàRL

Laurent Paquet
PricewaterhouseCoopers SàRL

Marleen Vandenput
PricewaterhouseCoopers SàRL

Michael Lockman
PricewaterhouseCoopers SàRL

Rene Beltjens
PricewaterhouseCoopers SàRL

Serge Saussoy
PricewaterhouseCoopers SàRL

Frank von Roesgen
Schroeder & Associés

Marc Hansen
SDV

MACEDONIA, FYR

Vladimir Vasilevski
Betasped International Freight Forwarding

Jovan Andonovski
Central Registry of the Republic of Macedonia

Kosta Gligorievski
Central Registry of the Republic of Macedonia

Nikola Dinevski
Central Registry of the Republic of Macedonia

Emmanuel Koenig

Benita Beleskova
IKRP Rokas & Partners

Theodoros Giannitsakis
IKRP Rokas & Partners

Valentina Jovanovska Vasileva
IKRP Rokas & Partners

Violeta Angelova Gerovska
IKRP Rokas & Partners

Dejan Knezovic
Law Office Knezovic & Associates

Valentin Pepeljugoski
Law Office Pepeljugoski

Tatjana Popovski Buloski
Law Office Polenak

Slavica Trckova
Law Office Trckova

Aleksandra Donevska
Lawyers Antevski

Katerina Jordanova
Lawyers Antevski

Zlatko Antevski
Lawyers Antevski

Nena Ivanovska
Macedonian Court Modernization Project

Makstone

Biljana Cakmakova
Mens Legis Cakmakova Advocates

Eva Veljanovska
Mens Legis Cakmakova Advocates

Ljubica Ruben
Mens Legis Cakmakova Advocates

Pavlinka Dameska
Mens Legis Cakmakova Advocates

Valerjan Monevski
Monevski Law Firm

Frosina Celeska
National Bank of the Republic of Macedonia

Zlatko Nikolovski
Notary Chamber of R. of Macedonia

Kristijan Polenak
Polenak Law Office

Bob Savic
PricewaterhouseCoopers

Goce Mojsoski
PricewaterhouseCoopers

Vesna Paunkoska

Zoran Cvetanoski
State Authority for Geodetic Works

MADAGASCAR

Aine Rakotondrazaka

Andrianaivo Harisoa

André Randranto
Ancien Bâtonnier

Njiva Razanatsoa
Banque Centrale

Lalaina Rakotoarisoa
Bureau Indépendant Anti-Corruption

Rene Ramarozatovo
Bureau Indépendant Anti-Corruption

Jean Marcel Razafimahenina
Cabinet Delta Audit Deloitte

Hanta Radilofe
Cabinet Félicien RADILOFE

Cabinet HK Jurifisc.

Fidèle Armand Rakotonirina
Cabinet Mazars Fivoarana

Natacha Adrianjakamanarivo
Cabinet Mazars Fivoarana

Volamiora Andriamaritafika
Cabinet Mazars Fivoarana

Isabelle Gachie
Centre d'Information Technique et Economique

Sahondra Rasoarisoa
Delta Audit Deloitte

John Hargreaves
Economic Development Board

Philippe Buffier
Espace Ingénierie

Ami Ravelomanana
FIDAFRICA / PricewaterhouseCoopers

Dominique Taty
FIDAFRICA / PricewaterhouseCoopers

Jacques Chareyre
FIDAFRICA / PricewaterhouseCoopers

William Randrianarivelo
FIDAFRICA / PricewaterhouseCoopers

Lalao Andriamanga
Guichet Unique des Investissements et du Developpement des Entreprises (GUIDE)

Sahondra Rabenarivo
Keyserlingk - Rabenarivo Associés

Lanto Ralison

Laingoniaina Ramarimbahoaka
Madagascar Conseil International

Raphaël Jakoba
Madagascar Conseil International

Anthony Rabibisoa
Maersk Logistics S.A.

Pascaline Rasamoeliarisoa

Florent Andriamahavonjy
Transparency International - Initiative Madagascar

Harimahefa Andriamitantsoa
Tribunal de Première Instance

MALAWI

Godwin Mwale
2PS Cargo Co.

Richard Chakana
2PS Cargo Co.

Edward Kaluwa
Combine Cargo

A. Rashid Jakhura
Fargo Group of Companies

Chimwemwe Kalua
Golden & Law

Dannie J. Kamwaza
Kamwaza Design Partnership

Alfred Majamanda
Mbendera & Nkhono Associates

Modecai Msisha
Nyirenda & Msisha Law Offices

Jim Ghobede
PricewaterhouseCoopers

Kevin M. Carpenter
PricewaterhouseCoopers

Misheck Msiska
PricewaterhouseCoopers

Andrews Katuya
Savjani & Co.

Davis Njobvu
Savjani & Co.

Duncan Singano
Savjani & Co.

Krishna Savjani
Savjani & Co.

Roseline Gramani
Savjani & Co.

John Dean
SDV Ltd.

Joseph Chavula
SDV Ltd.

Samuel Tembenu
Tembenu, Masumbu & Co.

Marshal Chilenga
TF & Partners

Bernard Ndau
The World Bank

Arthur Msowoya
Wilson & Morgan

D.A. Raval
Wilson & Morgan

MALAYSIA

Armeira Technologies Sdn. Bhd.

Dinesh Ratnarajah
Azman, Davidson & Co.

Zuhaidi Mohd Shahari
Azmi & Associates

Bank Negara

Brilliant Solutions

Tze Keong Chung
CTOS Sdn Bhd

Lee Hwa Furniture Industry Sdn. Bhd.

Lida Plastics Sdn. Bhd.

Loganath Sabapathy
Logan Sabapathy & Co.

Tharminder Singh
Logan Sabapathy & Co.

Chuan Keat Khoo
PricewaterhouseCoopers

Peter Wee
PricewaterhouseCoopers

Theresa Lim
PricewaterhouseCoopers

Wee Leng Lee
PricewaterhouseCoopers

Melina Yong
Raslan - Loong

S.G. Emas Sdn Bhd.

Geeta Kaur
SDV Sdn Bhd

Michel Barbesier
SDV Sdn Bhd

Tan Kee Beng
SDV Sdn Bhd

Chong Wah Wong
Skrine & Co., member of Lex Mundi

Koon Huan Lim
Skrine & Co., member of Lex Mundi

Kumar Kanagasabai
Skrine & Co., member of Lex Mundi

Liew Wei Ling
Skrine & Co., member of Lex Mundi

Hong Yun Chang
Tay & Partners

Christopher Lee
Wong & Partners

Zain Azlan
Zain & Co.

MALDIVES

Mohamed Hameed
Antrac Pvt. Ltd.

Ahmed Murad
Mazlan & Murad Law Associates

Hussain Siraj
Ministry of Higher Education, Employment & Social Security

Ibrahim Naeem
Monetary Authority

Nadiya Hassan

Shaaheen Hameed
Premier Chambers

Jatindra Bhattray
PricewaterhouseCoopers

Sriyani Perera
PricewaterhouseCoopers

Red Leaf Pvt. Ltd.

Dheena Hussain
Shah, Hussain & Co. Barristers & Attorneys

Fizan Shah
Shah, Hussain & Co. Barristers & Attorneys

Shuaib M. Shah
Shah, Hussain & Co. Barristers & Attorneys

MALI

Malick Badara Sow
Atelier d'Architecture et d'Urbanisme

Baya Berthé

Charles Ki-Zerbo
BCEAO

Ibrahima Makanguile
Cabinet I. Makanguile

Aboubacar S Diarra
Cabinet Lexis Conseils

Mahamane I. Cisse
Cabinet Lexis Conseils

Mamadou Moustapha Sow
Cabinet Sow & Collaborateurs

Madhou Traore
Centre National de Promotion des Investissements - CNPI

EcoBank - Mali

Alassne Diallo
Etude de Maitre Alassane Diallo

Adeline Messou
FIDAFRICA / PricewaterhouseCoopers

Dominique Taty
FIDAFRICA / PricewaterhouseCoopers

Evelyne M'Bassidgé
FIDAFRICA / PricewaterhouseCoopers

Fousséni Traoré
FIDAFRICA / PricewaterhouseCoopers

Jean Claude Gnamien
FIDAFRICA / PricewaterhouseCoopers

Aïda Niare Toure
Jurifis Consult Mali

Mamaidou Kanda Keita

Ahmadou Toure
Office Notarial Ahmadou Toure, Notaire a Bamako

Amadou Camara
SCP Camara Traoré

Djeneba Diop
SCP d'Avocat Diop-Diallo

Diop Mohamed Abdoulaye
SDV

MARSHALL ISLANDS

Anthony Tomlinson
Beca International Consultants Ltd.

Philip A. Okney
Land Registration Administration Authority

Philip Welch
Micronesian Shipping Agencies Inc.

Kenneth Barden
Ministry of Finance

Jerry Kramer
Pacific International, Inc.

MAURITANIA

Ahmed Cheikhsidiye

Aliou Sall
Assurim

Ahmed Ould Radhi
Banque Centrale de Mauritanie

Tidiane BAL
BSD & Associés

Youssoupha Diallo
BSD & Associés

Mohamedou Ould Hacen
Bureau TASMIM

Ahmed Salem Ould Bouhoubeyni
Cabinet Bouhoubeyni

Cheikani Jules

Yarba Ould Ahmed Saleh
Cabinet Me Sidiya

Cheikh Sall
Etude Hady Maouloudvall

Maouloud Vall El Hady Seyid
Etude Hady Maouloudvall

Dominique Taty
FIDAFRICA / PricewaterhouseCoopers

Raymond Any
FIDAFRICA / PricewaterhouseCoopers

Adama Demba Diop
Membre du Conseil Constitutionnel

Brahim Ould Daddah
Private Practice

Hamdi Ould Mahjoub
Private Practice

Mine Ould Abdoullah
Private Practice

Salimou Ould Bouhoubeyni

Hamoud Ismail
SMPN

Adou Ould Bahbana
Tribunal Commercial

Mustafa Ould Bilal
Tribunal Commercial

Zakaria Thiam
Tribunal Commercial

MAURITIUS

Artisco International

Yandraduth Googoolye
Bank of Mauritius

Ajay Bhurtun
Banymandhub Boolell Chambers

Urmila Boolell
Banymandhub Boolell Chambers

Vishwanee Boodhonee
Banymandhub Boolell Chambers

Andre Robert
Benoit Chambers

Rishi Pursem
Benoit Chambers

Thierry Chellen
Benoit Chambers

Iqbal Rajahbalee
BLC Chambers

D. Chinien
Companies Division

Marc Daruty de Granpre
Daruty de Grandpre Architects Associates Ltd.

Farfat Enterprise Ltd.

Gavin Glover
Glover & Glover Chambers

Catherine de Rosnay
Legis & Partners

Robert Ferrat
Legis & Partners

Jean Phillipe Chan See
Maersk Ltd.

Parikshat Teeluck
Maersk Ltd.

Reza Subratty
Maersk Ltd.

Thierry Koenig
Maigrot Koenig

Nand-MDI Group Ltd.

André Bonieux
PricewaterhouseCoopers

Didier Lenette
PricewaterhouseCoopers

Ram L. Roy
PricewaterhouseCoopers

Ramesh Doma
PricewaterhouseCoopers

Robert Bigaignon
PricewaterhouseCoopers

Damien Mamet
PricewaterhouseCoopers Legal Services

Fabien de Marassé Enouf
PricewaterhouseCoopers Legal Services

Primecom Ltd.

Ramdas Mootanah
Professional Architects Council

Deviantee Sobarun
Registrar-General's Department (Government)

MEXICO

Oscar O. Cano
Adeath Logistics S.A de C.V.

Mariano Enriquez-Mejia
Baker & McKenzie

Juan Francisco Torres Landa Ruffo
Barrera, Siqueiros y Torres Landa

Juan José López de Silanes Molina
Basham, Ringe y Correa, member of Ius Laboris

Monica Schiaffino Pérez
Basham, Ringe y Correa, member of Ius Laboris

Oscar de La Vega
Basham, Ringe y Correa, member of Ius Laboris

Eduardo Revilla
Calvo, González Luna, Moreno y Revilla, S.C

Enrique Nort
Comision Nacional de Bancaria y de Valores

Isis Anaya
Economic Development Ministry / Federal District Department

Exportim, Inc.

Alberto Avila
Federation of Interamerican Construction Industry (FIIC)

Pablo Alvarez Trevino
Federation of Interamerican Construction Industry (FIIC)

Alberto Saracho Martínez
Fundación IDEA

Diego Canales
Fundación IDEA

Arturo Perdomo
Galicia y Robles, S.C.

Héctor Kuri
Galicia y Robles, S.C.

Karla Baez
Galicia y Robles, S.C.

Manuel Galicia
Galicia y Robles, S.C.

Ana Tatiana Ortega Robles
Goodrich, Riquelme y Asociados, member of Lex Mundi

Eugenia González Rivas
Goodrich, Riquelme y Asociados, member of Lex Mundi

Jorge Sanchez
Goodrich, Riquelme y Asociados, member of Lex Mundi

Julio Flores Luna
Goodrich, Riquelme y Asociados, member of Lex Mundi

Teresa de Lourdes Gómez Neri
Goodrich, Riquelme y Asociados, member of Lex Mundi

Hector Munez

Gerardo Lozano Alarcón
Holland & Knight-Gallástegui y Lozano, S.C.

Juan Pablo Guerrero Amaparán
Instituto Federal de Acceso a la Información Pública (IFAI)

Alberto Balderas
Jáuregui, Navarrete y Nader, S.C.

Hans Goebel
Jáuregui, Navarrete y Nader, S.C.

Yves Hayaux-du-Tilly
Jáuregui, Navarrete y Nader, S.C.

Frida Alonso
Mexican Construction Chamber (CMIC)

Cristina Sánchez-Urtiz
Miranda & Estavillo, S.C.

Guillermo Piecarchic
PMC & Asociados

Carlos Montemayor
PricewaterhouseCoopers

Marco Nava
PricewaterhouseCoopers

Salvador Esquivel Bernal
PricewaterhouseCoopers

Yolanda Jaramillo
PricewaterhouseCoopers

Adriana Lopez
PricewaterhouseCoopers Legal Services

Alonso Montes
PricewaterhouseCoopers Legal Services

Alvaro Gonzalez
PricewaterhouseCoopers Legal Services

Fernando Santamaria
PricewaterhouseCoopers Legal Services

Gabriel I. Aguilar
PricewaterhouseCoopers Legal Services

Marcela Crespo
PricewaterhouseCoopers Legal Services

Mario Alberto Rocha
PricewaterhouseCoopers Legal Services

Wendolin Sanchez
PricewaterhouseCoopers Legal Services

Carlos Sánchez-Mejorada y Velasco
Sánchez-Mejorada y Asociados

Eduardo Solares
Solares & Ruiz Quintana, S.C.

MICRONESIA

Wayne Bricknell
E - CAD Project Management

Anna H. Mendiola
FSM Development Bank

Andrea S. Hillyer
Independent

Kenneth Barden
Ministry of Finance

Eric Emeka Akamigbo
Pohnpei State Government

Salomon Saimon
Pohnpei State Government

Stephen V. Finnen
Stephen Finnen's Law Corporation

MOLDOVA

Irina Moghiliova
Brodsky Uskov Looper Reed & Partners

Neli Panaiti
Brodsky Uskov Looper Reed & Partners

Serghei Auzeac
Brodsky Uskov Looper Reed & Partners

Irina Verhovetchi
BSMB Legal Counsellors

Cornelia Cozonac
Center for Journalistic Investigations

Eugen Osmochescu

Inga Grecu-Stavila
First Cadastre Project Implementation Office

Vitaliy Nikolaevich Bulgac
Independent Consultant

Politrans s.r.l.

Alla Cotos
PricewaterhouseCoopers

Corina Jumbei
PricewaterhouseCoopers

Cristina Muntean
PricewaterhouseCoopers

Mihaela Mitroi
PricewaterhouseCoopers

Nelea Moraru
PricewaterhouseCoopers

Sergiu Dumitrasco
PricewaterhouseCoopers

Svetlana Ceban
PricewaterhouseCoopers

Alexandru Munteanu
PricewaterhouseCoopers Legal Services

Andrian Candu
PricewaterhouseCoopers Legal Services

Marin Moraru
PricewaterhouseCoopers Legal Services

Silvia Grosu
PricewaterhouseCoopers Legal Services

Ruslan Pirnevu
Quehenberger-Hellmann SRL

Victor Burunsus
The World Bank

Lilia Carasciuc
Transparency International Moldova

Alexander Turcan
Turcan & Turcan

Carolina Parcalab
Turcan & Turcan

Mariana Stratan
Turcan & Turcan

Octavian Cazac
Turcan & Turcan

Roger Gladei
Turcan & Turcan

Evgeniy Untilo
Union of Employers in Building and Construction Materials Industry

Georghu Calugharu
Union of Employers in Building and Construction Materials Industry

Ion Railean
Union of Employers in Building and Construction Materials Industry

MONGOLIA

Tsogt Tsend
Administrative Court of Capital City

Batzaya Bodikhuu
Anand & Anand Advocates

Battsetseg Ganbold
Anderson & Anderson

David Buxbaum
Anderson & Anderson

Enkhbulgantamir Togtokhbaatar
Anderson & Anderson

Odmaa Khurelbold
Anderson & Anderson

Gansukh
GTs Advocates

Batbayar Byambaa
GTs Advocates

Badarch Bayarmaa
Lynch & Mahoney

Daniel Mahoney
Lynch & Mahoney

Bela Gutidze
PricewaterhouseCoopers

Courtney Fowler
PricewaterhouseCoopers

Matthew Tallarovic
PricewaterhouseCoopers

Rusa Sreseli
PricewaterhouseCoopers

Sergi Kobakhidze
PricewaterhouseCoopers

Khand Damdinsuren
Tsets Law Firm

MONTENEGRO

George Danilović
Azius

Vladimir Dasić
Bojovic & Dasic, PricewaterhouseCoopers Legal Services

Dragana Radević
Center for Entrepreneurship and Economic Development

Marko Tintor
Central Bank of Montenegro

Igor V. Stijović
Igor Stijović Law Office

Ana Krsmanovic
Institute for Strategic Studies and Prognoses

Jelena Ilincić

Radoš Kastratović
Kastratović Law Office

Vasilije Bosković
Law Firm Bosković

Nikola Martinović
Law Firm Martinović

Sasha Vujacić
Law Office Vujacić

Zorica Peshić
Law Office Vujacić

MBA Office Manager

Mike Ahern

Ana Karanikic
Montenegrin Union of Employers

Biljana Banovic
Montenegrin Union of Employers

Branislav Begovic
Montenegrin Union of Employers

Budimir Raičković
Montenegrin Union of Employers

Jovan Boljevic
Montenegrin Union of Employers

Mark Crowford
Opportunity Bank

Milena Roncević
Prelević Law Firm

Aleksandar Miljković
PricewaterhouseCoopers

Jovana Ilić
PricewaterhouseCoopers

Nenad M. Novaković
Private Practice

MOROCCO

Agence Med S.a.r.l.

Mehdi Kettani
Ali Kettani Law Office

Amin Hajji
Amin Hajji & Associés Association d'Avocats

Myriam Emmanuelle Bennani
Amin Hajji & Associés Association d'Avocats

Bank Al-Maghrib

Azeddine Kabbaj
Barreau de Casablanca

Rachid Benzakour
Cabinet d'Avocats Bensakour, Lahbabi

Younes Anibar
Cabinet Younes Anibar

Anis Mahfoud
CMS Bureau Francis Lefebvre

Abdessalam Aboudrar
Commission Lutte Contre la Corruption

Aziz Abouelouafa
Globex Maritime Co.

Bouchaib Labkiri
Globexline SARL

Azzedine Kettani
Kettani Law Firm

Nadia Kettani
Kettani Law Firm

Rita Kettani
Kettani Law Firm

Marc Veuillot
Landwell & Associés - PricewaterhouseCoopers

Michel Lecerf
Landwell & Associés - PricewaterhouseCoopers

Nora Djadoun
Landwell & Associés - PricewaterhouseCoopers

Lapirama Group International

Maria Belafia

Ahmed Bouhourrou
Ministère de l'Emploi et de la Formation Professionnelle

Nawal Jellouli
Ministry of Finance & Privatisation

Hicham Naciri
Naciri & Associés - Gide Loyrette Nouel, member of Lex Mundi

Richard Cantin
Naciri & Associés - Gide Loyrette Nouel, member of Lex Mundi

Azdine Nekmouche
Ordre des architectes de Casablanca

Rachid Senhaji
Ordre des architectes de Casablanca

Réda Oulamine
Oulamine Law Group

Azzedine Akesbi
Transparency Maroc

Houcine Sefrioui
UINL - IIHN

MOZAMBIQUE

Emilio R. Nhamissitane
Advogado

Alexandra Carvalho

Anastacia Chamusse
Banco de Moçambique

Eugénio Luis
Banco de Moçambique

Carlos de Sousa e Brito
Carlos de Sousa e Brito & Associados

Carlos Schwalbach

Marcelo Mosse
Center For Public Integrity

Auxílio Eugénio Nhabanga
Fernanda Lopes & Associados - Advogados

Lara Narcy
H. Gamito, Couto, Gonçalves Pereira e Castelo Branco & Associados

Pedro Couto
H. Gamito, Couto, Gonçalves Pereira e Castelo Branco & Associados

Telmo Ferreira
H. Gamito, Couto, Gonçalves Pereira e Castelo Branco & Associados

Jose Forjaz
Jose Forjaz Arquitectos

Katia Tourais

Jennifer Garvey
KPMG Auditores e Consultores

Magin Lda

Adrian Frey
Mozlegal Lda

Vânia Mahotas
Mozlegal Lda

Manuel Didier Malunga
National Directorate of Registry and Notaries

António Veloso
Pimenta, Dionísio e Associados

Firza Sadek
Pimenta, Dionísio e Associados

Nipul Govan
Pimenta, Dionísio e Associados

Paulo Pimenta
Pimenta, Dionísio e Associados

João Martins
PricewaterhouseCoopers

Malaika Ribeiro
PricewaterhouseCoopers

Rufino Lucas

Eduardo Calú
Sal & Caldeira - Advogados e Consultores, Lda

Ibrahim Agigi
Sal & Caldeira - Advogados e Consultores, Lda

José Manuel Caldeira
Sal & Caldeira - Advogados e Consultores, Lda

Julio Mutisse
Sal & Caldeira - Advogados e Consultores, Lda

Luís Filipe Rodrigues
Sal & Caldeira - Advogados e Consultores, Lda

Xiluva Rodrigues Matavele
Sal & Caldeira - Advogados e Consultores, Lda

Isabel Garcia
Silvia Garcia Advogados & Consultores

NAMIBIA

Axel Stritter
Egling, Stritter & Partners

Hans-Bruno Gerdes
Egling, Stritter & Partners

Frank Köpplinger
G.F. Köpplinger Legal Practitioners

Hanno D. Bossau
H.D. Bossau & Co.

Herman Charl Kinghorn
Kinghorn Associates

Josias Andries Agenbach
Koep & Partners

Peter Frank Koep
Koep & Partners

Renate Williamson
Koep & Partners

Richard Traugott Diethelm Mueller
Koep & Partners

Willem Carel Kotze
Koep & Partners

Onesmus Hanapho
Namibia Power (NamPower)

Ockhuizen Welbert
Namibia Water Corporation (NamWater)

Carina Oberholzer
PricewaterhouseCoopers

Dennis Hyman
PricewaterhouseCoopers

Erika Shikusinde
PricewaterhouseCoopers

Gerald Riedel
PricewaterhouseCoopers

Hennie Gous
PricewaterhouseCoopers

Mark Badenhorst
PricewaterhouseCoopers

Marius van Breda
TransUnion ITC

NEPAL

Parshuram Koirala
Advocate

Prem Shanker Shrestha
Credit Information Bureau Ltd.

Madan Krishna Sharma
CSC & Co. / PricewaterhouseCoopers

International Trading Concern

Megharaj Pokharel
Legal Research Associates

Sajjan B. S. Thapa
Legal Research Associates

Matrika Niraula
Niraula Law Chamber & Co.

Anup Upreti
Pioneer Law Associates

Bharat Raj Upreti
Pioneer Law Associates

Bijaya Mishra
Pradhan & Associates

Devendra Pradhan
Pradhan & Associates

Ramji Shrestha
Pradhan & Associates

Ram Chandra Subedi

G.D Udas
Registrar of Companies

Ashok Man Kapali
Shangri-La Freight Pvt. Ltd.

Jagat B. Khadka
Shangri-La Freight Pvt. Ltd.

Anil Kumar Sinha
Sinha - Verma Law Concern

Mahesh Kumar Thapa
Sinha - Verma Law Concern

Trinetra Business Concern Pvt. Ltd.

NETHERLANDS

Allen & Overy LLP

Annekarien van de Velde
Baker & McKenzie Amsterdam N.V.

Karin W.M. Bodewes
Baker & McKenzie Amsterdam N.V.

Piet Schroeder
Baker & McKenzie Amsterdam N.V.

Hylda Wiarda
Bronsgeest Deur Advocaten, member of Ius Laboris

Paul van der Molen
Cadastre, Land Registry and Mapping Agency

Jan Willem Schenk
CMS Derks Star Busmann

Jellienke Stamhuis
De Brauw Blackstone Westbroek

Margriet de Boer
De Brauw Blackstone Westbroek

Mark G. Rebergen
De Brauw Blackstone Westbroek

Sijmen de Ranitz
De Brauw Blackstone Westbroek

Stefan Sagel
De Brauw Blackstone Westbroek

Arjan Enneman
Expatax BV

Globe ITC

Glenn C. Haulussy
Haulussy The Law Company

Els Van der Riet
Houthoff Buruma Lawyers, Civil Notaries, Tax Advisers

Henri Bentfort van Valkenburg
Houthoff Buruma Lawyers, Civil Notaries, Tax Advisers

Jaap Koster
Houthoff Buruma Lawyers, Civil Notaries, Tax Advisers

Rolef de Weijs
Houthoff Buruma Lawyers, Civil Notaries, Tax Advisers

Rutger Schimmelpenninck
Houthoff Buruma Lawyers, Civil Notaries, Tax Advisers

Michiel Wesseling
Houthoff Buruma N. V., member of Lex Mundi

Marcel Willems
Kennedy Van der Laan

Jaap Jan Trommel
Nauta Dutilh Attorneys

Jeroen Holland
Nauta Dutilh Attorneys

Martijn Molenaar
Nauta Dutilh Attorneys

Richard Bakker
Ocean - Trans International BV

A.G.M. Hoogeveen
PricewaterhouseCoopers Belastingadviseurs N.V.

Fons Hoogeveen
PricewaterhouseCoopers Belastingadviseurs N.V.

Jan Bezem
PricewaterhouseCoopers Belastingadviseurs N.V.

Ralf Pieters
PricewaterhouseCoopers Belastingadviseurs N.V.

Remco Van Der Linden
PricewaterhouseCoopers Belastingadviseurs N.V.

Robert Van Galen

Robert Schrage
Royal Netherlands Notarial Organization

Hugo Reumkens
Van Doorne N.V.

Liane van de Vrugt
VédéVé Legal B.V.

NEW ZEALAND

Anna Cowie
Anderson Creagh Lai

Jeffrey Lai
Anderson Creagh Lai

Matthew Allison
Baycorp Advantage

Murray Tingey
Bell Gully

Rob Towner
Bell Gully

Russell Lawn
BuildLaw - Kumeu-Huapai Law Centre

Douglas Alderslade
Chapman Tripp

Geoff Bevan
Chapman Tripp

Jim Roberts
Hesketh Henry Lawyers

Michael McLean Toepfer
Hesketh Henry Lawyers

Richard Wilson
Jackson Russell

Robert Muir
Land Information New Zealand

Lowndes Associates - Corporate and Commercial Law Specialists

John Cuthbertson
PricewaterhouseCoopers

Kevin Best
PricewaterhouseCoopers

Wanita Lala
PricewaterhouseCoopers

John Powell
Russell McVeagh

SDV

Jania Baigent
Simpson Grierson, member of Lex Mundi

Andrew Matthews
Simpson Grierson, member of Lex Mundi

Ben Upton
Simpson Grierson, member of Lex Mundi

Shelley Cave
Simpson Grierson, member of Lex Mundi

World of Walls Ltd.

NICARAGUA

Minerva Adriana Bellorín Rodríguez
ACZALAW

Aida Maria Herdocia

Carlos Salinas
Alvarado y Asociados, member of Lex Mundi

Gloria Maria de Alvarado
Alvarado y Asociados, member of Lex Mundi

José Aníbal Olivas Cajina
Alvarado y Asociados, member of Lex Mundi

Edgard Torres Mendieta
Arias & Muñoz

Gustavo Adolfo Vargas
Arias & Muñoz

Roberto Argüello Villavicencio
Arias & Muñoz

Bendaña & Bendaña

Bruno Vidaurre
Camara Nicaragüense de la Construcción

Fabiola Miranda
Camara Nicaragüense de la Construcción

Humberto Carrión
Carrión, Somarriba & Asociados

Jorge Molina Lacayo
CETREX

Alfonso Sandino Granera
Consortium - Taboada & Asociados

Rodrigo Taboada Rodríguez
Consortium - Taboada & Asociados

Edgard Torres

Eduardo Garcia Herdocia

Ana Teresa Rizo Briseño
F.A. Arias & Muñoz

Bertha Argüello de Rizo
F.A. Arias & Muñoz

Francisco Ortega
Francisco Ortega & Asociados

Gerardo Gonzalez
Francisco Ortega & Asociados

Yali Molina Palacios
Palacios, Molina, y Asociados

Alejandro Fernandez de Castro
PricewaterhouseCoopers

Andrea Paniagua
PricewaterhouseCoopers

David Urcuyo Báez
PricewaterhouseCoopers

Edgar Mendoza
PricewaterhouseCoopers

Mariana Martinez
PricewaterhouseCoopers

Martha Solorzano
PricewaterhouseCoopers

Ruth Huete
PricewaterhouseCoopers

Sergio Noguera
PricewaterhouseCoopers

Ramon Ortega
PricewaterhouseCoopers

Sergio David Corrales Montenegro

Arnulfo Somarriba
TransUnion

NIGER

Charles Ki-Zerbo
BCEAO

Yayé Mounkaïla
Cabinet d'avocats Mounkaila-Niandou

Bernar-Oliver Kouaovi
Cabinet Kouaovi

Diallo Rayanatou Loutou
Cabinet Loutou - Architectes

Kharim Arzika
Conservation Foncière

EcoBank - Niger

Marc Le Bihan
Etude d'Avocats - Marc Le Bihan & Collaborateurs

Idrissa Tchernaka
Etude d'Avocats Marc Le Bihan & Collaborateurs

Souley I. Hammi
Etude d'Avocats Marc Le Bihan & Collaborateurs

Aïssatou Djibo
Etude de Me Djibo Aïssatou

Haoua Diaouga
Etude de Me Djibo Aïssatou

Adeline Messou
FIDAFRICA / PricewaterhouseCoopers

Dominique Taty
FIDAFRICA / PricewaterhouseCoopers

Evelyne M'Bassidgé
FIDAFRICA / PricewaterhouseCoopers

Fousséni Traoré
FIDAFRICA / PricewaterhouseCoopers

Jean Claude Gnamien
FIDAFRICA / PricewaterhouseCoopers

Marc Lebihan

Sahabi Oumarou
Themis International Consultants

NIGERIA

Samuel Etuk
1ST ATTORNEYS

Olaleye Adebiyi
Adebiyi & Associates

Gboalhan Agboluaje
Aelex, Legal Practitioners & Arbitrators

Oluseyi Abiodun Akinwunmi
Akinwunmi & Busari, Legal Practioners (A & B)

Ayodeji Olomojobi
Aluko & Oyebode

Barbara Akpotaire
Aluko & Oyebode

Gbenga Oyebode
Aluko & Oyebode

Kofo Dosekun
Aluko & Oyebode

Oludare Senbore
Aluko & Oyebode

Adedapo Omole
Asset Care Ltd.

Adeshina Oluwaji
Base4 Investment (Nig.) Ltd.

Olaniyi Ogunwole
Base4 Investment (Nig.) Ltd.

Dozie Okwuosah
Central Bank of Nigeria

Anse Agu Ezetah
Chief Law Agu Ezetah & Co.

Benson Olumekun
Clay & Potters

Barr. N.U. Chianakwalam
Corporate Affairs Commission

Churchill Williams
Corporate Affairs Commission

Dennis Ekumankama
Corporate Affairs Commission

Adenike laoye
EcoBank - Nigeria

Adamu M. Usman
F.O. Akinrele & Co.

Ike Mweje
Federal Inland Revenue Service

Temple Iheanacho
Federal Inland Revenue Service

Olufemi Sunmonu
Femi Sunmonu & Associates, Solicitors

Abraham Oyakhukime
First & First International Agencies

Fred Onuobia
G. Elias & Co. Solicitors and Advocates

Catherine Kadennyeka Masinde
IFC

Nouma Dione-Mbaye
IFC

Joanna Kata-Blackman

Sulaimon Alabi Yusuf
Lagos State Physical Planning & Development Authority

Benjamin Ikheloah
Nigerian Investment Promotion Commission

Patrick Okonjo
Okonjo, Odiawa & Ebie

Titilola Olateju
Okonjo, Odiawa & Ebie

Henrietta Onaga
PricewaterhouseCoopers

Ken Aitken
PricewaterhouseCoopers

Chiedu J. Ebie
Punuka Attorneys & Solicitors

Mathias Okojie
Punuka Attorneys & Solicitors

Okorie Kalu
Punuka Attorneys & Solicitors

Tochukwu Onyiuke
Punuka Attorneys & Solicitors

Babajide Ogundipe
Sofunde, Osakwe, Ogundipe & Belgore

Aniekan Ukpanah
Udo Udoma & Belo-Osagie

Daniel Agbor
Udo Udoma & Belo-Osagie

Oyinda Ehiwere
Udo Udoma & Belo-Osagie

Sandra Nyada
Udo Udoma & Belo-Osagie

Tunde Osasona
Whitestone Worldwide Ltd.

NORWAY

Aardal Mekaniske Verksted A/S

Amund Fougner
Advokatfirmaet Hjort DA, member of Ius Laboris

Anita Wirak
Advokatfirmaet Hjort DA, member of Ius Laboris

Bente Løvik Ulven
Advokatfirmaet Hjort DA, member of Ius Laboris

Christian Nyvold
Advokatfirmaet Hjort DA, member of Ius Laboris

Kaja Moen Welo
Advokatfirmaet Hjort DA, member of Ius Laboris

Mads Fuglesang
Advokatfirmaet Selmer D.A.

Svein Sulland
Advokatfirmaet Selmer D.A.

Christel Spannow

Stein Fagerhaug
DALAN advokatfirma DA

Vegard Sivertsen
Deloitte, member of Deloitte Touche Tohmatsu

Johan Ratvik
DLA Piper Norway DA

Espen Trædal

Ole Kristian Olsby
Homble Olsby advokatfirma AS

Jónar Transport

Karl Erik Nedregotten

Anne Ulset Sande
Kvale & Co. Advokatfirma ANS

Helge Onsrud
Norwegian Mapping Authority, Cadastre and Land Registry, Centre for Property Rights and Development

Magnar Danielsen
Norwegian Mapping Authority, Cadastre and Land Registry, Centre for Property Rights and Development

Oslo Kommune

Knut Ekern
PricewaterhouseCoopers

Morten Beck
PricewaterhouseCoopers

Odd Hylland
PricewaterhouseCoopers

Tove Ihle-Hansen
PricewaterhouseCoopers

Bård Ivar. Koppang
PricewaterhouseCoopers Legal Services

Christel Spannow
PricewaterhouseCoopers Legal Services

Carl Arthur Christiansen
Raeder Advokatfirma

Finn Rime
Rime Advokatfirma DA

Niels R. Kiaer
Rime Advokatfirma DA

Claus R. Flinder
Simonsen Advokatfirma DA

Berit Stokke
Thommessen Krefting Greve Lund AS, member of Lex Mundi

Jorgen Lund
Thommessen Krefting Greve Lund AS, member of Lex Mundi

Stig Berge
Thommessen Krefting Greve Lund AS, member of Lex Mundi

Thomas Nordgård
Vogt & Wiig AS

Jan Backer
Wikborg, Rein & Co.

Simen Smeby Lium
Wikborg, Rein & Co.

Tore Lerheim
Wikborg, Rein & Co.

OMAN

Ali Adam Mohd. Sulaiman

Ala'a Eldin Mohammed
Abu-Ghazaleh Legal

Sunil Jose
Abu-Ghazaleh Legal

John Alasdair Jeffrey
Al Alawi, Mansoor Jamal & Co.

Mansoor Jamal Malik
Al Alawi, Mansoor Jamal & Co.

Zubaida Fakir Mohamed Al Balushi
Banking Surveillance Department

Adam Mohammed Adam
Dr. Tariq Al Busaidi Legal Consultancy Bureau

Ahmad Attahir
Dr. Tariq Al Busaidi Legal Consultancy Bureau

M.O. Baidab
Dr. Tariq Al Busaidi Legal Consultancy Bureau

Sowsan Al Mnsoury
Dr. Tariq Al Busaidi Legal Consultancy Bureau

Hamad M. Al-Sharji

Mohammed Al Shahri
Mohammed Al Shahri & Associates

Mohsin Al Haddad
Mohsin Al Haddad & Amur Al Kiyumi & Partners

Naveen K. Amin

Jeff Todd
PricewaterhouseCoopers

Paul Suddaby
PricewaterhouseCoopers

Pushpa Malani
PricewaterhouseCoopers

Subha Mohan
Said Al Shahry Law Office

Christopher Knight
Trowers & Hamlins

Majid Al Toky
Trowers & Hamlins

Sean Angle
Trowers & Hamlins

PAKISTAN

Rashid Ibrahim
A. F. Ferguson & Co.

T. Ud-Din A. Mirza
A. F. Ferguson & Co.

Abdullah Enterprises

Cyril Almeida
Abraham & Sarwana

Farooq Abdullah
Abraham & Sarwana

Jawad A. Sarwana
Abraham & Sarwana

Khalid Habibullah
Abraham & Sarwana

Waqar Hussain
Abraham & Sarwana

Zaki Ahmed
Abraham & Sarwana

ACMC Logistics

Adam Fabrics Pvt. Ltd.

Al-Hadi Industries Pvt. Ltd.

Amir Sons

Apex International

Mohammed Ayaz
APLL Private Ltd.

Aroma Surgical Co.

Ash Traders International

Atara Tarpaulin & Textile Industries

Farooq Akhtar
Azam Chaudhry Law Associates

Maria Jamshaid
Azam Chaudhry Law Associates

Mohammad Qasim Qureshi
Azam Chaudhry Law Associates

Nadia A. Chaudhry
Azam Chaudhry Law Associates

Azgard-9 Ltd.

Bin Qutab Cargo International Pvt. Ltd.

Bright Trade and Industries

Bunker Logistics

Commerce International

Crown Movers Worldwide

Crown Trading Company

Tariq Nasim Jan
Datacheck Pvt. Ltd.

Javed Vohra
Fair Brothers International

Gankky Enterprises

Gemologica

Ali Adnan Ibrahim
Georgetown University Law Center

Shahzad Rasool
Globalink Transportation & Logistics Worldwide LLP

Golf & Sports

Greenfields International

Ghulam Haider Shamsi
Haider Shamsi & Co., Chartered Accountants

Image Garments Pvt. Ltd.

Ivon Trading Company

Jimpex Inc.

Kairas Kabraji
Kabraji & Talibuddin

Faisal Daudpota
Khalid Daudpota & Co.

Shumail Ahmad Butt
M/s Butt & Sohail LLP, Attorneys at Law

Huma Shah
M/s Sheikh Shah Rana & Ijaz

Mehmood Y. Mandviwalla
Mandviwalla & Zafar

Margala Enterprises

N. S. Chemicals

Proline Corporation

Abdul Rahman
Qamar Abbas & Co.

Abdul Razzaq
Qamar Abbas & Co.

Arif Khan
Qamar Abbas & Co.

Ikram Fayaz
Qamar Abbas & Co.

Tariq Mahmood
Raaziq International

Javaid Basini
Rangoonwala Group of Co.

Shahid Mughal
Rangoonwala Group of Co.

Tariq Rangoonwala
Rangoonwala Group of Co.

Rehan's Christ International Pvt. Ltd.

Sahil Freight Pakistan Pvt. Ltd.

Sami U. Zafar
Sami Zafar & Co., Advocates and Legal Consultants

Shamim & Shams Co.

Ali Jafar Abidi
State Bank of Paksitan

The Karachi Tannery Pvt. Ltd.

Trade Valley

Sajjad Raza
Transocean Shipping Agencies

Zeeshan Enterprises

PALAU

Kenneth Barden
Ministry of Finance

Erin E. Johnson
Office of the Attorney General

Frederick W. Reynolds
Office of the Attorney General

Jeffrey L. Beattie
Office of the Attorney General

David Shadel
The Law Office of Kirk and Shadel

Cristina Castro
Western Caroline Trading Co.

William L. Ridpath

PANAMA

Yadira Moreno
Aguilar Castillo Love

Alejandro Alemán
Alfaro, Ferrer & Ramírez

Alfredo Ramírez Jr.
Alfaro, Ferrer & Ramírez

Enna Ferrer
Alfaro, Ferrer & Ramírez

Jorge R. González
Arias, Aleman & Mora

José Miguel Navarrete
Arosemena Noriega & Contreras, member of Ius Laboris and Lex Mundi

Julio Cesar Contreras III
Arosemena Noriega & Contreras, member of Ius Laboris and Lex Mundi

Ramon Valdes
Arosemena Noriega & Contreras, member of Ius Laboris and Lex Mundi

Shanina J. Contreras
Arosemena Noriega & Contreras, member of Ius Laboris and Lex Mundi

Luz María Salamina
Asociación Panameña de Crédito

Maria Lourdes Chanis
CAPAC

Michael Fernandez
CAPAC

Ricardo Eskildsen Morales
Eskildsen & Eskildsen

Jorge Garrido
Garrido & Garrido

Mayra Obando
Garrido & Garrido

Luis Chalhoub
Icaza, Gonzalez-Ruiz & Aleman

Ramon Varela
Morgan & Morgan

Ivette Elisa Martínez Saenz
Patton, Moreno & Asvat

Angel Dapena
PricewaterhouseCoopers

Francisco Barrios
PricewaterhouseCoopers

Jazmin J. Solis
PricewaterhouseCoopers

Ricardo Madrid
PricewaterhouseCoopers

Ramon Ortega
PricewaterhouseCoopers

Erick Muñoz
Sucre Arias & Reyes

PAPUA NEW GUINEA

Tyson Boboro
Allens Arthur Robinson

Vincent Bull
Allens Arthur Robinson

Richard Flynn
Blake Dawson Waldron

David Caradus
PricewaterhouseCoopers

Esther Kendino
PricewaterhouseCoopers

Thomas Taberia
PricewaterhouseCoopers

Gaudi Kidu
Structon Architects, Ltd.

PARAGUAY

Hugo T. Berkemeyer
Berkemeyer, Attorneys & Counselors

Luis Breuer
Berkemeyer, Attorneys & Counselors

María Antonia Gwynn
Berkemeyer, Attorneys & Counselors

Maria Gloria Triguis Gonzalez
Berkemeyer, Attorneys & Counselors

Angela Schaerer de Sosa
Escribana Pública

Nestor Loizaga
Ferrere Abogados

Roberto Moreno Rodriguez Alcala
Moreno Ruffinelli & Asociados

Esteban Burt
Peroni, Sosa, Tellechea, Burt & Narvaja, member of Lex Mundi

Jorge Gomez
PricewaterhouseCoopers

Karina Lozano
PricewaterhouseCoopers

Larisa Guillen
PricewaterhouseCoopers

Leonardo Decarlini
PricewaterhouseCoopers

Nadia Gorostiaga
PricewaterhouseCoopers

Ruben Taboada
PricewaterhouseCoopers

Santiago Jure Domaniczky
Programa Umbral FAE

María Debattisti
Servimex SACI

Néstor Gamarra
Servimex SACI

Julio Gonzalez C.
Superintendencia de Bancos - BCP

Adriana Casati
Vouga & Olmedo Abogados

Perla Alderete
Vouga & Olmedo Abogados

PERU

Fernando M. Ramos
Barrios Fuentes Gallo Abogados

Luís Fuentes
Barrios Fuentes Gallo Abogados

Rafael Lengua
Benites, De Las Casas, Forno & Ugaz Abogados

Carlos Vegas Quintana
Camara Peruana de la Construccion

Herles Loayza Casimiro
Camara Peruana de la Construccion

Rafael Junco
Camara Peruana de la Construccion

Alfonso Alvarez Calderón
Estudio Alvarez Calderon

Marco Antonio Alarcón Piana
Estudio Echecopar

Anabelí González
Estudio Ferrero
Abogados

Gisella Domecq
Estudio Olaechea, member of Lex Mundi

Jesús Matos
Estudio Olaechea, member of Lex Mundi

José Antonio Olaechea
Estudio Olaechea, member of Lex Mundi

José Antonio Valdez
Estudio Olaechea, member of Lex Mundi

Lucianna Polar Figari
Estudio Olaechea, member of Lex Mundi

Manuel Villa-García
Estudio Olaechea, member of Lex Mundi

Martin Serkovic
Estudio Olaechea, member of Lex Mundi

Guilhermo Auler
Forsyth & Arbe Abogados

Libiak Corp.

Jimy Atunga Rios
M. A. V. Logistica y Transporte S.A.

Marisol Nieto Carbajal

Donato Hernán Carpio Velez
Notary Office of Donato Hernan Carpio Velez

Alonso Rey Bustamante
Payet, Rey, Cauvi Abogados

Raul Lozano-Merino
Peña, Lozano, Faura & Asociados

Peruvian Arts & Crafts de Jaime Zapata Espinoza

Diego Sanchez
PricewaterhouseCoopers

Humberto Allemant
PricewaterhouseCoopers

Javier de La Vega
PricewaterhouseCoopers

Walter Aguirre
PricewaterhouseCoopers Legal Services

Hugo Silva
Rodrigo, Elías, Medrano Abogados

Pedro Grados Smith
Superintendency of Banking, Insurance & Private Pension Fund Administrator

PHILIPPINES

Ace Anarem International Trading, Inc.

Emerico O. de Guzman
Angara Abello Concepcion Regala & Cruz Law Offices (ACCRALAW)

Gilberto Gallos
Angara Abello Concepcion Regala & Cruz Law Offices (ACCRALAW)

Lilia E. Lising
Banco de Oro

Villanueva
Banco de Oro

Manuel Batallones
BAP Credit Bureau

Fast-Tract Freight, Inc.

Alan Ortiz
Follosco Morallos & Herce

Jesusito G. Morallos
Follosco Morallos & Herce

Rachel P. Follosco
Follosco Morallos & Herce

Antonio T. Bote
International Consolidator Philippines, Inc.

Erich H. Lingad
International Consolidator Philippines, Inc.

Juana M. Dela Cruz
International Consolidator Philippines, Inc.

Herminio Liwanag
Jimenez Gonzales Liwanag Bello Valdez Caluya & Fernandez

Lory Anne McMullin
Jimenez Gonzales Liwanag Bello Valdez Caluya & Fernandez

Ma. Melva Valdez
Jimenez Gonzales Liwanag Bello Valdez Caluya & Fernandez

Maria Cristina Hernandez
Jimenez Gonzales Liwanag Bello Valdez Caluya & Fernandez

Melva Valdez
Jimenez Gonzales Liwanag Bello Valdez Caluya & Fernandez

Myla Gloria Amboy
Jimenez Gonzales Liwanag Bello Valdez Caluya & Fernandez

Victoria Limkico
Jimenez Gonzales Liwanag Bello Valdez Caluya & Fernandez

Rufo C. Venus
Metropolitan Bank & Trust Co.

Freddie Naagas
OOCL Logistics

Gwen Grecia-de Vera
PJS LAW

Alexander B. Cabrera
PricewaterhouseCoopers / Isla Lipana & Co.

Elmer R. Mitra, Jr.
PricewaterhouseCoopers / Isla Lipana & Co.

Genevieve M. Limbo
PricewaterhouseCoopers / Isla Lipana & Co.

Tammy H. Lipana
PricewaterhouseCoopers / Isla Lipana & Co.

Zayber B. Protacio
PricewaterhouseCoopers / Isla Lipana & Co.

Joseph Omar A. Castillo
Puyat Jacinto Santos Law Office

Roy Enrico C. Santos
Puyat Jacinto Santos Law Office

Janice Kae Ramirez
Quasha Ancheta Pena & Nolasco

Redentor C. Zapata
Quasha Ancheta Pena & Nolasco

Gil Roberto Zerrudo
Quisumbing Torres, member firm of Baker and McKenzie

Kenneth Chua
Quisumbing Torres, member firm of Baker and McKenzie

Rachelle Diaz
Quisumbing Torres, member firm of Baker and McKenzie

Connie G. Chu
Romulo, Mabanta, Buenaventura, Sayoc & de los Angeles, member of Lex Mundi

Jazmin Banal
Romulo, Mabanta, Buenaventura, Sayoc & de los Angeles, member of Lex Mundi

Joseph Donato Bernedo
Romulo, Mabanta, Buenaventura, Sayoc & de los Angeles, member of Lex Mundi

Ricardo J. Romulo
Romulo, Mabanta, Buenaventura, Sayoc & de los Angeles, member of Lex Mundi

Rovet International Enterprise

Rusvie Cadiz
RV Freight ABD Services

Jean Caillard
SDV, Inc.

Roland Bay
SDV, Inc.

Nicanor N. Padilla
Siguion Reyna Montecillo & Ongsiako

Rafael Khan
Siguion Reyna Montecillo & Ongsiako

Silveraxis Inc.

Cecile M.E. Caro
SyCip Salazar Hernandez & Gatmaitan

Emmanuel C. Paras
SyCip Salazar Hernandez & Gatmaitan

Uni-President Corporation

POLAND

Allen & Overy A. Pędzich Sp.k.

Bartłomiej Raczkowski
Bartłomiej Raczkowski Kancelaria Prawa Pracy, member of Ius Laboris

Aleksander Borowicz
Biuro Informacji Kredytowej

Zbigniew Skórczyński
Chadbourne & Parke LLP

Jan Niadzinski
DSV

Ewelina Stobiecka
e/n/w/c Attorney at Law

Ewa Wiśniewska

Anna Sowinskaya
Gide Loyrette Nouel Polska

Barbara Mycka
Gide Loyrette Nouel Polska

Dariusz Tokarczuk
Gide Loyrette Nouel Polska

Ewa Auleytner
Gide Loyrette Nouel Polska

Grzegorz Banasiuk
Gide Loyrette Nouel Polska

Marta Karmińska
Gide Loyrette Nouel Polska

Michał Kocur
Gide Loyrette Nouel Polska

Piotr Sadownik
Gide Loyrette Nouel Polska

Sylvia Petrovskaya
Gide Loyrette Nouel Polska

IWS

Dariusz Wojciech Rzadkowski
Kancelaria Notarialna S.C.

Tomasz Brudkowski
Kochański, Brudkowski & Partners

Dagmara Lipka-Chudzik
Magnusson

Aneta Laskownicka
Ministry of Justice

Jaroslaw Wysocki
Ministry of Justice

Maksymilian Norwa
Ministry of Justice

Dominika Rogon
Nikiel & Zacharzewski Law Office

Dariusz Okolski
Okolski Law Office

Panalpina

Iwona Smith
PricewaterhouseCoopers

Magdalena Śmigrocka
PricewaterhouseCoopers

Piotr Kaim
PricewaterhouseCoopers

Anna Maria Pukszto
Salans

Monika Czekalowska
Sołtysiński Kawecki & Szlęzak, member of Ius Laboris

Tamasz Kanski
Sołtysiński Kawecki & Szlęzak, member of Ius Laboris

Fidala Jaroslaw
Tokarczuk, Jędrzejczyk, Wspólnicy. Kancelaria prawna Gide Loyrette Nouel Polska

Rafal Dziedzic
Tokarczuk, Jędrzejczyk, Wspólnicy. Kancelaria prawna Gide Loyrette Nouel Polska

Vantis

Ewa Butkiewicz
Wardyński & Partners, member of Lex Mundi

Weronica Pelc
Wardyński & Partners, member of Lex Mundi

Lech Giliciński
White & Case W. Daniłowicz, W. Jurcewicz i Wspólnicy sp. k.

Barbara van der Mei
Wierzbowski Eversheds, member of Eversheds International Ltd.

Ewa Łachowska - Brol
Wierzbowski Eversheds, member of Eversheds International Ltd..

PORTUGAL

Acácio Pita Negrão
Abreu & Marques, Vinhas e Associados

Paulo Lowndes Marques
Abreu & Marques, Vinhas e Associados

Carmo Sousa Machado
Abreu Advogados

David Salgado Areias
Abreu Advogados

Duarte de Athayde
Abreu Advogados

Francisco Patrício
Abreu Advogados

Marta de Oliveira Pinto Trindade
Abreu Advogados

Miguel de Avillez Pereira
Abreu Advogados

Patricia Perestrelo
Abreu Advogados

Pedro Sousa Uva
Abreu Advogados

Rita Maltez
Abreu Advogados

Rui Peixoto Duarte
Abreu Advogados

Manuel Silveira Botelho
António Frutuoso de Melo e Associados - Sociedade de Advogados, R. L.

João Cadete de Matos
Banco de Portugal

Manuel P. Barrocas
Barrocas & Alves Pereira

Paula Alcântara Feliciano
Barros, Sobral, G. Gomes & Associados

Sónia Gonçalves Anjo
Barros, Sobral, G. Gomes & Associados

Mark Bekker
Bekker Logistica

Carlos de Sousa e Brito
Carlos de Sousa e Brito & Associados

João Pereira Marques
Carlos de Sousa e Brito & Associados

Susana Rua
Carlos de Sousa e Brito & Associados

Fernando Marta
Credinformacoes

António Luís Pereira Figueiredo
Directorate General of Registry & Notary Civil Service

Filomena Rosa
Directorate General of Registry & Notary Civil Service

João Moucheira
Directorate General of Registry & Notary Civil Service

Susana Cebola
Directorate General of Registry & Notary Civil Service

Inês Setil
Gabinete de Política Legislativa e Planeamento, Ministerio da Justiça

Daniel Parejo Ballesteros
Garrigues

Diogo Leónidas Rocha
Garrigues

Isabel Martinez de Salas
Garrigues

Miguel Marques dos Santos
Garrigues

Sara Gonçalves
Garrigues

Pedro de Almeida Cabral
Ministério da Justiça

Ana Margarida Maia
Miranda Correia Amendoeira & Associados

Rui Amendoeira
Miranda Correia Amendoeira & Associados

Susana Braz
Miranda Correia Amendoeira & Associados

Mondego Trading, Lda

Filipa Arantes Pedroso
Morais Leitão, Galvão Teles, Soares da Silva & Associados, member of Lex Mundi

Madalena Pizarro
Morais Leitão, Galvão Teles, Soares da Silva & Associados, member of Lex Mundi

Rui Patrício
Morais Leitão, Galvão Teles, Soares da Silva & Associados, member of Lex Mundi

Mouteira Guerreiro, Rosa Amaral & Associados - Sociedade de Advogados R.L.

Jorge Pedro Lopes
Polytechnic Institute of Bragança

John Duggan
PricewaterhouseCoopers

Jorge Figueiredo
PricewaterhouseCoopers

Lisa Helena Vaz
PricewaterhouseCoopers

Marta Elisa Machado
PricewaterhouseCoopers

Rita Marques
PricewaterhouseCoopers

Michel Boutrand
SDV

César Sá Esteves
Simmons & Simmons

Maria Valente
Simmons & Simmons

Terra Paralela

Maria Manuel Leitão Marques
UCMA

Paulo Henriques
UCMA

PUERTO RICO

Alberto Lastra

Camilo Almeyda

Juan Carlos Fortuno Fas
Fortuno & Fortuno Fas, C. S. P.

Myrna I. Lozada-Guzmán
Goldman Antonetti & Córdova

Thelma Rivera
Goldman Antonetti & Córdova

Javier Sánchez

Antonio Arias
McConnell Valdés

Antonio Escudero-Viera
McConnell Valdés

Jorge Ruiz Montilla
McConnell Valdés

Victor Rodriguez
Multitransport & Marine Co.

Griselle Lebron
PricewaterhouseCoopers

Victor Rodriguez
PricewaterhouseCoopers

Keila Ortega
Ralph Vallone Jr., Law Offices

Ralph Vallone
Ralph Vallone Jr., Law Offices

Myriam E. Matos-Bermudez
Sosa Llorens, Cruz Neris & Associates

James Arroyo
TransUnion De Puerto Rico

ROMANIA

Ados Trading

Alsunmarine & General Trading SRL

David Stabb
Anghel Stabb & Partners

Adriana Puscas
Babiuc Sulica Protopopescu Vonica

Dorín Coza
Babiuc Sulica Protopopescu Vonica

Veronica Grunzsnicki
Babiuc Sulica Protopopescu Vonica

Cosmin Anghel
Badea Asociatii in Association with Clifford Chance

Daniel Badea
Badea Asociatii in Association with Clifford Chance

Radu Ropota
Badea Asociatii in Association with Clifford Chance

Beton De Nice

Break Bulk Services SRL

Carpatica Invest SRL

Carmen Medar
D & B David si Baias S.C.A., PricewaterhouseCoopers Legal Services

Catalin Alexandru
D & B David si Baias S.C.A., PricewaterhouseCoopers Legal Services

Emanuel Bancila
D & B David si Baias S.C.A., PricewaterhouseCoopers Legal Services

Sorin David
D & B David si Baias S.C.A., PricewaterhouseCoopers Legal Services

Karman SRL

Neil McGregor
McGregor & Partners S.C.A.

Dominic Morega
Muşat & Asociaţii

Gelu Titus Maravela
Muşat & Asociaţii

Ileana Sovaila
Muşat & Asociaţii

Iulian Iosif
Muşat & Asociaţii

Marius Pătrăşcanu
Muşat & Asociaţii

Ion Dragulin
National Bank of Romania

Dumitru Viorel Manescu
National Union of Romanian Notaries

Tatiana Urimescu
National Union of Romanian Notaries

Adriana Gaspar
Nestor Nestor Diculescu Kingston Petersen, member of Ius Laboris, of Lex Mundi & of SEE Legal

Diana Emanuela Precup
Nestor Nestor Diculescu Kingston Petersen, member of Ius Laboris, of Lex Mundi & of SEE Legal

Laura-Adina Duca
Nestor Nestor Diculescu Kingston Petersen, member of Ius Laboris, of Lex Mundi & of SEE Legal

Manuela M. Nestor
Nestor Nestor Diculescu Kingston Petersen, member of Ius Laboris, of Lex Mundi & of SEE Legal

Patela Serv Com Srl

Anda Rojanschi
Pricewaterhouse Coopers Legal Services

Adriana Radu
PricewaterhouseCoopers

Alex Massaci
PricewaterhouseCoopers

Alina Manescu
PricewaterhouseCoopers

Alina Rafaila
PricewaterhouseCoopers

Cristina Clujescu
PricewaterhouseCoopers

Inga Tigai
PricewaterhouseCoopers

Irina Hirjoaba
PricewaterhouseCoopers

Irina Preoteasa
PricewaterhouseCoopers

Mihai Vintu
PricewaterhouseCoopers

Mirela Birlodeanu
PricewaterhouseCoopers

Oana Manuceanu
PricewaterhouseCoopers

Raluca Mocanu
PricewaterhouseCoopers

Rene Bijvoet
PricewaterhouseCoopers

Anamaria Corbescu
Salans

Cosmin Bonea
Salans

Cristian Mocanu
Salans

Obie L. Moore
Salans

Perry V. Zizzi
Salans

Raluca Radu
Salans

Tiberiu Csaki
Salans

Andrei Săvescu
Săvescu si Asociatii

Alina Badea
SCA Musat & Asociatii

Serban Epure

Alexandra Sova
Sova & Partners

Eugen Pop
Sova & Partners

Iuliana Negoita
Sova & Partners

Radu Cernov
Sova & Partners

Cristiana Stoica
Stoica & Asociatii Attorneys-at-Law

Razvan Dinca
Stoica & Asociatii Attorneys-at-Law

Sorin Corneliu Stratula
Stratula Tomosoiu Mocanu

Crenguta Leaua
Tanasescu, Leaua, Cadar & Asociatii

Gina Gheorghe
Tanasescu, Leaua, Cadar & Asociatii

Anca Danilescu
Zamfirescu Racoţi Predoiu Law Partnership

Nicolae Hariuc
Zamfirescu Racoţi Predoiu Law Partnership

RUSSIA

Allen & Overy Legal Services

Arsen Ayupov
ALRUD Law Firm

Lyudmila Merzlikina
ALRUD Law Firm

Irina Strizhakova
Andreas Neocleous & Co., Legal Consultants

Andrey Zhdanov
Baker & McKenzie - CIS, Ltd.

Evgeny Reyzman
Baker & McKenzie - CIS, Ltd.

Julia Borozdna
Baker & McKenzie - CIS, Ltd.

Valery Getmanenko
Baker & McKenzie - CIS, Ltd.

Dmitry Tarasov
Besedin Avakov Tarasov & Partners

Dmitry I. Melnikov
Cleary Gottlieb Steen & Hamilton LLP

Scott Senecal
Cleary Gottlieb Steen & Hamilton LLP

Yulia Solomakhina
Cleary Gottlieb Steen & Hamilton LLP

David Lasfargue

ESPRO Real Estate

Maria Gorban
Gide Loyrette Nouel, member of Lex Mundi

Gulmira McHale

Dmitry Kurochkin
Herbert Smith CIS LLP

Marat Agabalyan
Herbert Smith CIS LLP

Oksana Ulyanova
Herbert Smith CIS LLP

Tatyana Fokina
Herbert Smith CIS LLP

Vladimir Melnikov
Herbert Smith CIS LLP

Igor Artemiev

Dimitry Kafanov
Inmar Legal Co., Ltd.

JSC Orton

Alyona Kozyreva
Macleod Dixon

Igor Porokhin
Magnusson

OAO Pigment

Natalia Agafonova
Orrick (CIS) LLC

Ekaterina Chernova
Orrick, Herrington & Sutcliffe LLP

Olga Anisimova
Orrick, Herrington & Sutcliffe LLP

Evgeniy Gouk
PricewaterhouseCoopers Legal Services

Gennady Odarich
PricewaterhouseCoopers Legal Services

Konstantin Lapshin
PricewaterhouseCoopers Legal Services

Maxim Kandyba
PricewaterhouseCoopers Legal Services

Maxim Kuznechenkov
PricewaterhouseCoopers Legal Services

Anastasia Malashkevich
PricewaterhouseCoopers Russia B.V.

Andrey Shpak
PricewaterhouseCoopers Russia B.V.

Evgenia Shuplesova
PricewaterhouseCoopers Russia B.V.

Steven Snaith
PricewaterhouseCoopers Russia B.V.

Elena Subocheva
Russin & Vecchi, LLC

Tatiana Ponomareva

Stanislav Sheverdyaev
Transparency International Russia

Marlena Hurley
TransUnion CRIF Decision Solution

RWANDA

André Verbruggen

José Habimana
Banque Commerciale du Rwanda

Donatien Mucyo
Barreau de Kigali

Minette Mutoni
Barreau de Kigali

François Bikolimana
Cabinet Augeco Sarl

Isaïe Mhayimana
Cabinet d'Avocats Mhayimana

Christian Joseph Ndondera
Cabinet Haguma

Jean Haguma
Cabinet Haguma

Alain Kabeja
Consultant

Celestin Kaberuka
Electrogaz

Frederic Mutagwera

JB Nyibizi

Joseph Munyankindi

Benjamin Ntaganira
Kamanzi, Ntaganira & Associates

Désiré Kamanzi
Kamanzi, Ntaganira & Associates

Léopold Munderere

Marcellin Kamanzi

Olivier Nduhungirehe
Membre de la Cellule de Reforme du Droit des Affaires

Angélique Kantengwa
National Bank of Rwanda

Pothin Muvara

Annie Kairaba-Kyambadde
Rwanda Initiative for Sustainable Development / LandNet

Jean Havugimana
Rwanda Revenue Authority

Pierre Célestin Bumbakare
Rwanda Revenue Authority

Rodolphe Kembukuswa
SDV

Suzanne Iyakaremye
SDV

Jean Marie Vianney Mugemana
Société Cerede S.A.R.L

Theophile Kazaneza

Jean Claude Nsengiyumva
Tribunal de Grande Instance de Nyarugenge

Richard Mugisha
Trust Law Chambers

Emmanuel Abijuru
Union des Banques Populaires du Rwanda

Eric Nsengimana
World Freight S.A.R.L.

SAMOA

Murray Drake
Drake & Co.

Lawrie Burich
L. Burich - Building Contractors

Arthur R. Penn
Lesa ma Penn

Patea Malo Setefano
Ministry of Natural Resources & Environment

Shan Shiraz Ali Usman
Tradepac Marketing Ltd.

SÃO TOMÉ AND PRINCIPE

André Aureliano Aragão
André Aureliano Aragão Advogado

Agostinho Q.S.A. Fernandes
Directorate of Taxes

Frederico da Glória

Kiluange Tiny
JuriSTEP

Edmar Carvalho
Miranda Correia Amendoeira & Associados

SAUDI ARABIA

Aboud H. Saklou Trading Est.

Samer Pharaon
Abu-Ghazaleh Legal

Abdul Aziz Zaibag
Al - Zaibag Consultants

David K. Johnson
Al Juraid & Company / PricewaterhouseCoopers

Sami Al-Sarraj
Al Juraid & Company / PricewaterhouseCoopers

Soudki Zawaydeh
Al Juraid & Company / PricewaterhouseCoopers Legal Services

Jochen Hundt
Al-Soaib Law Firm

Juergen Villmer
Al-Soaib Law Firm

Mohammed Al-Soaib
Al-Soaib Law Firm

George Sayen
Baker & McKenzie Ltd.

Nasser Alfaraj
Baker & McKenzie Ltd.

Amgad Husein
Fulbright & Jaworski LLP

Anas Akel
Fulbright & Jaworski LLP

Mohammed Al-Ghamdi
Fulbright & Jaworski LLP

Majed Mohammed Garoub
Law Firm of Majed M. Garoub

Imad El-Dine Ghazi
Law Office of Hassan Mahassni

Muntasir Osman
Law Office of Hassan Mahassni

Adel Elsaid
Panalpina

Prabagaran Ramasamy
Panalpina

SAMTCO

Nabil Abdullah Al-Mubarak
Saudi Credit Bureau - SIMAH

Fayez Al-Nemer
Talal Bin Naif Al-Harbi Law Firm

Ali Abedi
The Alliance of Abbas F. Ghazzawi & Co. and Hammad & Al-Mehdar

Faten Abbar
The Alliance of Abbas F. Ghazzawi & Co. and Hammad & Al-Mehdar

Wisam Sindi
The Alliance of Abbas F. Ghazzawi & Co. and Hammad & Al-Mehdar

Ebaish Zebar
The Law Firm of Salah Al-Hejailany

Abdullah Al-Hashim
The Law Firm of Yousef and Mohammed Al-Jaddan

Abou Bakr Gadour
Toban Law Firm

Muhammad Lotfi
Toban Law Firm

Sameh M. Toban
Toban Law Firm

SENEGAL

Fallou Dieye
APIX -Agence chargée de la Promotion de l'Investissement et des Grands Travaux

Rita Da Costa Fall
APIX -Agence chargée de la Promotion de l'Investissement et des Grands Travaux

Fodé Diop
Art Ingénierie Afrique

Charles Ki-Zerbo
BCEAO

Cheikh Fall
Cabinet d'Avocat

Khaled Abou El Houda
Cabinet Kanjo Koita

Daniel Sedar Senghor
Etude de Me Sedar Senghor

Ibrahima Mbodj
Etude Me Ibrahima Mbodj

Ndjaye Mbodj
Etude Me Ibrahima Mbodj

Dominique Taty
FIDAFRICA / PricewaterhouseCoopers

Mahi Kane
FIDAFRICA / PricewaterhouseCoopers

Matthias Hubert
FIDAFRICA / PricewaterhouseCoopers

Pierre Michaux
FIDAFRICA / PricewaterhouseCoopers Legal Services

Mamadou Seck
Forum Civil, Section Sénégalaise de Transparency International

Gilberto de Barros

Jean Paul Didier Thibault
Ministère de la Justice

Oumy Kalsoum Gaye

Rita Dacosta Fall

Michèle Renous
S.G.B.S.

Mamadou Mbaye
SCP Mame Adama Gueye & Associés

Mame Adama Gueye
SCP Mame Adama Gueye & Associés

Magatte Dabo
Transfret Dakar

SERBIA

Rade Bačković
Association of Serbian Banks

Biro-Marketing

Mirko Kovac
Bojovic & Dasic, PricewaterhouseCoopers Legal Services

Snezana Minic
Bojovic & Dasic, PricewaterhouseCoopers Legal Services

Zorana Nikolic
Bojovic & Dasic, PricewaterhouseCoopers Legal Services

Dimitrije Nikolic
Cargo Team

Miodrag Milosavljevic
Fund for an Open Society, Serbia

Drazen Turujlija
Gide Loyrette Nouel, member of Lex Mundi

Sandra Simic
Gide Loyrette Nouel, member of Lex Mundi

Harrison Solicitors

Petar Stojanovic
Joksovic, Stojanovic & Partners

Dubravka Kosic
Kosic & Sutti

Igor Oljacic
Kosic & Sutti

Marko Repic
Kosic & Sutti

Marija Kostic
Law offices Jankovic, Popovic & Mitic

Nataša Cvetićanin
Law offices Jankovic, Popovic & Mitic

Nikola Janković
Law offices Jankovic, Popovic & Mitic

Lidija Djeric

Mike Ahern

Ana Stankovic
Moravčevic, Vojnović & Zdravković o.a.d. u saradnji sa Schönherr

Jasna Milosavljevic
Moravčevic, Vojnović & Zdravković o.a.d. u saradnji sa Schönherr

Relja Zdravkovic
Moravčevic, Vojnović & Zdravković o.a.d. u saradnji sa Schönherr

National Bank of Serbia and Montenegro

Durdje Ninkovic
Ninkovic Law Office

Ivan Krsikapa
Ninkovic Law Office

Olga Serb Gretic
Ninkovic Law Office

Aleksandar Dimitrov
Prica & Partners Law Office

Ana Calic
Prica & Partners Law Office

Jelena Edelman
Prica & Partners Law Office

Mihajlo Prica
Prica & Partners Law Office

Aleksandar Miljković
PricewaterhouseCoopers

Jelena Djokić
PricewaterhouseCoopers

Jovana Ilić
PricewaterhouseCoopers

Beba Miletic
Wolf Theiss

Bojana Bregovic
Wolf Theiss

Vidak Kovacevic
Wolf Theiss

Zorana Nikolic

Miloš Živković
Živković & Samardžić Law office

Nebojša Samardžić
Živković & Samardžić Law office

SEYCHELLES

Serge Rouillon
Attorney-at-Law

France Gonzalves Bonte

Shelton M. Jolicoeur
International Law & Corporate Services (PTY) Ltd.

Hughes N. Adam
Land Marine Limited

Alex Ellenberger
Locus Architecture Pty. Ltd.

Leslie Boniface
Ministry of Employment and Social Affairs

Marie-Pierre Lloyd
Ministry of Employment and Social Affairs

Conrad Lablache
Pardiwalla Twomey Lablache

Bernard L. Pool
Pool & Patel

SIERRA LEONE

Amy Wright

Susan Sisty
Basma & Macaulay

EcoBank - Sierra Leone

Darcy White
PricewaterhouseCoopers

George Kwatia
PricewaterhouseCoopers

Gideon Ayi-owoo
PricewaterhouseCoopers

Kelvin Abdallah
PricewaterhouseCoopers

Thomas Murega
PricewaterhouseCoopers

Mariama Dumbuya
Renner Thomas & Co.

Centus Macauley Esq.
Roberts & Partners

Emmanuel Roberts
Roberts & Partners

Lornard Taylor
Roberts & Partners

Mohamed Bangura
Roberts & Partners

Sadukia Investment Mining Group

Shipping Agencies Ltd.

Corneleius Max-Williams
Shipping Agencies Ltd.

Susna Sisay
Sisay & Associate

Rowland Wright
Wright & Co. Barristers & Solicitors

SINGAPORE

Angela Lim
Baker & McKenzie, Wong & Leow

Blue Oceans Venture Pte. Ltd.

Caledonian Commodity Trading Pte. Ltd.

City Developments Ltd.

Nish Shetty
Clifford Chance Wong Pte. Ltd.

Philip Rapp
Clifford Chance Wong Pte. Ltd.

Mark Rowley
Credit Bureau (Singapore) Pte Ltd.

Chi Duan Gooi
Donaldson & Burkinshaw, member of Lex Mundi

May Ching Ida Han
Donaldson & Burkinshaw, member of Lex Mundi

Manoj Sandrasegara
Drew Napier

Sushil Nair
Drew Napier

Global Trade Well Singapore

Audrey Ng
Kelvin Chia Partnership

Keppel Land International Ltd.

Kong Hwa Chan Trading Pte. Ltd.

Shi-Chien Chia
Ministry of Industry & Trade

Lui Hai Tan
Ministry of Trade & Industry

Hui Jia Ang
PricewaterhouseCoopers

Paula Eastwood
PricewaterhouseCoopers

QBB (Pte) Ltd.

Nanda Kumar
Rajah & Tann

Patrick Ang
Rajah & Tann

Airinn Loh
Schenker Pte. Ltd.

Andrew Seah
Schenker Pte. Ltd.

Cyril Dumon
SDV International Logistics

Service Point

Shook Lin & Bok (in joint venture with Allen & Overy)

Chia Shi Chien
Singapore Land Authority

Siu Ing Teng
Singapore Land Authority

Han Li Toh
Subordinate Courts

Kannan Ramesh
Tan Kok Quan Partnership

Kit Min Chye
Tan Peng Chin LLC

Shen Yi Thio
TSMP Law Corporation

Wan Sin Import & Export Agencies

Beng Hong Ong
Wong Tan & Molly Lim LLC

Cynthia Tan
Wong Tan & Molly Lim LLC

Yik Wee Liew
WongPartnership

SLOVAKIA

Allen & Overy Bratislava, s.r.o.

Andrea Jezerska
Čechová & Partners, member of Lex Mundi

Jana Borska
Čechová & Partners, member of Lex Mundi

Katarína Čechová
Čechová & Partners, member of Lex Mundi

Michal Zeman
Čechová & Partners, member of Lex Mundi

Tomáš Maretta
Čechová & Partners, member of Lex Mundi

Zuzana Gaalová
Čechová & Partners, member of Lex Mundi

Jana Brezinova
Dedák & Partners

Tomáš Kamenec
Dedák & Partners

Viktor Mišík
Dedák & Partners

Michaela Špetková
Geodesy, Cartography and Cadastre Authority of the Slovak Republic

Roman Turok-Hetes
National Bank of Slovakia

Panalpina Welttransport GmbH

Pavel Nechala
Pavel Nechala & Co.

Kristína Rúsková
Peterka & Partners

Lenka Očkaiková
Peterka & Partners

Ondřej Dušek
Peterka & Partners

Přemysl Marek
Peterka & Partners

Viera Gregorova
Peterka & Partners

Marcela Adamcova
PricewaterhouseCoopers

Radmila Benkova
PricewaterhouseCoopers

Todd Bradshaw
PricewaterhouseCoopers

Clare Vernon
PricewaterhouseCoopers Legal Services

Peter Mateja
PricewaterhouseCoopers Legal Services

Zuzana Dragúnová-Valerová
PricewaterhouseCoopers Legal Services

Jaroslav Škubal
Procházka Randl Kubr, member of Ius Laboris & Lex Mundi

Peter Varga
Procházka Randl Kubr, member of Ius Laboris & Lex Mundi

Michal Luknár
Squire Sanders s.r.o.

Jan Korecky
ULC Čarnogurský s.r.o.

Martin Javorcek
ULC Čarnogurský s.r.o.

Dagmar Zukalová
Zukalová Counselors-at-Law

SLOVENIA

Nataša Božović
Bank of Slovenia

Domen Neffat
Colja, Rojs & Partnerji

Saša Strahinič
Colja, Rojs & Partnerji

Drago Kos
Commission for the Prevention of Corruption

Barbara Kozaric
Deloitte & Touche

Export Center

Andrej Jarkovič
Janežič & Jarkovič Attorneys-at-Law & Patent Attorneys

Aleksandra Jemc
Law Office Jadek & Pensa

Pavle Pensa
Law Office Jadek & Pensa

Renata Šterbenc Štrus
Law Office Jadek & Pensa

Srečo Jadek
Law Office Jadek & Pensa

Urša Penca
Law Office Jadek & Pensa

Miha Velkavrh

Matjaz Nahtigal
Odvetniki Šelih & Partnerji

Mia Kalas
Odvetniki Šelih & Partnerji

Danijel Starševan
Panalpina Welttransport GmbH

Alan Maher
PricewaterhouseCoopers

Anka Pogacnik
PricewaterhouseCoopers

Beta Stembal
PricewaterhouseCoopers

Crtomir Borec
PricewaterhouseCoopers

Janos Kelemen
PricewaterhouseCoopers

Klemen Mir
PricewaterhouseCoopers

Laura Thomson
PricewaterhouseCoopers

Rada Djukic
PricewaterhouseCoopers

Špela Repič
PricewaterhouseCoopers

Jani Sorsak
Schönherr Rechtsanwälte GmbH / Attorneys-at-Law

Matthias Wahl
Schönherr Rechtsanwälte GmbH / Attorneys-at-Law

Tomaz Petrovic
Schönherr Rechtsanwälte GmbH / Attorneys-at-Law

Vid Kobe
Schönherr Rechtsanwälte GmbH / Attorneys-at-Law

Natasa Pipan Nahtigal
Šelih & Partnerji, member of SEE Legal

Bozena Lipej
Surveying & Mapping Authority

SOLOMON ISLANDS

Department of Finance and Treasury

James Apaniai
James Apaniai Lawyers

Phillip Tagini
Monash University

Don Boykin
Pacific Architects, Ltd.

Gregory Joseph Sojnocki
PricewaterhouseCoopers

John Sullivan
Sol - Law

Zarja Čibej

SOUTH AFRICA

Roelof Grové
Adams & Adams

Chris Todd
Bowman Gilfillan, member of Lex Mundi

Claire Tucker
Bowman Gilfillan, member of Lex Mundi

Heidi Bell
Bowman Gilfillan, member of Lex Mundi

Matthew Bonner
Bowman Gilfillan, member of Lex Mundi

Tim Gordon-Grant
Bowman Gilfillan, member of Lex Mundi

Unathi Kondile
Bowman Gilfillan, member of Lex Mundi

Jacques van Wyk
Cliffe Dekker

Llewellyn van Wyk
CSIR

Gabriel Meyer
Deneys Reitz

St Elmo Wilken
Deneys Reitz

Deutaimex International

Eamonn Quinn
Eamonn David Quinn Attorney

Gretchen De Smit
Edward Nathan Sonnenbergs Inc.

Ross Alcock
Edward Nathan Sonnenbergs Inc.

Gourmet Provisions

King Impex

Mari Monique's

Ormonde Import Export Services

Mark Badenhorst
PricewaterhouseCoopers

Paul De Chalain
PricewaterhouseCoopers

Sean Gilmour
PricewaterhouseCoopers

Q & N West Export Trading House

Peter Sands
SDV

Ralph Zulman
Supreme Court of Appeal of South Africa

T.T.C. The Transfer Company Pty. Ltd.

The Bureau

Renee Kruger
Webber Wentzel Bowens

Anastasia Vatalidis
Werksmans Inc.

Zinchem

SPAIN

Allen & Overy

Ana Armijo
Ashurst

Cristina Calvo
Ashurst

Ismail Fernandezanton
Ashurst

Juan Alonso
Ashurst

Nagore Corral
Ashurst

Alejandro Valls
Baker & McKenzie

María Gracia Rubio
Baker & McKenzie

Rossanna D'Onza
Baker & McKenzie

Alfonso Benavides
Clifford Chance

Carlos Vérgez Muñoz
Clifford Chance

Guillermo Rodrigo
Clifford Chance

Mercedes Olábarri
Clifford Chance

Nazaret Clemente
Clifford Chance

Juan Manuel Pardiñas Aranda
Equifax Iberica

Alberto Pimenta
Garrigues

Antonio Fernández
Garrigues

Antonio Merchan
Garrigues

Daniel Parejo Ballesteros
Garrigues

Fernando Vives
Garrigues

Gabriel Solís Pablos
Garrigues

Isabel Martínez de Salas
Garrigues

José Manuel Mateo
Garrigues

Lorenzo Clemente Naranjo
Garrigues

Agustin Del Río Galeote
Gómez-Acebo & Pombo Abogados

Cristina Soler
Gómez-Acebo & Pombo Abogados

Daniel Marín
Gómez-Acebo & Pombo Abogados

Fernando de la Puente Alfaro
International Relations

Carlos Valls
Iuris Valls Abogados

Eusebio Pujol
Iuris Valls Abogados

Agustín Bou
JAUSAS

John Coaley Plant SL

Antonio Sanchez
Landwell, PricewaterhouseCoopers Legal Services

Ernesto Benito
Landwell, PricewaterhouseCoopers Legal Services

Jaime Espejo
Landwell, PricewaterhouseCoopers Legal Services

Javier Garcia Camacho
Landwell, PricewaterhouseCoopers Legal Services

Juan Vazquez
Landwell, PricewaterhouseCoopers Legal Services

Julio Ichaso
Landwell, PricewaterhouseCoopers Legal Services

Sara Gutierrez
Landwell, PricewaterhouseCoopers Legal Services

Jaume Cornudella
Landwell, Abogados y Asesores Fiscales

Maria Davila
Landwell, Abogados y Asesores Fiscales

Siro Arias
Landwell, Abogados y Asesores Fiscales

Ana Gómez
Monereo, Meyer & Marinel-Lo

Ana Sacristán
Monereo, Meyer & Marinel-Lo

Andrés Monereo Velasco
Monereo, Meyer & Marinel-Lo

Juan Soravilla
Monereo, Meyer & Marinel-Lo

Mónica Regaño Aguirre
Monereo, Meyer & Marinel-Lo

Philipp von Wolffersdorff
Monereo, Meyer & Marinel-Lo

Sönke Schlaich
Monereo, Meyer & Marinel-Lo

Municipality of Leganés

Juan Bolás Alfonso
Notariado

Iván Delgado González
Pérez - Llorca

Pedro Pérez-Llorca Zamora
Pérez - Llorca

Roser Ràfols
Roca Juyent Lawyers

Iñigo Sagardoy
Sagardoy Abogados, member of Ius Laboris

Pilar Salinas Rincón
Sánchez Pintado, Núñez & Asociados

Alberto Núñez-Lagos Burguera
Uría & Menéndez, member of Lex Mundi

Alejandro Ferreres Comella
Uría & Menéndez, member of Lex Mundi

Ariadna Cambronero Ginés
Uría & Menéndez, member of Lex Mundi

Cristina Ayo Ferrándiz
Uría & Menéndez, member of Lex Mundi

Valentin Meriono Lopez
Valentin Merino Arquitectos, SL.

SRI LANKA

Capital Reach Holdings Ltd.

Clarion International Ltd.

N.P.H. Amarasena
Credit Information Bureau

Dharshika Herath Gunarathna

Savantha De Saram
D.L. & F. De Saram

Amalka Batepola
F.J. & G. De Saram, member of Lex Mundi

Ayomi Aluwihare-Gunawardene
F.J. & G. De Saram, member of Lex Mundi

Inoka Jayawardhana
F. J. & G. De Saram, member of Lex Mundi

Laksara Marapana
F.J. & G. De Saram, member of Lex Mundi

Priyanthi Guneratne
F.J. & G. De Saram, member of Lex Mundi

Shehara Varia
F.J. & G. De Saram, member of Lex Mundi

Tudor Jayasuriya
F.J. & G. De Saram, member of Lex Mundi

John Wilson Jr.
John Wilson Partners

Amila Fernando
Julius & Creasy

J.M. Swaminathan
Julius & Creasy

Kishani Jayasooriya
Julius & Creasy

Menaka Balendra
Julius & Creasy

Neluka Seneviratne
Julius & Creasy

Priya Sivagananathan
Julius & Creasy

Santushi Perera
Julius & Creasy

Shane Silva
Julius & Creasy

Shashi Weththasinghe
Julius & Creasy

Tilak Wimalagunaratne
Julius & Creasy

Kumudhini Jayasinghe

Microtec Computer Sytstems

Asiri Perera
MIT Cargo (Pvt) Ltd.

Jagath Perera
MIT Cargo (Pvt) Ltd.

Noamal Goonewardena
Nithya Partners

Paul Ratnayeke
Paul Ratnayeke Associates

Daya Weeraratne
PricewaterhouseCoopers

Mahes Jeyadevan
PricewaterhouseCoopers

Shamila Wijeratne

Chandrani Suriyaarachchi
Sudath Perera Associates

Charmalie Weerasekera
Sudath Perera Associates

Kumudika Gammanpila
Sudath Perera Associates

Sudath Perera
Sudath Perera Associates

Texco

Ramani Muttettuwegama
Tichurelvam Associates

Sithie Tiruchelvam
Tiruchelvam Associates

ST. KITTS AND NEVIS

Marcella Liburd
Bryant & Liburd

Anastacia Saunders
CaribTrans

Dahlia Joseph
Daniel Brantley & Associates

L. Everette Martin
Eastern Caribbean Central Bank, Securities Exchange

High Court Registrar

Michella Adrien
Michella Adrien Law Office

Nicholas Brisbane
N. Brisbane & Associates

Charles Walwyn
PricewaterhouseCoopers

Neil Coates
PricewaterhouseCoopers

Vernon S. Veira
Vernon S. Veira & Associates

Kamesha Graham
WalwynLaw

ST. LUCIA

Gillian Vidal-Jules
Attorney General's Chambers

Bradley Paul
Bradley Paul Associates

Carol J. Gedeon
Chancery Chambers

Thaddeus M. Antoine
Francis & Antoine

Andie A. Wilkie
Gordon, Gordon & Co.

Leandra Gabrielle Verneuil
Gordon, Gordon & Co.

Mary Juliana Charles
Gordon, Gordon & Co.

High Court Registrar

Mac Stephen Aubertin

Kimberly Roheman
McNamara & Co.

Candace Cadasse Polius
Nicholas John & Co.

Peterson D. Francis
Peterson D. Francis Worldwide Shipping & Customs Services Ltd.

Richard Peterkin
PricewaterhouseCoopers

Procurement Services International

ST. VINCENT AND THE GRENADINES

Arthur Williams

Agnes E. Cato
Cato & Cato

Mira E. Commissiong
Equity Chambers

High Court Registrar

Kay Bacchus-Browne
Kay Bacchs - Browne Chambers

Bernadine Dublin
Labour Department

Douglas L.A. Williams
Law Firm of Phillips & Williams

Moulton Mayers
Moulton Mayers Architects

Nicole Sylvester
O. R. Sylvester & Co.

Richard Peterkin
PricewaterhouseCoopers

SUDAN

Mohamed A.M. Osman
Darka for Trading & Services Co. Ltd.

Abdel Gadir Warsama
Dr. Abdel Gadir Warsama Ghalib & Associates Legal Firm

Mohamed Adam
Dr. Adam & Associates

Osman Mekki Osman
House of Legal Consultancies & Services Ltd.

Abdullah Abozaid
Law Office of Abdullah A. Abozaid

Ashraf A.H. El Neil
Mahmoud Elsheikh Omer & Associates Advocates

Hind Akasha Aboulela Hamid
Mahmoud Elsheikh Omer & Associates Advocates

Shireen Mohamed Hussein Ehmady
Mahmoud Elsheikh Omer & Associates Advocates

Tariq Mohmoud Elsheikh Omer
Mahmoud Elsheikh Omer & Associates Advocates

Omer Abdel Ati
Omer Abdel Ati Solicitors

SURINAME

Anoeschka Debipersad
A. E. Debipersad & Associates

Angèle J. Karg
BDO AbrahamsRaijmann & Partners

Anouschka Nabibaks
BDO AbrahamsRaijmann & Partners

Consuelo-Andrea Denz
BDO AbrahamsRaijmann & Partners

G. Clide Cambridge

Handels-, Krediet- en Industrie Bank (Hakrinbank) N.V.

Jos Steeman Shipping N.V.

Johan Kastelein
KDV Architects

Stanley Marica
Law Firm Marica

Jennifer van Dijk-Silos
Law Firm Van Dijk-Silos

Radjen Soerdjbalie
Notariaat R.A. Soerdjbalie

SWAZILAND

Bradford Mark Walker
Brad Walker Architects

C.J. Littler
C.J. Littler & Co.

Mangaliso Magagula
Magagula & Hlophe

Phumlile Tina Khoza
Municipal Council of Manzini

Andrew Linsey
PricewaterhouseCoopers

Paul Lewis
PricewaterhouseCoopers

Theo Mason
PricewaterhouseCoopers

José Rodrigues
Rodrigues & Associates

Service Magagula

Shadrack Mnisi
Sharp Freight SWD Pty. Ltd.

Vincent Galeromeloe
TransUnion ITC

Veli Dlamini

SWEDEN

Kjell Olsson
Advokatfirman Lindahl

Olof Hallberg
Advokatfirman Lindahl

Pernilla Carring
Advokatfirman Lindahl

Dain Nevonen
Advokatfirman Vinge K.B.

Jenny Dangre
Advokatfirman Vinge K.B.

Robert Wikholm
Advokatfirman Vinge K.B.

Carl Östring

Lars Hartzell
Elmzell Advokatbyrå AB, member of Ius Laboris

Karl-Arne Olsson
Gärde Wesslau Advokatbyrå

Petter Holm
Gärde Wesslau Advokatbyrå

Bengt Kjellson
Lantmäteriet

Johann Lannering
Magnusson Wahlin Qvist Stanbrook

Christoffer Monell
Mannheimer Swartling Advokatbyrå

Henric Diefke
Mannheimer Swartling Advokatbyrå

Jesper Kuschel
Mannheimer Swartling Advokatbyrå

Åsa Winblad
MAQS Law Firm

Mats Berter
MAQS Law Firm

Panalpina AB

Hedda Lapidus
PricewaterhouseCoopers

Hedda Stiernstedt
PricewaterhouseCoopers

Roger Gavelin
PricewaterhouseCoopers

Odd Swarting
Setterwalls Advokatbyrå

Til Trading

UC AB

Jesper Schönbeck
Vinge KB, Advokatfirman, member of Lex Mundi

Lars-Olof Svensson
Wistrand Advokatbyrå

SWITZERLAND

Peter R. Altenburger
Altenburger

Philippe de Salis
Borel & Barbey

Andrea Molino
Brunoni Molino Mottis Adami

Mauro Cavadini
Brunoni Molino Mottis Adami

Chamber of Commerce of Canton de Vaud

Ueli Huber
Homburger

Bernhard G. Burkard
Notariat Bernhard Burkard

Michel Merlotti
Notary & Consultant

Claire Le Fort
Pestalozzi Lachenal Patry, member of Lex Mundi

Jakob Hoehn
Pestalozzi Lachenal Patry, member of Lex Mundi

Michael Kramer
Pestalozzi Lachenal Patry, member of Lex Mundi

Oliver Widmer
Pestalozzi Lachenal Patry, member of Lex Mundi

Robert Furter
Pestalozzi Lachenal Patry, member of Lex Mundi

Sandra Habermacher
Pestalozzi Lachenal Patry, member of Lex Mundi

Urs Klöti
Pestalozzi Lachenal Patry, member of Lex Mundi

Pierre Natural
Pierre Natural, Notaire

Andrin Waldburger
PricewaterhouseCoopers

Daniel Schmitz
PricewaterhouseCoopers

Robert P. Desax
PricewaterhouseCoopers

SBI Gruppe der Schweizerischen Bauindustrie

Daniel Steudler
swisstopo, Directorate for Cadastral Surveying

Suzanne Eckert
Wenger Plattner

SYRIA

Kanaan Al-Ahmar
Al-Ahmar & Partners

Bisher Al-Houssami
Al-Israa International Freight Forwarders

Ali Ezzo Rhebani
Attorney-at-Law

Auditing Consulting Accounting Center

Mouazza Al Ashhab
Auditing Consulting Accounting Center

Karam I. Bechara
Bank Audi

Abdul Raouf Hamwi
Civil Engineering Office

Jacques El-Hakim
Hakim Law Firm

Lina el-Hakim
Hakim Law Firm

Youssef el-Hakim
Hakim Law Firm

Mazen Ibrahim
Ibrahim & Alousy Law Firm

Rana Habbal
Ibrahim & Alousy Law Firm

Joumana Jabbour

Fadi Kardous
Kardous Law Office

Fady Kardous
Kardous Law Office

Mazen N. Khaddour
Law Office of M. Khaddour & Associates

Nasim Awad
Legality - Lawyers & Consultants

Anas Ghazi
Legality Law office

Basmah Hafez
Ministry of Finance

Mohamad Khodar Alsaid Ahmad
Ministry of Finance

Osama Karawani

Raed Karawani

Housam Safadi
Safadi Bureau

Antoun Joubran
Syrian Arab Consultants Law Office

Gabriel Oussi
Syrian Arab Consultants Law Office

Hussein Khaddour
Syrian Legal Bureau

Nabil Sukkar
The Syrian Consulting Bureau

Faten Tibi
UNDP

Moussa Mitry
University of Damascus / Louka & Mitry Law office

TAIWAN, CHINA

Zue Min Hwang
Asia World Engineering & Construction Co.

Chaoh-Shinn Enterprise Co., Ltd.

C.F. Tsai
Deep & Far, Attorneys-at-Law

Everaise Supplier Trade Co., Ltd.

Chun-Yih Cheng
Formosa Transnational, Attorneys-at-Law

John Chen
Formosa Transnational, Attorneys-at-Law

Yuling Hsu
Formosa Transnational, Attorneys-at-Law

Jeffrey Lin
Joint Credit Information Center

Julie Chu
Jones Day

Jennifer Lin
LCS & Partners

Margaret Huang
LCS & Partners

Rich Lin
LCS & Partners

Victor Chang
LCS & Partners

Niken Automotive Accessories Co., Ltd.

Andrew Yeh
Panalpina Ltd.

Shing-Ping Liu
PricewaterhouseCoopers

Wen-Horng Kao
PricewaterhouseCoopers

Eric Tsai
Puhua & Associates, PricewaterhouseCoopers Legal Services

Ross Yang
Puhua & Associates, PricewaterhouseCoopers Legal Services

Catherine Liu
SDV Ltd.

Robert Hsu
SDV Ltd.

Sum-Gain Biomedical System Co., Ltd.

Edgar Chen
Tsar & Tsai Law Firm, member of Lex Mundi

Josh Fan
Tsar & Tsai Law Firm, member of Lex Mundi

Hui-ling Chen
Winkler Partners

Lloyd Roberts
Winkler Partners

Yeong Uong Enterprise Co.

Young-G Corporation

TAJIKISTAN

Bakhtiyor Abdulhamidov
Akhmedov, Azizov & Abdulhamidov Attorneys

Shavkat Akhmedov
Akhmedov, Azizov & Abdulhamidov Attorneys

Mansur Rakhimnazarov
CJSC "LEX"

Dilshod Kholmatov

Jienshokh Bukhoriev
IFC

Ministry of Labor & Social Protection

Natalya Ryashentseva
Pragma Corporation

Nigina Salibaeva
Pragma Corporation

Abdulkhamid Muminov
PricewaterhouseCoopers

Aliya Utegaliyeva
PricewaterhouseCoopers

Bakhytzhan Kadyrov
PricewaterhouseCoopers

Courtney Fowler
PricewaterhouseCoopers

Elena Kaeva
PricewaterhouseCoopers

Ilyas Jumambaev
PricewaterhouseCoopers

Natalya Revenko
PricewaterhouseCoopers

Sergi Kobakhidze
PricewaterhouseCoopers

Andrea Mario Dall'Olio
Tajikistan BEE - SME Policy Project

Djasurbek Teshaev
Tajikistan BEE - SME Policy Project

Madina Nurmatova
Tajikistan BEE - SME Policy Project

Tolib Alimatov

TANZANIA

Angelo Mapunda
FK Law Chambers

Krista van Winkelhof
FK Law Chambers

Vincent Mhina
FK Law Chambers

Bernard m. Luanda
High Court of Tanzania Commercial Division

Eliamani G. Mbise
High Court of Tanzania Commercial Division

Johnson Jasson
Johnson Jasson & Associates Advocates

Leopold Thomas Kalunga
Kalunga & Co. Advocates

Gilbert Nyatanyi
Mkono & Co.

Ngwaru Maghembe
Mkono & Co.

Nimrod Mkono
Mkono & Co.

Patrick Ache
Mkono & Co.

Shivani Patel
Mkono & Co.

Steven de Backer
Mkono & Co.

Wilbert B. Kapinga
Mkono & Co.

Duncan Owen
Phatisa - Innovative Financial Solutions

David Tarimo
PricewaterhouseCoopers

Rishit Shah
PricewaterhouseCoopers

Conrad Nyukuri
PricewaterhouseCoopers Legal Services

Shabani Mwatawala
PSM Architects

Alex Nguluma
REX Attorneys

Charles R.B. Rwechungura
REX Attorneys

Farija Ghikas
REX Attorneys

Sinare Zaharan
REX Attorneys

Frederick Ringo
Ringo & Associates, member of the Africa Legal Network

Mugftafa Tharoo
Ringo & Associates, member of the Africa Legal Network

Gilbert Marilhet
Sharbatho

Mohamed H. Sumar
Sumar Varma Associates

THAILAND

Allen & Overy Co., Ltd.

Suwat Kerdphon
Department of Lands

Exim Deccorner Company Ltd.

Steven Miller
Johnson Stokes & Master, member of Lex Mundi

Kanoksinpinyo Co., Ltd.

Niwat Kanjanapumin
National Credit Bureau Co. Ltd.

Pornsaran Sangsatra
Panalpina

Janist Aphornratana
PricewaterhouseCoopers

Ornjira Tangwongyodying
PricewaterhouseCoopers

Pauline Manzano
PricewaterhouseCoopers

Seetha Gopalakrishnan
PricewaterhouseCoopers

Thavorn Rujivanarom
PricewaterhouseCoopers

Salom Electric Co., Ltd.

Chalee Chantanayingyong
Securities & Exchange Commission

Picharn Sukparangsee
Siam City Law Offices Ltd.

Vira Kammee
Siam City Law Offices Ltd.

SPL NewEr@ Ltd.

Thamnu Vasinonta
Thai Contractors Association

Alongkorn Tongmee
Tilleke & Gibbins International Ltd., member of Lex Mundi

Chusert Supasitthumrong
Tilleke & Gibbins International Ltd., member of Lex Mundi

Cynthia M. Pornavalai
Tilleke & Gibbins International Ltd., member of Lex Mundi

Dussadee Rattanopas
Tilleke & Gibbins International Ltd., member of Lex Mundi

John Fotiadis
Tilleke & Gibbins International Ltd., member of Lex Mundi

Michael Ramirez
Tilleke & Gibbins International Ltd., member of Lex Mundi

Pimvimol Vipamaneerut
Tilleke & Gibbins International Ltd., member of Lex Mundi

Piyanuj Ratprasatporn
Tilleke & Gibbins International Ltd., member of Lex Mundi

Harold K. Vickery Jr.
Vickery & Worachai Ltd.

Chinnavat Chinsangaram
White & Case

Sakchai Limsiripothong
White & Case

TIMOR-LESTE

Ulderico Fernandes
Alfandega

Aderito LCA de Araujo
Archtimor Engineering Consultant

Gina Corte Real
Business Registration Unit, Directorate of Commerce

Consultoria de Lei

Hugo Nogueira Campanico
CRA Timor

Miguel Carreira Martins
CRA Timor

Pedro Sousa
Department of Land and Property, Ministry of Justice

Cornelio Pacheco
JVK International Movers

Jose Pedro Camoes
LBH-TL

Colin Heartwell
Ministry of Development

Jackson Lay
Palm Spring Estates

Felismino Garcia Cardoso
Prosecutor's Office, UN compound

Flavio Lorza
Prosecutor's Office, UN compound

Pedro Andrade
Public Defender

Cherryden Mazarado
Rocky Constructions

Rafael Ribeiro
SDV

Roberto Monteiro
SDV

Francisco Soares
Serviço do Imposto de Timor Leste

Marcia Dawes
Shearman & Sterling LLP

Tjia Soh Siang
Tjia & Tchai Associates

Maria das Dores Gomes
Tribunal Distrital de Dili

Rui Gomes
UNDP

Eusebio Guterres
UNIDO Business Regulatory consultant

Candido Conceicao
USAID

Vital dos Santos
VSP - Vital dos Santos & Partners

TOGO

Adjoavi Assogbavi-Gbedey

Romain Dansou
Agence EPAUC nouvelle

Coffi Alexis Aquereburu
Aquereburu and Partners Cabinet d'Avocats

N'Sarma Mabiba Douti
Assemblée Nationale

Foli Doe-Bruce
AUDEP International

Charles Ki-Zerbo
BCEAO

Bleounou Komlan

Denis Cordel
Bolloré DTI - SDV

Jean-Marie Adenka
Cabinet Adenka

Tiburce Monnou
Cabinet Akapo

Kodjo John Kokou
Cabinet d'Avocats John Kokou

Messan Raphael Ekoue Hagbonon
Centre d'etudes d'architecture et d'urbanisme

Kodko Cephas Keoula
Chambre de Commerce et d'Industrie du Togo (CCIT)

Samuel Sanwogou
Chambre de Commerce et d'Industrie du Togo (CCIT)

Adzewoda Ametsiagbe
Direction Générale de l'Urbanisme et de l'Habitat

Doe-Bruce Adama Ruben

EcoBank - Togo

Adeline Messou
FIDAFRICA / PricewaterhouseCoopers

Dominique Taty
FIDAFRICA / PricewaterhouseCoopers

Evelyne M'Bassidgé
FIDAFRICA / PricewaterhouseCoopers

Fousséni Traoré
FIDAFRICA / PricewaterhouseCoopers

Jean Claude Gnamien
FIDAFRICA / PricewaterhouseCoopers

Firmin Kwami Dzonoukou

Amessi Midiohouan
Fisc Conseil - Cabinet de conseil fiscal

Franklin Koffi Gbedey
Engineer

Galolo Soedjede

Koffi Yao-Gackpo

Da-Blece Afoda-Sebou
Ordre National des Architectes du Togo (ONAT)

Adjémida Douato Soededjede
SAFECO

Atchroe Leonard Johnson
SCP Aquereburu & Partners

Darius Atsoo
SCP Martial Akakpo, Société d'Avocats

Martial Akakpo
SCP Martial Akakpo, Société d'Avocats

Sonhaye Gbati

Yentroudjoa Kantati
Tribunal de 1ere Instance de Lome

Sronvie Yavoi
Tribunal du Travail

TONGA

Inoke Afu
Dateline Shipping & Travel Ltd.

Don Jacobson
Ministry of Finance

Nailasikau Halatuituia

Tomasi Fakahua
Sione Tomasi Naite Fakahua Law Office

Diana Warner
Skip's Custom Joinery Ltd.

Tony Ford
Supreme Court

Lee Miller
Waste Management Ltd.

TRINIDAD AND TOBAGO

Ronald Patience
Cargo Consolidators Agency Ltd.

Mark Ramkerrysingh
Fitzwilliam Stone Furness - Smith & Morgan

Alvaro Montenegro
HSMDT Ltd.

Stephen A. Singh
LEX Carribbean

Celeste Mohammed
M. Hamel-Smith & Co., member of Lex Mundi

Helen Ross
M. Hamel-Smith & Co., member of Lex Mundi

Jonathan Walker
M. Hamel-Smith & Co., member of Lex Mundi

Keomi Lourenco
M. Hamel-Smith & Co., member of Lex Mundi

Myrna Robinson-Walters
M. Hamel-Smith & Co., member of Lex Mundi

Nicole Ferreira-Aaron
M. Hamel-Smith & Co., member of Lex Mundi

Rena M. Mahadeo
M. Hamel-Smith & Co., member of Lex Mundi

Stacy-Lee Daniell
M. Hamel-Smith & Co., member of Lex Mundi

Deborah Ragoonath
PricewaterhouseCoopers

Peter Inglefield
PricewaterhouseCoopers

Ramdath Dave Rampersad
R.D. Rampersad & Co.

Steve Beckles
R.D. Rampersad & Co.

S. I. Primus & Sons Ltd.

Ramesh Lutchman
TransUnion

Trinity Chambers

Thomas Johnson
York University, Osgood Hall Law School

TUNISIA

Samir Abdelly
Abdelly & Associés

Mourad Abdelmoula
Abdelmoula & Associés

Salma Chaari
Abdelmoula & Associés

Monêm Achour
Achour & Associates

Mohamed Moncef Barouni
ACR

Adly Bellagha
Adly Bellagha & Associates

Elyès Ben Mansour
Avocats Conseils Associés

Faiza Feki
Central Bank of Tunisia

Abderrahmen Fendri
Conseil Audit Formation CAF SARL

Mabrouk Maalaoui
Conseil Audit Formation CAF SARL

Abdelmalek Dahmani
Dahmani Transit International

Abdelfatah Benahji
Ferchiou & Associés Meziou Knani

Noureddine Ferchiou
Ferchiou & Associés Meziou Knani

Amel Ferchichi
Gide Loyrette Nouel, member of Lex Mundi

Amina Larbi
Gide Loyrette Nouel, member of Lex Mundi

Imed Tanazefti
Gide Loyrette Nouel, member of Lex Mundi

Kamel Ben Salah
Gide Loyrette Nouel, member of Lex Mundi

Sami Kallel
Kallel & Associates

Faouzi Mili
Mili and Associates

Rafika Ben Aissa Bouslama
Ministère de la Justice

Rachid Tmar
PricewaterhouseCoopers Legal Services

Eric Douay
SDV

Wessam Ben Mahmoud

TURKEY

Rüçhan Derici
3E Danişmanlik Ltd. Şti.

Özlem Özgür Meriç
Abu-Ghazaleh Legal

Orhan Yavuz Mavioğlu
Alkan Deniz Mavioğlu Dilmen Law Office

AsRoyal

Bariyer Makina Kalip San. ve Tic. Ltd. Sti.

Erim Bener
Bener Law Office, member of Ius Laboris

Serkan Pamukkale
Birsel Law Offices

Bolero Socks

Ahmet İlker Doğan
Çakmak Avukatlik Bürosu

Ceren Kartari
Çakmak Avukatlik Bürosu

Naz Bandik
Çakmak Avukatlik Bürosu

Şebnem Önder
Çakmak Avukatlik Bürosu

Rıfat Günay
Central Bank of the Republic of Turkey

Aylin Yontar
Cerrahoğlu Law Firm

Banu Mert
Cerrahoğlu Law Firm

Begüm Ertabak
Cerrahoğlu Law Firm

M. Fadlullah Cerrahoğlu
Cerrahoğlu Law Firm

Müjdem Aksoy
Cerrahoğlu Law Firm

Onur Gülsaran
Cerrahoğlu Law Firm

Zeynephan Oğuz
Cerrahoğlu Law Firm

Devrim Çukur
Çukur & Yilmaz

Ebru Tuygun
Deloitte & Touche

Ekin Vukçuoğlu Özgülsen
Deloitte & Touche

Hayati Arman Gezer
Deloitte & Touche

Hülya Yılmaz
Deloitte & Touche

Sait Gözüm
Deloitte & Touche

Ufuk Soğütlüoğlu
Deloitte & Touche

Emine Devres
Devres Law office

Erdemler Otomotiv San. ve Tic. Ltd. Sti.

Egemen Karaduman
Ernst & Young Turkey

Feridun Güngör
Ernst & Young Turkey

İhsan Akar
Ernst & Young Turkey

Mustafa Çamlıca
Ernst & Young Turkey

Sadık Ferik
Ernst & Young Turkey

Himerpa A.S.

Alaattin Özyürek
Investment Support and Promotion Agency of Turkey

Alpaslan Hamdi Kuzucuoğlu
Istanbul Metropolitan Municipality

John's Coffee

Bülent Yiğit
Kadiköy 25. Noteri

Kekik Tarim Ltd.

Kinetik Biomedikal Tek. Sag. San. ve Tic. Ltd. Sti.

Başak Diclehan
KPMG

Fikret Çetinkaya
KPMG

Murat Emirhanoğlu
KPMG

Kazım Derman
Kredit Kayit Bureau

Yılmaz Nalçakar
Med Shipping Logistics Transport & Trade Ltd. Corporation

Bilge Saltan
Mehmet Gün & Co.

Melike Akan
Mehmet Gün & Co.

Şebnem Işık
Mehmet Gün & Co.

Yegan Üreyen
Mehmet Gün & Co.

Sadık Yamaç
Ministry of Public Works & Settlement of Turkey

Nilpar Ltd. Sti.

Ufuk Üçkardeşler
Norm Yapi Denetim Şirketi

Noyan Goksu

Elvan Aziz Bikmen
Paksoy & Co.

Selin Barlak
Paksoy & Co.

Ferhat Pekin
Pekin & Bayar Law Firm

Ceyda Tapsın
Pekin & Pekin, member of Lex Mundi, member of SEE Legal

Elif Evren Catana
Pekin & Pekin, member of Lex Mundi, member of SEE Legal

Fethi Pekin
Pekin & Pekin, member of Lex Mundi, member of SEE Legal

Gökben Erdem Dirican
Pekin & Pekin, member of Lex Mundi, member of SEE Legal

Hande Hamevi
Pekin & Pekin, member of Lex Mundi, member of SEE Legal

Koray Altunordu
Pekin & Pekin, member of Lex Mundi, member of SEE Legal

Şehnaz Güngör
Pekin & Pekin, member of Lex Mundi, member of SEE Legal

Sezin Gruner
Pekin & Pekin, member of Lex Mundi, member of SEE Legal

Şükran Kızılot
Pekin & Pekin, member of Lex Mundi, member of SEE Legal

Zeynep Akın
Pekin & Pekin, member of Lex Mundi, member of SEE Legal

Adnan Nas
PricewaterhouseCoopers

Ekin Altıntaş
PricewaterhouseCoopers

Esin Ertek
PricewaterhouseCoopers

Faruk Sabuncu
PricewaterhouseCoopers

H.Barış Yalçın
PricewaterhouseCoopers

Benek Gvenilir Erdemir
PricewaterhouseCoopers Legal Services

Burcu Tuzcu
PricewaterhouseCoopers Legal Services

Çağıl Şahin Biber
PricewaterhouseCoopers Legal Services

Ebru Yetişkin
PricewaterhouseCoopers Legal Services

Güzel Yıldırım
PricewaterhouseCoopers Legal Services

Nilgün Serdar
PricewaterhouseCoopers Legal Services

Nilgün Şimşek
PricewaterhouseCoopers Legal Services

Salkim Tarim Urunleri San. ve Tic. Ltd. Sti.

Selim Sarıibrahimoğlu
Sariibrahimoğlu Law Office

Luc Fourcade
SDV - Horoz Logistics

Serap Zuvin
Serap Zuvin Law Offices

Sumerman International

Aylin Tarlan
Tarlan & Pekyalcin Law Office

Derya Baksi Pekyalçın
Tarlan & Pekyalcin Law Office

Tektron Dis Tic. Ltd. Sti.

Ertaç Öner
The Chamber of Architects of Turkey

Torsan Automotive

Turkish Industrialists' and Businessmen's Association (TUSIAD)

Esin Taylan
Turunç & Savaşçin

Noyan Turunç
Turunç & Savaşçin

Selen Egeli Semiz
Turunç & Savaşçin

Simhan Savaşçın Başaran
Turunç & Savaşçin

Unimet Metal San. Tic. Ltd. Sti.

Mustafa Alper
YASED - International Investors Association

UGANDA

David F.K. Mpanga
A.F. Mpanga Advocates

Alan Shonubi

Henry Muguzi
Anti Corruption Coalition Uganda

Robert Kiggundu
Arch Forum Ltd.

Georgina Kugonza
Attorney-at-Law

Cornelius Mukiibi
C. Mukiibi Sentamu & Co.

F.M.S Egonda-Ntende
High Court of Uganda Commercial Division

Geoffrey Kiryabwire
High Court of Uganda Commercial Division

Kenneth Kakuru
Kakuru & Co. Advocates

Charles Kalu Kalumiya
Kampala Associated Advocates

Ronald Tusingwire
Kampala Associated Advocates

John Fisher Kanyemibwa
Kateera & Kagumire Advocates

Sim Katende
Katende, Ssempebwa & Co. Advocates

Muzamiru Kibeedi
Kibeedi & Co.

Kiryowa Kiwanuka
Kiwanuka & Karugire Advocates

Bernard Bamwine
Kwesigabo, Bamwine & Walubiri Advocates

Phillip Karugaba
MMAKS Advocates

Rachel Musoke
MMAKS Advocates

Walugembe Christopher
MMAKS Advocates

Masembe Kanyerezi
Mugerwa & Masembe Advocates

Godfrey Zziwa
Muwanguzi, Zziwa & Musisi Advocates

Jimmy M Muyanja
Muyanja & Associates

Ali Sengendo
Mwebe, Sebaggala & Co.

Alex Rezida
Nangwala, Rezida & Co. Advocates

Peter Mulira

Milton Turyaguma
P.M. Consult Ldt.

Jalia Kangave
PricewaterhouseCoopers

Osborne Wanyoike
PricewaterhouseCoopers

Paul Frobisher Mugambwa
PricewaterhouseCoopers

Plaxeda Namirimu
PricewaterhouseCoopers

Robinah Lutaaya
PricewaterhouseCoopers

Russell Eastaugh
PricewaterhouseCoopers Legal Services

Charles Mwebembezi
SDV Transami Ltd.

Clare de Wet
SDV Transami Ltd.

Fatuma Nabulime
SDV Transami Ltd.

Nicholas Ecimu
Sebalu & Lule Advocates and Legal Consultants

Parbat Siyani
Seyani Brothers & Co. (U) Ltd

Ezekiel Tuma
Shonubi, Musoke & Co. Advocates

UKRAINE

Sergej Vladimirovich Stepovoj
Absolut SV

Dmytro Korbut
Andreas Neocleous & Co., Legal Consultants

Andrey Astapov
Astapov Lawyers International Law Group

Olga Romanenko
Astapov Lawyers International Law Group

Tatyana Kuzmenko
Astapov Lawyers International Law Group

Yevgeniy Karpov
Astapov Lawyers International Law Group

Anna Putintseva
Chadbourne & Parke LLP

Sergiy Onishchenko
Chadbourne & Parke LLP

Sergiy Zheka
Chadbourne & Parke LLP

Konstantin Gribov
DLA Piper Ukraine LLC

Olena Bilozor
DLA Piper Ukraine LLC

Dmitry Martynenko

Zeeshan Wani
Globalink Transportation & Logistics Worldwide LLP

Sasha Androschuk
Grischenko & Partners

Savva P. Poliakov
Grischenko & Partners

Olexiy V. Pokotylo
Hannes Snellman, Attorneys-at Law Ltd.

Volodymyr Kuzminsky
Hannes Snellman, Attorneys-at-Law Ltd.

Florentin Blanc
IFC

Sanjar Ibragimov
IFC

Lyubomyr Drozdovskyy
Ilyashev & Partners

Maksym Kopeychykov
Ilyashev & Partners

Mariya Danchenko
Konnov & Sozanovsky

Natalia Dotsenko-Belous
Konnov & Sozanovsky

Olexiy Yanov
Law Firm IP & C. Consult

Olga Serbul
Law Firm IP & C. Consult

Oleg Y. Alyoshin
OOO IF "Image"

Igor Dankov
PricewaterhouseCoopers

Jorge Intriago
PricewaterhouseCoopers

Maxim Korsheniuk
PricewaterhouseCoopers

Ron J. Barden
PricewaterhouseCoopers

Slavyana Kamburova
PricewaterhouseCoopers

Adrian Opaits
PricewaterhouseCoopers Legal Services

Ivan Yurchenko
PricewaterhouseCoopers Legal Services

Kateryna Kokot
PricewaterhouseCoopers Legal Services

Olga Melnychenko
PricewaterhouseCoopers Legal Services

Yuriy Sorochynskiy
PricewaterhouseCoopers Legal Services

Oleksandr Padalka
Shevchenko Didkovskiy & Partners

Tatiana Buchko
Shevchenko Didkovskiy & Partners

Markian B. Silecky
The Silecky Firm

Maryana Yarmolenko
The Silecky Firm

Olena Brodovska
Vasil Kisil & Partners

Valeriy Lukinov
Venissa Ltd.

UNITED ARAB EMIRATES

Tarek Diab
Abu-Ghazaleh Legal

Adriatic Trading Establishment

Akhila Basith
Afridi & Angell, member of Lex Mundi

James Bowden
Afridi & Angell, member of Lex Mundi

Jiries Saadeh
Afridi & Angell, member of Lex Mundi

Shahram Safai
Afridi & Angell, member of Lex Mundi

Shahid M. Khan
Al Roken & Associates

Ishraga Abutaha
Al Suwaidi & Co.

Suneer Kumar
Al Suwaidi & Co.

Mohammed Kawasami
Al Tamimi & Co.

Sydene Helwick
Al Tamimi & Co.

Allen & Overy LLP

Theresa Abrefa
Berrymans Lace Mawer

Saeed Abdulla Al Hamiz
Central Bank of the UAE

Jassim Ali
Department of Economic Development - Dubai

Laila Bu Abdulla
Department of Economic Development - Dubai

Dolphin Manufacturing Ltd.

Ahmed Abdul Raheem Mahmoud
Emirates Advocates

General Enterprises Co.

Rania Yousseph
Habib Al Mulla & Co.

Walid Karam
Habib Al Mulla & Co.

Essa Al Zarooni
Hilal & Associates

Henrik Petersen
Maersk Kanoo LLC

Dean Rolfe
PricewaterhouseCoopers

Hunter Fullarton
PricewaterhouseCoopers

Salvatore Ruocco
PricewaterhouseCoopers

Ehab Lamie
Shalakany Law Office, member of Lex Mundi

Yasser Omar
Shalakany Law Office, member of Lex Mundi

Blaise Amikat
Trium Logistics LLC

Jennifer Bibbings
Trowers & Hamlins

Samer Hamzeh
Trowers & Hamlins

UNITED KINGDOM

Aerona (Air & Sea) Customs Clearing Agents Ltd.

Allen & Overy LLP

Andrew Wilson
Andrew Wilson & Co.

Simon Cookson
Ashurst

Bernadette Faulkner
Cleary Gottlieb Steen & Hamilton LLP

Shreya Damodaran
Cleary Gottlieb Steen & Hamilton LLP

T.A.R. Curran
Cleary Gottlieb Steen & Hamilton LLP

Techia Braveboy
Cleary Gottlieb Steen & Hamilton LLP

Companies House

David Crosthwaite
Davis Langdon LLP

Katherine Ashton
Debevoise & Plimpton LLP

Michael Steiner
Denton Wilde Sapte

Experian Ltd.

Farmlea Ltd.

Gregory A. Campbell

Jon Atkey
Her Majesty's Land Registry

IDC International Development Corporation TM

Interpower International Ltd.

James P. Sim & Co. Ltd.

Lyndon Norley
Kirkland & Ellis LLP

Richard Lister
Lewis Silkin Solicitors, member of Ius Laboris

Modelesque

Northern Dairy Supplies Ltd.

Olivex Ltd.

Becky Borman
PricewaterhouseCoopers

John Whiting
PricewaterhouseCoopers

Neville Howlett
PricewaterhouseCoopers

Nick Francis
PricewaterhouseCoopers

Richard Collier-Keywood
PricewaterhouseCoopers

Anjali Raman
PricewaterhouseCoopers Legal Services

Ian Carson
PricewaterhouseCoopers Legal Services

Kelly Griffiths
PricewaterhouseCoopers Legal Services

Leon Flavell
PricewaterhouseCoopers Legal Services

Nistha Jeram-Dave
PricewaterhouseCoopers Legal Services

Penny Bruce
PricewaterhouseCoopers Legal Services

Barry Mordsley
Salans

Amar Madhani
Simmons & Simmons

Charles Mayo
Simmons & Simmons

Hannah Botham
Simmons & Simmons

Helen Gorty
Simmons & Simmons

Nick Benwell
Simmons & Simmons

Lynn Hiestand
Skadden, Arps, Slate, Meagher & Flom

Skymart Worldwide

Christopher Mallon
Weil, Gotshal & Manges

Emma Malkin
Weil, Gotshal & Manges

Katherine Stones
Weil, Gotshal & Manges

Sally Willcock
Weil, Gotshal & Manges

UNITED STATES

Bellagio Foods, LLC

Bemex International

Centerload

Steven Horowitz
Clearly Gottlieb Steen & Hamilton LLP

Arthur Kohn
Cleary Gottlieb Steen & Hamilton LLP

Christopher Hale
Cleary Gottlieb Steen & Hamilton LLP

David Webb
Cleary Gottlieb Steen & Hamilton LLP

Desmond Eppel
Cleary Gottlieb Steen & Hamilton LLP

Fiana Kwasnik
Cleary Gottlieb Steen & Hamilton LLP

Lindsee P. Granfield
Cleary Gottlieb Steen & Hamilton LLP

Luke A. Barefoot
Cleary Gottlieb Steen & Hamilton LLP

Michael Lazerwitz
Cleary Gottlieb Steen & Hamilton LLP

Nathaniel Stankard
Cleary Gottlieb Steen & Hamilton LLP

Richard Conza
Cleary Gottlieb Steen & Hamilton LLP

Sandra Rocks
Cleary Gottlieb Steen & Hamilton LLP

Sarah Ten Siethoff
Cleary Gottlieb Steen & Hamilton LLP

Sean O'Neal
Cleary Gottlieb Steen & Hamilton LLP

Victor Chiu
Cleary Gottlieb Steen & Hamilton LLP

David Newberg
Collifr, Halpern, Newberg, Nolletti, & Bock

Dee's Designs

Donald Bernstein

Harmony Imports

Imke Ratschko
Imke Ratschko Plc.

Jacob Clothing Company, Inc.

Karen Wagner

MWTI Global Trade

My Chi To

NYS Department of State

Azniv Ksachikyan
Orrick, Herrington & Sutcliffe LLP

Rhea Saini
Orrick, Herrington & Sutcliffe LLP

Sam Miller
Orrick, Herrington & Sutcliffe LLP

Outlet Season LLC.

Panalpina Inc.

Parker's Wine Brokerage

Kelly J. Murray
PricewaterhouseCoopers

Penny Vaughn
PricewaterhouseCoopers

Robert Morris
PricewaterhouseCoopers

Stephen Anderson
PricewaterhouseCoopers

Rach Exports, Inc.

Samuel Nolen
Richards, Layton & Finger, P.A., member of Lex Mundi

Robinson Import Export Co.

Benjamin E. Gehrt
Seyfarth Shaw LLP, member of Ius Laboris

Bradford L. Livingston
Seyfarth Shaw LLP, member of Ius Laboris

Joshua L. Ditelberg
Seyfarth Shaw LLP, member of Ius Laboris

David Snyder
Snyder & Snyder, LLP

Frederick Turner
Snyder & Snyder, LLP

The Gear Spot

TransUnion

Stephen Raslavich
United States Bankruptcy Court

URUGUAY

César I. Aroztegui
Aroztegui & Asociados / Brons & Salas

Luis Baccino
Aroztegui & Asociados / Brons & Salas

Marcelo Femenías Vidal
Bado, Kuster, Zerbino & Rachetti

Richard Iturria
Bado, Kuster, Zerbino & Rachetti

Laura Barreix
Banco de la Republica Oriental del Uruguay

Milton Cohen
Banco de la Republica Oriental del Uruguay

Luz Calvo de Gross
Calvo-Lopardo-Prats & Asociodos

Matilde Milicevic Santana
Clearing de Informes

Ricardo Mezzera
Estudio Dr. Mezzera

Alma Kubachek
Estudio Juridico Notarial de Alma Kubachek

Flavia Gatti
Ferrere Abogados

Verónica Raffo
Ferrere Abogados

Diego Galante
Galante & Martins

Alejandro Miller Artola
Guyer & Regules, member of Lex Mundi

Alvaro Tarabal
Guyer & Regules, member of Lex Mundi

Carlos Brandes
Guyer & Regules, member of Lex Mundi

Corina Bove
Guyer & Regules, member of Lex Mundi

Patricia Regules
Guyer & Regules, member of Lex Mundi

Jorge de Vita
Jorge de Vita Studio

Juan Federico Fischer
LVM Attorneys at Law

Martín Prats Croci

Ricardo Olivera-García
Olivera & Delpiazzo

Alfredo Inciarte Blanco
Perez del Castillo, Navarro, Inciarte, Gari

Eliana Sartori
PricewaterhouseCoopers

Leonardo Decarlini
PricewaterhouseCoopers

Maria Noel Vidal
PricewaterhouseCoopers

Sergio Franco
PricewaterhouseCoopers

Sylvia Diaz
PricewaterhouseCoopers

Nelson Alfredo Gonzales
SDV S.A.

Andrea Medina
Shaw, Faget y Asociados Ltd., PricewaterhouseCoopers Legal Services

Dolores Storace
Shaw, Faget y Asociados Ltd., PricewaterhouseCoopers Legal Services

Sebastian Arcia
Shaw, Faget y Asociados Ltd., PricewaterhouseCoopers Legal Services

Ariel Imken
Superintendencia de Instituciones de Intermediación Financiera - Banco Central del Uruguay

Gerardo Vinoles
Vinoles Studio

UZBEKISTAN

Vera Ni
Anglesey Food

Zafar Khashimov
Anglesey Food

Petros Tsakanyan
Azizov & Partners

Alisher Inoyatov
Berad Group Co.

Mals Akhmedov
Biznes Advokatlik Servisi

Abduaziz Azizov
Booz Allen Hamilton

Jamol Askarov
Chadbourne & Parke LLP

Sitora Babadjanova
Chadbourne & Parke LLP

Alisher Shaikhov
Chamber of Commerce & Industry of the Republic of Uzbekistan

Bekhzod Abdurazzakov
Denton Wilde Sapte

Irina Gosteva
Denton Wilde Sapte

Mouborak Kambarova
Denton Wilde Sapte

Natalya Apukhtina
Denton Wilde Sapte

Timur Khasanov-Batirov
Derbes Brewery, Subsidiary of BBH

Khalid Farooq
Globalink Transportation & Logistics Worldwide LLP

Ravshan Rakhmanov
Grata Law Firm

Umid Aripdjanov
Grata Law Firm

Nodir Rasulov
Gravamen Fidelis & Fides LLP

Edwin Hyde
Idolec Pty. Ltd.

Nizomiddin Shakhabutdinov
Law Firm Leges Advokat

Alexander Samborsky
National Centre of Geodesy & Cartography

Abdulkhamid Muminov
PricewaterhouseCoopers

Akmal Rustamov
PricewaterhouseCoopers

Altaf Tapia
PricewaterhouseCoopers

Elena Kaeva
PricewaterhouseCoopers

Hairullah Akramhodjaev
PricewaterhouseCoopers

Vsevolod Payevkiy
Uzbekistan - SME Project

VANUATU

Mark Stafford
BDO Barrett and Partners

Christopher Dawson
Dawson Builders

John Malcolm

National Bank of Vanuatu

Dani Yawa
Pacific Lawyers

Arthur Victor Faerua
School of Law, University of the South Pacific

Silas Charles Hakwa
Silas Charles Hakwa & Associates

VENEZUELA

Carlos Velandia Sanchez
Asociación Venezolana de Derecho Registral "AVEDER"

Alfonso Porras
Baker & McKenzie

Carlos Plaza
Baker & McKenzie

Lubín Chacón
Benson, Perez Matos, Antakly & Watts

Eduardo Porcarelli
CONAPRI

Melissa Puga
CONAPRI

Mercedes Briceño
CONAPRI

Arturo De Sola Lander
De Sola Pate & Brown, Abogados - Consultores

John R. Pate
De Sola Pate & Brown, Abogados - Consultores

Thomas J. Pate Páez
De Sola Pate & Brown, Abogados - Consultores

Luis Fernando Miranda
Espiñeira, Sheldon y Asociados / PricewaterhouseCoopers

Ruben Gotberg
Espiñeira, Sheldon y Asociados / PricewaterhouseCoopers

Francisco Gámez Arcaya
Gámez & Vera, Abogados

Carlos Dominguez
Hoet Pelaez Castillo & Duque, member of Lex Mundi

Fernando Pelaez-Pier
Hoet Pelaez Castillo & Duque, member of Lex Mundi

Hector Garcia Corredor
Hoet Pelaez Castillo & Duque, member of Lex Mundi

John Tucker
Hoet Pelaez Castillo & Duque, member of Lex Mundi

Jorge Acedo-Prato
Hoet Pelaez Castillo & Duque, member of Lex Mundi

María Paola Donghia Inciarte
Hoet Pelaez Castillo & Duque, member of Lex Mundi

Bruno Paredes
Logistika TSM

Pedro Mendoza
Mendoza Davila Toledo

Pedro Azpurua
Pack Engenieros C.A.

Alex Grossmann
Panalpina

Alejandro Giolito
PricewaterhouseCoopers Legal Services

Bernardo Pisani
Rodriguez & Mendoza

Enrique Itriago
Rodriguez & Mendoza

Servio T. Altuve Jr.
Servio T. Altuve R. & Asociados

Francisco Aleman Planchart
Tinoco, Travieso, Planchart & Nuñez

Jeanette Villalta Rivas
Venezuelan Chamber of Construction

VIETNAM

My Linh Dao
Baker & McKenzie

Yee Chung Seck
Baker & McKenzie

Trang Vu
Credit Information Centre - State Bank of Vietnam

Isabelle Robineau
DFDL Mekong Law Group

Nasir PKM Abdul
Fléchеux, Ngo & Associés

Bernadette Fahy
Gide Loyrette Nouel, member of Lex Mundi

Jesse Lieberman
Gide Loyrette Nouel, member of Lex Mundi

Le Thuy Lan
Gide Loyrette Nouel, member of Lex Mundi

Nghiem Thi Bang Tam
Gide Loyrette Nouel, member of Lex Mundi

Nguyen Thi Thu Huyen
Gide Loyrette Nouel, member of Lex Mundi

Nicolas Audier
Gide Loyrette Nouel, member of Lex Mundi

Thi Bang Tam Nghiem
Gide Loyrette Nouel, member of Lex Mundi

Thi Hoang Trinh Ngo
Gide Loyrette Nouel, member of Lex Mundi

High Points City Co. Ltd.

Hoai Trung Tea Company

Dang The Duc
Indochine Counsel

Khanh Quang Lai
Indochine Counsel

Le Thuy Huy Nguyen
Indochine Counsel

Vu Anh Phan
Indochine Counsel

Hoang Anh Nguyen
Johnson Stokes & Master, member of Lex Mundi

Pham Thu Hien
Johnson Stokes & Master, member of Lex Mundi

Leonis Co., Ltd.

Phuc Le Hong
LuatViet - Advocates & Solicitors

Konrad Hull
Lucy Wayne & Associates

Mydang Tourist & Trading Co., Ltd.

Ngan Long Co. Ltd.

David Fitzgerald
PricewaterhouseCoopers

Dinh Thi Quynh Van
PricewaterhouseCoopers

Do Thi Thu Ha
PricewaterhouseCoopers

Nguyen Thu Thuy Vo
SDV

Thai Ha Granite Ltd.

Viet D. Phan
Tran H.N. & Associates

Van Anh Nguyen
Vietbid Law Firm

Vietnam Natural Stones Corporation

Vinacraft Co.

Pham Nghiem Xuan Bac
Vision & Associates

Tien Ngoc Luu
Vision & Associates

WEST BANK AND GAZA

Haytham L. Al-Zu'bi
Al-Zu'bi Law Office, Advocates & Legal Consultants

Nada Atrash
Architecture & Design

Karim Shehadeh
Attorney-at-Law

Hashem M. Khaleel
BDO National Brothers

Khalil Ansara
Chemonics International

Hiba Husseini
Husseini & Husseini

Mohamed Khader
Lausanne Trading Consultants

Muhammad Nassar Stone

Farouq Zaiter
PADICO

Ali Faroun
Palestinian Monetary Authority

Nancy Malki
Panorama

Riyad Maliki

Sharhabeel Al-Zaeem
Sharhabeel Al-Zaeem and Associates

Sami Shehadeh
Shehadeh Law Office

Tammam Trade

Fadi Kattan
Transjordanian Engineering Ltd.

YEMEN

Louai Al-Meqbali
Abdalla Al-Meqbali & Associates

Abdalla Al-Meqbeli
Abdalla Al-Meqbeli & Associates

Abdalla Qusai
Abdalla Al-Meqbeli & Associates

Assayad Fisherman Co.

Khaled Al Buraihi
Khaled Al Buraihi for Advocacy & Legal Services

Mohamed Taha Hamood Al-Hashimi
Mohamed Taha Hamood & Co.

Taha Husein Alhotybe

ZAMBIA

Barclays Bank

Robin Durairajah
Chibesakunda & Co.

Kanti Patel
Christopher, Russell Cook & Co.

Solly Patel
Christopher, Russell Cook & Co.

Deborah Bwalya
Corpus Globe Advocates

Elias Chipimo
Corpus Globe Advocates

Harriet Kapampa Kapekele
Corpus Globe Advocates

Chewe K. Bwalya
D.H. Kemp & Co.

Henry Musonda
Kiran & Musonda Associates Ltd.P591

Marjorie Grace Mwenda
M. G. Johnson-Mwenda & Co.

Chipo Munkombwe
PricewaterhouseCoopers

James Harley
PricewaterhouseCoopers

Jyoti Mistry
PricewaterhouseCoopers

ZIMBABWE

Innocent Chagonda
Atherstone & Cook

Beloved Dhlakama
Byron Venturas & Partners

Chris Venturas
Byron Venturas & Partners

Christos Venturas
Byron Venturas & Partners

Simplisius Chihambakwe
Chihambakwe, Mutizwa & Partners

Erle Koomets

Peter Lloyd
Gill, Godlonton & Gerrans

Harry Kantor
Kantor & Immerman

Paul Fraser
Lofty & Fraser

David Masaya
PricewaterhouseCoopers

Manuel Lopes
PricewaterhouseCoopers

Ostern Mutero
Sawyer & Mkushi

Stenford Moyo
Scanlen & Holderness

Richard Beattie
The Stone/ Beattie Studio

Vanani Nyangulu
V.S. Nyangulu & Associates

Doing Business 2008

STANDING ORDER FORM

Standing orders are available to institutional customers only.

If you or your organization would like to automatically receive each new edition of ***Doing Business*** *as it is published, please check the box below, complete your address details, and mail or fax this order form to us. This will establish a standing order for your organization, and you will be invoiced each year upon publication. You may also e-mail books@worldbank.org requesting your standing order for* ***Doing Business****. At any time you can cancel the standing order by sending an e-mail to books@worldbank.org.*

☐ *I would like to automatically receive each new edition of* **Doing Business**. *I understand that I will be invoiced each year upon publication.*

Name ____________________

Title ____________________

Organization ____________________

Address ____________________

City ____________________

State ____________ *Zip/ Postal code* ____________

Country ____________________

Phone ____________________

Fax ____________________

Email ____________________

Institutional customers in the U.S. only:
Please include purchase order. ____________________

Available for US customers only, international customers please contact your local distributor to establish a standing order.

Individuals interested in receiving future editions of ***Doing Business*** *may ask to be added to our mailing list at books@worldbank.org.*

Please indicate in your e-mail that you would like to be added to the ***Doing Business*** *e-mail list.*

By mail
World Bank Publications
P.O. Box 960, Herndon
VA 20172-0960, USA

Online
www.worldbank.org/publications

By fax
+1-703-661-1501

Questions?
E-mail us at books@worldbank.org

By phone
+1-703-661-1580 or 800-645-7247

DDBSO6